DA
689
.W 3
P 3
1964

ROOSEVELT UNIVERSITY LIBRARY
DA689.W3P31964   C001
PATTERSON, SHEILA, 1918-
DARK STRANGERS$ BLOOMINGTON

3 3311 00016 292 7

D0290375

WITHDRAWN

WITHDRAWN

DARK STRANGERS

Dark
Strangers

A SOCIOLOGICAL STUDY OF THE ABSORPTION
OF A RECENT WEST INDIAN MIGRANT GROUP
IN BRIXTON, SOUTH LONDON

SHEILA PATTERSON

INDIANA UNIVERSITY PRESS
BLOOMINGTON

Given in honor of
Bertha & Oscar Fineman
by the Fineman Family
Friends of the library of Roosevelt Univ.

© *Copyright by Sheila Patterson, 1963*
First published in the United States 1964
Manufactured in Great Britain
Library of Congress Catalog Card Number 64-11584

SEP 3 1964

DA
689
.W 3
P 3
1964

For Tadeusz

K 39453 H

Contents

Contents

viii

ix

Contents

Preface

THIS book has been such a long time in the writing that it virtually spans the whole period of unrestricted, large-scale immigration from the West Indies to Britain that ended with the Commonwealth Immigrants Act of 1962.

Such was far from being my original intention. The book's genesis was in a two-year research project carried out under the direction of Dr. Kenneth Little between late 1955 and early 1958, when I was a member of the staff of the Department of Social Anthropology, University of Edinburgh.

The project's main purpose was to round out the set of studies of race relations in Britain already carried out by Dr. Little and by his colleagues or students with a field-research study of what was then a new situation – that created by the presence of a large group of coloured working-class migrants in a central, urban industrial area in this country. Brixton was chosen as the area for field study as being more 'typical' of such situations up and down the country than such areas of social anomie and chaos as parts of Paddington and North Kensington. Although the latter area was to achieve world-wide notoriety in the late summer of 1958 as the scene of the Notting Hill 'race riots', it was and still is in areas like Brixton that the important long-term processes and problems of immigrant-host adaptation and acceptance are, with certain local variations, being worked out.

For although this inquiry was originally envisaged in terms of white-coloured relationships, the preliminary findings soon caused it to develop into a study of immigrant-host relations, with colour as one only of a number of major factors involved in the various processes of absorption. The basic field material was collected in the appointed period, but the processes of absorption continued inexorably, and coloured Commonwealth immigration grew into one of the major political issues of recent times. This made it difficult to cut the inquiry off tidily, particularly as I remained in contact with the local situation through many Brixtonians and West Indian settlers, and with the general issues through my work at the Institute of Race Relations. Additional material has therefore been added and the final major revision of the text was made in late 1961, with the exception of the Postscript dealing with social action, which was rewritten after the passing of the Commonwealth Immigrants Act in April 1962.

Preface

While I regret the delay in publication, something has perhaps been gained. For the additional years of observation have made it possible to provide a picture of a five-year span in the development of a particular migrant settlement, of the dynamic early stages of absorption in three main spheres of association – economic life, housing, and a whole range of formal and informal social relationships – and of the development of tentative forms of social organization within the migrant settlement.

This diachronic view, with its emphasis on actual immigrant-host behaviour and relationships in varying situations and on the varied factors that are influencing absorption, will, I hope, be of some interest and use at the present time. For since the coming into force of the Commonwealth Immigrants Act the emphasis in the public mind has subtly shifted away from *laissez-faire* policies and towards positive social action, both official and unofficial, to promote adaptation and acceptance on the side both of the newcomers and of the receiving society.

If such action is to be effective on both a short- and a long-term basis, it is essential to know as much as possible not only about people's attitudes and the occasional behaviour of mobs or extremist groups, but also about humdrum, everyday interaction over the whole range of social activities and roles.

Now it only remains to express my appreciation and gratitude to all those who have made this work possible and who have contributed so much to its progress and completion.

My thanks are due first and foremost to Dr. Kenneth Little for initiating the study, for his friendly encouragement, his tolerance of delays, and his invaluable comments and criticisms on the successive drafts of the manuscript. I also owe a debt of gratitude to my colleagues, Dr. Michael Banton, Mr. Anthony Richmond, Dr. Sydney Collins, and Mr. Harold Pollins for their valuable and constructive comments on the draft manuscript at various stages; to Professor George Simpson for his guidance on the Rastafari movement; to Dr. Malcolm Calley for his contribution on pentecostal sects among West Indian migrants; to Miss Janet Reid for her comments on the integration of coloured immigrants in industry; to Mr. Miles Wohlers for making available some unpublished material from a survey of Brixton Market stallholders' views of immigrant customers; to Mrs. Joan Maizels for some interesting comparative material; and to Dr. Ruth Landes for some enlightening comments on the contrast between the race relations scenes in Britain and the United States. My sincere appreciation is also due to the Nuffield Foundation for making the grant which enabled the original research project to be carried out and to the Institute of Race Relations for providing at a later stage information services and an environment which made it easier to extend the scope and time-span of the study.

It would be impossible to name here all the people and organizations which have given so generously of their knowledge and time to help this inquiry. I have thanked them all individually and take this opportunity of doing so once again.

Some particular acknowledgements are, however, due. On the official side I should like to express my special gratitude to the staff of the successive organizations concerned with the reception and welfare of West Indian migrants in Britain, the British Caribbean Welfare Service and the Migrant Services Division of the High Commission for the West Indies Federation; and more particularly to the Director, Mr. Ivo de Souza, and his colleagues, Mr. Frank Pilgrim, Mr. Stanley Johnson, and Mr. John Fraser; to Mr. Arthur Pickwood and Mr. W. L. Brewster of the Barbadian Immigrants Liaison Service; to various British government departments, notably the Ministry of Labour, both at head office and in various South London employment exchanges, and the National Assistance Board; to the Central Office of Information; to the Probation Service; to the Lambeth Rent Tribunal; to various departments of the London County Council and Camberwell Borough Council; and above all to Lambeth Borough Council, whose knowledgeable, patient, and friendly staff in themselves constitute an important factor in the integration of newcomers in the area.

On the industrial side I owe particular thanks to British Railways and the London Transport Executive, the GPO, the Gas Board, and the score or so of private firms in South London which were good enough to tell me of their experiences with immigrant labour. On the side of labour I must thank the Trades Union Congress, the National Union of General and Municipal Workers, the Transport and General Workers' Union, the National Union of Railwaymen, the Associated Society of Locomotive Engineers and Firemen, the Union of Post Office Workers, the National Union of Seamen, and other unions which were kind enough to put the viewpoints of organized labour, and also the Lambeth Trades Council for its courteous reception.

As for the non-governmental organizations and groups which have helped me over the years, their name is legion. I should, however, like to extend thanks to the following associations and individuals: the Family Welfare Association (Mr. Albert Hyndman); the London Council of Social Service (Miss Nadine Peppard); the British Council (Miss M. L. Harford, Mr. C. Dashwood-Evans); the Citizens' Advice Bureau (Miss M. E. Nicholson); the Southwark and London Diocesan Associations for Moral Welfare (Miss M. V. Raynes, Miss

Preface

J. M. L. Watson); the National Council for the Unmarried Mother and her Child; the Church of England Children's Society; and Dr. Barnardo's Homes.

I am also indebted to Social Surveys (Gallup Poll) Ltd. of London for their courtesy in allowing me to see and use the results of a number of surveys; to the *South London Press* and the *South London Advertiser* for permission to quote at such length from their columns; and to Melodisc for permission to quote the calypso on pages 341–2.

Of the many Brixtonians, West Indians, and others in public and private life who showed me so much courtesy and friendship during these years I should like to express particular appreciation to the following: Mr. H. Aking-Lewis, Mrs. Phyllis Allfrey, Mr. and Mrs. R. Arthurs, Mrs. Ashmead, Mrs. Elsie Boltz, Miss Dorothy Case, Mr. and Mrs. C. B. Edie, Mr. and Mrs. V. Forbes, Mr. George Greenwood, Sister Norah Harrison, Miss Jessie Hood, the Rev. Marcus James, Miss Claudia Jones, Mr. G. A. Leslie, Miss M. McDean, Mrs. J. Richardson, the Saunders family, and Mr. and Mrs. L. Selman. A rather special debt of thanks is due to those who had the appalling chore of deciphering my handwriting, typing and re-typing successive drafts, and checking references: Miss Muriel Thorburn in Edinburgh, Mrs. Juliette Hunting and Mrs. Kay Meletiou south of the border.

Finally, my most cordial wishes to the second generation of young West Indians now growing up as Brixtonians, and especially to Andrew, Dennis, Doreen, Jacqueline, Janet, Joy, Noel, Yvonne, Lorraine, June, and our godson Leslie John Tadeusz.

SHEILA PATTERSON

Hove
October 1962

Maps

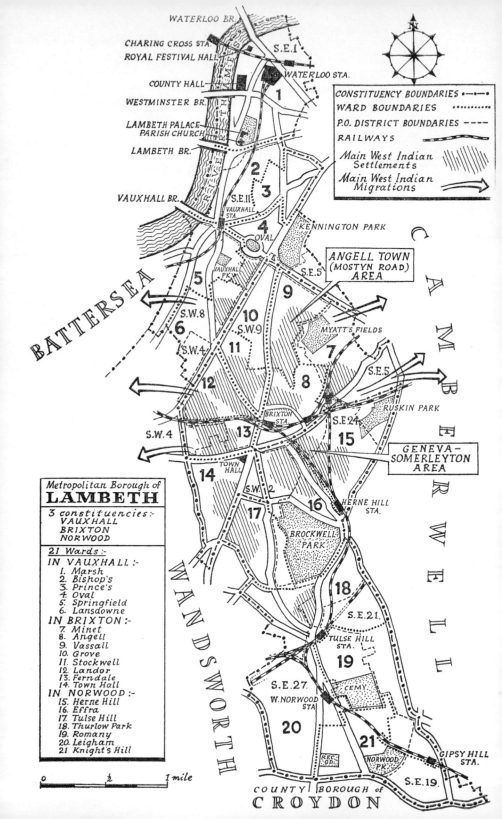

WATERLOO BR.
CHARING CROSS STA.
ROYAL FESTIVAL HALL
COUNTY HALL
WESTMINSTER BR.
LAMBETH PALACE
PARISH CHURCH
LAMBETH BR.
VAUXHALL BR.

WATERLOO STA.
S.E.1

S.E.11
VAUXHALL STA.

OVAL

KENNINGTON PARK

S.E.5

ANGELL TOWN
(MOSTYN ROAD)
AREA

MYATT'S FIELDS

S.E.5

RUSKIN PARK

S.E.24

GENEVA-
SOMERLEYTON
AREA

BRIXTON STA.

TOWN HALL

S.W.8
S.W.9
S.W.4
S.W.4
S.W.2

HERNE HILL STA.

BROCKWELL PARK

S.E.21

TULSE HILL STA.

CEMY

S.E.27
W. NORWOOD STA.

REC. GD.

NORWOOD PK.

GIPSY HILL STA.

S.E.19

COUNTY BOROUGH of
CROYDON

BATTERSEA

WANDSWORTH

CAMBERWELL

N

CONSTITUENCY BOUNDARIES ·—·—·
WARD BOUNDARIES ············
P.O. DISTRICT BOUNDARIES ----
RAILWAYS
*Main West Indian
Settlements*
*Main West Indian
Migrations*

Metropolitan Borough of
LAMBETH
3 constituencies:-
VAUXHALL
BRIXTON
NORWOOD

21 Wards:-
IN VAUXHALL:-
1. Marsh
2. Bishop's
3. Prince's
4. Oval
5. Springfield
6. Lansdowne
IN BRIXTON:-
7. Minet
8. Angell
9. Vassall
10. Grove
11. Stockwell
12. Landor
13. Ferndale
14. Town Hall
IN NORWOOD:-
15. Herne Hill
16. Effra
17. Tulse Hill
18. Thurlow Park
19. Romany
20. Leigham
21. Knight's Hill

0   ½   1 mile

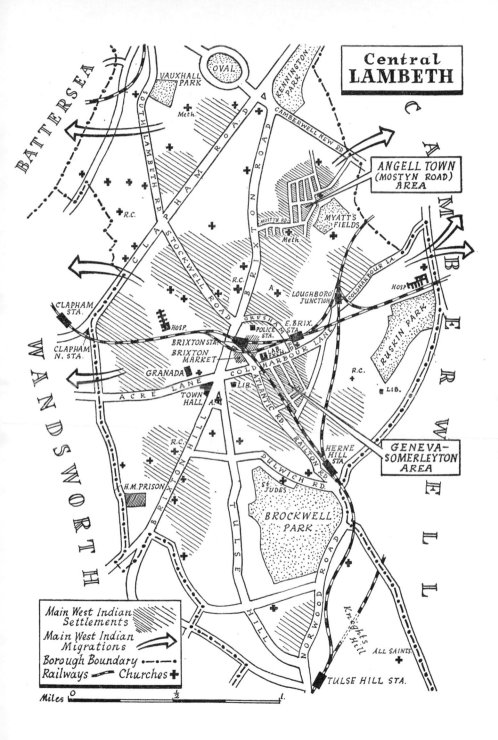

Central LAMBETH

BATTERSEA

CAMBERWELL

WANDSWORTH

OVAL

VAUXHALL PARK

Meth.

KENNINGTON PARK

CAMBERWELL NEW RD.

ANGELL TOWN (MOSTYN ROAD) AREA

SOUTH LAMBETH RD.

R.C.

MOSTYN RD.

Meth.

MYATT'S FIELDS

CLAPHAM RD.

STOCKWELL ROAD

BRIXTON ROAD

R.C.

LOUGHBORO JUNCTION

COLDHARBOUR LA.

HOSP.

RUSKIN PARK

CLAPHAM STA.

HOSP.

GRESHAM

POLICE STA.

E. BRIX. STA.

CLAPHAM N. STA.

BRIXTON STA.

BRIXTON MARKET

LIB.

LAB.

HARBOUR LA.

R.C.

LIB.

GRANADA

ACRE LANE

TOWN HALL

LIB.

COLDHARBOUR LANE

ATLANTIC RD.

RAILTON RD.

GENEVA-SOMERLEYTON AREA

R.C.

BRIXTON HILL

HERNE HILL STA.

DULWICH RD.

H.M. PRISON

ST. JUDES

BROCKWELL PARK

TULSE HILL

NORWOOD ROAD

Knights Hill

ALL SAINTS

Main West Indian Settlements
Main West Indian Migrations
Borough Boundary
Railways — Churches +

Miles 0 ½ 1

TULSE HILL STA.

PART I

The scope of the study

1

Aims, concepts, and hypotheses

'COLOUR SHOCK' AND 'STRANGENESS'

ONE afternoon, in May 1955, I went down to the South London district of Brixton to make a reconnaissance for the study of a recent West Indian migrant group which is the subject of this book. As I turned off the main shopping street, I was immediately overcome with a sense of strangeness, almost of shock. The street was a fairly typical South London side-street, grubby and narrow, lined with cheap cafés, shabby pubs, and flashy clothing-shops. All this was normal enough. But what struck one so forcefully was that, apart from some shopping housewives and a posse of teddy boys in tight jeans outside the billiards hall, almost everybody in sight had a coloured skin. Waiting near the employment exchange were about two dozen black men, most in the flimsy suits of exaggerated cut that, as I was later to learn, denoted their recent arrival. At least half of the exuberant infants playing outside the pre-fab day nursery were *café noir* or *café au lait* in colouring. And there were coloured[1] men and women wherever I looked, shopping, strolling, or gossiping on the sunny street-corners with an animation that most Londoners lost long ago.

Such a sight should have been familiar enough to me after years in Africa and the West Indies. I knew also from the press that several thousand West Indians had settled in Brixton since 1950. None the less, confronted with this street scene in the heart of South London, I still experienced a profound reaction of something unexpected and alien. In fact, I received what I was later to hear Professor Ira de A. Reid describe as a 'colour shock'.[2]

This first reaction of mine was, I think, similar to that of most people in the United Kingdom, following the recent large-scale immigration of West Indians and other coloured Commonwealth citizens into Britain. People in the United Kingdom knew that the

---

[1] 'Coloured' is used throughout in its colloquial English sense, although I realize that the term is open to criticism.

[2] During discussions on papers read at the Race Relations section of the Fourth World Congress of Sociology, Stresa, 1959 (reported in *Race*, 1960).

3

majority of inhabitants of the Commonwealth have coloured skins; some had encountered them on their own ground; many were even used to the idea that there are old-established coloured communities tucked away in dock and port areas in Britain itself. But to be confronted with coloured people in highly visible groups in the centre of its large industrial cities – this was something that at first seemed strange and even out-of-place to most people here.

The feeling of strangeness was not, however, confined to the natives of Britain. Let me illustrate this by another picture which my mind's eye snapped at Folkestone on a bleak February afternoon in 1956. It was one of those days when the sea and sky were a menacing grey, the wind cut to the bone, and the rain was almost sleet. The Channel boat had docked two hours late after a rough passage, and its few ordinary passengers had come ashore and settled with relief on the waiting train. On board, some six hundred West Indians of both sexes and all ages waited in apathetic misery for someone to tell them what to do. Some leaned over the rail or against the windows, staring with unbelief at the unimaginable prospect outside; others, overcome with *mal-de-mer*, lay back with their eyes shut. Almost all wore sandals or light shoes, straw hats, and pastel-coloured summer clothes, now stained and crumpled after three days of train and sea travel from Genoa. Several had wound towels round their necks or heads, or had put on two or more jackets, in a vain effort to keep out the dank chill.

This dejected mass of humanity was finally moved down the gangways into the waiting train. The train had no restaurant-car, but most of the migrants had only a pound or two in cash. They had either spent their meagre capital *en route*, or locked it into their trunks – these, it now emerged, had not accompanied them from Genoa and would not arrive for several days.[1] A few of the men brought out rum bottles and a certain animation developed in their vicinity. But the majority of the migrants remained frozen in apathy or apprehension, unable to give more than a bare account of themselves and their plans and destinations to the West Indian officials

[1] This was, of course, some years ago, and arrangements have greatly improved since then. I do not give any detailed account of the migrants' travelling arrangements and reception, since this may be found in a number of published works, including Ivo de Souza (1960, chapter on 'Arrival'); Ruth Glass (1960, pp. 7–10, 44G); and Joyce Egginton (1957, *passim*).

I should, however, add that for many migrants, particularly women and young children, the long sea and rail journey must have been an appalling, even a traumatic, experience. I myself spent four days on one of the immigrant ships plying on this run when it was returning westward with an over-full cargo of Latin immigrants to the Americas, and was at some pains to examine the dormitories, food, and other facilities provided for the immigrants, and their treatment by the ship's company. See also a series of articles by Anne Sharpley, an *Evening Standard* reporter who purposely travelled to Britain on a migrant ship (November 1961).

4

who now moved up and down the train, ticketing those students who were to be met by the British Council, and the women and young people who were travelling alone and had no contacts nor a precise destination. Some had the addresses of friends, but most of these, reflecting village patterns, were confined to surnames and streets – welfare officers would be kept busy seeing that the newcomers, if they were not met, got to the right Mr. Smith in the right King Street in London. Others had been told that it was best to take a taxi on arrival and had to be dissuaded from taking taxis from the London terminus to Manchester or Birmingham.

The newcomers were laconic enough with the West Indian officials. I found it almost impossible to draw them out at all. Most of them, I was to learn, did not follow my accent well, and a few from French-speaking islands did not speak much English. Some, especially the women, had been warned not to talk to white strangers; others were simply not used to talking to white people. I remember, however, two comments which I overheard in a number of groups: 'I still can't get over how strange it looks to see the white people working on the railway line, doing the dirty jobs, and cleaning out the toilet; and that white porter, he call me "Sir".'[1] And, as the train reached South London: 'Look at all those mean little houses and the hundreds of chimneys giving out that black smoke. I never think London she look so old and dirty and poor and so different from the way I picture.'

I have tried to emphasize the sense of differentness and strangeness felt by hosts and newcomers alike, because it seems to illustrate what I came to see as a basic difference between the present new and highly fluid situation in Britain and the old-established, more static situations in the American South, South Africa, or the West Indies. Another fundamental difference is obviously that of relative numbers. In Britain, with a population of over 52·5 million, there were, even in mid-1962, when the controls on Commonwealth immigration came into force, only about half a million coloured immigrants in all[2] (including up to 300,000 West Indians). At the time of this study the total was considerably less, and in September 1958 a Gallup Poll survey showed that only 42 per cent of respondents knew or had known personally any coloured people (this rose to 55 per cent in London). Even now it is still probably true to say that the greater part of the native population has had few or no first-hand contacts with the newcomers, and, in the majority of cases where there has

---

[1] I was later to hear this comment from many West Indians. George Lamming (1960, pp. 25–6) also mentions this impression.
[2] On 28 June 1962 the Home Secretary, Mr. R. A. Butler, estimated that about 450,000 coloured Commonwealth immigrants had come to Britain since 1955.

5

been contact, it has been peripheral and transient rather than a normal feature of everyday life.

AN IMMIGRANT SITUATION

When I undertook this inquiry in late 1955, I had carried out two full-length field-work studies – one of the Cape Coloured people and their relationships with Whites, Africans, and Asians in South Africa; the other of the gradual absorption of post-war Polish immigrants in Canada. At first, the colour factor and some cultural similarities inclined me to approach the Brixton inquiry as a racial situation analogous to that in the Cape. Very early in the course of field work, however, it became clear that this general approach was inadequate and usually inapplicable or misleading in the British setting, although it was often reflected in the immigrants' interpretation of their situation and problems. The immigrant-host framework, on the other hand, seemed to offer a far more satisfactory mode of interpreting the dynamic processes which were clearly taking place on both sides,[1] the complex motivations of behaviour, the fluid, undefined, and uninstitutionalized relationships, the marginal, peripheral nature of these relationships and the problem as a whole in the everyday life of the British population. Through this approach, in terms of the various stages of adaptation and acceptance on both sides, colour fell into what seems to me to be its rightful place as only one, albeit a very important one, of the manifold factors influencing and often complicating the particular immigrant-host relationship under investigation.

To summarize the situation of the West Indians in Britain, as I came to interpret it over nearly five years of field work and analysis: what we have in Britain at the present stage is not or not yet basically a colour or a race situation, however much it may appear

---

[1] In an excellent Senior Thesis ('Colour Prejudice in Britain') presented at Princeton University in April 1960, an American student, Robert Burt, admitted that he had been compelled to abandon his original project of comparing the racial situations in Britain and the American North, because he found the British situation very different from what he had expected, and virtually incomparable. He wrote: 'There is no simple or clear-cut explanation, or even characterization, that can be drawn of the British racial experiences. It may even be possible to deny completely the existence of a race problem as such—a concept which could not be possible in discussing the United States—and to assert that the present situation in Britain is an "immigrant problem", in which race is a complicating, but not defining, factor. One need not decide between the two concepts of "race" and "immigrant" problems; it is unnecessary legalism to place the social conflict under one rubric or the other. But it is very important to keep in mind that we are able to account in great measure for the present social conflict by disregarding the fact that West Indian or African immigrants into Great Britain are members of the Negro race.' See also p. 8 (footnote 2) for a similar view taken by Dr. Ruth Landes (1952).

so to many colour-conscious migrants – it is an immigrant situation. This immigrant situation is undoubtedly complicated by the factor of skin colour, which makes these particular immigrants, whether they are West Indians, West Africans, or Asians, more immediately visible and more strange than the thousands of other immigrants who have entered the country since the second world war. But the difference is at present one of degree rather than of kind. In Britain – that insular, conservative, homogeneous society – mild xenophobia or antipathy to outsiders would appear to be a cultural norm. It is extended in varying degrees to all outsiders, to Poles and coloured people, and to people from the next village or street.

It should also be emphasized that the West Indian newcomers differ from the British receiving society in social and cultural background at least as much as do such immigrant groups as the Italians, Latvians, and Cypriots. These social and cultural differences between the West Indians and the British in the United Kingdom are often obscured, not only by the more immediate and obvious difference of pigmentation, but by the facts of a common citizenship,[1] a common language, and a common adherence to Christian doctrine. It should, however, be realized that the bulk of the new West Indian migrants in Britain are drawn from a semi-rural colonial proletariat, with a background of slavery, poverty, and frustration which has left a distinctive mark on working habits, family organization, religious practice, and attitudes to authority. This historical background has also left most West Indians with a far stronger colour consciousness than is felt by most residents of Britain.

The social and cultural patterns of lower-class West Indian migrants are thus very often different from those of the contemporary lower and lower-middle classes in Britain with whom they are in most frequent contact.[2] It is only to be expected that situations of culture conflict should arise, as they in fact do, particularly in situations involving residential proximity, intimate social relationships, and sex and family life, and that the migrants themselves should often explain these conflicts in terms of colour. Such frictions would arise, however, as they do in the case of Southern Irish or Cypriot migrants, even if all visible differences were erased.

It is therefore erroneous to compare the new and fluid British situation with those in South Africa or the Southern States, where a

---

[1] That is to say, it is not a situation in which attitudes or behaviour on both sides are determined or structured in terms of real or assumed physiological differences (in this case, pigmentation) and the psychological, social, and cultural traits identified with these differences.

[2] These differences in social and cultural background, attitudes, and expectations are described in more detail in later chapters on housing and social life. Differences in patterns and attitudes at work are discussed on pp. 70–83.

colour bar has for generations been fixed in law, custom, and individual attitudes. The proper comparison is not with coloured-white relationships in Durban or Little Rock. It is with situations such as that arising out of the recent migration of Puerto Ricans to New York, where similar problems and conflicts, also complicated by the colour factor, have arisen in connection with employment, housing, and social and cultural differences.[1] The new West Indian migrants to Britain are, in fact, passing through the same kinds of dynamic process in their relationships with the local population as do all other working-class economic migrants – the same processes, for example, as the East European Jews and Irish in London in the last century, the Italians in Canada, the Puerto Ricans in New York, or even the southern rural Negroes in the urban north of the United States.

There has long been a tendency among students of race relations to approach the complex of situations and relationships that develops when a white and a coloured group live side by side as a special, even a unique, problem. The existence of socio-economic differences and cultural conflicts in many cases has often been almost overlooked in face of the overwhelming fact of colour; this is perhaps because of the subconscious feelings of responsibility and guilt that lurk in the minds of most white students of the subject, and because of increasing public preoccupation with racial problems and conflicts in general.

There is considerable justification for this particular form of colour consciousness on the part of the researcher in long-established and institutionalized situations, where there might be said to be a racial situation or a racial problem in the sense that the two groups are defined and define themselves in terms of racial criteria (in this case emphasizing pigmentation), and order their relationships accordingly in all spheres of association, as, for example, in South Africa or the Deep South. Moreover, the great mass of North American literature on such situations has tended to set the style or bias for later studies elsewhere. There is no valid reason, however, for retaining the smoked glasses when one is confronted with a new and dynamic situation, as in the northern cities of the United States, in metropolitan France, or in Britain today.[2] In such areas, the

[1] Cf. Fitzpatrick (1959–60) for a warning against confusing colour prejudice or discrimination with the conflicts of interests or cultures inevitable in an urban immigrant-host relationship.

[2] The difference in content between the situations of coloured people in Britain and in the United States has been stressed by Dr. Ruth Landes (1952), an American sociologist familiar with both areas: '. . . I grew increasingly sceptical of the generally accepted concepts, as applied to Britain, of prejudice, tolerance and acceptance. I felt that something else was going on, and it could be grasped if the

8

situation can more usefully be seen, not in black and white, but in terms of socio-economic class affiliations, of cultural contacts and conflicts, of rural and urban differences, of adaptation and acceptance between migrants or a minority group and the receiving society.

PROCESSES OF ABSORPTION

During the initial stages of field work, therefore, I found that the immigrant-host framework provided the most fruitful approach to the Brixton material. The general theoretical discussion that follows, although it precedes the detailed analysis of field material, was changed and rewritten several times, and represents the outcome of the study rather than its theoretical starting-point. I hope that social scientists will forgive some apparently tedious rehashing of general theory, and that other readers will excuse the inevitable incursion of sociological jargon.

In a homogeneous and peaceable society, as opposed to a conquest society, social relations are harmonious and voluntarily ordered among the great majority of the society's members. Migrant groups entering such a society usually expect and are expected to develop more or less favourable relationships with their hosts. Such terms[1] as 'adjustment', 'accommodation', 'integration', and 'assimilation' represent the goals recognized by both sides. Maladjustment, disintegration, and conflict are acknowledged as passing phases among individuals or small groups of migrants, but lasting group isolation or conflict does not conform to such a society's patterns. For instance, a migrant or minority group that refuses to accommodate itself to the receiving society's major norms, like the intransigent and uncompromising Doukhobor 'Sons of Freedom' in Canada, presents the receiving society with an almost insoluble problem.

Relations between an incoming group and a receiving society of the peaceable type to which we have referred above develop on an interacting, two-way basis which may be summed up in the rather

right questions were asked. . . . Prejudice seemed to muddy up the approach. . . . In America I knew it for a sociological reality . . . an organized system of values and orientation. In this sense, therefore, I would say there is no prejudice. . . . Britons could not follow the logic of black men profoundly integrated into the American social system because, in their land, black men *are not* so integrated. . . . Since such understanding does not bind the Briton and the Negro, the Negro's civil status and significance are similar to those of a foreigner.'

[1] For various definitions of these terms and processes see W. D. Borrie (1950). 'Absorption' is the overall term for all stages of adaptation and acceptance used by S. N. Eisenstadt (1954) in his studies of Israel. It should perhaps be made clear that the overall term and the particular terms used in this context apply both to a dynamic process and to a static or ideal end-product.

9

clumsy formula, 'adaptation and acceptance'. Adaptation,[1] in the form of resocialization and acculturation, is the part of the immigrant or minority group, while the more passive process of acceptance is mainly left to the receiving society. In the case of the latter, adaptation, where it takes place at all, is largely unconscious. It consists in an enlargement or modification of the receiving society's organizational framework or cultural patterns so as to include certain elements retained by the minority or immigrant group. This kind of adaptation by the receiving society has taken place steadily and perceptibly in countries of large-scale immigration such as the United States and Canada. It is less evident in homogeneous and old-established societies such as France and Great Britain.

The greater the social distance and cultural divergencies between the receiving society and the incoming group, the greater obviously will be the degree of adaptation and acceptance needed to achieve a satisfactory coexistence. It should, however, be noted that in many cases adaptation and acceptance do not march hand in hand. Some groups may achieve an almost total adaptation, but for a while at least remain only partly acceptable; whereas others may adapt themselves only partially, but may meet with a large measure of acceptance. As instances, one may cite American Jewry on the one hand and the Dutch or British immigrants in the States on the other.

Assimilation

The most complete phase of absorption is that of the assimilation of groups or individuals. Assimilation is understood to mean complete adaptation by the immigrants, or more usually by the minority group or by individual members of it, to the values and patterns of the receiving society; such complete adaptation is accompanied by complete acceptance of the assimilating group of individuals on the part of the hosts.[2] This ultimate social phase of assimilation may of course lead to the physical amalgamation of the minority group. Instances of this are the amalgamation of the Huguenots in Britain and elsewhere; of Dutch, Germans, and Scandinavians in the United States

[1] The term 'adaptation' is here employed, as by Carey (1956, pp. 6–7), to denote social and group change, in preference to the term 'adjustment', which in common usage is applied to individual change.

[2] This does not necessarily imply a 'one-way-street' relationship. Before complete assimilation is achieved, the host society may have moved a considerable distance towards the newcomers. The process of assimilation differs in each situation, but wherever it happens it is understood as a process leading to a complete end-product, in terms of full adaptation and acceptance by both groups (cf. Banton, 1952), and not in terms of Robert E. Park's definition of the concept in the *Encyclopaedia of the Social Sciences* (Vol. 2, pp. 281–2).

and Canada; of the Hottentots in the Cape Colony; and, it would appear, of over ten thousand former Negro slaves in the population of London during the nineteenth century.[1]

Apart from a minority of particularly energetic individuals, complete assimilation rarely occurs in the first immigrant generation. This is true even in the case of immigrants who are socially acceptable and culturally close to the receiving society, such as the British in the older Dominions, West Indians in New York Negro society, Latin immigrants in South America, or Jewish newcomers in Israel.

Integration

The process of assimilation can apply to individuals or to groups. There is, however, another stage or phase of absorption that applies to groups only. This is 'integration', or cultural pluralism, a stage in which the incoming group as a whole, through its own organizations, adapts itself to permanent membership of the receiving society in certain major spheres of association, notably in economic and civic life. On its side, the receiving society accepts the group as a lasting entity, differing in certain spheres that do not directly affect the overall life of the society, such as religion, and cultural and family patterns, and sometimes even in the retention of a mother-tongue or second language or of secondary loyalties to a country of origin.

Canada provides a good example of a country of integration. There the processes of integration are not only at work but actively encouraged by the authorities. Integration has long been the basis of the relationship between the two original ethnic groups in Canada, the Anglo-Canadians and the French Canadians. The nineteenth-century immigration of other ethnic groups was to a considerable extent based on the isolated bloc or group settlement, which made assimilation virtually impossible and favoured the development of organized ethnic groups and the retention of separate cultural patterns. For practical political reasons, the Canadian government has made the organized ethnic group the keystone of its post-war absorption policy.[2] The current development of the Canadian nation may be envisaged on a pattern not unlike the sections of an orange – separable, but similar in outer form and making up a harmonious whole. The fact that the organized ethnic group is aiming at integration does not of course prevent a minority of individual members from making assimilation to one or other of the two original ethnic groups their immediate goal.

[1] Cf. Little, *Negroes in Britain* (1947, pp. 170–90).
[2] Cf. Corbett (1957, p. 94) and Borrie (1950, p. 95).

11

Integration can proceed upon an equal basis where, as in Canada, Belgium, or Switzerland, there is no single majority society, or where, as in the United Kingdom or France, the majority society is willing to accept the minority groups on an equal footing in the economic, civic, and even the social spheres.

On the other hand, integration can develop on an unequal basis, as in the Southern United States or the Union of South Africa. In the Southern States, as in other former slave societies, integration was imposed on members of the slave group by force. Assimilation was barred to them and they were compelled to make a minimal adaptation to their limited, lonely role, the only one in which the ruling society was willing to accept them. The situation today in the Southern States represents a conflict between the former slave group, striving in the direction of equal integration or even assimilation, and the majority society, most of whose members are still unable to accept the Negro minority in any but its former inferior role. In the Union of South Africa, a conquest state as well as a former slave state, the processes of unequal integration continue as the rural and tribal Africans are gradually sucked into the state's modern urban economy. The conflict here is similar to, but more acute than, that in the Southern States, as a result of the Union's demographic structure and geographical situation. In both cases, and indeed in most societies where integration has occurred on an unequal basis, the situation contains elements of grave instability and conflict.

To be satisfactory, integration on an equal basis requires a strong and adaptable minority group organization, which can negotiate successfully with the majority society on behalf of its members and can lead these members towards a consciousness of their formal duties as members of the overall society. Such an organization is rarely evolved in the first immigrant generation.

Ideologically motivated immigrant groups, whether they are religious or political in orientation, usually form strong in-group associations at an early stage. But these associations tend, at least in the first period of settlement, to be focused on goals connected with the group's original motivations. They therefore tend to retard integration or assimilation instead of helping their members to adapt themselves to the new life and to gain acceptance from the receiving society. At a later stage, however, these 'traditional' associations enlarge or change their functions, or are superseded by new emergent 'integrative' associations.

Economically motivated migrant groups, on the other hand, tend to be less organized at the outset, whether because their members are impermanent in their intentions, or simply because they migrate at will in small, unorganized groups and are usually from a peasant

12

or urban proletariat with little experience of formal organization.[1] Where there is geographical isolation or where there are great socio-economic and cultural differences between the newcomers and the receiving society, the immigrants generally find it necessary to set up parish self-help and cultural associations in the first years of settlement. Sooner or later, most of these associations become 'integrative' in function, or new associations are created to meet the changing situation.

Migrant or minority group organization helps to fill the social void into which the individual migrant moves when he leaves his home, village, and neighbourhood; his friends and most if not all of his kinsmen; and all the familiar, everyday associations. For all migrants other than the few who are immediately acceptable in the new society and who are more or less adapted to it on arrival, the evolution of a strong internal group organization would seem to offer the best prospects of adaptation and acceptance in the new environment. First-generation assimilation usually takes place only in the case of particularly adaptable and acceptable individuals; it is often associated with intermarriage, although intermarriage does not automatically lead to acceptance and assimilation.

Integration can be either an intermediary phase in group relations, leading to ultimate assimilation, or a final phase in the absorptive process. The latter situation can arise either where the majority society withholds complete acceptance; or where the minority group itself continues to resist assimilation; or again where there are no majority or minority groups, but several large groups coexisting equally, usually with both a linguistic and a territorial basis. Such instances as Switzerland, Belgium, and Canada seem to indicate that assimilation and ethnic amalgamation are not a necessary or even a necessarily desirable sequel to integration. Indeed, these integrated pluralistic societies may provide a more satisfactory model for future political development in Western Europe and elsewhere than the unitary assimilationist societies.

Accommodation

In the first generation of migration, and certainly in the first years, we are usually concerned neither with assimilation nor with integration but with the phase of accommodation.[2] Like assimilation, this

[1] Some of the old bloc settlements in Canada and the Polish village settlements in France and Belgium constitute exceptions to this.
[2] This term is taken from Zubrzycki's study of Polish immigrants in Britain (1956, p. 76) and approximates to the process which he describes there, although I do not subscribe to his acceptance of 'conflict' as a separate stage in the process of absorption.

early phase of adaptation and acceptance is a process that can apply both to individuals and to groups, though members of the better organized groups are more likely to achieve a satisfactory preliminary adaptation and to be accorded a certain degree of acceptance by the receiving society. Like integration, accommodation can take place on an equal or an unequal basis, although the latter kind of process is unlikely to lead to satisfactory integration or assimilation.

Accommodation may be defined as the achieving of a *modus vivendi* between newcomers and the receiving society. The migrants establish themselves to an adequate extent economically and residentially, and conform at least outwardly to the new society's basic norms. For the receiving society, accommodation involves a limited acceptance of the newcomers. This acceptance is likely to be greater in some situations than in others. In egalitarian societies, for instance, it will be more complete in such universal and institutionalized areas of association as employment, public services, education, and legal and political rights; but in less defined and more intimate areas of association, such as residential proximity, private social intercourse, and intermarriage, the degree of acceptance is likely to be much less. The same considerations apply to the degree of adaptation by the migrants in the various areas of association.

Accommodation is thus the least degree of adaptation and acceptance that is consistent with peaceful coexistence between immigrants and the receiving society in the earlier period of contact. In the phase of accommodation, the newcomers are able to retain or rebuild their own social and cultural patterns. This helps to relieve the tensions set up among the newcomers by the compulsion to adapt themselves in other major spheres.

Group accommodation may pass over almost imperceptibly into the further phase of integration or assimilation, as economic migrants accept the permanence of their settlement, and political or religious exiles re-orient themselves towards their country of refuge. The transition may be said to take place when the migrant or the minority associations begin to devote most of their endeavour to acting as intermediaries between their members and the receiving or majority society rather than functioning as separatist, protest, or militant bodies.

In the foregoing account, these various phases of the processes of adaptation and acceptance have perhaps been made to appear too self-conscious and straightforward. In fact, they impinge on one another and overlap, or move at different rates in different spheres.

14

For instance, an accommodating group may often be more or less integrated in the economic and residential spheres, as the Southern Irish and the Poles are in Britain. Again, an individual may be fully assimilated in economic life, and even married to a member of the receiving society, and yet may continue to play an active part in his integrating or separatist group organization. In the first generation, this dualism of orientations and behaviour is very noticeable, particularly amongst younger European political exiles.

Moreover, as Douglas Manley (1958, p. 8) has pointed out, these stages do not necessarily occur in a tidy progression, but may proceed in steps and pauses; an immigrant group or a receiving society may make a major effort to adapt or to accept, and may then pause for years or decades. At times, there may even be the phenomenon of an apparent partial return to the old values and loyalties. We find an instance of this in Canada, where the many second- and third-generation Poles and Ukrainians have been re-imbued with 'old country' values by the new *élite* of political exiles. Such reversion may also be associated with limited acceptance on the part of the majority society.

I have already commented on the fact that adaptation and acceptance do not always proceed side by side. It should also be noted that the various processes of adaptation and acceptance may be consciously guided and furthered by the receiving or majority society. Such guidance is often found in countries of immigration, and even in Britain the initial reception of Polish ex-servicemen and European Voluntary Workers was carefully planned after the second world war. On the other hand, these processes may develop undirected and influenced only by the natural interplay of social and economic forces.

For many first-generation migrant groups, then, accommodation is the only phase of adaptation and acceptance that can be postulated. This is particularly true of habitual or transient migrants, such as the seasonal migrants of late nineteenth-century Europe, the Southern Irish in Britain, the Puerto Ricans in New York, and the West Indian migrants in the Americas; it is also true of migrants from a sociocultural environment that differs widely from that of the new society.

In the present study, accommodation was found to be the only useful concept to apply in analysing the relationships developing between West Indians and the receiving society. For the beginnings of the settlement are only a decade away, and the bulk of the newcomers are still oriented towards their home and their former way of life. They are preoccupied with dreams of a speedy and a rich return; and they are unwilling or unequipped to make more than a minimal adaptation to the new environment, although the English 'bias' in their social and cultural background does incline many of them to expect immediate and complete acceptance without any corresponding adaptation on their part. On the other hand, the majority of people in Britain still regard the West Indian newcomers as strangers and outsiders, as they do the Hungarians, the Italians, and at times the Southern Irish. This combination of high expectations with limited adaptability and limited acceptability is, as will be seen, a frequent cause of frustration and conflict among the immigrants, and tends to impede the process of accommodation.[1]

If many of the West Indian migrants become permanent settlers, the phase of accommodation will ultimately pass over into a further process. Whether that will be one of assimilation, as their socio-cultural background would suggest, or of group integration on an equal or an unequal basis, it is too soon to say. In this study we can only indicate trends which point in one direction or another.

ACCOMMODATION AND ITS INDICES IN BRITAIN

In this study I have set out to describe and analyse the processes of accommodation, that is to say of minimal adaptation and acceptance, in three main areas of association in Brixton. The first two are the areas in which an accommodating migrant group must make its major effort and in which it comes most closely and most often in contact and competition, and sometimes in conflict, with the receiving society – those of economic life and housing. In Britain, after all, everyone must gain his living in some way and find some place of shelter. The third area is one in which initial contacts between the two sides tend to be either casual or else formal and institutionalized – the whole range of social life, including religious association.[2] I have also included chapters on the migrant group itself, on its values and goals, its reactions to the receiving society around it, and its evolving internal social organization.

In a smaller-scale and more intensive investigation it might have been possible to measure more precisely the degree of migrant accommodation in the particular areas of association. In this work the aim has been to give a general, rather impressionistic picture of a very fluid situation, and to indicate certain trends.

[1] 'There is a certain confusion . . . on the part of the coloured immigrant. This is because he guides himself in terms of a logic of complete acceptance, whereas Britons act in terms of much more limited acceptance' (Ruth Landes, 1952).

[2] A fair amount of material was collected on contacts in other areas of association, particularly in political life and between the second migrant generation and their coevals and teachers at school. These aspects will be discussed in later publications.

It was, nevertheless, necessary to postulate some indices of accommodation in the various areas of association. These would obviously be modest and limited, and far from the thorough-going completeness of the indices to be applied in the stage of assimilation. In Brixton, therefore, it seemed unreasonable to expect more than a limited will to adapt among the West Indians, or a limited will to accept among the local population. Nor did it seem likely at this juncture that one would find any appreciable number of West Indians in supervisory posts or even in skilled jobs in South London industry, or in official positions in a trade union. Again, one would not expect to find large numbers of recent West Indian migrants owning one-family houses in middle-class residential areas, belonging to exclusive sports and social clubs, or serving as churchwardens in Anglican churches.

The gauges of accommodation seemed to be more modest, although they might go further in the economic sphere, for example, than in intimate social relationships. One might hope to find West Indian workers settling in a job with one firm; generally conforming to British workers' customs and accepting their viewpoints; joining the union where this is customary; being taken on by employers on merit and not as stopgap labour; not being laid off simply because they are regarded as outsiders; beginning to get promotion on grounds of ability and seniority. In the residential sphere, one might expect to find West Indian tenants being accepted by white landlords in a working-class area; and West Indian landlords enforcing certain standards of domestic hygiene and behaviour among their tenants, maintaining or improving their houses, and achieving a reasonable *modus vivendi* with their white tenants.

Turning to social relationships, one could hope to find West Indians observing such peculiar native habits as queueing; accepting local *mores* with regard to women met in the street; ceasing to regard ignorant but well-meaning remarks about their colour or way of life as deliberate insults to their race; becoming regular and welcome clients in the local pub. A few might vote in local elections or attend a local church regularly, although apathy in both these respects would perhaps be more indicative of full adaptation to local *mores*. One might also expect to find West Indian men marrying sooner, and taking a more permanent interest in their children's security and education.

On the other side, local people might be expected to be used to the presence of coloured people in public places, and not to stare at them or draw away from them in the streets, shops, or pubs; to offer new West Indian neighbours the customary welcome and cup of tea; to worship (if they go to church at all) side by side with the new-

17

comers; to judge individuals on their merits, without falling back on old preconceptions or generalizations based on superficial evidence. One might also expect the local press to stop lurid headlining of migrant misdemeanours, crimes, or antisocial behaviour.

SOME FACTORS THAT INFLUENCE THE PROCESSES OF ACCOMMODATION AMONG MIGRANTS AND IN THE RECEIVING SOCIETY

In discussing the processes of accommodation, I shall try to evaluate the major factors that assist or impede adaptation and acceptance in a given sphere. These factors are many and various.[1] They include the attitudes, preconceptions, and expectations of the migrant group and of the receiving society; differences of social class, religious and cultural background, and organizational methods; visible and audible differentiation;[2] personal idiosyncrasies; degrees of industrial skills and training; urban or rural provenance; the motivations and intentions of the migrant group; political ideologies; and such material situations as an economic recession or a housing shortage. Another factor that is often found to have a material effect on a given local situation is the existence or absence on the receiving side of highly prejudiced individuals or cliques in key positions, or of influential individuals or organizations who act as local sponsors[3] for the group or for individual newcomers. Also of importance are the degree of organization within the migrant group, and the presence of migrant leaders who are suited to act as intermediaries between their group and the local society. Adaptation and acceptance may also be greatly affected by historical events and traditional relationships between the two groups; by past economic experiences and existing economic pull-and-push factors generally; by ecological and demographic considerations; and by health and climatic factors.[4]

As Collins (1957, pp. 16–17) has pointed out in his study of various coloured minority groups in Britain, the interplay of so many factors can produce and has produced a large number of different local situations. In one district, for instance, a migrant settlement may become disillusioned and hostile as a result of discriminatory acts by the local population; in another, such a develop-

[1] Cf. Eisenstadt (1954, p. 10) on the variables that determine these processes.
[2] 'How would one explain race or ethnic prejudice to Helen Keller?' asked a linguist at a recent race relations conference. On the other hand, frequent misunderstandings and friction owing to differences of accent or English usage were noted during the course of field work.
[3] Cf. Collins (1957, pp. 30–2).
[4] See Appendix XI.

ment may not occur, perhaps because of previous good relationships or as a result of the intervention of a sponsor or the influence of a migrant or minority leader; in a third area, a small economic recession may evoke a wave of xenophobia among local workers; in yet another, which may lack the same bitter economic memories, and in which the unions and employees stand firm against discrimination, there will, on the contrary, be little or no local demand for coloured or foreign workers to be laid off first.

Motivations and expectations can be a particularly important factor.[1] The basic motivation of a minority or migrant group may be classified as economic or ideological. Ideologically motivated groups usually intend either to return to their own country when the situation changes or to preserve on alien soil the political or religious ideals which led or compelled them to migrate. Their expectations from the receiving society will be limited, their main wish being to be left in peace to pursue their own activities and goals. If they plan to return home they will merely accommodate themselves to the new environment; if they decide to settle they will ultimately move towards integration. Groups of this type rarely expect or demand complete initial acceptance in the early stage of settlement. And provided their goals are not inconsistent with the universal patterns and values of the receiving society, their hosts will not usually exert undue assimilatory pressure on them.

A similar evolution occurs in the case of certain economically motivated groups which are culturally or religiously distinctive. In Britain, this applies particularly to the Chinese, Moslem, and Hindu communities. Provided these groups conform outwardly in certain respects, the host society usually tolerates their presence and their distinctiveness. On the other hand, other economic migrant groups, such as the West Indians, lack any such distinctive and exclusive social organization and culture which might serve as a basis for group cohesion. In the absence of any strong group organization, their members remain impermanent in their intentions or are driven to seek assimilation before the receiving society is willing to accept them. If a migrant group combines impermanent intentions with a high expectation of acceptance, its relationship with the host society is even less likely to progress smoothly. On the migrant side, therefore, motivations, intentions, and expectations are important factors in conditioning the processes of adaptation and acceptance.

On the other side, the receiving society's attitudes and behaviour towards various groups of outsiders in different kinds of situation also exert an important influence on the migrant group and therefore on the development of migrant-host relations. Attitudes and be-

[1] Cf. Eisenstadt (1954, pp. 227–8 and 242–58) on motivations.

haviour towards outsiders are often favourable and helpful, as we shall see when we consider the activities of sponsoring individuals and organizations. But it is the unfavourable instances that attract attention and produce the difficulties and problems that are the *raison d'être* for so many sociological studies of immigration.

These difficulties and problems are often expressed in terms of such concepts as 'prejudice' and 'discrimination'; it therefore seems advisable at this point to clarify what I understand by these and other terms which I shall be using in this study, and to say a few words on the connections between them.

'Prejudice' is here understood as the emotional, irrational, and rigid disposition that exists in some individuals in relation to certain groups or things. Theoretically, a prejudiced disposition could be either favourable or hostile. In practice, however, the term is usually applied to a rigidly hostile disposition, one that is not amenable to reason or modification in the light of first-hand experience.[1]

The great majority of people in British society cannot be called prejudiced in this sense.[2] They do, however, have a number of rather unfavourable predispositions and attitudes towards certain groups of outsiders which may be derived from either second-hand information or first-hand experience, whether superficial or profound, misleading or relevant. These predispositions are not rigid but are potentially susceptible to rational modification, and they should be clearly distinguished from prejudice.

The term 'antipathy' has been put forward to describe this milder and much more widely encountered state of mind.[3] As will emerge later, the range of intensity of such antipathies is very wide, from a mild reaction of avoidance to a vehement hostility which in its manifestations in action may be superficially indistinguishable from

---

[1] In his Jaques Cohen Memorial Lecture on 'Prejudice', Ginsberg suggests 'prepossession' for this favourable disposition (1959, p. 1).

[2] In his book, *The Colour Problem* (1955, p. 240), Anthony Richmond, using the results of a still unpublished survey of British attitudes towards coloured colonials conducted in 1951, asserted that the population could be divided into three groups of roughly equal size according to their degree of prejudice, one-third being extremely prejudiced, one-third mildly prejudiced, and one-third tolerant. After criticism by Banton of the method of scaling used in the sample survey, Richmond modified his position (1958, p. 345), conceding that attitudes in Britain are probably more favourable and less rigid than he had supposed. The results of Banton's own smaller sample survey of attitudes in six British towns would suggest that only one in twenty-five of the British population would consciously subscribe to doctrines of racial superiority, though this would not mean that all of them were rigidly prejudiced by our definition, nor that all were prepared to translate such opinions into action (Banton, 1959, p. 37).

[3] Banton (1959, p. 30). (This is accepted by Henderson, 1960, p. 97.) Banton points out that the corresponding favourable predisposition would be one of 'sympathy'; we shall have occasion later in this study to consider the importance of such a predisposition in connection with the activities of 'sponsors'.

the manifestations of extreme prejudice. An effort should be made, however, to distinguish between the state of mind of a man who shows hostility to the Japanese in general because his family starved to death in a Far East internment camp and he himself was ill-treated while working on the Burma Road, and that of a prejudiced person who had no close or prolonged contacts with Asians but who instigates or takes part in an attack on a Chinese laundry in Limehouse 'just to show the yellow bastards'. In general, it is maintained that a mild and not a vehement degree of antipathy to foreigners and outsiders is the cultural norm in Britain.[1]

Having made this distinction between 'prejudice' and 'antipathy', we turn to 'discrimination'. In the sociological context, this may be defined as the differential treatment of persons ascribed to particular categories. Discrimination can be favourable, as when an employment exchange interviewer does not send a coloured applicant to a firm which he knows will refuse to take the man on. But since the term is customarily applied to unfavourable or hostile acts, it seems best to speak of 'differentiation' when the action is beneficent in intention.

Discrimination, then, is a way of behaving. There are no discriminatory predispositions, but only discriminatory actions. Prejudice and discrimination often go together, and each may encourage the other, but prejudiced people do not always or necessarily behave in a discriminatory way. And, what is more important for the sociological student of race relations, discrimination is not always or necessarily the outcome of prejudice. The study of race relations has long been bedevilled by what is called the 'prejudice-discrimination axis': [2] this is based on the erroneous hypothesis that behaviour is simply an outward expression of attitudes, and hence is to be studied and understood in terms of attitudes. Thus, discriminatory behaviour is seen as arising out of prejudiced attitudes and is equated with 'prejudiced behaviour'. This hypothesis lies behind the great bulk of research on Negro-white relations in the United States, and its persistence is easier to understand in that context. When, however, it is applied to the new and highly fluid situation in Britain, where migrant-host relations are usually not central but peripheral, its inadequacy becomes evident.

During the course of the Brixton study a considerable amount of discriminatory behaviour towards migrants was observed. But in the overwhelming majority of cases it seemed clear that this behaviour,

[1] Cf. Richmond (1958, p. 347).
[2] See Herbert Blumer's critical study of race-relations research in the United States since 1945 (1958, p. 420 and *passim*).

21

like most non-discriminatory behaviour, was primarily determined not by individual attitudes but by the nature and requirements of the particular social situation,[1] and by generally shared social orientations, values, and norms. Thus the widespread mild antipathy to outsiders to which reference has been made might be displayed without evoking social condemnation in a refusal to allow one's daughter to marry a coloured suitor. It would, however, evoke considerable disapproval if displayed in a refusal to allow a coloured worker to join a trade union, and for this reason the second kind of refusal would be less likely to occur.

Last-ditch defenders of the 'prejudice-discrimination axis' as a formula for explaining the racial situation in Britain are not daunted by the increasingly evident disparity between the relatively favourable attitudes towards coloured people expressed by the majority of British people and the obvious existence of a good deal of discrimination against them. One is frequently accused of naïveté for accepting more or less at their face value the explanations given by many individuals for acts of discrimination in which they disclaim any prejudiced or hostile feelings but advance economic fears, cultural differences, or considerations of social status for their actions. These, one is told, are rationalizations produced to cover the prejudiced attitude that was the true motivation of the discriminatory action.

I do not deny that some informants may prefer to explain their actions in terms which they think more acceptable to the interviewer and to society at large. A few informants may even be highly prejudiced persons who are cunningly disguising their own attitudes. But during the course of my field work I came to the conclusion that the majority of South London informants were giving the true reasons for their behaviour. When a landlady said that she politely refused coloured applicants because the other tenants would not like it and the neighbours would gossip, she was probably describing the neighbourhood situation as she saw it. When an employer set a quota for his intake of coloured labour on the grounds that to have more would slow down production and cause labour difficulties, he was usually speaking from his own experience or that of nearby employers. When lower-middle-class parents refused to allow their daughter to marry a coloured man because they objected to West Indian attitudes to marriage and sex and considered that the children of such a marriage would be socially handicapped, this was not usually a cloak for some rigid belief in racist doctrine but a

---

[1] The extent of discrimination against coloured people and, indeed, against outsiders in general, was in fact found to vary according to the nature of the situation, in a rank order of discrimination similar to that drawn up by Gunnar Myrdal (1944).

reflection of the highly conformist social climate in which they and their daughter are living.

It therefore seemed permissible to leave the study of the prejudiced attitudes and behaviour found among a small minority of individuals to the psychologists, and, instead, to concentrate on the social determinants of interracial behaviour and relationships, and on the group orientations, values, and norms that seem to condition and motivate this behaviour on either side over a whole range of situations.

THE 'COLOUR-CLASS' AND 'STRANGER' HYPOTHESES

Although discriminatory behaviour may have a number of motivations, two major hypotheses have been advanced to explain its prevalence and the varying forms it takes in varying situations in Britain. These are the 'colour-class' hypothesis first advanced by Kenneth Little (1947, p. 232) and the 'stranger' hypothesis supported by Michael Banton.[1] According to the first, British society is thought, largely as a result of its colonial past, to identify coloured people with the lowest social class; according to the second, they are seen as the archetypal strangers, both in appearance and in behaviour, in a society in which mild xenophobia is a norm.

Little's 'colour-class' hypothesis was formulated to suit the long-established, rather static situation which he encountered in the Cardiff dock area. Banton's 'stranger' hypothesis, on the other hand, emerged most explicitly in the analysis of his survey of racial attitudes in six inland areas, of which four had a settlement of coloured newcomers, while two had few or none. The two hypotheses are by no means incompatible, as Banton (1959, p. 81) saw, and each was found valuable in analysing the Brixton material.

In Brixton the West Indians are regarded as outsiders and strangers *par excellence*. This is not only because of their recent arrival and conspicuously different appearance, but because superficial observation suggests that many of them do in fact react and behave very differently from the majority of local people. The West Indians are also on the whole relegated to the lowest social class, not only because of preconceptions stemming from the colonial era, but because the great majority of them are observably in the lowest socio-economic bracket and because their behaviour patterns seem to conform to an outmoded nineteenth-century model of lower

---

[1] See, in particular, Banton (1958) and (1959, Chapter 5 *passim*).

working-class behaviour rather than to any current Brixtonian norms.[1]

Superficial first-hand observation by local people has on the whole supported the widely held preconceptions about both the strangeness and the low status of the coloured newcomers. These orientations undoubtedly condition the behaviour of Brixtonians to West Indians in many situations, particularly those which are intimate and uninstitutionalized, in which the relationship depends on acceptance by both sides of the same unwritten norms and values. As yet, however, such orientations are not particularly rigid, and in the majority of cases would be subject to modification as part of the overall process of accommodation. If for any reason such accommodation did not occur, attitudes could harden on both sides, the element of 'strangeness' and unexpectedness would decrease, and a 'colour-class' pattern could be established in the second immigrant generation, as it was in Cardiff.

---

[1] For a more detailed consideration of British attitudes to and preconceptions about outsiders in general and coloured people in particular, see pp. 228–35.

2

Field-work methods

THE FIELD researcher in the social sciences starts off with three main elements: his general terms of reference; his human material in the form of the group or groups whose organization or interrelationships are to be studied; and what Dollard calls the 'primary research instrument', that is to say, the researcher himself, with his own intellectual equipment and training, his personality, attitudes, and limitations. All three elements condition his working procedure and the third and personal element may influence his conclusions. The question of possible bias will be considered later in this chapter.

We have already discussed the terms of reference of the Brixton study and the main theoretical concepts and problems involved. The migrant group and the local receiving society will be described in the next chapter. It now remains to say something about the field-work methods employed, and about the researcher's personal approach to the situation.

Here it should be said that field work in a complex urban or race-relations situation is not always in practice the smooth and orderly procedure that is presented in the methodological sections of many sociological studies. Such elaborate methodological discussions would carry more conviction, and would make less depressing reading for debutant field workers, if they were accompanied by an account of the long hours and even days of apparently wasted endeavour; of the time spent in following false scents; in reading books, pamphlets, and other literature that yield only a few lines of valid information; in writing to people who do not answer or have moved without leaving an address; in telephoning people who either slam down the receiver or make an appointment and then do not keep it; of the hours spent visiting people who are suspicious and have no particular desire to talk, or others who talk like the ancient mariner but never on the desired subject; of the wear-and-tear on the digestion that results from eating large dishes of unfamiliar food, or from drinking neat proof rum or fizzy tepid soft drinks at odd hours; of attempts to conduct interviews, guided, open-ended or whatever they are subsequently called, with the tired informant's

25

children crying for food or a fresh nappy, with the radio or television on full blast, with the husband sitting suspiciously in a corner, or with the neighbours popping in and out.

On the more cheerful side, such an account of actual field work might also mention how much information can be picked up by shopping in the local market, strolling round the streets in the evening, sitting in a pub, or riding on buses; and how a chance remark may often open up a whole new line of inquiry, or illumine an old one, even to a point where the original terms of reference are seen to need some recasting.

THE SOCIAL ANTHROPOLOGIST'S APPROACH

The study of race relations has attracted social anthropologists, sociologists, and social psychologists. Each discipline relies on its accustomed techniques, though one may borrow from another when it seems useful. The main tools of the social anthropologist are direct observation and the interview. Most race-relations situations, however, occur in complex literate societies, where these tools can often be supplemented by the use of documentary materials, by quantitative data, and, if necessary, by such techniques as questionnaires and psychological tests.

The object of the present study was to ascertain to what extent a migrant group of several thousand West Indians had adapted itself to and become accepted in a South London borough with a population of nearly a quarter of a million. Had the inquiry been concerned only with the local population, a sample might have been constructed and a questionnaire applied. But in the case of the West Indian migrant group, the construction of a valid sample would have been rendered difficult, if not impossible, by reason of the recent arrival of most members (mainly after the last census report), of the changing demographic structure of the group, and of its high mobility.

In such a large-scale study of inter-group relationships, it seemed best to seek the point of contact in the various major areas of association, and to use the interview, supported by participant or semi-participant observation, as the main method of gathering firsthand material from the persons involved. Written questionnaires were not applied to the migrants, but sets of questions suitable for interviews with employers, personnel managers, trade union officials, welfare workers, ministers, and others were worked out in the early months of field work and were used extensively.

I was unable to live in the area for family and other reasons. I did, however, spend four or five days and often evenings in the Brixton neighbourhood each week over a period of two and a half years, interviewing, observing, or participating in various local or migrant activities.

During this period I interviewed some 250 local white people and about 150 coloured people. These interviews rarely lasted for less than one hour; many went on much longer. They were as informal as possible and, except in the case of officials, personnel managers, welfare workers, and others who were giving detailed factual information, written notes were not made till later. There is no need to dilate further on the inhibiting effect on relatively unsophisticated people of the sudden production of paper and pencil by the interviewer.

In both groups, about one-third of those interviewed were visited twice, and thirty white individuals and forty coloured individuals were seen on several occasions. About fifteen persons in each group fell within the category of informants who were aware of the general nature of the inquiry and took an active interest in it, sometimes to the extent of becoming gatherers of information themselves.

The choice of people for interview was not, as we have said, based on any sampling procedure, nor is there any guarantee that these informants were fully representative either of the receiving society or of the migrant group. Most of the white people interviewed were those found at various points of contact, official or unofficial, between the migrants and the bulk of the local population. They included housing and other local government officials; Ministry of Labour and National Assistance Board employees; probation, health, and youth officers; teachers; personnel managers, factory foremen, trade union officials; doctors, nurses, and almoners; ministers of religion; welfare and voluntary workers; political agents; house agents; publicans and shop-keepers in the nearby streets; neighbours; and white girls married to or living with coloured men.

The coloured people interviewed were those who could be found at any of these points of contact with white people, and their relations, friends, and fellow-tenants. Throughout, attempts were made to contact the average migrant rather than the unusual or biased individuals who tend to attract a researcher's attention most easily, and who are often more willing to give information or to express their frustration and grievances. All field workers face the problem of making initial contact with the group or community they wish to study. All the same, it is rare to find a migrant group so mobile and so unorganized that one has difficulty in meeting any of its members at all, save by the desperate expedient of knocking at doors or speaking to individuals casually encountered in the streets. These expedients would not, as it turned out, have been desirable ways of making contact with this unsettled and somewhat suspicious group of newcomers. In the Brixton inquiry, my task was rendered even more difficult by the fact that I had nothing tangible to offer the migrants in the form of assistance, work, or accommodation in the Brixton area, which might have served as an adequate introduction. The problem was eventually solved by means which are discussed in more detail in Appendix III. The extreme initial difficulty which I experienced in this respect had the additional consequence, as I have already explained, of causing me to modify my initial terms of reference: it was clearly futile to evaluate this kind of situation in terms of assimilation or even of integration, and so I was led to adopt the much more useful concept of accommodation.

THE INVESTIGATOR'S 'ROLE'

With the primary problem of making contact went the important problem of the investigator's role. As Banton (1955) wrote of his field research in Stepney:

'It very quickly became apparent that the analogy of the anthropologist working in a small self-contained society was not applicable, and that there was no ideal role for an investigator. . . . The anthropologist who works in an urban society can see only a fraction of its social life and the members of the society can keep him at a distance if they wish. Participant observation has to be complete if it is to be successful; the observer can ask only those questions appropriate to his role, and in urban living many more matters are thought to be a person's private business. On the other hand, valuable information can be obtained by the use of participant observation techniques in the urban situation by the worker who can give only part of his time to research and who is able to continue this for several years. . . . The investigator, be he white or coloured, will almost always stand out from his informers. The advantage which a coloured investigator will have in working with the immigrants is certain to be offset by reticence on the part of officials and by hostility by some elements of the coloured population itself' (p. 113).

In more stable and organized urban situations, the field worker is sometimes able to adopt the role of a welfare worker, or an evening class instructor, or other roles which give initial access to a fair number of migrants, without causing the investigator to be unduly identified with an officialdom which the migrants may regard with some suspicion or dislike.[1] If the inquiry concerns inter-group relationships, and is not simply a study of a minority or migrant group, the investigator must also, if he is to give an adequate picture of both sides, avoid being identified with the minority or migrant group by local officials and the receiving society in general. Role is of most importance at the beginning of a study, when a proper choice may enable the field worker to make a considerable number of satisfactory contacts. The adoption of too limited or defined a role can limit the type of contact; for instance, an investigator who has adopted the role of welfare worker will evoke some surprise and comment if he or she is seen in a shebeen or a jive club.

In the unstable, unorganized Brixton situation I could find no specific official or semi-official role that would have produced sufficient contacts or material to justify the additional time required for its performance. I therefore presented myself to initial sponsors and contacts under my true colours, as a university researcher carrying out a study of migrant-host relationships in South London. As the network of sponsors and contacts grew, explanations became increasingly perfunctory and personal, and most people interviewed, whether coloured or white, seemed to accept me as a person of good will, connected in some unspecified way with the academic or welfare world, as someone who 'wrote books', who had travelled a good deal, who made no value judgements or criticisms of conduct, and who was a good listener, interested not only in the newcomers but in the local people.

For many West Indians I provided a safety-valve, a channel for grievances and criticisms of the society to which I belonged. It soon became clear that a great deal of this froth of verbal aggression should be blown off and discounted as a serious expression of migrant attitudes and intentions. With the migrants I also acquired merit as a person who, unlike the majority of the whites who surrounded them, had been in the West Indies and understood, in part at least, the complexities and the standards of their culture. When meeting new West Indian contacts, indeed, I soon learned to open the conversation with a discussion of their home towns or

---

[1] Cf. Little (1947, p. 29). At the outset of his inquiry in Cardiff, Dr. Kenneth Little gained official permission to conduct an anthropometric study of the mixed blood children at the largest school in the district. Even this procedure, however, was found to be 'by no means ideal as an entrée'. This was, according to Little, 'mainly because of popular hearsay regarding the results of racial mixture. It was thought (and publicly suggested) by some of the coloured men that the anthropometry was an insidious, though not clearly understood, attempt to discredit them through their children. . . . One of the older men summed up the fairly general reaction of those who took any interest in the matter by asking: "What is it that makes us any different from anyone else?" '

islands, and to mention the fact that I had spent some time in the West Indies. The immediate increase in friendliness was usually remarkable. Some migrants, no doubt, regarded me as a spy of officialdom. Some local people, on the other hand, tended to receive me as an academic negrophile looking for evidence of colour prejudice or discrimination in the simplest acts or utterances. These charges were rarely made overtly, and seemed to emanate mainly from an inordinately colour-conscious, atypical, or antisocial fringe in either group.

Although I adopted no overall role for the purposes of this study, I found myself adopting many subordinate roles, some temporary, others more permanent. Such roles were those of adviser, chauffeur, guide to the sights of London, baby-sitter, confidante, 'our Mrs. P.', and in two cases the more permanent role of godmother. The performance of these subsidiary roles in relation to various individuals sometimes presented practical problems. For instance, a number of key informants lived in the same street and spent a good deal of their time watching what went on there. Since they were usually alien from one another temperamentally, or in regional or social origins, I had to exercise some ingenuity in timing my visits to individuals.

The difficulties which I encountered in making contact with West Indian migrants were not duplicated in the case of local people and officials. Indeed, to a researcher familiar with the caution, suspiciousness, or downright hostility with which so many South African whites, particularly officials, meet any inquiry into race relations, the friendly attitude of the majority of South Londoners of all capacities and classes came as a pleasant surprise. Only a minority of those in official positions showed initial apprehension about the objectivity of the study, on the assumption that academic investigators tended to be negrophile and to look for colour prejudice and discrimination everywhere. One of the main hazards in official interviews was the possibility that, where informants agree on a point, this might be because their information came from the same second-hand source and was not the product of their own experience.

LIMITATIONS AND POSSIBILITIES OF THE 'PRIMARY RESEARCH INSTRUMENT'

At the beginning of this section, we mentioned three elements in the field-work situation. The third element is that of the researcher himself, who can be his own best or his own worst research instrument. If he is to make proper use of this instrument, he must be aware of its possibilities and limitations. In research which is

30

primarily based on interviews and participant observation, such factors as the researcher's sex, age, class affiliation, and general attitudes and interests will clearly affect the nature of the contacts that are made and the type of information that is obtained.[1] The universal interviewer is a rare phenomenon, and one perhaps more likely to be found in the press world or among welfare workers than in academic life. Other interviewers must face the fact that they are able to establish rapport with certain groups and kinds of people more easily than with others, and that the material obtained from the former is likely to be more complete. It may not always be more accurate, however, since the informant may, because of his immediate liking for the interviewer, be more concerned either to give the interviewer the sort of information the latter is thought to be seeking, or to present himself in a good light.

So far as the present study is concerned, it may be said that I found myself more immediately at ease with the women migrants than with the men, with the settled than with the unsettled, and with middle-aged people and children than with adolescents and young adults. With local informants, these limitations did not apply to the same extent, presumably because one is more familiar and at ease with most sections of one's own society.

Some difficulties of contact with less settled male migrants, who tended to classify the white women with whom they normally came into contact either as welfare workers or as potential sex partners, were avoided by the frequent presence of my husband. In general, the latter, as a European 'foreigner' with no colonial background and no preconceived notions about coloured people, was sometimes able to establish a closer rapport with individuals who could not forget that I was both white and British. The fact that he was a 'foreigner' gave some migrants the opportunity to patronize him mildly from the standpoint of their British citizenship, while others tended to feel a certain underdog kinship with him. 'Yo' people and mine—they sho' know what it is to be exploited by an imperialist power', said one politically conscious British Guianian.

In so far as the age of the researcher affects his attitudes and relationships, it should be said that anthropologists usually do their field work in the earlier years of their career. This may well account for their tendency to study minority groups and the under-privileged generally, and their relative lack of sympathy with the conforming majority. Older field workers may be more objective and have

[1] To give an instance: many male personnel or works managers, especially those of the older generation, hesitated to mention to a woman inquirer instances of friction between coloured and white workers involving sex or personal hygiene. Consequently, I had sometimes to resort to leading questions to show that I was aware of the possibility of such friction.

31

more self-confidence in social relationships, and can approach officials with greater authority. On the debit side, however, they may be less flexible, more set in their attitudes and behaviour, and more apt to see patterns which earlier field work and reading have led them to expect, and to overlook or underestimate others of equal significance.

WHITE AND COLOURED INVESTIGATORS IN A COLOUR-CONTACT SITUATION

In a situation involving colour differences and colour consciousness, such as the Brixton one, the researcher must also appreciate the limitations imposed upon him by his pigmentation. In a study of race relations, the white researcher has an advantage over the non-white researcher only in relation to his own group. In South Africa, the Southern States, and perhaps in Britain, this may make it easier for him to get official information, cooperation, and support. The non-white researcher has an advantage over his white colleague in gathering information from other coloured people. In most colour-contact situations involving West Indians, Dr. F. M. Henriques, who describes himself as a 'dark, upper-class Jamaican', goes so far as to write (1953):

'. . . Because of the very nature of the material, and because of the colour-conscious personality of the individual involved, the European investigator is at a great disadvantage in gathering data. The acute colour-consciousness of the West Indian inhibits him from giving information to someone who represents the values he himself is lacking but trying to attain. Some information will be forthcoming, but much of it will be garbled and dressed to suit what the informant thinks are the ideas of the white investigator. This problem is met with in primitive societies but not to the same extent and degree, as the primitive informant does not necessarily feel that information given will affect his social status as so many West Indians do. . . . The real difficulty lies in the fact that the European is unable to discover whether his material is authentic or not' (p. 45).[1]

In plural coloured communities the coloured researcher has specific problems of his own. He is likely to be regarded with suspicion by sections of his own national group, because of class or political divisions. Other coloured groups will tend to regard him as almost as much of an outsider as the white investigator. In his study

[1] For a criticism of this viewpoint, see R. T. Smith (1956, p. 238).

of the Liverpool Negro community, Douglas Manley (1958, pp. 41–2) records that as a West Indian he had to obtain his information concerning the local African tribal unions at second hand rather than by means of direct observation. He also mentions the resentment caused by 'a well-meaning but tactless individual' who introduced an African into a private meeting of a West Indian organization. Manley adds that, even if he had succeeded in joining a tribal association, he would have 'run the risk of antagonizing the West Indians and of being identified with one particular tribe by all other Africans'. Finally, he mentions his own initial problem of contact. He was known to be of middle-class background, whereas nearly all the West Indians and indeed other coloured migrants in the area were of working-class status. This led to certain complications and required additional explanation.

In general, it is clear that both white and coloured researchers into race relationships suffer from disabilities of one kind or another. The coloured investigator's easier identification with one section at least of the coloured community or group is partially offset by suspicion of him on class and ethnic grounds within that group, and by the relative uncooperativeness or even hostility which he may meet from white officials and certain white individuals. The white investigator of colour-contact situations in which there is any friction is unlikely ever to gain full acceptance from any section of the coloured group, but will have a better chance of establishing a fair degree of rapport with all sections. He will, on the other hand, find contacts with white officialdom and individuals relatively easy, unless he is too emotionally linked with the cause of the minority or migrant group. In some cases a white outsider, for instance a North American or even an Englishman in South Africa, or an English-speaking European in Britain, will be able to establish a better rapport with both groups than will an indigenous investigator of either colour. In present circumstances, however, the same could not be said of a 'foreign' non-white investigator studying race relations in South Africa or the Deep South or even, perhaps, in Britain. Such an investigator would be identified with the migrant or subordinate group and his investigations would be regarded as a breach of the behaviour expected of his group.

THE RESEARCHER'S IMPACT ON THE SUBJECT-MATTER

Concern is often expressed about the impact of the investigator's personality and activities on the people studied. To put it bluntly – are they ever the same again? This concern is more relevant in the case of the conventional anthropological subject, the small, closed,

33

simple community. In complex urban situations, the researcher's impact is usually peripheral and impermanent. Unless he is particularly maladroit and aggressive, his presence should leave little or no more lasting trace than does the anonymous flow of local government officials, welfare workers, itinerant vendors, and others who knock on the doors of most dwellers in large cities. There is an additional reason for tact and circumspection in urban field work, where more than one study of a given area is likely to be made over a fairly short period. The urban investigator should bear in mind the plea to picnickers: 'Please leave this spot as unspoiled as you found it, so that others may enjoy it too.'

The need for tact and circumspection does not end with the period of field work, but is extended to the question of writing up and publication. The greater the rapport that has been achieved with informants of various groups, the more profound will be the confidences entrusted to the investigator. The student of a simple, non-literate society has to come to terms with his own conscience about publishing material so obtained. The urban investigator has also to consider the consequences of publishing material whose sources may be read and identified by the informants who placed their confidence in him and by those around them. In some cases, publication may not only be painful to the persons concerned, but may affect their jobs or wider social relationships within their group or with other groups. In this study, unlike that of Dollard in his anonymous 'Southern Town', it would be useless to try to disguise the particular London area investigated. It has therefore been necessary to withhold a certain amount of intimate material gathered from sources which could have been easily identified.

THE RESEARCHER'S BIAS

The study of race relations is comparatively new and uncharted, and one in which the attributes of the researcher are particularly important, not only as they effect the actions of the group studied, and the methods adopted, but also as they affect the way in which the researcher reacts to the situation and interprets the material. 'Racial' relationships engender more emotion than most others in the modern world, and the researcher, who is after all the product of a particular sociocultural background, cannot hope to approach them with full objectivity, however thorough his or her academic training may have been. The most that a researcher can do is to be aware of his own bias, to guard against it constantly, and to give his readers an opportunity of knowing what it is and judging his conclusions in the light of it.

34

An individual researcher's bias is not only a matter of individual personality. It may, like his field work, be affected by such factors as age, class affiliations, education, religious or philosophical beliefs, and familiarity with other peoples and cultures. So far as my own background is concerned, a brief note of the relevant data can be found on the dust-cover. It would perhaps be legitimate to record here, among elements that helped to form my present attitude or bias, a secure and conservative middle-class upbringing, the effects of which were partly modified by such liberalizing influences as Oxford in the late 1930s; five years of war work with an allied government; considerable travel, and contacts with people of most races, creeds, and convictions; five years of direct experience of a pigmentocracy in South Africa, which while it strengthened liberal attitudes also induced an inevitable colour consciousness in all spheres of life; and finally many years of academic and other work among refugees, immigrants, and minority groups.

In situations involving coloured peoples, researchers tend to be affected, not only by the frontierless egalitarianism and tolerance of their academic training, but, as I suggested earlier, by the somewhat negrophile and anti-white bias of most of the vast existing body of sociological and other literature on this subject.

In my own first book, for instance, which dealt with the disabilities of the Cape Coloured people in South Africa, I followed this black-and-white pattern or bias without much further examination. Later, a knowledge of other less acute situations, such as the colour-class hierarchy of Jamaica, Canada's pluralistic society, and class-conscious, mildly xenophobic Britain, helped me to see situations of race or colour contact less sharply, no longer in black and white, but in a variety of tones of grey. It was, therefore, in a spirit of attempting to understand rather than to blame, and with an unwillingness to make value judgements or blanket condemnations of groups, or to interpret every phenomenon in terms of colour prejudice or discrimination drawn from other contexts, that I carried out the present study. Such an approach may in itself be regarded as a bias by some, while others will assuredly detect evidence of bias of which I am not myself aware.

3

Background to the West Indian settlement in Brixton

THE HISTORY of earlier coloured migrant groups in Britain has been recounted in detail by a number of sociological writers. Here, therefore, it is necessary only to refer briefly to the main phases of this migration, the more so because the groups involved were small, transient, or isolated, had little or no direct connection with the present recent and large-scale migration from the West Indies, and exerted no great influence on the attitudes of the British population to coloured people, which until now have been largely acquired at second hand or in the colonial setting.

The first phase of coloured immigration into Britain began with the introduction of slaves in the seventeenth century to serve the aristocracy and the more socially ambitious merchant classes. At first, these slaves seem to have come direct from Africa but, later, returning nabobs from the West Indies would often bring their own slaves to ease their declining years.

This phase ended in 1772 with Lord Mansfield's decision in the Somerset case. Of about 14–15,000 slaves thus freed, some seem to have remained in the service of their former owners, while others who had a particular trade tried to live on their own in London. Considerable numbers of the latter group became a charge on the Poor Law authorities, and, in 1786, 411 indigent volunteers and some sixty white prostitutes were shipped to Sierra Leone to found the colony of Freetown. Of the remainder, some went to the West Indies as free labourers, but many others stayed on in Britain. 'Blacks' are recorded as being conspicious among London beggars as late as 1814. A parliamentary commission of this date recorded their poor condition, and also described the miseries of some hun-

---

[1] See particularly Little (1947, pp. 165–218) and Banton (1955, Chapter 2).

36

dreds of Lascar seamen stranded between ships in the riverside slums. Lascars and coloured seamen in general were to become a constant feature of Britain's dock and port areas. The former slaves, however, seem virtually to have disappeared from the scene by the last half of the nineteenth century. This was presumably as a result of intermarriage.[1]

The second phase of coloured settlement in Britain began at the end of the nineteenth century in the dock areas of London, Cardiff, Bristol, Liverpool, Hull, and North and South Shields. These settlers were usually seamen and they were rarely if ever accompanied by their womenfolk. Their numbers were augmented by stowaways and, after the first world war, by some of the several thousand coloured labourers who had been brought over to work in munitions, in labour battalions, and as replacements in the Merchant Navy. The great majority of these coloured immigrants were away at sea for long periods. When they came ashore they lived near their work, in rather isolated or self-segregating settlements. As a result, until the second world war, few untravelled inhabitants of the British Isles had ever come into face-to-face contact with a coloured person, although many were familiar with the activities of a small number of coloured entertainers, musicians, and sporting personalities, most of them West Indians or American Negroes.

Another category of coloured immigrants is that of the coloured students who have been coming to Britain in increasing numbers for the last 250 years. The first coloured students were a handful of chiefs' sons, who were sent to Britain for education and to cement trade and imperial contacts in 1710.[2] In the years between the two world wars, India sent by far the largest contingent, with the West Indian and West African groups in second and third places.[3] At no time, however, did the overall number of such colonial students at universities rise as high as 2,000 in a single year.

After the second world war, the number of overseas students of all origins rose steadily year by year, until by 1960–61 there were 35,729 British students from the Commonwealth and United Kingdom dependencies and 19,358 foreign students attending universities

---

[1] Little (1947, p. 190, n. 3) cites a report by a correspondent of the *Spectator* in July 1925 that ninety years before, i.e. in 1835, a Negro servant had served for some time in his grandfather's house as a footman. The fact that he was black never seemed at all strange, and Carlo (the Negro) was engaged to an English girl. Little also cites (p. 204) the Negro servant Gumbo in Thackeray's *The Virginians*, who married one of the housemaids, apparently without any objection being raised.

[2] See Little (1947, pp. 186–7 and 190–4) for a detailed account of these earlier students.

[3] This total did not include law and technical students. For a full account of the colonial students see Carey (1956, *passim*) and the P.E.P. Report (1955).

and other institutions of higher learning in Britain.[1] Of the former group, the great majority were Asian or Africans. The largest groups were from West Africa (11,771); India and Pakistan (4,645); and the British Caribbean (6,949).

Members of the coloured student group usually return home with very definite and often unfavourable impressions of their sojourn here, which can have an effect on Commonwealth relationships in years to come. The great majority of its members, however, are transient and are tied to one of a relatively few seats of learning. They come into close contact mainly with fellow-students, teachers, landladies, and minor officials, and therefore leave relatively little impression on the mass of the British population.

THE NEW WEST INDIAN MIGRATION TO BRITAIN

The second world war was the prelude to the third and most recent phase of coloured, and particularly of West Indian, migration to Britain. Thousands of West Indians came to Britain during the war years, either as volunteers in the armed Services, particularly in the Royal Air Force, or as technicians for Britain's man-starved war industry. About 7,000 Jamaicans served overseas in the armed Services, while smaller contingents volunteered from other parts of the West Indies. Some of the airmen served in R.A.F. units stationed near various provincial towns in Britain, particularly in the Midlands. Many of them were from the middle class, ambitious, and better equipped than those who came later to make contact with the British population and to perceive the economic opportunities that awaited them here. Although not all of them met with an unquestioning welcome in this country, some of the West Indian airmen chose to be demobilized here. In addition, many of those who went back found the economic situation at home so discouraging that they soon returned to Britain, despite the poor employment situation which obtained here immediately after the war.[2]

Another small group of West Indians came to the United Kingdom during the war to work in the Forestry Commission[3] or in munition factories. In all, 345 men arrived in Britain under the latter

[3] *Overseas Students in the United Kingdom—1960–61* (published by the London Conference on Overseas Students). Of the totals, 7,481 and 4,718 respectively were attending universities.

[2] During the war, unemployment in the building and construction industry in Jamaica was as high as 40 per cent; in transport and communications it was 34 per cent. The overall unemployment figure in 1942–43 was 25 per cent, without taking into account seasonal and other under-employment. In 1959 Douglas Manley reported a general unemployment level in the Caribbean of 15 per cent (1960, p. 14).

[3] These were experienced lumbermen from British Honduras, who worked in Scotland (Richmond, 1954, p. 23, n. 1).

38

scheme, of whom only about one-third were classified as skilled by the Ministry of Labour. The remaining two-thirds were found to be semi-skilled, whatever claims they might have made for their skills on enrolment (see Richmond, 1954, p. 34). These men worked on Merseyside and later in Manchester and Bolton.

The scheme was wound up in 1946 and some West Indian workers were made redundant after the return of the ex-servicemen and the economic crisis of 1947, which struck Merseyside with particular force. In 1951 Richmond estimated that only about one-third of all West Indians who had come to this country were still living in Britain, or serving in the Forces or the Merchant Navy. Nevertheless, this 'discovery' of the United Kingdom helped to turn the eyes of other work-hungry West Indians to Britain, as a possible alternative goal for migration. Later, when the McCarran Act of 1952 virtually halted West Indian immigration to the United States,[1] the United Kingdom became the only remaining wide-open territory for would-be migrants from the British Caribbean islands,[2] even though it was far away, expensive to reach, and difficult to leave in the event of failure.

In the immediate post-war years, economic conditions deteriorated in the West Indies as a whole, and particularly in Jamaica. Thereafter, West Indians began to arrive in Britain in small but steadily increasing numbers.[3] At first, there was no regular passenger-boat service and they came as stowaways.[4] Between 1946 and 1953, 898 stowaways, almost all Jamaicans, arrived from the West Indies; 131 of these were not landed.

The stowaway figures, however, were far lower than those of fare-

[1] Until 1952, West Indians entered the United States under the never-filled annual quota from Great Britain. After the McCarran Act became law, colonial dependencies located in the Western hemisphere received separate quotas of 100 per annum. The Senior–Manley Report (1955), however, suggests that there remain, apart from contract schemes, certain other opportunities for emigration to the States, and estimates that some 10,000 may have migrated from Jamaica to the States in the years 1943–54, in addition to a similar number of contract workers.

[2] Until 1 July 1962, every citizen of the Commonwealth, which contains nearly 617 million people, had unrestricted right of entry into and permanent residence in the British Isles, just as have the residents of the United Kingdom. The freedom to leave the realm or to return to it was laid down by Magna Carta for all men 'except the King's enemies', and 'saving only the duty they owed to the King'. In the last century it has been whittled away by regulations in respect of permanent migration to the colonies and Dominions, and there are now few territories in the Commonwealth which do not put up some barriers against unrestricted immigration from other parts of the Commonwealth, although most treat immigrants from the United Kingdom on a preferential basis. (On the legal and historical background of this, see Parry, 1957.)

[3] For an account of the early period of migration, see Banton (1955, pp. 59–60) and Egginton (1957, pp. 55–79).

[4] See Appendix I for table giving the annual numbers and geographical provenance of stowaways for the period 1946–60.

paying passengers, and they dropped as the latter rose. Prior to 1948, the number of fare-paying passengers from the West Indies to Britain had been limited by lack of accommodation. In that year, the s.s. *Empire Windrush* brought the first large group of migrants. They numbered 492 in all, and the majority of them were male, youngish, semi-skilled and skilled workers from Jamaica. Within three weeks they were all in work. In September 1948 the s.s. *Orbita* brought a further 108, who also found work without much trouble.

This fact received considerable publicity in Jamaica and the movement of migrants began to increase. It was limited only by the insufficiency of sea- and, to a lesser extent, air-transportation. Even as late as 1953, only three ships, two of them French and one British, were involved in the carriage of migrants from the West Indies to Britain. Between them, these three ships made only five sailings that year. In 1954 there were two British, two French, and two Italian ships which made seventeen sailings in all. By 1955, there were thirteen ships on the run (eight of them Italian and only one British); these ships made forty sailings during the year.

Between 1953 and 1955, the number of passengers per ship also rose considerably. In 1953 no ship carried more than 300 migrants. By 1955, only seventeen sailings had fewer than 300 passengers per sailing, and in twelve cases there were over 500 passengers per ship. Five years later ships were carrying up to 1,000 migrants at a time and there was an increasing number of charter flights.

Although the destination was new, this increasing efflux of Jamaicans and other West Indians to an overseas territory was no new phenomenon in the Caribbean.[1] Jamaica, Barbados, and most other islands have long suffered from over-population,[2] unemployment, under-employment, and lack of economic and other opportunities. In Jamaica, for instance, there was in the years between 1881 and 1953 a net outward movement of over 150,000,[3] mainly to Panama, Costa Rica, Cuba, and the United States. In Barbados, the population problem is grimmer than it is in Jamaica or indeed in a comparable area anywhere else in the world except Malta. As

---

[1] For a fuller account of West Indian migration as a whole, see Manley (1960). For an extremely detailed and valuable analysis which became available only after this section was written, see Davison (1961).

[2] In an article under the title 'Some Demographic Considerations', Roberts (1957b) records a total population of the British West Indian islands of 2,905,800 in 1954; a density of 370 per square mile (1,380 in Barbados, 785·3 in St. Kitts-Nevis, and 650 in Grenada); a birth-rate of 36·7; a death-rate of 10·6; and a rate of natural increase of 26·1. In 1960, according to the preliminary census count, the total population of the British Caribbean, including the mainland territories, was nearly 3,800,000, compared with just over 2,000,000 in 1921.

[3] See Maunder (1955). It should, however, be noted that these figures differ considerably from estimated net emigration figures given by Roberts (1957a, p. 139).

early as 1844, this island had a population density of 740 persons per square mile, or about half the island's 1954 density of 1,380. This may be compared with the population density of 790 per square mile in England and Wales. The total outward movement from Barbados of about 150,000 persons between 1861 and 1921 first reduced the rate of growth and later induced an actual decline in the population, which stood at only 156,800 by 1921. Since then, however, many immigration outlets have closed, and the population of Barbados has now reached the dangerous total of about 225,000.[1]

Both in the nineteenth century and today Barbados has so far been the only West Indian territory to embark on state-aided schemes of emigration. These have not affected more than a minority of the overall number of emigrants involved, but the 4,493 assisted emigrants who came from Barbados in the seven years from 1955 to 1961 may be said to have had an impact well out of proportion to their numbers on the British population. This is because so many of them are employed in public transport or in the hotel industry, where they come into frequent casual contact with large sections of the public, and where they have on the whole made a very favourable impression.[2]

SOME STATISTICS OF THE MIGRANT SETTLEMENT

Arrivals and Departures

It is impossible at present to give either a complete or an accurate statistical picture of the growth and character of the new West Indian migrant group in Britain. All alien immigrants were until 1961 required to register with the police, but this provision does not apply to West Indians or other Commonwealth immigrants.

The United Kingdom census takes no account of pigmentation, but it is reasonable to assume that the majority of those listed as 'West Indian born' would be coloured West Indians. Unfortunately for researchers, the last available census figures, published in 1951, were collected before the present migration got into its swing, and do not even remotely reflect the present position.

In 1951, some 15,000 persons born in the West Indies were resident in the United Kingdom.[3] This figure included, in addition to old-timers, several thousand post-war migrants or West Indian

[1] The information on Barbados is taken from Roberts's paper (1955). See also Lowenthal (1957). By 1960 the population had risen to 232,000.
[2] For a fuller account of the Barbadian scheme, see Davison (1961, Part II, pp. 10–11).
[3] The numbers in earlier decennial censuses were: 1911 – 9,189; 1921 – 9,054 (50 per cent male); 1931 – 8,595 (51 per cent male).

41

ex-servicemen who had opted for demobilization in Britain, and an unknown number of West Indian-born whites, who would presumably neither identify themselves nor be identified with the bulk of coloured West Indians in Britain. Of the total of 15,000, some 4,200 were resident in London, and of these 63 per cent were men.

Any estimate of the number of West Indian migrants in Britain at any time since 1951 must therefore be based primarily on statistics of arrivals and departures. For this purpose, the most detailed figures are those provided by the West Indian Migrant Services Division (formerly the British Caribbean Welfare Service) for arrivals or departures of substantial groups of migrants by sea or air. These figures are very approximate, but enable a minimum estimate to be made.[1] They do not, however, include those who travel individually or in small groups on ships or flights which do not normally carry migrants and are therefore not met by officials of the Migrant Services Division.[2]

Table A in Appendix II gives the approximate annual figures for the overall West Indian arrivals in Britain up to the end of 1961. Three main trends emerge clearly. First, the migration would appear to have been more or less self-regulating, probably in terms of the economic situation in Britain, and not to have been determined only by the amount of passenger-space available from the West Indies. During the years of full employment in Britain, the annual figure rose steeply by nearly 7,000 between 1953 and 1954, and again by over 15,000 in 1955. The first peak year for migrants, 1956, was also the year of the credit squeeze and the Suez crisis. The effects of these on industry and full employment, especially in the unskilled field, were being felt by the winter of 1956–57, and the number of migrants dropped by about 4,000 in 1957 and by 6,000 in 1958.

The drop between 1957 and 1958 was, in fact, of greater significance than the figures might suggest, because it was mainly among male migrant work-seekers. The number of women entering Britain remained constant in 1957 and dropped only by 1,600 in 1958, while the number of children under 16 continued to rise throughout this period. This is the second discernible trend in recent West Indian migration – the growing number of women and children arriving to

[1] The British Home Office has since 1955 kept records of all persons entering Britain who are in possession of a British passport issued in the West Indies (or other Commonwealth and colonial territories). These are the source of the estimates given in parliamentary answers from time to time. The figures for West Indians do not take into account the intentions of passport-holders and often differ from those collected by the Migrant Services Division.

[2] As a consequence of the dissolution of the West Indian Federation on 31 May 1962 this valuable and efficient Federal organization unfortunately had to be wound up, its functions devolving on various island and regional offices.

join their menfolk as soon as the latter have settled and saved sufficient money to provide passage-money and accommodation here. In the case of the children, the 'pull' factor for their parents is, of course, not employment but free and compulsory schooling. The moderate increase in the late-1959 arrivals and the record male immigration in 1960 would appear to reflect, with the usual time-lag, the end of the recession and the industrial boom in Britain in 1959. But the 1960 and, still more, the 1961 figures also indicate a third trend characteristic of most migrations.[1] This is their tendency to snowball among the friends and relations of successful migrants.

The same trends are discernible in the statistics giving the regional origin of various West Indian migrant groups. *Table B* in Appendix II shows the changing regional pattern of migration over the seven-year period, 1955–61. Jamaicans were the pioneer post-war migrants to Britain, and Jamaica still provides well over half the migrants. Both the absolute number of migrants from this island and the percentage which they constitute of the total decreased between 1955 and 1958. In 1959, however, the Jamaican figures showed an increase in the number of migrants, particularly men, which suggested that a new wave of migration might be starting from the island. This trend was confirmed in 1960 and 1961, over 18,000 men leaving the island each year. At the same time, the high figures for women (nearly 13,000 and nearly 18,000 respectively) suggest that a number might have been migrating on their own account or with their menfolk, rather than joining men who had migrated earlier.

Migration from Barbados, the other traditional island of emigration, tended to decrease over the period 1955–59, and the upsurge of migration, male and female, came only in 1960. This was also true of St. Kitts-Nevis and Antigua in the Leeward Islands, of the Windward Islands of Grenada and St. Vincent, and of Trinidad. Of the smaller islands, only Dominica and, to a lesser extent, St. Lucia (both in the Windward group) showed a significant increase in emigration as early as 1959, while from Montserrat (Leewards) and the mainland territory of British Guiana no major increase was noticeable even in 1960. No single reason can be given for these differing regional trends; in so far as they are precise,[2] they should probably be attributed to a combination of such factors as the economic position in each area, the availability of passenger-space locally in a given year, and the degree of success achieved by earlier

---

[1] The record 1961 totals may also be attributable in part, at least, to the impending threat of legislative controls, which stampeded many into migrating at once before the door should close.

[2] For instance, it is not entirely clear whether the data refer to the migrants' birthplace, the place where his passport was issued, or the port of embarkation, in cases where these do not coincide.

migrants and reported back home, or transferred back to dependants in the more tangible form of passage-money advances.

Table C in Appendix II gives the monthly breakdown of overall migrant arrivals since 1955. The annual variation in the peak month is not necessarily significant, because it may be dictated by the availability of shipping. It is, however, noticeable that the preferred months for migration are between April and October. For obvious reasons, shipping companies prefer to sail the Atlantic in the summer, and West Indian migrants, too, prefer to make their initial adjustment to the notorious English climate in the milder months, when they will not have to face immediate expenditure on warm clothing, stoves, and fuel. This element of choice may be more open to the more skilled or prosperous migrants.[1]

Until the new census returns are available, any estimate of the present size of the West Indian settlement in Britain must, as we have said, be based mainly on statistics of arrivals and departures. The immigration figures are, we have seen, only approximate, and the estimates of departures are even less precise. The Board of Trade statistics are of little assistance, since they include all passengers, including British sun-seekers leaving for the Caribbean by sea.

Towards the end of 1956, the British Caribbean Welfare Service began to keep a count of passengers returning in fairly large groups on the regular migrant ships. In late 1957, the Service's official report gave the rate of return, 'at a very rough estimation', as between 150 and 200 persons each month;[2] this rate seems to have been fairly constant, with a temporary upsurge in 1959 (4,500), perhaps because of the economic recession and anxiety over the disturbances in London in the Notting Hill area in 1958.

The great majority of these returning migrants paid their own fares, and were going back either because they thought that they would be better off at home, or because they had achieved their original object of accumulating sufficient capital to buy land or a business at home or of acquiring a skill or trade. About one-quarter of those returning were said to be women. Another substantial group among them consisted of young children and infants who were being sent back under escort to relatives at home while their mother or parents continued to work in this country. This arrangement is

---

[1] Cf. Roberts and Mills (1958, p. 48) for a note on the variation in seasonal patterns of migration between skilled and unskilled workers in the period 1953–55.

[2] B.C.W.S. Report, 31 October 1957. No breakdown is available of the regional destination of the returning migrants, although this could presumably be ascertained from the immigration statistics of the various regions. Roberts and Mills (1958) have some figures on re-migration to Jamaica in the years 1953–55, during which period 246 men and 168 women returned to the island from the United Kingdom (Chapter 8, Table A, p. 102).

fairly common. It is cheaper to feed and clothe a child in the West Indies than in Britain, and the working parents avoid the high fees charged by day nurseries or baby-minders in Britain. The children have to travel with an adult escort, usually a returning migrant who receives a fee of about £30 for this service.

It seems likely that some of those who returned home have since re-migrated to Britain. Some adults only went back for a holiday, while others thought better of their decision after they reached home. There is also an increasing number of cases where migrants who sent their young children home are bringing them back to Britain once they reach school age.

A small minority of returning migrants have been repatriated at their own request, either because of mental illness or because, as a result of age, ill health, illiteracy, lack of industrial skills, or temperamental factors, they could not adjust themselves to life in a British city. Over the four years 1957–60 these voluntary repatriants numbered some 280 in all. There were no deportations, since this measure did not until after 31 May 1962 apply to West Indians or other Commonwealth subjects.[1]

Vital Statistics

The net balance of arrivals and departures provides only a minimum total for the new West Indian migrant settlement in Britain. The number of children born to migrants in this country would have to be added to this figure, while the number of deaths here would have to be subtracted from it. Unfortunately, the gains and losses of the West Indian migrant group in Britain through births and deaths can be a subject only for conjecture, since the Registrar-General makes no differentiation with regard to any ethnic or immigrant group, and the census does not inquire into ethnic origins as is the case, for instance, in Canada.

The death-rate is obviously very low at present, and certainly does not balance the number of births. The birth-rate of the group is likely to be rather high, whether by comparison with the local birth-rate in Britain or with the West Indian birth-rate. This is because the majority of the migrants consist of men and women in their reproductive years, in a ratio which has gradually closed over the years until it is now in the neighbourhood of two women to every

---

[1] In a number of cases in recent years, however, the courts have sentenced Irishmen and a few West Indians or West Africans to suspended sentences, provided they leave Britain. This formula is tantamount to a sentence of deportation, unless the individual opts for gaol, but it cannot apparently be employed in more serious offences (see Griffiths, 1960, pp. 165–6). The deportation provisions of the Commonwealth Immigrants Act (1962) have since made such devices unnecessary.

three men. It seems probable that a considerable proportion of the women migrants have borne at least one child in this country. In addition, an unknown number of children have been born as the result of liaisons between West Indian men and white girls. These children are most likely to be drawn into the migrant group if their parents are married. The children born as the result of casual affairs between migrants and white girls have a more problematic future. They may be deserted by one or both parents, and many are likely to spend their youth in children's homes. When they grow up, however, the majority may drift into a coloured settlement unless they are able to pass as white.

No statistical data are available about the age-structure of the West Indian migrant group in Britain as a whole, other than that the percentage of West Indies-born children (that is to say, of the younger age-groups) in the total migrant group was approximately 5.7 per cent by the end of 1961. Apart from this, general impressions and expectations based on the usual age-structure of an economic migrant group would seem to support the findings of the Roberts-Mills survey of Jamaican migrants over the 1953–55 period: according to this, the average age of migrants was just over 30 years, nearly one-quarter of men and women were in the 25–29 age-group, and nearly three-quarters of both sexes were in the 20–39 age-group.[1]

Patterns of Migrant Settlement

The new migrants have not followed the old patterns of coloured settlement in docklands and ports. Instead, most of them have settled in inland urban areas with good possibilities of industrial employment. From 1955 onwards the British Caribbean Welfare Service and its successor published rough estimates of the geographical distribution of the new migrants. These were based on data such as the migrant's declared destination on arrival, on figures provided by employment exchanges and other local bodies, on visits by officials to the various areas of settlement, and so on. In view of the migrants' high mobility, and the fallibility of individual impressions, these estimates must be treated with extreme caution. In the absence of precise statistics, however, they can be of some use in indicating general trends and patterns of settlement.

Table D in Appendix II gives these estimates over a seven-year

[1] See Roberts and Mills (1958). These findings do not differ greatly from the data given by Maunder (1955) and derived from two surveys made in October 1954 of two parties of emigrants leaving for the United Kingdom, one by sea, the other by air. See also Davison (1961, Part I, p. 24). The London Sample taken by Mrs. Ruth Glass gives a rather different picture of the age-structure, largely because it was drawn from records of adult migrants (see Glass, 1960, pp. 18–20).

period. The migrants are distributed over at least forty towns and cities up and down the country – very few have settled in Scotland or in Northern Ireland. The largest settlements are in London, Birmingham, Manchester, Nottingham, and Wolverhampton; these settlements are not geographically concentrated but are split up into a number of nuclei, which often have little contact with each other.

The conjectural nature of the estimates makes it difficult to draw any general conclusions from them. It might be safe to say that West Indian newcomers are clearly attracted in the largest numbers to the largest and most highly industrialized cities with good employment possibilities, while numbers in the older maritime settlements remain relatively static. It would also appear that there is a greater mobility among migrants in the smaller, newer West Indian settlements in relatively small towns or centres. Few settlements apart from the 'big five' and the pre-war coloured settlements seem to be so well established that a decrease in economic opportunities or an increase in local hostility might not cause a considerable exodus to another more promising area. This may have happened in the case of Derby, Rugby, Hull, and Bradford-on-Avon between 1956 and 1957, a period in which all four towns show an estimated loss of West Indian settlers. In the case of Derby, if the 1962 estimate is accurate, there appears to have been a recent renewed influx of migrants, perhaps in response to improved economic opportunities. In general, these figures illustrate the difficulty of organizing and dispersing a 'free' migrant movement.

BRIXTON – PAST AND PRESENT

The West Indian newcomers have settled, then, in large urban industrial areas with a shortage of unskilled and semi-skilled labour. In such areas they have usually been compelled, as a consequence of the housing shortage and local antipathies, to cluster in the most dilapidated and socially undesirable districts.

One such district is found in Brixton, the place-name of an ancient administrative division and today of one of the three electoral divisions of the Metropolitan Borough of Lambeth. Throughout this study, however, the name will be used in the looser, and probably older, popular sense, and particularly in the geographical sense in which it has come to represent an established centre of settlement to the West Indian migrants themselves.[1] 'Brixton', for our purposes, is centred on Lambeth Town Hall and the Brixton market. It extends over the Angell, Vassall, Stockwell, Landor,

[1] But see p. 295 for a note on the changing significance of 'Brixton' among the more status-conscious migrants.

The scope of the study

Town Hall, and Ferndale wards of the Brixton division, with a heavy overspill south into the Herne Hill ward of Norwood division, which actually contains the most concentrated and central area of West Indian settlement. Other overspills are into the Tulse Hill and Effra wards of Norwood, and the Lansdowne ward of Vauxhall. Similar districts which may in part have originated in outward movements from Brixton are found in the roads between the north side of Clapham Common and the Wandsworth Road, in the poorer parts of Battersea, Lewisham, and Deptford, and in the Peckham area of Camberwell.[1] Brixton is the oldest and largest coloured settlement in this area and still provides the main focus and centre for the coloured people – particularly the West Indians, who live within a three- or four-mile radius.

The decline of Brixton, from a residential area for wealthy merchants and carriage-folk to a district which the remaining residents with any pretensions to middle-class status prefer to describe by other names, has been recent and rapid.[2] In this it provides a contrast to that area of earlier coloured settlement in London – Stepney.[3]

The history of the County of Surrey records that Brixton lies on former marshy ground where game abounded, and that it was not inhabited until the early 1800s. In the whole Parish of Lambeth there were in 1719 only 1,400 houses. By 1811 some building had taken place, and there were 7,704 houses and a population of 41,644 inhabitants in the parish.[4] The extension of the railways, of horse-drawn tram services, and finally of the underground railway led to large-scale speculative building and settlement south of the Thames, and the number of houses in Lambeth Parish nearly doubled between 1811 and 1822. South of Kennington Common there were few buildings before 1800. By 1816, however, the Vauxhall Bridge was opened and elegant buildings, mainly for the professional classes, began to be erected along Kennington Road, the Brixton Road, and Camberwell New Road, although Angell Town was still a single farm as late as 1826. On Denmark Hill, Champion Hill,

[1] In the analysis of her 'London Group', Mrs. Ruth Glass (1960) found that the postal districts S.W.9, S.W.2, and S.E.5 (approximately our Brixton-Peckham area) were the main areas of West Indian settlement in South London. Next came the postal districts S.W.8, S.W.4, S.W.11, S.W.12, and S.W.17 to the south and west, and S.E.15 and S.E.24 to the east (see maps, pp. xviii and xix).

[2] This brief historical sketch of the development of Lambeth and Brixton is taken from Allen (1826), Tanswell (1858), Malden (Ed., 1912, Vol. IV), the LCC *Survey of London* (1956, Vols. XXIII, XXIV, and XXVI), and Dyos (1952).

[3] See Banton (1955, p. 28).

[4] This rose to 87,858 in 1831; 139,325 in 1851; 208,342 in 1871; and to a near peak of over 300,000 in 1901. Since 1921, as in most London boroughs, the population has slowly but steadily decreased. The second world war with its bombardments and evacuations, and the post-war rehousing programme, gave additional impetus to the decline.

48

Herne Hill, and Dulwich Hill, detached and semi-detached houses or villas 'with fairly large gardens back and front' were built and sold on ninety-nine-year leaseholds for well-to-do London tradesmen of the better class.[1]

By contrast with the greater part of Brixton, Kennington, and Stockwell, Vauxhall began as and has remained almost entirely a working-class district of small poorly constructed houses. It is the area of Lambeth that has produced most of the property now scheduled for slum clearance, and has absorbed the fewest newcomers, coloured or otherwise. Its houses are too small for the reception of many lodgers and, unlike those of Brixton, they do not lend themselves for conversion into boarding- or rooming-houses. Many of them have remained in the tenancy of the same families since they were built. Somerset Maugham's *Liza of Lambeth* is located here.

After 1860 the type of building and the type of residents began to change for the worse in Brixton, Herne Hill, and other developing areas farther south. The gaps in development were filled in with undistinguished speculative dwellings by small local builders. These houses were taken by clerks, shopkeepers, skilled artisans, and the rank and file of commerce – either migrants from the country or refugees from the very poor districts of inner London. As Booth (1903) wrote: 'Southwark is moving to Walworth; Walworth to North Brixton and Streatham; while the servant-keepers of outer South London go to Croydon and other places' (Vol. IV, p. 166).

The process of social down-grading and material deterioration continued gradually but inexorably in the better-class areas. By the 1920s, the mansions of the carriage-folk had been cut up into single-floor flats,[2] often lacking in adequate modern conveniences and not fully self-contained. Their tenants were respectable artisans or white-collar workers. Even between the two world wars, rent control, inflation, rising repair costs, and the shortening leasehold tenure made most of these houses an increasingly unprofitable investment. A number of them became boarding-houses and, in others, vacant accommodation was let out on a more profitable but less socially acceptable furnished-room basis. Some undesirables moved in and the district began to acquire a bad name. The south-

---

[1] An interesting exception to this type of building is to be found in Sussex Road, which runs off Coldharbour Lane parallel with and next to Geneva and Somerleyton Roads. Here, twenty modest cottages were built in an attractive terrace construction as early as 1825. This road is one into which, despite its proximity to the main nucleus of recent West Indian settlement, no West Indians have so far moved. The small houses remain for the most part in single-family tenancy, often extending back for several generations to the original inhabitants.

[2] See Dyos (1952, p. 403 f.).

ward movement of resident owners into Sussex and Surrey gained impetus.

The second world war accelerated these changes. Today, virtually the only flat accommodation that remains in Brixton is controlled accommodation.[1] Wherever possible, landlords, few of whom still live in Brixton, have switched over to single-room furnished lettings. Despite the activities of the Rent Tribunal, this form of letting gives the landlord more profit and a certain freedom in his dealings with tenants. The outward movement of the 'servant-keepers' and much of the middle class may perhaps be illustrated by the changing political allegiance of Brixton voters. Whereas Vauxhall, in all but the exceptional 1931 elections, has always voted Labour, and Norwood, except in the 1958 LCC elections, always Conservative, Brixton voted Conservative in both the General and the LCC elections until the first post-war elections. Since then it has consistently voted Labour, though with a sizeable and increasing Conservative minority.

The present condition and reputation of Brixton may be inferred from the following comments made by local residents and officials during the years of my field work:

'Brixton has gone steadily down. My own mother-in-law remembers the time, sixty years or more back, when Acre Lane[2] had fields on each side. The Geneva and Somerleyton Road houses were single-family merchants' houses with servants on the top floor and carriages at the back. By the 'thirties they had been converted into artisans' flats. They were blitzed during the war, but some nice people still live there, especially in Geneva Road, which has a better reputation locally.' (A day-nursery matron.)

'Apart from its ordinary population, Brixton used to be the home of "regular" thieves, pick-pockets, etc. Now it is very uneven: middle-class, settled working-class, a sprinkling of Europeans, all sorts. Brixton has a lot of gangs, and teddy boys flourish more here among the respectable artisan and clerical classes than they do in tougher dockside areas.' (A police officer.)

'Brixton was almost fashionable within living memory as the residence of city merchants. Now Brixton and Kennington are one vast lodging-house. Apart from this shifting population, however, there is an important solid group of artisan flat-dwellers. Everyone meets in Brixton's large shopping centre. We have two

---

[1] Little, if any, of this accommodation was affected by the Rent Act of 1957, because rateable values were usually below £40.
[2] This is the wide artery leading from the Town Hall to Clapham Common.

concentrations of male Borstal licencees, one in Vauxhall, the other in Brixton, and we get a number of probation orders from the West End. A number of prostitutes live locally, but they operate, usually individually, in the West End, and there are no known streets or houses.' (A probation officer, before the Street Offences Act came into operation in 1959.)

'Brixton is the brothel area of Lambeth. The three areas are very different. Vauxhall is working-class and docks; Brixton, Bohemian, lower theatrical, shifting population, and criminals; Norwood, respectable middle-class.' (A Labour Party official.)

'You cannot set up the standards of Limehouse in Brixton. They do not fight their wives in the Brixton area. Brixton is just too good for you. If you want to use the language you admit using, you should go into a common lodging-house where there are people of your type, or live in the dockside area. The Brixton standards are higher.' (*South London Advertiser*, 8 December 1956, reporting a county court judge who was making an order for eviction against a man accused by his landlady of owing rent and using obscene language.)

'I have spent over twenty years trying to find out where Tooting ends and Balham begins, and I am still not sure about Brixton. And don't tell me it depends on the postal area; it doesn't. These place-names – Balham, Tooting, Battersea, Brixton – there are at least fifty of them in South London – are the names of old parishes or villages whose borders are now almost forgotten. The PO boundaries run across parishes, and the confusion grows worse because people think, for instance, that Balham is always S.W.12, or that all S.W.2 is Brixton. . . . I live in a neighbourhood that calls itself Streatham Hill, though the Post Office calls it S.W.2, which to them means Brixton. Then London Transport takes a hand. Their "Brixton" garage is next door to one of the most expensive blocks of flats in Streatham, and the residents flatly refuse to call themselves Brixtonians. We are in S.W.2, which is popularly called Brixton, but we pay rates in Wandsworth, a district that is far away. . . . We have to walk a hundred yards to post letters so that they are postmarked "S.W.16", which is Streatham. Brixton and Streatham are not so much places as a state of mind.' ('Wanderer's' column in the *South London Press* of 22 January and 20 September 1957.)

Underneath the shifting sands of modern Brixton, however, there is still a solid core of old-established white-collar and artisan resi-

51

dents, tenants of council flats, statutory tenants, and ratepayers. And it is this core that forms local public opinion about immigrants as about other matters.

Before the second world war, the population of Brixton and the surrounding districts seems to have been fairly homogeneous. A disgruntled reader in the *South London Press,* bemoaning the passing of the true cockney, placed the beginning of the end in the 1930s, when London was 'invaded' by 'hordes of Scots, Irish, and provincials' who came here during the depression and decided to stay.[1]

Until the post-war years the district did not contain many continental Europeans. Nor does Brixton or any part of the borough ever seem to have had a large Jewish community by comparison with some East London boroughs,[2] although a fair number of the regular market traders are said to be Jewish, most of them being non-residents.

Before 1948 coloured people were so rare in Brixton and the surrounding districts that they are remembered as individuals and personalities, not dismissed as an out-group. There was a handful of coloured doctors, of whom probably the best known and most notable was the Jamaican-born Dr. Harold W. Moody of Camberwell. He was an active and eminent churchman who founded the League of Coloured Peoples and did a great deal to fight economic and social discrimination against coloured people in pre-war Britain. There were also a few West Indian volunteers from the 1914–18 war who had settled down locally, usually as artisans. Some coloured people even achieved the status of being regarded as local

---

[1] *South London Press,* 4 October 1957. He added: 'Now the black races are following their pattern; the cockney . . . will be just a memory fifty years hence.' Another reader (20 September 1957) had suggested that any cockneys still left should be put into reservations to prevent them dying out completely.

[2] See *Fifty Golden Years* (a short history of the Brixton Synagogue, 1958). There was, however, considerable anti-Semitic activity by Sir Oswald Mosley's Black Shirts in the 1930s. Brixton is sometimes spoken of as second only to Bethnal Green for Fascist activities at that period, but this may be an exaggeration. In the 1937 L.C.C. elections two Fascist candidates in Bethnal Green (North-east) won over 3,000 votes each, compared with 15,533 Labour and 4,606 Liberal votes. No Fascist candidate stood for any L.C.C. or local borough election in Brixton in the 1930s, although the first Jewish alderman went on Lambeth Borough Council in 1937. After the war three Union Movement candidates stood for the Brixton L.C.C. election once only, in 1952, when they were bottom of the poll with a total vote of 2,054 (Labour 45,406, Conservative 25,877). At present, the Brixton Synagogue, which serves a wide area of South London from Camberwell to Clapham, Balham, and Croydon, has a congregation of nearly 1,000 members.

characters or eccentrics. One of these was a well-known ex-pugilist who worked for the Lambeth Borough Council for many years. Another was a chief's son from West Africa, known locally as 'Massa Johnson'. He kept several lodging-houses for coloured students, and was always seen around the streets in a top hat and morning coat. The nine or so houses which he owned are still known locally as the 'Johnson houses' and they remain in coloured ownership or occupation today.

In 1945 continental Europeans began to enter the borough in large numbers. The principal groups were Poles, Cypriots, and Maltese.[1] The number of Southern Irish migrants also increased considerably.

After 1948 an increasing stream of West Indian migrant newcomers began to move into Brixton. According to a Town Hall official, the influx became noticeable about 1952–53, but the local branch of Sir Oswald Mosley's Union Movement was already campaigning (unsuccessfully) on a 'Keep Brixton White' platform in the 1952 LCC elections in Brixton.[2]

Until the next census figures are available, the size of the West Indian settlement in this area must remain a matter for impressionistic conjecture.[3] When I began my field work in the district in late 1955, the figure generally accepted by local authorities and welfare workers was in the neighbourhood of 5,000. Of these, probably a quarter were transients, new arrivals staying with relatives or friends until they found work. This might take them elsewhere in London, or even into the provinces. Others would find a job nearby and stay on for good. As we have already noted, the larger coloured settlements tend to be more of a magnet to newcomers than the smaller ones, and therefore to grow more quickly.

Brixton's heyday as an unofficial reception centre is probably over. In the last few years, migrants have tended to go straight to other West Indian settlements, often outside London, where there are better opportunities for work, and most new arrivals in the district seem to be close relatives of earlier settlers who have

---

[1] According to the 1951 census, Lambeth had 1,325 Polish-born residents, 386 Cypriots, 194 Maltese, and 110 Gibraltese.

[2] Some months earlier, the Brixton branch leader of the Union Movement had told an audience of about fifty that 'black parasites are living on hard-working white people. Stowaways are met by a certain Prince [this may be the "Massa Johnson" referred to above] who invites them to live in Brixton and tells them how to live free on unemployment benefit' (*South London Press*, 4 September 1951).

[3] The 1951 census (London volume) recorded only 414 West Indian-born residents (307 of them male) in Lambeth at the time. Of these, 315 were from Jamaica (235 men, 80 women). There were, however, 366 men and 410 women born in India, and 24 men and 31 women born in Pakistan. It seems likely that the majority of these 'Indians' were in fact Anglo-Indians. In addition, there were 102 persons born in West Africa (85 males, 17 females) of whom nearly all were Nigerian born.

53

achieved sufficient economic stability to send for them. By 1960, therefore, the Brixton settlement was no longer growing very fast and seemed to be entering a phase of gradual consolidation. It was even losing small numbers of longer-settled migrants who, having achieved their nest-egg, were going home. If we accept the estimate of 5,000 at the end of 1955, then 9,000 to 10,000 or so would seem a reasonable estimate of the established settlement five years later. The only kind of check that can be made on these estimates is a rough residential one. For instance, well over half of the houses in Somerleyton and Geneva Roads are now owned or occupied by West Indians. Since there are about 190 such houses, each containing ten or twelve rooms, and since each room usually houses at least two residents, almost all of whom are West Indian, the migrant population of these two streets alone is probably at least 2,000. This area is, of course, a special case, but there are a fair number of other streets in the central area of settlement where one in every four or five dwellings appears to house West Indians.

There seem to have been a number of reasons for the West Indian migrants' choice of Brixton in the years after 1948. The district had long contained a large number of theatrical and other boarding-houses. The last local *raison d'être* of the theatrical boarding-houses ceased to exist with the closing of the Brixton Empress in January 1957.[1] Brixton is, however, central and cheap, and these landladies have continued to accommodate considerable numbers of rank-and-file 'pros' playing in the West End and elsewhere. It is said, though with what accuracy could not be ascertained, that even before the war some theatrical landladies were accustomed to accepting coloured professional entertainers.

Among the other boarding-house or rooming-house proprietors, a growing number since the war have themselves been newcomers, Southern Irish, Polish, or Cypriot; and some of these seem to have had less colour consciousness, and to have been rather more willing than the local landladies to accept coloured lodgers. There was also

---

[1] The account of its closing in the *South London Press* of 11 January 1957 illustrates not only the changing public taste in entertainment but the declining fortunes of the area: 'When the Empress opened fifty-eight years ago, extravagantly decorated in the French Renaissance style, it accommodated 1,500 with quite a sprinkling of boxes for the fashionable set of the day. But by 1930 the neighbourhood had become hardly the place for social graces and the boxes were more often empty than full. So the next year the Empress closed for extensive alterations. Floors, circles, stage, and dressing rooms were torn out and the whole place replanned. When it reopened in October 1931, the seating had been increased to 2,000, the largest and most modern theatre south of the river. The boxes had gone, and the accent was on cheaper seats, the gallery and circle being lengthened and widened. . . . The Empress . . . has been bought by Granada Cinemas and after it has been re-decorated and re-equipped it will reopen . . . as a cinema.'

a handful of coloured old-timer landlords in the Somerleyton and Mostyn Road areas whose houses were to form the nuclei of the future settlement.

An additional initial factor influencing West Indian settlement in Brixton may well have been the fact that, for a few years after 1948, many West Indian men arriving in London without a lodging or a friend to meet them were accommodated in the old Clapham air-raid shelters or in the LCC reception centre in Peckham. They were sent to the nearby employment exchange to register for work and, somewhat naturally, they tended to look first for accommodation and work in the neighbourhood.

Later, other factors encouraged the growth of the Brixton migrant settlement. The district contained many large short-lease Victorian houses, most of them dilapidated, some recently derequisitioned and containing statutory tenants paying uneconomic pre-war rentals. This type of property had ceased to be attractive to English home-purchasers, to property investors, and even to speculators. As a consequence, many leaseholders were willing to sell before the leases ran out and they became liable for large dilapidation pay-ments – to sell at any price to any bidder, Irish, Polish, Cypriot, or coloured.

Brixton has other advantages for residents. Although it is largely a dormitory area, with few local industries, it is cheap, centrally situated, and has good communications with central London and most peri-urban industrial areas. Most of the West Indian settlement areas are also near such focal points as the employment exchange, Brixton market with its excellent and low-priced wares, the Town Hall, and the principal large shops and places of entertainment.

These seem to have been the main reasons for the settlement of West Indian migrants in Brixton from 1948 onwards. In recent years, however, an additional reason for their continued settlement has been the magnetism of this growing coloured quarter, in which accommodation, companionship, and special marketing and recrea-tional facilities can be found with relative ease.

From the two original nuclei, the Somerleyton–Geneva Road area (which is, properly speaking, in Norwood, just south of the Brixton divisional border) and Angell Town (Mostyn Road, Angell Road, Wiltshire Road, Elliot Road, Akerman Road, Bramah Road, and so on), West Indians in search of accommodation have gradually spread through the whole of central Lambeth and beyond. They have moved southward (with a slight westward bias) up Herne Hill and Tulse Hill, and even as far as South Norwood over the Croydon border; eastward to Peckham, East Dulwich, New Cross, and Dept-ford; and westward to North Clapham and Battersea.

The scope of the study

Only to the residential middle-class south and to the north and north-east has this steady movement been contained. Residential accommodation in the solid working-class districts of North Lambeth and the boroughs of Southwark and Bermondsey is mainly restricted to dilapidated single-family terrace houses or to council flats. Neither type of accommodation offers much opening for newcomers and transients. In Bermondsey this barrier is strengthened by the steady conversion of former residential areas to industrial use. In addition, the people of Bermondsey form a particularly close community which does not easily accept outsiders.

The Camberwell coloured settlement seems originally to have been an offshoot of the Brixton settlement just over the border. It first became noticeable about 1955, and the coloured migrants are mainly to be found in Peckham and North Camberwell, between the Old Kent Road and Camberwell Green. Some of them would, in fact, come within the 'Brixton' settlement in the popular sense in which we are using the name. There are rather more Pakistanis and Indians in the Camberwell settlement than in Brixton.

This North Camberwell area consists mainly of dilapidated short-lease houses with two or three storeys. Many of them are scheduled for demolition and clearance. There has been no dense settlement of migrants as in parts of Brixton. Instead, the coloured newcomers, like the Cypriots and Poles before them, are dotted about wherever they can find accommodation. It is generally agreed that the Camberwell coloured settlement is considerably smaller than that in Brixton. Here again there are no official statistics, but an approximate minimum figure may be calculated for the year 1956, when 137 premises were known by the public health department to house coloured people, most of them West Indians. If one assumes that each dwelling housed a minimum of ten coloured people, one would arrive at a total of nearly 1,500 coloured migrants even at that early stage.

Other figures collected by local authorities in Camberwell in the years 1954, 1956, and 1958 give an idea of the growing number of West Indian and other coloured children, and therefore of elementary family units, in the borough. Whereas in 1954 there were no West Indian children in local schools, and only 17 in 1956, there were 93 in 1958. The fact that they were distributed in thirty schools, in only five of which were there more than 4 West Indian children (14 in one school, 7 in two, 6 in one, and 5 in one), seems to bear out the statement above that, except perhaps for one nucleus, the Camberwell settlement is more scattered than the Brixton one. These children were for the most part of primary-school age, and figures for attendance at child welfare centres (103 in 1956, 173 in 1958)

56

suggest that there were even more migrant children in the younger age-groups.[1]

According to a West Indian informant of the professional class who was working in the borough, Camberwell afforded a more favourable climate of opinion for coloured settlement than Brixton. This he attributed in part to the long association with the area of Dr. Harold Moody and his family, in part to the fact that the migrant settlement was less obtrusive, because of both its smaller size and its wider dispersal. He also contrasted the more positive attitude of the Borough Council with the studiously egalitarian and negative approach which in his view characterizes Lambeth.

Lewisham is more remote than Brixton or Camberwell from central London and has poorer communications. It has rather the character of a family residential area with a large proportion of black-coated workers. Coloured migrants have settled there in recent years, but at the time of this study the settlement was even less concentrated than that of Camberwell. A borough official interviewed in 1957 considered that the number of coloured migrants in Lewisham was small, even insignificant. He conceded, nevertheless, that there might be some 100 coloured-owned or -occupied houses in the borough. By the usual rough reckoning, this would in itself give a total of between 1,000 and 2,000 coloured residents in Lewisham as early as 1957.[2] In 1959, another local informant spoke of dispersed coloured settlement all over Lewisham, particularly in Lower Sydenham, Catford, Forest Hill, Hither Green, and, most recently, New Cross.

There was no time to collect more detailed information on the growing West Indian settlements in other South London districts. Fairly large groups would seem to be resident in Battersea and Wandsworth,[3] but the Brixton settlement remains the largest, oldest, and most stable. A new trend since 1957, after unskilled work became more difficult to find, has been for migrants to find a job

---

[1] Further light on the size of the Camberwell coloured settlement may also be thrown by the fact that about 150 wholly coloured marriages were conducted in the borough in the year 1958–59. It is interesting to note that in Mrs. Ruth Glass's breakdown of 4,691 addresses of migrants in Greater London up to 1960, 4·8 per cent were in Camberwell, as compared with 18·4 per cent in Lambeth. No detailed later figures could be obtained, but the situation in early 1961 was said not to differ greatly from that in 1958.

[2] This spokesman, incidentally, had the impression that there were few foreigners in Lewisham at all, whereas in fact the Polish community there is able to support a Polish priest and has a flourishing Polish-owned estate agency catering mainly for fellow-countrymen. The value of his impressions of the size and distribution of the coloured population must therefore be somewhat questionable, other than as an indication of official disinterest in this group at the time.

[3] Out of 4,691 London addresses, 6·5 per cent were in Wandsworth and 3·8 per cent in Battersea (Glass, 1960, p. 35).

where they could and then move nearer to their place of work to save travelling-time and fares. This has led to the setting-up of smaller nuclei of coloured settlement in North Croydon and Tooting, within easy reach of the light industrial areas of the Purley Way and Mitcham.

Another area of coloured settlement which has recently come into the news is the predominantly working-class borough of Deptford. Here the local press was in late 1960 writing of a 'Caribbean Quarter', and the M.P., Sir Leslie Plummer, was speaking of a 'boiling-up of racialism' over housing in the New Cross area. Some months later, the British National Party became active in the district; its three candidates polled 3,695 out of a total poll of 45,059 in the 1961 LCC elections. Despite loose talk of an 'influx', however, it seems unlikely that more than a few hundred coloured people were resident in the borough by the end of 1960; most of them were living in the area where the Old Kent Road, Lewisham Way, and Deptford High Street meet. This friction would, in fact, appear to be part of the usual teething-troubles of any new migrant settlement.[1]

Most coloured students lodge north of the river. A minority, however, live in South London, either because it is cheap or because they are attending one of the South London hospitals or technical colleges. As might be expected, most of these students avoid the working-class migrant settlements and congregate in areas with greater social pretensions such as Streatham and parts of Norwood.

A PRELIMINARY NOTE ON THE BRIXTON
WEST INDIAN GROUP

Brixton's coloured population is largely West Indian and, as a general rule, the present study will be confined to this group. Most of its members come from Jamaica, but there are smaller groups from British Guiana, Barbados, and other islands.[2] There is still a disproportionate number of youngish adult men, but wives, concubines, children, parents, and unattached women have in recent years been arriving in increasing numbers. By 1959 the proportion of women to men in the Brixton group seemed fairly high compared

[1] It is, however, interesting to note that Deptford may in fact have the oldest coloured settlement in South London. One informant who had known the area for years told me that its nucleus was a group of West African males, seamen or dock-workers, living in old houses run by English-speaking leaders or second-generation Anglo-coloured landlords. Unfortunately, it was not possible to pursue this inquiry further.

[2] See Glass (1960, p. 40) for the geographical distribution in London of migrants from various islands, taken from the addresses in her London Sample. Cf. also p. 346, n. 2 below.

with more recent migrant settlements, possibly as much as three women to every four men.

So far, Brixton seems to have attracted the more stable type of migrant worker, rather than the 'wide boys' or the drifters, most of whom find Paddington or Stepney more to their taste. The great majority of migrants in Brixton are semi-skilled or unskilled workers even by West Indian standards, and an increasing number are from rural areas. The Brixton West Indian settlement is almost entirely of lower-class background, although it has produced some small businessmen and multiple landlords. West Indian professional people usually live north of the river or in more attractive suburbs such as Dulwich or Streatham. *Bona fide* students, as we have noted, prefer to live in lodgings outside Brixton, and there are few old-timers.

The Brixton migrant settlement thus lacks a potential *élite* or internal leadership. Taking this into account in conjunction with its relatively recent origin, with the individualistic attitude and high residential mobility of many of its members, and with the fact that the main areas of settlement do not lend themselves to the creation of a firmly delineated and isolated coloured quarter, it is not surprising to find that the Brixton migrant group has not as yet developed any notable feeling of community, nor any strong and durable organizational bonds.

In its main features, the West Indian settlement in Brixton is fairly typical of the recent settlements of coloured people in this country, although it is longer established than most of them. It is therefore hoped that this study of its growth, its problems, and its evolving relationships with the local population and with the receiving society as a whole will prove of use not only to students of the more theoretical aspects of race relations but to a wider circle of readers.

PART II

Migrants at work

4

The British labour market and the immigrant worker

BRITAIN AS AN IMPORTER OF IMMIGRANT LABOUR

'The positive or negative contribution which the non-European immigrants make depends both on the nature of the services they are able to render and on the extent to which they are allowed to render them and are accepted by the community.'[1]

A JOB and a roof over his head – these are the main immediate needs of the newcomer in Britain. They are also the two main areas of competition and possible conflict between migrants and the local population, and therefore areas in which accommodation, though essential, is often difficult to reach on both sides.

The relations between natives and newcomers in the employment field cannot be studied in isolation from the regional and indeed the country-wide history of industrial relationships between British workers and immigrants, particularly when we are concerned with a dormitory area like Brixton, in which most people work elsewhere. This history has left workers and trade unions with certain fixed and generally hostile attitudes towards all outside labour: for expediency's sake, these attitudes are usually accepted or taken into consideration by employers and the government.

In Britain, the degree of immediate hostility to and discrimination against Irish, foreign, and coloured immigrants seems to be related to the degree of economic insecurity felt by the local working population.[2] Dr. Kenneth Little has shown how hostility towards and discrimination against coloured seamen in Cardiff swelled in the shipping industry's lean years from 1921 to 1938 and left an enduring mark on local attitudes.[3] Writing in 1955, Michael Banton

[1] 'The Positive Contribution by Immigrants' (Unesco, 1955).

[2] See *Report of the Select Committee on Emigration and Immigration (Foreigners)* (*1888*) and *Report of the Royal Commission on the Alien Immigration (1903)*, for complaints about employers' use of Poles and Lithuanians as strike-breakers and undercutters of wages in Lanarkshire and Cheshire.

[3] Little (1947, pp. 60–84). The writer also points out that even with the advent of better times the hostility engendered tended to retain its strength longer in Cardiff, where the coloured population was concentrated in a small, geographically isolated

pointed out that the only serious racial disturbances of the post-war decade occurred in Liverpool, where the level of unemployment was relatively high.[1] Since then, the disturbances in Nottingham in August–September 1958 have provided a further example of hostility and conflict arising at least in part out of economic insecurity.[2]

In the earlier post-war years, however, the shortage of unskilled and semi-skilled labour was so great in Britain (despite the regular presence of over half a million Southern Irish)[3] that the provisions of the Aliens Order (1920) were relaxed to admit individual foreigners under Ministry of Labour permits to work in certain branches of industry. In addition, the government and various public bodies were able to carry out certain recruitment schemes for importing labour into undermanned sectors of industry and trade. These sectors included agriculture, mining, building, brick-making, textiles, and domestic work. Trade union opposition was on the whole limited to the imposition of certain conditions and controls, such as redundancy priority clauses.

Chief among these recruitment schemes were: the Polish re-settlement programme of 1946–51, which was designed to resettle in Britain certain of those Polish soldiers and their families who did not wish to return to life under a Communist government; the EVW (European Volunteer Workers) programme for displaced persons of the same period; and some smaller schemes for German and Austrian domestic workers, Italians, and Belgians.

Together, the Ministry of Labour permit-holders, the EVWs, and the Poles totalled over 300,000, and constituted the bulk of immigrants from the Continent of Europe in the 1946–50 period. Other European migrants – students, dependants, and so on – brought the grand total up to 457,000, of which an unknown but substantial

area, than it did in Liverpool and London, where settlement was less concentrated. The implications of 'ghetto' settlement for the long-term processes of adaptation and acceptance are considered on pp. 213–14 below.

[1] Banton (1955, p. 127). Cf. also Richmond (1954, pp. 35–52), on the experiences of coloured workers on Merseyside during the 1947 recession.

[2] Cf. James Wickenden (1958, pp. 9–10, 24–6, and 30–1).

[3] The 1951 census showed 527,700 Southern Irish-born people resident in Britain, and another 188,100 from Northern Ireland. The majority of Southern Irish migrants are unskilled or semi-skilled workers and, as we shall see, they are often the group that comes into competition with coloured migrants for jobs. Although traditionally associated with building, personal service, and certain types of heavy industry, they have since the second world war entered a far wider range of industries. For the century and a half of British experience of Irish immigrant labour, see Jackson (1961, *passim*). Definite statistics are hard to come by until the 1961 census figures are published. Jackson has also estimated that by 1961 over one million Irish-born people were resident in Britain, the majority (perhaps five-sevenths) from the Republic of Ireland. The Economist Intelligence Unit (1) (1961) estimated that the net immigration into the U.K. from the Republic of Ireland alone between 1946 and 1959 was 352,600.

proportion may have returned to the Continent after a year or more.

Britain thus went to considerable trouble and expense to solve her post-war manpower problems; and a far larger number of outsiders entered the country and the labour force than had been the case for many decades. The Senior–Manley Report (1955), in a chapter on British attitudes to and experience of outsiders, compared the number of foreign-born residents in 1951 (597,500), plus an additional 268,700 foreign-born people classified as 'nationality not stated', with the figure of 268,400 foreign-born residents for the year 1931, and commented: ' . . . the British people have been subjected to an influx of foreigners on a scale much greater than they had previously experienced . . . the West Indian migration constitutes only a small proportion of this influx' (p. 15, para. 62).

The industries entered by the European Volunteer Workers and the Poles were those which were undermanned, by reason of their intrinsic unpleasantness, or because of low pay, long hours, or seasonal fluctuations. The jobs to which these workers gravitated when they were free of controls were less unattractive, but were still often characterized by one or more such features as low wages, low status, or insecurity. They were: building and construction; the production of seasonal consumer goods; food and soft drinks production; general labouring; the lower levels of the garment trade; the catering trade;[1] and public transport and communications. Such jobs are the traditional province of the recent immigrant in many countries, and they have on the whole continued to be the jobs which the recent coloured migrants must, despite their freedom from official controls, take on their first entry into the British labour market, although the extent of their penetration into any given industry varies considerably from area to area.[2] Agriculture[3], coal mining,[4] and domestic work[5] have, however, for a number of rea-

[1] See an article in the *Times British Colonies Review* (Third Quarter, 1957) on 'Colonials in Britain', under the title 'Room for Many More in the Catering Trade'.
[2] See Reid (1956, p. 205) for a comparison of coloured penetration of the building and catering trades in Manchester, Stepney, and Cardiff.
[3] There would seem to be a number of factors which deter West Indians from going on the land in Britain: chief among them are low wages, remoteness, climate, and a distaste for doing the work which many migrants were compelled to do before migrating. In addition, few migrants are equipped for work in the very different and highly mechanized agricultural industry in Britain.
[4] In May 1957 it was estimated that there were some two hundred West Indians employed in coal mining in various parts of the country (B.C.W.S. Press Release No. 11, 6 May 1957). In Press Release No. 21, dated 26 September 1957, the B.C.W.S. stated that, while there was no official limit to the number of West Indians that could be employed in coal mining, there was a limit to the hostel accommodation made available for West Indian miners. The majority of West Indians working in British mines were said to be in the lowest-paid grades.
[5] See below, pp. 82, 135.

sons failed to attract or receive any significant number of coloured workers at all.

THE BRITISH LABOUR MARKET AFTER 1956

In 1956 the overall labour shortage in Britain ended, following the cuts in government expenditure, the credit squeeze of early 1956, and the Suez Canal closure in late 1956. This year also saw the admission of some 11,000 Hungarian refugees, most of them young, single men, who had to be absorbed in the labour market, and the arrival of a few thousand Anglo-Egyptian refugees, who were to some extent cushioned by government welfare action and a privately raised relief fund.

During the years 1956 to 1958 no large-scale general recession in fact developed, and the shortage of skilled workers continued. In the semi-skilled and even more in the unskilled industrial market, however, the shortage of labour decreased or disappeared. This was also true to a certain extent in the textile, motor vehicle, wireless apparatus, and electrical goods industries. In consequence, employers became much more selective and the unions began to make their influence felt more than before. In addition, displaced British workers began to look with a more kindly eye at the jobs in basic industries, in public transport,[1] and other relatively low-paid occupations, jobs which they had hitherto scorned.

The attitudes of British workers and trade unions had never constituted a 'pull' factor in the same way as had purely economic factors. No organized body of labour, even in a country of immigration, welcomes large groups of newcomers. Until then, however, protests from this quarter had been more formal than real; these protests were based more on dark memories, hearsay, ignorance, and apprehension than on current reality.[2]

As we have seen, 1956 was a peak year for West Indian migration to Britain. After 1957 and until late 1959, the number of arrivals began to decline and increasing numbers began to return home. It seems likely that these changes were largely the outcome of the growing economic difficulties, underlined by the increasingly gloomy reports sent home by migrants already here, and by the warnings

---

[1] According to the Ministry of Labour annual report for 1956, published in late August 1957, there was a substantial redeployment of labour from manufacturing industries to basic industries. The number of men in employment in coal mining rose by over 3,000 (this would not affect West Indians, of whom only about 200 were so employed) and in transport and communications by 9,000. There were also increases in the numbers employed in building, contracting, and distributive trades, and in the chemical and allied trades.

[2] See pp. 143–9 for a more detailed discussion of the attitudes and reactions of British labour to coloured workers.

which the Jamaican and other West Indian governments began to issue in 1956 about the worsening employment situation in Britain. After September 1958 the disturbances in Notting Hill, London, may also, of course, have induced some migrants to return and deterred others from coming, although there is no definite evidence of this.

As early as May 1956 there was evidence that coloured workers were becoming more difficult to place in such centres as Brixton, Birmingham, Manchester, and Liverpool. By September 1956, Mr. Robert Carr, Parliamentary Secretary to the Ministry of Labour,[1] declared that the number of coloured unemployed throughout Britain was 6,800, or about 1,500 more than in the previous quarter. The total unemployed count in the country at this time was 208,000 (135,000 men and 73,000 women); there were 224,800 vacancies, 134,800 for men and 90,000 for women, but of these only 35,000 and 52,000 respectively were for unskilled workers. Mr. Carr, commenting on these figures, said that the situation was not critical; in the same period the total number of coloured workers in jobs had risen by 6,000[2] and there was no 'hard core' of unemployed coloured workers.

No regular counts of coloured unemployed have so far been published, but from time to time approximate numbers are given in parliamentary answers. While their use is limited in the absence of precise demographic data about the migrant group or its distribution, including the size of the working population, these estimates are given here as a rough illustration of the unemployment situation as it developed from 1956 to the end of 1960.

In June 1957 reports from areas of coloured settlement indicated a considerable if temporary improvement in the employment situation. At the same time, the Ministry of Labour reported that it was taking much longer to place migrant newcomers than in earlier years.

By the autumn of 1957 the overall number of coloured unemployed was about 7,500 (total unemployed in Britain 268,000), and over the winter this figure was doubled to 15,000 in March, when the total unemployed count was 433,000. The chief groups to suffer were Indians and Pakistanis, and the West Indian unemployed total rose only from 4,500 to 6,500.[3] At the end of July 1958 the coloured unemployment count was over 17,000,[4] and at the end of the year

[1] See *The Times*, 19 October 1956.
[2] It must also be taken into account that a steady stream of new arrivals (9,000 from the West Indies alone) was coming onto the labour market during the same period.
[3] Miss Pat Hornsby-Smith, *Hansard*, 4 April 1958.
[4] The Rt. Hon. R. A. Butler, *Liverpool Daily Post*, 6 September 1958. On 19 November 1958 these figures were presented in another form in the House of Lords: Lord Perth contrasted the coloured unemployment rate of about 8 per cent with that of the national average of under 3 per cent.

it was 14,300[1] out of an estimated total of 210,000 coloured migrants, of whom 115,000 were West Indians.

The winter of 1958–59 was a hard one and there was a peak figure of over 17,000 coloured unemployed in February 1959. After March, however, the employment situation improved radically, and no further reports of the number of coloured unemployed seem to have been published in 1959 and 1960[2] – this in itself is an index of the fact that the employment of coloured labour had ceased to be a major source of concern and friction.

Over the years since 1956 the South London labour market has experienced the same processes as the rest of the country, although the average unemployment figure may not have risen quite so high as in some undiversified industrial areas in the provinces. The customary seasonal variations due to the winter or post-Christmas drop in employment openings in catering, distribution, entertainment, transport, and such manufacturing industries as food production, clothing, and furniture, and also the curtailment of building projects, were greatly intensified by the general economic recession that was triggered off by the credit squeeze. Particularly hard hit were the labour-exporting dormitory districts of Brixton, Tooting, and Battersea, and it was there, in the years 1956–58, that employment for a time replaced housing as the main source of friction and potential conflict.

In the tabloid *South London Advertiser*, a highly emotive article appeared as early as 19 July 1956, headlined 'The Dole Comes to Brixton'. Alongside it was a photograph of West Indian men waiting by the employment exchange, and it stressed the fact that the 'biggest proportion of the men on the dole are coloured folk', and that 'twice a month regularly another shipload of West Indians pour into Brixton's 7,000-strong coloured population'. And by the autumn of 1958, just after the Notting Hill disturbances, even the more responsible, Labour-oriented *South London Press* was calling editorially for controls on the immigration of 'refugees from unemployment' of any colour during the current period of unemployment.

' . . . The fact is that white immigration is much more of a problem than the coloured one. . . . The reason West Indians, or other coloureds, are attacked is that they alone are recognisable

[1] *Hansard,* 5 December 1958. In mid-September of this year, the number of registered unemployed in Britain also rose to 476,000, the highest figure since the fuel crisis of 1958.

[2] By early 1961, however, Mr. Norman Pannell, M.P., was citing increased unemployment figures for coloured migrants in London following the peak migration year of 1960; a government spokesman, in answer, admitted that the coloured unemployment average was about 5 per cent, compared with the national average of 1·9 per cent. (*Hansard,* Vol. 634, No. 56, 17 February 1961).

to the thugs who take advantage of a general resentment among whites. . . . This resentment is due to a feeling that foreigners "come here and take the bread out of our mouths as well as our houses", and that feeling is well based. Over two-thirds of our population live by selling their labour, at the best prices their unions can get, and immigrants mainly come here to work, as is often said in their favour. They are forced to take low wages for long hours, and they lower the price of labour in the first place. In the second, with our Government now openly committed to a policy of creating unemployment to cheapen labour, foreigners are the first to be laid off, and they become a charge on the unemployment and welfare services paid for and built up by us as natives. . . . Many immigrants are valuable to the community they join, as we have seen since Einstein and other Jewish refugees from Hitler came to Britain or U.S. Most of the nuclear research in both lands is now being done by former Germans. But refugees from unemployment, like those who come from Eire, are seldom highly skilled workers – they would find work at home if they were – and this island, which lives by becoming a workshop to the world, needs skilled workers who can earn good money and are not willing to be cheap labour. . . . We can remain a home of freedom for political refugees but we cannot afford any longer to be a dump for the world's unemployed . . .' (*South London Press*, 12 September 1958).

South London unemployment figures reached their peak in March 1959. Thereafter recovery was rapid and coloured unemployment ceased to figure in the press. The experiences of the Brixton employment exchange over these years provide a good illustration of the situation as it developed, and also of the way in which a determined and positive approach could minimize the problem and prevent the formation of a permanent pool of West Indian unemployed, even at a very difficult period.[1]

WEST INDIAN MIGRANT WORKERS

'Push' and 'Pull' Factors

'Push' factors have shown themselves even stronger and more permanent in the situation under study than the earlier 'pull' factor of full employment. The 'push' factors have, as we saw in the last chapter, been in existence for over half a century and have sent stream after stream of West Indian migrants, particularly Jamaicans, in search of temporary and permanent work to the Panama Canal, Cuba, Venezuela, and the United States. And after the McCarran

[1] Described below (pp. 139–42).

Act of 1952 and the virtual ending of coloured immigration to the U.S.A., these pressures impelled a quarter of a million West Indians to make the relatively expensive journey to the only territory left open to them without restrictions – the United Kingdom – until even this door was partly closed in 1962.

The main 'push' factors consist of over-population; economic under-development resulting in large-scale unemployment; chronic under-employment; low wage levels; lack of economic diversity, opportunity, or incentives; and lack of adequate opportunities for education and vocational training.[1] Important, too, is the wanderlust characteristic of a frustrated and unsettled society.[2]

Between 1948 and 1956, and again after 1959, the major 'pull' factor stimulating migration to Britain was the fact of full employment in a diversified and large-scale economy. This full employment resulted in a flight from the less attractive and less well-paid jobs by British workers and a consequent shortage of labour. It also served to blunt the British workers' long-standing fears of dilution, undercutting, and lowering of living standards by foreign labour.

Other 'pull' factors for West Indian migrants were: year-round jobs; higher wages;[3] better opportunities for advancement and higher vocational training; the facilities offered by the welfare state and the more developed educational service; the increasing availability of cheap transatlantic transportation; Britain's open-door policy; a desire to visit the mother country and to see the city lights and gold-paved streets; possibly, too, the attraction of a white society to some 'white-biased' West Indians. All these 'pull' factors were underlined and re-emphasized by shrewd shipping agents in the West Indies, and later in letters written home by relatives and friends who were already in Britain and unwilling to admit to disillusionment or failure.

General Economic Background in the British Caribbean

The degree to which the West Indian newcomers adapt themselves to the new environment is affected not only by the labour situation,

[1] See Elizabeth E. Hoyt (1960) on the effect of the whole social and economic background on the employability of the lower-class Jamaican; and M. G. Smith (1960) for the 'formidable gap between reality and desire' in children's occupational aspirations and the occupations which they actually have to take up.

[2] Cf. this passage from a letter written by the Colonial Secretary of Barbados, Mr. Schomburgk, in 1863: 'A thirst for novelty and change, which is a prominent trait in the Negro character, induced a great number to leave the island . . .' (quoted by Roberts, 1955, p. 246).

[3] In 1946 the skilled wage differential ranged from 25–50 per cent less in Jamaica than in the U.K., while that for unskilled workers was 50–65 per cent lower in Jamaica. By 1952, however, the differential, though still considerable, had decreased to between 20–25 per cent for skilled workers and about 50 per cent for unskilled labour (Roberts and Mills, 1958, p. 4).

the opportunities, and the reception which they find in the British labour market, but also by the migrants' own economic background, skills,[1] expectations of and attitudes to work, degree of adaptability, and also by their expectations of the new society.

The West Indian economy is predominantly based on agriculture. In 1949, when the exodus to Britain was beginning, two-thirds of all wage-earners worked in agriculture and only 8 per cent in the manufacturing industries. Even the latter low percentage was about double that for 1939. Most rural wage-earners were dependent not only on their wages but also on the produce of a small-holding. This pattern of casual labour and hand-to-mouth domestic economy often continued to influence even the relatively small number of urban industrial workers.[2]

The economic situation of the islands from which the West Indian emigrants have come is characterized by a high degree of unemployment and under-employment, and by a high incidence of migrant and seasonal labour. This is especially true of Jamaica, from which the majority of migrants have always come, and it is the Jamaican situation that is most closely documented. In that island, the overall unemployment rate for recent years had been estimated at about 20 per cent. During the war years, however, this figure reached 40 per cent for building and construction, and 34 per cent for transport and communications.

Social and economic incentives are small in Jamaica, and the whole system is characterized by a high degree of instability. In a fairly recent study of Jamaican productivity, G. E. Cumper (1953, p. 3f.) cited the International Bank Mission's estimate that the productivity of Jamaican industrial labour was between 50 per cent and 70 per cent of that of the British worker. He added that the Jamaican worker was at a disadvantage *vis-à-vis* the British worker as regards spending opportunities, possibilities of promotion, social mobility, training, and general and specialized education.[3]

[1] In his study of West Indian male workers in Liverpool during the war, Richmond (1954) showed that a good adjustment seemed to be closely related to the individual migrant's degree of skill.

[2] See Maunder (1955, pp. 52–5).

[3] Douglas Manley (1960) gives some information on the general educational background in the West Indies (pp. 39–45). Illiteracy rates in the 1946 census varied from 29 per cent (Windward Islands) and 23·9 per cent (Jamaica) to 7·3 per cent (Barbados). There is, however, reason to suppose that these have been reduced since. Education is free but not yet compulsory. Very few children receive secondary education at all (3·5 per cent in Jamaica, 7·5 per cent in Trinidad, about one-third in Barbados). The Davison sample of 1960 migrants from Jamaica showed that 4 per cent of the men had no formal education, 16 per cent had reached primary grades 1–3, 78 per cent had reached grades 4–6, and only 2 per cent had received secondary education. The corresponding figures for women showed a rather higher level (0 per cent, 9 per cent, 88 per cent, 3 per cent). (Davison, 1961, Part I.)

71

In the West Indian industrial system, there is relatively little specialization and there are few large-scale establishments. Even skilled men tend to be jacks-of-all-trades rather than master of one in the Western or United States sense. Apprenticeship is a more flexible concept and a man may become a skilled worker in West Indian terms in a considerably shorter time than in Britain.

In a report on industrial training methods in Jamaica, Ella Campbell (1953) wrote:

'For all practical purposes there is no apprenticeship system in Jamaica. . . . The Apprenticeship Committee report stresses that the present law is for all practical purposes obsolete, points out how unsatisfactory is the state of affairs with regard to apprentices (especially in the smaller industries and enterprises) and gives as reasons the lack (in most cases) of any system of training or well-defined conditions of employment; the lack of co-ordination with the training offered by technical and vocational schools, little or no regard being paid to the basic educational qualifications of apprentices or learners; the exploitation of juveniles by some employers, who utilize nominal apprenticeship as a means of securing cheap labour; the attitude of some parents and guardians who are more interested in the immediate increase of family income than in a career for the boys and girls whom they seek to place under apprenticeship; the tendency of apprentices and learners under such conditions to shift from one employment to another, or to open up business on their own in a small way before completing training; and the frequent abuse of the system by partially trained apprentices who, in the absence of regulations requiring certification of apprentice and master, are able, when they set up for themselves, to employ apprentices of their own' (p. 13).[1]

Miss Campbell also gave figures, taken from the 1950 report of the Education Department, for the number of students at the only technical school (the Government Technical School, Kingston) then in existence in Jamaica to provide technical and commercial training: total number of day students, 638—commercial 173, domestic science 122, technical 149, trade 194; total of evening students, 707 —commercial 147, domestic science 213, technical and trade 347.

In Britain, a strong and old-established trade union organization guards skills and standards. In the West Indies, however, the trade

[1] In his study of religious cults in Morant Bay, Jamaica, Moore (1954) gives the following list of accepted apprenticeship periods in that area: tailor, 1–1½ years; carpenter, 3 years; painter, 18 months; barber, 1–18 months; automobile mechanic, 5 years; dressmaking, 1–1½ years.

union organization is only forty years old. It has until recent years been weak, confused, and bedevilled by individual political ambitions. A number of unions, some of which may be company unions, compete for the workers in a given industry. Miss Campbell gave the following information about Jamaican unions in 1953:

'In the trade union field . . . it is generally found that organization amongst agricultural and domestic workers is slowest and most difficult. These groups form the majority of the Jamaican wage earners and this has meant that the whole pattern of union activity has been subject to special difficulties. The high incidence of seasonal and casual employment, and the nature of the estate system impose additional local handicaps on stable union organization. The development of craft unions has also been negligible, due to the low level of skill demanded in the majority of occupations. The growth of trade unionism and the current upsurge of political activity date from about 1938, and trade union and political activity have been closely linked. Each of the major political parties is closely allied with a trade union organization which attempts to cover all types of workers and to gain political support from the workers for the party to which it is linked. Trade unionists in 1938 were 0.41 per cent of all wage earners; in 1950 they were 24.13 per cent. Gross union assets rose from £150 in 1938 to £20,160 in 1949, suffering a decline in 1950 and 1951.'

Since then, the percentage of trade unionists to the wage-earning population has risen (it was estimated to a possible 40 per cent in 1957), but the highly personal link with rival political leaders seems to remain, as does the subordination to politics.[1]

Migrant Occupational Background and Skills

It is almost certainly true that the West Indian migrants who have arrived in Britain since the war are above the British Caribbean average in economic skills,[2] and probably in terms of such intangibles as initiative and the desire for self-improvement. They are nevertheless hampered by a poor educational background and a lack of specialized vocational training or modern industrial experience in

[1] See O. W. Phelps (1960) and C. P. Bronley (1960).
[2] See Roberts and Mills (1958, p. 124); Maunder (1955, p. 59); Luke (1954); and Davison (1961). See also Roberts (1957b, pp. 279–80) on the possible disadvantages of this movement to the West Indian territories, in the event of large-scale economic development there.

73

British terms. Far from enriching the new society to the same degree as they impoverish their home economy by migrating, the majority must start at the bottom of the industrial and occupational ladder and, as will be seen in the individual industrial case histories given below, strive hard to attain even minimum standards.

No overall statistics of the migrants' occupational background or training are available, but the results of several detailed surveys provide a picture that corresponds well enough with the impressions I formed over these years of field work. For instance, the surveys carried out by W. F. Maunder and by the Institute of Social and Economic Research of the University College of the West Indies in collaboration with the Central Bureau of Statistics in Kingston, Jamaica, over the years 1953–55 gave some useful data about the labour history of the migrants leaving for Britain at that time. This included the information that 34 per cent of two groups of emigrants totalling 794 people had left their jobs a year or more before emigrating, while 7 per cent (mainly women) had not worked for three years or more (see Maunder, 1955, p. 54).

Statistics relating to the industrial classification and earnings of this particular group of emigrants showed that, of the males, 23 per cent had come from agriculture and fishing, 31 per cent from manu-facturing, 10 per cent from building and construction, 15 per cent from commerce and public utilities, 10 per cent from services, 4 per cent from transport, storage, and communications, and 8 per cent from unclassified occupations. Average earnings ranged between 37*s.* and 86*s.* per week, the mean being 57*s.* Of the women, 8 per cent had come from commerce and public utilities, 23 per cent from services, 8 per cent from unclassified occupations, and 61 per cent from 'manufacturing'. According to the article, this last high pro-portion was accounted for 'in major part by those whose occupation was defined as "handicraft workers"; the majority in fact were dressmakers and milliners'. Average earnings among the women ranged narrowly between 31*s.* and 37*s.*, the mean being 35*s.* per week (Maunder, 1955, p. 51, Table 10).

Roberts and Mills (1958) also gave further information on the economic and residential background of female migrants to Britain over the years 1953–55. The percentage of women classifying them-selves as 'dressmakers' remained steady at 50 per cent in all three years, although the actual number in the group rose steeply each year. On the other hand, the percentage of 'domestic workers' (few or none of whom, as we shall see, would agree to take up this occu-pation in Britain) rose from 13 per cent in 1953 to 18 per cent in 1955, while the percentage of women declaring themselves outside the labour force on departure rose from 14 to 19 per cent over the

The British labour market and the immigrant worker

same period.[1] Few women migrants were illiterate: only six in 1954 and thirty-three in 1955. Women also continued to migrate from the urban areas in larger numbers than did males: 39 per cent came from Kingston in 1953 and 29 per cent in 1955; from Kingston–St. Andrews, 60 per cent in 1953 and 49 per cent in 1955.[2] This is probably due, first, to the time-lag in the migration of wives and other female relatives to join male migrants from urban areas already established in the United Kingdom; and second, to the spread of the migratory impulse to many enterprising single women, following encouraging reports from Britain.

There is a wide difference of opinion as to the distribution and degree of skills among the West Indian migrants in Britain. This is due mainly to the considerable divergence between the requirements and training opportunities of the two economies,[3] which has resulted in contradictory estimates, according to whether these are based on the migrant's own statement of his skills and former occupation (which in turn may be slightly embellished in the telling), or on the actual work being done in Britain by migrants – or, again, on British assessments of their abilities (in which case one must allow for the fact that recent immigrants usually start at the bottom of the work ladder and that local assessments may be somewhat more pejorative than the facts justify).

The figures given by Roberts and Mills (1958) reflect the former extreme, being based on forms filled in by male migrants before they left Jamaica in the years 1953–55. The writers, however, warn readers that the 'occupational classes designated skilled in terms of conventional West Indian standards bear little relation to the classes of skilled workers as understood in Great Britain.[4] According to their own unverified claim, 65 per cent of all male migrants leaving the island in 1953 were skilled or semi-skilled (the 1954 and 1955

	1953	1954	1955	Total 1953–55
Dressmakers	417	1,480	2,780	4,677
Domestic workers	116	353	1,087	1,556
Housewives	95	255	835	1,185

[1] The classification 'dressmaker' does not necessarily imply any particular skill or industrial background but simply indicates that the individual concerned could use a hand sewing-machine and would earn a little pin-money at home by running up dresses for her family and neighbours. The 'housewives' were presumably going with or to join their husbands. The steep rise in 1955 probably reflects the increasing prosperity of male migrants, which enabled them to send for their womenfolk.

[2] These are the percentages of all women migrants resident in the area before migration. Comparative figures for men were 309 from Kingston in 1953, falling to 178 in 1955; and from the total urban centre of Kingston–St. Andrews together 51 per cent in 1953 and 37 per cent in 1955. See Roberts and Mills (1958, pp. 44–57) for further analysis of these trends.

[3] Cf. Senior–Manley Report (1955, p. 30).   [4] Cf. also Glass (1960, p. 7, n. 26).

75

percentages were 66 and 61 per cent respectively). Unfortunately, these occupational categories had to be deduced from the entries made by all migrants on the routine Embarkation–Disembarkation cards. There was therefore little possibility of singling out the genuinely skilled from the undoubtedly far larger and more amorphous group of 'semi-skilled', which probably included an unknown number of 'unskilled' who hoped that such up-grading might in some way advance their prospects in the United Kingdom.[1] These returns did not include the relatively small professional and white-collar class. An indication of the divergence between British and Jamaican standards of skill is perhaps afforded by the fact that in 1954 about thirty illiterate migrants claimed to be 'skilled' and another sixty-five in 1955. Over the three-year period, as we have seen, the number of unskilled emigrants from rural areas and of illiterates showed a steady increase,[2] and the writers anticipated that this trend would continue in later years.

Another set of figures, embodying migrants' evaluations of their skills and background, appeared in a paper which gave the results of a sample survey of the records of 200 male West Indians who had applied to the British Caribbean Welfare Service for assistance in 1957.[3] From this it appeared that 43 per cent of respondents had claimed some training in a trade before coming to England, while 22.5 per cent had been doing white-collar jobs and 1.5 per cent had professional qualifications (mainly in teaching and nursing). Thirty-three per cent were said to be unskilled or to have had no previous occupation. This paper also analysed the occupational background of 1,025 passengers who arrived on the s.s. *Irpinia* on 24 August 1956: 43.3 per cent were said to be skilled, 4.8 per cent to have done white-collar jobs, 1.7 per cent to be professionally qualified, and 35.6 per cent to be unskilled. As no 'semi-skilled' category was

---

[1] Cf. Roberts and Mills, 1958, p. 19.

[2] The number of male illiterates, who were appreciably older than the majority of migrants and who mostly came from rural areas, was 69 in 1954 (the first year in which the count was made) and 261 in 1955. Though comparable statistics for more recent years are not available, it is generally agreed by officials, particularly from the Ministry of Labour, and by welfare workers who have interviewed incoming immigrants over a period of years in the London area, that the percentage of unskilled, rural migrants has steadily increased, as one would expect in view of the arrival of increasing numbers of migrants from the smaller islands, which are rural and less industrialized even than Jamaica. The regular Employment Report (No. 4 of 1960) issued by the Migrant Services Division also reported on the plight of many illiterate migrant work-seekers in Britain in February of that year. The Davison articles already cited give a picture of the occupational background of migrants from Jamaica and Dominica in 1961. The Jamaican data show *inter alia* that 45 per cent of the male sample were working on their own account (28 per cent of the total in agriculture or fisheries), 36 per cent were working for wages, and 19 per cent were unemployed (Table 15).

[3] 'Some aspects of West Indian migration' (B.C.W.S., 31 October 1957).

76

provided it seems likely that a number of respondents hopefully up-graded themselves in both inquiries. As for the very high percentage of white-collar workers in the first survey, this can probably be attributed to the fact that this group would tend to concentrate in London, would have difficulty in getting similar work in England, and would be more likely to ask for official assistance than would less sophisticated migrants.

In 1959 Mrs. Ruth Glass carried out a much more detailed and refined analysis of a London Sample of migrants drawn from the same records. This showed that, according to their own statement on application to the agency, the previous occupational status of those men whose previous occupation was known (608 persons) was as follows: professional – 1 per cent; other non-manual – 23 per cent; skilled – 46 per cent; semi-skilled – 5 per cent; unskilled – 13 per cent; agricultural – 12 per cent.[1] In assessing these proportions, allowance must be made both for the very natural tendency of manual workers to up-grade their status, particularly when seeking work or a better job, and for the very real differences in skilled levels and standards between the Caribbean and the British economies. As for the minority of men in the London Sample[2] (330 persons) who had some experience of the London labour market and whose occupation (on their own affirmation) was thus recorded at the time of their visit to the agency, Mrs. Glass found that 6 per cent were working in non-manual occupations and the remainder in manual work (34 per cent skilled, 17 per cent semi-skilled, and 43 per cent unskilled). A further table[3] suggested that there had been considerable occupational down-grading among the 236 men whose occupations in the West Indies and London were known. This down-grading may, as we shall see later, be more formal than real, particularly in the case of black-coated workers who prefer the high wages of industry to the low-paid security of a London office or shop. As Mrs. Glass pointed out, 'a lowering of status, as a result of migration, does not necessarily imply a decrease of income'. As for the down-grading of genuinely skilled men, there may have been some instances with an unimaginative employer or a xenophobic shop-steward, but it is difficult to accept that this could have taken

---

[1] Glass (1960, pp. 21–5). In a further breakdown by territory of origin, considerable regional differences emerged. For instance, professional and other black-coated workers predominated in the migrant groups from Trinidad and British Guiana, skilled workers in the contingent from Barbados.

[2] Fifty-one per cent of the male sample were said to be 'mainly not yet employed' (see Glass, pp. 28–30).

[3] Glass, pp. 30–4, and Table II: 41 per cent occupied the same status as before, 5 per cent had a higher status, and 54 per cent a lower status than in the West Indies.

place on any large scale in view of British industry's chronic need of skilled men, which persisted throughout the 1956–58 recession.[1]

The London Sample affords one example of the kind of work actually being done by West Indian migrants in London. A second set of figures is provided in an earlier survey (1955), based on a sample drawn from Brixton, Paddington, Stepney, and Birmingham, by the British Institute of Public Opinion.[2] According to this, 40 per cent of West Indians interviewed were holding skilled or semi-skilled jobs in Britain; 53 per cent unskilled jobs; the remaining 7 per cent consisted of students, housewives, and others. Disregarding the last category, this would mean that 43 per cent of those in employment were doing skilled or semi-skilled work, 57 per cent unskilled work.[3]

The difference between the proportions in the London Sample and those in the Public Opinion survey may perhaps be accounted for by the fact that the former sample might be somewhat over-weighted at the top and also because it covered a situation several years later in the migration process, when earlier arrivals had begun to make their way up the industrial ladder.[4]

A third source of information about the migrants' skills is based on assessment at the British end. For instance, a memorandum sent to the Trades Union Congress by the Ministry of Labour Staff Association[5] gave the following rough estimate of the division of skills among West Indian work-seekers: skilled – 13 per cent; semi-skilled – 22 per cent; unskilled – 65 per cent. How this estimate was arrived at is not clear, but it seems to have been based on a country-wide consensus of estimates and placing experience drawn from members at local labour exchanges in 1954.

None of these sets of figures is definitive or even easily comparable. I have given them here principally in order to show how the

---

[1] One group of skilled migrants, too small to be distinguishable statistically, consists of West Indians who have already worked in industry in the United States. I came across a few such men and in no case had they experienced any difficulty in finding or holding a skilled job in Britain.

[2] Published in the *News Chronicle* in February 1955.

[3] Roughly the same percentages were arrived at by Janet Reid in her study of *Negroes in Industry in Manchester* (unpublished report): she found that the 735 coloured workers involved in her survey (just under 15 per cent of the estimated coloured population of Manchester in 1954–55) were distributed in industry as follows: 1 per cent skilled; 44 per cent semi-skilled; 55 per cent unskilled. These figures were, of course, based not on the migrants' own statements but on other people's statements about their status. In a forthcoming study of immigrants in Croydon industry (carried out for the Institute of Race Relations) I also hope to provide some detailed figures of the distribution of West Indians and other immigrants by occupation and skill-levels in all factories employing over one hundred workers.

[4] Cf. Glass (1960, p. 27).

[5] Published in the *Civil Service Argus* of February 1955.

migrants' estimates of their own industrial value and job expectations may often outstrip the possibilities open to them in Britain. Unless they come to terms with this situation, the resulting disillusionment and sense of injustice are likely to exert an adverse effect on their general adaptation to life in this country.

Migrant Intentions, Attitudes, and Expectations

The migrant's difficulties in adapting himself at work are often intensified not only by real differences of industrial background and training but also by more subjective factors – by impermanent intentions; by a lack of adaptability; by the exaggerated expectations of which we have already spoken; by a set of acquired attitudes to work, to trade unions, to white people in general; by the particular circumstances of his initial reception by local people. There are also such impersonal factors as climatic differences which may affect his health and working efficiency (see Appendix XI).

The West Indian migrant is often said to be more mobile than the British worker, and so in a better position to take advantage of shifts in the economic situation here. This observation is only partly true. Most West Indians do not, at least for some years after their arrival, intend to settle permanently, and many are used to the idea of migrant work and travel. In Britain, however, most lower-class West Indians prefer to live near their relations or friends, and dislike pioneering in any new town where they will be lonely and may have difficulty in getting accommodation. For instance, a number of those migrants who were engaged in Brixton by Northern and Midland employers in earlier years have gravitated back to London or to the large coloured communities in Manchester, Liverpool, Nottingham, and elsewhere.

Those migrants who are the most mobile may also be the least likely to make a good first impression,[1] consisting as they often do of the unemployed, of the unsettled, and of single men. Their mobility is also likely to be limited to areas in which there is already appreciable coloured settlement and therefore no shortage of unskilled labour. The psychological restlessness that is often associated with the mobility enforced on so many seasonal labourers by the West Indian economic situation is, in any case, unlikely to help their accommodation to British economic life.

In the eyes of British employers mobility could be an asset – impermanent intentions are usually not. The majority of the recent migrants from the West Indies have come to England in search of work and good wages. A minority have also come to acquire skills

[1] Cf. Banton (1955, pp. 134–5).

or training which they may use to advantage back home.[1] For the majority, therefore, a job in England is the means to an end, that of acquiring the means to return to a better life at home. There is, however, an element, consisting mainly of younger single men and women, who have come here out of wanderlust, as they formerly went to the United States and South America. This wanderlust is characteristic of many West Indians. It is particularly prevalent among Jamaicans, among whom the tradition of migrant labour has for long been established. For such migrants the prestige of having been overseas is sufficient reward on their return.

Whatever their motives for coming, few of the migrants who have arrived in Britain over the last few years will as yet admit to themselves or others that they intend to stay on in this country permanently. Some of the more thoughtful, however, add that they do not know when they will achieve their ambition to return home in style. The frequently expressed desire or intention to return home may in part be a reaction to the difficulties or rebuffs that individuals have experienced in this country. For the most part, however, it seems to be a continuation of the migrants' original plan. In either event, this impermanent approach to the English environment not only inhibits many migrants from trying to adapt themselves, but also works against their acceptance as employees or workmates.

Despite the migrants' impermanent intentions and consequent lack of incentive to adapt themselves to the British way of life, many of them have, as we have seen, high expectations of immediate acceptance by the English on the grounds of common British citizenship.[2] Migrants also have high and often excessive expectations in the economic sphere, in such matters as wage-levels, the acceptability of their skills, and so on.[3] In a large number of cases in South London it was found that migrant men and women without any pretensions to skill expected an immediate wage of £10–£12 and £7–£9 respectively, and that men who lacked documents to prove their skill or did not have their own tools were taken aback or resentful when they were directed to a semi-skilled or unskilled job. Even warnings from earlier migrants against thinking that the streets are paved with gold, or that the newcomers would be able to walk into the job they prefer, were usually regarded with suspicion, as an

[1] Cf. the figures given by Stephens (1956, pp. 7–8).

[2] Joyce Egginton (1957) quotes the words of Vincent Brown, a 38-year-old stowaway from a rural Jamaican town, to an English magistrate: '. . . I stowed away – to come to England and find work. As British subjects we think we should be given preference for work in this country over Germans and Poles' (p. 54).

[3] In an interesting article on 'Education and Occupational Choice in Jamaica', M. G. Smith (1960) argues that unrealistic job expectations are already present in rural children, fostered by the ambitions of their frustrated parents and by the urban-oriented curriculum of the primary schools.

The British labour market and the immigrant worker

attempt on the part of those issuing them to keep a good thing to themselves. The subsequent disillusionment caused many new-comers to move from job to job in search of the expected higher wages, and thereby earned them a reputation of instability and unreliability in many firms.

This disillusionment has also found expression among many migrants in a 'chip-on-the-shoulder' attitude which explains all set-backs and disappointments in terms of colour discrimination by British employers, fellow-workers, and employment exchanges. As we shall see, the answer is rarely so simple, and the attitude contri-butes nothing to the processes of accommodation on either side. This touchy or 'chip-on-the-shoulder' attitude is not entirely a reaction to direct experience of Britain and the British. Usually it is a product of their home environment.

Colour-class consciousness is very acute in the West Indies, and particularly in Jamaica (see below, pp. 223–5). This colour con-sciousness is, however, all too often intensified for the migrant in London by incidents at work, in the streets, or while he is looking for accommodation, until he comes to explain every cool answer, refusal of accommodation, leg-pull by his workmates,[1] and refusal or loss of employment as due simply and solely to the fact that he is coloured. This rationalization absolves him from the need of self-criticism, and from the need to make a profounder effort to under-stand and adapt himself to the environment in which he now finds himself. It also evokes an unfavourable reaction among the majority of employers and fellow-workers who are not actively colour-prejudiced but judge the newcomers in terms of working ability and willingness to 'fit in'.

During my interviews with management and employment agencies in South London, I found that certain traits and attitudes to work were often mentioned as being characteristically West Indian, although it was recognized that these traits were by no means absent in the local labour force as a whole. They included slowness; lazi-ness unless under firm supervision; irresponsibility; and a disinclina-tion to regard hard work as creditable in itself[2] or the job as more than a source of wages.

Such attitudes to work, as we have said, are by no means confined to West Indians. The average British worker, however, apart from being on his own ground, has the additional advantage of having been brought up since childhood to the idea of a regular fast

[1] See pp. 146–51 for a more detailed discussion of working relationships.
[2] Banton (1955, p. 136) notes the African immigrant's surprise at the 'English puritan belief that there is a virtue in working'; a similar surprise was expressed by several West Indians in Brixton.

81

routine at work. Many West Indian migrants have, on the other hand, been used to unemployment, or to casual work for a few days a week, punctuated by agricultural chores on a small-holding. Time is not money in such circumstances, and the idea of clocking in or out and of high-geared production lines is quite alien, while irresponsibility and lazy working are often the outcome of casual labour with no incentives. The need to adjust to a type of work in which one rarely sees the finished product may also be an added burden on the migrants; much of the work or chores done at home involved seeing a particular job through to the end; the same applies to the Jamaican craftsman, in contrast with his more specialized counterpart here. West Indians are also used to smaller and more informal working units, and to more familiar relations with a supervisor than prevail in the large mass-production units in Britain.

Another West Indian attitude to work which is usually dormant at home emerges sharply in the migrant situation. Dirty work and cleaning chores are regarded by many migrants not only as unpleasant in themselves, but as menial and degrading. This attitude seems to be part of the heritage of West Indian slavery, and also to be associated with the low wages which such occupations still command in the West Indies.[1] Some migrants also seem to fear that the British regard such work as most suitable for coloured people.

'I didn't borrow and save and come all this way just to scrub and clean. I can do that back at home.' (Jamaican woman on National Assistance, justifying her refusal to take a cleaner's job in a café.)

'When I first arrived here I had nowhere to go and they put me in a reception centre. The manager told me I must work for my keep and set me to scrub the floors. After an hour I told him what he could do with his work and walked out.' (Mechanic from British Guiana.)

'When I told one coloured woman I could only offer her domestic work right away, she said: "Housework – that's a white woman's job." ' (Employment exchange official.)

'West Indian women will only take cleaning work in a hospital. They seem to associate it with nursing, which is one of the most desirable professions in their eyes, though few have the right

[1] It may also be connected with the fairly widespread disinclination to work for anyone else; this is characteristic of the Jamaican peasant proprietor and of the many women who act as 'higglers' (middlemen) for agricultural produce (see Henriques, 1953, p. 69; Kerr, 1952, pp. 107–8; and Sydney W. Mintz, 1955, pp. 98–103).

educational qualifications to start training.' (Employment exchange manager.)[1]

The situation of the West Indian women migrants is more difficult than that of the men. Few have worked outside their homes before, and the majority are used only to home chores and to home dressmaking, mainly on hand machines and in their own time. They are, moreover, used to living in a large family and household unit in which child-tending and housekeeping can be shared. Few have had any experience of routine work, industrial discipline, time-keeping, and regular attendance at work regardless of minor ills or domestic troubles.

In this account of the West Indian workers' economic background, training, attitudes to work, and expectations, there has possibly been too much emphasis on the factors that impede adaptation and slow down acceptance. This is because they were more stressed by informants at this relatively early stage of accommodation, whereas comparatively harmonious relationships tended to go unrecorded. Factors that often assist West Indian workers are their desire to earn good money,[2] their ability to perform boring routine jobs for long periods, their courtesy and cheerfulness (particularly noticeable among London Transport workers), their love of sport, and their admiration for England and many English ways. Given a firm, sympathetic, and patient works manager or foreman, such factors can, as we shall see in the following chapters, further the processes of accommodation on both sides.

[1] The final statement may seem to be at variance with the fact that there are several thousand West Indian nurses or student nurses in Britain. It reflects, however, the experience of a South London employment exchange, which deals mainly with working-class migrants.

[2] I found little or no justification in Brixton for the widespread stereotype of the 'won't-work' migrant, who comes to Britain simply to live off the welfare state. The great majority of West Indians whom I met were either in work or looking for it very energetically. The only exceptions were a minority of unskilled women with young children who had, like many local women, found that they were better off drawing assistance and making extra money by baby-minding, dressmaking, and other untaxed jobs than they would have been in a low-paid unskilled job. Local National Assistance Board officials confirmed these findings, and pointed out that fewer West Indians applied for assistance than would have been entitled to do so and that many had expressed a reluctance to 'take charity'. There was also an increasing tendency for migrants in need to be helped by friends or relations within the group.

5

The employer's angle—the public sector

THREE main agencies are involved in the processes of integrating West Indian migrant labour into British industry. They are the migrant worker himself, whose background, capacities, and attitudes have just been discussed; the employer or management side; and the existing local labour force. Auxiliary agencies are the employment exchanges, which are involved with the employer, and the trade unions, which lead, follow, or canalize the views and actions of the organized section of labour.

Of these three elements the employer calls the tune, and therefore exerts by far the most important influence on the accommodation and ultimate integration of migrant labour. This may well hold good in most immigrant situations, but it emerged with particular strength in South London, where full employment had at least temporarily blunted the working men's profound fear of, and hostility to, outside labour, and where the unions were relatively weak in a number of the industries studied. This does not mean that the employer would disregard the views of his workers, but simply that these would often be expressed informally to a supervisor and not through a union representative.

Field work in the industrial sphere presented certain difficulties. Brixton is not, as I have pointed out, industrially self-sufficient, and a very large proportion of its whole working population has to travel some distance to work. Brixtonians work in the City, all over South London, in the East End, in the West End, in North London, and in the new industrial areas in Acton and Croydon. The small amount of work available locally tends to go to members of old-established local families, although some West Indians have found work in industries and firms with a high turnover.[1]

Clearly, there was neither time nor facilities for conducting a

---

[1] It is perhaps worthy of record here that only four out of 120 firms represented in the Lambeth Employers' Federation were in 1957 said to be employing any appreciable number of coloured workers.

systematic survey of Brixton West Indians at work all over London or of the policies and practices of the firms that employed them.[1] I therefore decided to make a somewhat arbitrary selection of about thirty establishments in the South London area which met the following criteria:[2]

1. The firms should fall within the main categories of industry operating in South London.

2. Within each category, establishments of different size should be chosen.

3. These establishments should employ or at one time or another have employed coloured labour.

A list of suitable firms was compiled with the help of the managers of the Brixton and other local employment exchanges, who were in the best position to know where appreciable numbers of West Indian workers had been placed. A few firms were added to the list because one or more of my West Indian informants worked there, or because these firms were constantly advertising for unskilled or semi-skilled labour in the South London press. This informal introduction from the exchange also served to ensure a reception in most cases. Out of thirty-five firms approached, I had only two outright refusals. One came from a large firm of contractors which has for years employed Irish, coloured, and other migrant labour, but which was the terrain of a series of well-publicized strikes for most of the period of my field work. The other came from a small firm which had experimented with a handful of West Indian workers but had 'now dispensed with their services' and saw no reason 'to take up our or your time with academic discussion'. Three other medium-sized firms with a similar experience of West Indian workers adopted delaying tactics and were not in the end visited.

Over the years 1956 and 1957 I visited several publicly owned

[1] In 1958–60 I was able to carry out a more detailed inquiry into the integration of coloured and white immigrants in Croydon industry. Its findings will be published shortly and will include a more elaborate version of the questionnaire used in this inquiry.

[2] The inquiry was confined to that part of South London adjacent to Brixton: (a) because most West Indians resident in Brixton try to find work as near home as possible; (b) because this is intended as a study of migrant integration in a particular locality, and it seemed probable that South London employers and workers were more likely to know the Brixton area and to be influenced by off-the-job contacts with Brixton West Indians than would be the case in, say, North London or Acton; (c) for reasons of geographical convenience. The 21 private firms were distributed as follows: Brixton, 2; Stockwell, 2; Camberwell, 2; West Norwood, 2; Streatham, 1; Wandsworth, 1; Battersea, 3; Bermondsey, 3; Borough, 1; Lewisham, 2; West Dulwich, 1; North Croydon, 1.

and twenty-one private industrial establishments in South London. Since then, an attempt has been made to revisit or recontact firms previously visited in order to find out whether any changes in policy or practice concerning West Indian migrant labour have occurred. This follow-up seemed advisable because in the earlier period a number of informants seemed to regard West Indian workers as stopgap, unsatisfactory labour which would be expendable in the event of any recession and consequent redundancy. There have been at least two such minor local recessions in certain industries, and it seemed worth while to check whether such viewpoints were in fact translated into action when the occasion arose.

The information obtained was uneven in quality because of the differing viewpoints and approach of individual informants. Each interview lasted an hour or more. In smaller firms the informant was usually the owner or managing director. In medium-sized firms he might be the works manager, perhaps with the participation of a welfare officer or nurse. In larger firms the principal informant was usually a personnel or public relations officer, who might call on various departmental heads to give more detailed information. The material also varied quantitatively. A questionnaire was prepared and used, but in interviews with busy managers of small firms it could not always be applied systematically nor could full or detailed answers be obtained to every question. The general purpose of the questionnaire was to get an impression of the firm as a functioning whole, and of the way in which migrants were adapting themselves to and being accepted in this whole. Information was therefore sought on such variables as the type and status of work involved, wage levels, the local manpower situation, the size and age of the firm, the degree of unionization, labour turnover, the attitudes of individuals on the management side and of long-term local employees.

With regard to coloured workers, the inquiry was concentrated on management policy and experience, and on impressions of white and coloured employees' attitudes and behaviour as observed by the informants. The second-remove material thus obtained on employee attitudes and behaviour was subsequently compared with and checked against first-hand information provided by various union officials and shop-stewards, and by individual white and coloured workers. On the whole there were few discrepancies, and most personnel officers, perhaps because of their training and the nature of their work, seemed to present a particularly fair and accurate picture of local workers' attitudes to and relationships with coloured fellow-employees. In general, biased attitudes seemed to increase at the lower levels of management and administration and to reach

86

their peak among foremen and supervisors, who are usually forth-right individuals who have been promoted from the shop floor.[1]

No attempt was made to interview individual workers, either white or coloured, during these visits to factories. I felt that any such *ad hoc* interviews would be conducted in a highly artificial and not very productive manner, whether or not a representative of the management was present. Some personnel managers suggested that such interviews could be arranged, but seemed relieved when the suggestion was not accepted. The representatives of several firms with a large proportion of coloured workers expressed the hope that I would not seek such interviews, on the reasonable grounds that coloured-white relationships were developing without undue friction and that any questioning of individuals might cause them to focus on underlying potential problems and so exacerbate the situation.[2]

The general picture that emerged from these interviews is obviously not typical of South London industry as a whole, but only of a minority of establishments which were induced by specific need and possibly by a less conservative approach to try out a new type of labour at this period. The inquiry was in fact concentrated on those sectors of industry that were and still are chronically short of labour – particularly unskilled and semi-skilled – because of low wages, difficult hours, seasonal fluctuations, or hard or unpleasant working conditions. Such industries are: public transport and communications, other public services, food and soft drinks manufacture, laundry work, some sectors of light and heavy industry, the garment trade, building, and so on.

Because of the small number of firms involved and the somewhat arbitrary method of their selection, and also because of the impossibility of presenting the results of the inquiry in a statistically satis-

[1] There was, however, one exception among the personnel officers, an ex-service-man who had served in the R.A.F. as an officer in the Middle East and who showed a high degree of what we have elsewhere called 'the wog complex'. ('Some niggers can be very unpleasant. Personally, I wouldn't like to touch one or get too close to him. In Cairo I had a lot to do with wogs but if I touched them it was only with the tip of my boot.') This 'wog complex' was also noticeable to a lesser extent among several other personnel managers and works managers, most of whom had, in fact, seen service overseas in the last war. Few representatives of managements interviewed were without the usual aversion to close social contacts with coloured people frequently found among the English middle classes, but this attitude only emerged in such asides as: 'One has to draw the line somewhere, and personally I wouldn't want them living in the same house'; 'Intermarriage is where I draw the line'; 'I don't support a colour bar but when my wife was asked to take a coloured student as a lodger I vetoed it. Somehow I feel a difference'. These remarks were qualified, however, not in terms of any belief in racial inferiority, but rather on social and cultural grounds. Such attitudes did not seem to influence unduly the informants' professional attitude towards labour problems, which was a utilitarian one.

[2] Cf. Stephens (1956, p. 6) for a similar attitude among some Birmingham employers.

factory manner, it seemed best to avoid possibly spurious tabulations and to summarize the situation in each establishment as it emerged from interviews, follow-ups, and sometimes from additional information given on other occasions by union officials, individual white or coloured employees, and others.

PUBLIC SERVICES AND UTILITIES

The great majority of the West Indian migrants in Brixton are not equipped to enter public or private employment except at the semi-skilled or unskilled level. So far as public employment is concerned, a small minority have been able to find clerical, technical, or professional posts in national or local government offices, but the bulk of coloured workers are to be found in the lowest grades of such establishments as the Post Office, British Railways, London Transport, the Regional Gas Boards, and local government service.

A considerable number of West Indian migrants have been called up and have done their national service, and a small number have signed on for the regular army. Unfortunately, no information could be obtained on this subject, on the familiar ground that the Services make no colour distinctions. Two young West Indians from Brixton known to me were called up during the period of this inquiry. Their reactions differed in no significant way from that of the average national serviceman; they made no complaint about special discrimination, but complained a good deal about food, cold, ill-fitting uniforms, and 'bull'. One of them later signed on as a regular.

Neither the regular armed forces nor the police force are, however, likely to appeal to the majority of recent migrants, to whom relatively low pay, distant pension rights, security, and rigid discipline are less attractive than higher wages, the possibility of change, and independence after working hours. On 16 February 1958 the *Sunday Express* quoted an official Metropolitan Police statement to the effect that, though there was no bar against coloured people becoming policemen, none of the applicants who had so far appeared had been able to satisfy the very high standards required.[1] From a few off-the-record conversations with police officers, I gleaned the general impression that, as in the matter of promotion or contact with the public in some other types of job, certain doubts

---

[1] Three years later the Metropolitan Police view was reported to be that 'it would be unfair to a coloured man to act as a policeman in a predominantly white community where he might be resented'. In opening a national campaign for 10,000 new police recruits the day before, the Home Secretary, Mr. R. A. Butler, had said that while the recruitment of coloured policemen had so far been found neither necessary nor expedient there was 'no bar on it' and he certainly would not exclude it (*Guardian,* 24 and 25 January 1962).

were felt in the force as to the possible reactions of the public to a coloured policeman 'ordering them about'. No coloured policemen have yet appeared on South London streets, although local police have established unobtrusive contact with various members of the migrant group and are usually adequately informed by migrant 'narks' of what occurs in their midst. From time to time it has been suggested that coloured policemen should be taken on to help to patrol areas with a large migrant population, but nothing further has come of this, and it might be considered an undesirable precedent to appoint coloured police specifically for employment in coloured areas.

THE POST OFFICE

Since the second world war the Post Office has suffered from a chronic labour shortage, the consequence, I was told, of full employment, the inconvenient hours, and the relative decline in pay compared with the wages paid in private industry,[1] for which the security and status which the work still offered were inadequate compensation. My informant contrasted the situation in 1957 with that prevailing before 1939. At that period, he said, the Post Office was still a career and a way of life for most of its employees. There were many 'Post Office families' with traditions, loyalty, and a pride of craft and service, and outsiders would not then have been accepted easily.

The recruitment of coloured (mainly West Indian) workers for the Post Office began in London about 1948, following an agreement with the union concerned. By 1957 nearly 10 per cent of all applicants were said to be coloured, but of these only about one in ten finally came to work in the Post Office. A number of reasons were given for this. One or more out of every ten coloured applicants was rejected on the initial aptitude tests; some of those rejected were found to be virtually illiterate, while others had, quite understandably, no knowledge of British geography. After the aptitude tests all applicants go to a regional interviewing board where a further 10 per cent or more of total applications are usually turned down. Next comes a medical test and finally the taking up of references for those who have survived the course. The latter procedure caused the greatest wastage among West Indian applicants, since the taking up of references from the Caribbean might last two months or more, by which time the applicant would probably have settled himself in a job elsewhere.

[1] In the lowest recruiting grade, that of postman (PM), the basic pay was £10 3s. in 1957; that of the higher recruiting grade (PTO), for which a school leaving certificate is required, was a little over £13.

Coloured postmen were not evenly distributed throughout the London postal area at this time. Each district recruited its own workers and the variation in numbers was probably to be attributed to the availability of coloured and other labour locally, and also to varying attitudes towards coloured workers among those responsible for recruitment.

As a consequence, the majority of coloured postmen were to be found in three central postal districts in 1957. In one district there were 130 coloured postmen; the second had 13 coloured postmen (higher grade),[1] 67 coloured postmen, and 11 coloured cleaners; and in the third there were 3 coloured postmen (higher grade), 94 postmen, 44 postwomen, and 1 counter man. The third district was thought to have the highest proportion of coloured workers in any district, over 5 per cent of the total number employed.[2]

When I asked about the working performance of coloured employees, I was told that their discipline compared well with that of many white workers, but that many had been found less efficient. On the welfare side, they were said to present 'no great problem'. They did not mix much socially with fellow-workers except in sports activities, notably cricket. The main troubles which they brought to the welfare staff arose out of housing difficulties. From white workers there had been a few complaints over hygienic habits and body odour, but most cases of friction had been found to arise between coloured and coloured and not between coloured and white.

Inquiring about the possibilities of promotion for coloured people, I was told that the union had been consulted about this as early as 1953, when a number of coloured postmen became eligible for consideration in this respect. The union, as will be seen, made no formal objection, but in the case of promotions to supervisory posts the administration appeared to be moving with care at the time of my interview. It was stated that one of the qualifications for such posts was the ability to get the best out of subordinates, and there seemed to be a certain implication that coloured employees might not yet be sufficiently accepted for this to be possible. This official

[1] After two years' service a postman may become a postman, higher grade (PHG), by virtue of seniority if he passes a simple aptitude test. Alternatively, he may try to pass an examination for promotion to the higher recruiting grade (PTO).

[2] The great majority of coloured Post Office workers were, as we have seen, in the wage grades. In 1956, however, a few coloured women clerical workers were taken on to ease the shortage. I was told that the clerical staff, who are even more status-conscious than Post Office workers in the wage grades, had been unenthusiastic about this move initially but that they had 'got used to the coloured newcomers'. Little mixing, however, seemed to occur off the job. The recruitment of coloured, as of all other, clerical workers was said to be subject to the requirement that they should have a smart and attractive appearance.

caution was all the more noteworthy in view of the increasing unwillingness of Post Office workers as a whole to accept promotion.
For instance, I was told that in recent years about 50 per cent of
postmen and over 30 per cent of postmen (higher grade) in London
had refused promotion because of the greater responsibility involved.

A few years later coloured employees were still concentrated in
the three central districts, where it was said to be more difficult to get
good staff than in the suburban districts. Working relations between
coloured and other staff were, I was told, satisfactory. No coloured
employees had yet reached a direct supervisory position but no
trouble was anticipated from other workers when this should happen. My informant drew attention to a definite change in one aspect
of the situation over these years – whereas there had been some
adverse public reaction to coloured counter staff and even to postmen delivering at the door, this stage was definitely over.

BRITISH RAILWAYS

The railways are a nation-wide public service with a long and fine
tradition. Unlike the Post Office, most of the work is 'dirty hands'
rather than 'white collar' but the railway service has until recently
been able to count for the backbone of its staff on a large nucleus of
'railway families' up and down the country; for generations members of these families made the railways their life, a vocation rather
than a job. Since the war, however, with full employment and
the five-day week, recruitment of new railwaymen has become
increasingly difficult. New recruits have been deterred by the relatively low wage levels in relation to private industry,[1] by the long
and irregular hours, and by the possibility of round-the-clock or
week-end work. Nor is the job one of such cast-iron security as it
was, because of competition from road and air services, and also
because of increasing dieselization, electrification, and rationalization within the industry.

In recent years British Railways has therefore had to cast its
recruiting net much farther afield. Poles and Balts were taken on in
the earlier post-war period and, as every traveller by rail must be
aware, large numbers of West Indians have for several years been
working on the railways in London and elsewhere.[2] Lack of time
made it impossible for me to gather information from all four
London Regions, which in any case stretch well beyond the London

[1] See W. John Morgan's article 'Gloom on the Iron Road' (*New Statesman*, 16
January 1960) for a detailed discussion of wage levels and railwaymen's morale at
that time.
[2] Up to the end of 1961, 598 had been brought from Barbados under the special
recruiting scheme.

area proper. The material that follows is therefore drawn from one Region only. Interviews at head office and a number of stations and depots took place in the summer of 1957 and again in the summer of 1959,[1] and so it was possible to get an impression of the situation as it developed over a period of time.

In 1957 this Region was employing some 68,000 persons, almost all of them on the permanent staff, and had some 2,000 vacancies at all levels, though there were fewer in the starting grades than in earlier years. Of the 68,000 staff, just under 1,000 were coloured. Most of these were men, and over 75 per cent of them were in the starting grades, the majority being employed either on operating (porters, etc.), in motive power (as shed staff), or on the permanent way (as labourers or platelayers). In the aristocracy of the footplate section, by contrast, there were only fourteen in the fireman grade and three fitters and boiler-smiths.[2] There were relatively few coloured staff in the commercial section (checkers, etc.) because, it was said, few had the necessary knowledge of geography, and also because of 'language difficulties' ('difficult accents slow all work down'). This latter consideration was also said to make most West Indian applicants difficult to employ as booking-clerks, where 'mutual intelligibility' was essential. There were a few coloured clerks, but these were usually students who would leave the service as soon as they had qualified professionally. A number of West Indians, mostly Barbadians, were also working in the catering section, usually behind the scenes in buffets or below stairs in railway hotels.[3]

The management's general experience of coloured workers was that the majority of recruits had little initiative or sense of responsibility, and that they did not develop these traits with time. They had shown themselves slow workers (possibly as a consequence of climatic differences), and this slowness emerged most noticeably in the few all-coloured gangs. If coloured workers were dispersed in ones and twos, however, they caught the faster local tempo and worked better. Their turnover was not particularly high, but they were thought to make a lot of fuss about minor illness and to absent themselves unnecessarily. Most seemed to expect too much at the

[1] This later inquiry was conducted in connection with a survey of the employment of West Indian migrants in stores, hospitals, and public transport in the London area, carried out by a study group for the West Indian Advisory Committee of the London Council of Social Service in that year.

[2] See below (pp. 157-63) for an account of the policies and attitudes of the National Union of Railwaymen (NUR) and the Associated Society of Locomotive Engineers and Firemen (ASLEF).

[3] See *Times British Colonies Review* (Third Quarter, 1957, p. 15) for an article on colonial workers in the catering trade in Britain. The British Transport Commission initiated a colonial training scheme with a fortnight's course in 1955.

outset and showed little willingness to 'work their passage' to acceptance. A distinction was made by some informants between the majority of coloured railwaymen recruited in London and the small group of Barbadians specially selected and recruited in their home island, the comparison being strongly in the latter's favour.

Most of the objections raised by railwaymen to coloured workers were economic in origin, as described by my management informants. These objections arose out of fears of redundancy, and resentment at the possibility of losing overtime pay (now regarded as virtually part of the wage) as vacancies were filled, and of lowered piece-work earnings by teams owing to coloured workers' slowness. There also appeared to be a certain feeling that the status of the job was lowered by the recruitment of coloured workers, and some anxiety was noted among old-timers lest the standards of service and safety should be lowered. Personal status considerations also emerged in objections to the promotion of coloured workers to any kind of supervisory position. On the footplate, fears were expressed about coloured workers' reliability and fitness for this particular work on the grounds that they reacted more slowly, were not always easily intelligible, and often did not themselves immediately understand the accent and phrasing of British supervisors; some accidents arising from factors of this kind had in fact occurred.

There was also a certain amount of off-the-job friction, particularly in earlier years. The management had received some objections about 'different habits' in mess-rooms and lavatories, and some large stations and depots were said to have introduced separate facilities, particularly in mess-rooms where old-timers objected to the very highly seasoned and pungent food which the coloured men cooked up for themselves. It had not however been thought necessary to appoint a special welfare officer to deal with coloured workers. The union was said to have cooperated fully in trying to secure acceptance for the newcomers, and, on the whole, after a troublesome start, bad relations between coloured and white were the exception rather than the rule. A prevailing attitude was said to be 'He's not so bad – he can't help his colour', and when a coloured employee was a good worker he got credit for it.

Station-masters are responsible for taking on their own staffs in the starting grade, and a nucleus of long-service railwaymen can still have a considerable influence on the general climate prevailing at certain stations and depots. These features help to account for the considerable variations in attitudes and behaviour reported at different depots and stations over the last few years.[1] In 1957 I was

[1] For major reported cases of local friction over the employment of coloured railwaymen see Appendix IV.

told that there were some pockets of resistance to the entry of coloured workers, mainly in certain goods depots in the Region. With the exception of one station, the passenger station staff were said to be more tolerant. Coloured workers were also to be found at a number of the smaller stations and on the permanent way.

Visits to two large passenger stations suggested that each situation varied according to the attitudes of a minority with firm opinions one way or the other. In one, where there were twelve coloured workers in a staff of 780, it was stated that the station-master would not stand for 'any display of colour prejudice'. The other station was one at which there had been considerable well-publicized friction, resulting in the departure of all coloured workers. At the time of my visit four more coloured porters had just been accepted rather grudgingly, but the men in charge at this station clearly shared the unfavourable views of their staff on the matter. An informant said: 'I doubt whether they will ever fit in. They're not like us and they won't learn. A crowd of 2,000 immigrants arrived from the Continent last weekend and just went berserk in the station. The railwaymen see them coming in and they form their own opinions about them. Where's it all going to end?'

In 1957 I raised the matter of promotion for coloured workers, and was told that this presented a problem in terms not only of their acceptability but also of their suitability. In the wage grades the Commission was bound to promote on seniority if a man was suitable. In the Locomotive Department, in particular, it was obligatory for a man to attend classes and go on to higher grades. Here, however, there had been cases of drivers refusing to work with coloured firemen. In other departments, however, a few coloured workers had been promoted to positions where they were over white men. It was thought that the situation would develop favourably if the coloured workers made an effort to adjust themselves and get accepted. The railways wished to train them to fill gaps left by wastage at higher levels and to see them progress like all others. Very few, however, attended the voluntary classes which might help their promotion. If the bulk of them were going to remain in the starting grades in most departments, an unassimilable and untrainable core of coloured labour, this would, it was thought, be bad for the service. It would lower the status of the job, and would interfere with the established mode of recruiting from the ranks.

By the summer of 1959, when I paid my second round of visits to this Region, I found that the recruiting position was somewhat easier, and that there had been a major redundancy of over 2,000 in 1958. This redundancy had been handled by normal wastage, by going slow on recruiting, and by putting off over-age workers and temporary female labour; the regular staff had not therefore been affected. The overall number employed in the Region was down to 66,000 and the number of coloured workers to 903. The breakdown by departments showed that the drop in the number of coloured workers was evenly spread over the Motive Power, Chief Mechanical and Electrical Engineer's (CMEE), and Chief Civil Engineer's (CCE) Departments. Like the overall loss of over 2,000, this drop was said to be due to normal wastage and curtailment of recruitment, and I was told, apparently with justice, that 'in this respect no distinction has been drawn between coloured and other employees'.

An encouraging feature was noted in the fact that in 1959 a greater proportion of coloured railwaymen appeared to be in grades above the starting grade than in 1957.[1] A more detailed breakdown of the numbers of coloured workers in the various higher grades was unfortunately not available. In 1959 it was also noted that a considerably larger number of coloured clerks (72) were being employed than two years earlier. There were also four coloured employees on the technical staff.

Little change in the attitudes of English railwaymen to coloured workers was noted over the two-year interval. The complaints that were raised were, I was told, still concerned mainly with reduced overtime, slowness, and promotion of coloured railwaymen. Many local railwaymen did not care to put in for jobs involving more responsibility, but they objected if a coloured worker did so and was accepted. Such matters were usually dealt with in conjunction with the NUR at local level. Two at least of the big goods depots still refused to take any coloured men at all, although in one there was a pre-war immigrant ('completely black') on the local committee. The main reasons for these refusals seemed to be that big goods depots mainly relied on local labour, which was very clannish, and had also evolved rapid team techniques for handling the work, which was tough, irregular, and intensive while it lasted. It was unlikely that slower outsiders of any kind would be well received in such depots. I was told at the regional office that experience had shown that, in general, coloured workers fitted in best when scattered in ones and twos in small or medium-sized stations.

LONDON TRANSPORT

This consolidated and highly centralized public service involves work that is more varied and of a less manual type than that avail-

---

[1] In 1957 about four-fifths were in the starting grade, and in 1959 two-thirds. These figures are not strictly comparable, since the 1957 ones included workshopmen of various grades of skill, whereas the 1959 figures gave a separate and undifferentiated total for all workshop employees.

able on the railways. Like the railways, it is or was something of a life vocation, though for a much smaller nucleus of employees; the work has also, since 1939, lost status by comparison with jobs in manufacturing industry,[1] and has suffered from a chronic labour shortage. As with the railways, West Indian workers were taken on after consultation with the unions. The engagement of West Indians began on a small scale in 1950 and has continued in increasing numbers. In 1956, by arrangement with the Barbadian government, an interviewer and medical officer from the London Transport Executive (LTE) visited Barbados, where they engaged 50 male conductors, 20 female conductors, and 70 stationmen, and also arranged for local officials to recruit further staff of the standard required. More Barbadians (2,112 in all by the end of 1961) have since been recruited and brought over. In addition, several thousand coloured migrants have been recruited through the normal channels in London itself.[2] In the same year (1956) the LTE appointed a West Indian welfare officer to assist in the welfare and problems of the Barbadians and other coloured staff.

By 1957, and still more by the time of my follow-up interview in 1959, it was clear that the LTE had amassed considerable experience in the engagement and employment of West Indians. I was told that greater care in selection was required than in the case of local applicants, since West Indians applied without having much idea of the requirements of the job. The interviewer had to make sure that the applicant had the right sort of temperament to deal with the public, and, in the case of conductors, that he could handle money and give change easily and correctly. He had also to probe the new arrival's background carefully, since references from the West Indies were difficult to obtain.

Once selected, West Indians were distributed evenly throughout the service, where this was possible, and the union was kept

[1] Here are some busmen's illuminating views as reported in the press before the London bus strike of 1958: 'The job's not what it was; we were the second best paid on the industrial list, now we're fifty-seventh. Before the war it was a hell of a job to get on the buses. Once on, you were set for life. The trouble started during the war when we accepted a wage freeze to help the war effort.' 'Before the war the police and the buses were the two best jobs in London. Now it's deteriorated out of all recognition. If Lord Ashfield [first chairman of London Public Transport Board] could come back and see this lot, he'd turn in his grave. . . . It's sunk to rock bottom. *And* the *types* on the buses. Before the war it was definitely respectable' (*Observer*, 4 May 1958).

[2] LTE informants would not give any precise and detailed figures for the numbers of coloured workers employed in 1957 and 1959, on the grounds that no discrimination was made and no such statistics were kept. On 14 May 1961, however, the *Sunday Times* reported that there were some 1,200 coloured men and women in the total labour force of 37,000, or just over 3 per cent. In a few garages, notably West Ham, Stockwell, and Walworth, the proportion could go as high as 10 per cent (*Daily Mail*, 15 May 1961).

informed of such allocations. In the early 1950s there was some trouble at a few London centres, but this was resolved and by 1957 there were no garages with a definite bar against coloured workers. Much of the work involved team work, between a driver and conductor or a motorman and guard, and white and coloured were said to work well together under such arrangements. The deciding factor in the acceptance of coloured by white staff was thought to be the former's 'ability and willingness to do the job'. The fact that West Indians were participating in sporting events was also regarded as conducive to better working relations.

From the management angle, it was noted that the turnover rate among West Indians tended to be lower than the overall figure, and that their performance and relationship with the public were 'usually nothing but good'. The specially selected Barbadians were singled out for particular praise in all these respects and also for their smart appearance and the pride and interest which they showed in their work.

Redundancy policy for all employees was, I was assured, 'last in, first out'. This rule was applied in the only major case of redundancy after the war (the South London conversion from trams in 1952, which had no effect on coloured staff). Other redundancies were dealt with by normal wastage.

During my second interview in 1959 I was told that promotion of West Indians was proceeding on the normal basis of seniority and ability. Such promotion was, however, usually to positions of greater responsibility and skill rather than to positions of direct authority over others. On the underground side, which many West Indians preferred until the bus wage-rates were equalized, promotion was said to be faster. Only seventy-five out of 634 coloured workers taken on were still in the starting grade, and a few station foremen (more or less equivalent to charge-hands in industry) already had some white workers under them. None had so far been employed long enough to qualify for full supervisory positions. The buses offered fewer opportunities for promotion, but every year a number of West Indians were trained as drivers.

Looking to the future, it was said in 1959 that London Transport was still recruiting West Indians and intended to continue such recruitment on a basis of individual suitability and a 'last in, first out' redundancy policy.

Over the years of relatively full employment, therefore, it would seem that the West Indians working for the LTE have achieved a certain measure of integration in that they are regarded as part of the permanent labour force by employers, unions, most fellow-workers, and the public. Even if the economic situation were to deteriorate greatly, it seems likely that this position would remain unchanged. On the other hand, more care has to be taken in selecting West Indian workers and allocating them to particular areas or jobs, and there is still considerable resistance among most English workers to the idea of promoting West Indians to positions of authority over white workers.

Clearly, therefore, the integration of West Indians in transport in the London area has by no means been fully achieved. To those familiar with immigrant situations in Britain and elsewhere, however, it would be surprising to find any immigrant group, whatever its colour, fully integrated in any sector of the new country's economic life after so short a period as six or seven years. The situation, so far as the LTE and also British Railways are concerned, would in fact appear to be fairly encouraging by comparison with many other sectors of industry.

Comparing the position in the two transport services, it may be said that the less traditional, more centralized LTE, in which so many employees work in scattered couples and small groups, is perhaps better fitted for the integration of large numbers of immigrant workers than the more clannish, traditional, and decentralized Regions of British Railways. In both services, however, policies have been evolved for intake, training, and ultimate integration, and the most satisfactory results have been achieved by careful pre-selection as in the Barbadian schemes.

THE GAS INDUSTRY

Since the war the gas-works have, like the three public services already described, suffered from a grave labour shortage. This may be attributed less to the wage-scales than to the heavy, hot, and seasonal nature of the work and the fact that much of it involves shift-working.

At the time of my visit seventy coloured workers were employed out of a labour force of 3,000 in gas-works in South London. The great majority of these were stokers in the retort houses, where they were said to stand the heat well. While management described their working abilities as 'variable', the main problems seemed to arise in connection with their acceptance by other workers. This varied considerably from one gas-works to another. In one in which the men were described as 'progressive-minded', relationships were said to have developed well with the coloured workers, apart from one small 'fracas'. At another works, however, the local men were older and more 'conservative', and there had been a few clashes. Complaints had also been made about personal habits, the eating of

Kit-e-Kat sandwiches, and so on, but similar criticisms were made of the other main group of newcomers, the Southern Irish, by this compact, clannish group.

Joint consultation plays an important part in this highly unionized industry, and there had in consequence been some 'minor difficulties' and effective union opposition to the recruitment of coloured workers in certain sectors.

By contrast, my informant told me that coloured girl clerks had been accepted without difficulty by the clerical staff. Management had not, however, recruited any coloured workers on the maintenance side of the organization, where formal skills were necessary. An additional reason given for this was: 'A husband might resent a coloured man going into his house when his wife was at home alone.'[1] No evidence to support this supposition was adduced, and it seems that here again we have to do with the phenomena of uncertainty and the attribution of stronger bias or hostility to others than one claims to feel oneself, which play such a great part in blocking avenues of employment to coloured and other newcomers in the society.

In a follow-up some years later it was learned that the whole gas industry in South London had been radically reorganized and in part closed down, so that no useful information about the development of working relationships in particular units was available. It seemed, though, that the change had tended to strengthen the 'clannishness' of long-term local workers in the industry. Young Anglo-Indians and West Indians were applying and being considered for apprenticeship as gas-fitters, but it was said that so far they had had to be turned down because of their inadequate educational background. Anglo-Indians and Indians were employed on the clerical staff, as before, but no coloured employees were as yet working in contact with the public.

LOCAL GOVERNMENT

Few of the Brixton migrants are, as we have seen, qualified for salaried posts or skilled work. Nor do those who are so qualified necessarily seek relatively low-paid, permanent, pensionable work, at least in the earlier years of their migration. A handful of coloured professional persons, including one public health inspector and a district nurse, were found to be in the employ of various local

---

[1] In the Electricity Board most of the work is skilled or involves contact with the public, either over the counter or in their homes. These facts would, it was indicated, preclude the employment of any considerable number of coloured people at the present time.

authorities in the area, and an increasing number of local government and technical students from West Africa and the Caribbean were being temporarily attached to the appropriate departments for training. For the most part, however, migrants were being employed as labourers or on such social services as street-cleaning and refuse-collecting – work which they disliked and usually took on only as a stopgap.

In one of the South London boroughs there was a very popular West Indian old-timer, who had worked in the parks section for many years. He had long been married to a local woman and kept a little aloof from the newcomers. Nevertheless, many migrants asked him to help them to get work and he did so, acting as a sort of sponsor, until about thirty were being employed by his department. By late 1956, however, none was left except the original old-timer. Said the supervisor: 'The newcomers carried knives, and the Londoners began to carry them too, so we had to get rid of them. But old Sam's different. He's one of us, and quite one of the nicest people I've ever known.' 'Old Sam', incidentally, had been a well-known boxer and local people were very proud of him. Work was always found for him although his sight was said to be getting very bad. The local union representative also said of him: 'Old Sam's different. He belongs to the job.'

6

The employer's angle—the private sector

OVER the period 1955–58 I visited five privately owned establishments in South London which produce soft drinks, fruit products, conserves, and biscuits. In size they ranged from the giant multiple firm Pan-Provisions Ltd., which combined catering and food production; through Cracker-Snaps, with 2,500 full-time women and almost an equal number of part-time workers of both sexes; Orlando Preserves, with about 1,000 employees, 90 per cent of them women; Nutty Fruits Ltd., with 400 employees, mostly women; down to Fizzo Soft Drinks, with a total labour force of 110, of whom 60 were women.

Pan-Provisions

Pan-Provisions has since the early post-war years been one of the main employers of West Indian and other immigrant labour, both male and female, chiefly on the food-processing side. At the time of this study some coloured women were also employed in the cafés, usually on cleaning or kitchen-work behind the scenes. At this time, however, virtually no coloured women were employed as waitresses or in other jobs involving contact with the public in South London middle-class residential areas, or indeed in Brixton itself. The reason for this was one that was frequently given to me by representatives of retail firms and catering trade managers in a later and more detailed inquiry into the integration of immigrants in industry – the firm's uncertainty about possible public reactions.[1]

On the food-processing side at Pan-Provisions, several thousand workers were employed. At the time of my visit 5 per cent of the total labour force was made up of coloured men and 2.5 per cent of coloured women, and the firm was continuing to take on suitable coloured applicants. The regular practice appeared to be to main-

[1] At this period and later, however, an increasing number of coloured women were employed in view of the public in Pan-Provisions' city cafés

tain a limit or 'quota' of about 10 per cent, and to suspend recruitment of coloured workers temporarily if the percentage rose above this figure, until wastage brought it down again. The proportion of coloured workers had a tendency to rise because this group had a relatively low turnover. This the firm's spokesman attributed to the fact that coloured employees, realizing that they had a good job and that they faced more difficulty than others in finding employment, were reluctant to leave it. Southern Irish workers, by contrast, had a very high turnover but, notwithstanding, were regarded as very good workers.

Like most large firms, Pan-Provisions attempted to disperse its coloured workers through as many departments as possible. As a group, however, they had been found slower than the average and they could not be placed in certain departments where speed was essential. Care had therefore to be taken to avoid undue concentrations in the remaining departments: 'If there is more than 25 per cent, it looks like a "coloured department", and the other girls don't like it.'

Pan-Provisions has employed coloured workers since about 1949, and when I visited the firm some seven years later I was told that the 'main teething troubles' were long since over. In earlier years certain problems were said to have arisen: notably over the dating of white girls by coloured men and, on the coloured side, over a strong tendency to attribute reprimands or notices to quit to colour discrimination. Later a number of 'old stagers' emerged, as they had done among the Irish and East European immigrants; these individuals acted as informal leaders and helped to smooth things out within the group. My informant added that his department had found it best not to put coloured people of different national or geographical origin together, since most disputes and friction seemed to arise not between coloured and white employees but between coloured and coloured.

With memories of the South African situation and of food advertisers boasting that their products had been touched only by 'white hands', I asked whether any of the many visitors who are conducted over Pan-Provisions' model factory had commented adversely on the use of coloured labour for food production; only a bare handful had done so, I was told, out of many thousands of visitors.

Redundancy appears to be an academic question for Pan-Provisions Ltd. No redundancy rules or agreements on priorities exist, and my informant pointed out that any conceivable temporary reduction could be dealt with by a temporary cut in recruitment and the normal process of wastage. As for promotion, at the time of my visit it was felt that suitable coloured workers could be put on to more skilled work but that promotion to such a position as charge-hand was unlikely.

Pan-Provisions has clearly accepted coloured workers as a permanent, albeit limited, element in its labour force and has evolved selection, training, and personnel procedures to minimize or eliminate any special problems or frictions that might arise. In this it appears to have been motivated by enlightened self-interest. Unionization is rather weak in this firm, except among a minority of skilled male workers, so that the attitude of the unions to coloured workers has played little part either way in influencing their situation. The views and reactions of the local labour force have however been taken into account, within reason, to avoid provoking unnecessary friction.

Cracker-Snaps

Cracker-Snaps, the second largest firm in this group, is situated in a highly industrialized area that has lost many of its residents since the war. The firm still has a fair-sized nucleus of long-term local cockney labour, and has in recent years built up a fairly stable additional labour force from people resident outside the district. These include some Cypriots and a large group of Polish ex-officers and men, many of whom work together on night shift. About one-third of the firm's labour force, however, continues to show a very high turnover.

To help solve its labour problem Cracker-Snaps some years ago instituted its own private recruiting scheme for girls from Southern Ireland. Later, in 1955, after consultation with the works committee, the firm began to take on West Indian workers for those departments (about half of the total) which had agreed to accept them. One year later the proportion of West Indians (all full-time workers) had risen to 10 per cent of the total labour force. At this stage considerable friction developed and it was decided to suspend any recruiting of West Indians until the percentage was brought down by normal wastage. At the time of my visit in 1957, the proportion was down to just over 7 per cent, and the firm had just notified the employment exchange that it was ready to interview West Indians again. The 10 per cent maximum was, however, to be retained.

My informant told me that the firm was fairly well satisfied with its West Indian male workers from the viewpoint both of their working performance and of their relations with other workers. The majority of West Indians employed by Cracker-Snaps were, however, women. Management found them on the whole slow and child-like on the job, with a tendency to complain over trifles. Some appeared lazy, but this laziness usually disappeared if they were put

103

on to piece-work that they could do. A chip-on-the-shoulder attitude over colour had been observed among many, and one group had organized a 'go-slow' campaign among West Indians for higher wages and had been sacked. It was thought that turnover was likely to be high, since many had already left to have babies.

I was further told that intense friction had blown up between local women and West Indians some months after the latter were first taken on. This friction arose not from economic resentments or fears but from behavioural differences. The majority of complaints received from white women employees about West Indians at this time concerned body odour, spitting, unattractive table-manners, and unhygienic habits in the canteen (that hardy perennial, the Kit-e-Kat sandwich, recurred) and in the toilets. A personnel officer told me that she had also received a number of protests about West Indian women washing their feet or their false teeth in the hand-basins and then using the communal towels to dry them. Some of these episodes were, I was told, definitely proven, but in other cases rumours and exaggeration had probably played their part; once or twice there was even a possibility that somebody had tried to 'frame' a case against the coloured women.

On their side, a few West Indians had complained to the management that they were being cold-shouldered by fellow-workers. Others had expressed considerable indignation about the special induction course which had been introduced for West Indians; this was said to stress the need for personal hygiene in food production.

By mid-1957, when I visited the factory, the worst of the trouble was thought to be over. The labour force included intelligent West Indian women who had been employed for some time and who would, it was hoped, advise and give an example to newcomers.[1] It was added that West Indian women were becoming less 'bizarre' in their dress and were thus 'standing out less' than they had done in earlier days. Personnel officers, however, still expressed some concern about the latent attitudes of the local labour force: 'I don't know how much our girls will stand, and we can't afford to lose our white labour.' A hopeful augury here was the very liberal and positive attitude to the employment of foreign and outside labour taken by the area secretary of one of the main unions represented in the firm.

[1] Personnel officers here said that they had evolved some rough-and-ready selection procedures: 'We've had a lot of experience now and we can tell pretty well from the way they walk in whether they will do. If they walk in lazily and giggle too much we reject them; we also reject the "coal-black-mammy" types. We're taking on a better type now but they get restless after a few months. We were too soft at first. Now we tell them they must adapt themselves and behave like everybody else.'

At the time of my visit West Indians had not worked long enough for Cracker-Snaps to be taken on the permanent staff, so that the question of promotion did not arise and they would be among the first to be put off in the unlikely event of redundancy. Some years later I learned that a West Indian who had been a shop-steward in 1957 had been promoted. In general, accommodation seemed to be proceeding, though slowly; the quota was still observed, and one or two departments still did not accept coloured workers. Little change was noted in the management's attitude, but a 'hardening of attitudes' was reported among some employees, particularly part-time women workers. This was attributed mainly to 'prejudice and ignorance', but in a minority of cases to resentment over lowered group earnings as a result of West Indian slowness.

Orlando Preserves

Orlando Preserves, which lies south of Brixton, is an old-established, rather conservative firm, barely unionized, with a large nucleus of long-term local labour, consisting mainly of married women. Additional seasonal labour, including students, is taken on temporarily each summer. In 1955 there was a shortage of labour and the management decided to try about thirty 'coloured ladies' on the permanent labour force 'by way of insurance'. Work is organized on a group basis at Orlando, and trouble soon arose with local workers because the coloured workers were slower and bonuses were consequently less. The coloured workers were then put in groups of eight or nine with a white supervisor. Since the coloured groups worked more slowly than the other workers this meant that they were paid less per hour, which gave rise to misunderstanding and resentment. One group charged the firm with colour discrimination ('one rate for whites, one for blacks'), demanded a higher rate, and turned off their machines. The manager told me: 'We have had trouble-free labour relations here all along and we couldn't stand for that sort of thing. As a result we decided to stop taking on coloured labour except as temporaries in the summer, and we can now afford to pick and choose from those who apply.'

Orlando's welfare officer told me that there had been little resistance from the long-term local labour when the coloured women started work: 'South London working-class women are a pretty tolerant lot and most were neutral to begin with. But they became much more hostile later as a result of the experience, first over lowered bonuses and then over habits in the canteen and toilets. Like us, they found them difficult to understand and stand-offish. On the other hand, we still have one or two Anglo-Indian girls and

105

they've fitted in just like the Spanish or Italians. And there's an Indian girl who they've made quite a pet of.'

Nutty Fruits; Fizzo Soft Drinks

Nutty Fruits and Fizzo Soft Drinks, the two remaining firms in this group, are organized on the basis of a small permanent labour force, consisting mainly of local residents, and an annual seasonal intake of temporary workers, which they have trouble in finding. In both firms wages are rather low, although some jobs offer bonus possibilities. In neither are the unions at all strong. At the time of my interview Nutty Fruits was employing a larger proportion of what my informant referred to as 'dark labour' or 'Jamaicans' than any other firm in this group (and also one or two coloured clerical workers), whereas Fizzo employed about eleven coloured workers in its total labour force of 110.

At Nutty Fruits, management had come to regard West Indian workers as slow in training and at work. The normal practice was to put them on such jobs as packing and selecting, which are usually done by older local labour. These jobs are slow, repetitive, and boring, and the West Indians could be trained to do them adequately. Some minor criticism had occurred with other workers over 'alien personal and eating habits' but it had not been allowed to develop. The question of promotion was regarded as academic, since none were considered good enough workers.

At Fizzo Soft Drinks, the manager opened the discussion by stating: 'There's no discrimination in race, religion, or anything else here. Most workers are local cockneys but we've had almost every nationality here except Germans. I'm Jewish myself and I won't have them.' He had employed coloured men and women for some years and found them no slower than local labour at picking up the job. The women, however, were not very popular with fellow-workers on the following grounds: body odour ('you can't get away from it'); a tendency to refuse their turn at cleaning jobs which all normally did in rotation; excessive exuberance and aggressiveness in groups. My informant told me that he had tried an experiment in the early days of coloured labour by putting a rather intelligent West Indian woman in with a particular group where the shop-stewardess 'had her knife into coloured girls'. He had hoped that personal contact might break down this feeling, but unfortunately this did not happen. The group sent the coloured woman to Coventry and 'ganged up on her' during the toilet breaks until she could stand it no longer and left.

LAUNDRY AND DRY-CLEANING

A considerable number of Brixton migrants have at one time or another found work in the labour-hungry and highly competitive laundry and dry-cleaning industry. I visited two firms in this group.

Wash Whiter Laundry

Wash Whiter Laundry is an old-established laundry situated in an artisan residential district south of Brixton. The bulk of its labour force is still local; many workers have been there for a quarter of a century or more and representatives of two or even three generations of a family may still be found working there.

Apart from its nucleus of more or less permanent workers, Wash Whiter has had considerable trouble in keeping its labour force up to strength. In 1955 the situation was particularly difficult and the firm decided to take on coloured labour. 'Hundreds have been through my hands since then,' said the personnel manager. By late 1957, when I visited the laundry, the labour shortage had eased, and the firm had become more selective. At this period there were over a dozen coloured women and ten coloured men in a labour force of nearly 200 (170 women and over twenty men). All the coloured men had been with the firm for more than a year, and on the whole they were regarded as satisfactory. One man was illiterate but was said to be very willing and a 'hard slogger'.

Among coloured women there had been a much higher turnover, although those still with the firm had been there for six months. The women presented rather more personnel problems than the men.

'The other women don't really like the way they bring in their own food and eat it in the canteen, nor their habit of keeping their hats on indoors [the men do this as well]. We still get the odd complaint about West Indians having dirty toilet habits but I rather ignore this. It's difficult to pin down and I couldn't have them up as a group to lecture them about it.[1] There's no active hostility, however. We've only had one fight and that was between two West Indian girls.'

The manager at Wash Whiter was one of the few informants who had noticed the operation of the 'uncle' or 'aunty' system among coloured work-seekers,[2] perhaps because his office faced the entrance and he paid a good deal of attention to what was going on there. He usually refused to take on applicants who arrived in such

---

[1] Contrast the special induction course at Cracker-Snaps.
[2] Stephens (1956, p. 11).

'bunches', and preferred to get them from the employment exchange.

Redundancy seemed an unlikely contingency at this time, but my informant was prepared to state his policy:

> 'It would be a tricky problem but we wouldn't listen to demands for all coloured workers to go first. It would be "last in – first out".'

Asked about the possibility of promotion, the manager said:

> 'They're not positive or forceful enough. In any case, although promotion isn't based on seniority here it would be tricky with so many old-established white workers: they're a clannish lot, and can make things difficult for newcomers or management. Public opinion is very easily felt via the supervisors. I've never tried coloured workers as clerks or vanmen. The public might object and a coloured girl in the office might feel awkward on her own. It's easy enough to get clerks, anyway.'

While he was not enthusiastic about coloured workers, this informant gave the impression of being fair-minded and sympathetic in his day-to-day approach to their problems:

> 'I don't really approve of their coming into the country in such numbers, but as they're here I take on those who are suitable. After they've worked here for some time, they open up a bit. We usually help them with loans for accommodation and so on. There was a religious problem with two of the girls, who are Seventh Day Adventists and can't work after sundown on Friday nor on Saturday. Head office agreed to this as long as we don't pay them for the time. Many of them leave to have babies, but some come back again afterwards.'

Jeeves Cleaners

Jeeves Cleaners is situated in the same district as Wash Whiter Laundry, but differs from it in being smaller and more highly mechanized. It has recently come under the management of two lively and efficient young men, who are less involved with the old-established local labour force and less concerned with its views. Like Wash Whiter, Jeeves Cleaners is not unionized at all.

In 1955 this firm was experiencing extreme difficulty in getting labour, and the managers, after consulting the existing staff, decided to try coloured workers. About twenty-five men and two women were taken on. After a year most had left or been dismissed, and the management had decided to recruit no more for the time being. My informant was anxious to convince me that this decision was not due to racial prejudice:

'We're only concerned with efficiency here. We employ one Indian, two Italians, and a Pole. We also still have two coloured men from the original batch. The rest just weren't up to it. They never seemed to understand why we white people should rush about so much. They were still living where the coconuts fall into their laps. At one time there were almost as many dark people as whites, but we operate a very narrow profit margin in this trade, and every employee must pull his weight all the time. With the best will in the world, we couldn't keep on people who would stay away for several days without notice and then say: "Why you worry? I no come in, you no have to pay me." '

At Jeeves the main objection to coloured workers was on grounds of efficiency. My informant told me that, apart from some complaints about minor illnesses and tired feet (the work involved a lot of standing), he had not found them difficult to deal with. Nor had he received many complaints from other workers about their personal habits or behaviour. The firm would still be willing to give a try to any 'likely-looking' coloured applicants ('some of the men who've applied are really vicious-looking and would terrify the girls, so I wouldn't take them'). At the end of my visit this informant, who lived in a distant middle-class suburb, emphasized once again that he had no objection to employing West Indians but that he would 'draw the line at having them as neighbours or in the family'.

LIGHT ENGINEERING

Visits were paid to four establishments in this sector.

Audio-Communications Ltd.

The largest of the four was Audio-Communications Ltd., established some forty years ago and situated in a working-class residential area with a growing population of coloured and other immigrants. Wages here are low-average, and most of the work is unskilled machine-minding. Other jobs involve machine-operating, inspection, and assembly. The core of the labour force consists of long-service, local married women, but since 1945 the firm has faced an acute labour shortage and has experimented with various untried types of labour.[1] For this reason Audio was one of the pioneer employers of coloured female labour in the South London area, accepting its first half-

[1] Despite its labour difficulties, Audio does not recruit juveniles, because of their high turnover, nor Southern Irish immigrants, for reasons which I could not elicit.

dozen from the employment exchange in 1954. In consequence, it attracted more and more coloured applicants 'over the grapevine', until by the time of my first visit in 1956 they were said to make up 75 per cent of all applicants. At this time, over 11 per cent of the full-time male labour force of about 600, and about 20 per cent of the full-time female labour force of 650, were coloured.[1] Some time before my visit the proportion of coloured women had reached 30 per cent, but their turnover rate was higher than average (often because of pregnancy) and wastage had brought the numbers down. A personnel officer told me that as a result of this high turnover the firm had had over 200 coloured men and 350 coloured women through its hands in the past two years.

The great majority of coloured workers were, I was told, doing unskilled work, and the management's general impression was that nine out of ten were slower than the average local worker. Their main objection, however, was high turnover and absenteeism for 'petty aches and pains'. Management was also disturbed by the aggressiveness of coloured women in groups:

> 'They gang up and throw their weight around in the cloak-rooms, and our white girls are getting quite frightened. At the bus stop they push their way past the queue, and one old-timer had her glasses broken with an umbrella when she remonstrated. Still, these have only been isolated incidents. Some coloured employees attend the firm's socials and seem very well-behaved; and a few white workers were recently invited to attend a coloured wedding and quite enjoyed themselves. They were rather impressed to find that the wedding cost £200.'

One of the welfare officers at Audio made further comments about West Indian women's health and their relationships with other workers:

> 'The pregnancy rate's colossal, but there's also some abortion. I think there must be at least one abortionist operating locally. They have a lot of gyne [gynaecological] troubles but very little V.D., and the Mass Radiography unit uncovered no T.B. I give them a pep talk about not "making a baby" as they call it, but they just smile and say they'll try not to. I find a lot of them great liars. There's a sort of stone-walling attitude and you can't tell from their faces where you are with them. The main trouble with the other workers is their aggressiveness, though there have been

---

[1] Like most firms depending on unskilled or semi-skilled female labour, Audio also employed a large proportion (500 workers) of part-time labour on 'married women's shifts'. No West Indians were to be found among part-time workers in this firm or any of the others visited.

110

some complaints about B.O. and spitting. They do seem to sweat more but they keep their body and underclothes clean. I keep a spray here for the bad cases and prescribe Amplex where I can. As for spitting, they do seem to do it a bit more than the others.'

At this period Audio clearly still regarded coloured labour as an undesirable necessity, temporary and expendable in the event of a recession. I was told that the management would change to white labour any day if it became available and that it was greatly concerned by the decreasing number of white applications, fearing that this might be because the factory was getting a name in the district as a 'coloured factory'.

By the time I revisited Audio two years later, there had in fact been some redundancy and the firm had put off several hundred full- and part-time workers, mainly women. As my informant had prophesied, coloured workers had borne the brunt of the redundancy, and now constituted 9 per cent of the male labour force and 13 per cent of the female full-time workers.

Despite this reduction, it was obvious that management had moved a long way towards accepting coloured labour as a permanent component of its labour force in the two years since my first visit:

'We got rid of the trouble-makers and the most aggressive types. Now we are building up an established nucleus of good types, just as good as the whites. Some have been with us for as long as three years, and have moved out of Brixton to nicer houses near the factory. The turnover for pregnancy is still high but some come back. They mix well and are much better accepted now by the other employees. If a coloured girl leaves to have a baby the rest hold a collection for the layette. I hear very few complaints about personal habits these days and I notice they've adopted our way of dressing. I think most of our troubles are over but I wouldn't put any of them in a supervisory position yet.'

Air-Tight Containers

The second of the four was Air-Tight Containers, which employs nearly 900 workers, two-thirds of them women, and most of them unskilled or semi-skilled. The factory is sited in an industrial area and the firm has since the war been forced to import its labour from surrounding boroughs.

Air-Tight still has a solid nucleus of long-term local workers but has had to explore a number of new avenues to make up its labour force. It runs a private recruiting scheme in Southern Ireland, and employs a considerable number of Cypriots, and a few Poles, Balts,

111

Hungarians, and Anglo-Indians. In 1954 the firm began to recruit West Indian men in some numbers. By 1957 this recruitment had ceased. My informant, a personnel officer, said that the firm had given the West Indian men a fair try, but that they were not sufficiently 'machine-minded' and their turnover was too high. The firm had also taken on some African and Indian men but a mixed Afro-Asian group led by some students had created 'a lot of bad feeling', and applicants from these groups were no longer taken on.

Air-Tight continued to employ an average of thirty to forty West Indian women on unskilled machine-minding. In 1954 an all-West Indian production line had been tried but this was a 'hopeless failure'. The works manager had, at that time, refused to take on any more; but the continuing labour shortage had compelled him to change his mind. West Indian women were now dispersed over the various production lines, as they were thought to work better when there was only one to a line. They had been found slow, and needed a good deal of supervision; some were regarded as defiant and uncooperative ('dumb insolence'), while many were said to be difficult to understand. Pregnancies were very frequent and turnover was therefore high.

Air-Tight's male workers are about 90 per cent unionized, the women only about 10 per cent. The union does not seem to have played any significant part in the reception or rejection of coloured workers. About the reactions of local workers, I was told:

> 'There is the occasional petty complaint about spitting, cliqueyness, heating up smelly curries on the soldering machines, eating Kit-e-Kat sandwiches, and so on. But on the whole feeling among our own people isn't very acute. I can give you one instance of a coloured van-driver who's very popular but a hopeless driver. He would have gone long ago if he weren't a coloured man, but I don't want to be accused of victimization. The lack of bad feeling here may be due to the fact that there's no room for outsiders to live in this area and therefore no competition for housing. In the office, however, attitudes are more rigid. I tried to put an Anglo-Indian male clerk in there but the man in charge refused to keep him.'

In addition to its West Indian women, Air-Tight at this time employed nearly 100 recently recruited Southern Irish girls. Newcomers of both groups were given induction 'pep talks' by the nurse on the subject of basic hygiene ('the Irish are as bad as Jamaicans in the toilet anyway'). These talks had apparently aroused particular resentment among the West Indians. It was clear that both Southern Irish and West Indians were at this stage regarded as short-term,

112

stopgap labour. In support of this, my informant pointed out that the West Indians regarded themselves as temporary migrants. They did not usually join the superannuation fund or take advantage of the opportunity that was open to all workers of buying shares in the firm.

Petroff Engineering Company Ltd.

The third employer in this group, Petroff Engineering Company Ltd., is a precision engineering firm, over half of whose labour force of 700 is made up of skilled men and which suffers from a shortage not of unskilled but of skilled labour. It thus presents a very different picture from the two mass-production firms just described. At the time of my visit the wages for all grades of skill were described as a little higher than the district average, and the labour force was almost entirely local and permanent. Two-fifths of the skilled men had been with the firm for more than fifteen years, and at least one-third of the 150 women employees were wives or daughters of male employees. They were described to me as 'steady locals – not the biscuit-packing type'.

It was somewhat surprising to find that coloured workers had been employed in this large, close-knit, highly specialized concern since 1951. In 1957 the firm was employing seventeen coloured men, most of them West Indians; of these, ten were skilled, three semi-skilled, and four were working as labourers. There was also an Anglo-Indian apprentice, and an Indian male clerk in the offices. There was only one coloured woman in the female labour force. I was told that the women's work was highly skilled and that the firm's experience with other coloured women had been disappointing. They had been found to lack the requisite ability and application for the work.

The somewhat individual situation which I found at Petroff Engineering was attributed by my informant to a definite employment policy emanating from the top level of management, which included a number of Europeans who had come to Britain as refugees between the wars. This policy stressed individual skills or aptitudes, as against differences of race, colour, or creed. In detail, it was the firm's policy to disperse coloured workers in ones and twos through the many small departments, and the personnel department avoided taking on more than 8 to 10 per cent of coloured labourers in the relatively small unskilled group, in order to avoid giving the impression that such work was reserved for coloured workers.

I was told that the firm was quite satisfied with its West Indian

113

skilled workers. At the outset their skills and training were not up to local standards, but they were good enough to serve as a groundwork for further specialized training. Most West Indians took longer to acquire speed, but with patient training they did so. Two departments were so satisfied that they had expressed a preference for coloured labour and one Jamaican was actually the highest earner in the factory. A minority of foremen, supervisors, and fellow-workers were still biased, but experience had shown that this bias tended to decrease with increased contact. No incidents or complaints on either side had been reported for a very long time. My informant considered that this might be due to the fact that craftsmen are more interested in an individual's basic skills and feel more economically secure than do unskilled workers, and also to the good type of West Indian recruited ('not the Brixton type, our men all live locally'). Petroff Engineering was not a closed shop but it was 70 per cent unionized, and most West Indians joined the union and were active members; they had participated in the recent strike like all other workers, and one of them was a branch official of the Amalgamated Engineering Union (AEU). They were also said to be integrating well on the social side, and participating in the firm's club activities. The only department where friction still seemed possible was the office, where objections seemed to stem from status considerations. The management wished to take on more coloured office workers but was proceeding with caution for the time being.

In the event of redundancy, I was told that the principle of 'last in, first out' would apply. Nobody had ever suggested that West Indians should be included in the proviso agreed with the unions that 'foreigners' should be made redundant before British workers. As for promotion, skill and length of service were the main criteria: 'The factory manager started on the shop floor twenty years ago, so the sky's the limit.' The management would at present probably think very carefully about promoting a West Indian to a charge-hand's job but he would have the same basic chance. One Indian with technical qualifications was already running a test section.

Jovian Products Ltd.

The position at the fifty-year-old firm of Jovian Products Ltd. was very different. Unlike Petroff Engineering, Jovian has since the war, when it employed 4,000 workers, been struggling to switch its production to peace-time demands and has experienced a series of major redundancies. By the mid-1950s the total number of employees was down to 1,000 and since then, particularly in 1956 and 1958, there have been temporary large redundancies of several

114

hundred, usually the unskilled or non-productive workers. This firm is, unlike most others visited, a closed shop (AEU and fourteen other unions) so that the unions have a good deal to say about the way in which redundancies and other labour problems are handled.

I visited Jovian some months after 450 workers had been put off. Of those who remained, nearly 50 per cent were skilled men, 5 per cent were labourers, and the remainder were semi-skilled. The majority of workers were said to be local but the firm had retained ten coloured men, who were either in semi-skilled work or on labouring. I was told that other coloured workers had been included in the redundant group on the 'last in, first out' principle.[1]

The management at Jovian was not very enthusiastic about coloured workers. A personnel officer told me:

> 'We've found them slow and there've been complaints from the other men over their toilet habits. I'd rather have a strapping Irishman any day than a darkie, even if the Irish don't stay long. After the last redundancy, it would cause a lot of trouble among the men if we took on any more coloured men or even swarthy British subjects from Egypt, so we're not doing so.'

HEAVY INDUSTRY

In the heavy industrial sector, four firms were visited.

Gallotherm Ltd.

By far the largest was Gallotherm Ltd., which had 2,500 employees (1,800 men, 700 women) in early 1957. Of this number, 20 per cent were skilled (all men), 60 per cent semi-skilled, and 20 per cent unskilled. The labour force was mainly local and turnover was very low. This old-established but streamlined firm had a tradition of family service, ranging in some cases over three generations: 'It's a dirty-hands job but wages and conditions are good and we don't get the bottom of the barrel here as far as labour is concerned.' The firm was highly unionized (Transport and General Workers Union (T & GWU), Amalgamated Engineering Union (AEU), Electrical Trades Union (ETU), and others).

Gallotherm employed fourteen West Indian men, semi-skilled and unskilled, one coloured woman, and some Anglo-Indians; in the

---

[1] One of my coloured informants, who later got a skilled job in a London Transport repair shop, was sacked by Jovian at this time. He admitted to being a bad timekeeper but claimed that the sacking was due to colour victimization and that the unions did nothing to help him. I found this difficult to accept because I learned that another West Indian whom I knew in Brixton, and who had worked at Jovian a little longer than the first man, was not made redundant at this time.

office there were one or two West African clerks. The firm also employed a dozen or so Poles, who were regarded as 'very satisfactory'. The West Indian men were considered slow, but were preferred to the Irish because they stayed longer. Many had come from farm work or sugar refineries and were physically strong. They were employed 'in quiet corners where they would not run into trouble'. There had been no complaints from the other men about personal habits, but some foremen were opposed to coloured labour and refused to take them.

I was told that the firm had tried out West Indian women in larger numbers at the outset, but had found them 'capricious' and unsuitable for the piece-work and inspection that are women's work at Gallotherm. There was no set policy or agreement with regard to eventual redundancy, but a general feeling existed in management that there was 'an Englishman for most jobs' and that the 'Jamaicans' would go first, although the unions had not opposed the introduction of coloured labour or attempted to introduce a specific redundancy clause.

Short and Crane

Short and Crane, which produces boilers and a variety of heavy products, is much smaller than Gallotherm. The firm has always drawn its labour from the settled local working class and still has a low turnover and a long-term nucleus. Since the war, however, a number of skilled men have moved out and there has been difficulty in getting a supply of boys or even of apprentices; it has therefore been necessary to make up the deficit from other sources. Short and Crane has tried Poles, Irish, and, since 1950, coloured workers. When I visited the firm in mid-1957 some forty coloured workers (mostly West Indians) were employed out of a total labour force of about 225 men, of whom just over one-third were skilled workers. There were two coloured skilled workers, twenty-three were on semi-skilled work, fifteen were labourers, and one was employed in the office. This was the largest number of coloured workers that had ever been employed, the average number in previous years having been about twenty.

The works manager told me that he found most coloured workers slower than others. This had been the main source of complaints from fellow-workers, because it pulled down group earnings. In consequence, some had been put on a separate night-shift. Much of the work was done in a warm atmosphere and coloured workers seemed to like this and to work better as a result.

Slowness on the job was the main complaint made by the other workers about West Indians, and there were few complaints about personal habits ('a live-and-let-live atmosphere prevails here'). There was however a certain social distance, notably in the canteen, where the groups ate apart. Some West Indians had played cricket for the club and one had even captained it for a while, but most others did not take part in the social club's activities at all. My informant had noted some attempts by 'the factory's Communists' to approach coloured workers, whom he characterized as 'an easy target'.

Although Short and Crane had employed coloured labour for seven years, West Indian workers were far from being fully accepted by management. My informant said: 'We only accept coloured labour because there is nothing better. If there is a slump, the coloureds will go first, good or not.'

Some years later the situation did not seem to have changed greatly. West Indians were still regarded as a 'floating population', suitable only for a limited number of unskilled and semi-skilled jobs:

'Local labour's difficult to get and beggars can't be choosers. We had one who was an honest-to-God worker but he got a call to move on. We haven't any redundancy yet, but if it happened I think the AEU stewards would try to close down on them. The "last in, first out" rule might be awkward if it meant a local man going before a coloured. Whatever we decide, we'd work it out round the table with the shop-stewards first. We're not a closed shop but we're heavily unionized and it's no good trying to start a man unless he's got a union card.'

My informant added that even this rather limited union acceptance of coloured workers was greater than in an affiliated firm in Yorkshire, where the unions 'won't entertain the idea of them being taken on at all'.

Heavy Ores Ltd.

Heavy Ores Ltd. is a metal-processing firm situated in the dock area and recruiting most of its regular labour force locally. The work is hot, heavy, and organized on a three-shift basis. It is, however, well-paid and offers plentiful overtime possibilities. Like most other firms in this sector, Heavy Ores is highly unionized. When I went to visit the firm in the autumn of 1957, it was employing some ninety men on processing work: of these about twenty-five were coloured (most of them West Indian). Some had come from the employment exchange, but others had been recommended by friends or relatives already employed there. All were working as general labourers but for one, who was the furnace-hand of what was described as an 'all-darkie' team. The others worked in mixed teams. Occasionally a white man

117

would be put in the coloured team temporarily and he would then be expected to take orders from the coloured furnace-hand. The works manager told me that in this small, compact working community he left it to the furnace crews to 'sort out slackers'. He himself had no adverse comments to make about the performance or turnover of coloured workers. As for other sources of friction between workers, he said: 'I have had some complaints from the local men about dirty habits and eating odd food, Kit-e-Kat, and so on, but I told them to sort it out for themselves and the complaints died down. In my view, the darkies are no less clean than the rest.' My own impression after this interview and a tour of the processing works was of a rough-and-ready but fairly tolerant working community, in which the coloured workers appeared quite well integrated. The small professional staff also included one coloured chemist.

Pneumastic Company Ltd.

The fourth establishment in the heavy industrial sector, Pneumastic Company Ltd., differs considerably from the other three. It is situated in a residential area to the south of Brixton. The work is hot and not too pleasant; it also involves shift-working. The demand for the product fluctuates heavily and this has resulted in relatively low wage-rates and lack of job security. The firm is not strongly unionized. There was a major redundancy in 1952, when several hundred workers were laid off. When I was there some four years later, the firm employed 400 men and 550 women (the latter on lighter work). The majority of these were still local residents but the total included twenty-five Polish men and about the same number of coloured men, most of whom were West Indians. Coloured workers had been taken on since 1954, when the firm's orders began to improve. Said the personnel manager:

'We prefer them to the Southern Irish, whom we find too mobile and won't employ. We can't afford to be particularly selective and have to take what comes on the whole. But a large proportion of coloured applicants have to be turned down. Some are right out of the jungle – barely literate.'

Pneumastic Ltd. had one coloured skilled engineer and a few coloured men on semi-skilled work; the remainder were on unskilled jobs. My informant made the following comments on their working ability:

'The darkies are usually pleasant and willing in disposition. They seem a little slower at picking up the job because of lack of

industrial experience and language difficulties (i.e. intelligibility).
They like to make a meal of a job and enjoy repetitive piece-work.
On two-handed jobs the whites get impatient and resentful. They
feel they're being slowed down and earning some of the darkies'
money for them. We got over this by putting two darkies together,
giving them an allowance for steady work, and paying the other
whites in the group a small allowance to compensate for lowered
earnings. Though we put them together in twos we try to spread
them throughout the departments. I don't like more than 25 per
cent of Poles or coloured in one shop.'

Apart from resentment over lowered earnings, I was told that
there had been little opposition by local workers to the arrival of
coloured workers and no trouble at all had been reported over
differences of personal habits.

Pneumastic's experience with coloured women had been less
satisfactory. The firm had experimented with both all-coloured and
mixed teams. In neither case had their performance been adequate
and they had shown themselves aloof, difficult, and capricious. The
supervisors had been unwilling to continue and the experiment was
dropped: 'We wouldn't try West Indian women again except in a
job they couldn't spoil.'

Redundancy was by no means an academic issue at Pneumastic
and my informant held very definite views on policy:

'If we have any more redundancy the principle of "last in, first
out" certainly won't apply. Efficiency is the prime consideration,
but we also have to consider the intangibles. If I had to decide,
I'd keep the English as against the Poles and coloured. After all,
blood's thicker than water.'

AUTOMOBILE SALES AND REPAIR

A fair number of West Indian men find employment in automobile
servicing and repair shops, and indeed this is one of the few skills
which could be acquired with relative ease in the West Indies. I
visited one large old-established firm of this type (Omega Automobile Service) in the Brixton neighbourhood in late 1957. A spokesman told me that his firm had employed West Indians for three years,
mainly on semi-skilled and labouring work. They had never formed
more than 10 per cent of the labour force. A few who claimed to
be tradesmen had been tried out as mechanics, but they needed
considerable supervision. One or two had come from other London
firms with proper references and they had been given skilled jobs.

119

Migrants at work

The unskilled men were not noticeably slower than the average local worker, and the firm preferred them to the Irish as labourers.

I was told that there had been, shortly before this interview, a period of trouble between different coloured groups. This had culminated in a crow-bar fight which was broken up by the police, and as a result the firm had sacked many workers and suspended further recruitment of coloured labour. It had just begun to take them on again for temporary jobs.

There was no union organization at Omega, I was told, nor had there been any definite decision or consultation with other workers about their initial employment. If redundancy occurred, dismissals would be decided on the basis of seniority plus workmanship and time-keeping record. Skin colour would play no part and, if white workers objected, this would make no difference. The management had received no complaints from other workers about the personal habits of West Indians, possibly because the type of work offered the minimum of opportunities for contact on or off the job and there was no canteen. Some West Indians had complained that they were being victimized by receiving lower pay-packets. These complaints were quite unfounded, according to my informant, because every employee was paid the same basic wage, and extra according to his experience.

Omega Automobiles also employed some coloured clerical workers. These were all Asians and were described as excellent workers. The men were usually part-time students. No suitable West Indians had applied for clerical jobs, I was told. There were vacancies on the sales side, but it was not the firm's policy to accept coloured applicants in positions where they would come in contact with the public, for fear of possible objections and loss of trade.

THE GARMENT TRADE

The mass-production garment trade is centred on Oxford Circus and Aldgate, but I found two firms in South London which had some experience of coloured workers.

Dandy Chemises

The first, Dandy Chemises, was a rapidly expanding, go-ahead, post-war creation, which employed 100 unskilled men and 850 women, the majority of whom were skilled. Skilled work for women involved operating power-machines, while semi-skilled work consisted of cloth-inspection, pressing, trimming, and packing. The average wage for a skilled piece-worker was said to be over £9, and machinists who could not earn a weekly minimum of £7 8s. lost their jobs. Unionization was nil and labour turnover high.

At the time of my interview, this firm had eight coloured men among its labouring force of fifty and a few coloured clerical employees (mainly students) in the office. The labourers were said to present no particular personnel problems, while the coloured clerical workers had been accepted without trouble. A personnel officer suggested that this might be due to the fact that most of the office staff had been promoted from the works and 'lacked the status-consciousness and prejudice of the average white-collar worker'.

As a result of its steady expansion and high labour turnover, Dandy Chemises' main problem was to ensure a steady intake of skilled women machinists. All applicants were considered, irrespective of colour. A personnel officer said:

> 'We require ability or a capacity for training, and also a smart appearance. From coloured applicants, after long experience, we also require intelligibility and an appearance attractive enough not to give offence to the rest of the staff. By this I mean that they should not be unkempt or too dark or negroid-looking.'

At this time there were twelve coloured women in the total of nearly 600 machinists. Their turnover rate was lower than average and some of these women had been with the firm for three or four years By contrast with most other management informants whom I interviewed, this firm's spokesman had no complaints to make about coloured workers' slowness. This was probably because only the really fast and efficient machinists survived the initial trial period. When they were first taken on, coloured women were often found to be demanding, quick-tempered, and prone to attribute any setbacks to colour discrimination. Those who stayed on mellowed and became more courteous. My informant commented on the fact that only one coloured woman had come through a recommendation from a friend already working there. He thought that this might be due to a realization that few 'home dressmakers' of the West Indian type could hope to meet the firm's high standards. Most coloured applicants still came from the employment exchanges, but some were brought in batches by smartly dressed coloured women. The latter were thought to be acting as informal employment agents, since they came back quite often.[1]

Large-scale redundancy was said to be unlikely at this firm, but there were seasonal fluctuations. There was a simple formula for

[1] Cf. Stephens (1956, p. 11) for the 'uncle' system in operation.

laying off workers – the least efficient must go whatever their colour.

When I made a check-back some years later, an informant reported no significant change in the performance, behaviour, or turnover rate of West Indian women. Most were said to be too slow to stand the pace and it was interesting to note that all applicants were still new arrivals, although it might be supposed that some West Indian women would by now have accumulated some London experience and references.

Teen Cottons

The second garment firm, Teen Cottons, was also a post-war, non-union establishment. It was far smaller and, perhaps for this reason, seemed to be run in a cosier and less impersonal and streamlined manner than Dandy Chemises. Some years before my visit in 1957 the firm was so short of machinists that it decided to try coloured labour. The manageress told me that she first asked the existing staff for their cooperation and all but one agreed. There was some initial friction, due, my informant thought, to 'the feeling of strangeness'.

'But once the girls got to know one another they became more tolerant. One coloured girl from Panama became particularly popular and the girl who had objected most at the start became her close friend. At the beginning I had some complaints over body odour and dirty habits in the toilet, but I got over this by letting the coloured girls use my own private toilet. Personally I found them rather cleaner than the others.'

So far as working capacity was concerned, however, the experiment had been unsuccessful, I was told. Though the coloured girls were nice and 'a good type' they had no experience of power-machining. To train them needed time and patience, and only two ever 'made the grade', while the rest never got fast enough to earn even the basic £5 10s. ('they tried but couldn't lose their languid ways'). By comparison, an average machinist earned £8 to £9, and top machinists could make £12 to £13. At the beginning, the experiment had been tried of putting the coloured girls together on a machine bench, but this did not seem to affect their speed one way or the other. Others were tried out on finishing work, but they were slow at this and never became much faster. Another disadvantage was that most of the coloured girls had been found to be pregnant immediately after they began work.

By the time of my interview, no coloured women remained on the machinist strength of just under 100. Said the manageress:

'We still need machinists but not so badly as before. I really tried hard with the West Indian girls but they just were not up to the work. I feel guilty when I turn away coloured applicants who've seen the "vacancies" notice outside, but it's a matter of efficiency, not colour bar.[1] I'm not prepared to try any more unless they can show British experience. At the moment we've got seven or eight Cypriot girls who are very good at this sort of work, and some Irish girls who lack experience like the coloured women.'

BUILDING AND CONSTRUCTION

The building industry is one of high labour turnover and high rewards for workers. In addition, it is an industry of constant flux and change, in which permanent hostilities or difficult personnel situations rarely build up to a climax. Despite the climatic hardships involved, it has attracted many West Indian migrant workers. I interviewed one large and one smaller firm of contractors, Atlan Construction Ltd. and MacMortar Brothers.

Atlan Construction Ltd.

Since policy and practice in the very large firms vary from site to site, I concentrated on a site near Brixton where building operations were in progress for about three years. At the time of my first visit some 2,000 men were working on the site but this number decreased as the work drew nearer completion. The contractor's agent, an able and ambitious man who had started life as a carpenter and worked his way up to his present position, had decided views on many subjects and a more forceful and blunt way of expressing them than most of my management informants:

'I've had 300 blacks through my hands in the last two years. As workers I find them slow, lazy, and aggressive – the West Indians much more so than the West Africans. Occasionally they're violent – twice I've had a knife pulled on me in my office. I rely on Irish labour for the real hard work.[2] There's no friction over personal habits between the West Indians and the other workers,

---

[1] Cf. article on 'Training and Employment in the Garment Industry' in the *Times British Colonies Review* (First Quarter, 1957, pp. 11–12) for a survey of colonial workers in the London garment industry in which similar views are expressed.

[2] This is a fairly common feature in the building and civil engineering industries in London, which have used a great deal of Irish labour for over a century. Many foremen are Irish; somewhat naturally they tend to take on their own countrymen and to get more cooperation from them than they do from other workers.

123

but there's been a lot of bitterness because they slow up work so much and cause loss of pay. Now I put most coloured workers in their own gangs under a white supervisor. I am sorry for them, but they are not up to the work here. They are only a generation away from the jungle, trying to be Western and failing. They're cunning and have an inborn animal instinct. Those who do well do so by preying on their own people. They make money by graft, letting rooms, and living off women, and the smart ones take jobs as a cover. Several turn up at this site in Zephyrs and Cadillacs each morning but otherwise they live like pigs. One man brought his girl friend when he was applying for a job and she urinated outside the office in full view of everyone.'

This informant claimed that his views, which became increasingly unfavourable at each visit, were entirely based on his first-hand experience of coloured labour over these few years. In fact, I learned later that he had served as a non-commissioned officer with colonial forces during the war and his attitude seemed to be an extreme example of what may be called the 'wog complex' (see pp. 233–4).

MacMortar Brothers

A rather less extreme picture was given by the spokesman of MacMortar Brothers of Stockwell. This firm was much smaller than the firm which had contracted for the public housing site. Its practice was to recruit workers on the site and to pay them by the hour. These workers usually included a large number of Irish, who were regarded as excellent navvies, and some Poles, who were considered good workers. MacMortar Brothers no longer found it economic to retain a permanent nucleus of skilled men, but most labour was resident locally; quite a number would turn up for work regularly and they were given priority.

Coloured labour consisted mainly of West Indians. They had begun to apply for work in 1955. The firm had not made any policy decision but had simply begun to sign them on. There had been no trouble with the unions over the employment of coloured labour, but half-way through one job the unions had got together and made it a closed-shop job, presumably to avoid any lowering of trade standards and wage-rates. Standards of skill were undoubtedly different and my informant said that he had experienced some difficulty in sorting out 'the real craftsman among those who claimed to be skilled, particularly in the case of carpenters'.

MacMortar Brothers had found the majority of coloured workers slower than local labour. Their method was to find a 'good black tradesman' and to give him his own gang, rather than to put

124

coloured workers under a white foreman. This sort of 'national' gang was common in the building industry and suited employers, I was told, although the unions were usually against it. Coloured gangs were generally slower, but this arrangement was preferable to putting coloured men in a mixed gang where they would slow down work and arouse white bitterness over lost bonuses.

This firm had not found any more absenteeism among coloured workers than among others, but noted that they did not seem as keen as the local workers to go on National Assistance. If there were any complaints about them from other workers they did not get as far as head office: 'The men are a rough-and-ready lot anyway, and most unlikely to be finicky about their own or other people's personal habits.' This spokesman had not come across any evidence of touchiness or aggressiveness among the coloured workers. On the question of redundancy policy, he said: 'In a slump, the coloured workers will go first, and quite rightly. There should be job priority for local people.'

SOME GENERAL COMMENTS ON THE INDUSTRIAL CASE HISTORIES

These interviews with private firms covered a wide variety of industrial establishments, employing in all about 18,500 workers, of whom approximately 1,500, or less than 1 per cent, were coloured at this period. The case histories show that, while an acute labour shortage was virtually the only consideration that induced firms to agree to accept coloured or indeed any immigrant labour in the first place,[1] a large number of factors could influence the subsequent development of relations between migrants and management, and migrants and fellow-workers. Apart from such elements as the nature of the work involved and the working capacity of the migrants, an important or even decisive part could be played by such variables as the size, age, and 'personality' of the firm; the character and size of the permanent local labour force; the degree of identification between management, labour force, and locality; the policy of the unions; the duration of a given firm's experience with coloured labour; and such intangibles as the traditional status of the job and the firm, and the views of key individuals in management and the permanent labour force.

The interaction of such variables can perhaps best be illustrated by a brief glance back at the firms which appeared reasonably successful and those which had been particularly unsuccessful in

---

[1] But see pp. 132f. for an account of the role of the employment exchanges in 'selling' migrant labour to labour-hungry firms.

employing coloured labour. It should perhaps be stressed here that such success is not necessarily synonymous with successful production and good labour relations in general. For instance, a small, close-knit, old-established firm with a permanent local labour force may function like a big, happy family, but it will not necessarily take kindly to the introduction of outsiders.

The more successful firms on our list were: Pan-Provisions, Nutty Fruits, Wash Whiter Laundry, Audio-Communications, Petroff Engineering, Heavy Ores, and Dandy Chemises. These firms differ very widely in most objective criteria, but it is possible to discern certain features which may have furthered the integration of coloured workers in each case. Each suffered from a chronic labour shortage, each had persevered for several years with the employment of coloured labour, and each had evolved special procedures for selecting and training coloured workers and for allocating them to suitable work.[1] In the case of Dandy Chemises, indeed, the firm's success could be attributed almost entirely to its policy of retaining only the best coloured workers.

In most cases the firms were not the medium-sized, traditional type of firm with a large nucleus of long-term local labour. Petroff Engineering was an exception, but here the most important factor appeared to be the positive, almost sponsoring policy laid down at the highest level. In all cases management seemed to have adopted a fairly firm attitude towards objections to coloured labour by other workers, although where these were valid efforts had been made to meet them.

In six out of the seven firms union organization was weak or non-existent, so that the trade unions' influence on coloured integration was negligible. Three of the firms (Pan-Provisions, Wash Whiter, and Audio-Communications) had established a formal or informal maximum quota of about 10 per cent of coloured labour, a percentage which seems to have been widely adopted by larger firms in this and other areas.[2] But two firms which were particularly short of labour and lacked a large nucleus of permanent local workers (Nutty Fruits and Heavy Ores) employed more than double that percentage, while the two firms with a largely skilled labour force had less than 2 per cent of coloured labour, although both would undoubtedly have taken more had it been available. Coloured workers seemed

---

[1] At another local light industrial firm which was not employing coloured workers at the time of my field work, a new manager in 1960 reported great success in the employment of West Indian women on packing. He said that, given initial training and the incentive of a bonus, he preferred them to other workers, who tended to become irked with the routine nature of the job.

[2] This was confirmed in my later study of the integration of immigrants in Croydon industry. See also J. A. C. Brown (1954, p. 115).

to have been accepted as part of the permanent labour force in all these firms, and would be treated on the same basis as other workers in the event of redundancy. Only in the matter of promotion were certain reservations evident, which suggested that full acceptance had still to come.

The three most unsuccessful cases occurred in an old-established, traditional, and status-conscious firm, Orlando Preserves, which gave up coloured labour altogether after a fairly brief experiment; and in Jeeves Cleaners and Teen Cottons, both of which were too small and too much involved in cut-throat competition to waste time and money on special selection and training procedures. The latter instance showed that a sponsoring attitude was not by itself enough to secure the permanent integration of a particular group in the labour force.

From the remainder of the case histories, it seemed fairly clear that the great majority of West Indians had not, at least in the years of full employment up to late 1956, adapted themselves, or been accepted by management or fellow-workers as much more than inferior, unskilled, stopgap labour, slow, alien in habits, and often difficult to deal with, a group that would be expendable in the event of a recession.[1] Some employers, however, made an exception of individual West Indians, usually skilled or semi-skilled old-timers who had been with the firm for some years and who were accepted as part of 'our own people'.

This term 'our own people', used to denote the long-term nucleus of local workers who could, with their families, be relied on to keep the firm going, recurred frequently in almost all interviews, and it was clear that their interests would come first in the event of a recession.[2] At this time coloured workers were regarded neither as part of the permanent labour force nor as part of the local community[3] (in which most, in any case, did not live), and this view was reinforced by such factors as high turnover, mobility, and the reiteration by so many migrants of their intention to return home

[1] But see p. 142 below for a general change of attitude among local employers by 1961, in the direction of accepting West Indians as a component of the permanent local labour pool.

[2] Modes of referring to coloured labour stressed the group's out-group character. The contrast was between 'our own people' and 'the West Indians', 'the Jamaicans' (which usually included all West Indians), 'dark labour', and sometimes, towards the end of an interview, 'the darkies'.

[3] Cf. Banton (1952): 'It is important to recognize that the discriminatory policy practised by many employers is not based upon racial prejudice, nor upon the personal whims of the man who engages staff, but upon a preference for local labour which, whether justified or not, can be rationally defended . . . employers have what one of them called "a leaning towards our own folks", a feeling that workers who have been living in the country all their lives and who "belong" there have a stronger moral claim to employment than have recently arrived immigrants.'

within a few years. Nor had their working capacity in most cases been impressive enough to counterbalance these unfavourable considerations and induce managements to override conservatism and bias among their supervisors and permanent labour force.[1] How far managements were justified in this ascription of conservatism and bias to local workers should emerge more clearly in a later chapter.

CLERICAL, COMMERCIAL, AND PROFESSIONAL OCCUPATIONS

In view of the educational and industrial background of most West Indian migrants in the Brixton area, no systematic investigation was made into the extent of their employment in clerical, commercial, and professional occupations. The South London employment exchanges confirmed that they placed few coloured work-seekers in any of these occupational categories except as labourers or cleaners behind the scenes in retail firms. Since such work was usually lower paid than industrial work, it was also little in demand among coloured migrants.

From my interviews with private industrial employers, it emerged that few West Indian applicants were accepted for clerical or staff jobs, both because there were few applicants and these usually of poor quality, and because of possible or actual objections by existing staff, particularly women, on what appeared to be status grounds. In about half-a-dozen cases, however, coloured individuals, usually of the student class, were working in clerical or technical jobs. Indians and, still more, Anglo-Indians, seemed to have less difficulty than West Indians in getting such work, presumably because of their lighter colour, more European appearance, their reputedly higher cultural background, and their lesser degree of 'strangeness'. There was also widespread feeling on the management side that 'the public might not like it' if West Indians were put behind the counter, or in other jobs such as those of roundsmen and meter-readers, where they came into direct contact with the public. This feeling was almost invariably based on supposition rather than on actual experiment, and it is difficult to say to what extent, if at all, it was a projection of the informants' own views, or simply a reflection of established norms.

In Brixton itself a handful of coloured people were found working in commercial jobs which brought them into contact with the public. This seemed to occur mainly in firms which had some reason to

---

[1] Stephens (1956, p. 12) points out that at times of full employment employers are particularly 'employee conscious'—a factor which can tell against the coloured worker.

expect that this move would stimulate West Indian trade, either in the large cut-price chain stores or in the smaller trading establishments near Brixton market. In other retail establishments, it seemed that the relatively low pay of shop assistants was to some extent counterbalanced by a strong feeling of the job's superior social status in relation to a factory job, and managements appeared to feel that to take on even a suitable West Indian would cause more trouble than it was worth. 'In one large local store they recruit their girls on a family basis,' I was told at the employment exchange: 'They are afraid of taking on coloured people, especially men, and having the mothers say that the job's not what it was.'

Clerical workers are even more jealous of their status than shop assistants, and only a few coloured people were found working in Brixton offices. Most of these were male students from India or West Africa who were working temporarily, usually at low salaries, to augment their grants or to fulfil certain practical qualifications for their studies. The fact that their presence was temporary appeared to make them more acceptable among the regular staff. In offices such as those of solicitors, house-agents, surveyors, and accountants, who had considerable professional dealings with the West Indian public, there was perhaps a greater willingness to override or assuage staff objections and to employ at least one coloured person in a clerical or professional capacity.

A considerable number of coloured women are employed in the nursing profession in South London, and a certain number of male coloured teachers are also to be found there, although the latter have had to face considerable opposition within their profession and from parents. As only a handful of these professional workers live near or have any social connection with the Brixton migrant group, however, no detailed inquiry was made into their numbers or conditions of work.

The wide distribution and general popularity of West Indian and other coloured nurses[1] do throw a rather strange light on the general belief that 'the public might not like it' if they were to be served by coloured shop assistants and counter clerks, or even waited on by coloured waitresses. Indeed, the whole question of the social content of such direct contacts needs careful and detailed examination. Why, for instance, will the public accept coloured doctors, nurses, post-

---

[1] Over the whole period I came across only one instance of expressed hostility to coloured nurses; the woman chairman of Blackheath Chamber of Commerce was reported as saying that she thought the idea of employing coloured hospital staff was 'revolting' and that she would refuse to be treated by coloured doctors or nurses if she were seriously ill (*South London Press*, 29 March 1957). Moreover, matrons at three South London hospitals told me that they had encountered only a bare handful of such cases over a ten-year period.

men, ticket collectors, and sanitary inspectors while flinching, or being supposed to flinch, from coloured teachers, policemen, meter-readers, shop assistants, receptionists, and even garbage collectors? It would be hard to construct any scale based on gradations of authority or intimacy or other criteria which would account for these seeming anomalies.

7

The role of the employment exchanges

APART from a small minority whose friends or relations find jobs for them on arrival, the vast majority of newcomers register for work with the local Ministry of Labour employment exchange on arrival. As one manager said: 'Even without reading the papers I can always tell when a new shipload's arrived. Next morning there'll be seventy or more round at the exchange bright and early. You can't say they're not keen to work.' It is also thought that proportionately more coloured work-seekers than white continue to use the exchanges if they lose their jobs.

In these circumstances, the policy and practice of the employment exchanges can clearly exert an important influence in the early stages of the migrants' integration into British industry, although this influence cannot always run counter to the local employers' views and requirements or to the overall economic situation. The exchanges' capacity to place work-seekers is also, of course, somewhat limited by the fact that since the revocation of the Notification of Vacancies Act in 1956 employers are no longer compelled to notify exchanges about vacancies.

The general policy of the employment exchanges, as of all other government agencies, is very clear. They provide a public service and exercise no discrimination on grounds of race, colour, or creed.[1] At district level, however, a number of specific local factors may cause this official egalitarianism to be modified in the direction of some kind of discrimination or differentiation, not necessarily unfavourable, towards various categories of worker, including coloured migrants. Such modifications and variations emerged quite clearly in the course of interviews which I had with officials at eight South London employment exchanges.

[1] For this reason, no statistics of coloured workers were regularly published or officially kept at this period, although from time to time a minister would give approximate figures for the number of coloured unemployed or of those in receipt of national insurance in answer to questions in parliament; many employment exchanges were also able to give a rough estimate of the number of coloured applicants, placings, and unemployed in their area at a given time.

131

Migrants at work

The first part of the employment exchange's work is to interview the work-seekers and to assess their capacities. The interviewing clerk is usually familiar with the qualifications, background, and probable idiosyncrasies of local applicants. In this he is helped by the fact that such applicants may have certificates or references, and also an awareness of the general requirements of local employers and of their own suitability for particular jobs.

These considerations do not necessarily apply in the case of immigrant applicants, coloured or other, and most exchanges go through a difficult initial period when such applicants begin to register for work in large numbers. In the case of West Indians the major sources of misunderstanding have arisen over ignorance of economic background and skilled requirements on both sides;[1] over difficulties of communication (both South Londoners and West Indians say that they find it difficult to understand the other group's accent); and occasionally because of truculent or aggressive behaviour by West Indian work-seekers or because of an unsympathetic or impatient reception by an individual clerk.

By 1956–57 several of the South London employment exchanges which I visited had got over these teething troubles and had acquired considerable experience in handling and assessing coloured applicants, and also, as we shall see later, in placing them. Coloured work-seekers were becoming accepted as a permanent part of the exchange's work, and in one or two cases, where numbers justified this procedure, arrangements had been made for all West Indians, or at least for new arrivals, to be interviewed and placed by one of a particular group of clerks, who could devote more time and sympathetic interest to these particular applicants and to their placing in industry.[2] Such arrangements undoubtedly paid off in practical terms, but they provided a pretext for charges of segregation even from some of the coloured workers whom they were intended to assist. After a few years they ceased to be necessary, as local employers accepted or became resigned to the presence of West Indian workers in the labour force, as the migrants themselves acquired a more realistic appreciation of local industry's require-

---

[1] 'So many come in claiming to be skilled carpenters, but it turns out that they haven't done anything but the roughest sort of outside building work. "Have they got their tools?" is our rough criterion now. If so, we give them a chance at a skilled vacancy . . .'

[2] Cf. Banton (1955, p. 134) for a similar arrangement after the war in Stepney. It should also be noted that, apart from the other formal types of differentiation applied to these alien groups, arrangements were made for Polish ex-servicemen and East European EVW workers to be interviewed by specially chosen officials in the early stages of their industrial settlement in Britain. In this case, however, the main objections came from British workers, who felt that such arrangements 'discriminated' in favour of the newcomers.

132

ments, and as all employment exchange officials became more familiar with migrant applicants.

Understanding the migrant worker and evaluating his capacities are only the first part of the employment exchange's work. Next and equally important comes the matter of placing him in employment. In practice, as in the case of all new and untried sources of labour, this involves intensive and far-ranging canvassing and cajoling of employers, few of whom, except for the dying minority of old-time exploiters who welcome immigrants as likely to be more docile and willing to accept lower wages and poorer conditions, regard the prospect of employing any outsider with anything but reluctance and suspicion.[1] In South London, as I have already shown, no examples of such 'sweated trades' were encountered, and the majority of establishments visited were medium or small, long-established family concerns with a strong sense of association with the local community, which was in most cases not in Brixton itself.

Among such employers, the South London exchanges noted a fairly consistent sequence of employer reactions to coloured labour over the period of my field work. In the first place, there was a general unwillingness to try out a new and unfamiliar type of labour. This was usually based on preconceived notions about coloured or colonial peoples and on the anticipation of opposition from the permanent labour force. After some persuasion, however, most employers with a persistent labour shortage, particularly employers in poorly paid or otherwise unattractive industries requiring a large unskilled, semi-skilled, or seasonal force, would agree to try out coloured workers. In areas such as Brixton, where coloured settlement began some years earlier than elsewhere, most of these possibilities had by 1957 been exhausted. Some employers had, after what they considered to be a fair trial, rejected coloured labour as unsuitable. Others had refused to take coloured workers after hearing about the experiences of dissatisfied colleagues. A third group continued to employ coloured workers, but often, as we saw in the case studies, regarded them as stopgap labour, expendable in the event of major redundancy. At this date the general scarcity of semi-skilled and unskilled labour had eased, so that employers were more in a position to pick and choose than they had been in the early 1950s. This did not necessarily affect those coloured workers already

---

[1] In South London it has apparently long been a general practice to ask prospective employers 'Will you take coloured (or West Indian) labour?' The purpose of this is to save the coloured applicant the humiliation of being refused a job at the place to which he has been sent. This apparent discrimination or differentiation sometimes brings unjustified odium on the employment exchange, if a coloured work-seeker happens to know that there are vacancies in a given factory to which the employment officer does not send him.

in employment, but it made employers less willing to take on new coloured applicants.

At the eight exchanges visited, officials attested to the existence of an unofficial though varying quota in most factories. This they attributed mainly to trade union or employee resistance, although it was recognized that firms with a long local tradition usually preferred to preserve the original character of their labour force, and would not take on too many outsiders. It was also suggested that both employers and unions were becoming increasingly adept at throwing the responsibility for any discrimination that might exist onto the other side.

In the course of these interviews, I found that a fairly consistent general picture of the capacities and traits of West Indian work-seekers seemed to prevail among informants. This was a composite picture, derived both from first-hand experience of interviewing and from later employer reactions. As will be noted, this picture coincides fairly closely with that given by most management informants in the detailed case histories. The image of the average West Indian male worker was the following one:

'West Indians are semi-skilled at best, but most are only suitable for rough labouring jobs. Their professional standards are lower and they have an exaggerated idea of what they can earn. We ask them for apprenticeship papers or testimonials. Usually they have none so we adopt a rough-and-ready test; if a man has his tools we give him a chance at a skilled job if one is available. They have come here to make money and are keen to get work and to do overtime. They like factory work and building for this reason, although the latter involves outside work in a climate which they dislike and find trying. They will not stay long in a low-paid job and will leave without explanation if they find a better one.[1] They're not anxious to receive National Assistance and many don't even apply for it. Employers find them physically and mentally slow, but usually able to learn a dull repetitive job; most prefer to scatter them in ones and twos in departments rather than place them together in larger groups, when they are believed to become trouble-makers and also to arouse hostility among white workmates. Employers tend to take on members of one coloured group only, as it has been found that West Indians, West Africans, and Asiatics quarrel among themselves. Some employers prefer them to the Irish, others the reverse. Coloured workers are said to need more supervision than white workers

[1] This tendency was much less noticeable by 1958, after the effects of the recession were felt.

and are sometimes said to be childish and irresponsible. They dislike English food and avoid jobs where food is included in the wage. Their eating and personal habits sometimes attract un-favourable comments from fellow-workers. Many are touchy and a minority have a definite chip on the shoulder and are verbally aggressive both in the exchange and after they get to work. Only a handful of instances of physical violence have, however, occurred in the exchanges and these could be parallelled by instances of similar white misbehaviour. Few West Indians are used to the tempo and discipline of modern industrial life and they find the climate and the long hours of travel difficult. This applies particularly to the women.'

Officials at all exchanges visited had evolved a rather more unfavourable image of West Indian women work-seekers, and agreed that their placing presented a much greater problem than that of the men. In most cases women migrants formed a much higher proportion of the total female unemployed register than the West Indian men did of the total male register, reaching 45 per cent on several occasions. The general impression of informants about West Indian women may be summarized as follows:

'Like the men, the West Indian women arrive with the expecta-tion of high wages and find it difficult to accept that they have not got the skill or training to command such wages. Many of them claim to be dressmakers by trade, but they have never operated a power-machine and only the young and intelligent can learn to work at the speed required in the workshops over here.[1] They won't travel far to work, nor accept shift-work or residential jobs. Above all, they won't accept domestic work or charring, which is the only kind of work we could fit them into at once. They came here to a better life and regard domestic work as demeaning and poorly paid. They will take catering work at a pinch, but they don't like putting their hands in hot water or detergents and they won't get down on their knees and scrub. They dislike the food that is often included in such jobs, and will throw the jobs up at any time for seasonal factory work. If they lose two jobs, they're pretty well unemployable. The women rather than the men are likely to constitute a labour problem. Employers find them slow, touchy, unadaptable, choosy, hypochondriac, and lacking in stamina. Many refuse to take more after one experience. They say

---

[1] 'Some have been very successful,' said an official on the women's side in mid-1957, 'but the majority are only stopgaps. Those who make the grade find their own jobs later, and we don't see them here again. Once they have a good English reference they are all right.'

that they need more supervision than white workers. Many employers prefer the lighter-coloured ones and ask for them in preference to "black-mammy types" and "dark ones". Some employers find them not worth training because of their habit of "making a baby" every year or so. Employers also claim that their white women employees object to working side by side with them for personal hygienic reasons (more so than in the case of male workers). There is no evidence that their objections to domestic work and cleaning are lessening as other jobs become more difficult to get. Some accuse officials of "keeping the good jobs for white people".'

My interviews at all these exchanges confirmed the general claim of the employment service that no discrimination existed or would be tolerated so far as the exchanges were concerned. In most cases, indeed, it was obvious that managers and staff went out of their way to persuade doubtful employers to try coloured labour, often including a proportion of coloured people in 'bulk orders' for labour, and to help individual coloured applicants, sometimes in matters well outside the employment sphere. On the other hand, it was evident that over the years of interviewing and experience of employer reactions, most informants had come to regard the average coloured worker as a poorly qualified, unadaptable, not particularly efficient, poorly educated outsider, who could be integrated into the British economy only with some difficulty and at the less skilled levels. It was realized that there were exceptions (old-timers, ex-R.A.F. men, and students were usually mentioned)[1] but there seemed to be tacit acceptance that these exceptions were few and far between.

Despite this view of the average West Indian worker, all exchanges nevertheless felt competent to deal with current registrations and with continued immigration, unless there were to be a large-scale economic recession. By 1957–58 coloured workers were taking six or seven weeks to place, in comparison with a fortnight or so in earlier years, but no pool of permanent coloured unemployed was building up in any area. Only two managers used the word 'problem' in connection with coloured workers. Several others vehemently condemned the wholesale use of this word 'by the press

---

[1] There was a certain tendency to differentiate between Asians and West Indians or West Africans. Asians were considered to be better educated and more intelligent. Within the West Indian group several informants also appeared to associate greater intelligence and better qualifications with a lighter skin and less Negroid appearance. This may have been due to preconceived notions, but could be partially justified in terms of the colour-class stratification that still prevails in the West Indies.

and you academic people' (although I had not in fact used it), on the grounds that it tended to attract unnecessary attention to a fairly normal and manageable situation and often to create a problem where none had existed.

The officials whom I interviewed began by talking of 'them', 'the coloured people', 'Jamaicans', or 'West Indians'; but by the end of the interview several of them had slipped into what seemed to be more natural terminology and were talking of 'darkies', 'blackies', or even, in one or two cases, of 'blacks'. Like the management informants, most informants in this group drew a distinction between the coloured group and 'our own people'; this term appeared to refer to English work-seekers who were long-term residents of the district. Other outsiders were the Hungarians and the migrant Irish. Poles, however, after ten years of economic integration and settled local residence, were felt to merit inclusion among 'our own people'. 'The Poles are one of us now,' said one exchange manager. 'We don't have any trouble placing them – they're known to be good workers – but actually hardly any of them register these days. They are all in settled jobs or find their own.'

In general, the reactions to coloured work-seekers of the personnel in employment exchanges such as Brixton, with a long and intensive experience of interviewing and placing West Indians, seemed more favourable than those encountered at other exchanges whose staff had not at that time had much experience of dealing with West Indians in large numbers. The main attitude encountered was one of sympathy, tempered at times with slight exasperation or amused patronage.

Officials in the higher posts in employment exchanges were usually found to be more favourable in their attitudes to coloured work-seekers than were lower-grade officials. It should be remembered, however, that higher officials are in less constant direct contact with work-seekers and their problems than are the counter staff; that they live in middle-class areas with few coloured residents, or in areas well away from the district, and consequently may feel less identified with it or its problems; and that they have probably learned to be more cautious over generalizations than have their subordinates. At counter level, officials could at times become exasperated by applicants, coloured or white, who took up more of their time than usual; who hung around the exchange;[1] who blamed

---

[1] Here is an instance of the sort of misunderstanding that arises in exchanges. In late January 1957 I was visiting a Jamaican acquaintance. In came a fellow-lodger, a pleasant middle-aged man with several skills but no formal apprenticeship papers. He complained about the local employment exchange, saying that a Jamaican had made a scene there some days ago, so as a result coloured men were no longer allowed to wait about outside. There were 'certainly some preju-

137

the official for not finding them a skilled job; who might become aggressive and on a few occasions even violent; and who sometimes spoke in such a dialect or with such an accent that the less well-informed officials could not understand them and concluded, usually erroneously, that English was not their mother tongue.[1]

Instances of such friction or irritation could be and usually are cited as evidence of colour prejudice in the official concerned, rather than as the normal lapses of a harassed clerk. My impression was that such incidents could usually be explained in the latter way. A spokesman of the Ministry of Labour Staff Association, whose membership covers about 90 per cent of Ministry of Labour employees in grades up to and including Grade V, supported this impression; he emphasized that the letters and reports from members on which the memorandum concerning coloured labour was based[2] showed a strong feeling for official fairness, even though a minority of individuals had displayed personal bias in comments on outside matters, such as friction over housing or social amenities.

When I first wrote up this material in 1958, I concluded that the South London employment exchanges were, within the limitations imposed by the labour situation and the needs of local employers, playing a considerable part in easing and accelerating the initial processes of the West Indian migrants' accommodation in local industry. The mild personal antipathy felt by a few officials was more than offset by the official policy of no discrimination, by the professional desire for efficiency in placing applicants, and in some exchanges by the very positive, sponsor-like attitude of the

diced people in that exchange', he said. He had been told that there was no work by several interviewers, then white men had come in and been sent off to jobs. On 8 February, the *South London Press* published a statement by the manager of the Brixton exchange saying that visiting hours had been staggered to stop congestion outside the exchange (where up to fifty men, most of them coloured, might regularly be seen waiting for work): 'We have limited accommodation here and one of the heaviest unemployment figures in London. When people are dealt with we like them to go as soon as possible. If they do not go at once we get firm with them. Coloured men are no worse than white . . . but it is very difficult for them with nothing to do.' Later I was told that the sight of so many coloured migrants waiting for jobs in a time of unemployment was arousing some local resentment and that this was yet another reason, in the migrants' own interests, for trying to disperse them quickly if there was no job to which to send them. A similar incident was reported two years later in the *South London Press* (20 February 1959).

[1] A few might also be consciously or subconsciously influenced by status considerations. Employment exchange officials take a natural pride in their speed and efficiency in placing applicants and in the fact that they can supply employers with a 'good type of labour'. A few South London employment exchanges, however, handle so many West Indian applicants that some local work-seekers call them 'darkie exchanges' and go to register elsewhere. This applies particularly to skilled or white-collar workers.

[2] Cf. p. 78 above.

manager. The widespread 'discriminatory' process of ascertaining in advance whether an employer would consider coloured applicants[1] also operated as a shield which protected coloured work-seekers from the sort of rebuffs and rejections which might have stimulated a colour-conscious, chip-on-the-shoulder attitude and thus have retarded their personal adjustment to life in this country.

In revising the original manuscript for publication, I should have liked to check back with all eight South London exchanges to find out how the situation had developed over the intervening years. These years, of course, covered the moderate recession which lasted until the early spring of 1959, and the second migrant wave which began in 1960 and continued through 1961.

Unfortunately, there was no time to revisit all exchanges. But I had remained in touch with the exchange that 'pioneered' coloured labour in this area, and it may be of interest to record briefly its experiences from the early 1950s to the spring of 1961.

The Brixton exchange is in an area in which at least half the working population is employed outside the borough. The local association of industry and neighbourhood is therefore limited, and there are no strong communal memories of past unemployment in the immediate area, as there are in many single-industry towns that suffered heavily in the Depression. For decades this exchange has been accustomed to export much of its labour to other London boroughs and to the provinces. It was thus better equipped than many others to take the West Indians in its stride. By the time of my first visit in 1955, a large proportion of West Indian applicants had become a regular feature of the day's work, and the somewhat specialized task of interviewing and placing new arrivals had become a routine.

Undoubtedly this development had been helped and was to be helped in the future by the fact that over the whole crucial period this exchange had a series of particularly energetic and sympathetic

[1] This initial policy of what he calls 'structural shielding' was attacked as discriminatory, by contrast with the policy of the United States Employment Service, by Professor Frank F. Lee in a paper 'A Comparative Study in Race Relations: Negroes in the American North and West Indians in Britain' read at the Fourth World Congress of Sociology, Stresa, 1959 ('The Government, in effect, approves of and strengthens the already existing tendencies in Britain to discriminate against coloured or West Indian workers').

Burt (1960, p. 101) commented that this statement was not valid: 'The criticism is derived from an American perspective of race relations. The Ministry is not attempting to bring together workers of different social categorizations, of different colour-castes; it is attempting to bring the West Indian immigrant into the British working population. If we regard the problem as it is seen by the employment exchanges, if we acknowledge the similarity between the West Indians' problems and those of prior foreign working-groups within Britain, we must recognize the strong grasp which the Ministry has on the reality of the problem.'

managers, who took a more than professional pride in their handling and placing of the steady migrant influx. The first of these managers may have had his task eased by the fact that he had, as manager in a provincial dockside area, with an old-established coloured quarter, already experienced most of the problems that were likely to arise in this new district of migrant settlement. But if it was he who set the tone, his successors maintained it, virtually qualifying as sponsors in their persistent efforts[1] to persuade employers all over London to try coloured labour and to persevere with it, and in their endeavours to direct a stream of hand-picked coloured 'pioneers' out of the South London area into undermanned industries as far afield as Ipswich, Aldershot, Nottingham, Coventry, and even Yorkshire.

These efforts to disperse coloured work-seekers were partially frustrated, first by the tendency of West Indians to return to the Brixton area, where they could so easily find accommodation and companionship, and second by the 1956–58 recession and the consequent falling-off of demand from provincial employers, who no longer needed to look outside their own areas in order to fill their vacancies. The recession also caused many coloured and other unemployed in the provinces to return or move to London, where the unemployment rate remained lower than elsewhere.

Thanks to the energetic approach of its manager and officials, the Brixton exchange was able to prevent the formation of a permanent pool of West Indian unemployed even in the worst of the recession. However, the unemployment figures for the district did reflect the vulnerability of the unskilled West Indian worker in times of economic stress. The overall number of unemployed rose from just over 1,100 in September 1956 to about 3,000 in the autumn of 1958, while the proportion of coloured unemployed rose from approximately one-quarter to one-third of the total. In late 1958, moreover, placing of West Indians was taking considerably longer than it had done in 1955 and 1956, when a fortnight or less was the average.

It should be noted that all through this recession period a considerable number of notified vacancies for skilled men remained unfilled for lack of suitable applicants, as they did before and have done since. But it was increasingly difficult to place any unskilled work-seekers in South London, and demand for labour from districts outside London, which were harder hit by the recession, ceased altogether.

[1] 'So many times I have said we have reached saturation point, but each time the boatloads arrive we seem to find them jobs' (the then manager, quoted by *South London Press*, 16 October 1956).

The recession had one indirectly favourable consequence in that it induced West Indians who had jobs to sit tight rather than leave after a few weeks or at short notice; this disposed of one of the main criticisms levelled at them by employers. An informant at this exchange also confirmed the impression I had received from my follow-up of some of the case histories that very few managements had in fact carried out their verbal threat to put all West Indians out first in the event of a recession, although most had been more cautious about taking on newcomers.

By the spring of 1959 retrenchment appeared to be over in most of South London's industries, particularly in building and civil engineering, and by July the overall unemployment figures in Brixton for that month showed much more than the average seasonal improvement. The position was not yet back to that of September 1956, but the exchange was finding it possible to place more West Indians than were registering for work, and so cut down its backlog. It was also noticeable that at Brixton there were only about twelve new West Indian registrations a week in the summer of 1959, compared with the mass registrations of 100 or so that were a feature of earlier summers, every time a migrant ship arrived. This suggested that the West Indian settlement in Brixton was becoming stabilized, and was no longer a major reception centre for new migrants.

About a year later signs of a minor and temporary local recession were noted. This coincided with increased arrivals of men and women migrants in the all-time peak migration period of 1960–61. Once again, however, the placing machinery worked smoothly, the 'block orders' from the provinces were coming in again, and by the summer of 1961 the position remained roughly as before: the exchange was 'about holding its own against the new arrivals'. There was no permanent pool of West Indian unemployed, the average time taken to place newcomers was about six weeks, and the number of coloured unemployed was about one-third of the total unemployed. As in earlier years, migrant women constituted a disproportionate number of the coloured unemployed total, and actually made up nearly 70 per cent of the total female unemployed register. The earlier comments on the general work capacity of coloured women still held good. I was also told that, though single applicants could still be placed even as clerical workers, provided that they were qualified, there was an increasing number of migrant women 'with men behind them'; this was said to make them extremely 'choosey' and difficult to place in regular work.

The general position at this time had indeed changed for the better in certain ways. No particular deterioration in the working quality of new arrivals had been noted, and a fair minority of skilled men were applying for work. These could be placed within a day. There was also a growing number of applicants who had been in Britain for some years, and whose working history could therefore be checked. 'If they have good references they get back into work very quickly.' It was believed that some workers in the latter category no longer came to the exchange for work but were able to find a new job on their own. Employers were also willing to take newcomers on the recommendation of a friend or relation who was already working for them and giving satisfaction.

Perhaps the most important and significant change noted over this near-decade was that employers who looked to Brixton and the surrounding districts for their labour force were said to have accepted the fact that West Indians were a permanent feature of the local landscape; thus it was no longer necessary for the exchange to exercise its persuasive powers with such zeal. There were fewer and fewer blanket refusals to take coloured labour, and the main point at issue was the matter of numbers. As we saw in the industrial case histories, few firms were willing to have more than 10 per cent of West Indians in their labour force at any time. It was also interesting to note that several large firms had adopted the policy of sending personnel officers to the employment exchange to make their initial selection of West Indians there.

The experiences of the Brixton employment exchange over these years illustrate the workings of the process of accommodation among the three groups involved: the intermediary employment service, the migrant work-seekers, and, lastly, the employers themselves. They also illustrate the way in which an exchange can, by adopting a firm and positive policy towards migrants, play an almost sponsoring part in promoting their ultimate acceptance as part of the permanent local labour force.[1]

---

[1] On the contribution of employment exchanges in other areas see Richmond (1954, pp. 36–7, 47–8, and 159); Stephens (1956, p. 11); and Banton (1955, p. 134).

8

The local worker's angle

TRADITIONAL HOSTILITY TO FOREIGN LABOUR

BRITISH workers usually display a strong hostility to the employment of all 'outside' or 'foreign' labour, in which category they place not only Europeans but also coloured Commonwealth immigrants, and often even the Southern Irish. This hostile attitude is the understandable result of generations of struggle for better working conditions and wages, in a very different atmosphere from that which has prevailed in Britain since 1939.[1] Undercutting, strike-breaking, deliberate importation of outside or foreign labour with lower living standards – all these weapons have been used by employers in the past. And there are few older workers who do not remember the dark times of the nineteen-thirties, while many younger men were bred in homes which existed on the dole, homes in which 'Mum pawning her wedding ring' is a remembered symbol of extreme poverty and insecurity.

The present antipathy or hostility of English workers to newcomers in the labour market would seem to arise out of two kinds of fear. The first fear is primarily economic; the second is associated with non-economic factors and often with preconceived ideas about the particular group of outsiders involved. Elements in economic fear include the basic fear of unemployment, the fear of lowered economic standards, and the dog-in-the-manger fear lest 'our' welfare cake should be cut too thin because there are so many outsiders there to share it.

Of these three elements, the immediate fear of unemployment dwindled in most parts of Britain with the post-war years of full employment, as the memories of past insecurity faded. This was particularly true in London, with its low unemployment rate and great industrial diversity. In the years immediately after the war, however, the country-wide fear of future unemployment was still

[1] This economic xenophobia and its causes are so established that they hardly require documentation here. Illustrations of widespread initial hostility to European and coloured immigrant labour can, however, be found in the cited works of Zubrzycki, Tannahill, Little, Banton, Richmond, Stephens, and Reid.

strong enough to induce the government to impose severe restrictions on European Volunteer Worker immigrants over a period of three to four years, and in some cases to make union membership obligatory so that the unions could exert some control over their wages and conditions of work. In addition, redundancy clauses and other restrictive agreements in many industries kept EVWs and even, in some cases, Polish ex-servicemen in unskilled jobs and employed on a temporary basis, so that they would be the first to leave in the event of unemployment.

Such safeguards enabled the government to allay the misgivings felt by organized labour over the importation of non-British workers. They could not however be applied against Commonwealth coloured migrants, all of whom had, until mid-1962, the free and unconditional right of entry into Britain. Their British passports were to prove a two-edged weapon. On the one hand, they made entry possible and controls invalid; on the other, they constituted no automatic ticket to local acceptance and indeed marked the West Indian and other coloured newcomers as a potentially more dangerous and unmanageable group of competitors than the other foreigners who were subject to controls. Moreover, the newcomers' high visibility singled them out as a target for the economically insecure, as they waited outside the employment exchange for work, or in cases when large numbers were employed in a particular factory.

Economic Fears

By the early nineteen-fifties, however, when West Indian migrants began to enter Britain in increasing numbers, full employment had prevailed for several years and local competition for unskilled and semi-skilled jobs was at its lowest. British workers' reactions to the newcomers therefore tended to reflect not so much the basic fear of unemployment as the second kind of fear. This was the fear, not of losing their jobs, but of being forced back to lower living standards, either by undercutting or by the loss of the overtime pay and bonuses which many had in the years of full employment come to regard almost as part of their basic wage.

Union and national wage agreements have made the fear of undercutting largely illusory except among those employed by a minority of small employers in under-unionized industries. No definite evidence of it was found in South London during this investigation. The fear, nevertheless, persists among many rank-and-file workers. Like the fear of unemployment, it is a reflection of a grimmer past, when employer-employee relationships were less regulated or enlightened than they usually are today.

144

On the other hand, loss of overtime pay or bonuses was found to be a very real issue. Until 1957, it was probably the most frequent basis of objections to the employment of coloured labour made by South London workers. A slower worker can materially effect the earnings of his workmates in a shop where employees work in groups or pairs on a piece-rate or bonus basis. In many cases, as we have seen, coloured workers have been found slower than local workers; but the managements concerned have usually been able to dispel the resulting ill-feeling either by forming all-coloured groups under a white supervisor, or by giving the faster workers in the group a bonus, variously named, to compensate for their losses, or by moving coloured workers to slower time-rate jobs. Even on time-rate work, however, trouble could arise if the work was organized on a group basis, on the ground that the coloured worker was slower and 'did not pull his weight', so that others were earning part of his money for him.

In the chronically undermanned industries of transport and communications, the situation was a little different both in South London and elsewhere. Until 1957–58, employees tended to feel more secure about their jobs than workers elsewhere, but they had as a result of the chronic labour shortage come to take their regular overtime earnings for granted. These overtime earnings were threatened by the prospect of the large-scale introduction of West Indian labour, proposed by many local transport authorities in the hope of bringing the transport services up to adequate strength. Against this transport workers argued, through their unions or individually, that if the basic wage were increased the job would attract enough Englishmen, and there would be no need to bring in outsiders.[1] Their opposition was translated into strike or go-slow action in many parts of the country, notably in Wolverhampton, Birmingham, and Sheffield. In the London area initial trouble was confined to a few depots, one of these being Stockwell in the immediate vicinity of Brixton.[2] It was smoothed over with relative ease and speed.

The third element in the British workers' economic fear of outsiders is the 'dog-in-the-manger' attitude, as a trade union official

[1] This underlying motive emerged very clearly in the overtime ban by Wolverhampton T & GWU in September 1955, and in a statement made by the West Bromwich unofficial bus strikers in early 1955:

'Owing to our low level of wages we know that if we accept an influx of coloured labour we shall be brought down to a 44-hour week by which it would be impossible for a family man to exist. This means that men and women who have been on the platform staff for many years will have no alternative but to seek other employment. Therefore we say that an influx of coloured labour will not solve the transport department's labour situation.'
[2] See p. 156 below for a fuller account of this from the trade union's viewpoint.

145

called it. This was one of the most widespread reactions I found during my field work. It was variously expressed:

'Look at all those darkies at the exchange; they get sent out to jobs while local people are unemployed' (an elderly Brixton machine-operative).

'The British working class fought for seventy years and more to drag itself up to a decent standard of living; now they come in and reap all the benefit of it without any effort on their part' (a Labour Party constituency worker).

'I don't think it's right all these foreigners and blacks should get all the benefits of the welfare state and the health service straight away, without paying anything towards it' (a local government clerk).

'A lot of them just come over here to live on National Assistance; and we have to pay for them to hang around the streets doing nothing'[1] (a factory foreman).

'I hear there's talk of special hostels and training schemes for blacks. Nobody suggests doing that for our own people' (an unskilled labourer).

'Why should they be able to come over and work here on an equal basis with our own men? We can't go over there and take their jobs' (a trade union branch official).

These impressions are highly subjective and often inaccurate. They do however represent a very widespread attitude, one that arises not only out of economic insecurity but out of a more general apprehension about social status. Such apprehension would appear to constitute an important element in the British worker's aversion to outsiders in general and to coloured people in particular.

Considerations of Social Status

The fear of losing status at work is obviously the product of the whole set of preconceptions and impressions held by the British working class about coloured people. In the South London area this fear appeared to be considerably stronger in relation to coloured people than in relation to European workers or to the Southern Irish. Here it must be stressed that the Southern Irish are a constant feature of the local labour scene, while the Europeans have been settled in the South London area for several years longer than the

---

[1] Here again the West Indian's high visibility works against him. The majority of those seen 'hanging around the streets' in daytime are likely to be night-shift workers.

West Indians; both groups have therefore adapted themselves to a greater degree to local *mores* and are more accepted by local people.

Apprehension over status was shown by South London workers when they objected to an excessive proportion of coloured labour in any one department or shop, lest it should be regarded as a 'black shop';[1] in a certain tendency to regard some rough, unpleasant, and low-paid jobs as 'darkie jobs' and to shun them even more than before; and in the very widespread unwillingness to contemplate taking orders from a coloured man. It should be noted, however, that these objections did not necessarily include the few old-timers, some of whom were in skilled and responsible positions; for most of these had come to be accepted as individuals irrespective of their colour.[2]

This desire on the part of white workers to maintain their own status and that of their jobs is as yet far from the rigidity of the 'Kaffir work' complex developed over the generations by white South Africans. In South London it is, as has been stressed, the product of second-hand preconceptions, reinforced by first-hand observation, often superficial, of coloured newcomers. There is, of course, some danger that hardening attitudes among local workers and employers could result in the establishment of certain categories of unskilled work as 'black men's jobs' which an Englishman would avoid, and in the creation of a pool of unskilled coloured labour which would be more or less restricted to such jobs. Such a development does not seem very likely, but it could be facilitated if the majority of coloured workers fail to establish themselves as indi-

---

[1] Cf. *Manchester Guardian* (12 July 1956): 'The fact that a job can be and is done equally well by a coloured man as a white is held by many workers to depress its status. Consequently, the white man resents the coloured for showing the job for what it is and this resentment can be expected to increase as men used to good jobs are forced into poorer ones.'

[2] To gain acceptance in an industrial community where the coloured worker is still roughly equated with unskilled labour requires more than adequate craft qualifications. This point was made by a West Indian artisan who has worked in the same repair shop for several years:

'You got to be patient with them, man. They sho' ignorant but it no good letting them rile you. Most don't mean no harm. My difficulty come with the unskilled ones. I had a white apprentice who was a good boy. I handle him with kid gloves at first, then he ask me home to meet his family. A year ago I was in line for the foreman's job in my old shop but they move me to the special repair shop to avoid trouble. Working there supposed to be an honour. That's a very cliquey shop but they not against me, just putting me on trial. The foreman had a bloody-minded mate he wanted to get rid of so he put him with me. He was with the R.A.F. in India and claims to have been a fitter but there's nothing to show it. He talk about wogs. I handle him very carefully, avoid giving him direct orders, and always say "Please". I don't want a row where he'll call me a "black bastard" and I'll have to hit him. I can wait till they put us on piece-work. He's so slow he'll bring down the pay for the rest and the whole shop will turn against him. Patience, man, that's what you need.'

147

viduals of varying capacities in their places of work, or as members of the local community rather than of a culturally and visibly alien ghetto.

Another non-economic reason for aversion to coloured workers is often cited by English workers. This is the widely held belief that coloured men are highly sexed and promiscuous. In cases where men and women work in close contact this has sometimes led to protests about the employment of coloured men from the white women themselves or from white male fellow-workers. Again, the belief that coloured people have unpleasant personal habits has helped to strengthen this aversion, which is part of the general antipathy to the different and the strange which governs the Englishman's reaction to outsiders, particularly in his social life.

VARIABLES AFFECTING WORKING RELATIONS

Aversion or hostility to foreign or coloured labour in general is modified in South London by the cockney's live-and-let-live attitude towards individual newcomers and by what Leslie Stephens (1956) in his Birmingham survey called 'the everyday decency and friendliness of the ordinary British worker, which leads to a helpful attitude to strangers'. Among many trade union members and politically minded individuals, these favourable attitudes are reinforced by the creed of world-wide brotherhood among workers, by the trade unions' high-level stand against any form of racial or other discrimination, and by the Labour Party's emphasis on Britain's responsibility towards the peoples in colonial or under-developed territories.[1]

A further extremely important variable in determining in-group reactions to coloured workers and other newcomers in a particular

[1] In Gallup Poll Survey No. 427 (March 1955) 79 per cent of British respondents felt that it was wrong for people to refuse to work with coloured men or women (12 per cent answered that it was 'right', 9 per cent 'Don't know'). Three years later, however, in answer to a somewhat differently phrased question ('Do you think that coloured people from the Commonwealth should be allowed to compete for jobs in Great Britain on equal terms with people born here?') 50 per cent of respondents in London answered 'Yes', 36 per cent 'No', and 14 per cent 'Don't know'. Women and young people in the 16–20 age group tended to answer less favourably than the average. Field work for this poll was done during the time of the Notting Hill disturbances, when most people seemed on the whole to be trying to understate any hostile views about coloured people, but it is arguable whether the public condemnation had yet had time to make respondents more cautious about voicing hostility. Perhaps the phrase 'on equal terms' influenced the answers negatively. In her further analysis of this poll, Ruth Glass (1960) found that those who knew or had known coloured people expressed less bias than those who knew none (60 per cent of those with personal acquaintance with coloured people answered 'Yes' to the above question on employment, as opposed to 48 per cent in the nation-wide sample).

department or shop is the lead given in the direction of acceptance or rejection by a particular individual of strong views, be he manager, trade union official, supervisor, foreman, shop-steward, welfare officer, or simply a respected fellow-worker. It is to these unpredictable interventions of 'sponsors' or their opposites, who might be called 'anti-sponsors' or 'black-ballers', that the great variation of viewpoints and behaviour in seemingly similar situations can often be attributed.

In the same way, relations between migrants and local people at work may be influenced by variations in the labour or residential situation. For instance, the milder reactions of local workers in a South-East London light industrial plant to the large number of coloured workers employed could, as we saw in the case histories, be attributed to the fact that few if any coloured people lived in that particular borough, where there was little or no furnished or other accommodation for outsiders. Local and coloured workers therefore met only at work, and the former had no first-hand experience of the coloured newcomers as rivals for housing or as close neighbours.

One of the most important factors influencing relationships at work is, of course, the migrant's will and capacity to adapt himself to his new human environment. Good working relationships usually arise on an individual basis between Jim and Winston or Mary and Doreen, and not between a white and a coloured worker as such. Aversion and hostility are undoubtedly present among the local workers, but they are felt much more towards the unknown, undifferentiated, and threatening out-group than towards those who have become familiar workmates.[1] As has been said, there is a growing minority of coloured individuals, mainly old-timers, or early post-war arrivals, who have made a little niche for themselves and who are not usually included by their workmates in the 'coloured' category. If there is no major recession, one may expect the number of such accepted individuals to grow, so that the name-less mass of coloured labour will gradually be broken up and absorbed piecemeal in the local labour force.

[1] The British Institute of Public Opinion poll published in the *News Chronicle* in February 1955 showed that while 50 per cent of West Indians polled felt that off-the-job social contacts with British people were 'all right' or better, the percentage rose to 78 for workshop contacts. In a similar situation, a white busman wrote to the *Wolverhampton Express and Star* on 5 September 1955, during the T & GWU overtime ban of that month, to say that individual relationships between coloured and white workers were good but that collectively the coloured workers threatened the union. The history of the gradual integration of Poles and other East Europeans into British industry over the last decade or so has also shown how the traditional hostility to 'foreign' labour is broken down by increased knowledge and proximity.

At the present time, however, as a high trade union official who had been a factory worker for years pointed out to me:

'Men spend most of their working lives in the factory environment and a feeling of community is evolved. The West Indian is a worse outsider than most. He may be more intelligent – but often he doesn't smoke, he doesn't stand his round of drinks in the pub after work, he may work too hard, he doesn't know or learn the factory gossip or protocol of behaviour, or accepted forms of swearing. Factory life is a hard one and each newcomer is judged and classified before he realizes it. And in times of unemployment all outsiders are barred. My own Tyneside accent nearly caused a riot in a labour exchange queue in Birmingham in the early 'thirties!'

One might add to this that the West Indian often resents the London worker's well-meant but rough humour, and takes the Londoner's off-handedness and ignorance of other peoples and countries for a deliberate insult to his colour and his cultural background. Nicknames such as 'Sambo' and 'Darkie', jocular references to 'Jungle Jim', jokes about 'just off the trees', 'no shoes', 'pidgin English', and 'doesn't it come off when you wash?' can be duplicated by similar expressions in relation to the Scots, the Welsh, the Irish, and the Poles. But most coloured workers have not yet learned to distinguish between the majority of well-meaning though ill-informed fellow-workers and the small minority of deliberately offensive and prejudiced persons.

This ignorance and insensitivity among English workers undoubtedly do not further the accommodation of West Indian workers in the work situation. They are, however, fairly permanent features to which all newcomers have to accustom themselves. The most liberal trade union branch secretary to whom I spoke made no bones about this:

'We won't tolerate colour bar or discrimination among our members. But the West Indians can't expect feather-bedding just because of their colour. They'll have to learn to mix in and adapt themselves to our ways if they're to be accepted. They must lose their chip-on-the-shoulder attitude and realize that if someone calls them "Sambo" or "Blackie" he doesn't usually mean to be offensive. They should answer them back in the same spirit as "Ginger" or "Shortie". A factory isn't a school for young ladies and nicknames are usually personal.'

It was technically impossible to carry out a systematic inquiry into the attitudes or behaviour of Brixton or South London
150

workers. The material for this section was derived from a variety of sources, chiefly from general interviews with local informants, from the press, and indirectly from personnel officers and employment exchange officials. Fortunately it was possible to check this rather miscellaneous body of information by interviewing a number of officials in the unions most concerned about their policy and practice in relation to coloured workers. It should however be remembered that the union informants could speak for only a proportion of South London workers. As the case histories show, several firms were not unionized at all and in a number of others, particularly those with a large female labour force, the union organization was weak.

TRADE UNIONS – PRINCIPLES AND PRACTICE

When one considers the trade unions' policy and reactions towards coloured and indeed all outside labour, one finds that the ambivalence which so often characterizes the ordinary worker's viewpoint is at times intensified almost to the point of schizophrenia. This ambivalence arises out of the need to reconcile the principles of universal brotherhood and non-discrimination with the fears and antipathies of a large and vocal proportion of rank-and-file trade union members. About a century ago Ben Tillet, himself the son of an Irish immigrant, expressed this recurrent dilemma when he told newly arrived Jewish immigrant workers: 'Yes, you are our brothers and we will do our duty by you. But we wish you had not come to this country.'[1]

In considering union attitudes to any large immigrant group one should not forget that trade unions *qua* unions must regard with suspicion any non-union-minded labour force that enters or is introduced into the country's economy, because it may be used either to undercut local workers and throw them out of employment, or to lower standards and working conditions, or to show up restrictive practices by working harder and longer.[2] In this connection it should not be forgotten that the trade unions' own position is by no means fully secured even today. The total working population is just over 24,500,000, of whom only about 9,600,000 are union members.[3]

[1] Quoted by Banton (1955, p. 30) and taken from *The Jew in London* by C. Russell and H. S. Lewis (1900, p. 13).
[2] The last process was more conspicuous in the case of the Poles and EVWs. Few West Indians can work faster or better than local workers but 'hogging the overtime' is a complaint sometimes raised about them. This caused a strike of building workers in Southwark in 1960. (*South London Press*, 10 June 1960.)
[3] Information supplied by Trades Union Congress (TUC) Library in March 1961. Of the union members, over eight million belong to the 184 unions affiliated to the TUC. It was pointed out that some categories of the working population would not be eligible for union membership.

151

Fewer than one out of every two male workers and one out of every four female workers, therefore, belong to a trade union.

As we have said, Brixton is basically a dormitory area for West Indians, and most of its coloured residents work scattered all over London. Some West Indian workers join unions near their place of residence, but the majority of those who join at all do so at their place of work, as do most Brixtonians. It therefore seemed advisable, where possible, to interview trade union officials at both the national and the local level, in order to get a wider perspective, and also to compare viewpoints at various levels of the hierarchy.

It was interesting, though hardly surprising, to find that viewpoints at different levels of the hierarchy varied considerably but consistently. At higher levels general principles and policies have greater influence. In addition, most higher officials have learned the need for circumspection when making statements on controversial issues. Branch and local officials are, of course, more likely to share not only their members' economic fears, but also any local hostility arising out of housing and social problems. Thus at lower levels in the hierarchy I noted an increasing tendency to express uninhibited and often unsympathetic views on the subject of coloured and other outside labour.

The Trades Union Congress

In recent years the Trades Union Congress (TUC) has tended to soft-pedal any discussion of coloured immigrant labour or of colour discrimination or bias among British workers. Where such discussion could not be avoided altogether, the TUC has taken the view that any hostility felt or expressed by British workers is primarily attributable to economic fears of all outside labour deriving from past experiences. For instance, at the 1957 annual conference of the Nottingham Consultative Committee for the Welfare of Coloured People, Miss Marjorie Nicholson of the TUC Colonial Section maintained that, 'regardless of colour, the British worker feared any reduction of bargaining power or full employment for which he had striven hard and simply wanted to protect his position. Most of the difficulties arose from this, not from colour. Indeed, she found it quite extraordinary that the colour problem in this country should be "so very little". She advised the coloured immigrant to join and become an active worker in his union.'[1]

[1] *Manchester Guardian*, 8 April 1957. Later in her talk, Miss Nicholson went further, suggesting that the colour of a man's skin was, by and large, 'almost irrelevant' if he wanted a job (at this, a vague murmur of disagreement was reported from the audience).

Two years earlier, at the 1955 Trades Union Congress, Mr. T. J. O'Dea of the Civil Service Clerical Union had moved the following motion, which was considered to have been carried unanimously:

'This Congress condemns all manifestations of racial discrimination or colour prejudice whether by government employers or workers. It urges the General Council to lose no opportunity to make the trade union attitude on this issue perfectly clear and to give special attention to the problems emerging in this country from the influx of fellow-workers of other races with a view to removing causes of friction and preventing exploitation.'

In his speech Mr. O'Dea gave an admirable exposé of the high-level trade union viewpoint on coloured immigrant labour from the Commonwealth:

'We are concerned with the principle, and the principle of the trade union movement is quite simply this, that we believe in helping the working man in any part of the world irrespective of race or colour. . . . We must see that never if a slump comes these fellow-workers from other countries be used as a form of cheap labour to depress our standards. . . . We feel that this immigration must be considered to see that the immigrants are not directed to unsuitable work. We feel that these coloured people, when they do get work, should be recruited and indeed welcomed to the trade unions. We feel too that when their skill has been evaluated by British standards they should get the rate for the job. Finally and simply, we believe that they should be given the opportunity to advance like other workers in the industry. Quite briefly we feel that they should be treated in exact equality with white workers who work with them. If we do that we will not merely avoid this danger of cheap labour but we will do something more important: we shall show to the world, and to the coloured races in particular, that the British trade union movement in its relations with coloured people in this country puts into action the principles in which it believes.'[1]

[1] *Report of Proceedings at the 87th Annual Trades Union Congress,* Southport, 1955, p. 458. Two other resolutions against racial discrimination were also passed at this congress. It should perhaps be recalled that, at this precise period, the Transport Section of the T & GWU was objecting to the taking on of any coloured labour in Wolverhampton, while the National Union of Mineworkers (NUM) had just rejected the suggestion that labour should be imported from Austria and Italy. This rejection was not, said the NUM General Secretary, Mr. A. Horner, on the ground of racial prejudice but because ill-trained labour 'not liable to be organized' would delay the reforms and improvements that the miners needed (*Manchester Guardian,* 5 September 1955). Mr. Ernest Jones, the President of the NUM, added that the miners would reject Italians because of the language difficulty. Some miners put their objections rather more bluntly.

153

Migrants at work

At the next two Trades Union Congresses, on the other hand, all discussion of coloured labour in Britain was avoided.[1] But after the Nottingham and Notting Hill disturbances the TUC General Council did issue a forthright statement denouncing colour discrimination, which was submitted to the 1958 Congress and circulated to all delegates. This expressed the TUC's feeling of shock at the recent outbreaks and called on all trade unionists to help to prevent any recurrence.[2] At the 1959 Congress this was followed up by a resolution deploring the recent outbreaks, which were attributed to fear and ignorance; supporting anti-discrimination legislation, and pressing for progressive education and a positive contribution by the radio and television services to foster good race relations.

The General Unions

As an advisory body, the TUC can speak with an even more liberal voice than the majority of its member-unions. At top level, however, most unions have indicated their refusal to countenance discrimination against coloured immigrants of British nationality. But the general unions involved in industries which coloured workers have entered in great numbers, such as transport and communications, have been forced to take account of the views of various sections of their membership. A popular way of doing this was, particularly in earlier years, to advocate some unspecific type of control over all immigration or to suggest that economic conditions and opportunities should be improved in the colonial territories.

A resolution with such a content was adopted by the T & GWU's Biennial Delegate Conference[3] in 1955 and reaffirmed in 1957. It ran as follows:

'That this Biennial Delegate Conference of the Transport and General Workers Union:

reaffirms its belief in the universal brotherhood of men and its endorsement of the Human Rights Charter of the United Nations

[1] In his 1957 presidential address, however, Sir Thomas Williamson made a brief reference to the matter:

'We cannot ignore the vast and growing world population, increasing at the rate of 30,000,000 a year. Probably a little more than a quarter of mankind today enjoys what we regard as a decent standard of living; the remainder exist in varying degrees of poverty, squalor, and starvation. In the under-developed lands there are too many of our fellow-men who are unemployed or under-employed. In the countries of the Colombo plan alone, each year there are 10,000,000 more mouths to feed. In the Caribbean, hundreds are still boarding boats for Britain because their own land does not offer them a living.'

[2] *Report of Proceedings at the 90th Annual Trades Union Congress,* Bournemouth, 1958, p. 459.

[3] This Conference is the governing body of the union and its decisions are binding on all officers and members.

154

Organization; declares that discrimination on the grounds of race or colour is un-Christian and contrary to trade union principles; and reaffirms its opposition to any form of colour bar.

Conference recognizes, however, the grave situation which is revealed by uncontrolled immigration from any source. Especially when emigrants leave home because of the persistence of widespread unemployment, they often arrive ignorant of and unprepared for the great differences in climate and in social custom which greet them. They have no assurance of securing suitable work, or of finding anything but the most wretched living conditions, and they are only too likely to be exploited by their own countrymen or others. Not only is this exploitation wrong in itself; it is also a grave menace to existing social standards in this country.

For this reason Conference calls upon the government to work out a policy, in conjunction with the TUC, based upon: the control of immigration in such a manner as will overcome these evils; and, above all, a programme providing for substantially increased capital investment in the West Indies and other colonial territories so as to provide, on a long-term basis, full employment with decent living standards for the peoples of these territories, thereby eliminating the need to emigrate merely for the purpose of securing the right to live' (Stephens, 1956, p. 16).

At district and branch levels, attitudes in this immense pantechnicon of a union varied considerably. Of the ten resolutions down for discussion on coloured labour at the 1957 Conference in Blackpool, three advocated some restrictions on coloured immigration or employment, two suggested that the unions should urge a colonial policy that would give coloured workers a chance to earn a living in their own countries, and five wanted the union to confirm and reinforce its opposition to any colour bar. As the *Manchester Guardian* commented at the time: 'It takes all sorts of branches to make a union as big as the T & GWU.'

At T & GWU national headquarters in late 1957 a spokesman emphasized that friction in the provinces as well as in London had died down and that attitudes at local level were much less hostile than they had been. A slump might put the union in an awkward position *vis-à-vis* some of its members, whose attitudes towards coloured labour were contrary to union policy, but it was hoped that no large-scale recession would occur before a considerable number of West Indians had settled down and been accepted as individuals rather than as members of an alien group.[1]

[1] At the 1961 Conference, however, eight motions (four from the London area) were tabled advocating various curbs on immigration. Mr. Frank Cousins had to

So far as the T & GWU is concerned, the South London district has been relatively free of friction by contrast with some Midland areas. The district is highly unionized, which may have helped local members to feel more secure. In South London, 500 busmen at Stockwell Garage objected to working with two coloured men in November 1954,[1] but the ban was lifted some days later and no further overt trouble seems to have occurred until May 1961.[2] Coloured busmen participated like everybody else in the 1958 bus strike. In the other major industrial action of the last few years, the strike in the engineering industry, coloured members of the T & GWU (and the AEU) came out with the rest. A district official of this union said that individual members' complaints about coloured migrants' working ability and personal habits had died down over recent years. He considered that things would be all right unless there was a major slump. In that case, the men would probably expect the 'foreigners' to go first; this would include the coloured workers, who were believed to be a potential danger because they could live more cheaply and therefore manage on lower wages if need be.

The National Union of General and Municipal Workers (NUG & MW), over 800,000 strong, shares labour agreements with the T & GWU and draws its membership mainly from workers in the brick industry, gas and electricity, local authorities, and the heavy metal industry.

A substantial number of coloured workers are to be found in these industries but a spokesman from national headquarters could give no precise idea of coloured union membership ('certainly thousands'). So far as was known there are still no coloured union officials. The union has negotiated agreements relating to the employment, redundancy, and promotion of non-British workers (notably Poles and Italians) but these do not apply to Commonwealth workers. The union has no differential policy towards coloured workers and, in general, unlike the T & GWU, takes a

---

quell a 'sizeable revolt' but avoided a vote by making an 'executive statement' setting out the case against controls. One delegate from Poplar seemed to echo Ben Tillet's words a century earlier: 'We know we have to have regard to humanity, decency, brotherhood, and all the rest of it. I know, brothers, we have to go on being brothers, but there is a limit to which brotherhood can go.' (*Guardian*, 13 July 1961.)

[1] See *South London Press*, 5 and 13 November 1954.

[2] At a conference of delegates from London Transport's eighty bus depots a resolution opposing the 'influx of immigrants into this country and their employment in London Transport' was passed by a majority of two. The resolution was moved by a delegate from West Ham, with support from Walworth and Stockwell. It was subsequently declared invalid by the T & GWU on the ground that it conflicted with previously determined national decisions. (*Institute of Race Relations Newsletter*, June 1961, p. 7.)

rather quietist line, avoiding discussions and resolutions on the subject. National headquarters is aware of some friction 'just below the surface', particularly in the radically reorganized South London gas industry, but my informant stressed that over more than a decade only two incidents had arisen of sufficient importance to reach national level. One concerned the workings of the seniority rule, and was caused by the fact that West Indians had to be given precedence over non-naturalized European workers with longer service; the objections came from shop-stewards and fellow-workers but were finally settled on the 'Britons first' principle. The second incident was said to have arisen in the mess-room where night-shift workers heat up their food: some men objected to the smell of dishes brought in by West Indians and refused to share the mess-room with them until the union intervened. My informant pointed to the virtual absence of motions concerning coloured workers on the annual conference agenda as an indication of the lack of strong feeling at branch level.

Most other unions in the country are more closely identified with a single industry, trade, or skill than are the T & GWU and the NUG & MW. There are considerable variations in attitudes and behaviour towards coloured or other outside labour not only within but between these unions. These variations depend on such factors as: the strictness of craft requirements for union membership; the degree of unionization within the industry (high unionization makes for a greater feeling of security among members); the status which the members ascribe to the job; the past economic history of the particular industry or locality; political orientations (usually favourable in the case of West Indians but operating in earlier years against Poles, EVWs, and Italians); the number and quality of outside workers who have come into a given industry, their intentions, and the duration of their stay in the country; and the extent to which these newcomers are union-minded and take an active part in union organization.

Some Public Service Unions

In the National Union of Railwaymen (NUR) we have an example of a highly organized union associated with an industry that is a public service and has traditionally been regarded as a vocation by many employees.[1] The high degree of unionization in this industry

---

[1] In August 1957 the NUR had 371,000 members out of 589,000 temporary and permanent employees in the railway industry, including the London Underground. Of the remainder, 150,000 were members of the Associated Society of Locomotive Engineers and Firemen (ASLEF) or of various unions within the Confederation of Shipping and Engineering Trades. Quite a number of railwaymen belonged to more than one union.

might be expected to give members a feeling of security in relation to newcomers, but this has been offset by in-group clannishness, status considerations, and the fact that coloured workers (like Southern Irish migrants) are not yet generally felt to be 'railway-minded'[1] or 'union-minded'.

A general statement of NUR policy was made by its late General Secretary, Mr. Jim Campbell, writing in the *Railway Review* of 28 September 1956. This was shortly after a rather difficult television interview with Christopher Chataway;[2] Mr. Campbell claimed that this programme gave a disappointing and misleading picture of the problems of employing coloured labour on the railways, and continued:

'The union has made its policy known in unambiguous terms – no discrimination whatever against men or women whose skin is a different colour from our own. It does not matter two hoots to us whether a man has a red skin, a brown, black, or bleached skin. The overwhelming majority of railwaymen have tried to live up to that policy and deserve every credit for doing so. . . . First and foremost, I believe, there is a natural fear and resentment towards any influx into the labour market. Every worker naturally prefers a state of affairs where there are more jobs than men to fill them. With the recent automation sackings in the motor industry and with the railway modernization plan gaining momentum, is there any wonder that many railwaymen are apprehensive at the flooding of the labour market by workers from overseas? Their colour is beside the point.'

He went on to qualify this statement by saying:

'Not all coloured men are suitable for employment on the railways, and the safety of the public must be protected by insisting on standards of efficiency, such as the ability to understand verbal orders. Experience has shown that it is far easier to absorb coloured workers where their numbers are not excessive.

[1] The NUR organ, the *Railway Review*, has been attempting to combat these attitudes. For instance, a report in the issue of 16 August 1957 told in a very cosy style the story of West Indian shunter Hilton Pink ('Pinkie to the lads') who became a hero to his fellow-workers at the station by taking rapid emergency action to help an English shunter involved in an accident. The account continued: 'We are proud to tell this story if only because it helps us to counter the poison that is being injected by the popular press, the films, and the cheap television that men are vicious and evil-minded towards each other. . . .'

[2] In 'Panorama', 17 September 1956, Mr. Chataway confronted the NUR representative and the goods agent in charge of Smithfield depot, who had said that he had vacancies for porters, with four Jamaicans whom the interviewer had sent there the next day and who had been told there were no porters' vacancies. Mr. Campbell was also interviewed on this programme (BBC television).

158

Where there is large-scale recruitment the coloured men themselves tend to form their own cliques, thereby creating a barrier between them and their white colleagues.'

In November 1957 the London District Council of the NUR called a special meeting of 'colonial' railwaymen and their colleagues to discuss mutual problems and to encourage better relationships at work. Grievances and troubles were aired on both sides. One organizer, Mr. Johnny Matheson, addressed a plea to coloured members to play a bigger part in union work and to realize that many of their difficulties were those which have to be faced by any immigrant, irrespective of colour. The basic problems of all workers were the same, he pointed out, being concerned with the improvement of wages and conditions of service. He asked coloured workers not to go round with a chip on their shoulders. If they were rebuked for a poor job, they should not complain that they were being 'picked on' because of their colour. They should understand the outlook of their white colleagues, who still had bitter memories of the unemployment and misery of the 1930s and feared that any influx of labour from overseas might undermine hard-won working conditions.[1]

Union officials at various levels attributed most of the isolated cases of friction not to any colour bar but to economic fears of bonus losses, or to the railwaymen's fear that safety, both the public's and their own, was jeopardized by the employment of any outsiders, European, West African, or Asian, who did not speak or understand English adequately. Of West Indians it was said that their accent or dialect was often unintelligible to local railwaymen, and it was thought that the Londoner was equally unintelligible to the newcomers. One union official made a distinction in favour of the group of Barbadians who had been selected and brought in under the special recruiting scheme.

Non-economic causes of friction mentioned by union officials whom I interviewed included divergences in personal habits and diet (many railwaymen bring their food to work and heat and cook it up in mess-rooms), and violent behaviour. It was said that the old-

---

[1] Continuing this discussion in the correspondence columns of the *Railway Review*, two railwaymen wrote (4 October 1956) that there was no danger from unsuitable or 'diluted' labour, provided that full use was made of the existing machinery to ensure that all such labour was properly trained or else removed. They believed that with 100 per cent trade unionism, determined leadership, and the closest union between all railwaymen regardless of colour, conditions of employment could be transformed out of all recognition. It was their own experience that 'where a coloured man is treated normally and patiently he turns out as good as the rest. It is where the coloured lad is treated with hostility, barred, and ostracized that the rot sets in. How could it be otherwise?'

established nucleus of railwaymen in most depots and stations was not likely to tolerate aggressive manners or the use of knives and other weapons from any group of newcomers.[1] There had also been some objections from women cleaners when coloured male cleaners were assigned to work on the same job. But it was felt that this type of friction was dying down as local workers and newcomers became more used to one another.

Railway union officials foresaw a major source of friction in the future over promotion, which on the railways was largely bound up with seniority. There was widespread opposition to the promotion of coloured railwaymen, however well qualified, to positions where white railwaymen would be working under them. My informants considered that there would probably not be such strong opposition to serving under Poles or other European railwaymen, provided that they were naturalized and spoke the language well; this they attributed to the fact that Poles had been working on the railways since shortly after the war and were therefore more established and accepted.

Since these interviews, opposition to the promotion of coloured railwaymen, while it has certainly not disappeared, seems to have abated slightly. As we saw earlier, a greater proportion were by 1959 in ranks above the starting grade, although it was difficult to ascertain how many were in positions of authority over other workers. There have also been some cases of union refusals to support threats of strikes over this issue.

Like the NUR, ASLEF agreed in 1954 to accept coloured workers of British nationality 'into the line of promotion', in order to overcome the labour shortage. ASLEF is the union of the aristocracy of the footplate, both for British Railways and for the London Transport Executive; its fully paid membership is about 73,000 out of the 82,000 drivers, firemen, cleaners, and motormen employed by the British Transport Commission.

During my visit to ASLEF national headquarters, I was told that most coloured railwaymen on the locomotive side were 'union-minded' and that the union welcomed them as British subjects. My informant said that his members were cliquey, status conscious, and still imbued with a certain sense of vocation, and that there had been resistance to coloured newcomers at a few depots. Such resistance arose not out of personal objections ('This type of work attracts the cream of all recruits and they usually know how to behave') but out

---

[1] See letter in *Railway Review* of 30 August 1957, in which the writer demanded control of West Indian migration: 'These people must not be allowed to brandish knives at Englishmen while on duty.' He added that West Indians were weakening railwaymen's bargaining power.

of status fears and concern for safety. These matters were raised at the May 1957 Annual Assembly of Delegates at Blackpool,[1] at which two London branches, Nine Elms and Stratford,[2] moved for restrictions on promotion. The former asked bluntly that 'coloured labour should not enter the line of promotion', while the latter requested, in more general terms, that 'the recruitment of British Colonial and Foreign labour for footplate grades on British Railways cease forthwith', and that 'those already working in footplate grades be considered as not in the line of promotion'. Plaistow added an amendment that such workers should be removed when sufficient white men were available at depots and that they should go first in cases of redundancy.

Despite the wording of his motion, the Stratford delegate was at pains to deny the accusation that he was asking for a colour bar. He based his case on working experience, claiming that the great majority of coloured workers had proved to be slow, virtually unintelligible, and also to have difficulty in understanding instructions and orders. This was likely to be dangerous to public security in an emergency. He and other speakers also mentioned cases of aggressiveness and their conviction that coloured workers were receiving preferential treatment from management.

Stratford's motion was finally lost by 49 votes to 6 after a fighting speech by the General Secretary, Mr. A. Hallworth. This included the following passage:

'No matter which way you look at this question, it is a colour bar. Stratford can put all the trimmings round it that he likes, but it makes not the slightest difference. It is a fine thing to stand anywhere and say you are a socialist and that you stand by the ideals of socialism, and then when it comes to applying the principles of socialism on your doorstep to deny them. Is that socialism? Not as I know it. . . . I would say that elementary socialism is the uplifting, not just of the men in the line of promotion on the ASLE & F, but uplifting the workers of the world, without regard to colour, creed, or race. On that basis I would say that during the first war I slept with coloured men and I am not ashamed to say so. During the last war the men at Stratford and Hornsey did not object to fighting shoulder to shoulder with these men. They never questioned whether these men, regardless of their dialect, were able to fight Nazism and Fascism. We welcomed them. The policy of this Organization is that any man, mother's son that he is, no matter where he comes from, who is a

[1] See *Report of Proceedings of the Annual Assembly of Delegates*, Blackpool, May 1957, pp. 517–29.
[2] See Appendix IV.

161

British subject, can enter the line of promotion. That is right. . . . We have heard a lot about what took place in June 1955, when we were fighting the management to establish the principles of this Organization. During that fight every coloured lad in the line of promotion was on strike. In other words, regardless of the colour of skin the heart was not black. There were some white men at work.'

It is instructive to note that the next and successful motion at this conference, whose deliberations were largely concerned with technical matters, came from Kings Cross: it criticized the total inadequacy of the present methods of recruiting, selecting, and training applicants for entry into the line of promotion and asked for a far more comprehensive scheme 'in the interest of the Society and the efficient working of the railways'.

Another union that is linked with a public service is the Union of Post Office Workers, with a membership of about 80 per cent of the total number of General Post Office (GPO) employees below the managerial level. Here again the union and the management seem to have cooperated over the admission and integration of coloured workers. In about 1949 the GPO approached the union to ascertain its views on the recruiting of coloured workers to ease the labour shortage, and received a favourable response. At the national headquarters of the union I was told that the main reason for this acceptance was the fact that they were British subjects and in many cases ex-servicemen.

Since that date, according to my informant, there had been no trouble over coloured labour that was in any way comparable to that reported elsewhere. He attributed this to the type of worker that entered the Post Office: 'I reckon that we have a better lot of members than some other unions – more disciplined and objective. They get the point about the need for the union to take an impartial and world-wide view when it's put to them.' Minor difficulties had of course arisen, but these were less over working ability or personal habits than over differing attitudes to the job. 'There are still a lot of Post Office families, and the ideal is to make it a lifetime job. Coloured workers are often birds of passage, and if there were to be a depression there might be some feeling against all outsiders. There have also been a few complaints that coloured staff are over-sensitive about their colour.'

Coloured postmen were not at this time (1957) particularly active in the union, but it was thought that this might change as they became more union-minded and better known in their local branches. On the subject of promotion, the union's spokesman told

162

me that the GPO administration had asked for the union's views in 1953, after a considerable number of the 500 or so coloured postmen on the staff had become eligible for promotion on seniority. Once again the response had been favourable. Here my informant added that promotion to a truly supervisory rank rarely came in less than ten years of service, and that the promotion referred to was usually to better-paid and more responsible work.

Some years later a union representative confirmed that the integration of coloured postal employees was proceeding smoothly; the national headquarters had no recorded case of either staff or management trying to 'apply a brake' to the up-grading of coloured workers at these lower levels, nor had there been any complaints from coloured workers in this respect. (My informant privately wondered whether this situation would continue at the supervisory level.) Coloured workers joined the union but so far did not appear to be playing a very active part. The union's line on immigration was said to be 'progressive', and it was stressed that, unlike some other unions, it had passed no resolutions calling for controls or restriction.

Four Unions Concerned with Private Industry

In the private industrial sectors in which large numbers of coloured workers were employed, it was not possible to interview representatives of all the unions concerned. Interviews were therefore restricted to three large industrial unions which had begun as craft unions, and to the appropriate union for the London garment trade.

The three former craft unions are associated with the building, engineering, and food-processing industries, and their policy and practice with regard to coloured workers were found to vary considerably.

The first union has a membership of about four craftsmen to every labourer; and despite the migratory nature of the work it has achieved 80 per cent unionization in its sector of the building industry. It is therefore able to enforce apprenticeship and craft standards strictly.

The building industry has long been accustomed to a cosmopolitan labour force, traditionally including large numbers of Southern Irish, and more recently Poles, Italians, and other Europeans. Coloured workers have been employed in considerable numbers for some time and many have joined the union, although a spokesman at national headquarters was unable to tell me how many were in the skilled or the labouring categories. By 1957 the various newcomers were regarded as active and acceptable union members. One South London branch secretary was Polish and there was at least one coloured shop-steward.

163

At its Annual Conference in July 1955, this union passed a resolution condemning any attempt to bring a colour bar into British industry. The resolution stated: 'The common enemy of working men is the employer, and rather than seek out each other in dispute may we go forward in a united struggle to improve our standards of living.' Since then the union has made no public pronouncements on the subject, regarding them as unnecessary. The fluctuating and migratory nature of the job, I was told, prevents situations of any kind from building up on a permanent basis and any minor frictions that arise between white and coloured workers do not get beyond local level.

The second union in this trio has a more complex structure, based on degrees of skill, acceptance by other craftsmen, differing contributions and benefits, seniority, and sex. The craft tradition lingers on and the skilled men are said to exercise a disproportionate influence in the union. I was also told that craftsmen in this industry feel themselves to be particularly vulnerable to undercutting because of the number of small firms involved; in 1957 over two-thirds of the firms in this industry employed fewer than 250 employees.

No figures or estimates of coloured membership in any grade were available for this union, but it was said that relatively few coloured workers seemed to possess the required skills or formal qualifications to get a craft grading on arrival, and that coloured men were usually too old to meet the age qualifications for apprenticeship in Britain. There were no coloured full-time officials at this time; my informant said that it was too early for such a development, since there was a seven years' membership qualification for full-time office-holders. Only a year's membership qualification was required of minor branch officials, and there were already a few coloured branch officials.

This union is a lively, politically minded body whose policies have often been dictated by left-wing activists. In 1956 the National Committee adopted the United Nations Declaration of Human Rights, and the union has given a much better deal to coloured workers than it did to political refugees from Eastern Europe; even if the latter possessed impeccable craft qualifications, these did not outweigh their anti-Communist views, and I have several times heard them dismissed as 'fascists', 'landlords', and 'reactionaries'.[1] On relations with coloured workers, I was told at district level:

---

[1] This was one of the craft unions that for years refused to admit Poles and European Volunteer Workers, however good their craft qualifications. Finally it did so only because rival unions were accepting them and so weakening the union's bargaining position. But as late as 1958 I found several closed shops in South London which were refusing to admit Poles and Hungarians, even if they belonged to the skilled section of the union.

'There is no discrimination on grounds of colour in our union. If it happens in individual cases we don't hear of it. It wouldn't be tolerated and our members know it. If there were to be a slump the men would undoubtedly feel that outsiders should go first, but we'd take a firm line.' My informants found coloured workers very union-minded, and stressed that all coloured members had come out with the rest in industrial action in the South London area.[1]

The last union in this trio also retains a large number of skilled members from its craft-union days. The industry has however changed and developed as a result of mechanization and automation, and as a result of the introduction of an increasing proportion of women and of foreign or outside labour. One section of the industry in South London is only about 50 per cent unionized, and the other section far less so.

Increased mechanization, dilution with female and outside labour, and low unionization are all factors that have produced a general sense of insecurity among workers in the industry. After the second world war the union negotiated redundancy agreements with many firms, which provided that foreign workers should go first; these agreements are only now being changed and modified. Later the union was compelled to recognize the feelings of local workers about the entry of coloured labour, and negotiated several agreements with large firms providing that coloured workers would be employed only in departments where employees had agreed to accept them.

At the higher levels officials were forward-looking, progressive, and entirely opposed to any colour discrimination. I was particularly impressed by one informant, who had been born and brought up near the Tiger Bay area of Cardiff. Having seen the gradual integration of the coloured settlement there as individual families were moved out of the coloured quarter by post-war rehousing programmes, he had no general misgivings over the future development of relationships between the West Indian newcomers and the local population. He regarded as 'routine' the complaints which he received from members about coloured workers' slowness, which affected earnings, and about unhygienic personal habits, sexuality, and aggressiveness. Nevertheless, he considered that West Indians would have to make a major effort to adapt themselves to British ways if they were ever to be fully accepted. From the union's viewpoint, they must also learn to be more union-minded and, once they

---

[1] In an unofficial strike by building workers in late 1958 on a South London site where this and other unions were involved, a number of coloured workers were particularly active. Three were photographed by the *South London Press*, which commented: 'When pickets were chosen to parade the South Bank building site this week the boys with the blackest skins were chosen to advertise that it is "black" in the eyes of those who are locked out' (10 October 1958).

165

joined, to take a more active part in union affairs. There would be no opposition to their holding union office; the union had already appointed a coloured shop-steward in a mixed shop in South London, and had one young coloured member who was taking the lead in organizing European workers in a small factory where the union had previously made no headway.

The garment trade in Britain, and particularly in London, is traditionally associated with Jewish and other minorities. There is therefore relatively little feeling among workers against 'outsiders', who in London include Cypriots, Poles, Italians, and latterly West Indians. The industry has also in the past been associated with insecurity and sweated labour and has proved a very difficult one for unionization. Today four out of every five workers are women, and only three out of eight workers are unionized. Unionization is uneven, and strongest in the men's clothing and women's outer-clothing sections.

At top level, a spokesman of the union concerned with the garment trade in London displayed a realistic and liberal attitude to the employment of coloured workers. In some unionized firms, I was told, management had consulted the local branch before starting to employ coloured workers, and there had been no objections. The union's main concern was to get the West Indians to join the union, and those working in unionized factories had shown no resistance to this. There were already several coloured shop-stewards in London, one in an all-white shop, but so far none had become a full-time official. On the question of redundancy, my informant said: 'Despite the feelings of insecurity prevalent among garment workers, I think the principle of "first in, last out" could be made to apply in organized factories, even in the event of a slump.'

Rank-and-file union members' attitudes to coloured workers were said to be tolerant, except for an occasional young ex-serviceman with a 'wog complex'. Head office had received complaints about the obnoxious personal habits of coloured workers, but I was told: 'We feel that head office can't get involved in that sort of thing. We put it down to ignorance on both sides. But the West Indians' welfare people[1] should try to instil in them the idea of being extra specially careful to represent their race well, like the Jews.'

Like the two garment-trade employers interviewed, the spokesman for this union saw the main problem for West Indian labour in terms not of personal relationships with fellow-workers but of their low working capacity. In Britain, he said, the garment trade was one of

---

[1] This union was at that time one of the few which seemed to be in regular contact with the British Caribbean Welfare Service (later the Migrant Services Division).

high productivity, and most employers would not retain workers who could earn only the minimum wage. Neither West Indians nor West Africans were used to the tempo of work here. Many expected to earn more than they were worth. They were jacks-of-all-trades rather than specialists, and few or none had the long craft training required for the best tailoring work. Most West Indian men had gradually been transferred to pressing, which they liked and at which they were fairly successful. They were willing to work hard, and the minority who made the grade became as good as the average local worker with time.

The National Union of Seamen

Very few of the coloured working population in South London, with the exception of some old-timers in Deptford, follow the occupation so long associated with coloured workers in the older dockland settlements. By way of postscript to this section, however, a brief reference should be made to the National Union of Seamen (NUS), since the membership of this union is about 25 per cent coloured (African, Asiatic, and West Indian) and it has had longer and more detailed experience in this sphere than any other British union. Indeed, unlike most other unions, the NUS had actually had to face, in the period between the two world wars, the mass unemployment, undercutting, and displacement by unorganized coloured or foreign labour which in this century have been only vague and potential threats to most other unions.

In the early 1930s, one out of every three registered seamen in Britain was unemployed. The main economic threat to British seamen came not from the British-domiciled coloured seamen but from the 40,000 or so Lascars (British and foreign) who were in the shipping industry in 1935. These Lascars were taken on in foreign ports, and were paid wages much below the National Maritime scale. Soon, however, coloured seamen resident or domiciled in Great Britain became identified in the eyes of white fellow-seamen with this alien coloured group that menaced their livelihood and living standards. In fact, these coloured seamen were in a doubly difficult situation. Being registered in Britain, they were unable to sign on at lower wages, while employers, knowing the unpopularity of the coloured crews, were likely to choose a white man rather than a coloured man who had to be paid the same wage.[1]

[1] At national level, the NUS rejected any imputation of discrimination. It appears, on the other hand, that at local level a number of union officials discriminated in their application of the Aliens Order of 1925, which officially referred only to alien coloured seamen. In the Cardiff area, for instance, this order was taken by police officers and union officials to apply to all coloured seamen, and many

167

In 1957 a high official of the NUS who remembered those times assured me that the attitudes of white union members were greatly changed: 'Prejudice would not be countenanced now and coloured members of the NUS (i.e. those who are British-domiciled) would not be classed as "colour" in the event of a slump.' In the full-employment conditions of recent years I was told that the NUS had agreed to controlled employment of seamen from African, Asiatic, and Caribbean ports on 'Indian articles' (i.e. two years' service at lower wages, with the employer taking responsibility for repatriation). By 1957 the total number of seamen on 'Indian articles' was nearly 50,000; this represented an increase of 15,000 over the 1952 total. At a NUS conference the next year concern was expressed at this increase; one delegate was reported as saying that he had no objection to Lascars, Chinese, or West Indians earning a living, but that when his own standard of living was jeopardized it was a different matter. The union's secretary, Mr. T. Yates, pointed out that the union had at no time practised a colour bar, and that 15,000 to 20,000 coloured seamen had been members for a long time. He was concerned only with the practice of employing Asiatics in latitudes where they were normally not engaged. 'In no circumstances will any ship that has come in "white" or United Kingdom manned be changed to any other manning.'[1]

coloured British seamen suffered from the restrictive stipulations of the British Shipping (Assistance) Act of 1935 regarding the employment of non-British seamen. For a fuller account of the 1920s and 1930s, see Little (1947, pp. 55–77) and Banton (1955, pp. 34–5).

[1] *Lloyd's List*, 17 April 1958.

Summary of the employment situation

To SUM up the employment situation generally, it may be said that the utilitarian approach of most employers faced with a chronic labour shortage has on the whole been a factor promoting the early stages of absorption of West Indians, as of other newcomers, in the South London labour market. On the other hand, the traditional hostility of the local labour force, organized and other, to all outsiders, has tended to work against their acceptance. In practice, however, this hostility has been modified, and in some firms even dispelled, by sponsoring action not only by management but by union officials. Where a particular union has come out firmly at national level for non-discrimination, this attitude tends to percolate gradually downwards to all but a few outposts of resistance. Such acceptance is of course furthered by evidence of adaptability among the immigrants and by their joining and playing an active part in the unions.

The minor recession of 1956–58 showed that in practice many employers had accepted West Indian workers as part of the local labour force to a greater extent than could have been inferred from their statements on eventual redundancy policy; it also showed that, despite their frequently voiced hostility or apprehension, union branches and local workers had not in most cases demanded or enforced any discrimination against migrant workers in the matter of redundancy.

This seems to point to the attainment of a certain degree of accommodation on both sides in working relationships.[1] Such accommodation is however still limited and tends to be confined to the work situation, and there is little or no carry-over of these relationships to the neighbourhood or to informal social life. In the work situation, too, status considerations remain a strong factor, usually operating against the migrants in questions both of skill-levels and of promotion.

A minority of exceptional individual migrants have begun to move

[1] In the Gallup Poll conducted by Social Surveys Ltd. for the *Daily Telegraph* in the summer of 1961, 60 per cent of respondents considered that coloured people from the Commonwealth should be allowed to compete for jobs in Britain on equal terms with people born here, and 68 per cent said that they would not mind working with coloured people; 49 per cent of male respondents and 21 per cent of female respondents had in fact worked at some time with coloured people, and in both cases five out of seven thought they were about the same as white people at their work.

up from the bottom of the industrial ladder and to undermine the British workers' notion of coloured workers as Lascars, coolies, and cane-cutters in far-away lands. Such progress is limited by the low industrial capacity of the majority of today's migrants. It could be speeded when the locally educated second generation enters the labour market. The latter will no longer be strangers, but they will still have to strive against the 'class' notion that coloured workers are on the whole suitable only for unskilled and semi-skilled work, just as their parents have to combat the 'stranger' notion to win acceptance as a permanent part of the local labour force.

PART III

Strangers and neighbours

9

The housing situation in Lambeth[1]

PUBLIC HOUSING, SHORTAGE, AND OVERCROWDING

HOUSING, or accommodation in its literal sense, was until the 1956–
58 economic recession the coloured migrants' main problem in
Brixton, as in most other parts of England. It also was, and has
again become, the chief source of competition and potential conflict
with the local population. There are two aspects to this question of
housing: the one is concerned with actual living space, the other
with social and cultural contacts and conflicts.

Like most South and East London boroughs, Lambeth suffered
greatly from enemy bombardment during the 1939–45 war. Despite
the overall decrease in population in latter years (from a rough total
of 300,000 in the years between 1900 and 1930 to 230,000 in 1951,
an estimated 224,200 in 1955 and 221,960 in 1961), the housing
shortage was in the late 1950s still very serious.

In January 1955, some months before I started on this study, the
borough's waiting-list contained the names of some 10,000 families.
By late 1957 this peak figure had been reduced to some 5,500,
but less building was being done. The borough had by then more
or less exhausted its reserves of empty buildings to rehouse families
displaced by slum clearance and was relying for extra accommodation on the small percentage of council dwellings that were falling
vacant each year. Since then slum clearance has remained a priority
and the compulsory derequisitioning of nearly 3,400 requisitioned
properties[2] has involved the rehousing of some 1,500 former tenants
and their families. Consequently, very few families on the waiting-
list have been rehoused. By the end of 1959 this list stood at 5,250
and by the end of 1960 at 4,700, but some of the reduction came
about because of families who had moved or found alternative
accommodation by their own efforts. The council had at this time

[1] The local housing authority for the Brixton area.
[2] Under the Requisitioned Houses and Housing Act of 1955. Despite widespread
local apprehension about the consequences of the new Rent Act, which caused
an increased number of applications to be made for rehousing in late 1957, only
three compulsory purchase orders had in fact been made by the end of 1960.

some 5,000 dwellings, of which about 4 per cent were falling vacant annually, and another 500 were under construction.

The qualification for inclusion on the Lambeth housing-list is three years' residence in the borough, while no applicants for permanent rehousing are considered until they have been one year on the list. In fact, most applications wait far longer than that. Under the system of priorities, the main points are given for room shortage, family separation, illness, and physically bad conditions. Supplementary points which bring the case forward for earlier consideration are war service, loss of house by enemy action, and the lack of a separate kitchen.

Because of the Borough of Lambeth's *laissez faire*, non-differentiatory policy towards its migrant population in recent years,[1] it was virtually impossible to get any precise official information about the number of West Indian families on the waiting-list or the number who had been rehoused. In 1958 a borough official hazarded a guess that there might be some fifty West Indian families on the waiting-list, about one-tenth of them urgent cases. Two years later I was told that no separate figures were kept but that the number of West Indian applicants was probably increasing as more qualified under the three-year residence rule.

As for rehousing, it was suggested by various non-official informants that applications from coloured families were often so marked and were therefore distinguishable when they went up before the Housing Committee for consideration. This allegation was officially denied, although I was told that a certain amount of discretion was exercised in this as in other boroughs as to the type of accommodation offered to any families that qualified for rehousing, on the basis of the Octavia Hill categories and standards.

Allegations of official discrimination in the routine rehousing of coloured families were and remain academic and unproven. No significant number of coloured families could have qualified even for entry on the waiting-list until 1957, when rehousing practically ceased.

In March 1956 the then mayor, Alderman Nathan Marock, was quoted as saying: 'Despite all that may have been read or heard about what has gone on in Lambeth, during the past year only six West Indian families have been rehoused in the worst type of requisitioned property – because no one else would take it – and two

[1] 'In Lambeth we have tried to be fair to everyone. As a Council we have frowned on attempts to provide special facilities for one section of the community' (Alderman Nathan Marock writing in *London News* [organ of the London Labour Party] October 1958). But see *South London Observer* (28 June 1951) for an earlier and less impartial report passed by the General Purposes Committee, complaining of coloured 'loafers' and bad housing and overcrowding among the newcomers.

174

or three in council flats.'[1] And by the end of 1957, the number who had been housed was said to consist of less than a dozen families placed in requisitioned property, a handful in hutments, and two or three in older-type council flats.

In the rather explosive local atmosphere created by the post-war housing shortage, the local council seems to have been concerned not so much with discriminating against the few coloured applicants on the housing-list as with persuading local ratepayers and voters that they were not in fact discriminating against local applicants in favour of recently arrived coloured migrants. This belief was fairly widespread and appears to be based on a handful of instances in which coloured people gained priority on the borough or London County Council[2] waiting-lists because they had been displaced by slum clearance or were living in grossly overcrowded conditions. In Lambeth very few West Indians live in scheduled property but the overcrowding prevalent among them was by 1955 a matter of common belief or knowledge. An unusually outspoken comment on the Labour-controlled council's predicament and reactions over this matter was made in April 1956 by Alderman Wilfred Laverick, who had resigned from the Labour Party in the preceding May:

'When the matter [i.e. of coloured overcrowding] was brought before the [Lambeth Council Labour] Group eighteen months

---

[1] *South London Press*, 30 March 1956. Presumably the borough council has since had to find other accommodation for these six families under the derequisitioning process. I visited one of these requisitioned houses which had been a boarding-house for coloured students before the war. In theory it housed single males in single or double rooms, but an unknown number of female 'cousins' and relations of both sexes also seemed to live there from time to time. The house was kept in reasonable order, and rents were collected by a West Indian woman caretaker, who lived in one room with her husband and two children and paid a lower rent in return for her part-time services. This house has since been demolished.

[2] The LCC is responsible for about half of London's housing, and an estimated 25 per cent of Lambeth families were said to be registered on both the LCC Southern District and the borough waiting-lists at this time. But few were rehoused from the waiting-list, again because of the priority being given to slum clearance. Some families of coloured applicants had been rehoused because of the overcrowded conditions in which they lived and a second group had qualified as a result of slum clearance. This had not gone unnoticed. In 1957 an official told me: 'There is confusion in the public mind when they see the waiting-list increase. Coloured families may come to the top of the waiting-list faster and this gives rise to a lot of unthinking animosity. People are ready to accuse them of fiddling themselves into scheduled property with the aim of getting themselves rehoused ahead of the queue, but this device is not peculiar to coloured people and we try very hard to rehouse only the *bona fide* families, whatever their colour.' The accommodation made available to West Indians varied considerably, from requisitioned property to the older blocks. I did, however, come across one case of a family of model tenants who, after a few years in an old block where the flats were shabby and had no baths, were moved to newer and far more attractive accommodation. By 1961 there was said to have been little change in the number of West Indian families housed by the LCC.

ago, one of the leaders said that to handle the problem would be dynamite. Why? Because, had the Council taken it in hand, they would have been forced to apply the Public Health Act in taking action on overcrowding in many of the homes of coloured people. That in effect would have meant that any coloured person evicted would have gained priority on the housing-list' (*South London Press,* 10 April 1956).[1]

Some months later the Labour M.P. for Brixton, Colonel Marcus Lipton, made a more cautious statement on the same lines:

'. . . Emigrants from the West Indies stand no chance of being rehoused by local authorities. . . . Emigrants have to make their own arrangements, frequently buying dilapidated property with only a few years to run on the lease. There is much overcrowding which local authorities have to overlook because they have no alternative accommodation to offer if an overcrowding notice were to be served' (*Racial Unity Bulletin,* July 1956).

In the two years that followed, normal rehousing, as we have seen, virtually ceased. In pursuance of their general quietist policy, local dignitaries seem to have avoided making any further published statements on the problem of West Indian overcrowding or rehousing. In October 1958, however, Alderman Marock wrote an article in the *London News* (official organ of the London Labour Party) in which he commented favourably on the 'clean, sober, and industrious coloured people in Brixton'. This article included the following passage:

'We do not find them very much different in behaviour from the rest of the community. Because of economic conditions they crowd together, and when you find twenty or so in one house there is an outcry. Yet I will show anyone who cares to come here white people living in exactly the same conditions; none of them are on the housing-list because they do not want to move. They are content to be overcrowded because they have a low rent to pay. Less than 100 yards from where I live in Wiltshire Road, Brixton, there is a house where forty-two white people live – most of them Irish. The local council is not in a position to rehouse all or even a few of these people and if they take action under the Public Health Acts they would have a moral obligation, if not a legal one, to rehouse the people they displace.'

---

[1] The Labour-controlled council was attacked by the Conservative Party in the 1961 LCC elections for alleged failure to enforce existing legislation to prevent overcrowding in connection with 'the flood of immigrants into this part of London in recent years' (from election leaflet *Build a Brighter Brixton*).

In general, it would appear that the Lambeth and other South London local authorities have for years turned a Nelsonian eye upon mild overcrowding[1] in certain areas predominantly inhabited by coloured people.[2] They step in only in particularly blatant and protracted cases of 'gross overcrowding'. This is a non-statutory term, but it might be held to apply to cases of 'indecent occupancy', where members of the family of both sexes over the age of 10, or persons of different sexes who are not related to each other, must sleep together.[3] Most West Indians live one family to a room, and the majority of their household units probably contravene the statutory regulations about overcrowding to a greater or lesser degree. On the other hand, most children are still very young and there are probably relatively few cases of 'gross overcrowding' among them as yet.

It is not definitely known to what extent the Brixton coloured migrants are overcrowded compared with the local population. The only available Lambeth figures (for 1957) showed an average of 9·2 persons (7·7 adults and 1·5 children) of all colours per house in Geneva Road; the permitted number for each house if let as a single unit was 13·5. In Somerleyton Road, which was even more heavily settled by West Indians, and where the permitted number per house if let as a single unit was 16, there was at the same period an average of 12·2 persons of all colours (9·9 adults and 2·3 children). A similar check on 13 houses inhabited by West Indians in the Crown Road

[1] The Housing Act of 1936 aims first at securing proper separation of the sexes, second at restricting the number of 'units' occupying a dwelling-house. Under the first requirement: 'A dwelling-house shall be deemed to be overcrowded if any two persons, being 10 years old or more, of opposite sexes, and not living together as husband and wife, are obliged to sleep in the same room.' So far as the second requirement is concerned, the Act allows 2 units to 1 room, 3 units to 2 rooms, 5 units to 3 rooms, 7½ units to 4 rooms, and 10 units to 5 rooms; 2 units are allowed for every room over that total. Bathrooms and kitchens are excluded and certain minimum sizes are laid down for the rooms. Any individual over 10 years of age counts as one unit; under that, he or she counts as half a unit; while babies under 1 year of age are not counted at all.

[2] The blind eye of officialdom has not been turned only towards coloured migrants. For instance, there was until quite recently a fire-trap caravan site not half a mile from Lambeth Town Hall whose existence was for long not officially recognized by any local authority; on it lived some thirty families in mouldering and dangerous caravans, serviced by a single filthy toilet and one cold-water tap.

[3] For instance, Battersea welfare and sanitary officials complained of overcrowded conditions in a case which came before the South-Western Rent Tribunal in June 1956. In this case two female cousins and their four children, including two older boys, slept together in one room. The chairman of the Rent Tribunal told the cousins: 'Whether on moral or sanitary grounds I don't know, but in this country we just don't live like that. We would put women and children in one room and the boys in the other' (*South London Press,* 27 June 1956).

177

neighbourhood of Camberwell at the end of 1957 showed a total of 79 persons (49 men and 30 women) to 79 rooms.[1]

These official counts seem rather low, probably because they were taken at times when most of the residents were out at work or shopping. The figures therefore depended to a considerable extent on hearsay and on the statements of landlords or tenants who would be apprehensive about giving information with regard to any overcrowding that might exist. During my field work over the same period I visited a large number of these houses after informants had returned from work, and I formed the impression that the average West Indian-tenanted house in Somerleyton Road contained a minimum of 20 residents.[2]

Since the migrants were British subjects, they could settle and work where they pleased. Thus no special provisions were made for them on a national basis, as had been done earlier for the members of the Polish Resettlement Corps and the European Volunteer Workers. It is difficult to see how any such provisions could be made at a national level for British immigrants, since they would involve certain controls which might well be interpreted by the immigrants as discriminatory. Only in one case is there any record of official action designed to ease the general British housing situation, and this was taken not by the British government but by the colonial government involved. This was the Cyprus government, which at this period was issuing passports only to those intending migrants who could prove that they had a sponsor in Britain.

Not surprisingly, in view of local housing difficulties, no efforts were made at a local government level in Lambeth or elsewhere in South London to provide hostels or any other special accommodation for the West Indian migrants.[3] Nor were there any unofficial

---

[1] A survey made in 1956 by the Medical Officer of Health in West Bromwich, in a similar area of recent coloured settlement, yielded the following comparative figures (the immigrants at this time consisted of 505 West Indians, 248 Indians, 85 Pakistanis):

	Immigrants	Town as a whole
Persons per household	11·69	3·56
Persons per room	1·77	0·84
Percentage of persons living more than two to a room	50·22	4·66

[2] See below (pp. 182-4) for a more detailed description of the average house in this district.

[3] During the 1954–55 mayoralty of Councillor H. N. White, J.P., founder of the Racial Brotherhood Association, a delegation from the Lambeth Borough Council visited the Colonial Office. This delegation proposed that reception centres be set up for West Indians at the ports of disembarkation or at the main points where the transients congregated, to ease the burden on such unofficial 'reception centres' as Brixton. As reported, the Minister's reply reflected the widespread official egalitarianism, which was under later mayors to characterize the policy of Lambeth

non-profit-making housing associations in the area[1] at this time or up to the end of 1960. The only evidence of voluntary endeavour was the setting up of two specialized hostels for women migrants, and the use of two West Indian-owned lodging-houses as reception hostels for the organized Barbadian immigrant groups. A number of local welfare workers who were consulted on this point felt indeed that any housing scheme initiated specifically for coloured migrants might well increase local ill-feeling and thereby defeat its own ends.

MIGRANT SOLUTIONS TO THE HOUSING PROBLEM

The West Indian migrants in Brixton were left, then, to find their own living space. This they did first of all by crowding into the few boarding- and lodging-houses that would accept coloured lodgers. Soon, however, the more energetic and resourceful began to buy up dilapidated short-lease houses, and then, as they became more knowledgeable and prosperous, longer leaseholds or even freehold houses. In a large number of cases, houses were bought with one or more white sitting tenants; the consequences of this will be discussed later.

The majority of coloured migrants, particularly in the earlier years of the Brixton settlement, seem to have been induced to purchase property because of the need to find accommodation for themselves and their relations or friends, rather than for any profit motive.[2] However, an increasing number have gone into the house-owning and furnished room-letting business because it promises excellent returns.[3] Whatever their initial motivation, house-owners and land-lords soon find it necessary or expedient to charge high rents in order to cover the considerable mortgage and other costs, and to see their capital back with interest in the short period in which the lease has yet to run, or in which they reckon that they will have accumu-

Borough Council itself, and which makes so many chary of introducing special legislation in this respect: 'He felt bound to come to the conclusion that there were serious objections to the setting up of centres which would provide facilities which did not exist for other British subjects who might come over to work in this country, which would be expensive to run, and might, it was thought, tend to hinder the absorption of coloured workers into the community, by identifying them as a class apart from the time they enter the country.'

[1] See Conservative Commonwealth Council's 'Report on West Indian Accommodation Problem in the U.K.' (18 March 1957) for an account of the activities of various housing associations in the provincial towns.

[2] A considerable number of West Indian landlords still find themselves before the Rent Tribunal because they have given notice to a tenant, allegedly on the ground that they require the room 'for a relative who is to arrive shortly'.

[3] In one case which I heard discussed by the Rent Tribunal in 1957, the total outgoings on an eight-roomed leasehold property which the owner bought for £1,000 were (apart from Schedule A and D taxes) under £140, while the gross annual income was about £1,000.

179

lated a sufficient nest-egg to return home. In these circumstances, they consider it reasonable to let off every available room or cubby-hole, and will sometimes even partition larger rooms without concern for ventilation or light.

Once a certain room-rent becomes established for a West Indian tenant, it becomes more or less customary and obligatory, and few landlords, coloured or white, would ask less. In the Brixton area the average rent for a small room was about 25*s*. to 30*s*. per week in the 1955–58 period, and 50*s*. was the usual charge for a large room. Usually this rental entitles the tenants to the joint use of the house's toilet and bathroom (if such a facility exists) and of a gas-cooker on the landing or in an improvised kitchen, and to a change of bed linen and possibly towels once a fortnight.

At that time these rents were high for the Brixton area as a whole, and were almost invariably slashed by up to 50 per cent if a West Indian tenant took his landlord to the Rent Tribunal. Tenants regard such rents as in the nature of a 'colour tax';[1] nevertheless, this 'tax' does assure them of freedom from rebuffs in seeking accommodation and of the opportunity of living among familiar and congenial people without undue outside interference. So far, therefore, the majority of West Indians have paid up, philosophically or angrily, without attempting to get the 'tax' abolished by mass appeals to the Rent Tribunal. Most are still deterred by a fear of getting involved in unfamiliar official procedures, of losing the room, and, in some cases, of the possibility of 'black-listing' by coloured landlords and even of a beating-up by strong-arm squads. A few West Indian middle-class informants suggested that tenants might also be deterred by a feeling of *esprit de corps,* an unwillingness to show up West Indian landlords in an unfavourable light and attract adverse publicity, but I found no evidence of such motivations among Brixton migrant tenants.

Unlike most local landlords, West Indian landlords rarely stipu-

---

[1] Up to 1960 there was some evidence that the 'colour tax' was shrinking, since local rents rose while those charged by coloured landlords remained static. But large numbers of West Indian newcomers began to enter Brixton later that year, and the increased demand for rooms enabled coloured landlords to put up their rents above the local average again.

Cf. Carey (1956, pp. 68–71). The 'colour tax' was rather cynically justified by a white chartered surveyor giving evidence for a coloured landlord at Lewisham Rent Tribunal in December 1956. He said that the same sort of thing happened in Ruislip and Newmarket, where Americans were charged more for accommodation. It was 'perfectly fair' for a landlord to charge more rent for accommodation from a coloured person than from a white person. 'It is a matter of supply and demand,' he added. There was a risk attached to letting to coloured people because it would lead to difficulties with other people living nearby. The speaker stressed that he was 'distinctly against the colour bar' but had to state the facts as he saw them. (*South London Press*, 14 February 1956.)

late the number of persons who should occupy each room, although they may put the rent up if the total rises beyond what they consider reasonable.[1] In Brixton, it was usual to find the smaller rooms occupied by a man and woman, or by a woman with one or two small children. Larger rooms usually held a minimum of two adults, and often one or more children. When relatives or friends arrived from the West Indies, it was generally accepted that they would be put up for a week or so, until they found work and a lodging.

During the years of my field work I heard many reports of 'coloured dormitories' in the area, containing six or eight beds or mattresses, for which single men were said to be charged one pound per head per week. In actual fact, out of the hundred or so houses which I visited during this period, I found only a few houses of the men's dormitory type. In none of these did any room contain more than three single beds. Local officials and welfare workers whose work takes them into many West Indian-tenanted houses were also of the impression that the overcrowding stories were greatly exaggerated, at least as far as Brixton was concerned. Additional corroboration on this point was supplied by a Lambeth housing supervisor, who wrote in January 1956:

'The general impression [among officials whose duty it is to investigate living conditions] seems to be that there is little serious overcrowding; men frequently sleep three in a room, but as there is a great deal of movement, it may be reasonably assumed that most families, reunited in this country and having regular employment, improve their conditions of living, so that it is usually the new arrivals whose physical environment is most unsatisfactory.'[2]

Nevertheless, there were a considerable number of bad cases. A social worker told me of one 'Box and Cox' arrangement in which the room and double bed were shared by a mother and baby who slept in it at night, and a male relative and his friend on night-shift who had the use of the bed during the day. This case came to light when the mother contracted pneumonia and was taken into hospital after sitting in a chair nursing the baby for two days. She also had notes of the following cases: a girl of 26 with a baby, sleeping in the same room and on the same bed as her brother, aged 30; another woman living in one room with her father; and a pregnant woman living with a young married couple. I came across several such cases myself. For several months one small room with one bed housed a West Indian father and adult son and the latter's Irish

---

[1] See Hyndman (1960, pp. 96-105) for comparative material on West Indian housing problems in London.

[2] Society of Housing Managers, *Quarterly Bulletin* (January 1956, pp. 4–6).

mistress. In another house I found the West Indian landlady living with her 6-year-old daughter and her married sister and brother-in-law in a medium-sized room.

Towards the end of my field work, however, there were certain signs of improvement in the migrants' housing situation. By the end of 1958, there were several hundred coloured-owned houses in Brixton and the total has undoubtedly increased since then. This means that several thousand rooms are available for coloured tenants. In consequence, a certain competition has arisen among the more established landlords in latter years for good and steady tenants.[1] This competition has brought about a corresponding improvement in the standards of cleanliness, decoration, and facilities in quite a number of houses, but has not yet resulted in lowered rents. On the other hand, there has been little or no tendency for rents to rise, even in houses where landlords have spent a lot of money on redecoration or improvements; while rooms that were particularly unattractive or expensive, or rooms in houses with a bad name, might actually stand empty for a week or more before finding a new tenant. One multiple landlord told me at the end of 1958: 'I thinking of selling up. It so much work and the tenants getting so particular now.'[2]

In spite of the gradual tendency for earlier arrivals to start improving their houses, it would still be true to say that the majority of houses owned by West Indians in Brixton conform to the following composite picture of an average West Indian-owned house in the Somerleyton–Geneva Road area. A few houses in these streets are of course well above this standard, while a number of others, particularly those run by male landlords for single male migrants, are considerably worse.[3]

> The houses in these roads are large, ugly, dilapidated, Victorian structures, semi-detached, with neglected and rubbish-strewn back gardens. There are a few gaps in the rows due to bombardment. The freehold was formerly held by the Ecclesiastical Commissioners but it was bought in October 1957 by Lambeth Borough Council. The leases have only a few years to run and are held by a large number of individuals, coloured and white; some hold

[1] It is not always so easy to find such tenants. In 1957 I interviewed a middle-class couple from Kingston. After showing me over every foot of their house and garden, on the improvement of which they had spent several hundred pounds, apart from furnishings, the wife said: 'We have a hard time trying to educate the tenants to keep things nice. They're not used to good conditions at home or in the other houses here.'

[2] For a recent reversal of this trend, see p 180, n.) above.

[3] See Appendix V for some more widely differing examples of West Indian-tenanted houses in the Brixton area. See also p. 295 for a note on the three main stages of migrant settlement.

more than one lease. The majority of white landlords do not live on the premises. The exteriors are for the most part dingy, unpainted, and crumbling. Front steps and windows are grimy and most windows are hung with sleazy, unlined rayon curtains that are drawn across day and night. Dustbins and junk stand in front of most houses. Many front doors have lost their knockers and bells, and their wooden or glass panels are broken or cracked.

Inside the front door of such houses one may expect to find a number of unclaimed letters, pools coupons, and circulars, and several large, new, gleaming prams. There is also a vague, all-pervading smell of ancient dirt, of inefficient and overworked plumbing, unaired rooms, cooking, paraffin stoves, sometimes of mice, and always of many people congregated together. The visible shared parts of the house are usually unswept and unscrubbed, with cracked lino ingrained with dirt, peeling wallpaper, and unshaded lights that do not always function. In the shared kitchen or on the landings there is an assortment of unwashed utensils and crockery, and one or more old and grease-splashed stoves. In the communal bathroom and lavatory there is usually similar evidence that tenants feel that their cleaning is the landlord's responsibility. In such houses, too, the plumbing is often out of order for considerable periods, the hot-water geyser does not work, and the lavatory door bolt may have been torn away.

By contrast, the individual rooms are usually clean. In a number of cases tenants have repapered the walls and put down new linoleum at their own expense. West Indian women usually keep their own rooms spotless and are particular about clean bed-linen and hygienic handling of their own crocks and cooking utensils. Since their arrival in large numbers, living standards have risen considerably among the migrants in Brixton. The worst-kept rooms are usually those in which live single men, or men with transient white girls. In such houses the individual rooms tend to be almost as dirty and untended as the shared parts, and tenants add little of their own, whether linoleum, wallpaper, pictures, or radiograms. The house is regarded merely as a place in which to sleep. In one such dormitory-house, a middle-aged Jamaican with a bad leg told me indignantly: 'The Welfare Officer come round and say I must go to work and I say to him: "You think if I not truly in pain and unable to walk I wish to stay all week in this cold sad house and not earn money to help my wife and children I leave behind in Kingston?" '

Standard equipment for individual rooms is one or more large beds, a big table and some upright chairs, a wardrobe and chest of drawers, and the cheap curtains mentioned earlier. Most tenants add their own portable paraffin stoves, ornate bedspreads, family photographs, lampshades, and, at a later stage, radiograms and sewing-machines. In only a few cases did I come across a television set. West Indians for the most part seem able to provide their own entertainment.[1]

This type of house differs from those in more stable areas in that tenants do not usually stay long enough to know their neighbours or even their names. If one is looking for a particular person, one must bang several times at the front door until somebody gets tired of the noise and answers, and then make inquiries from room to room. Such a house is usually more overcrowded than those in other districts. In general, however, it was very difficult to ascertain the precise number of regular tenants of such a house, as opposed to those who might be visiting or those recent arrivals who were camping out with friends or relations and would move on again as soon as they found their own accommodation. Only one type of tenant is constant in these houses, and that not by choice. This is the white statutory tenant, usually elderly, who remains on a single floor in many such houses, the flotsam and jetsam of an earlier era.

This area is the reception centre for new arrivals, and for the unsuccessful, the single, the adventurous, the 'wide boys', and the white girls who live with them. The usual lively hum and warmth of a West Indian-tenanted house, with its open doors, its friendly room-to-room visiting, its blare of radios and gramophones, its hymn-singing and group prayers on Sundays, its smells of codfish, pork, peppers, and cabbage frying in coconut oil, combined with the stuffy heat of paraffin stoves in each hermetically sealed room, may in such houses be augmented or replaced by loud and often quarrelsome voices from rooms in which gambling, ganja-smoking, and drinking are going on; in latter years the organized turbulence of the basement club has also played its part.

The Somerleyton–Geneva Road area calls to mind Zorbaugh's description of parts of Chicago's near North Side in the nineteen-twenties: 'an area of transition, an anonymous rooming-house area without community traditions or much informal social control, a world where behaviour is impulsive rather than social . . . a world of atomized individuals, or spiritual nomads' (Zorbaugh, 1929, p. 86).

---

[1] By 1961 this was no longer true. A forest of H-aerials had sprouted at roof level in these two streets and a 21-inch television set had become a widespread status-symbol among the migrants, and an indicator of the process of culture contact. Sometimes, however, the television set and the radiogram would be playing together, with a rather distracting effect.

THE ROLE OF THE RENT TRIBUNALS

Although only a minority of unusually energetic or vengeful West Indian tenants go to the trouble of lodging a complaint against their landlord before the Rent Tribunal, cases involving West Indians have since 1956 formed an increasing proportion of all South London Rent Tribunal cases. This growing use of an agency of the receiving society to remedy hardships largely incurred with the migrant group may be regarded as indicating the early stages of migrant accommodation in the housing sphere.[1]

During 1956–57 I attended a number of hearings and collected all locally published reports of proceedings involving coloured tenants or landlords. Although these cases obviously reflected the least tolerable living conditions and the most bitter landlord-tenant relations, they corroborated and enlarged my own impressions of the way in which a very large number of West Indian migrants were living in Brixton and the neighbouring districts at that time.

Eleven such Rent Tribunal cases were reported in the *South London Press* in the year 1956, and in 1957 the figure rose to two dozen. All the tenants and all but two of the landlords involved were coloured, most of them being West Indian. The main charges against landlords were excessive rents, giving no rent books, disregarding previous Rent Tribunal findings, or failing to keep the house clean and in good repair. In some cases tenants had clearly got together and were charging their landlords collectively.

In only one case was the tenant occupying more than one room. Room-rents ranged from £3 down to £1 10s.; most were in the neighbourhood of £2 10s. In almost all cases the rent was reduced by the Tribunal to a figure varying between £1 15s. and £1. In about one-quarter of the cases the Tribunals gave maximum security of tenure (three months), thereby ensuring that the tenant might return after that period and apply for a further extension.

Usually the Rent Tribunal took a strong stand on the tenant's side against the landlord.[2] In a number of cases, however, its protec-

---

[1] A decrease in Rent Tribunal cases in years to come could also be interpreted as an index of increased accommodation both within the immigrant group and between migrants and the host society. Cf. the comment by a retiring Rent Tribunal chairman on Polish landlords, of whom there have been a considerable number in Brixton since the war: 'We used to get a tremendous number of Poles at this tribunal but now they seem to have vanished. As landlords they are very clean and efficient and run their houses well. They are very quiet, sober people and always have perfect records.' (*South London Press*, 20 December 1957.)

[2] In one case, however, an apparently a-typical coloured landlord in Tooting was highly praised by the Wimbledon Rent Tribunal. 'People make remarks about the living standards of people coming from the Commonwealth, but Mr. W. has a splendid little house,' commented the chairman. He continued: 'Although it is

185

tion was more formal than real. Some West Indians had moved out before a hearing and others moved afterwards. Some claimed that the landlord made life impossible for them, either by brute force[1] or by more subtle forms of persecution. Others (five reported cases) alleged that West Indian landlords were sufficiently in touch and in sympathy with each other to ensure that different tenants were 'black-listed'. One West Indian landlord accused certain tenants of being vindictive and trouble-makers. Here are some reports of the tenants' views:

'We find it difficult to get accommodation except in houses owned by West Indians. But we are black-listed. All the coloured landlords have this system of charging £2 10s. to £3 a week for one room, and if they know you will take them to the Tribunal they will not take you in.' (Mr. W., quoted in the *South London Press* of 7 September 1956.)

'I swear by Almighty God that I have made no representation to Battersea Council, and that I am quite satisfied with my rent.' (An oath alleged to have been drawn up by a coloured landlord, Mr. J.B.L., for his tenants to swear to – cited at Battersea Rent Tribunal and reported in the *South London Press* of 2 March 1957.)

'I want to bring to the notice of the Tribunal and other authorities the present condition of overcharging and overcrowding in these houses. My people are afraid to come to the Tribunals, because if they do, they will find it impossible to find another place. The landlord will pass the word around to his friends not to let

---

one of the smallest complete houses I have ever visited, it was a pleasure to go there. A real bijou house with lots of rooms, it was very clean and well decorated.' Mr. W. complained that the tenant was always 'jazzing and drinking in the evenings'. 'It is too small a house for jazzing and dancing,' commented the chairman, adding that the rent was very fair and the Tribunal could not reduce it. (*South London Press*, 3 September 1957.)

[1] A case of this type came up before the South-Western court in early September 1957, when a landlord, his son, and another man were committed for trial at the Old Bailey accused of causing grievous bodily harm. According to the reports in the *South London Advertiser* and *South London Press* of 6 and 7 September: 'M. said that seven weeks ago he was lodging in one of G.H.'s houses, when H. and other men burst into the bedroom and told him to get out because he owed three weeks' rent. Although he only owed one week's rent he left, and they threw his belongings out after him. He was walking home from work when the accused and other men got out of a car and attacked him. He was hit many blows on the head and face.' To the detective-inspector who served the warrant on him, H. was reported to have said: 'It is all because of that fellow M. We will drive him out of the country'; and the son to have said: 'This man should not have gone to the police. He deserved what he got. This won't be the last.'

you in if you go to a Tribunal.' (Mr. O.P., asking for a cut in his rent at Kennington Lane, after having left there – reported in the *South London Press* of 11 January 1957. Similar cases were reported in the *Clapham Observer* of 8 February 1957, and the *South London Press* of 31 August 1956, 23 August 1957, and 6 September 1957.)

A Rent Tribunal official who was questioned on this point said that the idea of a more or less formal landlords' association which could black-list trouble-making tenants was probably exaggerated, but that undoubtedly individual landlords met together informally and could pass the word around. My own observations confirmed that a grape-vine existed, not only between landlords in relation to the most difficult tenants, but among tenants with regard to the most difficult landlords.

In general, the Rent Tribunal evidence confirmed first-hand observations made over the period of study. Rent books are rarely, if ever, given by West Indian landlords to West Indian tenants, and notice is often given abruptly and incorrectly. Rents are customarily high, services are minimal, and landlords' profits considerable. Rent Tribunal findings are frequently ignored, and ignorance with regard to rates, sanitary and overcrowding provisions, and statutory tenancies is still widespread.

In spite of their generally beneficent influence, the Rent Tribunals' proceedings are sometimes marked by misunderstandings and even clashes between West Indians and others, including members of the Tribunal. These may leave the West Indians with a feeling of resentment, the non-West Indians with a feeling of impatience and alienation. Such misunderstandings are usually caused by sheer inability to communicate – resulting from considerable differences of vocabulary and accent. They also arise out of ignorance on either side of the other group's customs and living standards, while the West Indians, most of whom are simple people, are often inhibited and apprehensive in the presence of white authorities whose position and function they do not fully understand.

I was present on several occasions when members of a Tribunal, after making considerable efforts to achieve understanding, spoke impatiently and sharply to West Indian witnesses, who may have appeared to be adopting an attitude of 'dumb insolence' or 'evasiveness'. To an observer more familiar with West Indians, however, it appeared that the witnesses in question were benumbed with apprehension and understood little or nothing of what was being said to them in legalistic language and with an alien accent. On one occasion, a local reporter who had listened to a case commented:

'They wouldn't dare talk that way with most local people. I'd have walked out if they tried it on me.'[1]

Some Rent Tribunal members are inclined to pontificate on the wretched lot of tenants and the iniquities of landlords. They do not restrict such observations to West Indians, but remarks about West Indians tend to be more widely reported in the press. While the reader's sympathy is usually aroused for the tenant, the main impression left is often a derogatory one about the group's low morals and living standards and its members' lack of charity towards one another. Characteristic examples of such reported observations are:

'It grieves me to see what the people of your colour have to put up with in this district in accommodation, and when one of their own colour is involved it grieves me even more.' The report continued: 'One of the tenants admitted she had an illegitimate 10-week-old baby boy, and another tenant said he was living with a woman. . . . He denied the [landlord's] charge that another woman was also living with him in the same room' (*South London Press*, 25 September 1956).

'A West Indian tenant slept on a chair outside his room for five nights after his landlord had locked him out, he told Battersea Rent Tribunal. . . . Said the Rent Tribunal chairman: "I didn't think West Indians treated each other like this." Told . . . that all the other tenants had been paying excess rents, he added that the papers should be sent to Battersea Council. "A thoroughly bad case," he remarked' (*South London Advertiser*, 26 September 1957).

'A case where excessive rent was being charged for rooms for which "one could not imagine more than a token rent being paid" was described by the chairman of Battersea Rent Tribunal as: "a sordid, squalid, depressing case, ranking with the worst in the ten-year history of Rent Tribunals" ' (*South London Press*, 17 February 1956).

[Headline 'One of the Worst Homes in Battersea'.] 'This is a slum in the technical, non-abusive sense of the word . . . it is one of the worst dwellings in the Borough of Battersea. We take a very serious view of this case; it is very bad. The conditions really are

---

[1] On the other hand, the Tribunal's patience is at times tried by behaviour such as that reported in the *South London Press* (24 April 1959). A West Indian landlord accused the Tribunal of taking account of colour when making decisions and somewhat rashly interrupted the formidable lady chairman with the words: 'Just a minute, Sis . . .'

frightful, and I am afraid that the tenant's parts are not kept clean. The tenant, his expectant wife, and his two sub-tenants live in two damp rooms. A nice place for a baby to arrive in the next month. The landlord . . . is one of those happy non-resident land-lords. He is not living where there is no light in the lavatories. The Borough Council has been consulted, and they say there is bulging and broken plaster, defective flooring, and a leaking roof. That is the kind of place you coloured people come from the sunny West Indies to live in' (*South London Press*, 1 February 1958).

On the whole, however, the Rent Tribunals in South London have helped to ease the lot of West Indian tenants, albeit indirectly. Few tenants, West Indian or otherwise, remain for longer than they need in the house of a landlord whom they have taken to the Tribunal, even if they have been given maximum security of tenure. Yet the obligation to appear before the Tribunal and give detailed informa-tion about the condition and management of a house does help to impress some landlords with the advisability of conforming to local living standards and patterns, although they may still ignore the rent fixed by the Tribunal when taking new tenants.

10

Economic and social aspects of housing

THE MERE presence of so many highly visible newcomers in an area suffering from an acute and chronic housing shortage is likely to set up tensions and evoke local resentment. But competition for living space is not the only source of friction between newcomers and natives. There are economic and social aspects to the housing question which can give rise to even more misunderstanding and conflict.

In Brixton, for instance, there is a widespread belief that the arrival of coloured residents in a street or neighbourhood causes property values to depreciate. 'Our street is getting "hot" – the blacks are beginning to move in and we'll have to sell and move while the going's good,' a woman was overheard to say in Marks & Spencer's in Brixton Road in the summer of 1957, and this sort of remark was made fairly frequently to me by other local householders.

In 1956 there were several appeals by local ratepayers against the rateable value of their property, on the ground that property values were being lowered by the 'influx of Jamaicans'.[1] These appeals came from more or less middle-class areas. In each case other reasons for appeal were given (poor drains, erection of a large LCC housing estate, increased traffic). One appellant made a statement fairly characteristic of local attitudes: 'Of course we don't want a colour bar, but there is an objection to too many Jamaicans in our road. We cannot help Jamaicans coming into the country and they must have homes – but they do lower the tone of the road.'

The chairman of one Valuation Panel suggested that the objection was in fact based on class distinctions and not on colour: 'If the Aga Khan came to live in Herne Hill Road the property would go up in value.' In each case, however, the Valuation Panel admitted

---

[1] *South London Press*, 26 October and 6 November 1956.

190

the force of the various grounds adduced, and reduced the rateable value by a few pounds.[1]

Sociologists generally point out that the public is wrong to associate coloured migration to a district with the lowering of property values, and that in fact coloured immigrants move only into areas that are already deteriorating. This is, of course, perfectly true of the main areas of lower-class West Indian settlement in Brixton and the surrounding districts, but its applicability is less clear in the peripheral middle-class areas.

South Londoners tend to associate colour with low social status and undesirable cultural traits,[2] and the arrival of even one coloured family in a middle-class street is therefore likely to evoke feelings of social and economic insecurity among its white inhabitants.[3] The outcome depends mainly on the behaviour of the coloured new-comers and the extent to which they are followed by others.

In some cases, the coloured family has a class affiliation or aspirations similar to those of its new neighbours, adapts itself outwardly at least to local *mores,* and is ultimately accepted by its neighbours. An elderly woman civil servant who has lived for forty years in Brixton gave me an instance of this process:

'There are two coloured families living in our street now. One is a professional man with a Scandinavian wife. After a few weeks of uncertainty and apprehension, people have almost ceased to notice his colour. But the other family! . . . They shocked the neighbours for months after they moved in. The house was dirty, with uncleaned windows, unscoured steps, and over-filled dustbins in front, and the man liked to sit with his feet out of the window. People preferred to pass this house on the far side of the street. Recently, however, the house has been spruced up. The windows are clean and there are lace curtains at them. Altogether you cannot tell the difference – so maybe gradually they'll learn our ways and fit in.'

[1] This was in contrast to the action of the Birmingham authorities who, when faced with an appeal for a reduced rating assessment on the ground of coloured movement into the neighbourhood, announced that such appeals were unlikely to succeed (*Birmingham Mail*, 28 and 30 November 1956).

[2] See pp. 197-8 and 230-5 below for a more detailed discussion of such preconceptions about colour and class.

[3] H. J. Dyos (1952) quotes a nineteenth-century writer's picture of an apprehensive middle-class suburbanite in South London faced not with the arrival of coloured strangers as neighbours but with the expansion of that other nation, the poor tenement-dwellers. 'He gazes darkly from his pleasant hill villa upon the huge and smoky area of tenements which stretches at his feet. . . . Every hour he anticipates the boiling over of the cauldron. He would never be surprised to find the crowd behind the red flag surging up his little pleasant pathways, tearing down the railings, trampling the little garden; the "letting in of the jungle" upon the patch of fertile ground which has been redeemed from the wilderness' (p. 393).

Coloured middle-class or artisan families are quite as status-conscious as their English neighbours. They move into such 'select' streets with the intention of escaping and dissociating themselves from the 'ghetto' areas. Such families deprecate large-scale coloured settlement in 'their street', sharing the fears of their white neighbours that both the social tone and the economic value of their property will go down. Therefore the presence of one or two such families in a street does not necessarily precipitate a decline in property values.

A local columnist corroborated this when he wrote:

'It is known that so long as the coloured folk keep to spots like Somerleyton Road, there is no trouble. It is when they reach the middle-class suburbs that there is talk of lowering the tone of the road. That is also economic, not social, friction, I think. People who are buying their own house are very sensitive to anything that lowers the value. A "common" family is equally detested. As it happens some coloured folk have arrived in my own suburban road. There has been no trouble, so far. But there would be, of course, if it was found to lower the value of the property. A neighbour who has met one of the coloured men says he is a "perfect gentlemen". The others also seem to me to be very civilized – which is more than I can say for some of the white neighbours, unfortunately' (*South London Press*, 13 April 1956).

Most West Indian migrants in South London do not belong to this status-conscious middle class, and they are not at present greatly concerned with the long-term social and economic aspects of private home-ownership. For the majority of migrants a house in London is still not a home. It simply represents accommodation for several years, and the opportunity of getting a quick return on one's money by sub-letting rooms to a large number of compatriots. But those who have accumulated sufficient capital from rents or from other sources and those who pool their resources may try to buy houses in better-class areas, where the property is less dilapidated and is held freehold or on a long lease. Through their indifference to, or ignorance of, the intangible social values in such areas, they may then cause a general exodus from the street or district by local residents and a consequent decline in property values.[1]

In the majority of South London areas in which the West Indian migrants have settled *en masse*, these considerations do not apply. In these areas property had already become a liability for most landlords as a result of such factors as the following: the age and

[1] See *South London Press* (26 July 1957) for a petition sent by owner-occupiers in a Clapham street to their M.P., asking for his help in averting such a process.

size of the premises; war damage and neglect; the increasing disparity between low controlled rents and the high post-war costs of repairs; and the social deterioration of the property as a result of residential changes. The owners of short leases also faced the prospect of having to meet large dilapidation claims from the ground landlords when the leases expired.

By the early 1950s property of this kind had become almost unsaleable as an investment or a home, for few local people would take on the statutory tenants even for the sake of a free flat. Even the statutory tenants themselves usually refused to buy such houses when they were offered to them at a rock-bottom price. Some South London landlords, in fact, preferred to disappear for good, thereby avoiding the payment of rates, repairs, and other outgoings, which, after the damage and enforced neglect of the war years, often exceeded the rents.

The West Indian newcomers were attracted to these houses because of their size and apparent cheapness. In the early 1950s West Indian house-hunters in Brixton were often naïve and uninformed. Many of them did not understand the distinction between freehold and leasehold, nor realize that the local authorities could order certain expenditure on repairs and maintenance, and that a heavy schedule of dilapidations might be presented at the end of the lease by the ground landlord of such neglected property. At the outset, moreover, the meaning of a statutory tenancy was not widely understood, and a number of West Indian buyers failed to protect their interests by using the services of a solicitor or surveyor.[1]

'COLOUR PREMIUMS'

The growing demand from West Indians for this type of property caused shrewd leaseholders and agents to demand higher prices than they could otherwise have hoped to obtain. No building society would grant a mortgage on short-lease property, whoever the prospective purchaser might be (see below, p. 196), so that local people were often puzzled to know how these poorly paid migrants financed their house purchases. The initial deposit was low, and the vendor would often grant a short-term, high-interest mortgage, to which the West Indian buyer, unlike a local purchaser, would agree in the certainty that he could meet repayments by filling the house with

---

[1] It is claimed that a few unscrupulous agents took advantage of this naïveté and ignorance to unload a number of otherwise unsaleable properties. On more than one occasion, West Indians who bought houses to obtain accommodation for themselves actually became the owners of premises fully occupied by statutory tenants.

his compatriots and charging high rents. In other cases, it seems that more prosperous West Indians gave mortgages to their compatriots on similar terms.[1]

The existence of this sort of 'colour tax' or rather 'colour premium' in house purchase as well as in rents is widely recognized by West Indians in Brixton. On two occasions I was myself asked to act as nominal buyer: 'If they think they are selling to a white person, they'll take £50 to £100 less.' Some white vendors are willing to forgo the higher price for the sake of their white sitting tenants, and instruct their agents to sell only to white purchasers. Their decision may weaken if it is found that no white person will purchase the property. Where there are no sitting tenants, most local vendors usually take the highest bid. A few are even known to have stipulated that the house must be sold to a coloured buyer, usually because they expect to obtain a higher price.[2]

As West Indians acquire more capital and knowledge of local property conditions, the 'colour premium' may cease to operate so flagrantly in house purchase. By 1959 there was already some evidence of this in the central area of migrant settlement in Brixton, where several short-lease houses were on the market for months without finding a buyer. One of these properties even had a vacant flat, but its price came down from £750 to £200 before one of the many coloured people who inspected it was induced to buy. Both of the two white sitting tenants in this particular house had refused to buy it, since they intended to move away from the area as soon as they found other accommodation.

The large-scale West Indian purchase of houses in the Brixton area has also evoked resentment and envy among a number of local people who may not otherwise be directly involved. Observations of the following nature were heard fairly often:

'Whenever a house becomes vacant in this street, the black people buy it and pack them in four or five to a room. Where they get the money from I don't know. They prey off their own people

---

[1] The *South London Press* of 1 April 1960 reported on the activities of a British Guianian resident in Battersea who specialized in buying up poorer property, repairing it, and selling it to purchasers, many of them West Indians, for whom, through a banking company managed by himself, he would arrange a mortgage in cases where a building society would not lend enough. At any one time this individual owned up to 100 houses, according to his own statement.

[2] In one rather special case, vouched for by a local government official, the motive behind such a stipulation was not economic. Two old ladies stated that they had asked an agent to sell their house to a coloured purchaser because the white sitting tenant had made their own lives a misery for decades and they hoped that he would now be repaid manifold! The assumption behind this and similar reported cases (e.g. *The People*, 19 March 1961) is far from being complimentary to the West Indian migrants.

and make a lot more than a white landlord could, and the local authorities let them get away with worse conditions.' (An elderly working-class widow.)

'We have a couple of those coloured landlords on this building site. They come to work in their flashy new Zephyrs but they only take the job to fool the income-tax inspectors.' (A building contractor.)

'They are like anyone else – good and bad as in all races. I have only one charge against them. I am sure they are getting away without paying income tax on those rents, and that's unfair.' (An estate agent.)

In general, the economic aspect of the housing question has operated against the acceptance of the West Indian migrants by local people. Not without some justification, owner-occupiers in middle-class streets and statutory tenants are particularly apprehensive and potentially hostile to the movement of West Indians into the neighbourhood. Among the migrants themselves the purchase of houses may ease their immediate anxieties about living space, but the reactions of local people and the 'colour premium' are naturally resented.[1]

THE ESTATE AGENTS' VIEWPOINT

Like the local tradesmen and other providers of professional services, the estate agents have a rather special attitude towards the West Indians who have moved into the area. Expediency rather than apprehension is the keynote, and the agents I interviewed, all of whom, incidentally, lived in middle-class suburbs outside the area, were able to give a detailed and objective picture of the gradual adaptation of the migrants in the housing sphere. The notes of one of these interviews are perhaps worth giving in full:

'We sell more houses in this area than any other agent. The Jamaicans aren't a large percentage of our clients yet, but are increasing all the time. Their first requirement was somewhere to

[1] As a West Indian correspondent wrote to *South London Press* (5 July 1957): 'Their [i.e. the West Indians'] right to buy houses is the inalienable privilege conferred by prudence. It is perplexing to contemplate that the same people who object to the West Indians renting rooms are also against West Indians buying homes to make themselves prosperous. English people own some of the best houses in Jamaica. In the majority of cases it is the English who force the Jamaicans to buy houses, and there should be no envy against Jamaicans who pay two or three times the normal prices of the houses they buy and are forced to rob their tenants in order to recover their investments.'

live – not profit-making. They had to pay heavily for it, and to let rooms. This was not only to make money but to help their relations and compatriots. As the English house-owners became aware of the possibilities, house prices went up. At this stage the profit motive got much stronger among the West Indians. When they started buying they could get mortgages on a 20-year repayment basis. Now money's tighter and only the vendors will lend on such property. They want quick repayment of their capital. The Jamaican view is a short-term view, so this doesn't worry them unduly.

They don't mind leaseholds, though I wonder whether they fully appreciate the significance of the dilapidation claim that will be made at the end. Now they are getting more money they prefer freeholds, which are easier to resell. Few have resold as yet. They're mainly interested in the number of rooms, though a few are buying small houses now. They don't like Geneva and Somerleyton Roads, and some even refuse to buy in the Brixton area. I try to dissuade the few who want to band together to buy a house. Sometimes a man and woman buy jointly. They can save faster than the locals, and club together for this. On the whole I prefer to deal with coloured clients. They don't play you about and are prompt and much better payers. A few buy several houses. There are a few real exploiters and some of these are white.

After an initial spurt, property values do decrease, for the house can then only be resold to coloured people. I wonder if we shall ever get to the stage when we can sell a coloured house back into white ownership. I try to avoid selling a house with white tenants in it to a coloured purchaser. I don't feel they should live together in the same house. If we can't avoid it, I do something to find other accommodation for the white tenants. I don't know of any restrictive covenants in this area. Some white vendors won't sell to coloured people. It has happened that a vendor takes a lower price from a white buyer who promptly resells at a profit to a coloured purchaser. We hesitate to sell the first house in a nice area to a coloured buyer. Some ground landlords have tried to resist coloured infiltration but it's useless. As they are here, we're lucky they've had the guts to find their own solution. They're mainly in accommodation that most of our own people won't look at.

We won't manage mixed houses at all, but we manage a few Jamaican houses, just the business side, not the tenants. Jamaican tenants are good payers, but as white agents we would have trouble in the courts if we had to sue West Indians,'

The other two agents I visited gave a similar picture, but added one or two additional points. One agency, which was nearest to the central area of settlement, already had a 50 per cent coloured clientele ('Their money's as good as anyone else's, and Saturday mornings especially it's like a doctor's waiting-room here. Perhaps they think we are fairer to them than other agents.') This informant added:

'They prefer not to buy houses that have been in coloured ownership as they think that their compatriots let a house run down. But usually a coloured house is rebought by a coloured man in the end. Some come back to sell, saying they're going home. Most coloured clients are men, but there are a few women and some joint purchasers. They pay fairly good prices provided they get a high mortgage, and don't argue about the price like the Poles. Private vendors usually give them a mortgage. They are good payers. Their main interest is in the returns of the house, not capital appreciation. They are not choosy about property, nor after a home, like the Poles. The latter bought just after the war. They would snap up a house, then argue over the contract. They wanted homes, nice houses where they could get a mortgage. Now they've moved to better areas and we don't see much of them as clients. We have an occasional Cypriot or Maltese, but no Irish – they don't usually buy houses. We manage eight or ten houses with coloured tenants for white landlords. They're good payers as tenants. It's easier to get rooms now and they're more choosy about what they want. Some don't want Brixton, and will go farther afield to Clapham or Camberwell, but they're always interested in areas with convenient communications.'

The third agency had formerly handled rather more select and expensive property than the other two, and its West Indian clients appeared to have continued this tradition. While the other agencies spoke of coloured clients having a few hundred pounds to put down, this informant dealt with cash deposits ranging up to £1,500. He also knew of no restrictive covenants in the area but spoke of an attempt by one large ground landlord to prevent coloured infiltration by buying up the leases at a higher-than-market price. This had proved too expensive and the attempt had been dropped.

SOCIAL AND CULTURAL DIFFERENCES

Inherent in the economic fear of lowered property values is a factor that would continue to influence local behaviour towards West

197

Indians even were there no housing shortage. This factor is rooted in a combination of preconceived notions associating colour with alienness, low status, and 'uncultivated' behaviour, and an increasing awareness among local people of certain real social and cultural differences between themselves and the newcomers. These notions and these differences will be considerd in more detail in the chapters on social life and associations. They are also a very important factor in the housing sphere, in which competition for a scarce commodity is often exacerbated by enforced proximity and intimacy between uncongenial groups of people.

Brixtonian *mores* are on the whole those of the respectable upper-working class, or of the even more status-conscious lower-middle or white-collar class. There are many local people and transient residents who do not conform fully to these *mores,* but their voice is rarely heard at the Town Hall, in the local press, or at the local M.P.'s office, although their bad example may serve to reinforce the *mores.*

What, then, do these respectable residents expect from their street and their neighbours?[1] They expect a tolerable and at least superficial conformity to 'our ways', a conformity to certain standards of order, cleanliness, quietness, privacy, and propriety. Clean lace curtains are hung at clean windows, dustbins are kept tidy and out of sight, front steps are washed, front halls are like band-boxes, and house fronts are kept neat. Houses do not give the impression of being packed to the brim with temporary and noisy strangers of both sexes, and basements are not turned into drinking or gambling clubs.[2] Except for the children, people do not fraternize noisily and for long periods in the street or on doorsteps.[3] They 'keep themselves to themselves' and life is lived quietly within the house, often in front of the television set. Doors are kept shut, and wirelesses or radiograms are played discreetly. Overt violence, whether verbal or physical, may occur but is not approved, particularly in public. Family respectability is maintained, although not every gold wedding ring denotes an actual ceremony. Marriage is the norm for decent girls, and the unmarried expectant mother usually feels shame and is regarded as bringing shame on her family. Moral nonconformity

[1] See Gorer (1955, Chapter 4) for an analysis of English attitudes to and complaints about neighbours in general—lowering the neighbourhood by personal habits, noise, failure to control children and pets, gossip, were major complaints.

[2] The rapid increase of basement drinking and dancing clubs with a West Indian management and clientele in residential areas has provided a new source of friction since 1958. See p. 365 below for a more detailed account of these clubs.

[3] In the more congested lower-class streets of South London this 'sitting-out' habit was more prevalent in the past than it is today, and an attempt to revive it was made by the LCC on a new Southwark site by providing a roof-deck. (*South London Press,* 9 October 1959.)

is tolerated so long as it is discreet and causes no inconvenience to others.

No immigrant group has in the mass so signally failed to conform to these expectations and patterns as have the West Indians. The Cypriots, Maltese, and Italians are often held to infringe the criteria of neatness and quietness, but most are thought to live respectable family lives, or at least to keep themselves to themselves. This also applies to the Poles who, after a doubtful start, have earned respect as conformists and solid householders interested in conserving and even improving their property. Southern Irish migrants are often said to be 'as bad as the darkies'; but they are not so easily identifiable, and the criticisms are therefore not so sharply focused. In the case of the Southern Irish and the West Indians, of course, the differences and frictions are intensified by the fact that these are lower-class migrants moving into a highly status-conscious, upper-lower- or lower-middle-class local society.

CORRELATION BETWEEN CLOSER PROXIMITY AND INCREASED RESENTMENT

Local attitudes and reactions towards West Indian neighbours usually become more focused and more critical with increasing proximity. The most critical views are usually found among those who share the same house, the least critical among those who live at the other end of the street or a few streets away.[1] Fairly typical of these relatively uncritical reactions was the remark of a Clapham warehouseman in early 1957: 'The area round Brixton Hill is thick with them now. But they're not so bad. There are good and bad among them just like the rest of us.'

The only informants who were indiscriminately critical were found among those who had shared a house with West Indians and based all their judgements on this experience, or among middle-class people who did not live in any proximity to West Indians at all, and were therefore basing their views on hearsay and superficial observation.

The opinions I heard tended, on the whole, more towards the unfavourable than towards the favourable. The main emphasis was laid on differences in social and cultural patterns so noticeable as to

[1] The September 1958 Gallup Poll found that, of Londoners questioned as to their reactions if coloured people came to live next door, 11 per cent would definitely move, 16 per cent might do so, and 73 per cent would not move. In answer to the question: 'Would you move if coloured people came to live in great numbers in your district?' the percentage answers were respectively 28 per cent, 28 per cent, and 44 per cent. The 1961 Poll showed little or no difference in attitudes.

199

arouse aversion and even fear, and on the immigrants' general failure to conform to the neighbourhood standards of house-proudness, cleanliness and hygiene, and quiet and seemly behaviour. One woman informant, who worked in the Town Hall and lived in a middle-class street into which a few coloured families had recently moved, outlined the main categories of objectors and objections:

'There are three groups of objectors to the coloured people: first, the tenants in houses bought by coloured people; secondly, people in areas where there are a lot; thirdly, people in better-class areas into which they are beginning to infiltrate. The first group's main complaints are about dirty toilets, noise, and food smells. Sharing a house usually works only when the toilet isn't shared. A few West Indian landlords do deliberately try to frighten white tenants and run them out. Some come to us and say they are frightened of being murdered in their beds. The second and third groups, especially the latter, are house-proud and object to the tone of the area going down. Most coloured people don't wash their windows, and they put their dustbins in the front garden. Some of them carry knives too. Of course we only get the bad cases here. There must be many where there are no complaints, but most of them just don't live as we do.'

The variety of individual viewpoints about West Indian neighbours can perhaps best be illustrated by a series of direct quotations:

'Even the coloured people won't buy this house and certainly I wouldn't now – not in this street. We've been here thirty years, but now everyone who can is moving away, and so will we when we get something. Those local women who are left won't go down the street alone at night. My friends are frightened to visit me here unless I meet them and take them to the bus stop. It's the noise, and men and women coming and going at all hours of the night. I've had men scratching at the front windows trying to get in, so I daren't leave the window open at night.' (Middle-aged, lower-middle-class woman in basement flat in all-white house in Somerleyton/Geneva area. A local official described her as 'not particularly prejudiced, but goes along with the crowd and repeats what they are saying'.)

'Can't you do something about it? The black men next door do their business in the garden, in full view of my little girl. I can't always keep her in or away from the window.' (Middle-class young housewife in Atlantic Road district, speaking to a local government official.)

'We've got Jamaicans next door now. It's terrible. They are so noisy. They don't greet us, but one made passes at our Shirley. He was a great big tough. In the end I went for him with a broom. They put out their dustbins and milk bottles in front and block the way. There are dozens of them in there. Up the road, though, there are some other coloured people – Nigerians, I think – who are quite different. A real king and queen. They are doing nicely and you wouldn't know they were there.' (Cheerful, rather slatternly middle-aged woman in untidy requisitioned basement flat in Angell Town.)

'Don't be frightened. The dog won't go for anyone white. He only goes for blacks. We had to share a house with them and had a bad time.' (Middle-class woman, aged about 45, with bull-dog, in well-decorated ground-floor flat in Angell Town.)

'Of course their ways are very different from ours. It's so difficult to compare social class. They are usually very clean in their own rooms (which most people don't see), but don't clean the steps or public ways. They always keep their curtains drawn. They go in and out of each other's rooms without knocking and often visit regardless of who is there. I find the men less easy to get on with than the women. Their manners are sometimes arrogant and I can't get used to the way they keep their hats on indoors.' (Woman social welfare worker.)

'Those niggers just petrify me. First I used to have a flat in Somerleyton Road, and after they moved in they made life hell for me, knocking on the door at all hours; then they killed one of my cats by throwing lighted cigarettes at it. Then the Council moved me to —— Road but it was almost as bad there. Now I am here, but there are blacks across the road – in and out at all hours, shouting, racing their cars. I wish they would move me to a decent area.' (Old, rather difficult woman living alone in one half of small working-class house behind Geneva and Somerleyton Road.)

'It's a question of different standards and cultures. The philanthropists talk about racial brotherhood, but it is usually someone else who has to clasp the black brother to his breast in practice. The British working class has fought a bitter fight for years for better living standards and a public health service. Even in the poor years between the wars the working class kept high standards. They don't like people urinating in public and keeping their dustbins foul, and they have a feeling about white girls going with coloured men. There is a bitterness over the Southern Irish too.

201

They breed like rabbits and so get high on the housing list.'
(Active Labour Party member who was born and bred in the
district.)

Verbal criticisms and comments were seldom, if ever, as virulent
as those made by the minority who write letters to the local press.
Here is one example:

'We as a nation must be slightly insane or we would not tolerate
thousands of Negroes, many of them little more than animals,
dumping themselves in this country to enjoy the conditions we
have worked and fought for. White people might be more tolerant
of Negroes if they had not ample proof that they debase the life
of any white community they move into.' (Letter to the Editor,
South London Press, 5 July 1957.)

About the most favourable comment I heard was made by a
variety act performer whose caravan was temporarily camped on a
bomb-site off Somerleyton Road between shows. He had a young,
good-looking, intelligent wife, and a well-mannered, lively daughter,
aged ten. He said:

'We find the coloured people O.K. They mind their own business and are kind neighbours. They don't worry my wife or the
little girl either, but then we are show people, used to getting on
with all colours and races.'

Fairly common among local people were the attempts at objectivity, the expression of the Londoner's 'live-and-let-live' attitude:
'But after all, there are good and bad in all races'; 'It will be all right
once they get used to our ways'; 'I feel sorry for them really; after
all, they probably wouldn't choose to live packed together in such
conditions if they could get better accommodation in decent houses'.
'I took her a cup of tea when they moved in, just to be neighbourly.
I didn't know what to expect at first but she seems a nice quiet type
and house-proud. We sometimes have a little chat on the way to the
shops.'

In many local judgements about coloured fellow-residents and
neighbours there was, however, a tendency to generalize from particular unfavourable instances and to apply higher standards than would
be applied to the living patterns of local lower-class people. Relatively few critics of 'the way these darkies live' had in fact been
inside a West Indian's home. Their views were therefore frequently
based on superficial observation and neighbourhood gossip, on the
reports of social welfare workers whose work usually takes them
into the poorest and worst-kept houses, and on stories derived from
202

the unhappy experiences of white tenants who have acquired coloured landlords. Nevertheless, by 1960 a certain neighbourly rapprochement was noticeable. Local and migrant children appeared to play together without any reservations, at least up to the early 'teens, and to walk to and from school in mixed groups. White and coloured men were sometimes noted returning from work together, while an increasing number of West Indian and local women were observed gossiping together in a spontaneous, neighbourly way over their prams and shopping-baskets.

COLOURED LANDLORDS AND WHITE TENANTS – A SPECIAL CASE

Local criticism of West Indian fellow-residents is greatly intensified among the minority who share a house with them. This situation has long been admitted to be the one most likely to cause immediate ill-feeling and friction.[1]

In practice, apart from white wives, girl friends, and prostitutes, and a minority of white landlords or landladies, this minority consists of the statutory tenants who live in houses which have been bought by coloured landlords. The security of tenure and the low controlled rent provide a considerable motive for such tenants to stay on, particularly in the case of elderly pensioners, who may have put a great deal of money and work into decorations and improvements, or may quite simply be attached to their homes. But in Brixton it is rare to find furnished tenants, the young and enterprising, or settled families with unmarried children, particularly daugh-

[1] (a) 'There has been a noticeable increase in the type of case which is nominally a dispute between landlord and tenant, or a dispute between neighbours, but is actually a colour bar row. In several such highly untoward incidents, the centre has been consulted by persons of both African and European descent, and the outstanding feature of these law suits has been the high state of feeling engendered among the parties, their relatives, friends, and acquaintances on each side. This fierceness is not a problem that can by itself be dealt with effectually by legislation or by the legal aid service.' (Cambridge House Annual Report, 1954–55.)

(b) 'The coloured landlord and the English sitting tenant is the worst situation that we have to face at present.' (British Caribbean Welfare Service official, September 1957.) See also *South London Press* (5 April 1957) for a similar statement by the magistrate at London South-Western court.

(c) The 1957 Report of the Medical Officer of Health, Camberwell, stated that fourteen people applied to the Council for rehousing on medical grounds caused by friction between tenants, and 'in six instances inquiries revealed incompatibility with coloured landlords'. 'On the other hand,' the Report continued, 'it is a pleasure to record that many coloured and white families are living in the same houses quite harmoniously.'

(d) 'We are getting more and more complaints in this office of the behaviour of Jamaicans who purchase property and proceed to make life a misery for any white sitting tenants in the house.' (Political party official, late 1960.)

ters, remaining for long in a house with a coloured owner or fellow-tenant. As one informant from a nearby community centre told me:

'Local people still have noncomformist ideas about behaviour. They may do these things, but they still feel that drinking, gambling, adultery, and illegitimacy are wrong and a disgrace. The West Indian patterns seem alien and shocking to the locals. They think that the Negroes have more uncontrolled sexual appetites, and they've noticed their proneness to irregular unions so they don't want their daughters in the same house as black men. Only the old, infirm, and inefficient get left behind in houses into which black people have moved, and they are filled with apprehension and sheer fear. The elderly women often think they are likely to be raped or attacked. The worst cases occur when the statutory tenant has a flat on an upper floor. Those in a basement flat usually have a separate entrance and facilities so that contact is not so frequent.'

Old people tend to be less adaptable than others, particularly in their home life, and most of their distress and apprehension is probably due to nothing more than the close proximity of large numbers of strangers whose behaviour seems alien, unattractive, and intrusive. In a minority of cases there has been evidence of pressure and even deliberate intimidation by West Indian landlords, who saw no reason why these two or three rooms should not be furnished and let far more profitably to other West Indians.

Until the general decrease of such reporting in 1958, the press both local and national, devoted a great deal of space to such cases. A local case involving an elderly statutory tenant was heard before Judge Clothier at Lambeth County Court on 6 December 1954:

Miss M. said she had been a tenant in the house since 1914. F. bought the house last year. Whenever she entered, F. barred her way. When visitors called, he and his lodgers told them that she did not live there or that she was not in when she was. Coloured men came upstairs to her flat and onto her landing at night. F., who denied all the allegations, said there were four other coloured men and two white women living in the five rooms in the lower part of the house. He agreed he would like possession of Miss M.'s flat for his brother to live there.

Judge Clothier said: 'This is another of those cases in which a coloured man, having bought a house in which white people are tenants, seeks to evict the white people as soon as he gets his foot inside. C.F. came to this country in 1948 with £2 in his pocket, and in 1953 he had contracted to pay £1,700 for this house. He paid

204

£850 down. It must be heart-breaking for him to have a tenant paying 10*s.* a week for three rooms which he could let at 30*s.* a week each. He seems to think it is a grievance that this spinster, living alone on a separate floor, should have refused to let him have one room for a dark gentleman to live in. . . . I do not know what the remedy will be, but I hope there will be a remedy found quickly . . . one remedy would be to send back to Jamaica anyone found guilty of this practice, or to forbid black people buying a house containing white tenants.'

He granted Miss M.M. of Mayall Road, Herne Hill, an injunction against her landlord, C.F., ordering him to abstain from any interference with her rights as tenant of the top floor. He also ordered him 'to refrain from abusing her, or, indeed speaking to her on any occasion except when it is absolutely necessary to speak to her as her landlord. He must refrain from telling visitors that she is not in when she is in, and he and his tenants, sub-tenants and friends must keep off the stairs to her flat'. He awarded Miss M. £2 damages because offensive language had been used. . . . Ordering F. to pay the costs, he said to him: 'You have done your countrymen no good by conduct of this sort.'[1]

Although most reported cases were of this type, the West Indian landlord did not always emerge as the villain. In another case, from the same street, which came before the same judge some years later the outcome was quite different. A Jamaican landlord who had bought a house in Mayall Road in 1955 was seeking to evict his 60-year-old tenant, on the grounds that he deliberately damaged property and used obscene language. The landlord told the judge: 'I am tired of being mistreated by an Englishman because I am a nigger.' The tenant replied by complaining that he was constantly annoyed by the music of fifteen Jamaicans living in the house. There was a trumpet – described by the judge as 'a weapon' – an organ, a piano, and a radiogram, all in the rooms below. The judge called the two families quite incompatible, and in a lyrical passage commented:

'The landlord and his family come from Jamaica, a land of sunshine. They are filled with a desire to be joyful and play musical instruments. In this more sombre country their feeling of joyfulness has been somewhat stifled. It may be that, in time,

[1] *Daily Telegraph,* 7 December 1954. There was a rider to this case in parliament. The Attorney-General, Sir Reginald Manningham Buller, stated in a written reply that he did not propose to take any action to implement the recommendation regarding Jamaican landlords in this country. 'It would be deplorable if it were supposed that the application of the law in this country depends on the colour of a person's skin' (*Daily Telegraph,* 14 December 1954).

Jamaicans in this country will become as depressed as whites, and there will be no more blowing of trumpets.'

Judge Clothier then ordered the tenant to leave the house within three months, saying: 'If only half of the allegations against him are proved, I should think there can be no doubt he was a nuisance.'[1]

Over the years 1955–58 I talked to many local people who had a West Indian landlord and also to officials who had to deal with the friction that so often arose in such cases. Only twice did I meet white families who got along well with their West Indian fellow-tenants and landlords. Neither of them was local: one family was from Southern Ireland and the other had recently moved over from North Kensington. The following statements taken from my interview notes give a fair picture of the prevailing attitudes at the time:

'I am one of the few white men left in the street. The black people began to move in three to four years ago. My landlord owns the two adjoining houses as well. He is a gentleman, but it's the others in the house. He is not trying to get me out but I would like to move. The toilet and public ways are always dirty, and the Jamaicans jabber away in their own language (*sic*) when I complain. So mostly I clean it up myself. They're noisy, though they stop at 11 p.m. since I spoke about it. They often sleep six to a room, and a dozen or so are in and out all the time between 6 and 12 p.m. The front door is always open and I have been burgled twice. The people around don't like them. I don't talk to them much myself.' (Cheerful, philosophically-minded 73-year-old pensioner, a bachelor described by a welfare worker as 'the life and soul of the Darby-and-Joan Club'.)

'The darkies downstairs keep the toilet insanitary and there are at least sixteen of them using it, plus uncounted extras at the weekend. They rarely trouble to bolt the door and often come out unbuttoned. My wife and I never use it now. We've bought a special commode. There ought to be another toilet for the house. . . . No, there has been no actual attempt to get us out.' (Rather aggressive, elderly, lower-middle-class tenant of well-decorated, three-room flat on top storey of three-storey house bought by Jamaican couple. On checking, it was found that he was exaggerating as to numbers; not more than eight to ten coloured people lived regularly in the five downstairs rooms.)

'We pay 18s. a week for two ground-floor rooms and a kitchen – no bath. The other tenants are English and we have all been

[1] From report in *South London Advertiser*, 16 March 1957.

here since the war. Last year the basement flat fell vacant and a Jamaican bought the house. He lives in one room and rents the other to his friends. I don't think he realized at first that he couldn't get us out legally. Then he tried everything he knew to make us leave – noise, late parties, tough men friends blocking the wives' way when we were at work, appearing at their doors half nude. We and the English tenants fought back and took him to court. It's quiet now; he knows he can't win. Our main complaint is the smell of their food.' (Middle-class Polish typographer.)

'There was an axe fight last week in that house; two coloured men and a woman ran out into the road. A few houses down there was an old lady in a top flat who was scared stiff of the coloured people who took over the house. When her friend, Mrs. W., in the basement, was rehoused, the old lady just kept to her room and died in a couple of weeks. Just round the corner, however, there is a house where, after a lot of trouble between the coloured section and the white section, all the whites have gone but for a pleasant rather sluttish Irish girl and her children. They're on very good terms with the landlady. The landlady keeps the house cleaner than it was before. My policy would be to separate the West Indians from the locals in the same house. I'd rehouse the whites and leave the coloured people to it, just keeping them up to the mark and teaching them our ways slowly. In a few years the short leases will be up and they'll be qualified for rehousing. But things are quietening down and the locals are resigned to having them about.' (Local government official.)

'The worst problem we have is the bad black landlord who buys the remaining lease of old poor property and makes the white tenants' life impossible with dirty toilets, noise, remarks to the women, and so on. These tenants come to us, decent working-class people, and we have to say we can do nothing for them because they are technically "housed". I can give you at least a dozen cases.' (Labour Party official.)

'I've got eleven cases of this type on hand. In five of them the white tenants have been driven to leave; the other six have remained thanks to my stiffening. Decent English working-class people literally fear the West Indians. Most of them have vile habits. If only they behaved like us it would be all right. The local feeling isn't a colour bar; it's a question of different cultural levels. It seems to me that some coloured landlords may even be pleased at getting whites into their power and humiliating them, after being treated like natives back where they come from.' (Conservative Party official.)

West Indian informants whom I interviewed on this subject were usually more reticent, although one or two landlords went out of their way to stress their good relationships with their white sitting tenants. Few had any complaints about these tenants other than to deplore their aloofness. Most of these coloured landlords seemed to have accepted the legal obligation and the consequent economic loss.[1] Only a handful of them appeared to regard such tenants as convenient targets on which to vent anti-white resentments.

A small number of white tenants were found living in coloured-owned houses by choice. These were usually transients of either sex who rented a furnished room for the same high rent as the coloured tenants. In their case, coloured landlords often complained of noisy or immoral behaviour, dirty habits, dishonesty, and failure to pay the rent regularly. It seems likely that some at least of the white tenants who chose to live in coloured-owned houses in Brixton did so because they did not expect the landlord to enforce local stand-ards of behaviour as strictly as most white landlords would do.

WHITE LANDLORDS AND COLOURED TENANTS

Today the exclusive white landlady who turns away the coloured room-seeker because of 'what the other tenants (or the neighbours) would say' is more familiar to coloured students north of the river than to West Indian newcomers in Brixton.[2] As we have seen, the majority of new arrivals now go straight to relatives or friends, and there are so many rooms available in coloured-owned houses or in those of white landlords who let only to coloured tenants that no West Indian need risk a rebuff by knocking at the door of a local landlady whose reactions are unknown, but may well be negative.[3]

This does not mean that the migrants in Brixton feel no uncer-

---

[1] In 1958 a local housing official told me: 'We've had a number of coloured landlords in since the new Rent Act wanting to know if they can get their sitting tenants out or how much they can increase their rent. But, despite the Rent Act, there are very few cases where the tenants can be given notice, as most of these flats have a rateable value of under £40 per annum.'

[2] Even at the beginning of 1955 it appears from a Gallup Poll survey that most West Indians (694) in Paddington, Brixton, Stepney, and Birmingham were experiencing little trouble in finding a place to live, while over half had a place to go to on arrival. Of those interviewed, 58 per cent had a West Indian landlord, 22 per cent had an English landlord, and 16 per cent had a landlord of another nationality (4 per cent 'didn't know').

[3] In fairness to London's landladies it should be said that those who keep a 'respectable' house, a house with a good name, do not usually accept couples who make no pretence of being married; that they do not like couples with babies or young children (because of noise and other possible nuisance-value); and that they are likely to give notice to any single tenant whose visitors of the opposite sex stay overnight. These forms of discrimination have nothing to do with colour but they would affect a large number of West Indian migrants in Brixton either at the outset or later in the tenancy.

tainty or apprehension about the reactions of local white landlords. Most informants who arrived before about 1955 had the experience of being refused a room more than once. Such experiences cut deep, and there are always the 'Sorry, no coloured' or 'English only' notices on the tobacconists' boards to revive them. For the majority of migrants today the fear of such discrimination is probably strong enough to keep them within the coloured quarter and paying the 'colour premium'; but actual knowledge of it is only a derived opinion and, as we have seen, they often feel a sharper and more direct hostility towards the West Indian landlord (see above, pp. 185–9).

Of latter years relationships between white landlords and coloured tenants in Brixton and the neighbouring districts have been restricted to three types of white landlord or landlady: first, the white landlords who let only to West Indians and charge a 'colour tax'; second, the minority who do not object to taking coloured tenants who meet their general requirements; and third, the non-professional landladies, usually wives or widows of professional status, modest means, and liberal views, who have been recruited by such organizations as the British Council and Methodist International House to take in coloured students.

The third group, like the students for whom they cater, does not fall within the scope of this study. The first is mainly composed of house-owners of depreciated property who have seen a chance of making it pay at last. Many West Indians seem to prefer these white landlords, despite the fact that they charge the same high rentals as West Indian landlords. It is considered that, although they are usually less easy-going about tenants' morals[1] and behaviour, they give better value for money in services by keeping the house cleaner and by not neglecting repairs. Lodging in a well-run, white-owned house also seems to confer a certain social *cachet* on the West Indian tenant within his own group, particularly if the landlord is English. For these advantages some are willing to give up the cosy, *laissez-faire* life of the all-coloured household.

[1] This is how the famous calypsonian, Lord Kitchener, then a Clapham resident, saw the London landlady:

> *My landlady's too rude,*
> *In my affairs she likes to intrude.*
> *This is how she start*
> *A lot of restrictions to break your heart.*
> *After ten o'clock*
> *Tenants must know my front door is lock,*
> *And on the wall she stick up a notice*
> *'No lady friends not even a Princess'.*
> (Calypso composed and sung by Lord Kitchener in *A Man from the Sun*, a play given on BBC television in 1956.)

209

The second group tends to merge into the first, because a West Indian tenant, once accepted, will try to introduce friends. Ultimately the other white tenants move out and the house becomes a 'coloured' one. These less colour-conscious landlords are usually not local people but are themselves newcomers – Irish, Cypriot, or Polish. One Polish landlady told me how this transformation took place in her Stockwell house, which was in a street now heavily settled by West Indians. She continued to own this house but moved with her family to middle-class Norwood,[1] where she also rented rooms: 'I took them in down there because I was sorry for them, but I won't take them in this area. They're not nice to have in the same house with a little girl and they definitely do have a different smell. But I've got a nice Indian lady and her niece living upstairs – they're different and so clean.' A West Indian who lodged in a Polish-owned house in Peckham told me that Polish landlords had the general reputation of being good and cheap, but strict about visitors.

Although non-British landlords may be less colour conscious than local people, they often conform to local practice for the sake of expediency, and it is probably only a minority who accept West Indian tenants. In a set of interviews with Polish landlords in South London, published in the *Polish Daily* of 15 March 1957, the following fairly representative viewpoints emerged: 'It is very unpleasant to refuse a room to Negroes. Often they are nice, polite students, but the English tenants wouldn't stand for it. The Chinese are fine tenants, clean, reliable, hard-working. . . .' Another Polish landlord, asked what sort of tenants he preferred, said: 'The best tenants are single, working people, compatriots. . . . The English regard themselves as masters of the house, and treat foreigners in a superior way. Each time I advertise a room Negroes come after it at once. I can't take them, because they spoil the good name of the house.'

[1] See my paper on 'The Polish Exile Community in Britain', presented at the 1961 Annual Proceedings of the British Association for the Advancement of Science at Norwich, for a more detailed account of changing Polish settlement patterns in South London.

Conclusions and future trends

A TEMPORARY AND MAKESHIFT SOLUTION

As WE have seen, the West Indians have evolved their own solution to the problem of living space by buying up deteriorating property, much of which has ceased to seem a sound investment proposition to local investors, and by filling it with fifteen to twenty-five people instead of the two to three English families who formerly lived there. So the arrival of 10,000 newcomers, mainly in the Brixton area, has not aggravated the housing shortage in Lambeth as much as might have been expected, or as much as many local people still believe.[1]

This solution is a temporary and makeshift one – one that may contain the seeds of future problems. If the migrants cease to regard their stay as short, many will tend to adapt themselves more to local living patterns and will become dissatisfied with their present accommodation, high rents, and degree of overcrowding. Within a few years, most of the migrants will be entitled to apply for council housing, and the housing authorities may be faced with a more difficult situation than they are today. Their difficulties will also be greatly increased by the fact that many of the houses owned and occupied by West Indians are, as a result of overcrowding and poor maintenance, degenerating into actual slums far more rapidly than they would normally have done.

In considering the administrative problems that are likely to face the housing authorities in the future, and the frictions and conflicts already generated by competition for scarce living space and enforced proximity between two groups of differing social and cultural background, we have perhaps dwelt more on the experiences and reactions of the receiving society than on those of the migrants. The conditions in which the majority of West Indians have to live, however, have also an obvious effect on the overall process of migrant adaptation to life in this country.

[1] The position can however be over-stated. Recently, the *Church of England Newspaper* (24 February 1961) quoted the Rev. F. H. Sisley, Vicar of St. Paul's Church, Brixton: 'Housing is one of the tremendous headaches in an area such as this. In order to get in they pack, literally pack, multitudes in one room. A house which previous to the coming of the migrants about six years ago held six people now holds up to thirty. Very many of the coloured people in the South will soon become eligible for enrolment on the housing-list and this is troubling the housing authorities considerably.'

It is generally assumed by the British public that West Indian migrants have been used to poor living conditions and that they congregate together in numbers by choice. So far as the bulk of the recent working-class migrants in this area are concerned, this assumption may be reasonably accurate. On the other hand, climatic conditions in the West Indies make overcrowding under the family roof more tolerable than it can possibly be in Brixton. In the West Indies, the lower-class family's hut or bungalow serves mainly as sleeping-quarters. Cooking is done in an outside kitchen, children play in the yard, and visitors may sleep on verandahs.[1]

In the urban environment and inclement climate of Britain, such overcrowding is only tolerable so long as it is regarded as temporary. Some of the more settled families have already spread out into two or three rooms, despite the extra expenditure entailed. But for the majority of West Indian migrants in Brixton, the private enterprise housing solution means dirt, discomfort, and often ill health. The single-room unit impedes the development of settled family life, and holds back schoolchildren and those who would like to study and so work their way out of the unskilled category. The whole system encourages bad living conditions and so helps to perpetuate the local view of the migrants as an alien and socially undesirable group. Once established, this solution also restricts the coloured worker's mobility, which could be an asset to him in worsening economic conditions, by making him afraid to go to a city or town where there is no established coloured settlement. The 'colour tax' encourages single women earning a low wage to live with men for the sake of a lodging. It also means that the rent represents a much higher proportion of the migrant's weekly income than is paid by most working-class Londoners. Added to the remittances sent home, re-payments of debts incurred for passage money, PAYE[2] deductions, and unexpectedly high expenditure on food, travel, warm clothing, and fuel, these high outgoings on rent mean that a large number of migrants find themselves financially marking time rather than accumulating sufficient capital with which to return home according to their original plan.

As a way out of this deadlock, the desperate and the astute have resorted to house purchase and room-letting. In this they have followed the practice of most immigrants in a new country, and that of their immediate predecessors in Brixton, the Poles and the

---

[1] Cf. Henriques (1953, pp. 111–2) for living conditions in Portland Parish in 1943; also Kerr (1952, pp. 57–8), and Elizabeth E. Hoyt (1960, pp. 134–5). The 1953 Jamaican Sample Census showed that 46 per cent of all homes had only one room (p. 89).

[2] 'Pay As You Earn': the system for collecting tax on earned income, introduced in the U.K. in 1943.

212

Cypriots. The pattern of such buying among migrant groups with a peasant or property-owning background is usually to buy cheap, improve, fill with steady tenants, and sell as a going concern, then to move to a more desirable area and repeat the process. With this goes the process of setting up an attractive home, particularly in the case of political exiles like the Poles, who have little hope of returning to their own country. Imperceptibly, of course, this process of property-improvement and home-building turns the immigrant or exile into a settler, a citizen, and a good neighbour, and so speeds the process of absorption.

It is too early to see whether house purchase will have such a stabilizing effect on the West Indian migrant group in Brixton. As yet it is rare to find a house-owner or landlord (the two terms are really synonymous) who regards his property as anything more than a short-term source of income, and as long as such high profits can be made with so little outlay it is hard to see why this attitude should change. There is evidence of an increasing appreciation of the economic aspects of property-owning, but there is less perception of the social intangibles among the local population that determine a district's status, while the idea of making a 'home' is not often encountered as yet.

The chief result of the migrant landlords' activities so far has been to establish and extend a set of coloured or partly coloured quarters with Brixton market as their hub. This coloured settlement is not so geographically defined or isolated as was the coloured dock-quarter in Cardiff in the 1920s and 1930s, nor is it so compact as the coloured quarter in Stepney. The Brixton coloured settlement consists of one heavily settled area in the Somerleyton–Geneva Road district, a less compact area in Angell Town, and a dozen or more less-concentrated nuclei within a few miles' radius of Brixton market. There is increasing evidence of the development of three zones or stages of settlement (see p. 295 below).

THE 'GHETTO' AND ITS CONSEQUENCES

I was often told by Brixtonians, 'They're happier living together in their own way.' Though this is undoubtedly in part a rationalization of most local residents' aversion to close residential proximity with coloured people, there is at present some truth in this assertion.

In spite of overcrowding and physical discomfort, the incipient 'ghetto' in which most West Indians live in Brixton eases the immediate processes of adjustment and adaptation for the newcomers. It provides something of an oasis where they can relax among their own people after the strain of coping with everyday life

213

in an unfamiliar and highly industrialized urban environment. The process of accommodation is also helped by the presence of an increasing number of West Indian women and of family units.

Within the coloured area, further patterns and distinctions develop. Certain streets become the dormitories of the restless, the unsuccessful, the unattached, the antisocial, and the newcomers who have nowhere better to go, together with the white misfits who have drifted into the coloured orbit. These are the streets of the nameless, of the undelivered letters, of the lodgers who do not know the names of those on the floor below, of the migrants who change their rooms as they change their jobs, for the difference of half-a-crown a week, for a brusque word, or because of some inner restlessness. Other districts acquire a better name, and the inhabitants of certain houses form themselves into informal social units which may hold together for months or years, and may serve as a substitute for the family and even for the village at home.

Life within the West Indian settlement is described in later chapters. Here, however, attention may be drawn to the dangers inherent in the consolidation of a coloured settlement into a ghetto. In all minority group settlements, such a ghetto tends to perpetuate minority group values and traits, to limit social and cultural contacts between newcomers and local people, to reinforce local views on the alienness of the newcomers, and so to retard ultimate integration or assimilation.

But a coloured ghetto is also likely to be self-perpetuating because of its high visibility. Long after Polish, Italian, and Jewish ghettos have blurred and merged in the rest of the city, a coloured ghetto can remain. It can remain, not as an area where temporary migrants or people of a different sub-culture prefer to live, but as a depressed area regarded by the majority society as suitable for people who, however much they may have come to share the same living patterns and cultural values, are still visibly different and socially unacceptable to that society.

The pattern of the further evolution of the coloured migrant settlement in South London will depend very much on the extent of new migration, on the number of those already here who decide to stay and to accommodate themselves to local life, and on the number who actually carry out their present intention of returning home within a few years. If a large number of migrants turn settler, one may expect a gradual movement into single-family houses and flats in non-ghetto areas by the most successful and established settlers. Such a spatial and social dispersal may to some extent offset the similar centrifugal movement of white families away from the main coloured concentrations. This movement is at present limited by shortage of accommodation, but may be expected to increase if the housing situation eases in South London as a whole.[1]

In the event of further large-scale migration some of the potential ghettos around Brixton may be consolidated. Any large-scale permanent increase in Brixton itself is unlikely, because of the lack of local employment openings and the existing degree of residential 'saturation'. But the main West Indian concentrations in Brixton will almost certainly remain as they are until some official housing programme disposes of them. In this connection the Lambeth Borough Council's purchase of the freeholds of the whole area of Geneva and Somerleyton Roads, Atlantic Road, Vining Street, and a portion of Coldharbour Lane from the Ecclesiastical Commissioners in October 1957 was a bold step. This is the main reception area, the area known locally as 'Little Harlem', and the district with the greatest number of coloured lease-holders. It will be interesting to learn what plans the Council has for it once these leases fall in in the early 1960s.

[1] See *Quarterly Bulletin* of the Society of Housing Managers (January 1956) for the observation by a Lambeth housing supervisor that local authorities tend to re-house white statutory tenants from West Indian-owned houses, thereby indirectly helping to consolidate existing migrant settlements.

PART IV

Social and cultural life

11

West Indian and British patterns and preconceptions

PROCESSES OF ABSORPTION IN THE SOCIAL AND CULTURAL SPHERE

THE INITIAL phase in the development of migrant-host relationships is usually one of limited accommodation in work and housing. These are two areas of more or less compulsory association, for all migrants and some local people, involving competition and sometimes conflict. Accommodation in the social and cultural sphere is not – except for those migrants and local people who are forced into close residential proximity with one another – so much a matter of competition or conflict as of voluntary cooperation or avoidance.

This is particularly true of a migrant group with a fairly well-balanced demographic structure, which makes it unnecessary for most males to compete for the favours of local women. Local acceptance is likely to be at its least in this sphere, particularly in the most intimate and least institutionalized sectors of social life. Migrant adaptation is also minimal here and, except for superficial and casual public contacts, occurs largely within the migrant group itself. Exceptions are found in the rare cases where immigrants and a receiving society share the same social and cultural patterns to a very large degree, so that the need for adaptation is limited, and the newcomers' degree of acceptability is high; for example, in the case of British immigrants in the older 'white' Dominions, or Jewish immigrants from Europe in Israel.

Most other immigrant groups make interim social and cultural arrangements within their own group. These arrangements gradually become institutionalized, and may subsequently be modified or adapted to suit the new environment. Such adaptation is usually an indication of the immigrants' transition from the stage of accommodation to one of overall integration or even of assimilation. The arrangements which the West Indian migrants are in process of making within their group will be considered later.

West Indian migrants in Britain share the same language, religion,

219

Social and cultural life

and citizenship as the British receiving society.[1] Unlike most other coloured migrants from the Commonwealth, moreover, they come from an English-oriented sub-culture, and lack any distinct and separate culture of their own. On the surface, this common heritage may seem to many migrants and to well-meaning sponsors to be adequate to facilitate easy adaptation and acceptance in all spheres. But the apparent community is often superficial and masks very real divergencies and sometimes incompatibilities between contemporary British and West Indian social and cultural patterns, as well as some important divergencies between the attitudes and expectations which each group holds in relation to the other. Both objective and subjective factors are on the whole likely to slow and hamper the processes of adaptation and acceptance for the recent working-class West Indian migrants, particularly in the area of social and cultural association, in which this 'assimilating' group is more likely to expect early acceptance than are such 'integrating' groups as the Chinese or Pakistanis. Discussion of actual contacts in the social and cultural spheres will therefore be preceded by a brief account of the main patterns and preconceptions involved on either side.[2]

WEST INDIAN SOCIAL AND CULTURAL PATTERNS

In the British West Indies, historical, economic, and climatic factors have, in conjunction with the mingling of a number of diverse cultural and ethnic components, British, French, Spanish, African, Asian, perhaps even Amer-Indian, and latterly North and South American, produced a new social and cultural amalgam. Not yet fully set, this amalgam is English-oriented but none the less recognizably different and specifically West Indian, although it contains many regional variants, and a number of unresolved and often conflicting elements deriving from the upper-class 'European' and the peasant 'African' extremes.[3]

An interesting illustration of this diversity and conflict was given recently in a Kingston editorial under the heading 'This West Indian Personality':

'. . . We no longer regard ourselves as a number of imported peoples the significance of whose existence depends on the use which the metropolitan country makes of our lives. We are now largely reconciled to our presence in these islands. The search is

[1] With the exception of some Hindu, French-speaking, and other minorities.
[2] See also Manley (1960, pp. 18–48) on the social and cultural background of the migrants.
[3] See Madeline Kerr (1952) on the conflict between peasant and middle-class culture patterns in Jamaica, on the frustrations inherent in the society, and on the unintegrated basic personality type that often results (pp. 95, 105, 113, 193, 202).

220

now for an identity. We, who are just at about the beginning of this serious search, are in danger of developing a few easy attitudes, a few angry or embarrassed stunts of behaviour, and presenting them through display as the national personality in its total validity. . . . We tend to make claims which are in the nature of dispensations.

On one side of the line there is what might be called the Dispensation Through Being a West Indian. It is used, in public life, to excuse lack of dignity, boisterousness, crudity of behaviour, childish wilfulness, question-begging, and mediocrity of performance. It tends to make the person who claims it self-righteous; to make him suspect that any rebuffs which he suffers are on account of his colour or his race; to make him forgive incompetence, so long as it is the incompetence of "my own people"; to make him regard non-West Indians with an automatic suspiciousness.

On the other side of the line there is the Dispensation From Admitting The Non-European Influences. The persons who make this claim want to exclude all that the claimers of the other Dispensation insist on including. They tend to have difficulty with their speech, because their imitations are inaccurate. Their personalities sometimes give the impression of falseness and calculatedness. They have a hyper-sensitivity which may be deeply resentful of direct reference to the non-European part of their tradition, on the suspicion that such a reference is intended as an insult.

Both claims are the result of a paranoia, of a belief that the coloured West Indian is one of the persecuted types of humanity. In the one case, the belief that members of European races do not accept him makes him a boisterous and non-self-assessing individualist, trying to substitute aggressiveness for his basic lack of self-respect. In the other case, the same belief makes him self-effacing and sham, trying to substitute a shallow practice of shallowly comprehended European values for his basic lack of self-respect. Both gestures are facile. In both cases the attempt at self-realization has been arrested before it has been completed. In both cases the truth has been simplified. But the other, and obvious, truth is that until we attain a self-respect based upon full and unblinking comprehension, we will neither receive nor deserve the respect of others which it is so dangerous to be without.'[1]

Henriques (1953, p. 171) describes Jamaican society as being in a state of dysnomia, whose major causes are poverty and colour, and the Jamaican personality type as being filled with internal con-

[1] *Public Opinion*, 7 June 1958.

flict and anxiety, as a consequence of the society's 'white bias'.[1] Moreover, West Indian social organization and culture are also still primarily rurally-based, and this again does not make it easier for West Indians to adjust or adapt satisfactorily to the highly complex and integrated sociocultural environment that they encounter in a British city.

The differences between present-day British and West Indian social and cultural patterns emerge most clearly among the large lower-income majority in the West Indies. It is from this group that the great majority of present-day migrants to Britain come. And the differences in such basic elements as norms and values relating to sex and kinship, the determinants and attributes of social class, and religious belief and practices, are among the most significant for the development of relationships in the social and cultural spheres between an 'assimilating' migrant group and local British society. Nor should one overlook a virtual polarity and incompatibility in behaviour patterns over a wide range of situations, between the uninhibited spontaneity and mettlesome directness of most West Indians and the extreme orderliness and reserve which a number of observers consider characteristic of the public behaviour of the contemporary British.[2]

The West Indian patterns relating to sex and kinship were set in slave days. At this time, families and tribal groupings were split up in transit or even before; tribal marital and kinship patterns were overridden or fell into abeyance because there were no cohesive groups to maintain them.[3] On the plantations, slaves were property

[1] Hyman Rodman, in an article 'On Understanding Lower-Class Behaviour' (1959, pp. 441–50), cautions sociologists and social workers against viewing lower-class behaviour in middle-class terms. 'Illegitimacy' and 'promiscuity', for instance, are, he suggests, middle-class terms for what may be not 'problems' but 'solutions' in lower-class circumstances. 'Dysnomia', too, may be a middle-class term for a middle-class judgement. This contention may be true in the Caribbean context, but the unresolved conflicts and frustrations and the 'solutions' which the migrants bring with them undoubtedly hinder their accommodation to English urban society, with its middle-class-oriented norms and values.

[2] Cf. Gorer (1955, p. 13); Renier (1931, *passim*). A picture of accepted British middle-class norms of behaviour can often be gleaned from the comments of the Bench when sentencing immigrants for various misdemeanours or crimes. The comment begins: 'You must learn that in this country we don't . . .' and continues with a variety of disapproved ways of behaving from carrying knives to smoking marihuana, beating up one's wife, or making a noise after midnight. It should of course be remembered that migrants often behave more laxly in the migrant situation than they would at home, since there are few group social controls or persons who know one's home circumstances.

[3] Henriques (1953, p. 7) points out that among the Akan people, from whom many of the slaves were drawn, family patterns were in any case matrilineal and polygamous, although it would be impossible to ascertain the degree to which this influenced later developments. See pp. 298-303 below for a more detailed discussion of West Indian family patterns.

and could set up no permanent conjugal or family ties. Parents had no rights over their own children; indeed, men might not always know which children they had sired. Slave women were liable to be taken as concubines by planters or their overseers. They were encouraged to breed promiscuously, and to produce further slave property for their owners, particularly in the final period of slavery after the abolition of the slave trade in 1807.

The formal marriage customs of the planters were adopted by their mixed-blood sons and daughters. Among the coloured upper and middle classes, therefore, marriage became the norm, and shame was felt if a kinswoman committed the lower-class act of bearing an illegitimate child. Yet marriage was often accompanied by casual infidelities, and even though decreasingly in later years, by concubinage.[1]

The formal marriage tie was an index of high economics as well as social status. This has remained the case. Between 60 and 70 per cent of the children in most West Indian islands are born out of wedlock, roughly half of these being the issue of informal but relatively permanent unions. There are no figures to show how many of these unions are subsequently formalized, but the usual reason for such formalization is to mark the fact that the couple have attained economic security. This improved economic status is displayed in the elaborate and expensive paraphernalia of the marriage ceremony, which is witnessed and celebrated by as many relatives and friends as can be assembled together. The fact that the marriage takes place in church is usually to be associated less with regard for marriage as a religious sacrament than with the status-conferring aspect of church-going. After marriage, the male partner assumes greater responsibility and authority in relation to his children. Among the great majority of West Indians, however, the matrilineal or matricentral patterns of slave days still persist, and the father-child tie remains weak and impermanent or even non-existent.

At most social levels, West Indian attitudes to sex and procreation remain relatively untouched by puritanical teachings or northern hypocrisies. Sexual intercourse is regarded as a natural activity, with procreation as its natural outcome. Fecundity in a woman is seen as natural and desirable, while barrenness and artificial prevention are thought of as unnatural, unhealthy, even wrong.[2]

Like the kinship system, the contemporary West Indian colour-class system derives from slavery and the hierarchy based on it. In

---

[1] The stereotype of the promiscuous white planter who debauched coloured womanhood still persists and is often advanced by apologists as a main reason for infidelity or sexual licence among West Indians today.

[2] Cf. Madeline Kerr (1952, p. 107); and Edith Clarke (1957, pp. 95–6).

Jamaica, this colour-class system was represented by Henriques in the form of a pyramidal structure, topped by a small white or fair-coloured upper class, which largely monopolizes high civil service jobs, the professions, and such occupations as that of planter. Below this class comes a middle class, composed of coloured people and some aspiring blacks, whose preserves are the clerical, lower super-visory, shopkeeping, and teaching occupations. At the bottom of the pyramid is the vast, mainly black, lower class of labourers and peasants.[1]

Lightness and high social status are still approximately associated, and darker individuals who succeed in making good economically marry 'lighter' to 'improve the colour' of their children and so reinforce their newly improved status in the second generation. West Indian society, particularly in the upper, middle, and upper-lower classes, appears to be affected by a 'white bias': that is to say, by an association of whiteness or lightness with everything that is socially or culturally desirable, and of blackness with the contrasting back-ward, primitive, and undesirable qualities. In a society where the great majority of the population is black, this colour-class system with its white bias is obviously likely to produce a profound frus-tration among the black lower-class majority, to evoke inter-class tensions and hostilities, and to work against group or community solidarity. It also produces a preoccupation with colour in the majority of its members and a tendency to interpret everyday situa-tions, and particularly setbacks, in terms of colour.[2]

[1] Henriques (1953, p. 42). The lower class is of course proportionately far larger than the others; probably nearly 80 per cent of the Jamaican population belong to the peasant and labouring class, and about the same percentage (78 per cent) were listed as 'black' in the 1943 census returns. Henriques follows the census in restricting the term 'coloured' to people of intermediate pigmentation. In this study we have been using the term with reference to all non-whites in Britain. In a recent article, M. G. Smith (1961) discusses the widely differing norms and values of these three 'sociocultural sections' in Jamaica. No classification according to colour is available from the 1960 census returns, but there is no reason to think that the colour-class divisions have altered significantly.

[2] A front-page story in the progressive Jamaican weekly *Public Opinion*, on 20 February 1957, affords an interesting illustration of several aspects of Jamaican life, notably the preoccupation with colour and the easy-going attitude to sex and illegitimacy. Under the headline 'Black Girl Turning White' the report gave the story of an unmarried mother, formerly a 'black Negro woman' with a black mother and a black father (not married). Two years earlier she 'started turning white'; the white spots spread until they came together and only a few spots were left on her legs and neck. Before the change she had borne one black baby. Of her second child it was said: 'His mother started turning white when she was pregnant with him. And he has come fair.' Photographs illustrated the contrast between the black brother and the white brother (both of whom had different sur-names) and the newly-white Miss Pringle (aged 20) and her black mother. The neighbours' reaction was said to have been hostile, Miss Pringle being thought to have 'an infection'. Her 'boy friend' was quoted as saying: 'I am satisfied nothing is wrong with her. She has a child for me.'

224

The white bias includes a cultural bias towards a nineteenth-century colonial version of British culture. This has been strengthened by a long period of English-oriented education, during which generations of children learned about the rivers of England and King Alfred and the cakes, or wrote essays on how to build a snowman at Christmas and the production of beet sugar. They also learned from liberal-minded and nostalgic English teachers and ministers that they were members of a proud Empire or Commonwealth of which Britain was the centre and 'mother country'.

Migrants who come to Britain with this 'white bias' often find themselves confused and confounded by the social and cultural patterns which they find in contemporary Britain, and also by their first contacts with a white lower-middle- and lower-class society which does not conform to their expectations of a white élite nor appreciate the newcomers' white bias or their expectations of complete acceptance. In the early period of settlement many lower-class migrants also find it difficult to associate unselfconsciously with white people on an equal social basis.

There is an inevitable obverse to the West Indian white bias. This is the frustrated, hypersensitive, chip-on-the-shoulder attitude which often arises in the West Indies, where light colour and an imported and not fully assimilated set of values are set up as an ideal, but an ideal to which the majority of those to whom it is purveyed are totally unable, by virtue of both their skin colour and their inadequate cultural background, to aspire. In the United Kingdom this chip-on-the-shoulder attitude hinders adaptation and acceptance, and is often evoked or intensified by disillusionment and failure to change the patterns of economic frustration and social rejection. Carried to aggressive extremes in the West Indies, this attitude has produced the 'black bias' of Garveyism, Ethiopianism, and Ras Tafarism; in Britain it is more likely to evoke the protest-type migrant association (see pp. 362–4 below).

Another important sphere in which West Indian values and patterns (especially among the lower socio-economic class) differ from those of contemporary urban Britain is the religious one. Here again the overall framework of Christianity tends to mask considerable differences of attitude and behaviour.[1] In general, religious belief and practice—orthodox, sectarian, or cultist—play a much larger and more significant part in the life of the majority of West Indians than they do in British urban society.

The orthodox Christian churches serve one important social function in the West Indies which is no longer served by most urban churches in Britain. They act, according to Henriques (1953, p. 76),

[1] For a further account of religious life in Jamaica, see pp. 349-54 below.

225

as a binding force in society, by bringing together in a single congregation members of various social classes. West Indian informants claim that at home these services are fully attended, so that worshippers get a feeling of warmth and community with fellow-worshippers. They also get a feeling of universal Christian brotherhood, stretching over colour divisions. This feeling is sometimes rudely shaken among migrants to Britain, who expect to find the same sort of fellowship in the country in which their church originated.

The orthodox churches also provide a situation in which status and prestige may be gained by regular attendance in one's best clothes, by elaborate ceremonies connected with marriage, christening, and so on, by office-holding, and by the regular attendance of one's children at Sunday school. Membership of the Anglican and Roman Catholic denominations carries a particularly high status. The majority of upper-class people belong to these churches, most of whose ministers have until recently been white and British born.

No precise correlation of religious affiliation with colour group is available, but it can be said that the membership of West Indian nonconformist churches, sects, or cults is drawn largely, if not exclusively, from the black lower class. The sects and cult groups do not fulfil the same solidarizing function in the total West Indian society as do the orthodox churches. Instead, they satisfy in a very large measure the feelings of frustration and the emotional needs of the majority of the impoverished and socially frustrated black lower class.[1] As purveyed by such agencies, Christianity offers a means of satisfaction in the present and a certain future, for neither of which could the poorer West Indian otherwise hope in his home circumstances. Migrants, on the other hand, may find other outlets in the new country for their emotional and recreational needs, particularly if their economic circumstances are greatly improved.

BRITISH PATTERNS

On the British side,[2] patterns tend to be more complex and varied, as one might expect in a large, diversified, and industrial society. Social stratification is determined not by the unchangeable determinant of colour, with wealth and education as adjuncts, but by the relatively acquirable determinants of education, occupation, and

---

[1] Madeline Kerr (1952, pp. 134–5) lists the following most important functions of religion in Jamaica: (a) as wish-fulfilment; (b) as an emotional outlet; (c) as a substitute for recreation; (d) as an outlet for potential leaders.

[2] There would seem to be some differences of values and norms as between the English, Scottish, Welsh, and Irish. Here we shall be primarily concerned with those of the English, with whom the recent migrants are mainly in contact.

226

wealth.[1] The stratification is similar in the two societies, but in Britain the values and norms of the upper and middle classes have —as a result of earlier industrialization and universal education, the homogeneity of the native population, the wider spread of prosperity, and the unifying effects of such mass cultural media as the press, radio, and television—been extended at least in a modified form further into the lower socio-economic class than has yet been the case in the West Indies.[2] In addition, the middle class itself is proportionately far larger in this country than is the corresponding class in the British West Indies. It is, incidentally, often into lower-middle-class and upper-lower-class areas in British cities that the lower-class West Indian newcomers move, and this can produce inter-class tensions.

In the sphere of family and sex relationships, these British middle-class values and behaviour patterns stress monogamy, premarital chastity, sexual restraint, marital fidelity, and the importance of formal marriage as a social contract.[3] The indiscriminate procreation of children has come to be regarded as improvident and uncontrolled; illegitimacy is a matter for shame and contempt; and the act of sex itself is usually invested with a puritan feeling of innate sinfulness.

In Britain birth is a non-acquirable status determinant of diminishing importance, though membership of an aristocratic, county, or wealthy professional or industrial family obviously helps an individual to acquire the other determinants. Indices associated with class membership, which may help an upwardly mobile individual to gain a footing in a higher class or to secure his position there, are certain approved forms of speech, manners, dress, social display, and membership of approved organizations.

Patterns of religious belief and practice in Britain again differ greatly from those found in the West Indies. Works rather than faith, the approach of Martha rather than of Mary, seem to be the main characteristic of the majority of urban non-Roman Catholics in this country. In Gorer's sample, taken in 1950, nearly a quarter of the

---

[1] See T. S. Simey (1956) for a review of recent research on the analysis of the class structure of British society.

[2] See Ralph Samuel (*New Left Review*, **1**, 1960) on working-class Tories in Clapham and Stevenage.

[3] See Gorer (1955) for an inquiry into English attitudes towards love, sex and marriage, class, and religion. Recent studies have, it is true, established the strength of the mother-centred extended family in urban working-class areas in Britain, but this is rarely associated with a total absence of the father and there is evidence that the pattern is changing in the direction of greater responsibility of the male; it thus seems doubtful whether this 'Mum'- and 'Nan'-dominated complex is fully comparable with the matricentral West Indian family unit which is discussed in Chapter 16 below. For British lower-class family patterns, see Young and Willmott (1957), Madeline Kerr (1958), and Firth (Ed.) (1956).

population of England (26 per cent of the men, 18 per cent of the women) gave no denominational affiliation at all. Only 6 per cent of the population visited church more than once a week, and another 9 per cent went regularly once a week. Forty-five per cent were intermittent church-goers, the majority of whom attended only once or twice a year, presumably at Easter and Christmas. The non-worshippers or those who attended only for weddings and funerals were heavily concentrated in London and other cities. Of those claiming any denominational affiliation, nearly 60 per cent aligned themselves with the Church of England. Of this group, only 3 per cent attended church more than once a week and 10 per cent once a week, compared with, for instance, 19 per cent and 35 per cent respectively for Roman Catholics and 17 per cent and 15 per cent for Baptists (Gorer, 1955, Chapter XIV).

BRITISH ATTITUDES TO OUTSIDERS

In the two universal and more highly institutionalized spheres of work and housing, behaviour and relationships on the side of the receiving society are often, as has been shown, determined by various factors unconnected with individual or even group attitudes to outsiders or coloured people. However, the social and cultural sphere is one in which such preconceptions and attitudes can at times play a more important part in determining behaviour towards and relationships with newcomers, particularly as the type of association becomes less institutionalized, more intimate, and more subject to individual temperamental variations. At this point, therefore, it may be useful to consider the nature and content of British or rather English attitudes to outsiders in general and to coloured people in particular.

Every group or society appears to define its own identity in terms of insiders and outsiders, those who belong and those who are strangers and foreigners. Group identity seems to be protected by the development of attitudes that are more or less antagonistic to foreigners. As Max Gluckman has said, 'We must assume that this sort of hostility is an essential part of group existence [although it] does not imply that there must be actual fighting between groups'.[1]

Xenophobia, defined in the *Oxford Dictionary* as a 'morbid fear of foreigners', is really not the proper word for the traditional antipathy to outsiders which has been described as a cultural norm in Britain. The term's derivation stresses an element of fear and implies a consequent aggressiveness that do not seem dominant in the contemporary British attitude, strong though it is. 'There's a

[1] See Gluckman, 'How Foreign Are You?' (*Listener*, 15 January 1959).

foreigner. Let's heave a brick at him,' is no longer the general reaction in Britain. But 'There's a foreigner. Let's keep our distance', is a fairly general reaction for which 'xenophygia' or 'flight from strangers' might be a more precise term.[1] Here it should be added that this aversion to and avoidance of outsiders do not operate only in relation to people from outside the United Kingdom, but are characteristic of relationships within the society. The same feeling operates to a lesser degree between English and Scots, between Northern English and Southerners, between different counties, villages, boroughs, and even streets. Each village or small town has its stock character, the 'foreigner' or outsider from the next county who has only lived there for twenty-five years or so, and this attitude to outsiders still holds good, very little modified, among the settled residents of such districts as Brixton and Camberwell.

The antipathy felt towards non-Britons may be attributed to a series of historical and economic factors that have accentuated the customary tendency of a homogeneous, old-established, and geographically isolated community to entertain feelings of aversion, superiority, or apprehension towards all outsiders. For many centuries the majority of Britons have met non-Britons in time of war—as enemies, or occasionally as rather unwelcome allies[2]—in the colonial situation, or when groups of foreign workers with a low standard of living were imported to threaten their jobs and living standards. Such encounters have almost invariably served only to evoke or strengthen feelings of hostility, superiority, or apprehension towards all foreigners. These reactions have crystallized into a set of preconceptions, usually mildly derogatory but not necessarily rigidly stereotyped, about former enemies such as the French and Germans, about cheap immigrant labour such as the Southern Irish[3] or the Poles and Lithuanians in the nineteenth century, and about 'colonial' peoples like the Negroes, Asians, and Arabs.

Such images and attitudes form a part, though often a peripheral and unconsidered part, of the national cultural heritage. They are

[1] Cf. Gorer (1955, pp. 18 f.) on English people's shyness and loneliness. It may be noted that whereas ξενος in Greek means both 'guest' and 'stranger,' these two English terms are widely separated in connotation.

[2] The British have rarely liked, trusted, or admired their allies. One has only to recall Wellington's views on the Spanish guerrillas, the British army's image of Brazilian and Portuguese troops in the first world war, and the wave of quite unreasoning relief that swept the country after the capitulation of France in 1940.

[3] The only reference to ethnic hostilities in Lambeth in earlier times that could be found was in Thomas Allen's *History and Antiquities of Lambeth* (1826). He reports (p. 159) that in 1736 mobs collected in Lambeth 'interrogating the people whether they were for the Irish or not, who were at that time very obnoxious'. Huguenot hatters settled in Lambeth, Wandsworth, and Battersea in 1685 but they seem to have been absorbed in the local population without trace.

perpetuated down the generations by word of mouth, in school text-books, in literature and popular mythology, and more recently via the cinema, radio, and television. Sometimes they retain sufficient force, long after the events that evoked them, to hamper objective judgement of new arrivals.

Among the majority of Britons these preconceptions would appear to be susceptible to revision, depending on the degree of close personal contact that occurs and on the nature of the resulting first-hand experiences. Such a change is obviously more likely where individuals or small groups of strangers are involved. When large groups arrive together, the derived ideas are more likely to persist, because of the lack of opportunities for close personal contacts and reappraisal, or because the group constitutes a genuine economic, social, or cultural threat to the majority society, a threat which may seem to justify the content of the original image. This is particularly so if there is anything in the real social and cultural endowment of the newcomers that conforms to the existing preconceptions current in the receiving society. Superficial contacts may then reinforce the preconceptions, and among a minority even raise them to the strength of rigid stereotypes.

BRITISH IDEAS ABOUT COLOURED PEOPLE

In the case of non-white newcomers, the usual British insularity and antipathy to outsiders seem to be intensified by the newcomers' visible alienness. The coloured migrant, and particularly the Negro, appears to be the supreme and ultimate stranger. And his visible strangeness is, as has been said earlier, accentuated by a whole set of preconceptions associating dark pigmentation with alien cultural traits and with the lowest social and economic status.

These preconceptions about coloured people are found not merely in the former 'ruling classes' but in all social classes in Britain. They are for the most part the left-overs of nineteenth-century colonialist attitudes, perpetuated in outmoded history and geography textbooks and in much of the classical and other fiction of the last century.[1] Such preconceptions are reinforced in the more sophisticated sections of British society by survivals of the pseudo-anthropology of

---

[1] Notably in the writings of Rudyard Kipling, and after the turn of the century in such diverse publications as the novels of Edgar Wallace and John Buchan, the *Boy's Own Paper,* and the jingoistic *John Bull.* An unusually out-spoken instance of such views was voiced by a Labour peer in the House of Lords in April 1958. Speaking of the registration of ships under 'flags of convenience', he said: 'I do not know whether there exists a Liberian who knows the stem of a ship from the stern. I understand that they mostly live in the bush.'

the nineteenth century, with its glorification of the Nordic 'race' and 'culture' and its condemnation of racial mixture on alleged 'biological' grounds.[1] In addition, the overseas missionaries, those enemies of slavery and friends of the coloured oppressed for so many decades, have sometimes helped to perpetuate the concept of coloured people as backward, primitive, and incapable of self-help, through their paternalistic approach and continuing appeals for funds to convert the 'poor benighted heathen'.

It may be, too, that the common religious habit of thinking in terms of opposed categories, of a dichotomy between good and evil, God and Satan, and the identification of good with whiteness and light, evil with blackness and dark, has caused a whole set of adverse traits to be associated more or less subconsciously with a dark skin.[2]

Another interesting though unexplained element in the formation of second-hand notions about coloured people among the English urban lower-middle and lower classes was, even as late as the 1930s, the threat used by mothers to naughty children: 'Now then, Johnnie, you stop being naughty or the black man will come and get you.' A considerable number of adult South Londoners recalled such threats when asked about their own attitudes to coloured people before the coloured immigrants came to Brixton. One informant added that if he dropped a sweet on the floor his mother would say: 'Don't pick food up off the floor. For all you know a black man might have spat on it.' It is impossible to say whether the presence of several thousand coloured men in the lower socio-economic levels of London society in mid-Victorian times was responsible for this unsympathetic image, or whether the reference was to the homely sweep or to some undefined power of darkness.

To some extent the aversion and apprehension which this image aroused in children may have been counteracted by the equally

---

[1] The argument of the Negro race's biological inferiority was rarely used by Brixtonian informants of the lower or lower-middle class, with the exception of two pathologically prejudiced supporters of the Union Movement, the British National Party, and some regular correspondents in the South London press. It was, however, used in my hearing by a local upper-middle-class committee woman, by a senior reporter on a national paper, and by an educationalist with a psychological training. The argument of the possible genetic disadvantages of race mixture was also used in connection with the West Indian immigration to Britain in a broadsheet issued by the Eugenics Society in 1958.

[2] '. . . Many (of us) have absorbed the oft-preached doctrine of the superiority of the white races which has crept into our vocabulary in verbal symbols. "White" stands for purity, "black" for evil. Angels are white, devils are black. Heaven is the abode of the white-robed, hell is gloomy with dark-clad demons. No doubt there will come a change in our symbols in the future, but at the moment it comes as a surprise to many that a person with dark features should be a skilled surgeon, an understanding nurse, an able barrister, a first-class mechanic' (*Your Neighbour from the West Indies*, published by the British Council of Churches, 1955, p. 16).

231

widespread belief that to touch a Negro brings good luck, by the homely and well-beloved golliwog, by children's rhymes like 'Ten Little Nigger Boys' and 'Eeny-meeny-miny-mo', by books such as *Little Black Sambo* or *Uncle Tom's Cabin* which present coloured people as inferior but agreeable, and by the popularity of 'nigger minstrels'.

Contemporary notions about coloured people are also drawn from the minor Negro characters, usually comic servants or sexy girls, as portrayed in some American films; and from popular press presentations of the exotic, violent, and primitive aspects of life among former colonial peoples.[1] Preconceptions derived from such sources often provide a certain satisfaction for both writers and readers, and therefore may be the more difficult to change. For there is considerable confusion and insecurity among all classes in Britain as the erosion of imperial power and national prestige continues, and it becomes necessary to adopt new attitudes and to form new relationships with other nations and with former colonial dependants.[2]

One other element in the creation of attitudes towards peoples of different physical appearance is rarely discussed but may be of considerable importance. This is the subjective aesthetic aspect. In Britain the ideal of physical beauty and consequently of a desirable marital or sexual partner, male or female, has long been based on the classic Graeco-Roman model, which approximated fairly closely to the dominant Anglo-Norman, upper-class type. Until the advent of the cinema, permissible deviations were more or less restricted to Celtic, Scandinavian, and other North European 'types'. Thereafter, Slav and Mediterranean 'types' were added to the amalgam.[3] More

---

[1] Instances of such presentation are so frequent that any reader can collect a substantial sheaf in a single month's reading of the more popular daily and Sunday press. Appendix VIII gives a selection of reports dealing with relationships between coloured men and white women, taken from the South London press. A typical presentation of the savage element in the image of the Negro was the *Daily Express*'s front-page coverage of the Watutsi-Bahutu war in Ruanda-Urundi in late 1959. It ran 'JUNGLE MASSACRE—The first full story of the fiendish dwarf killers of Africa. The pygmies, torturers and executioners for the giants, swarmed from the trees to kill and burn in a frenzy' (*Daily Express*, 13 November 1959). A few weeks earlier (1 October 1959) the book-review column in the same paper was headed: 'The not-so-far-fetched world of Ernest the educated engine-driver who killed and ate his little brother.'

[2] These 'post-colonial blues' are sometimes translated into group action. Edward Crankshaw, writing in the *Observer* on 29 June 1958, made this discerning comment: 'The Suez affair, at bottom, was the outcome of a wave of irrepressible boredom, weariness and frustration on the part of a people sick to death of leaning over backwards to be "progressive", trying with much determination but little grace and less conviction to treat "the lesser breeds" as equals—and getting no thanks for it.'

[3] Some of these terms are used in their colloquial sense, although properly speaking they are applicable only to linguistic and cultural groupings.

recently, there has been a definite trend to admire more exotic 'types', such as mestizos, Anglo-Asians, Polynesians, Japanese, and the fairer Indians. This has however been largely confined to the women of these groups; as yet it is barely reflected in the findings of British- and American-organized international beauty contests, where the great majority of finalists still tend to be drawn from the representatives of the Anglo-Saxon and Scandinavian countries.

Very recently, there has been an increasing vogue for 'Negro beauties'[1] but so far these have almost invariably been women of mixed ancestry, with brown skins and not conspicuously Negroid features, such as the American singers Dorothy Dandridge, Lena Horne, and Eartha Kitt, and the British-born stars Shirley Bassey and Cleo Lane. Negroid features, far more than dark colour *per se,* still seem alien and unaesthetic to many Britons, just as the jutting bone-structure and pinkish pallor of the European 'foreign devils' struck the Chinese as the ultimate in ugliness. It is also probable that the British tend to associate flattened noses and thick lips with pugilism, in which many Negroes have excelled, and that thereby the association of the Negro with primitive brutality is strengthened.

Apart from these second-hand sources, there is one rather specific type of contact situation which has had a considerable influence on the views and attitudes of a minority of lower-class and lower-middle-class Britons towards coloured people, and through them on the views of many within their circle of friends and relations. This is the sort of temporary 'white man boss' situation that arises when British troops or technicians are stationed in colonial territories or when British sailors go ashore in Middle East or Asian ports. Such contacts are usually superficial, transient, and unrepresentative, but they produce vivid and often derogatory impressions which are the more difficult to correct because they are gained at first hand.[2] Indeed, in South London the only people, apart from a patho-logically prejudiced handful, who displayed uncompromising verbal hostility towards the coloured newcomers seemed to be those who had had such first-hand contacts with coloured people overseas during the war. This 'wog complex' was not evident in all who had

---

[1] At the end of 1959 Mrs. Sam Goldwyn was quoted as saying: 'Negro beauties next in Hollywood vogue' (*Daily Express,* 5 December 1959).

[2] It may be that such attitudes are inculcated in some servicemen even during training in this country. A photograph in the *Daily Express* of 23 March 1956 showed a riot exercise at Dearbolt Camp, County Durham, carried out by 3,000 men belonging to a special brigade kept in readiness for transfer to trouble-spots anywhere. The 'rioters' had their faces blackened, and the mob was quietened by shooting. The commanding officer was reported as saying: 'We go through this routine once a month. It is to teach the men restraint—to shoot only when it is necessary.' This incident led to a question in the House of Commons by Mr. Fenner Brockway on 16 April 1956.

served overseas, but it was reasonably widespread,[1] and of course tended to influence the views of others to some extent.

What, then, are the major preconceptions that help to make up the attitude of the average Briton towards coloured people? As has been said, a coloured skin, especially when combined with Negroid features, is associated with alienness and with the lowest social status. Primitiveness, savagery, violence, sexuality, general lack of control, sloth, irresponsibility – all these are part of the image. On the more favourable side, Negroid peoples are often credited with athletic, artistic, and musical gifts, and with an appealing and child-like simplicity which is in no way incompatible with the remainder of the image.

These preconceptions, which have until recently been unverifiable at first hand for most Britons, are usually buttressed by a formidable ignorance about the Commonwealth and its peoples.[2] It is no desire to wound that makes most Britons unable to distinguish between West Indians and West Africans, or to appreciate the differences in their history and cultural background. But the frequent: 'British Guiana, is that the same as Ghana?', 'Did you wear shoes at home?', 'I suppose you lived in a thatched hut,' or, to a West Indian: 'How did you manage to learn English so quickly?' are, as has been shown in the industrial context, a powerful source of irritation and offence.

When a migrant group enters a new society, sometimes not one but two types of interaction develop. In the first place, there is the contact, interaction, and sometimes conflict of two cultures and two social systems. In the second place, there may also be interaction and sometimes conflict between the preconceptions and expectations which each group holds about the other. This second more subjective kind of interaction tends to affect and complicate the first type.

In Britain, face-to-face association between local people and

---

[1] The 'complex' was often selective. One local government official in Brixton, a clever cockney who had moved far from his working-class origins and acquired a tolerant and humane approach towards people on the way, said (before the Suez incident): 'I learned to respect and like Indians when a Sikh saved my life in the army. But the months I spent in Egypt only made me despise the wogs more. Familiarity bred contempt there all right!'

[2] 'In Great Britain, where the people should know more of their colonial responsibilities, the extent of public ignorance was revealed by a survey of opinion made in 1948 on behalf of the Colonial Office. From this survey it appeared that a surprisingly large proportion of those asked were unable to distinguish between the self-governing countries of the Commonwealth and the dependent territories, few could name more than two or three of the colonies, and some even believed that various foreign countries were British possessions. It was made obvious that even the better-educated sections of the population knew very little on the subject, while the population as a whole lacked fundamental geographical knowledge about the Commonwealth and Empire. In these circumstances it is scarcely surprising that in foreign countries even less should be known, and that the facts should be misunderstood and distorted by prejudice' (Sir Allan Burns, 1957, p. 14).

coloured migrants is so recent that the overall situation remains highly fluid and undefined. Nor is it uniform throughout the country. Conditioning factors vary from district to district, and local attitudes and reactions also vary according to the contacts and situations involved. In public and economic life, for instance, relationships are more or less limited and defined. In private life there are fewer rules, as has been noted, and individuals have greater freedom to translate their personal attitudes or apprehensions into behaviour.

In the next chapters I shall try to show how the two forms of interaction have developed in the Brixton area in a wide range of social situations: from the usual casual and fleeting contacts of everyday urban life to formal associational life, and to the most intimate and enduring relationships between individuals or families. The role of local sponsors in furthering the processes of social and cultural adaptation and acceptance will also be considered.

12

Casual and 'categoric' contacts between migrants and hosts

CONTACTS IN THE STREET AND PUBLIC PLACES

THE STREETS of London have seemed depressing or unfriendly to many other strangers before the West Indians came.[1] During the week these streets are full of hurrying, harassed entities, intent on getting to work on time or on escaping from the rain. At night or on a Sunday, the streets away from the city's entertainment centre are empty but for the occasional church-goer, the groups of raucous teenagers waiting for the cinemas to open, and the police. Few people in these London streets have the time or the inclination to stroll or to lean against a building, to smile or sing, or even to bid passers-by good-day.

In such surroundings the coloured migrant feels lost, uneasy, even rejected. If he in addition sees a chalked or painted sign 'K.B.W.' (meaning 'Keep Britain [Brixton] White') or 'Nigger Go Home' scrawled on a wall,[2] his feelings of insecurity, indignation, and rejection are heightened out of all proportion to the actual significance of the sign as an index of widespread local feeling. The great majority of local people will not chalk up such a sign but equally they will not consider it their duty to remove it. If the migrant, walking home one evening, chances on a loud-speaker van of the Union Movement, whose speaker is declaiming on the evils of overcrowding, unemployment, and miscegenation, and on the desirability of deporting all immigrants, he will not usually stop to reflect. He will blame the society that allows such things to be said about those

[1] Cf. the reactions of the Italian exiles, Pecchio and Mazzini, of the Russian Herzen, and of the French Communard Jules Vallès, cited by Francesca Wilson (1959).

[2] During the years of this study, a handful of such signs appeared from time to time near streets heavily settled by West Indians. In 1952 a man was prosecuted and fined £1 for writing 'K.B.W.' on the Town Hall and on a wall in Coldharbour Lane (*South London Press*, 9 May 1952). Such signs have been appearing rather less frequently in recent years, although one exceptionally indelible one, painted in about 1957, can still be seen in the Kennington area. In June 1961 the *West Indian Gazette* reported a recurrence of such signs in Railton Road and elsewhere.

236

who consider themselves members of it, rather than consider that the licence granted to such a movement is regarded as the measure of its insignificance and harmlessness.

From the local point of view, the presence of large numbers of highly visible and often audible newcomers may serve only to reinforce derogatory preconceptions. Said one middle-aged artisan: 'I'd be frightened to let my daughter walk along Coldharbour Lane alone at night now – there are so many blacks about, the place looks like darkest Africa, and they say most of them carry knives.' Some local people appreciate the newcomers' cheerful greetings to passers-by, but many resent the uninhibited interest which a loitering group of coloured men will usually show towards a personable female passer-by. A social worker told me in 1959:

'Local people don't like the coloured men's attitude to women. You can't go along certain streets, even in broad daylight, without every second one making remarks and suggestions, whether you look the type or not. And local people say they're getting more noisy and aggressive as the numbers go up. They now feel so established in Brixton that they can do what they like.'

After a few years, local people get used to seeing a large number of coloured faces about in the streets and public places, but this does not of itself necessarily lead to closer acceptance. And anti-social groups such as teddy boys usually regard the newcomers as the easiest targets for their aggressive behaviour towards the outside world. In most reports of assault cases, individual or group, involving coloured people and whites in South London it has usually emerged that the aggressor or aggressors were white.[1] But the fact that coloured people were involved and sometimes fought back has been widely reported by the press and over the local grape-vine, and this has tended to link coloured people in the popular mind with undesirable and antisocial whites and to reinforce the preconception

---

[1] Such assaults seemed to increase in number just after the Notting Hill disturbances. The *South London Press* reported at least three cases, on 12 and 26 September, and 17 October 1958. The incidents did not, as in Notting Hill, lead to mass disturbances, but otherwise they reflected the same sort of pattern. In one case, a group of fifteen to twenty youths on Clapham Common (until 1959 locally notorious as a resort of prostitutes and their ponces and clients, of teddy-boy gangs and rough characters generally) just before midnight began to jostle, push, and punch a coloured man. One youth then shouted, 'There goes one of them. After the black ——.' When told he would be arrested, one of the two accused, a Balham dairyman, aged 18, said: 'I'll get three months for this and when I get out I will get the first black wog I see and do him in' (*South London Press*, 26 September 1958). Earlier local cases of attacks by gangs of white youths on coloured people were reported in the *Daily Telegraph* (20 September 1955) and the *South London Press* (23 March and 30 April 1957, and 11 July 1958).

of primitive violence. In one of the relatively few reported cases where the initial aggression came from a coloured man, the deputy chairman at the Sessions increased the sentence from six weeks to three months on appeal, and made the following generalizing comment: 'This is a type of assault that is not looked upon favourably in this country' (*South London Press*, 30 August 1957).

Some casual contacts involve a closer though limited relationship. These are the contacts that occur on public transport and in public buildings[1] or stores. There are two main types of contact in this sphere – those between members of the public on an equal basis, and those between customers or members of the public and staff or officials. The latter type has been called the 'categoric' type of contact.[2] In the former case, relationships tend to be conditioned by general attitudes on both sides; in the latter they are usually defined and limited by the respective roles of the two parties, a situation which often makes for a more harmonious development of relationships.

A very large number of contacts between coloured newcomers and local whites occur on buses or in tube-trains. Here some friction can be generated by the recent arrival's ignorance of and possibly temperamental aversion to the queueing system, which has since 1939 developed into a cardinal principle of British communal life. Queue-jumping and pushing by energetic young coloured men and women at rush-hours was commented on adversely by a number of Brixton informants. Some West Indians claim that fellow-passengers often change seats so as to avoid proximity, but I saw no instances of this myself.[3] It did however seem to me that on some occasions women avoided taking a seat next to a coloured man if another seat was available. Though it was clearly not possible to verify motivation in such cases, some of my local women informants admitted that they practised such avoidance. Reasons given were: 'I don't want to hurt their feelings but I don't want to get mixed up with one of them' and 'If anyone I know saw me sitting next to a darkie there might be talk'.

---

[1] These, of course, include public lavatories and baths. In South London a handful of complaints were said to have been received about unhygienic behaviour (in public conveniences), but officials felt that this was not necessarily attributable to West Indian users. One local health department had received a number of complaints from male users of the public baths, who refused to take a bathroom which had just been used by a coloured man 'in case the colour comes off'.

[2] Cf. Little (1947, p. 251).

[3] In only one case did an informant (middle-class, male) express any strong feelings in the matter, and this was on the ground of body odour: 'I can understand why in some hot countries there are special buses for them. I had three round me in a crowded train to Charing Cross and it wasn't pleasant. I thought I'd be sick before I got there.'

'CATEGORIC' CONTACTS

Contacts on public transport vehicles can, of course, lead to casual conversation and an increased familiarity and understanding between locals and newcomers. In the case of coloured people, such familiarity has also been fostered by their large-scale employment as conductors, inspectors, and drivers in public transport. Their selection and employment in this service are described elsewhere, but it may be generally stated that almost without exception these coloured transport employees have evoked sympathy and admiration among the London travelling public.[1] The general image of the coloured bus conductor includes cheerfulness, courtesy, especially to the old and to women, humour, and patience. This first-hand image is now fairly widespread and has gone some way towards dispelling or countering derogatory preconceptions about coloured people.

'Categoric' contacts between white officials and coloured members of the public have not always been so happy.[2] Patience and imagination are not obligatory qualifications in the lower ranks of the public service, and it is at this level – in the buses, over the counter, with the police patrol, in the employment exchange, or in the post office – that most initial contacts occur. It is in such situations that a group of informal, easy-going yet prickly, unpunctual, unsophisticated people come into contact with a vast, rigid, impersonal bureaucracy which is right outside their experience or their expectations of the mother country. On their side, the officials' attitude may range from

---

[1] On several occasions it has been suggested to me, by both white and coloured informants, that coloured people enjoy taking these service jobs because it gives them a chance to feel important by (*a*) wearing a uniform, and (*b*) ordering white people about. The possession of a uniform undoubtedly carries prestige in the present situation of coloured immigrants because it indicates that the wearer has a steady and relatively well-paid position, to which not all coloured immigrants can aspire. As for the second observation, one can only say that, if this is the case, the ordering about is done unobtrusively and with remarkable courtesy so far as white members of the public are concerned, though sometimes less so in the case of coloured passengers. In a talk on the migrants' background and expectations to the Royal Commonwealth Society, Frank Pilgrim, then Information Officer in the Migrant Services Division, attributed this special politeness to the fact that some West Indian bus conductors had been white-collar workers in the West Indies: 'I can assure you that bus conductors in the West Indies are true to character.' (*R.C.S. Journal*, 1958, **1**, 3, p.230.)

[2] Contrary to official expectations, contacts between the few coloured officials and the white public have been for the most part smooth and uneventful. A West Indian public health inspector in South London attributed this to the fact that such West Indians are usually well educated, English-oriented, and lack the chip on the shoulder that characterizes so many working-class migrants. Only one minor instance of friction was mentioned by informants, when a health department sent a coloured worker to spray some verminous flats with disinfectant. This was apparently regarded by the tenants as adding insult to injury.

exasperation to an often patronizing sympathy. Some may also feel a certain sense of resentment that their particular office has lost status because coloured people have come to constitute the bulk of its clients (see p. 138 above).

'Categoric' relationships between white businessmen or professional persons and coloured clients or customers, or vice versa, in Brixton are for the most part based on simple expediency. Relatively few of the thousands of local trading establishments cater exclusively for what used to be called the 'carriage trade', and coloured customers are acceptable as replacements for local customers lost as a result of bombing and rehousing elsewhere. So far, however, relatively few establishments have attempted to cater specifically for coloured customers. Those that have done so are mainly grocers, greengrocers, butchers, and other stallholders in or around Brixton market.

The old-established firm of grocers that pioneered this development some years ago is one that used in earlier years to do a considerable middle-class trade in the district. The manager said: 'The arrival of the West Indians was a shot in the arm for local trade. We pioneered the idea of stocking their own foods, and others are now copying us as they find white custom decreasing. But the Jamaicans are loyal – they stick to a place that pleases them. They are good spenders and very particular. We now sell 10 cwt. of rice a week, dried cod fish, dried pork and ackee, and all kinds of beans, spices, tinned yams, coconut butter, etc.'

A small Jewish tailor in the same area, stocking a gay selection of men's clothes, had an advertisement in the window that read: 'Material made up in any style: English, American, Edwardian, and West Indian.' He said: 'I personally like them. They spend well, take a long time over their choice, and are particular about their purchases. They like bright colours and wide peg-top trousers, not Edwardian suits.'[1]

In the market a toy-stall owner said: 'We have a lot of West Indian customers. They buy good-class toys to send home to their children, but they won't look at a coloured doll. It has to be a blonde with blue eyes, and we've learned not to suggest the others.' This observation was confirmed by a salesgirl in a multiple store in the main street.

Several vegetable stalls in the market have greatly increased their

---

[1] On the other hand, another Jewish businessman who ran a small dry-cleaning business nearby said he could not stand the bad manners and rudeness of his coloured clients; they were always losing their tickets and complaining. This informant planned to emigrate to South Africa, where he had relatives and 'where they keep the coloured people in their place'. (He returned in late 1959, considerably disillusioned.)

sales of cabbage, green and red peppers, onions, and pineapples, and have started to stock green bananas, mangoes, and avocados in season. Butchers and fishmongers have found an increase in their sales of chickens, the cheaper cuts for stewing, and such items as pigs' knuckles. One enterprising butcher even stocks goat meat 'specially slaughtered on our own farm in Surrey' for the festive 'curry goat and rice'. A record stall that was recently opened in the market does a large trade in West Indian calypsos, West African 'High Life', and pop music among coloured buyers. Furniture and clothing stores with hire-purchase facilities are also attracting an increasing volume of trade.

A number of hire-purchase wholesale firms which operate on a considerable scale from door to door in areas of close West Indian settlement have also adapted themselves to this new and increasingly lucrative type of trade. These firms use either their own white agents or, increasingly, coloured agents who work on commission in the evenings and at weekends as a sideline to their normal jobs. Chief among these firms is one whose catalogue includes everything from motor-cycles to radios and oil-stoves to baby clothes. A thriving business on a smaller scale is also done by a publishing firm which sells ornately bound and illustrated Bibles, cookery books (although there is no great sale for the latter among West Indians), editions of the classics, and so on.

All parts of Brixton market and the surrounding streets are patronized by coloured customers, but the stalls nearest the Cold-harbour Lane entrance tend to attract the majority of coloured shoppers. White people are more in evidence in the other sections, but many now avoid shopping on a Friday or Saturday, when almost all West Indians do their shopping. Some local Brixton women claim that the coloured women shoppers are pushing and aggressive, and that there are men around who take the latter's part if there is an argument.[1] Such incidents may have occurred, and two or three have actually been reported in the local press,[2] but I have had no personal

[1] A local factory manager who lives in a middle-class district near Brixton said in 1958: 'They reckon Brixton belongs to them. My wife doesn't like going to the market any more. The noise and the B.O. are the worst things about them.' A West Indian professional woman who lives nearby and shops in the market once a week also told me that she avoided these days because she disliked the 'market habits' of most migrants and could understand that stallkeepers and local people might also find them annoying.

[2] See *South London Press*, 6 March and 30 October 1959. The earlier report gave an objective account of what was later blown up by some other papers, local and national, as the 'Brixton Market Riot'. An altercation between a woman stall-keeper and a West Indian woman customer began over the issue of handling toma-toes. The customer hit the stallkeeper and the dispute spread. The customer left and returned with her husband and some friends. The fight was quelled after half an hour by the police.

experience of them. Nor, in the course of several years of shopping and walking about in Brixton, did I detect any differential treatment of coloured clients. They were served in turn, and were addressed as 'Sir' or 'Madam', 'dearie', or by their proper names in the same way as anybody else, whatever the vendors' private opinions might be.[1]

Only a few firms have actually come into existence to meet the newcomers' needs, and most of these are coloured-owned (see p. 382 below). There is, however, a grocery business run by a young and enterprising local businessman some miles away from the Brixton centre which has an almost entirely West Indian clientèle. This grocer's West Indian trade began when he noticed that after migrants moved into the area stocks of rice and chick-peas were selling out much faster than usual, and he made it his business to ascertain and stock their preferred foods. Most of his business is done through deliveries of regular weekly orders; unlike most other firms, this firm employs coloured staff behind the counter.

In general, the presence of a large number of West Indian migrants has so far done little more than give a fillip to local trade and commerce. Brixton is the main shopping centre for a wide surrounding area which includes middle-class Norwood and Dulwich, and the bulk of local trade is still done with white people. In the good-class establishments there is still a feeling that the local public would not like to be served by coloured staff, and coloured employees are rarely seen in Brixton, despite the difficulty of obtaining staff at all. One multiple cut-price store has a few coloured assistants, and they are also to be seen behind the counter of a large local cafeteria, as usherettes in a large local cinema, and in one or two small shops in the market area.

In some other areas of coloured settlement in Britain it has been claimed that coloured people pay more than locals, not only for houses and rented rooms, but for other types of service and even for food and clothing. Undoubtedly a 'colour tax' operates in housing in Brixton, but I found no evidence there of consistent over-charging for goods. In view of the fact that many of the smaller traders do considerable business with coloured customers and that prices of

---

[1] A wide variety of attitudes among a hundred Brixton market stallholders or assistants emerges in an as yet unpublished survey by Miles Wohlers. A fairly large minority considered the West Indians more difficult than local customers or than other white immigrants in the area. Main objections were to buying habits (bargaining, fingering perishable goods, slowness in buying) and to rude, aggressive, and noisy behaviour. The attitudes of those with a larger proportion of coloured customers were more favourable than the others, which might suggest either that closer acquaintance improves relationships, or that coloured people tend to buy from a sympathetic vendor.

goods in the large firms are usually clearly marked, it is difficult to see how such a 'colour tax' could operate or persist. It is also difficult to imagine that the large group of coloured people now established in the area would tolerate it. On the contrary, West Indian newcomers tend to bargain and expect a makeweight or *braata* on their purchases, as at home – an attitude which on occasion is said to lead to friction with stallkeepers and impatient local customers.[1]

The reception accorded by local tradesmen in Brixton to the coloured newcomers is on the whole sufficiently cordial to ease their accommodation to everyday life in Britain. These shopkeepers and their staffs are among the migrants' most frequent white contacts, and the friendly, almost joking, relationships so often observed between them may go far to mitigate the effect of the unexpected or unintentional snubs encountered by the migrants elsewhere.

The only local businessmen for whom the coloured migrants have brought any particular problems are landlords and boarding-house keepers,[2] publicans, café and restaurant owners, and dance-hall proprietors. Usually their reactions are dictated by similar considerations of economic expediency: they are based on the anticipation of public objections and loss of trade, and on the belief that if any or too many coloured people are allowed in the establishment it will become known as a 'coloured' one and thereby lose its character and status.

The question of status again emerged during investigation of the relationships between white professional men, particularly doctors and dentists, and coloured clients in the area. Two general practitioners with a partly middle-class practice have found it expedient to set up a second consulting-room in the area nearest the largest coloured settlement and to request their coloured patients to attend there along with other local working-class white patients. A coloured doctor long settled in an area some miles to the south has adopted the same practice, also to avoid antagonizing his middle-class white patients. The latter come to the consulting-room at his private house; all others, white or coloured, go to his other surgery in a working-class district.

There is not much material to be drawn from the Brixton area on the subject of the 'categoric' relationships between white customers and coloured businessmen or professional men. Before the arrival of the recent migrants, quite a number of coloured medical

---

[1] Cf. *Going to Britain?* (BBC publication, 1960, p. 29) in which migrants are advised on suitable behaviour in a London street market.

[2] See pp. 195-7 above for the attitudes of house agents with a large number of coloured clients.

men, Indian, West Indian, and African, succeeded in building up a white practice in South London, though not in Brixton itself. This does not seem to have been done without difficulty and unpleasantness, but those interviewed were well established professionally and were highly regarded members of local society. Most of their patients were said to be from the working class. Two of these informants suggested that any aversion to colour among such patients was more than outweighed by the prevalent belief that Indian or Negro doctors might possess not only Western professional skills but also some magical formulae or 'secrets of the mysterious East'.[1]

The handful of coloured small tradesmen who have recently set up in business to cater for the needs of the growing coloured buying public appear to attract a certain amount of white custom, but do not go out of their way to do so. An exception to this was found in a tailoring establishment in Battersea. It is owned and run by a West Indian old-timer with a small white staff. He built up a local trade long before any number of West Indian migrants arrived in South London, and his firm makes no particular attempt to cater for coloured clients. Asked about relationships at work, this informant said that neither among his staff nor among his clients did he notice any awareness of his colour. He regarded himself and felt that he was regarded as a Londoner.

CONTACTS IN PLACES OF RECREATION

A more intimate kind of casual contact between migrants and local people occurs in public places of recreation,[2] such as cinemas, billiard halls, dance halls, cafés, pubs, and hotels.[3] Local cinemas apply no bar, and indeed some managers single out their coloured clients as being particularly quiet and orderly. There were at the time

---

[1] This was the main reason advanced as late as the early 1950s in race-conscious South Africa for the continued attendance of large numbers of white patients, usually of the poorer classes, on Malay, Indian, and African doctors. See Patterson (1953, p. 256).

[2] An increasing amount of contact is also taking place in establishments where betting or gambling is permitted, such as greyhound tracks (Catford is the nearest to Brixton) or, more recently, bingo halls in the district itself. Bingo has attracted many West Indian adherents, and here again their visible success has aroused resentment among some. As the *South London Press* columnist wrote: 'I heard the other day the latest in race prejudice from an embittered poor white: "These coloureds", she said, "they win all the prizes at bingo" ' (1 September 1961).

[3] There are few residential hotels in Brixton. From the accounts of the few coloured people in Brixton who have spent any period away from home on holiday or business it would seem that they try to make advance reservations at a hotel known to take coloured people.

of my field work no local dance halls,[1] so coloured men usually went to the Locarno on Streatham Hill or to the big West End dance halls. At none of these is there at present any official bar against entry, but some coloured men complain that white girls frequently refuse to dance with them, only to accept offers from white men immediately afterwards. Such statements are difficult to verify. In some cases they may be accurate, in view of the widespread local disapproval of association between white women and coloured men. In August 1958 there was a brief period of colour discrimination at the Locarno, following a ruling by the nation-wide Mecca chain that coloured men would not be admitted without their own partners on rock-and-roll nights (Mondays). The measure was said to have been introduced because of rivalry between coloured and white dancers over girls, which resulted in fist and knife fights at some halls. Street brawls of this kind had occurred in July 1958 and on earlier occasions outside the Locarno.[2]

Contacts between migrants and local people in cafés and restaurants are relatively few, since West Indians prefer where possible to eat their regional food at home. Those who are forced to eat out tend to go to cheap and unpretentious eating-places where objections to their presence would probably not be raised. A handful of coloured youths frequent the various local cafés patronized by white teddy boys or near teddy boys. An informant claimed that they mixed amicably, except for an occasional squabble or fight, but

---

[1] 'It is a pity Lambeth Council gave up its mixed dancing some years ago. I met plenty of coloured folk then, and have kept in touch with some of them. What strikes me and everyone who actually meets foreigners or Britons of other colours is not the differences but the similarities. We have far more resemblances than differences, I find' ('Wanderers's' column, *South London Press*, 24 October 1958). As an index of increasing acceptance, it is instructive to compare this comment with the leader in the same paper four years earlier (20 August 1954) attacking the idea of holding a 'Jamaica Night' at the Town Hall.

[2] See *South London Press*, 8 and 15 August 1958, and *West Indian Gazette*, September–October 1958. The later *South London Press* report contained the information that some years earlier there had been a total colour bar at the Locarno, which was built and first run by a South African. A Gallup Poll (58/33) was taken in June 1958, following the introduction of a colour bar at the Scala ballroom, Wolverhampton. The overall results were: Approve—22 per cent; Disapprove— 62 per cent; Don't know— 16 per cent. Breakdowns by sex, age, class, voting intention, and region showed interesting variations. More men than women disapproved; disapproval was highest in the two younger and the oldest age-groups, lowest in the 35–44 age-groups. Upper-class respondents had very definite views pro or con (Approve—40 per cent; Disapprove—58 per cent; Don't know – 2 per cent); while the middle class was more approving than the lower class. Voting intention made relatively little difference to attitudes, except that more Conservatives and those who were uncertain of their voting intentions were uncertain about their attitude over the dance-hall ban. Of the geographical regions, London and the North of England showed a high response for 'Approve' (27 per cent and 31 per cent respectively), while the South, Midlands, and Scotland were below the overall total.

that most cliques or gangs were all-white or all-coloured.[1] During the 1956–58 period I myself did not see any coloured people in the few middle-class cafés and restaurants in the area, but after some discreet questioning I got the impression that middle-class, well-dressed, coloured people entering these places with an air of assurance would not be treated any differently from other clients.[2] A few visits with middle-class coloured friends to such establishments just outside the Brixton area were entirely uneventful, but no conclusions can be drawn from this in view of the presence of a white sponsor. It can, however, be said that the relatively few middle-class coloured people in the area seem to avoid attending local places of entertainment or recreation where they might be identified with the mass of working-class coloured migrants. Instead, they go to the West End or to the Kensington, Earls Court, and Bayswater districts, where coloured students and professional people are more established and accepted. Often they prefer to go to Indian or Chinese restaurants, either because they can be sure of a correct reception, or because they find the food more inviting.

In Britain, contacts in pubs have always involved a certain process of voluntary selection. There is no constraint on the artisan in working clothes to drink in the public bar, nor on the clerk or commercial traveller to choose the saloon bar, nor the old ladies the private bar. Yet most habitual pub-goers have their preferred place in their preferred local, where they regularly meet an informal group of associates whom they may not necessarily meet elsewhere. The unwritten protocol of such groupings is rarely infringed by those British strangers who drop in casually and unobtrusively for a drink and who are thoroughly familiar with the unspoken rules. But these rules may be trampled on unwittingly by groups of half-apprehensive, half-aggressive West Indians, who are more used to the conviviality of the village rum shop.

In the early years of the Brixton coloured settlement, there were

---

[1] In late 1960 and again in 1961, I was told that the teddy-boy problem in Brixton had become much less acute, and that the majority of those who wore black jackets and other currently fashionable gear were not particularly vicious or aggressive. They were beginning to frequent the coloured basement clubs. A new development was that white teenage youths on motor-scooters were said to be coming into the area to fraternize with local coloured teenage girls, of whom an increasing number could be noticed. My informant thought that this development might cause some initial friction but might in the long run be conducive to assimilation. He added, significantly: 'All the coloured girls and boys speak with a cockney accent now – that helps, because the locals really can't understand the older ones.'

[2] A light-coloured, self-assured nurse living in Camberwell said that during her eight-year stay in England she had never encountered any discrimination in such places. She added that she was not on the look-out for it and thought that this might influence the reaction of the restaurateur or waitress.

several incidents in which coloured people were refused service or asked to leave public houses. These have almost ceased, partly as a consequence of the action of a group of middle-class coloured people and white sponsors, including an LCC member, who took a few test cases before the licensing authorities. At present, the position seems to be that those West Indians (usually men) who drink outside their homes or the coloured clubs[1] have established their own 'locals'. Here they are sure of a reception, and have accepted local pub *mores* sufficiently to enable them to instruct newcomers.[2] This infiltration has undoubtedly caused some former habitués to go elsewhere, but the licensees have accepted the situation with reasonable grace, helped possibly by the knowledge that the coloured men are good spenders who usually prefer short expensive drinks to the Englishman's beer or ale.

Even in the 'locals' favoured by coloured migrants, the principle of voluntary selection usually holds good. Let us take for example a pub which is in the heart of the coloured settlement area, on a street corner where a dozen or more coloured men habitually congregate. This large, old-fashioned house has a saloon bar with a snack counter, an upright piano, red leather seats, and some palms. It also has a small private bar, and two public bars separated by partitions. All bars are served by the same staff from a circular

[1] Some contact occurs between migrants and local people in the coloured-owned clubs. This can lead to friction and conflict but is on the whole amicable because the whites are self-selecting and go because they enjoy the atmosphere, music, and company. The main impact of the increasing number of coloured clubs on local people is of course through their frequent nuisance value (noise, crowds, parking of cars, and lowered residential amenities). See p. 365 below for a further discussion of coloured-owned clubs.

[2] The highly publicized 'colour bar' at the Milkwood Tavern, Herne Hill, which was brought up by the Lambeth Trades Council as a reason for opposing the renewal of the licence at the licensing session on 16 February 1959 (see *South London Press,* 17 February 1959), turned out to be only a partial bar. The licensee claimed that he continued to serve coloured people known to him, that he served West Indian busmen, employed a West Indian woman, and that two coloured men were members of the loan club and one of the darts team. He had, however, refused to serve coloured people unknown to him after 'undesirable coloured men', sometimes accompanied by 'white women of dubious character', started using the Tavern in 1955. The licensee agreed that he would make no further distinction on the basis of skin colour, and the Bench renewed the licence. If the licensee's contentions are accepted, this case would appear to support both the 'colour-class' and the 'stranger' hypotheses. An interesting sidelight on the case emerged when a local family protested that they had been 'embarrassed by the case because the reference clearly referred to them and they are English'. The *South London Press* (20 February 1959) went on to say: '*The family are dark-skinned because from 1921 to 1932 they lived in India* (my italics). Mr. N., an auditor on the Bengal Railway then, died in England a few years ago. He was English. His widow, Mrs. F. N., was born in Brixton.' See also *South London Press* (25 July 1958) for a reference to the ban imposed on coloured patrons by the landlord of the Robin Hood and Little John in Deptford Church Street, after fights involving coloured men.

central counter. The saloon bar always contains a majority of local whites, ranging from artisans in their best clothes to clerks, market traders, and businessmen, with a sprinkling of raddled old ladies, said to be former theatrical 'pros', drinking pink gins and nursing lap dogs. There are usually a few prosperous and well-dressed coloured men in groups, and occasionally a coloured man with a white girl. The small private bar is entirely filled by elderly women of the superior charwoman type, drinking Guinness or a port and lemon. The smaller public bar is usually filled with coloured men, while the larger public bar is divided about equally between elderly white artisans, usually in working clothes, and rather flashy white women, usually with coloured men. Coloured and white men rarely seem to drink together.

The coloured penetration of the pubs has gone sufficiently far for some West Indians to be accepted as regulars and supported by the licensee against white outsiders. An incident at a Loughborough Junction pub in June 1956 provided an example of this. On leaving the pub on a Saturday night, a West Indian was attacked by a white man with a knife. The police arrived in time to prevent the growing crowd of white and coloured onlookers from joining in, and the licensee was quoted as saying: 'The attack was unprovoked. The Jamaican is a regular and I would call him a gentleman.'[1]

Casual contacts in such places of recreation as bars, cafés, and dance halls do of course provide the main opportunities for friction and open clashes between migrants and local people, just as they do between local people. Such places tend to attract a fair proportion of the young, the lonely, and the maladjusted of both sexes, and it is inevitable that from time to time incidents should occur, particularly if competition for a desirable commodity such as a dancing partner flares into overt conflict. But whereas in Nottingham one such incident led to the mass disturbances of August 1958, such friction in Brixton has not so far spread beyond the immediate actors and locality.

In all casual and superficial contacts, preconceived ideas may still be more potent than the experience itself, or may condition its interpretation. Local people who have never spoken to a coloured person may be firmly convinced that coloured people are indolent or aggressive, simply because they have seen a group of them waiting outside the employment exchange or sat behind a truculent individual on a bus. Coloured people, on their side, often find it difficult to understand that abruptness and the lack of any greeting or smile may be due not to their colour but to the general reserve of

[1] See *South London Press*, 28 June 1957, for a similar defence of a coloured 'regular' by a landlord.

British urban life, or to the fact that the individual is naturally grouchy, has a hangover or toothache, or quarrelled with his wife the evening before.

It would be difficult to indicate any general trend arising out of these innumerable casual contacts. The main effect in an area of large-scale settlement such as Brixton is, as was said earlier, to accustom the local population to the migrants' presence. 'There are so many darkies about now that Brixtonians take them for granted. While the majority cannot be said to accept them fully, they are resigned to their presence,' said one local informant. A Jewish tailor in the district illustrated this attitude further by citing a rueful local joke, later heard from several other sources.[1] This concerned a stallholder in Brixton market who, seeing a white customer among the Saturday morning crowd, greeted him with 'Dr. Livingstone, I presume?'

The following comment by an elderly office cleaner in 1958 seemed to sum up prevailing local attitudes fairly well:

'I've got a nice new flat in the Trust Buildings. No black people there yet anyway, though some of the women mind black babies. The babies are very pretty. But people here don't like it – everything's so crowded. The dark people fill the markets up, especially on a Saturday. They push and make others wait. They're often rude on the buses. At London Bridge my daughter says no one can get on and there are sometimes fights.

In Brixton they stand about and talk in crowds and no one can pass. The Black Maria's down Geneva and Somerleyton Roads most nights about 10. The black men fight over these white girls. You can see what *they* are. There's a man in Somerleyton Road who sits on the step playing his banjo and the children gather round. Another lies in bed every weekend with his feet out of the window. Funny, isn't it? Two men come along our street each morning to work regular as clockwork. One's dressed in all colours, pink cap, green shirt, etc., the other in a trilby. You should hear the first one laugh. Some of them really look quite nice.'

The bright colours and exotic styles of clothing affected by the immigrants, particularly by recent arrivals, and their resonant, differently accented voices and frequently uninhibited deportment in public have undoubtedly contributed to the general effect of strangeness and differentness which the immigrants' pigmentation tends to create. This does not necessarily evoke hostility. As a

[1] This joke later appeared in the *South London Press* (25 November 1960).

middle-class welfare worker from an adjacent borough said: 'I really enjoy coming to Brixton. It's pleasant to see the coloured folk around, young and lively, and brightly dressed. But I think local people's stand-offish attitudes arise out of a sense of strangeness and alienness, because of their different appearance and behaviour.'

Since 1958, however, there has been a noticeable changeover to drab, dark colours and to English-style clothing among migrants seen around in Brixton. Among the second generation audibility is also less, since most now speak with a cockney accent. A welfare worker with over ten years' experience of the area commented in late 1960 on the probable consequences of this decreased audibility and increased intelligibility: 'It furthers good relations and acceptance, because most of the locals really don't understand what the older ones are saying. I had trouble myself at first until I got used to the accent, but I still can't follow if they switch into dialect. Small wonder that some locals think that English isn't their mother tongue.'[1]

[1] On differences of accentuation, enunciation, and dialect, see Hyndman (1960, p. 92).

13

Associational contacts

IN BRITISH towns and cities organized social and cultural activities
are dwindling with the rise of the media of mass entertainment,
particularly television. The latter has driven its devotees out of the
pubs, the cinemas, the spectators' seats at sporting events, and the
political meetings, into innumerable small darkened rooms, where
social intercourse is limited to arguments about the choice of programme. 'Wanderer' wrote sadly in his column in the *South London
Press* of 5 April 1956:

> 'Old friends may live near each other nowadays and still never
> meet or know of each other's existence. . . . Why is local life so
> impersonal now? It seems a new population has come to the old
> villages and a rootless mass of us are living in "dormitory"
> suburbs as they do in Greater London. In fact I see more signs
> of social life out there in the long grass. Dances, whist drives,
> amateur theatricals, church socials, election controversies, are all
> shown in posters that have almost disappeared from our own
> asphalt jungle. We have lost so many street markets, music halls,
> and small picture palaces, and the pubs don't teem with life now.
> You won't see people dancing in the streets on Bank Holiday
> now. They're off in coaches to the coast. It may be a good loss,
> but now we are all very middle-class, in uniform collars and ties
> – and neighbours don't meet so much in multiple or chain stores.
> So we all sit at home looking at TV and "hardly see any of the
> old crowd any more". We see more people than ever, of course,
> but we don't know them. What I think we need is some new
> social life to take the place of the comradeship of the old days,
> when everyone knew everyone else in the street.'

The organizations of the receiving society fall into two main
categories as far as the immigrants are concerned: those already in
existence to meet local needs; and those interracial associations that
have arisen, usually at the instigation of one or more sponsors, to
cater for the needs of the newcomers or to promote inter-group
contact and cooperation. The associations that have arisen within
the coloured group itself are described in Chapter 17 below.

251

Social and cultural life

In spite of the decline of organized social activity and community feeling in the area, a surprising number of local organizations are in existence, catering for a wide range and variety of spiritual and secular needs. The *Lambeth Guide,* for instance, lists over 319 local organizations: of these 14 are concerned with the arts; 18 with sport; 24 with hobbies (aquarists, pets, flying, photography, gardening, magic, model railways, and philately) and 'miscellaneous pursuits' (British-Soviet friendship, film technique, nuclear disarmament, savings); 20 are social and general, including community settlements; 34 are concerned with welfare; 28 are old people's clubs; 36 are youth clubs and organizations; 15 are women's clubs; 7 are concerned with the voluntary defence services; 14 are service and ex-service clubs. The remainder of the list consists of 79 churches; 13 political party branches;[1] and 17 professional, trade, and industrial associations.

It was clearly impossible to cover this vast field of inquiry adequately, so I confined my interviews to those spiritual and lay organizations which, because of their functions and their geographical proximity to the main areas of settlement, seemed most likely to play some part in the early years of migrant-host accommodation. On the whole these tended to be the a-symmetrical type of association where something is done *for* an applicant, rather than the symmetrical assemblies of the like-minded where members cooperate *with* each other for certain ends.

The chief voluntary associations with which I was in contact in the Brixton area were: local churches of various denominations, secular welfare associations, children's societies, youth clubs, community centres, ex-servicemen's associations, sports clubs, and interracial associations.

THE CHURCHES

In many immigrant situations it has been found that of all associations the churches could play the most important part in aiding the early stages of accommodation. At that time of loneliness, frustration, and often poverty, immigrants, particularly those from simple backgrounds, turn in greater degree to their faith as a support. Most churches have a supra-national and universal message; and they are open to all, even the poorest. They offer not only a place of individual worship but one where spiritual and social communion may be sought with like-minded people, and where guidance and perhaps material assistance may be obtained from an established leader of the local community.

[1] At the time of this study most migrants were not concerned with British local or national politics, although various party organizers were already aware of their potential either as voters or as a local political issue.

252

As increasing numbers of West Indians began to arrive in Britain, the churches showed full awareness of their responsibilities towards the newcomers. As early as April 1950 the British Council of Churches urged the churches and their congregations to take every opportunity of promoting the welfare of non-European students and workers, and recommended that the government set up a national advisory panel to coordinate all voluntary work on their behalf. Since then there have been relatively few public policy statements from any of the churches, but after the Notting Hill disturbances in 1958 the Executive Committee of the British Council of Churches issued a downright statement on behalf of all its member churches condemning colour prejudice and hostility and expressing its opposition to any restriction on immigration.[1] The Council and member churches have also set up a number of high-level special committees to promote the welfare and integration of the newcomers.

The welcoming attitude and policy of church leaders are not in doubt. But it is at parish and individual level that the welcome has to be translated into action. The main tasks facing the parishes have been: first, to make contact with the migrants; second, to get them to church; and, third, to induce them to attend regularly and participate actively in parish life after the initial contact has been made.[2] This third task involves the additional problem of ensuring that the local congregation will receive the newcomers in a friendly and understanding way.

Some ministers have tackled these tasks energetically, while others, perhaps the majority, have adopted a *laissez-faire* attitude. In the Brixton area only a handful of ministers were reported to be apathetic on the matter, or actively unwilling to accept coloured people as regular members of their congregation.[3] It was not possible to track down to its source the story frequently repeated by West Indians, about a friend, or the friend of a friend, who after his first visit to a church was asked by the minister not to come back as the white congregation would not like it. On the one occasion on

[1] See the Institute of Race Relations' collective publication, *Coloured Immigrants in Britain* (1960, pp. 148-50), for the text of these and for a detailed account of statements and action by the British Council of Churches and individual churches over the 1950s. See also the Council's pamphlet *Your Neighbour from the West Indies* (1955), and the Church Information Office's handbook *Together in Britain* (1960), for church initiatives to provide information to local parishes about the newcomers and their background.
[2] In 1955 the British Institute of Public Opinion asked a West Indian migrant sample: 'Do you go to church or chapel? Or has anyone invited you to attend?' To these questions, 33 per cent replied that they attended, 8 per cent that they had been asked but did not go, and 59 per cent that they had not thought about it.
[3] Cf. *Church of England Newspaper* (24 February 1961) for the views of the vicar of one Brixton parish, who was reported as advocating immigration restriction.

which an actual name and church were stated, these turned out to
be those of a minister who had started the first interracial social
club in Brixton. The story continues to crop up from West Indian
informants, however, and has, in the view of a West Indian minister
with whom I discussed the matter, become a rationalization of the
immigrants' own failure to attend church as regularly as they did in
the West Indies.

West Indian informants usually gloss over the practical reasons
for not attending church in the new environment, and prefer to give
reasons which shift the responsibility away from themselves. 'I went
into church the first Sunday I was here but everybody stared so I
never went back.' 'At home the minister stand by the door and
shake hands with all the congregation and everyone greet one
another, but here nobody say a word of welcome.' 'Why should I
go to church here when the white people themselves don't go? When
in Rome do as the Romans do.' 'I can't enjoy my church here, the
church so cold and empty and nobody sing.'[1] 'When I go in the
minister ask everyone to welcome our black brother as if I some
wild man from the jungle. I never go back there.'[2] 'In Jamaica the
minister tell us we all brothers in Christ, and Great Britain a
Christian country. But here they don't treat us in a Christian way.'[3]
'Some people say the English people wrote the Bible so that they
can keep we coloured people under.' 'The men in the factory think
of Sunday as "double time", not God's day.'

These statements reflect a combination of disappointed expectations about Britain and of initial reactions to the strangeness and
complexity of a new environment. These reactions may be strengthened by an existing chip-on-the-shoulder attitude in the immigrant
himself. Only rarely do they seem to have been provoked by active
rejection on the part of local ministers or congregations.

In Brixton the initial response of local congregations to the
migrants was usually rather more benevolent, as befitted practising
Christians, than that of the average local resident. But this response
was not always devoid of a mildly patronizing flavour, thanks to

[1] This lack of warmth was borne out in a statement by the Archdeacon of Derby,
the Ven. A. F. Richardson, quoted by the *Daily Express* on 17 May 1957:
'A public house provides more fellowship than any church in England. People go
to church as individuals and leave as individuals with no feelings for others at all.'

[2] West Indians are particularly sensitive about anything that smacks of the missionary approach. A West Indian minister said to me: 'After all, we've been
Christians for hundreds of years. We even send missionaries to Africa ourselves!'

[3] 'No wonder there is general bewilderment among those who come to England
– England where the missionaries come from. Many have been brought up in places
where Christianity means something very real, and they cannot understand. . . .
There is, fortunately, sometimes another side to it. It is thrilling when we do see
people from overseas welcomed into a Christian fellowship' (the Rev. David Shep-
pard writing in the *Daily Mail*, 28 December 1956).

254

generations of missionary activity, which is strongly fostered in South London. For the most part local congregations did not envisage the need to adapt or enlarge their own ideas, or to provide a less reserved reception than they would normally give to any newcomer.

By the time a few West Indians appeared in church, most members of the congregation had already had occasion to acquire some superficial first-hand notions about them, their way of living, and in particular certain family patterns which did not conform to local patterns, much less to Christian patterns as these local people understood them. There were some stares at the newcomers in a congregation, for the most part friendly but not without some reserve or even apprehension. Some of the more staid and formal nonconformist congregations were a little taken aback by the bright clothes, informal behaviour, and energetic way in which the newcomers sang and otherwise participated in the services.

In this area, as elsewhere, the Anglican Church has felt it a particular duty as the established church to make contact with the newcomers. Through its moral welfare organization it has been active in helping women in need, and it has set up coordinating committees to cover other aspects of migrant welfare. At parish level, however, it has been found that only a small number of migrants are regular attenders. These are usually relatively well-educated persons from the skilled artisan, clerical, or professional classes which made up the bulk of the Anglican congregations in the West Indies.

Anglican worship in the West Indies differs little from that in this country, except perhaps in the size of the regular attendance. Anglican immigrants do not, therefore, find any great differences here as do sectarian worshippers, except that some Brixton churches tend to be 'Low', while the tendency in the West Indies is towards the High Church ritual. For West Indians, however, attendance is primarily a community activity with a status value. Where there are no communal ties, as in England, they tend, like the English themselves, to stay away except for the great annual festivals, marriages, and christenings. The truly devout minority, however, usually find their way to the nearest church and establish themselves as members of the congregation.[1]

A good example of the function of the orthodox churches in

[1] An elderly lady who has been in England for some years, and who spends much of her week at the church, had some scathing comments to make about compatriots who explained their non-attendance by the fact that people stared and they felt out of place: 'Most of them didn't go to church at home anyway. Godly people go to church and pray and listen to the minister. They don't have to look around and pay attention to other people.'

creating or reinforcing social solidarity among Jamaicans of all classes in the migrant environment as well as at home was provided after the appalling Jamaican train crash in late 1957. At the initiative of Sir Hugh Foot, the then Governor of Jamaica, who was on leave in London, a memorial service was held in Clapham Parish Church. Although this service was arranged at very short notice, messages were sent out all over London over the usual unofficial migrant grape-vine, and a congregation of between 600 and 800 Jamaicans of all classes attended the service. One elderly Jamaican woman, a regular Anglican church-goer here, commented: 'It was the finest service I ever did attend here – the church full and everyone singing lustily. Afterwards we talked with our friends outside. Sir Hugh and his Lady shake hands with us and say they remember me from home – and I meet all sorts of people I never know to be here in England at all.' The vicar appealed to those migrants resident in the neighbourhood to attend regularly in the future. This appeal apparently went unheard, for the West Indian attendance on succeeding Sundays reverted to the usual small number of regular members of the congregation.

Anglicans are in a minority among recent immigrants but most Anglican churches in the area have their handful of West Indian regulars; some of these act as servers, sing in the choir, or even serve on parochial councils. Those who were interviewed seemed to be fairly well settled economically and residentially; they were formally married and in general well accommodated to British society. A parish priest described them as 'the settled type who live in more than one room'. Their participation in church life would seem to be both an affirmation of their relatively high socio-economic status in the West Indies and a means of maintaining or even improving it here. Regular church-going, apart from its status value, provides an opportunity for further infiltration into local society. Informants of this type usually claim to be on visiting terms with a number of white families, and invite the minister to attend major social functions at their homes.

A problem for local ministers is to attract not only this relatively well-adapted and acceptable handful, but also the great majority of the unsettled, the maladjusted, and the transients. For this purpose, the faithful handful are not necessarily their most helpful assistants, since they are likely to regard the introduction of such people as damaging to their own position. In several parishes, however, ministers and coloured parishioners have over the last few years actively attempted to attract these others into the fold. The history of two such attempts in the Brixton neighbourhood is worth recording.

The first one was made several years ago by an energetic and ambitious young West Indian professional man who had been in the Air Force during the war and wished to start a social club for migrants. The local vicar encouraged the plan and gave him the use of the church hall, in the hope that some members might be induced to attend services as well. The organizing was left entirely to the West Indian, and for some months there was a regular club attendance of from twenty to thirty. During the next winter the organizer was away for several weeks. When he came back he found that the group had fallen apart, after a life of only six months. He attributed this to the members' fatigue at the end of the working day, to the hard winter, to members' frequent changes of lodging which took them away from the vicinity, and to internal quarrels. He was anxious to try again, but felt that at that stage West Indians probably preferred to be left alone; to attend a social club of their own was something that most of them had not done back home, and it represented an extra effort. The big city 'stupefied' many of them, and their main aim was simply to make money and to go home. The majority did not fulfil the vicar's expectations by joining his congregation. A comment in the *Church Times* (18 March 1955) attributed the failure of this particular club to the fact that it 'degenerated into a dance hall for coloured men and white girls'.

This indirect attempt to attract West Indians to the church having failed, the vicar tried again. He allowed a non-ordained West Indian preacher to hold regular sectarian meetings in the church hall, in the hope that the group, which was a branch of the American-oriented Church of God,[1] might ultimately be brought into some kind of communion with the parish. When he made this request, however, the group went elsewhere. This reaction is not particularly surprising, for there could never have been much hope of persuading any regular adherents of this lively sect to desert it for the formality of Anglicanism. At this stage the vicar gave up further efforts and simply accepted those immigrants who came to services. His experience served as a deterrent to other ministers, most of whom had quite enough to do with their normal parish work.[2]

In another South London parish a young curate of exceptional energy, ability, and imagination, himself not English-born, initiated a drive to gather in the newcomers. He too worked through a group of potential coloured leaders. In this case, however, they were West African students, whom he organized into a regular discussion

[1] See Chapter 17 for a more detailed account of this sectarian group.
[2] In late 1959 I learned that another social and cultural club had been started at this church on the initiative of some West Indian members of the congregation. This was still in existence in 1961.

group. Finding little response to notices and appeals, the curate and his helpers conducted a door-to-door search for coloured people in the parish. 'We would mark the houses where the curtains were drawn all day and then go along to call on them at night.'[1]

As a result of these door-to-door exhortations, a small number of West Indian migrants were induced to attend services, and several dozen came along to the two socials organized by the parish and attended by the Bishop, the Mayor, and other local dignitaries. I attended the second of these functions and was impressed by the unforced friendliness of the local parishioners, mainly artisan and lower middle class, who had turned up in strength. The coloured people present were divided between the student group and their friends, mainly West Africans, and the more settled West Indian artisans, elaborately dressed, and hiding their uncertainty behind a formal manner. The curate later deplored the fact that his efforts had not succeeded in bringing in the group of lonely and unsettled recent arrivals who were probably most in need of advice and help. He also commented on the way in which the West Indians and West Africans kept apart at the socials, and thought that the fact that his action group was West African and of the student class might have had a deterrent effect on those West Indian working-class migrants whom they had approached.

A few weeks after the second social the curate was transferred and the most active student returned to West Africa. The rest of the group fell apart, no further socials were held, and coloured attendance at the church fell off as people moved out of the area. This pattern was to be duplicated in a number of other interracial enterprises, whose continuance was found to depend almost entirely on the ceaseless efforts of a sponsor.

One or two similar attempts at promoting active religious integration were noted in South London. But, in general, local Anglican vicars, like the ministers of most other denominations, have adopted a more or less benevolent *laissez-faire* attitude towards the bulk of the newcomers.[2] With this sometimes goes a somewhat patronizing toleration of what one minister called 'their tendency to moral weakness', by which he meant their unstable conjugal patterns. The

---

[1] The permanently drawn curtains, combined with an absence of net curtains, are a good rough guide to West Indian tenancy, originally pointed out to me by a public health inspector.

[2] For instance, the vicar of St. Saviour's Church, Brixton Hill, wrote in his parish magazine in 1958: 'Italians and Cypriots have all moved into the parish quietly. Immigrants must, if they hope for a welcome, move discreetly and adapt themselves to our ways and standards.' A more positive attitude was displayed in the *Camberwell Chronicle*, parish newspaper of St. George's, Camberwell (see issue for mid-February 1960).

minister usually welcomes those who attend service, gives advice or help when asked, marries or christens those who present themselves. 'If the couple calling the banns give the same address, I don't trouble them with my usual little pre-wedding talk,' said one vicar; 'and I've got used to the fact that the bride will wear white even if she is six months with child. But, oh, how I wish they'd turn up punctually! It's always half an hour afterwards and usually more, however much you warn them not to be late.'

The reactions of a local congregation seem to be conditioned by the individual minister. If a minister acts as a sponsor he can dispel uncertainty and apprehension among his congregation. It is in such parishes that one finds more regular coloured church-goers, particularly if the minister has avoided the sponsor's pitfall of appearing to patronize the migrants. Yet the welcome accorded cannot go far beyond the normal behaviour of the local people. It may therefore continue to strike newcomers as reserved and cool until they understand it better. The reception accorded to the migrants may also be modified by other factors. To quote the vicar of a parish long identified with the group that carried through the abolition of slavery: 'In this church of all churches we must do something for the coloured people. Everyone is friendly and willing to help, but, you know how it is today, they are all too busy to go out and offer their help without being asked.'

The church authorities are not entirely satisfied with the situation. For years there has been talk of appointing a coloured curate or even a coloured vicar in areas largely settled by West Indians, such as Brixton, but most authorities are afraid that such a move might be construed and condemned as segregationist. One coloured West Indian minister to whom I talked, however, thought it would be a realistic and acceptable move. Meanwhile a positive step has been taken with the appointment of a chaplain to West Indian immigrants in the London area.[1]

Other denominations have also made similar efforts and had similar experiences with the migrants.[2] The Methodist Church evolved an excellent system of introductory postcards for migrating members of West Indian Methodist congregations. These would, it was hoped, enable Methodist migrants to be brought into the local congregations as soon as they settled down. The plan was to some extent defeated by the fact that most migrants, except for the extremely devout, mislaid their cards or forgot to send them in. And

[1] This is a priest seconded from the Kingston see, whose stipend, residence, and travelling expenses are covered by the dioceses of Southwark and London.

[2] For the rather special experience of the local Unitarian congregation, see p. 357 below.

most of those who did come in are said to have reacted with the same apathy or avoidance as the Anglican migrants.

Relatively few Brixton migrants are Roman Catholics.[1] Those whom I encountered seemed to be fairly perfunctory in their church attendance, but, as a local parish priest said, 'no more than the rest of my flock'. A few had arrived with letters of introduction from West Indian priests, and it was thought that more could be done in this direction. A local section of the Legion of Mary also contains a special 'West Indian Praesidium', concerned with the spiritual and material needs and problems of the migrants.

Because of their style of worship, the Baptist churches have been rather more successful in attracting and holding coloured worshippers than have most other demoninations. Nevertheless, even in the congregation which would appear to have the most attractive service and the most lively minister, a 'saved woman' of about 40 years from Brown's Town in Jamaica lamented: 'I can't enjoy my church here. It's half empty and they don't sing heartily. There's no choir either. Back home in Brown's Town the church was like heaven, with the choir singing like angels.' The minister of this church, a youngish and energetic North American, gave a fairly optimistic picture of his work among West Indians. He had about ten coloured members, of whom two were sidesmen, and many more adherents or casual attendants, particularly on special occasions such as Easter, when fifty or more coloured worshippers might attend.

'We set a high standard for all our members, and require six months for full acceptance. One West Indian woman, a nurse from Barbados, is on our Executive. I have married a good number and have dedicated a number of coloured children. Some West Indian adults come for baptism, and I lend the church to them for their own meetings, though I don't approve of some of their practices.[2] We have had a coloured Evangelist to preach. There's a lot of immorality among the West Indians, but probably no more than among the whites. South London is a great mission field. Many whites and coloured people are just formal Christians. It's faith, not only works, that counts. Hell is real, the right path is narrow, and only a few are saved. Repentance, and making a decision for Christian salvation, are the only right way for coloured or white.'

[1] Trinidad, British Guiana, and the Windward Islands (formerly French) have a far higher proportion of Roman Catholics than Jamaica, Barbados, and the Leeward Islands have. On published statements by the Roman Catholic hierarchy see *Coloured Immigrants in Britain* (Institute of Race Relations, 1960, pp. 151–2).

[2] These were meetings of one of the Church of God sectarian groups (see pp. 355-60 below).

The Salvation Army has been active among the migrants in some areas of Britain, notably Birmingham, but reported little contact with the migrants in Brixton because of their high mobility, although small groups were said to attend services. It was not possible to make contact with all the other denominations in the Brixton area, but it was learned that some West Indians attend local Congregationalist churches,[1] whose evangelical flavour they find appealing. Of the local pentecostal sects, it was interesting to note that the Elim (Four Square Gospel Association) had attracted few West Indians, although it is strong in the West Indies. On the other hand, the local Seventh Day Adventist church drew large numbers of West Indians, and by 1960 it had virtually 'taken over' and become a separatist sectarian group (see p. 355, n. 1). In general it was noted that the Adventists have been most successful in transferring and holding their migrant members, probably because of their extreme door-to-door proselytizing zeal and the warm welcome extended to new-comers not only by the pastor but by members of the congregation.

On the whole, the churches in South London have not so far succeeded in becoming a major agency for promoting closer migrant-host relations in the religious and social spheres. They have, however, done a good deal to modify ignorance and antipathy among their own congregations, thereby preparing the ground for later acceptance. This work is, of course, limited by the fact that the regular church-goers are themselves a minority in South London as in other urban areas. In the near future the churches may find it easier to make and maintain contact with West Indian migrants by persuading them, if not to attend services themselves, at least to send their children to Sunday school, as was the almost universal custom in the West Indies.[2]

It is in their ancillary welfare services that the churches, and particularly the Anglican Church, have come into most direct contact with the immigrants. These services have included assistance for unmarried mothers,[3] the provision of hostel accommodation for women, and so on. In such activities, members of the Society of Friends, whose austere form of worship would be unlikely to appeal to most migrants,[4] have also played an important part.

[1] Cf. Clifford S. Hill (1958), a Congregationalist minister, for a vivid account of his work with West Indian migrants in North-West London.

[2] In 1960 an energetic Anglican vicar made a move in this direction by starting a Sunday school class in a Somerleyton Road room.

[3] The National Council for the Unmarried Mother and her Child has also helped a number of such cases in the Brixton area.

[4] This lack of doctrinal appeal was recognized by one Quaker social worker, who said: 'Something should be worked out for them on a natural and spontaneous basis; outdoor services with singing, testifying, and Bible reading would be a good thing.'

Among the most active of church welfare organizations in South London is the Church of England Moral Welfare Association. This organization is concerned with the moral aspect of family welfare. A major part of its work is with unmarried mothers, who are often referred to local moral welfare workers by hospital almoners. In practice it may involve a great deal more than moral welfare counselling. It may, for instance, include advice, material help, and mediation in getting allowances and arranging adoptions, affiliation orders, and similar services. Such work fills a number of gaps between the various state and local welfare agencies, and supplies the personal touch that these may lack, thereby furthering the individual's accommodation within the local group. Moral welfare workers are usually middle-aged women with a middle-class background. They are not necessarily in possession of a recognized social work qualification. Considerable variety of individual attitude towards the migrants and their problems was noted, from apprehension and avoidance to sponsorship. One moral welfare worker in the area became such a noted sponsor that her name is still recalled with nostalgia by the women she helped, although it is some years since she moved to another post out of London.

Moral welfare workers have increasingly been called upon to act as intermediaries between West Indian newcomers and local society. At the end of 1955 about 10 per cent of all maternity cases handled by the Southwark diocesan organization involved West Indian women. By 1957 this proportion had risen to nearly 25 per cent but thereafter it dropped to an average of about 15 per cent of the increased overall total. This drop was not necessarily significant; some moral welfare workers suggested that as the migrants became more established more of the women had somewhere to go and therefore did not come to the organization for help. The number of cases in which West Indian mothers were helped in the Southwark diocese over these six years was 1,102, but in some cases the same individual was helped on two or three occasions.[1]

VOLUNTARY WELFARE ASSOCIATIONS

Of the lay voluntary associations that already existed to cater for the needs of the local population, those concerned with welfare have, as one would expect, so far played a larger part in migrant accommodation than those concerned with more purely cultural and recreational ends. The major part has of course been played by the agencies of the welfare state, but a considerable number of voluntary associations have acted as intermediaries and advisers, providing

[1] See Appendix VI for a tabulation of the work done for West Indian mothers by the two diocesan organizations south and north of the Thames.

legal and other advice, clothing, hostel accommodation, and other material assistance to the migrants. Some associations and some individual social workers have even acted as sponsors.

It should be stressed that these facilities are in most cases supplied not as part of a deliberate absorptive programme, as in many countries of immigration, but as part of the normal pattern of local life. They are usually available to all migrants who apply, but in practice only a small minority take advantage of them, either because the majority are ignorant of their existence or because not all migrants are willing to apply for assistance of any kind. Difficulties may also arise in the case of smaller local welfare associations, if organizers feel a certain reluctance to extend a full measure of assistance to migrants, on the grounds that 'our own people' have first claim on the resources of the association which was originally set up to serve local needs. This attitude was encountered on two occasions in Brixton. In two larger voluntary organizations trained social workers spoke of encountering similar attitudes among their committee members, and of the possibility that a number of substantial subscriptions might be cancelled if the association were thought to be 'unduly favouring an exterior group'.

A rather special case was that of the special Citizen's Advice Bureau opened in Lambeth between the years 1955 and 1957 by the Family Welfare Association as part of its 'Project for the Welfare of Coloured People in London'. This served local residents as well as migrants, the latter constituting about 8 per cent of the 12,467 calls made at the Bureau over the three-year period. It was unfortunate that the Bureau had to close down when the project and special funds were exhausted, but it undoubtedly performed a considerable service in easing tensions during this crucial period of migrant-host accommodation, at a time when relatively little was being done in the area by most other agencies.[1]

The 'categoric' type of contact mentioned earlier includes that between welfare workers and migrants. The value of the welfare associations' contribution to the accommodation of the migrant group depends not only on the material assistance provided but also on the nature of this 'categoric' contact or relationship, which can exert considerable influence upon the life of an individual migrant. Among the untrained voluntary workers in this area, personal bias, ranging from antipathy to negrophilism or old-fashioned paternalism, seemed to play a greater part in relationships with migrants than among the trained welfare workers, whose training tended to inhibit the display of such bias and to impose a more uniform and

---

[1] For a detailed account of the varied and valuable work done by this Bureau and of the main case-work problems encountered, see Hyndman (1960).

263

'categoric' approach. The more personal approach of the untrained voluntary workers could of course make the situation a good deal more difficult for the migrants who needed assistance, but in other cases it might be more effective than impersonal assistance.[1] Indeed, as I have already pointed out, several local sponsors emerged from this group of untrained voluntary workers.

One particularly useful service that can be rendered to new-comers by a welfare association is the provision of hostel accom-modation.[2] In the Brixton area, this has so far been limited to the establishment of two hostels, one restricted to single coloured work-ing women, the other catering for coloured women and their young children. The latter has a high turnover of 'hard cases', women who have just left the maternity hospital, women who have lost their jobs or their rooms, or who are in difficulties for other reasons.[3] The other hostel fulfils a very different purpose: with its rather austere house-rules and its fairly high charges (£3 12s. 6d. per week for a bed in a shared room in 1958) it draws most of its residents from the established and 'respectable' women migrants. Usually they stay in the hostel for fairly long periods and, unlike the transient residents of the second hostel, they are not necessarily those most in need of material assistance. They are however better able to take advantage of the opportunities for social contact with local people afforded by the hostel, with its 'respectable' address and its small sitting-room where guests may be entertained. Most of the residents of this hostel were found to have some social contact, formal or informal, with local people, either through local churches which take an interest in the hostel or through other organizations. Even here, however, such contacts appeared to be superficial and to be sought for prestige purposes, while the greater part of the residents' social life was lived within the coloured group.

CHILDREN'S SOCIETIES

Children's societies such as Dr. Barnardo's Homes and the Church of England Children's Society (which has its head office in Ken-nington) are playing a considerable part in this early period of West

[1] On the merits and demerits of trained and untrained social workers see the Younghusband Report (1959) and the debate on this report in the House of Lords (17 February 1960).

[2] In many areas, the British Young Men's Christian Association (YMCA) has done a great deal to provide accommodation and assist newcomers from the colonies and elsewere to adapt themselves to British life. The local YMCA in Brixton, however, has only a half-dozen or so coloured residents, mainly young men of the student or white-collar background for which it primarily caters.

[3] Owing to lack of funds and staff this hostel was entirely reorganized in 1960 and no longer caters exclusively for West Indians or accepts unmarried mothers and babies.

Indian settlement, because so many West Indian mothers find it difficult or impossible to keep children with them, or to save enough money to send them back under escort to relatives in the West Indies.

The homes visited during the course of this study had all housed a succession of coloured children from various backgrounds: for several decades there was a regular sprinkling of children with white mothers and Negro or Asian fathers, usually from dockside areas; these were followed by a fair-sized group who were the product of war-time and post-war miscegenation between British girls and American Negro servicemen. In most cases, neither parent was heard of again once the child was placed in the home. The most recent group was fairly large, and consisted of the children of West Indian unmarried mothers; these usually maintained contact with their children, intending to take them back when circumstances permitted. There was also a small inflow of the children of white girls and coloured men, usually West Indians. Most of these children were usually deserted in the end, it was said; in a few cases the coloured father might display some interest for a year or so, but the white mother rarely reappeared.

The four homes which I visited were either in the outer suburbs or some miles south of London, but most of the coloured children in them came from the South London area. In all these children's homes there was a very definite attempt to assimilate the coloured children by splitting them up in ones and twos in different houses. Coloured children were not sent to houses where the house-mother or house-father was suspected of bias or had expressed any unwillingness to take them. Informants in all four homes stressed, however, that there was no real evidence of prejudiced attitudes among staff or white children or of friction on grounds of colour. In one home it was admitted that during quarrels between children epithets denoting colour (for instance, 'Nigger', 'Blackie', or 'Sambo') were sometimes used, but this was interpreted as no more than the common tendency to single out distinctive traits during childish altercations (such as 'Taffy', 'Freckles', or 'Fatty'). In three homes it was said that colour consciousness seemed to strike the coloured children themselves first of all, and that this was often associated with contact with the outside world[1] or with puberty.

[1] To illustrate this colour consciousness, one informant cited the case of two brothers, one dark and one nearly white, who came in together; the lighter coloured one tried to avoid his brother from the start, and even to pretend that they were not related. In another case the young daughter of a white mother who had abandoned her child was taken out each weekend by her coloured father, who stated frequently in front of the child that he wanted her brought up with white children; on these excursions he would take her to a special hairdresser to have her hair straightened.

Informants said that the young coloured children were usually extremely popular and received a good deal of petting from other children. Relatively few were then in the teenage group, where all relationships seemed to become more self-conscious. In one home it was said that white teenage boys appeared to avoid the coloured girls at dances and other social functions. Coloured teenagers themselves were regarded as a particularly difficult group, likely to present more problems than the local teenage boy or girl. This was attributed to the earlier physiological maturity noted among most of them, to their almost invariable lack of any family or outside connections, and to their growing awareness of being 'different', not only in status as institution children in the outside world, but in appearance from the rest of the group. It was also suggested that when they went out of the relatively unbiased isolation of the home to a secondary school the realization of colour differences and differentiation might come as more of a sudden shock and disturbance to them than to other coloured children living with their families in an ordinary mixed neighbourhood. To ease this situation, it was the custom to send coloured children along with another child who already attended the school and who was instructed to act as sponsor.

Children's homes would afford an interesting field for studying the development of colour consciousness and attitudes to colour on both sides. They provide a uniform situation in which the dozen or so children in a house have a close but not exclusive relationship to each other and to the house-mother or -father. It is also a field in which extraneous influences are at their minimum, unless they emanate from those children who come in at a later age or from those who are visited frequently by biased relations.

Most children's associations are also concerned with finding adoptive or foster parents for the children under their care. The homes are in fact intended to serve as places where the children can wait for adoption or until their parents reclaim them, or where they can be brought up if no other solution can be found. Coloured children are more likely than others to remain in the homes, either because their parents rarely reclaim them or because it is extremely difficult to find adoptive or foster parents for them. The extent to which coloured children have become a regular feature in the welfare landscape[1] is indicated in a recent Central Office of Information poster appealing for foster parents with the caption: '30,000 of us need foster homes.' It shows five small children playing in a ring, four of them with pinkish white faces, the fifth cocoa-brown.

[1] For instance, there were 569 coloured children in the care of the LCC in June 1958. (*Hansard*, 27 June 1958, p. 830.)

The housing and economic situation of most recent coloured migrants is such that coloured foster parents are hardly to be found. The associations have therefore to look to white foster parents in order to place coloured children. In 1957 one large association found that 80 per cent of its applicants were refusing to take coloured children for fostering, the usual reason being: 'What would the neighbours say?' The minority who were willing to take coloured children had various motivations: some gave as a reason their desire to take a stand against colour prejudice and discrimination; others said that they enjoyed having children in the house and counted on the coloured child remaining with them longer.[1]

This organization carefully scrutinized the motives of the minority of applicants for coloured children, discarding the most exalted negrophiles and not sending coloured children to a family which specified light colour or other physical traits or to a community which was altogether unaccustomed to coloured people. Rural communities had been found to be the most biased; ports, seaside towns, and cities the most tolerant. Examples of successful placings included: a woman in a small Devon town, who had begun by fostering one coloured child, had asked for others, and now had three in all; a grandmother who could not bear having a house empty of children and had taken four coloured girls (she had asked for 'the ugly ones whom no one else will love'); and a couple in a seaside town with one boy of their own, who had taken a coloured boy to bring up with him. I was told that this couple had cancelled plans to emigrate to Australia when they found that they could not take the coloured boy with them; finally they adopted him.

One informant made the additional comment that most foster parents with children of their own preferred not to take coloured children of the other sex. Once made, however, placings of coloured children with foster parents were successful and only a handful had been sent back; one of them was a particularly difficult girl in her teens.

While it is difficult to find foster parents for coloured children, it is far more difficult to get them adopted. Few of the recent migrants have as yet achieved the economic and social stability required by the adoption societies, and such adoption of children as occurs is entirely informal. The rare childless woman will sometimes take her

---

[1] British foster parents are drawn from all socio-economic classes in society. The allowance made barely covers basic food and clothing, so that foster parents are unlikely to be animated by financial motives in offering a home to children. More applicants are turned down than are accepted, and those who are accepted must have a solid religious background and a stable family circle. In addition, they must also be registered with the local authorities.

husband's child by another woman, and a settled middle-class couple will sometimes take over a good-looking baby from a female relative or acquaintance who cannot contrive to keep it and continue working under migrant conditions (see below, Chapter 16, p. 309). As late as 1958 there were no recorded applications for formal adoption from West Indian couples, although one association had placed a few coloured children with suitable childless 'mixed' couples, and another specialized in the placing of the children of coloured Americans with their fathers' relatives in the United States.

A fair number of white would-be adoptive parents express willingness to adopt the more attractive coloured babies, but adoption society officers view this enthusiasm with a certain scepticism: 'It's all very well to pet a little chocolate boy doll, but will they feel the same when he grows up into a great husky fellow making friends with the neighbour's daughter? That's when some of them try to push him back to us, and what effect is that rejection going to have on him?' said one. He continued: 'Then there are the types who have a guilty conscience about their poor downtrodden black brothers and want to make it up by adopting a coloured child. We don't think that's an entirely healthy motive for adoption.'[1]

The situation facing the adoption societies at the time of this study was that they had both a surplus of white couples seeking to adopt a child of their choice and a growing surplus of coloured children whom few otherwise suitable white couples wished to adopt.[2] The policies of the various voluntary societies differed slightly, but all handled the placing of coloured children with

[1] One such adoption, which took place in Middlesex in 1951, was reported in the *People* of 18 September 1953 under the heading 'Such a Happy Family—and a Lesson to all Narrow-Minded People'. 'They adopted him, they say, as their own small and humble protest against the colour bar', said the report. 'But would YOU have the courage. . . . Could you face the pointing fingers, the nodding heads and the tongues touched with innuendo?' See also Institute of Race Relations U.K. Press Summary and *Newsletter* for a number of reports and articles dealing with the care of unwanted or illegitimate coloured children.

[2] An article in the *Daily Mirror* (30 January 1957) gave the position in the main agencies at the end of 1956. The Church of England Children's Society reported that only 15 of the 2,000 adoptions arranged in the period 1951–55 had been of coloured children. In 1956 Dr. Barnardo's Adoption Department reported that legally approved parents had been found for 180 white children but for only one coloured child (a half-caste). During the same period the National Children's Homes had negotiated 160 adoptions, of which only one involved a coloured child. In recent years, however, resistance to fostering or adopting coloured children seems to have decreased slightly. For instance, 18 children of coloured or mixed parentage out of a total of 178 were placed in foster homes (some with a view to adoption) in 1958 by the Church of England Children's Society; in 1959 and 1960 the corresponding figures were 23 out of a total of 147, and 34 out of a total of 169.

268

extreme caution, usually insisting on a prolonged period of fostering before agreeing to an adoption.[1]

The difficulties faced by the adoption societies arise out of British attitudes towards miscegenation and mixed marriages, and out of the identification of colour and 'strangeness', which makes it difficult for those involved to regard a coloured child as a full member of a white family.

YOUTH ORGANIZATIONS

Unlike their parents young white and coloured children appeared to mix freely and unselfconsciously in informal street play-groups, in day nurseries, and in nursery and primary schools. Few West Indian children in Brixton were, however, old enough to participate in the activities of youth organizations in the 1955–58 period. For the small minority of older boys and girls, most of whom had only been in Britain for a year or so, the same considerations that prevented the vast majority of their parents and elders from participating in local associational life held good.

In the ten or so local youth clubs or associations visited, the organizers were, with one exception, anxious to extend a welcome to coloured boys and girls. Most said that they had tried to bring them in, but none had been able to attract more than one or two or to keep them as regular members. The main difficulty was thought to be that at this stage of migrant settlement the children shared the social and cultural patterns of their parents and found the club members alien and the activities uninteresting.[2] A further point which was not particularly stressed but which emerged from interviews was the question of class-affiliation. Some of these associations catered mainly for lower-middle- and upper-lower-class boys and girls, and their activities involved expenditure on uniforms, outings, and other extras that a working-class migrant family could not afford, even if the parents were anxious to advance their children's status.

The general feeling of youth association organizers was that it would be difficult and perhaps undesirable to introduce special programmes for West Indians boys and girls at this relatively early stage. It was hoped that after the parents had become more settled in the district and the children had attended local schools for some

[1] An article in the *Guardian* (3 March 1961) headed 'Caring for the Unwanted Coloured Child' suggests that these policies have not changed significantly in recent years.

[2] Informants added that this *ennui* was fairly widespread among South London boys and girls as well, particularly among those who left school early and took dead-end but well-paid jobs.

time they would emulate the more energetic of their schoolmates and join of their own accord.

The organizers interviewed said that they had not encountered any particular resistance to the idea of introducing coloured members from existing members. But I was told that there had been some objections from parents of girl members when the idea was discussed, on the ground that they 'didn't want their daughters going with darkie boys'. One youth club organizer, whose club had several excellent jazz bands, said that as soon as the club moved into its new premises he hoped to attract coloured teenagers by holding a calypso or steel-band concert, and by encouraging those who attended to set up their own ensembles within the club. This seemed likely to prove an interesting experiment, but nothing came of it because this organizer left the club some months later.[1]

The local Scout organization reported the presence of only a few coloured Scouts scattered through the area. The South Lambeth Division of the Girl Guide Association had rather more coloured members, to the total of about a dozen Guides and a dozen Brownies. For a while there had been a coloured Guider, but she had moved out of the area. Local Guide officials were anxious to attract coloured children,[2] but found that their attendance was fitful, and that they often moved with their families at short notice and without leaving any forwarding address. Both Scout and Guide organizations felt that any special arrangements for migrant children would be undesirable.

COMMUNITY CENTRES

There are a number of community centres operating in Brixton and the surrounding district. These are mainly old-established religious or university missions, in which the initial work of dispensing charity or material and spiritual welfare has developed into the provision of educational and recreational facilities for a variety of local groups.

---

[1] The situation in teenage clubs had changed little as late as 1959, to judge by a survey of 32 clubs in the London area made by a Royal Commonwealth Society junior study group and reported by Margaret Bowerman (1960). Of the 32, only 13 had coloured members.

[2] In the autumn of 1958 all Commissioners in whose areas large coloured settlements had grown up met at Guide headquarters to discuss ways in which the movement could promote migrant integration. Afterwards, each Commissioner was given a list of the names and addresses of all West Indian girls of Brownie or Guide age who were known to be living in the area. In South Lambeth Guiders visited all these children, but this initiative did not produce many recruits. One should, however, remember that the Guide and Scout organizations have a somewhat middle-class orientation and are often associated with the local Anglican parish. This tends to limit their membership range to a status-conscious or upwardly mobile minority among the local population as well as the migrants.

Because they are organized to cater to the needs and tastes of a section of the local community, these centres have been unable to do much more than adopt an open-door policy in relation to the migrants and to provide immediate advice and assistance wherever possible.

One centre in Kennington tried to get coloured people to join its choir ('we know they love to sing and that might overcome the initial strangeness they feel'), but after six months had to admit defeat. The choirmaster said that two coloured people had come in at different times but neither had stayed. He attributed this to lack of interest:

'It wasn't because they were made to feel out of it. Our members haven't a grain of prejudice. But the songs we usually sing, while they aren't highbrow, also aren't rock-and-roll, which is what they seemed to want. I get the general impression that West Indians are individualists and prefer singing solo and impromptu to choir work. And there was another snag. One of them actually expected to be paid for coming!'

In another community centre an organizer referred to the additional problem of making the club or centre known to migrants, few of whom read national or local papers or go to public libraries and other public buildings where notices can be displayed. This difficulty of making contact is of course a basic one for all associations in the early years of migrant settlement. It is complicated by the migrants' general unfamiliarity with the area or with transportation routes, which makes it difficult for them to locate club premises and other meeting-places.

EX-SERVICEMEN'S ASSOCIATIONS

Many of the West Indian newcomers are too young to have fought in the last war and so to qualify for membership of ex-servicemen's organizations. Most of the old-timers who fought in the 1914–18 war did however belong to the British Legion, and one was even secretary of a branch. This informant told me that he had not been able to persuade any of the West Indians who served in the R.A.F. in the 1939–45 war and subsequently settled in the Brixton area to join the organization. This lack of enthusiasm is paralleled locally among the younger generation of ex-servicemen.[1]

[1] Cf. *Clapham Advertiser* (4 December 1959) on 'Apathy in the British Legion'.

LEISURE ASSOCIATIONS

Migrant participation in organized leisure activities in South London is, as one might expect, still very small. In the first place, most migrants have neither time, inclination,[1] nor money for such participation. Moreover, this is a fairly intimate area of association in which there is considerable reluctance to accept outsiders whose tastes and behaviour may be different and uncongenial. In the handful of cases where migrants had joined local recreational associations this was usually in the field of sport and could be attributed to the support of a sponsor.

No middle-class social clubs were found in the immediate Brixton area but there were indications that a social colour bar prevailed in some clubs elsewhere in South London.[2] On the whole, members of middle-class organizations and clubs tended to display a paternalistic desire to 'do things for' coloured people and a reluctance to 'do things with' them.

As was noted earlier, there are a number of small leisure organizations in South London, concerned with a wide range of specific cultural pursuits from drama to photography. In these there seemed to be less resistance to the admission of outsiders, but there was little desire to participate among the migrants themselves. A handful of coloured people belonged to such groups, but most of them were Asian or West African students. South London also has a number of jazz clubs, which might be thought more likely to attract the working-class migrants. But many West Indians have radiograms and can listen to their preferred forms of jazz and calypso music in their own homes or in one of the mushrooming coloured clubs or shebeens.

Migrant participation in local leisure associations is therefore mainly confined to sport. In a few cases, West Indians have been brought into local sports clubs by sponsors. These 'pioneers' are

[1] Madeline Kerr (1952, p. 81) writes of the absence of recreational possibilities in the Jamaican village: 'The boys will play cricket perhaps occasionally but there is nothing comparable for the girls. In fact, the only recreation is sexual activity.'

[2] In a discussion of the colour bar in June 1957 Balham Rotary Club members are reported to have agreed that a social colour bar existed even within Rotary, especially where strong colour bars were already applied in the community. This colour bar was felt to be linked with other kinds of professional and class barriers. Most speakers agreed that they would base their decision on whether to admit a man to their homes mainly on his education and attitude to life rather than on his colour, but at the same time would not be so happy if coloured men asked to take out their daughters. It was felt that Rotary could best help by working for a higher standard of living in the migrants' home countries and by becoming more truly international in outlook (*Balham News*, 21 June 1957). A Toc H informant told me that similar views were voiced by some Toc H members at the same period.

usually carefully selected, rather a-typical migrants, who have something to offer the club in the way of sporting prowess. For instance, a coloured doctor, settled in the area for thirty years and married to a local middle-class woman, had sponsored three West Indians for membership of a Dulwich sports club, where they proved a valuable accession to the cricket eleven.

A number of cases were also noted of West Indians joining works cricket teams in South London. Informants on the management side felt that this contributed greatly to the migrants' acceptance by the other men. For the most part, however, keen cricketers among the migrants in South London were forming their own teams,[1] and the process of social integration was taking place indirectly, as the teams began to make regular fixtures with local cricket clubs.

Other sports in which a small minority of West Indians were participating as members of local or works clubs were running, athletics, boxing, weight-lifting, and even soccer. It may or may not be significant that these were sports in which virtual sexual segregation prevails.

In the sphere of sport and other leisure pursuits, the British are as yet less accustomed to participating with coloured people than to being entertained by them. Coloured boxers, athletes, cricketers, singers, dancers, and jazz musicians have for decades been a part of the British scene. The prestige won by outstanding coloured sportsmen and entertainers has undoubtedly helped to enlarge the image of the coloured person in British eyes, as it has done in the United States. It has also enabled such personalities as Paul Robeson and Learie Constantine to conduct status-raising campaigns for their own group. But proficiency in such fields as boxing and jazz music has also tended to reinforce local preconceptions associating colour with violence, sensuality, and uninhibited behaviour in general.

Professional excellence in the sporting and entertainment world confers prestige but not necessarily status on the individual. While a South Londoner will be proud to shake hands with or seek an autograph from a personality in the sporting or entertainment world, irrespective of his colour, this does not mean that he will necessarily be willing to have him as a permanent visitor in the home or as a husband for his daughter. Coloured professional achievements in sports and entertainment are not therefore likely to secure a greater immediate social acceptance for the coloured group as a whole, although a common interest in the same sports and types of entertainment may ultimately do so.

---

[1] For an account of the importance of cricket clubs in local community organization in Jamaica, see M. G. Smith (1956, p. 301).

273

INTERRACIAL ASSOCIATIONS

Since 1955, white sponsors in the Brixton area have initiated various interracial social clubs and associations.[1] Reports from other London boroughs and urban areas elsewhere suggest that such clubs and associations have in some cases been successful in attracting and keeping both newcomers and local people. In Brixton, however, the two interracial enterprises which survived until the end of 1958 had become primarily recreational clubs catering for their coloured members, with a few liberal-minded, middle-class white sponsors sharing responsibility for the running of the clubs.

Such a development was only to be expected, for these clubs began by trying to bring people together not because they were likely to be congenial socially or culturally, but simply because they were of different colours. However, goodwill and a desire to reach over the colour barrier are not by themselves a sufficient basis for regular social intercourse. This was realized by the secretary of a club in eastern England, who wrote to me in 1958:

'Our aim has been to help British West Indians sufficiently to fit them into local life. We hope to put ourselves out of business. We are keen, but originally not very well-informed, amateurs. We now feel that with many more women over here our social programme may well collapse. The men have homes to stay in, folks to go to the films or pub with, etc., and therefore less need for a clubroom. We keep this club open for those who are new. Our other work, welfare, etc., is still important and we find that all individual cases come to our notice by personal contacts.'

The two longest-lived clubs in the Brixton area, then, were compelled to adapt their social activities to the tastes of their coloured members, who opted for such activities as jazz, dancing, cricket, dominoes, and billiards. One club held weekly meetings in a cheerful church hall offering a wide variety of recreational facilities. When first visited in late 1956, its membership consisted of a steady nucleus of about ten settled middle-class West Indian couples, and some forty or fifty others, most of them young, single men of the better-

[1] A different type of interracial association has also been noted. This is the local coordinating committee on which sit representatives of the council voluntary welfare organizations and the migrants themselves, sometimes with a liaison officer attached. Such committees have proliferated since the Notting Hill disturbances, and many of them have been grouped together into the Standing Conference of West Indian Leaders for Community Development (see *Coloured Immigrants in Britain,* Institute of Race Relations, 1960, pp. 36–7; Glass, 1960, pp. 208–9). Lambeth Council has so far maintained the even tenor of its *laissez-faire* egalitarian policy in this respect.

paid artisan group. Attendance was irregular and varied between ten and fifty from week to week.

Apart from the club organizer and his friends, there were few regular white members. From time to time the rector of the Anglican parish whose hall the club used would issue a reminder to his congregation, and a few members would come in for a week or so. Occasionally other whites would drift in but they rarely came more than once. On one occasion, a coloured member brought in two young Irishmen who were his workmates. Their visit coincided with the presence of a press photographer, who insisted on photographing them as they jived with two West Indian girls. The photograph was subsequently published as an illustration of goodwill between black and white, but the two exponents of goodwill are thought to have resented the fuss and publicity. At all events they did not come back a second time.

This club provided excellent facilities and a comfortable meeting-place for its members, but there were complaints about the total ban on alcohol and gambling, and about the scarcity of female dancing partners ('nice coloured girls find most of these boys too aggressive, and one or two of the men admit that they only come in here to pick a girl up'). Friction also arose as a result of the paternalistic approach of the organizer, a former policeman and youth club organizer, and of the firm discipline which he enforced. This led to difficulties with the more active members, which were temporarily resolved by setting up a committee on which coloured officers predominated. But friction continued and in late 1958 this club ceased to function, after a life of approximately three years.[1]

Another interracial enterprise was initiated some years ago by a local Labour mayor. It was grandly conceived as a community centre for all local citizens. A committee of eight white and eight coloured people was appointed; it was under the chairmanship of a successful local coloured businessman and had an imposing list of supporters. Sufficient sums for the large-scale centre envisaged were not, however, forthcoming, while the publicity with which the project had been surrounded alienated a number of prominent local people and even aroused some opposition among the white sponsor's opponents in his own political party and elsewhere. With no

[1] In the summer of 1959 another interracial club was started in the same area, this time by a West Indian post-office worker who had served in the R.A.F. At the time of writing this club had successfully survived two winters, thanks to the efforts of a committee of settled middle-class migrants. Like the others, however, it had few white members, despite the 'interracial' tag. On the informality characteristic of almost all West Indian associations and the difficulty of organizing lower-class West Indians into voluntary associations at all, see Douglas Manley (1958, p. 299); and M. G. Smith and G. J. Kruijer (1957, pp. 29–30).

premises and no firm plans, the association's membership dwindled and fell away to a handful. Thereafter its only activities for a year or more were to hold a couple of fund-raising dances at the Town Hall. These dances were usually attended by several hundred people, mostly coloured, from the borough and elsewhere, who were attracted by the West Indian band and cabaret. The small minority of white people present consisted of some borough dignitaries with their wives, some welfare workers and sponsors, a very few working-class people, mainly men, and some white women who had come with coloured men. These included students or nurses who came with coloured students, some young girls dressed in Left-Bank or beatnik style, and a few older professional prostitutes. There were also a few white wives of coloured professional men and old-timers.

After the original white sponsor of this organization had left the area, a group of Quaker sponsors began to work with the West Indian chairman of this group, with the aim of setting up a modest recreational club intended primarily for the migrants. The committee was re-formed to include some more coloured businessmen and a coloured lawyer.

When I last visited this club, in late 1959, it was still functioning and its regular membership was growing slowly but steadily. It was open several nights a week in a basement in Somerleyton Road, the centre of migrant settlement. Activities included dancing, current affairs debates, youth groups, and sport. The club had two established cricket elevens, which played regularly against other coloured and local teams. Of all the South London recreational clubs for migrants, this seemed the most vigorous and likely to survive.[1] Perhaps one of the main reasons for this was the attitude of the Quaker secretary, who once told me:

> 'I've never had to make an effort to like or get on with West Indians. I just liked them and all their ways from the start. The main difficulty is to keep them interested without being patronizing or bossy. You have to keep after them all the time or the whole organization would fall apart in a few weeks, but you mustn't let them think you're nagging or bullying.'

On the whole, it would seem that the majority of West Indians do not respond to these interracial or community activities. Fatigue, apathy,[2] lack of common interests or community feeling, colour

---

[1] A setback occurred in 1960 when this club found itself without a regular meeting-place but it retained a nucleus of steady members, particularly cricketers, at the time of writing.

[2] Another interracial association which ran for over a year with considerable success in Battersea broke down when the white organizer was away for a few weeks, as a result of apathy and defections by its coloured members.

consciousness, expectation of encountering prejudice or patronage, dislike of being singled out for special treatment, lack of money for non-essentials – these are among the factors that help to keep migrants away from interracial organizations or the white-organized socials that are sometimes held by borough community associations, churches, and other bodies. For instance, only three coloured people, all nurses, turned up at a well-advertised dance held by the Camberwell Community Association for 'newcomers in the borough' in April 1956.

Experience in Brixton and elsewhere in South London with interracial clubs and enterprises[1] suggests that their value has lain less in any direct contact between coloured and local people from the same social background than in the example and guidance provided for the migrants by tactful sponsors, not only in the clubs but in informal social encounters in their homes. The experience of such groups as the Somerleyton Road club does, however, suggest that as the migrants develop their own associations and leadership interracial social contacts may gradually evolve on a group basis, for instance between cricket clubs or jazz units. Such contacts may ultimately lead naturally to closer and more informal contacts between individuals of congenial tastes.

[1] A different type of interracial initiative was tried out by the Rank Organization at the Camberwell Odeon in late October 1958, shortly after the Notting Hill disorders, at the *première* of the film *The Defiant Ones*. This film tells the story of a Negro-hating Southern white and an American Negro who escape from a chain-gang but cannot break the handcuffs that bind them together. Without any great advance publicity, some sixty white and coloured guests were invited and paired off with their opposite numbers; they included actors like Edric Connor and Frances Day, public health inspectors, models, nurses, boxers, busmen, and an English and a Jamaican Anglican minister. This initiative, the declared aim of which was to assuage some of the prickliness and uncertainty aroused on both sides by the Notting Hill disturbances, was well received by the guests and the local press.

14

Informal social relations

SOCIAL CONTACTS

IN THE EARLY years of a migrant movement social adaptation and acceptance are, as has been stressed, minimal on both sides. The receiving society may be fairly willing to open factory gates,[1] church doors, welfare agency doors, pub doors, and so on. But few of its adult members are willing to open to strangers that ultimate door, the door to their homes. In Brixton this unwillingness is reinforced by the reserve, lack of sociability, and fragmentation that characterize informal social life in large English cities.[2]

Of all the settled Brixtonians whom I interviewed only a handful had ever visited a coloured home socially or invited a coloured visitor to their own home. Each of these instances involved a woman: two were baby-minders for coloured women,[3] one was a primary school teacher who visited the parents of a favourite pupil,

[1] It will be recalled that, according to the 1955 Gallup Poll findings, the proportion of West Indians who were satisfied with relationships with fellow-workers was considerably higher than the proportion who recorded good social relationships with the local population. In London, where work-places are often at great distances from the place of residence, there is in any case little opportunity for acquaintance on the job to be carried over into leisure hours, or extended to the family, and it would be erroneous to attribute a man's failure to ask a coloured workmate home in terms of colour discrimination only. The same Gallup Poll found that only 42 per cent of respondents knew or had known any coloured people personally. By 1958 this percentage had risen to 49 per cent over the whole of Britain (55 per cent in London), of which 58 per cent were men, 42 per cent women, suggesting that contacts at work were still the main ones.

[2] Cf. Gorer, 1955, Chapter 4, on 'Friends and Neighbours', in which he describes the typical relationship of the English to their neighbours as one of 'distant cordiality' (p. 52). By 'fragmentation' here I mean the widespread urban practice of having friends or companions for one particular social context or activity but not necessarily permitting an overlap. Thus a man may have pub friends or workmates of twenty years' standing whom he has never invited home. On the rather similar attitudes towards social contacts with coloured people found in Willesden in 1959-60, see Mrs. Joan Maizels's report for the Willesden Borough Council (1960, Chapter 6). This also showed that personal contacts made for more favourable attitudes.

[3] One of the few intimate relationships so far achieved between local people and migrants, apart from those between children in the schools and street play-groups, has been between local adults and migrant babies or young children. 'Petting the

278

and a fourth was landlady in a house catering for West Indian tenants. Among the various factors inhibiting such acquaintance was one mentioned by quite a number of local people: this was the difficulty of recognizing individual West Indians who 'all tend to look alike'.[1] West Indian informants, incidentally, claimed that they had a similar difficulty.

Fairly typical of the attitudes of other informants was the remark of an elderly pensioner of the artisan class living in Kennington: 'I keep myself very much to myself, and I do not know any coloured people although I see plenty around in the streets.' The newcomers, too, usually prefer to shut themselves away in their own makeshift homes and to recreate as far as possible the environment in which they have always lived. This is particularly true of those migrants who have hopes of returning home after a short period.

In Brixton subjective antipathy to social and sexual intimacy is often reinforced by observed social and cultural differences between the newcomers and Brixtonians, and particularly by the contrast between local reserve and control and the uninhibited spontaneity of the newcomers' behaviour. Informal social intercourse between newcomers and local inhabitants, particularly when it involved both sexes, was usually found to be limited to 'dress' occasions such as weddings and christenings. The more settled coloured people would usually invite a few whites to this type of party. Most of the latter were not neighbours with whom they lived on terms of social equality, but ministers of religion, sponsors, and other persons whose presence brought prestige to the hosts. A certain artificiality and restraint tended to prevail and the real party, according to my informants, usually started only after the white guests had left (see Appendix IX). Such social contacts were not on a reciprocal basis and the hospitality tended to be returned not by a counter-invitation but by presents and various services.

Another kind of informal social intercourse was noted in the case of a small minority of white people, mostly unattached men and, in later years, teenagers, who were regulars at the various local coloured clubs and shebeens. This was usually because they found the atmosphere more easy-going and uninhibited, and could drink, dance, or gamble in peace. In the teenagers' case the main attraction seems to have been jazz. These contacts are not socially approved

piccaninnies' is widespread in streets and shops, and a considerable number of local women mind coloured babies. The main element in the relationship would appear to be one of patronage, and it often fades as the child grows into his or her teens and nearer to equal status with the local admirer.

[1] Cf. Banton (1959, p. 131). I mentioned the problem of 'audibility' and difficulties of verbal communication on p. 250 above.

by the settled local population, which regards the coloured clubs as a major neighbourhood nuisance.

Among the few middle-class migrants, students, and old-timers, especially those with English wives, social contacts with whites were not always so limited or formal. For instance, a British Guianese teacher on the staff of a South London church school said that many parents invited him to parties and dances in their homes, although he qualified this by saying that most of his teaching colleagues were aloof or even hostile, and made no attempt to help him at work or to see him after school hours.

On the other hand, an old-timer who had lived in the same Stockwell street for twenty-five years said that, apart from his wife's family, he and his wife had only one real set of friends, an English couple who had lived in the flat above them during the war. Like other old-timers interviewed, this informant felt that his social acceptability in local white society had been jeopardized by the recent large-scale influx of lower-class migrants. This influx had, in his view, reinforced the English tendency to classify all coloured people together at the very bottom of the social scale and to judge the white women who associated with them accordingly.

INTER-GROUP SEXUAL RELATIONS AND INTERMARRIAGE

In Brixton the degree of social distance observed by the local population towards the migrants seems to be directly correlated with the degree of informality and intimacy inherent in a particular kind of contact. There is some kind of rank order of avoidance.[1] Local people are more willing to talk to coloured people, as indeed to all strangers, in a bar, to meet them at a sports or cultural club, to meet or even dance with them at socials, than to invite them home, have

---

[1] Banton (1960, pp. 180–1) suggests an analysis of 'social distance' in terms of *ego*, the actor whose position is taken as a starting point; *alter*, the man towards whom his behaviour is directed; and the *onlooker*, a member of *ego's* group who appraises his conduct and who may cause *ego* to be rewarded or punished for it. Six hypotheses are then posited.

That *ego* will observe greater social distance towards *alter*:
1. The more *alter* is thought to be unaware of the norms governing social relations in *ego's* group;
2. the more *alter's* group is of low prestige;
3. the less public justification *ego's* social role gives him for associating with socially inferior persons;
4. the more *ego* feels vulnerable to criticism or challenge from members of his own group;
5. the more the relationship in question is regulated by implicit modes of communication;
6. the weaker are the sanctions for bringing the stranger into line if he behaves inappropriately.

them as permanent friends, have them as in-laws or marry them and have children by them.

There is little doubt about the existence of this aversion to inter-marriage or miscegenation among a large section of the British population. Banton's survey of attitudes in six provincial centres gives the proportion of those disapproving of intermarriage as over 45 per cent.[1] Only a small number of these objectors were positively opposed to intermarriage on biological or other grounds. The others seemed to feel a vague aversion to racial mixing which they des-cribed in social and cultural terms. The main reason advanced was that intermarriage or miscegenation was unfair to the children in the present social climate. It was also felt that differences of class-affiliation and culture patterns, and such elements as the differing status and treatment of women in the two groups, would give mixed unions less chance of success. One other reason cited was that it looked 'peculiar' and 'not natural'. This may reflect current aesthetic standards as well as a deeper aversion to the different and strange. In general, however, objectors seem to have felt that such unions were the affair of the people concerned. Their objections grew stronger when they were asked to contemplate a possible mixed union in their own family circle.

Banton's survey was carried out in six areas less heavily settled by coloured migrants than Brixton. Only 45 per cent of respondents recorded any first-hand contact with coloured people. In the Brixton district it seems likely that almost all local residents have by now had a number of face-to-face contacts, though usually of a casual and transient nature, with coloured migrants. As a result, their views on miscegenation and intermarriage may be somewhat sharpened by superficial first-hand observation and the greater possibility of being drawn into closer social relationships with the newcomers.[2]

Yet in Brixton white wives or consorts are in a small minority among the migrants, in contrast to such earlier coloured settlements

---

[1] See Banton (1959, Appendix II). In September 1958 a Gallup Poll (58/53) showed that only 13 per cent of respondents approved of mixed marriages between white and coloured, while 71 per cent disapproved and 16 per cent were undecided. Londoners were slightly more tolerant than the rest of Britain. More women dis-approved than men, although their attitudes in other situations were often more tolerant than those of male respondents. In a later poll carried out in May 1961 for the *Daily Telegraph*, the percentage of 'Don't knows' had increased to 25, while percentages of those approving and those disapproving had decreased to 7 and 68 respectively.

[2] A young male clerk living in the Somerleyton Road area told me in 1957: 'The locals have more or less accepted the presence of the coloured people, but people are afraid of going down Somerleyton and Geneva Roads at night, and my Dad won't let my sister out alone in the evenings any more. Still, there's good and bad in all races, and there are a lot of white teddy boys around who behave worse.'

as Cardiff or Stepney. Consequently, the attitudes of the local Brixton population towards such relationships are still based mainly on preconceptions, augmented by hearsay and casual observation. Local attitudes seem to range from mildly disapproving *laissez faire*: 'Well if they want to do it, it's their own business'; to outright distaste: 'Disgusting. I don't know how a decent woman could let a blackie touch her.' *Laissez-faire* attitudes tend to harden when the possibility of intermarriage or cohabitation is considered in relation to a daughter or other female relative. I was often asked towards the end of an interview, by both men and women: 'Well, would *you* like it if it was *your* daughter wanting to marry one of them.'[1] The most defined and hostile attitudes were usually found among those parents of young girls who were living in enforced social proximity to West Indians, as statutory tenants of West Indian landlords. A number of these informants based their objections on their observations of West Indian men's behaviour to their own womenfolk: 'They don't seem to feel any responsibility for the woman or their own children. Just "make a baby", and off they go to another one and leave her to cope. It's not right and I don't want my girl mixed up with one of them.'

It was rare to find any Brixtonians who accepted intermarriage and sexual intercourse between white women and coloured men as part of the normal course of events, without making any judgements about its general desirability or the reverse. The main exceptions were some of the white women partners in mixed marriages, who usually volunteered the information that they had after a while ceased to be conscious of any difference in skin colour. The great majority of local people interviewed remained colour conscious, and seemed to feel that sexual intercourse between black men and white women was something alien and abnormal. No significant difference in attitudes was noted between the two sexes.

Informants often speculated as to the underlying motives of the partners concerned. The motives of the West Indian men were thought to be loneliness, a lack of sexual control, and a desire to demonstrate social equality with the white women who had been out of reach in their homeland. As for the white women involved, it was generally considered that they must be of a bad type or so unattractive that they were unlikely to get anyone else. Of one attractive middle-class girl whose action could not be dismissed in

[1] Cf. *South London Press* (22 July 1960) for a report of the dismissal of two senior girls at a South London school for talking to workmen who were repainting the school. The mother of one heartily concurred with the headmistress's action, saying: 'I wouldn't want my daughter to talk to these workmen—they are not steady family men. I am not against the Irish—I am Irish myself—but some of them are casual men and there are a lot of Jamaicans employed too.'

this way, a neighbouring housewife said: 'She looks such a nice, quiet girl. I wonder how she came to marry a coloured man.' Some informants considered that the girls might be intrigued by the coloured men's reputed sexual prowess and superior sexual equipment, or be looking for more attention and respect than an Englishman would accord to girls of their type.

At least twenty local informants commented that the women they had seen with coloured men usually seemed to be extremely fair, with either blonde or red hair and a white skin, and speculated on the possible attraction of opposites. But one or two added that this impression might be due to the contrast between dark and light skins. The majority disliked seeing coloured men and white women together in public; most jumped to the conclusion that the couple must be sexually involved, a conclusion which they would not necessarily have drawn in the case of a young English couple walking together. The more prejudiced found the sight 'disgusting', while a number of those whose general attitudes were tolerant and sympathetic admitted that they could not get used to the sight and found it unaesthetic.[1]

Informants sometimes made a distinction between different ethnic groups and types of features, finding the sight of a white girl with an Indian or a Chinese less unattractive than that of a white girl with a man of Negroid appearance. This would support the thesis that the coloured Negroid migrants are the ultimate strangers to the insular British. They are strangers whose appearance is outstandingly different not only in pigmentation but in facial and physical traits. These features are also, as was said earlier, associated with the inferior and primitive traits long ascribed to Negroid peoples, and with the ultimate in the unaesthetic by many whose taste has been formed on Graeco-Roman and Northern European patterns.

Few local informants had any very defined attitudes in relation to the reversed situation, that of intermarriage or cohabitation between white men and coloured women. Only two cases of such mixed marriages were encountered.[2] In the first case the wife, a light-

---

[1] In early 1957 a rent collector said: 'To the British they seem different, frightening, even strange, and they've a different culture and different ways. People in Brixton are used to seeing them around but don't really accept them. Colour prejudice is something more than just class feeling. I myself have got used to seeing them around with white girls but I used not to like it. When it comes to intermarriage and cohabitation I'm basically opposed to it. The Negro is only fifty years from the jungle and it's taking a bit of a risk to marry one. They've got a different attitude to women. Still, what has to happen will happen. Ultimately I suppose we'll have homogenization of the human race.'

[2] Several other cases were culled from the local press. One concerned the lonely Japanese wife of an ex-serviceman, who was portrayed by the reporter with great sympathy and approval. A note about the return of a regiment from some years

coloured West Indian, seemed to have earned a respected place for herself in the neighbourhood The other was a well known and popular variety artiste. Local men who had been abroad or served overseas were presumed to have taken advantage of local facilities in Asiatic and African ports, but no great indignation was expressed. This comparative local indifference to intermarriage or mixing between white men and coloured women may be attributed to several factors. In the first place, such cases are comparatively rare.[1] In the second, white males usually have a wider choice of coloured partners; and their choice, at least in marriage, tends to fall on lighter-coloured girls of some social standing who are fairly acceptable to the receiving group. Thirdly, women are expected to and usually do adapt themselves to their husband's environment, so that neither the man nor his children are necessarily lost to or rejected by the group, as may happen to the woman in the reverse case.

Local attitudes towards white girls who consorted with coloured men were until 1958 reflected and maintained, or magnified and stimulated, by items in both the local and national press. To quote a local reporter: 'Sex and colour are always news. When they come together, the effect is more than doubled.'[2]

Most of these press reports presented either the white women involved, or the coloured men, in a derogatory light. The women were shown as common prostitutes, promiscuous teenagers, or unstable and shiftless amateurs. Sexuality, violence, heavy drinking, and poncing were recurrent themes. The reports seemed to be given in rather more detail than those of similar cases involving local white people. Since 1958, however, the South London papers, and particu-

of duty in British Guiana added that a number of the men would be bringing West Indian wives home with them. There were also several reports of local marriages where the brides were clearly Anglo-Indian or Anglo-Burmese, and one where the bride was even more evidently a very light Cape Coloured. These cases were reported in the normal way as local weddings, and the good looks and smartness of the brides were praised. The 'mixed-blood' groups involved were light-coloured, lower-middle-class people of the assimilating, 'pass-for-white' type, and it seems likely that many South Londoners would not regard such marriages as intermarriage in the full sense of the word. Indeed, I have heard a number of working-class South Londoners attribute relatively dark or sallow skin to long residence in a hot climate. Others speak tolerantly of people as having a 'touch of the tar-brush', without any of the almost pathological revulsion to 'black blood', even in the smallest admixture, that one finds among some South Africans and American Southerners. On fraternization between the second generation and white teenagers, see p. 246, n 1).

[1] Between 1955 and 1960 only 26 cases of West Indian mothers in which the putative father was English or European were reported by the Southwark Diocesan Association for Moral Welfare. In the London diocese the figure was considerably higher, with a total for the six years of 83, of which 47 occurred in 1960 (see Appendix VI).

[2] See Appendix VIII for a selection of such reports.

larly the widely read bi-weekly *South London Press*,[1] have tended to omit the words 'Jamaican', 'coloured man', and 'white woman' from most headlines, characterizing the participants only in the text of the report, and playing down the more lurid aspects of the case. This change, whether deliberate or unconscious, is undoubtedly both an indication of increasing accommodation between migrants and the local population and a factor that helps to carry this accommodation still further. It has not so far extended to the majority of national dailies or Sunday papers, or to local papers in many areas of more recent West Indian settlement.

What is the relationship between local Brixtonian attitudes to mixing or intermarriage between white women and coloured men and the facts? It has already been said that the actual number of local mixed marriages and liaisons, other than impermanent ones, is far lower than in earlier areas of coloured settlement elsewhere in Britain.[2] Of the dozen or so which I encountered, about one-half involved old-timers, usually skilled artisans or clerks. The marriages were of long standing, usually dating from the years immediately following the 1914–18 war. The children of these unions were grown-up, and most of them were married to white husbands or wives and settled successfully in a socio-economic niche slightly above that of their parents. The old-timers' white wives usually came from a settled upper-working-class background. They were energetic, aware of political issues and, in one or two cases, militant about the colour question. Most wives had passed through an initial period of rejection and disapproval by their own families and friends, but this had usually been partially or wholly resolved. In all cases, however, there was an unwillingness on the part of husband and wife to incur unnecessary social snubs and slights; this had resulted in a somewhat restricted social life and had made the couple more dependent on one another.

The friends and acquaintances of such couples were usually white people, perhaps because of the very small number of old-timers settled in South London. Their cultural life was that of the people

[1] Its Friday edition has a circulation of over 76,000. The readership is obviously considerably higher. It is also worthy of note that this particular paper, however colourful its earlier news-reporting about the migrants, has since 1951 remained consistent in its opinion that the problems they posed were not connected with 'so-called race' but with overcrowding, bad housing, profiteering, unemployment, and the like (e.g. in the issue of 29 May 1951).

[2] This statement is based on observation and the impressions of all informants. Obviously not all casual mixed affairs result in the birth of children, but it is perhaps significant that according to the annual reports of the Southwark Diocesan Association for Moral Welfare the number of English girls giving coloured putative fathers for their illegitimate children was only 110 for the six years 1955–60. (The figure for London north of the river was approximately three times as high.)

around them, possibly as a result of the acculturative influence of the wife in earlier years. In one case, however, the husband had had a strong cultural influence on his wife, teaching her, as he said, 'to read serious books and to think about serious matters'. On the whole, the acculturative process may not have been a hard or long one for the husbands. These particular old-timers, all of whom had had war service and who had struck out on their own, away from the accepted centres of coloured settlement in slums and dock areas, seemed to have had more than average ability, personality, and character. Without exception, their marriages appeared to be successful and they themselves to be fully adapted to local ways and accepted in local society. The husbands had ceased to desire to return to the West Indies, although most of them maintained contact with their families and cherished a certain pleasurable nostalgia for their birthplace. These old-timers usually remained socially aloof from the recent migrant group, although they acted as occasional sponsors or 'interpreters' for the newcomers in a variety of situations.

Most other cases of mixed marriages encountered in Brixton involved younger coloured professional men. The majority did not live locally but were frequently present in a professional or welfare capacity among the working-class newcomers. These men had usually met their wives during the war or their years of study, and the wives appeared to come from a similar social and economic background to that of their husbands. Even more than the wives of the old-timers, the 'professional' wives were militantly opposed to any form of colour bar and were strongly identified with their husband's group. While their husbands acted as interpreters between newcomers and the local population, the wives often acted as sponsors. These couples spent much of their leisure time with coloured people or liberal-minded whites from a similar socio-cultural background, but avoided too close identification with or too much informal association with the mass of the newcomers. These wives had little need to act as interpreters of local culture to their husbands, who were already familiar with English ways. Those who came from liberal backgrounds were able to act as sponsors and to secure their husband's acceptance in their own group, but the others tended rather to leave their former environment for that of their husbands.

I came across a few mixed marriages where the husband was neither an old-timer nor a professional. One was between an American Negro living in Somerleyton Road and a young English girl with several convictions for petty fraud and shop-lifting. The others were nearer to the old-timer pattern; white women of a more stable type, and upwardly mobile coloured men, who seemed to have acquired prestige within the migrant group from such a union.[1]

This handful of mixed marriages, successful as they have been on the whole, has not so far succeeded in changing the generally unfavourable local attitudes to mixed marriages and miscegenation. These attitudes are, it has been stressed, based mainly on second-hand notions, and are more likely to have been strengthened by a few casual glimpses of white prostitutes walking with coloured men than modified by personal acquaintance with one of the successful mixed marriages. Until the Street Offences Act of 1959 Clapham Common afforded a fertile terrain for such encounters, and also an area of potential friction and conflict between local and migrant men.

While the majority of recent West Indian male migrants in Brixton form permanent or temporary liaisons with West Indian women, or bring their wives or common-law wives over to join them, there are a certain number who have casual and short-lived affairs with white girls, very few of whom are locally born. Some of these white 'casuals' are ageing, low-class, professional prostitutes. Most, however, seem to be young girls, usually from the rural areas of England or Ireland. A few are girls from the European continent who originally came to Britain to do domestic work. In the majority of cases, these 'casuals' appear to have adopted this way of life before they came to the area or began to live with coloured men.[2]

The white 'casuals' were so mobile and often so hostile[3] that it was possible to establish some sort of enduring contact with only two of them. An attempt was made to reinforce these and more casual observations with information drawn from the experience of social workers and others who provided useful services and were

[1] See Appendix VII for brief biographies of two white wives of West Indians in Brixton. One local welfare worker said that most of the more permanent white consorts of coloured men seemed to be the 'bossy type', who enjoyed the role of senior partner which they were enabled to play as a result of their West Indian partner's relative ignorance of local ways. This view did not coincide with the position as I found it, except in one rather exceptional case of a handsome middle-aged ex-prostitute who easily dominated a *ménage à trois* consisting of her Irish husband, a punch-drunk boxer, and her lover, a well-to-do Jamaican club-owner. There was no evidence of white wives occupying positions of leadership *within* the coloured group in Brixton, by contrast with the Tyneside situation recorded by Collins (1957, p. 56).

[2] There is a fairly general feeling that only the lower-grade prostitutes would take coloured clients or live with coloured men. One housewife in Stockwell said of her neighbour: 'She's a bit of all right. A different hubby each week; but she's on the way down. She's not particular about colour any more.'

[3] Michael Banton (1955) was much more successful in his Stepney field work. He suggested (p. 169) one possible reason for this success: 'The women were glad of the company of a white *man* [my italics] who showed no dispositon to be hostile.' In Brixton, most women welfare workers claimed that the 'casuals' were more hostile to them than to their male colleagues.

therefore able to maintain contact with individual girls for fairly long periods. Most of them seemed to feel an initial need to justify their association with coloured men. They usually did this rather aggressively as if to *épater les bourgeois*: 'Now I've had coloured men, I'll never bother with a white man again. They look after you and are exciting to live with.' Further inquiries supported the view of a male welfare worker that most of the 'casuals' he had met locally were in search of affection and security under their defensive mask of truculence.[1]

A moral welfare worker cited several cases of white unmarried mothers who claimed that they had associated with coloured men because they felt impelled to make a thorough-going gesture across the colour barrier. Since such statements were usually *post factum*, it is possible that they were rationalizations. On the other hand, girls initially holding such views would be far more likely to find themselves in social contact with coloured men. Some white wives of coloured men also professed this motive, and had actually met their future husbands at meetings of protest and political organizations concerned with human rights or anti-colonial aims.

Clearly, few of the 'casuals' are equipped to help their coloured partners to adapt themselves to local behaviour patterns, while their mere presence in any numbers serves to buttress local preconceptions associating a dark skin with sexual promiscuity.

It is coming to be realized by the more established migrants that these casual affairs, which are particularly 'visible' because the partners spend much of their time in clubs and pubs, give the whole West Indian group a bad name in the district and consequently tend to make it less acceptable to the local population. At present there is no responsible public opinion within the group strong enough to apply effective sanctions. But it was noted that several coloured landlords outside the Somerleyton–Geneva Road area were giving notice to tenants who brought in white 'casuals', although they continued to tolerate the ordinary short-lived West Indian *ménages*.[2] In one licensed coloured club, too, the manager was by 1958 refusing to admit unescorted white women.

---

[1] 'Probably the only happy time in Joan's life,' said a probation officer about a 16-year-old girl in a remand home, 'was when she went to live with some Jamaicans. They gave her affection and a sense of belonging. Unfortunately she had to be brought back here because she was found on the streets soliciting.'

[2] There seem to be very few coloured women prostitutes plying their trade in Brixton, although before 1959 a few cases were reported in the press of coloured women prostitutes with Brixton addresses operating in Hyde Park, mainly among a white clientele. One house was noted in Brixton in which lived three generations of mixed-blood women whose clientele was reported to be either white or Indian. This family was Anglo-coloured and had no connection with the recent migrant group.

Most Brixtonians do, as we have said, dislike the idea of miscegenation or intermarriage between white and coloured people, and few respectable local girls will be seen out with or court a West Indian man. This local antipathy has remained moderate and unfocused, probably because of the relatively low incidence of such unions. In Brixton, by contrast with the older areas of coloured settlement, the proportion of West Indian women to men is probably as high as three to four, and is likely to rise even higher as more male migrants settle and send for their families. Brixtonians are therefore more accustomed to see West Indians walking out with their own womenfolk, and often with their children, than to see them associating with white women.[1]

The presence of so many West Indian women, most of them obviously highly respectable, has not only helped to allay local apprehensions about the potential threat to respectable white women; it has also furthered the processes of accommodation on the migrant side. These women have helped to improve living standards and have brought a certain order and stability into migrant life. The more settled among them have also begun to establish contacts with neighbouring white housewives, shopkeepers, officials, ministers, and others. These spontaneous local contacts, particularly those with neighbours, may gradually, in conjunction with the indirect leisure contacts through sports clubs and others, and the increasing contact between migrant and local children in day nurseries, schools, and street play-groups, provide a firm basis for migrant-host accommodation in the sphere of informal social life.

---

[1] One alderman who had in his time helped many coloured people said in early 1957: 'Local people feel strongly about the housing shortage, and more recently about their jobs, but they've got used to the West Indians. Besides, the West Indians have brought their own ladies, which means there isn't so much trouble in that direction.'

PART V

The migrant settlement from within

15

Introductory

DEMOGRAPHIC COMPOSITION AND SETTLEMENT
PATTERNS

THE APPROXIMATE demographic composition of the coloured migrant settlement in Brixton was outlined in Chapter 3, but may be recapitulated at this point.

It is still true to say that the settlement contains more men than women; but the proportion of women has steadily increased as migrants have found accommodation and sent home for their families. The number of young, locally born children is also increasing as migrants set up conjugal unions.

The size of the group waxes and wanes according to the arrivals of immigrant ships and the availability of accommodation and work. The more or less settled nucleus has grown to about 10,000; at first the increases were steep, but in the last few years they have been more gradual, caused mainly by the arrival of women and children to join their menfolk. The losses by re-migration home are very small but seem to be gradually rising.

The relatively settled migrant nucleus is by no means an organized community. It may be said to consist of those who have come to regard the Brixton area, in the loose popular sense defined earlier (see pp. 47–8), as at least a temporary home from home, and who have established themselves residentially to an extent that would cause them to hesitate before moving out of South London or even out of range of Brixton market.

The Brixton settlement consists almost entirely of West Indians, the great majority of them being from Jamaica. There are some West Africans, but most of these are students, here only for a few years. These students in any case tend to dissociate themselves from the Brixton group on class grounds. The small numbers of Indians, Pakistanis, and Anglo-Indians living in the area usually keep aloof from the West Indians and from each other. A few are in contact with the West Indian group in the role of landlords, but this is more characteristic of Camberwell than of Brixton. The account of the

293

'Brixton migrant settlement' that follows therefore relates to West Indians unless otherwise stated.

Although the settlement first became noticeable in about 1951, the majority of West Indian migrants in Brixton did not come to England until 1955 or later. There is no significant group of old-timers, as for instance in Tyneside, although a handful of West Indians and West Africans, both professional people and artisans, have been living in the area since the 1920s and 1930s. Because of their small numbers, however, and the fact that they have married white local women, these earlier arrivals have been more or less assimilated into local society. They do not therefore play, and indeed avoid playing, a direct or full-time role as leaders among the newcomers. Such leadership, in so far as it exists, is usually assumed by the earlier arrivals among the new migrant group, particularly by landlords, club-managers, or those whose superior training, qualifications, and knowledge of British ways acquired in the Royal Air Force or in war industry give them a certain initial advantage over the rest.

The Brixton district has, as I said earlier, tended to attract the more settled type of migrant, and the settlement contains a large number of fairly young couples, legally married or otherwise, of babies and young children, and of unattached women, with a fringe of bachelor cousins, friends of both sexes, parents, and older children brought out from the West Indies as the parents become more prosperous. As we have seen, it also contains a small number of white wives and consorts of West Indians, and their children.

Brixton attracts relatively few migrants from the West Indian intelligentsia and middle classes. Nor until recently, with the increase of the coloured clubs, has it attracted many of the more lively and antisocial, café-society elements so sharply painted by Samuel Selvon (1956) in *The Lonely Londoners* and by Colin MacInnes (1957) in *City of Spades,* although some people of this type are certainly to be found in the Geneva–Somerleyton area. The majority of West Indian residents in this area are from a fairly settled urban or rural working-class background, with a sprinkling of skilled artisans and lower-middle-class migrants, some of the latter working in a lower occupational grade than they did at home.

The views of most middle-class and upper-class West Indians about Brixton and other districts were expressed by a West Indian house agent operating in the West End of London. His clientèle was, he said, drawn from a higher income-group than those migrants who lived in Brixton. In the early years of the war, only Kilburn, Brixton, and Camden Town had been open to coloured residents, but now that accommodation was to be had in better areas his clients

294

regarded Brixton as *infra dig.*, and would not go there if they could afford better accommodation elsewhere.

Among the Brixton coloured migrants, settlement can already be divided into three zones or stages, corresponding in a less-developed way to those described by Kenneth Little (1947, pp. 45–6) for the Cardiff of the 1930s and by Sydney Collins (1957, pp. 36–44) for Tyneside.

First come the original unofficial reception areas in the depressed central streets, where relatively few of the former local residents are now left.[1] Such are the Geneva–Somerleyton area and the Mostyn Road area. Here live, or rather lodge, the newcomers, the impoverished, the unsuccessful, the lonely, the restless, and the minority of antisocial or criminal types. Those West Indian migrants who become settled and financially secure usually leave these over-crowded areas after a year or so. They move to streets with a better social standing and a lower concentration of coloured residents within a two- or three-mile radius of the centre. Some buy their own houses and set up as landlords. Finally there is a small third group, consisting of a handful of professionals, white-collar workers, old-timers, and artisans, living with their families in suburban houses or private or council flats in predominantly white areas.

These stages or types of settlement do more or less reflect the social and economic status of their residents within the coloured group, and, particularly with the third group, their degree of adaptation to the local environment. Towards the end of my field work I noticed that more status-conscious migrants in the third group and even some in the second group were beginning to dissociate themselves verbally from 'Brixton', which they used when referring to the central reception area and the market vicinity in much the same way as other local residents.

CONDITIONING FACTORS

Before describing the organization of the Brixton migrant group, we should perhaps stress once more certain factors that must of necessity condition intra-group social relationships, just as they condition economic and social relations between the migrants and the local population.

In the first place, apart from some of the earlier arrivals, most West Indians are still migratory in intention. All their efforts and hopes are directed towards accumulating sufficient capital or acquir-

---

[1] Brixton ceased to be a large-scale reception area by the end of 1956, when the local shortage of work caused new arrivals to go elsewhere. Nowadays, most new-comers are relatives or close friends of migrants already settled in Brixton.

ing a new skill so that they may return to a better future in the West Indies. There is little will or energy left over for other purposes, such as making a pleasant home, participating in local social and cultural life, or endeavouring to adapt themselves to local *mores*.

Such an attitude is characteristic of many economic migrants, although the history of such groups as the Irish and Italians in the United States shows that hopes of return are not always realized. By contrast, large numbers of West Indian migrants to Central, Southern, and North America have in the past drifted back home, whether or not their ambitions were achieved, but this was perhaps due in some measure to the relatively small distances and low return fares involved.

A second factor that slows the development of intra-group organization is that most of the migrants are unfamiliar with the tempo and complexity of life and work in a large city. Such essential processes as earning a livelihood to provide oneself and one's dependants with the basic needs of food, shelter, and clothing are, as we have seen, far more complicated in the London setting than in the rural Caribbean, and take up most of the individual migrant's time and energy. One West Indian social worker said that he found many of his countrymen 'dazed by the big city', and another suggested that their difficulties were often enhanced by lack of imagination, arising out of the narrow set of 'life situations' in their home environment. This, he considered, made most of them unadaptable and caused them to seek sanctuary in the coloured quarters of British cities.

Another factor that impedes migrant accommodation to urban life in Britain is the climate (see Appendix XI). This is rarely appreciated by the British, although, as we have noted, it is one of the principal complaints made by migrants. Their shock and discomfort are usually augmented by a lack of warm clothes, by an inadequate diet based on carbohydrates, and by the rigours of life in a single room, usually shared with others, in a badly built, damp, and draughty house with no adequate lavatory facilities. This single-room existence has also, as we shall see, a considerable effect on the development of family relationships.

The difficulty of adjusting to the new climate is often not only physical but psychological. The lack of sun and warmth is enhanced by the migrants' translation from surroundings which, however poor or squalid, are usually not out of reach of trees, mountains, and the sea, to grimy treeless streets that offer little inducement to continue the lively outdoor life of the Caribbean.

Yet another factor that has obviously hampered the development of more permanent social ties is the high economic and residential

296

mobility characteristic of most recent migrants. Finally, there is the allied factor of the lower-class West Indian migrants' social and cultural background, which does not indicate any particular need for a highly integrated or formal communal and associational life.[1] As an ex-R.A.F. officer from Trinidad who canvassed coloured migrants in Brixton during the 1955 general election said: 'Most of them live just as they did in the West Indies; on a low level, with rough food and no comforts. They are dead serious about saving, though. They may go to a cinema or have a drink-up once a week. Otherwise they lie on their beds when they get home from work or maybe talk on street corners if the weather permits.'

[1] Cf. M. G. Smith (1956).

16

Family, kinship, and household

TRADITIONAL AND MIGRANT TYPES OF CONJUGAL UNIONS AND ELEMENTARY FAMILY GROUPINGS

THE BASIC social unit within the Brixton migrant group can be classified in three different ways, according to: the type of conjugal union; the type of elementary family grouping; or the composition of the domestic or household unit.

In the migrant situation, classification according to the type of union would be misleading and inadequate, unless the unions are associated with or result in the formation of family groupings. In the earlier years of migration, many migrants arrive alone or ahead of their families, and contract one or more casual or unstable conjugal unions. These have little lasting social significance unless children result, and not always then.[1]

Similarly, closer study of the simple domestic or household units found in the mainly single-room society of the Brixton migrants suggests that these units often fail to satisfy the individual's basic social and economic needs. They rarely contain all the members of an elementary family grouping. At times they are not even economically self-supporting or self-contained. The links with close kin at home are often as strong as or stronger than any bonds between the members of a Brixton domestic unit,[2] and are maintained by a

---

[1] In this connection, it was noted that the unmarried migrant mother tends to refer to her temporary partner as 'the children's father'. Terms such as 'common-law marriage' and 'concubinage' are not used by ordinary migrants, but the latter term is less misleading than the former in the West Indian context. Where there is no issue, the partners may refer to each other as 'my friend', and the woman sometimes speaks of 'my man'. The 'friending' system, formal or non-cohabiting, is described by J. G. Moore (1954) in his study of religious groups in the Morant Bay area of Jamaica in 1950.

[2] The large sums of money sent home to Jamaica (either as repayments or aid) by these working-class migrants are an index of the close trans-Atlantic consanguineous links between migrants and their kin at home. The Jamaican GPO reported that postal money orders received from the U.K., almost all from relatives, totalled £1 million in 1955; this rose to over £4 million in 1960. On their side, kin in the West Indies send photographs, news, and local foods and spices that are difficult to procure in Britain. Cf. Lloyd Braithwaite (1957, p. 563) for a note on the ties between kin in Britain and at home.

298

frequent exchange of letters (despite the heavy airmail charge), by the exchange of presents, and by the news brought by recent arrivals.

It therefore seems more profitable to characterize the elementary family grouping as the basic social unit among the migrants, whether all its members are at present members of the same domestic unit or whether they are geographically far apart.

The term elementary family is here used, perhaps rather more loosely than it should be, to include all varieties of family grouping that are concerned with the birth and upbringing of children, whether they are based on a conjugal or a consanguineous bond. In Brixton, such family groupings range from the legalized patricentral or egalitarian unit, through the units based on faithful concubinage or 'unstable' or 'housekeeper' concubinage, to the matricentral or matrilineal unit. Casual or promiscuous non-cohabiting unions, common though these are, do not in my view come within the classification of significant conjugal units, unless they result in the birth of a child and the consequent setting-up of an unstable family or matricentral family unit.

This classification of family groupings stresses the basis of authority and responsibility in the family grouping. The patricentral or egalitarian and the matricentral or matrilineal types are self explanatory. In the various forms of concubinage or non-legal union, authority and responsibility are shared by both partners, but usually with a bias towards the maternal side.

This typology is adapted from the West Indian literature, which was found invaluable in analysing the Brixton material. For in the early stages of settlement immigrants tend to reproduce their customary patterns of family and domestic organization in so far as current circumstances permit. This continuity or *vis inertiae* is particularly marked in the case of the migrants who intend to return home after a few years. Their associations will therefore tend either to be casual and impermanent, or to be a continuation of home groupings, or to be entered into with an eye to the future at home. So the conjugal and family patterns found among the migrants are not simply a response to the new circumstances, although they may gradually and unconsciously be adapted to suit these circumstances whenever the old patterns prove inadequate. For instance, the lack of other formal and informal associations in the migrant environment could conceivably increase the value and importance of the conjugal link and the family grouping for male migrants.

Various classifications have been made of conjugal unions and family patterns in the West Indies. These are usually correlated with economic and social status, colour, land ownership, and to a lesser

299

extent with rural and urban residence. The present classification is derived mainly from those used by Simey (1946), Henriques (1953), and Edith Clarke (1957) for Jamaica,[1] whence most of the Brixton migrants have come. Possibly the fact that analysis of the Brixton material has suggested modifications indicates that conjugal and family patterns among the migrants have already undergone more change than was evident to me. This could be established only by a comparative study of the home and migrant situations.

The types of conjugal union found in the West Indies, and particularly in Jamaica, may be divided into legal marriage, faithful concubinage, unstable or housekeeper concubinage, and casual or promiscuous unions. Legal marriage is, according to Henriques (1953), the norm of the upper and middle classes, but is only an unattainable ideal to the majority of the lower classes. He writes:

'Although no social stigma attaches to the unmarried state and "living in sin" is not a term of reproach, marriage is often regarded as an ideal which is not within the woman's reach. Marriage to the lower-class woman means a better home and above all a servant. . . . In other words the economic factor is of some importance in determining legal marriage. The majority of cases of monogamy were found among the better-off members of the lower class. . . . Another economic aspect is the actual cost of the wedding. The Jamaican insists on a "show" at his wedding. People must be entertained with music, rum and food: if this cannot be done it would not be a "proper" wedding' (p. 107).[2]

The term 'concubinage' may refer to the type of union traditionally contracted by planters and by upper-class West Indians in addition to legal marriage. Among the lower-class urban or peasant West Indians, on the other hand, it is used to describe cohabitation between a man and a woman without legal and religious sanctions, usually in lieu of marriage. In the case of what Simey and Henriques call 'faithful concubinage', this union receives full social sanction in the lower-class society in which it is so often found; if

[1] Edith Clarke's book, *My Mother Who Fathered Me*, came to hand after the first draft of this chapter was written, and stimulated some further thoughts and considerable re-drafting. Studies of family organization elsewhere in the West Indies give a basically similar picture to the Jamaican one, although the East Indian communities constitute an exception (see R. T. Smith and C. Jayawardena, 1959; and C. Jayawardena, 1960). *Social and Economic Studies*, the Journal of the Institute of Social and Economic Research, University College of the West Indies, has published a considerable number of studies of West Indian family and kinship patterns. One of the most interesting of these from the point of view of this analysis is based on field material from a Barbadian village (S. M. Greenfield, 1961).

[2] See also Greenfield (1961).

it is economically successful it may lead to legal marriage and a rise in social status. In these accounts faithful concubinage would seem to be distinguished from unstable concubinage (the 'keeper' or 'housekeeper' union) mainly by its duration and by the economic situation, compatibility, and aspirations of the partners. Edith Clarke (1957) found a type of union in the three areas which her team studied – Sugar Town, Orange Grove, and Mocca – which she called 'purposive concubinage'. This she distinguishes from other forms of concubinage by the fact that it involves a formal courtship in which the man promises both the girl and her parents to look after her as if she were his wife. He may even promise marriage or give some indication of a serious intention to make her his wife if the trial period is satisfactory. 'While the couple do not set up house at once, and may not do so even after the birth of two or more children, a relationship begun thus formally will, more often than not, develop into a domestic unit and may culminate in marriage' (p. 105).

Edith Clarke's 'purposive concubinage' appears to refer to a far smaller group than Henriques's 'faithful concubinage', and since no evidence of the first type of union came to light in Brixton it seemed better to adopt the latter term. It may be noted here that, while both writers stress the freedom and independence enjoyed by the woman in the more stable forms of concubinage, Henriques extends this feature to the more unstable or 'housekeeper' type, whereas Edith Clarke states that the latter implies a lower status for the woman, who is referred to by the man as a 'housekeeper' or 'servant', who 'provides for him'; who is not permitted to have her 'outside' children with her; who may not know her temporary partner's economic affairs, or even claim his exclusive sexual attention. In the Brixton situation, as will be seen, the man's authority and status in the non-legal unit seem to depend largely on his economic circumstances, intentions, and individual personality.

These types of union and the family patterns to which they give rise, or which precede them, must be understood in relation to the historical and socio-economic background in the West Indies. All types of grouping but that based on legalized marriage arose primarily as a consequence of slavery, with its disregard of conjugal and kinship ties and its encouragement of sexual promiscuity and rapid breeding. This process may possibly have been facilitated by the prior existence of matrilineal and polygamous institutions among some of the West African people who formed the bulk of the slave labour force. Today the various types of union coexist, associated with different levels of occupation and income, with the ownership of land, and with the colour-class hierarchy.

So far as the types of elementary family grouping, consisting of

301

children and parents or persons *in loco parentis*, are concerned, it seemed sufficient for the purposes of this study to classify them according to three main types. These types appear to correspond both to the groupings described explicitly or implicitly in the West Indian literature and to those found in Brixton. They are:

A *Legalized Monogamous Units*
  1. Patricentral
  2. Egalitarian

B *Units based on Concubinage[1] or Non-Legal Unions*
  1. Faithful
  2. Unstable or Housekeeper

C *Maternal Units*
  1. Matricentral
  2. Matrilineal

In Type A units the stress falls mainly on the conjugal link between man and wife; in Type B it falls to a lesser or greater degree on consanguineous ties; in Type C it falls entirely on consanguineous bonds. In Type C1 the mother keeps most or all of her children with her; in Type C2 she goes away to work and leaves them with her own mother, grandmother, sister, or cousin.

Type A1 is in the West Indies found only in the upper and middle classes, and in a small, upwardly mobile section of the lower class.[2] Types B and C in all their variations are normal lower-class patterns. An idea of their prevalence is given in the 1943 Registrar-General's report for Jamaica, cited by Henriques (1953, p. 85).[3] This showed that of all mothers, 33·1 per cent were legally married, 2·5 per cent and 0·1 per cent respectively widowed or divorced, 29·4 per cent 'common law' (faithful concubinage), and 35·6 per cent single.[4] In Jamaican terms, therefore, about 70 per cent of children were born to women in some form of fairly permanent union. In Jamaica the official illegitimacy rate for the year 1942 was 69·93 per cent; other figures at the same period were: for Trinidad 65 per cent, for Grenada 64 per cent, for British Guiana 48·4 per cent, and for the more economically secure island of Bermuda, 19·08 per cent.

The majority of recent West Indian migrants in the Brixton area

---

[1] The term 'concubinage' is loaded with conflicting associations and is used here only in place of a more satisfactory one. For a discussion of other terms used by students of the West Indian situation see Hyman Rodman (1959, p. 445).

[2] Type A2 is virtually restricted to the younger professional minority.

[3] See also Manley (1960, p. 32) who also shows how the proportion of legalized unions increases in the older age-groups.

[4] Cf. Clarke (1957, p. 113 f.) for striking regional variations on these proportions; and Ibberson (1956, p. 95) for an analysis of the all-island figures.

are of lower-class antecedents. Legal monogamous unions were not therefore the norm among them at home, and legal marriage may even have been a less attainable goal than informants newly conscious of English ideas of respectability would have an English inquirer believe. For most, the normal conjugal and family patterns were and are associated with the non-legal union or the maternal family. Each adult migrant has probably experienced more than one type of relationship, for, despite the statistical persistence of certain proportions between family types, individual relationships change frequently, particularly in the younger age-groups.[1]

The units arising out of unstable concubinage meet the migrants' immediate biological and social needs, though not always adequately. In the man's case, there is the need for a sexual partner whose fertility will demonstrate his virility,[2] and for a housekeeper. In the woman's case, there is the similar need for a sexual partner, and for a protector and supporter for herself and her child or children.

The migrants are chiefly concerned with the attainment of certain economic goals, and there is as yet little deliberate effort to conform to local *mores*. There are, however, certain factors in the new situation which are imperceptibly but inevitably influencing and changing the patterns of family organization within the migrant group.

First comes a set of factors already mentioned. These include isolation, now that the migrant is cut off from the lively social intercourse and mutual aid of his island kinship group and local

[1] The 1961 Jamaica Sample Survey gives a picture of the marital status and family responsibilities of migrants at that time: 43 per cent of men and 34 per cent of women were single with no children; 36 per cent of men and 44 per cent of women were single with children (most men claimed to have a stable union, more women an unstable one); 22 per cent were legally married and almost all of these had children (Davison, 1961, Vol. 4, Nos. 1 and 2, p. 24).

[2] All studies of West Indian lower-class society emphasize that frequent gratification of the sexual urge is considered right and natural for women and men. Madeline Kerr (1952, p. 87) stresses that it is regarded as a physical need and is not necessarily associated with any feelings of romantic love. Earlier she refers to the almost universal belief that if a woman does not have her destined number of children 'she will be nervous, have headaches, or even go insane. . . . Another belief is . . . that a child is God's gift and must as such be welcomed under all circumstances' (p. 25). See also Henriques (1953, p. 88). A West Indian minister in London explained to me that the birth of children outside wedlock was not regarded as contrary to religious precepts since they could be justified in the Old Testament: 'God said—go forth and multiply.' My most striking experience of this widespread attitude came one Sunday in 1957 at Speakers' Corner, where I had accompanied three West Indian women from Brixton. Two of them were carrying buxom babies. A distant male acquaintance of the third woman came up and asked after her children, complimented the other two on their babies, and then addressed me: 'What, you've no babies? Aren't you married? Yes—and you haven't a young baby? You must be slipping!'

community; the perplexity of the small-town or rural migrant plunged into the cauldron of a big city and into the tempo and complexity of a highly developed industrial system; and the bewilderment of the coloured individual suddenly faced with the different values and unpredictable attitudes of an all-white society after the static complexities of a colour-class hierarchy. Such factors affect both men and women migrants; but the absence of a wider family group falls particularly harshly upon the women.

A further factor is the general improvement in the economic situation of individual migrants. As studies of the West Indies have shown, legal marriage is usually associated with the attainment of economic security by the cohabiting couple and particularly by the male partner. The new economic emancipation of the more self-reliant women migrants also makes for change. In the lower-class group in the West Indies only the 'higglers' or market-women seem to have been independent. Others eked out the meagre and desultory assistance provided by their menfolk by domestic work, as home dressmakers, or in the fields. In England a considerable number of lower-class West Indian women have found themselves better off on their own, either as wage-earners or even with the help of the National Assistance Board. Such assistance is usually augmented by various tax-free payments for such services as baby-minding, rent-collecting, home dressmaking, caretaking for a landlord, acting as a hire-purchase company's agent, arranging weddings, or catering.

This new factor of female emancipation can influence the evolution of the elementary family grouping in one of two directions. A unit based on faithful concubinage may develop into an egalitarian legal monogamous unit, particularly when the male partner is in a better economic position than he would have been at home.[1] An unstable family unit may, on the other hand, become more unstable, until the male partner disappears and the woman sets up a matri-central unit, with the day nursery, the school, and possibly the migrant neighbours and the National Assistance Board taking the place, however inadequately, of the matrilineal, matrilocal unit on which she might have relied in the West Indies. Sometimes, however, the West Indian pattern may be repeated, with the mother

[1] A West Indian middle-class informant with several years' experience of migrants in London agreed about the possibility of such a development, but not about its permanency: 'I think that our people's stronger sexual urge and need for its expression will prevent much change. I don't think the new situation will make them more willing to marry. Temporary legalized monogamy *might* emerge as a result of the constraining effect of economic and housing difficulties. But these legal marriages could break up as easily as the informal liaisons. The emancipation of women could bring considerable changes but not in the direction of more settled and formal marriages, in my opinion.'

304

sending the children home to her family while she remains here to work for their keep. A small number of lower-class women migrants have succeeded in achieving financial stability and even prosperity by their own efforts, and it is noticeable that for the present at least they usually prefer to remain independent, taking and discarding male consorts in a 'queen bee' fashion.[1] This pattern would seem to be an inversion of the unstable concubinage generally encountered in the West Indies, and a response to the new economic situation.

Improved earnings, economic opportunities, and income tax concessions may help to incline ambitious male migrants as well as their womenfolk towards legal marriage, which is associated with a higher socio-economic status both in the West Indies and in the new environment. There may be a certain conflict here, however, since the traditional form of the middle-class patricentral family unit requires the woman to stay at home and look after the children, usually with the assistance of a servant. In the migrant situation, the economic security that leads to legal marriage can often be maintained only if the wife continues to work.

Local *mores* constitute yet another factor that may be expected to have an increasing influence on the migrants' family patterns. It has already been pointed out that the local norm is the legal conjugal family and that deviations, however frequent, are neither approved nor publicized. Despite the lack of close social contacts between migrants and local people, these norms gradually become known to the migrants, and particularly to the women, through their contacts with local officials, ministers of religion, schoolteachers, and social workers.[2] Another powerful incentive may be provided when the migrants' children are sufficiently old to compare their own and their schoolmates' family circumstances and

[1] I came across three or four such cases during the course of my field work. All the women owned one or more houses. The *South London Press* of 14 May 1957 records a case in which a male concubine did not acquiesce meekly in the situation: 'E.B., aged 41, of Deptford, was sentenced to three years' imprisonment for attacking Miss F.C., the girl with whom he had been living since 1953. Jealousy was said to have come between them after the first six months, and when in July 1956 Miss C. bought a house she made up her mind not to live with him any more. In November, B. told her that he had lost all his money, and out of sympathy she allowed him to return. He became more and more jealous of the lodgers, and in March started battering her with a hammer when she was asleep. Before he was arrested he said: "She has done wrong. She is dead. She deserved it." '

[2] Mrs. Helen Judd, tutor for overseas students at the London School of Economics, writing in an article in *Moral Welfare* cited in the *Manchester Guardian* of 22 January 1957, expressed her belief that the change in the West Indian conception of marriage and parentage would come about through various social pressures, but 'those workers who have impressed on their clients the desirability of getting married have wisely used economic rather than moralistic arguments, e.g. entitlement to benefit on the husband's insurance'.

to exert pressure on their parents or parent to conform to local patterns.[1]

A further factor that must obviously affect the relationships between migrant men and women, and thereby perhaps shift the centre of gravity within a family grouping, is the relatively favourable ratio of West Indian women to men in Britain as compared with the home situation. This is not entirely compensated for by the presence of white women. The number of white women available for such relationships with coloured men is limited, and many of these are not the kind of women with whom most male migrants would wish to contract anything more than the most casual alliance.

The West Indian woman has thus acquired a certain scarcity value in the migrant situation, although the ratio is slowly becoming less favourable in older settlements such as Brixton. This scarcity value may influence her own attitude to her male partner and give her increased bargaining power in her endeavour to attain a more stable and secure type of union. The widespread cry 'I must seek a man to be responsible for me' quoted by Edith Clarke (1957, p. 102) is even more urgent in Britain, where the woman is usually cut off from all her kin. Collins[2] suggests that the bitterness and violence shown by male migrants over their relationships with women indicate the greater importance of these relationships as a source of emotional security in an insecure migrant situation. This increased need among the men may, in conjunction with a more demanding attitude among the women, lead to more stable forms of union. Against this, of course, must be set the lack of any public opinion within the group to compel the man to conform even to the undemanding norms expected of him, and the greater ease with which he can evade legal obligations by losing himself in another migrant settlement.

Yet another important factor in conditioning the development of migrant family patterns is that of living space. As a result of accommodation problems, high rents, and impermanent intentions, the almost invariable housing unit among the migrants is the furnished room. The family unit associated with such housing facilities is therefore the 'one-room family', rather than the extended families which can be housed in West Indian bungalows and shacks. Shortage of accommodation may influence the partners in an unstable union to remain together for longer than they would otherwise do. On the other hand, family life in a single room does

[1] Cf. Henriques (1953, p. 133) for a similar situation in Jamaica.
[2] Collins (1957, p. 25). He is of course referring to the Tyneside situation, where most of the women involved are white, but a fair number of cases of domestic violence between West Indian couples have been reported in the South London press.

306

not conform to the pattern of legal marriage as it is traditionally seen by West Indians, quite apart from the inevitable frictions which it must cause between conjugal partners and between parents and children.

SOME BRIXTON CASE HISTORIES

The elementary family typology that has been used in this analysis of migrant family patterns in Brixton is, as I have said, based on the identity of the parent or person who regularly provides for the family and who is the person of authority in that family. These roles are usually associated. The migrant family type is, as in the West Indies, correlated with various degrees of economic security, of social status, and of social aspirations. The different types may be illustrated in more detail by reference to the following set of case histories of sixteen West Indian migrant women with whom I was able to maintain contact for periods of varying length ranging up to five years. It will be noted that contact lasted longer when the individuals concerned had a more settled and adjusted family relationship, even if this was not based primarily on a conjugal tie. In some cases only a few facts could be ascertained before contact was lost.

1. MRS. BEULAH F

Beulah was born some forty-three years ago in a small town in St. Anne's Parish, Jamaica. She was brought up there in a semi-rural environment, living in a modest house with a yard, fruit trees, and a small piece of land on which coffee is grown. Her background is aspiring upper-lower class. Her mother and father were married in church and brought up their family as staunch Baptists. Dancing and theatre-going were not permitted and drinking was frowned upon. Beulah received elementary schooling and was then apprenticed to a dressmaker. Before leaving home she worked as a home dressmaker, and sometimes took young girls for training. She married a local craftsman (also in church) when she was about 22, and lived with him in their own house until he died in 1953. They had three children, a boy who is now 19, a girl who is now 12, and a boy of 8. After her husband's death, she began to live with another man; some months later he emigrated to England, saying that he would send for her later. Meanwhile she bore another child, a girl, by this man. She was helped by Jamaica Welfare until the man sent for her to join him in England. She sold her house and borrowed from the minister

307

to raise her fare, left the four children in the care of her parents, who were by now old and poor, and came over by sea to England in late 1955.

She spent the first few weeks in her fiancé's room in Somerleyton Road and got a job as a packer. Within a few weeks he deserted her. She found she was pregnant; the Jamaican landlord soon found out and told her to leave. She tramped the streets looking for rooms and after a few days was desperate enough to stop a West Indian stranger in the street and ask if he could help her. He knew of a small vacant room in a Jamaican-owned house in Herne Hill and took her there. She got the room for 25s. a week after agreeing to keep the landings and upstairs kitchen clean for the landlord. This house is one of the congenial 'cellular households' described later, and Mrs. F lived happily there with her new baby. She kept herself on National Assistance grants, augmented by unofficial baby-minding and services for the other tenants, who at times helped her out with food and small gifts of money. She was even able to send a regular modest remittance home to her parents for the maintenance of the children. Mrs. F calculated that she was better off at home looking after the baby herself, than if she went out to work to earn £5 or so a week, and had to pay her fares and possibly hire someone else to look after the baby. In her present circumstances she was self-sufficient, and was not compelled by economic need to go and live with a man for the sake of a lodging. She and the baby were always well and even smartly dressed, the pram was new and expensive, and the room was increasingly filled with good-quality cooking utensils, a new electric iron, a radio, and finally a £40 treadle sewing-machine bought on hire-purchase.

Mrs. F comes from the respectable church-going lower or middle class and, unlike most of her fellows, often spoke of the shame that she felt over having an illegitimate baby: 'That Eustace he done me a big wrong! A respectable married woman all those years and he promise for to marry me.' She had little free time, but enjoyed the visits of a young West Indian evangelist who held prayer meetings in her room or in that of another Baptist family in the house. At times she and this family would attend a local Baptist church together, taking the babies with them, but Mrs. F found the English services cold and uninspiring. She never visited a cinema or danced because of religious scruples, although she would take an occasional alcoholic drink and also 'did the pools'.

Mrs. F made several abortive attempts to get the boy baby, born in Brixton, adopted, fostered, or put in a home. Nevertheless, she refused to give him up to his father, who appeared several times and demanded him, using threats and on one occasion physical violence.

308

After he left her, he had married another woman legally, was earning a skilled wage, and was anxious to claim the income-tax allowance for the child. He never paid any regular maintenance to Mrs. F for the child; but although she consulted the Children's Officer, she never actually got to the point of sueing him for it.

The next year Mrs. F met an old acquaintance, a Jamaican, who was earning good money in a building gang just outside London. She agreed to marry him and the wedding was fixed for the summer. He visited her at week-ends, paying a pound or so towards expenses, and probably cohabiting with her despite her later denials. By July she found herself pregnant again ('I always refused him to stay, but once he bring some rum and I let him stay that night'). The man then claimed that he had never 'made any babies' in his life and was in fact sterile, so that the expected baby could not be his and was probably that of the man in the next room, who had always been very friendly with Mrs. F. This allegation was flatly denied by both parties, but the man refused to marry her. He came to see her occasionally, in response to pleading letters, gave her an occasional pound, but refused to admit in writing that the baby might be his. Finally he ceased to come or to answer letters.

Mrs. F, deeply mortified, moved from the no longer 'happy house' to an unattractive windowless cubicle in a house near the Somerleyton Road area. During her pregnancy she also ceased to attend church, apparently feeling some shame at displaying her condition publicly in front of 'godly' people. After a quarrel with the landlord (coloured) she moved to a room in Somerleyton Road, and after another similar quarrel to another room in the same road. This was a well-furnished first-floor front room in a very clean and well-decorated house owned by a light-coloured man with a white wife; for this she paid £2 10s. She was initially on good terms with the other tenants but after her return from the maternity hospital with the new baby in the spring was disposed to find fault with them. Shortly afterwards she again moved to another house across the road.

Later in the year Mrs. F 'gave' the second baby to a childless, middle-class, coloured couple. When questioned about this entirely informal transaction she claimed to have lost the foster mother's address but added: 'Don't worry, Mistress P. She a nice lady who couldn't get conceive herself but has plenty of money and bought nice clothes for the baby. She give me five pound when she take him and send me a pound a week since.'

At present Mrs. F lives on National Assistance, augmented by whatever she can make from unofficial baby-minding (20s. to 30s. per week per child), home dressmaking, and cooking and mending for single male tenants. She has no regular man friend, although the man from the 'happy house' still visits her and advises and helps her with everyday problems. She has no wish 'to make another baby' and so far has not done so. She often feels depressed and hopeless. She has no anti-white feelings ('I have had good luck with my white people') but considers that 'her own people' over here have treated her shabbily. If she 'won the football pools', she would return home and buy a little house and a dressmaking business in Kingston.

She does not, however, wish to go home at present (even by means of free repatriation) because there is no work there for her and she can from here better help her children and her parents, who are too old to work except on their patch of land. The oldest boy has only recently been apprenticed back home and will not be earning enough to help out for some years. After that, she thinks it may be worth bringing him over here, now that national service is lifted. The oldest girl is still too young to be of much help to her mother here, either in the house or as a wage-earner. In any case, Mrs. F spends a fair amount on the youngest child and herself and has so far been unable to save up any money for fares. She has spent her share of 'partners' cash (a form of savings, see p. 348) on items like the electric sewing-machine.

2. MISS THELMA L

Thelma is just over 30 years old and comes from a middle-class family in St. Ann's Parish, Jamaica. Like many families in this area, her family claims a considerable admixture of 'white blood'. Thelma and her cousin Derrick, whom she came to join in London, are both tall, very slim, and mid-brown in colouring, with small delicate features and few Negroid traits. Thelma is extremely attractive, and has a gentle, gay, and resolute personality.

The L family live fairly comfortably on their own land in Jamaica. Thelma was trained as a dressmaker. She was to marry a prosperous older man, but when she became pregnant the man withdrew his offer. To avoid social embarrassment Thelma was sent to her cousin in England in 1956. During the latter part of her pregnancy she was told by the landlord to leave her room in Somerleyton Road. She went to work as a resident domestic in a denominational mother-and-baby home, and after the baby was born in 1957 she found a basement room in an Irish-owned house in Somerleyton Road, next to her brother and sister-in-law. Despite the embarrassment felt by the older generation at home, Thelma is
310

generally respected by her relatives and friends here for her independence, and is thought to have received extremely shabby treatment from the baby's father.

The baby was baptized in the local Methodist church to which Thelma belongs. The lavish baptism party was attended by forty or more guests, drawn from the most settled and respectable Jamaican residents of Brixton. For a year after that Thelma worked as a power-machinist for a central London garment firm and made extra money by home dressmaking. The baby, whose name is Gloria, was cared for during the day at the local London County Council day nursery.

When the garment firm went out of business Thelma got a lower-paid job with another firm, but was again laid off in the recession. After a few weeks of unemployment she moved up to Nottingham, having heard from friends that work was easier to find there. She failed to find a job, however, and the child became ill. In early 1958 she came back to Brixton, saying that she had been lonely and homesick away from it. She was out of work for several more months, but in the summer found another job which she still has.

Occasionally she would say that she found life here too much for a woman on her own, but she did not set up a *ménage* with any of the West Indian men who hung round her.

Recently, however, after four years of life on her own, she married a Jamaican artisan of whom she said: 'He's a good man and a good provider, and wants to take care of me.' This seems to represent a reversion to the middle-class pattern prevailing in her home environment, with perhaps a tendency to the newer egalitarian monogamous form. The wedding was celebrated in great style, with six bridesmaids, the bride in white and the bridegroom in midnight purple.

The couple have settled in a large attractive room in an exceptionally well-kept West Indian-owned house in a 'second-stage' or peripheral area. Both are in steady well-paid work; they have a good deal of expensive new furniture including a radiogram, cocktail cabinet, and television set, and are considering the purchase of a car. There are no new babies as yet but Thelma's daughter Gloria has been fully accepted by her stepfather, whom she calls 'Daddy'. Thelma now says that Brixton is her home and seems happier and better adjusted than ever before in Britain, although she is not robust and finds the climate trying. Unlike many other migrants, she has from the start got on well with and been liked by English people. This may be attributed both to her own personality and good looks and to her middle-class background and aspirations.

3. MRS. AMABEL L

Mrs. Amabel L is related by marriage to Thelma L. The L and H families were on friendly terms in Jamaica. Amabel married Thelma L's cousin, Derrick, in London in 1954, with the usual lavish ceremony in an Anglican church.

Mrs. L came to England from the United States, travelling first-class by sea ('not in one of the immigrant ships' – as she is careful to stress). One of her brothers and two sisters also live in London. The brother works as a skilled mechanic (he worked in an engineering plant in the United States for a while and has experienced no trouble in holding a skilled job here). He is married and has one child. After living in Brixton for some years the brother and his family moved to Croydon, which they find cheaper and quieter. Mrs. L's first sister, who arrived three years ago, has had one baby in London, but has not as yet married its father, with whom she has lived for most of that period. Before the baby was born she worked as a machinist in a garment firm in the Old Street area. The second sister arrived in 1957 and took a job in a catering firm for some months, until she found 'something better'. Mrs. L and the first sister both received secretarial training in Jamaica, but have worked here as machinists.

Mrs. L has had one miscarriage and has two children born in London. Since the miscarriage she has not been able to work. Her husband, however, earns a skilled mechanic's wage, and the couple live comfortably, have a second-hand Hillman Minx, and are saving up for the deposit on a house. They change accommodation quite often, for Mrs. L has high standards and is also moody and quick-tempered with landlords and fellow-tenants. During the 1956–58 period, the L family moved from one room to another in Somerleyton Road, then went further afield to Norwood, moved back to Brixton because Mrs. L found Norwood too isolated and lonely, made three more moves, and ended up in two rooms in Geneva Road, for which they paid £4 10s. Later they found this too expensive and gave up one room. Since then they have moved twice, the second time to a 'better' road, but have not yet bought their own house because their savings were recently stolen from a suitcase by a fellow-tenant.

Mr. L is gay and sociable, and goes out a lot, with or without his wife. Neither belongs to any associations, nor do they attend church regularly (they are both Anglicans). They intend to return home in a few years.

4. MRS. GEORGINA W

Georgina W was born near Montego Bay, Jamaica. At the end of the 1939–45 war she married a man from the same district. They are both Anglicans, come from the lower-middle class, and at home were relatively well-to-do. The husband had a small farm, which employed about twenty hands in the season, and also owned a shop in the neighbouring town. He describes himself as a roving type. He went to the United States to work for a time and made an attempt to get into Canada. According to his own statement, he failed to do so because of his dark colour. (Canada does accept a small number of West Indian immigrants, but in practice most of these are drawn from the fairer minority or the 'poor white' group.)

Mr. W came to Britain in 1954, not, he says, only for the money, but because 'we Jamaicans like to travel'. He left his wife in Jamaica to look after their six children and the farm. Mrs. W was in poor health and the farm deteriorated. Mr. W has, however, retained the land. Two years later Georgina came to join her husband in Wolverhampton, leaving the children in the care of her mother and father. She did not like the Midlands climate and the couple soon moved to London. She works in a tailors and he, after a period as a labourer in a steel factory, works in the same firm as a learner-presser. He gets only a 'boy's' wage for this, but says that prospects are good once he is trained. Another baby has been born to them in England, and it is looked after during the day by a West Indian baby-minder.

The Ws live near Clapham Common in a small house owned by a West African. They have a large clean front room to which they have added some furniture of their own. They pay £2 10s. a week. 'It's not what we're used to, but housing is the biggest difficulty. The Africans live differently from us. They dress up smart to go out but at home all eat out of one pot and don't clean their rooms.'

Mrs. W does not like London any better than she did Birmingham, and wants to go home as soon as possible. Mr. W enjoys moving about the world, although he plans to settle at home once he has gained skills and saved up some capital. Both attend the nearby Anglican church, and Mr. W takes an active part in church affairs and is very well liked by the vicar and parishioners. He is a balanced, lively, and cheerful individual with no chip on his shoulder, who can, as he says, always get on with people wherever he goes. He is nevertheless a little disappointed with England and the English. In the mass he finds them self-centred and reserved, and unlike the English whom he knew in Jamaica. He speaks rather

313

proudly of the latter acquaintanceships. The Ws send money home for their children's keep and are saving to make the down-payment on a house. This will, they reckon, make it easier and quicker for them to collect the capital necessary for their planned return.

Postscript. – A year after this was written, Mr. W's roving nature got the better of him again and he returned to Jamaica. Although he had not saved as much capital as he planned, the return was eased by the receipt of a legacy from a deceased relative at home, which has enabled him to start farming his land again. Mrs. W stayed on in London for a year, during which time she substantially improved her economic position, bought a house in which she let rooms, and worked in a hospital as a nursing auxiliary. She then returned home to her husband with the youngest child. The case of the Ws was the only one I encountered of a successful return according to the original plan; but Mr. W again returned to England on his own a year later to earn some more capital.

5. MRS. TOMASINA M

Tomasina was born in Trinidad about forty years ago. Her family is Negro with some Indian admixture.

At twenty she set up a union with Mr. M, and their oldest daughter was born the following year. While Tomasina is of lower-middle-class antecedents, Mr. M's family are wealthier and lighter coloured, and generally regard themselves as socially superior to hers. They were opposed to any formal marriage between Mr. M and Tomasina and seem to have made her life rather difficult. The couple remained together but did not cohabit; she lived with her family and worked as a dressmaker. A boy and two more girls were born to them. Mr. M did not volunteer for the Services during the war ('I kept the home fires burning! '). Instead, he worked as a mechanic in Port of Spain.

After the war, good jobs were few in Trinidad and Mr. M came over to Britain in 1950. He admits to being restless and adventurous, and says that these traits as well as the desire to make money influenced his decision to emigrate. Like many of the earlier migrants he had no money, no contacts, and no accommodation to go to on arrival; he spent his first few nights in a London County Council reception centre. This unpromising start was followed by a period of sleeping rough on benches, after which he found shelter in a condemned basement in Paddington in which an old woman kept her dogs and cats; she gave him newspapers on which to sleep.

After this he moved to Brixton, which he found cheaper and

314

quieter. He got a good job with a large car-parts firm, and was soon able to send for Tomasina. Shortly afterwards he married her in a local Roman Catholic church. The three girls and the boy remained with Tomasina's parents in Port of Spain; a fourth girl was born here in 1953. Tomasina got a good job as a power-machinist in a West End firm, at which she earned up to £9 a week. Mr. M was declared redundant in his job when the car industry underwent a mild recession. He claims that the 'first in, last out' rule was not applied to him or other coloured workers and that the union did not take up their case sufficiently strongly. Soon, however, he found a secure and well-paid job as a skilled mechanic, which he still has.

Apart from his regular income, Mr. M makes extra money as a commission agent for insurance and hire-purchase firms among other West Indians, as a middle-man in all kinds of deals, and as part-owner or manager of several houses which accommodate West Indians. He used to work as a part-time solicitor's clerk in Brixton on Saturday mornings, and sometimes used his large second-hand car as an unofficial taxi for American Negro servicemen leaving the West End coloured clubs late at night. He explains these activities by saying: 'I got a family to keep. You got to hustle, man!'

For several years the M family have not had to worry about high rents or unsuitable accommodation. They are among the few migrants to have been allocated a council flat; this was a three-roomed flat with a kitchen and inside toilet but no bath. In 1956 they sent for their two younger daughters at home, and later the oldest daughter arrived. The older son was left in Trinidad to finish his schooling. Meanwhile another boy was born, and some months later the family of seven was given a larger and more modern council flat in the same neighbourhood.

Before the birth of her son, Tomasina gave up her machinist's job. The drop in income was partly compensated for by the £4 5s. a week brought in by the oldest daughter, who within a week of her arrival found a job in a Battersea factory. After some months of housekeeping, Tomasina, who has worked all her life, decided to put the baby in a day nursery and took a nearby factory job; this enables her to go home at lunch time and to be back soon after the children arrive home from school.

The Ms live well, and spend a lot on food and on entertaining their many friends and new arrivals from Port of Spain, who regard Mr. M as an unofficial advice bureau. They rent a telephone and own a lot of new furniture, an upright piano (one daughter has lessons from a paid private teacher), a radiogram, and also an elaborate, illuminated, and well-stocked cocktail bar (symbol of the successful migrant); a 21-inch television set was added in 1960.

315

Tomasina makes all the children's and her own clothes at home and also runs up some of Mr. M's shirts. He is a smart dresser and has several expensive tailor-made suits. The earlier ones were cut with an American drape but latterly they have been made in the Italian style. Tomasina rarely goes out except when Mr. M takes his family for a week-end drive. Mr. M is quite a young-man-about-town and goes out to drinking and dancing clubs or to the greyhound track fairly often on his own or with male friends. He is a keen cricket fan and takes his annual holiday to coincide with any outstanding Test match at the Oval (not excluding the South Africans). Both the Ms are nominal Catholics and the baby was baptized in a local Catholic church. They do not, however, attend services regularly. The children are bright, well mannered, well dressed, and speak with a London accent.

Mr. M is politically minded and sometimes attends protest meetings ('I even used to speak in Hyde Park in my younger days') organized by coloured groups in London. He used to have rather a 'chip-on-the-shoulder' attitude and on occasion provoked incidents in pubs and other public places when he suspected colour discrimination or heard prejudiced views expressed. Tomasina is less easily roused and says that she has encountered little prejudice or discrimination. The couple have several 'respectable' English friends and are also on good social terms with their children's teachers. Mr. M, however, finds the mass of the English working class among whom he lives and works dull, reserved, ignorant, and insensitive. He says: 'You don't know where you are with them, unlike the States where there's a colour bar and that's that. At work they were surprised when I told them I wore clothes at home, could speak English and read and write. As for the people in the old flats, they were a rough lot. It wasn't safe to park the car there at night. It was stolen twice. I didn't like the kids playing too much with most of the children there – they were just like hooligans.'

The Ms do not intend to return to Port of Spain for a long time, although they often feel homesick and would not like to stay here for ever ('English life is so colourless'). In Britain, however, they consider that the children will have a better education, and they themselves have achieved a higher economic and social status among their own people and even locally than they might have done in the complex colour-hierarchy at home. Mr. M would like to go back for a holiday soon, to show his family and friends how well he is doing here. His family are now reconciled to the marriage, and several close relatives have visited them in London. Mr. M likes to play the part of unofficial doyen for newcomers from Port of Spain, and frequently lends money for lodgings or warm clothes.

316

But he does not keep open house so often as he used to do, saying: 'I'm tired of some of these West Indians who drink up my money. They think because I own two houses and have a pound for drinks in the pub I getting rich, and they don't take their turn or pay back what I lend them. I've got a car now, and I'd like to have a servant for Tomasina and stop her working. Then I move out some tenants from one of the houses, and we move in there and spread out.'

6. 'MRS.' MIRIAM W

Mirian W was born in 1918 in St. Andrews, Jamaica. Her background seems to have been on the borderline of the lower and the middle classes. She worked as a dressmaker in Jamaica, and for more than ten years lived intermittently with Mr. F, who is lighter in colour, somewhat better educated, was working as a clerk in a local export firm, and has far-reaching but somewhat ungrounded political and social aspirations. By him she has three living children, two boys now in their teens, and a younger girl.

In 1953 he left her, and the next year she came to England with the girl; the boys remained in Jamaica, and have not so far joined her. Miriam W settled in Stockwell and soon found a reasonably well-paid job in a local light industrial plant. She is energetic and resourceful, and quickly found ways to augment her wages by home dressmaking, acting as a hire-purchase company agent, and organizing West Indian weddings. She also runs a 'partners' bank, which is a non-profit-making savings device (see p. 348). In 1956 her 'husband' (as he was introduced to white people) rejoined her in London, bringing a small capital sum for investment. Using this and her savings they made a down-payment on an old two-storey house in Herne Hill, which was for sale cheap because it has a white statutory tenant in the ground floor. Of the remaining three rooms, Miriam W, Mr. F, and the child (registered here under his surname) took one; and the others were let to two West Indian families, one with one child, the other with two.

Mrs. W (the 'Mrs.' is a concession to English susceptibilities) is a vast, exuberant, capable woman, who has managed to cope excellently with life in England despite a number of illnesses and the ineffectualness of her socially ambitious partner, of whom she is, however, tolerantly fond and almost proud. He has been in and out of work several times since he arrived, mainly in unskilled and low-status jobs.

He continues to affect great social consequence, patronizing Mrs. W, ordering her about, and explaining to white acquaintances that

317

he remains with her only for the child's sake. ('In Jamaica I would never have lived in such a way.') He spends a number of evenings out at clubs and political meetings. ('Of course one couldn't possibly invite one's friends home to a place like that. When I go home I shall stand for the Legislature.') He is always about to start evening courses of one kind or another, but so far has not found the time. On several occasions he moved out and took a room on his own. ('I had no room for my books there, and it was quite impossible to do any reading.') During one such outing the woman whom he took to live with him became pregnant. He accepted responsibility for the child and has now sent it home to his mother to be cared for.

Mrs. W is very sociable and usually has a number of West Indian friends in for a chat in the evenings. She does not drink for religious reasons, unlike Mr. F who drinks away much of his pay. She has adjusted well to life in this country, but had one setback in the recession period, when she was laid off and could not find work again for over six months.

Janet, Mrs. W's little daughter, is highly intelligent and has found a sponsor in a white teacher, who often takes her away for weekends, keeps an eye on the whole family, and is intent on furthering her scholastic career. Mrs. W sometimes feels unhappy about the effect this has on the child's affection for her mother and her home, but is ambitious for the child and accepts the help offered. Janet already shows signs of developing a strong colour consciousness, and has been found trying to 'wash the nasty black colour off' several times. She has joined the Brownies and is a keen member (the only coloured one in the pack). Brown Owl apparently welcomed her accession as a 'real brown Brownie'. Her easy-going mother does not fully live up to Janet's new standards of behaviour and wardrobe. A crisis arose on her last birthday when Janet invited some white school-friends and fellow-Brownies to tea and her mother forgot the date and went out, leaving the house locked. Disaster was only averted by the prompt action of the white sponsor and a friend, who bought cakes and presents and drove all the children to the sponsor's flat.

Postscript.– This unstable *ménage* was terminated in 1960 when Mr. F returned to Jamaica, where he is said to be living with another woman by whom he had several children before migrating. Before leaving he made it clear that he did not wish to retain close links with Mrs. W or his daughter. He has not written since leaving, not even in answer to a letter from his daughter. The latter now says : 'My father no want me. I no want him.'

7. MISS FLORENCE D

Florence was born in 1927 in a poor district of Kingston. She worked intermittently as a domestic servant in Jamaica. She came here on her own in 1954, found work as a cleaner, and began to live with a fellow-Jamaican in Brixton. In 1955 a boy was born. Initially she wanted to 'give him to the government' but she was unable to get him fostered or taken into a home. After the baby's birth she subsisted either on the low wages paid in various un-skilled jobs, or on National Assistance, or on a fluctuating allow-ance doled out by the child's father.

Her whole life after arriving in England was unsettled. She found or had found for her over a dozen jobs, but left or lost them all in a matter of days or weeks. Despite her lack of qualifications for any other work, she turned down or walked out of a number of cleaning jobs because scrubbing was involved ('my back have a misery') or because she considered the hot water and detergents bad for her hands. The one job that she liked, in a fish-and-chip shop, she lost because, she claims, other Jamaican women came to the proprietor 'and told tales on her'.

Between 1954 and 1957 Florence changed her accommodation seven or eight times. This is of course nothing out-of-the-way for the migrant group. What was perhaps unusual is that it was usually she who was asked to leave by the landlord. She claimed that wherever she went her own people were against her and made trouble for her. In the one case where this could be checked, how-ever, it appeared that most of her difficulties might be of her own making. Two other tenants and the landlord described the loud quarrels between the couple, the bad language used to other tenants, and Miss D's quarrelsomeness over the use of the kitchen and bath-room. ('This is a happy house, and we can't have a real trouble-maker like her in it any longer,' said the landlord.)

Florence left her 'man' three or four times during the three years that I knew her, on the grounds that he beat and abused her, and did not give her enough money even for food. In her opinion the National Assistance allowance was both larger and more regular, and it was better to live alone and draw it. Her 'friend' visited her infrequently and rarely stayed for more than a few days or weeks at a time. He earned at least £10 a week, according to Florence, but had seven children by another woman at home to whom he was sending money; he was also saving up to buy a business after his return. When last seen, in late 1957, Florence was living by herself in Somerleyton Road, but the man had found her and was offering to marry her because he was very fond of the baby, and also because 'he would get a better code number on his income-tax return'. She was not sure what her decision would be. After this she moved again, but left no forwarding address, possibly because she wished to avoid the child's father. I was unable to find her again.

Florence is an unprepossessing, slow-thinking, and melancholic individual, and it is difficult to imagine her well established in life either in Jamaica or in Britain. She feels little resentment against the English or white people; those whom she has met she regards as having taken her side or been less unkind to her than 'my own people'. She has succeeded in keeping her child clean, healthy, well fed, and well clothed, but beyond that seems incapable of planning her life or of adjusting herself in any way. She will presumably drift along as at present for an indefinite time to come, unless the marriage has actually taken place and the man is taking responsibility for her and the baby.

8. MRS. LAUREL N

Laural N was born near St. Ann's Bay, Jamaica, in 1930. Her family background is on the margin of the middle and lower classes, but she is intelligent and ambitious. In Jamaica she worked as a dressmaker, acquiring sufficient skill to enable her to work as a power-machinist in London.

She came to this country alone in 1955, her reason for migrating being to improve her economic position. In 1956 she met and began to live with a fellow-Jamaican from St. Andrews; she married him a year later, when they had achieved the requisite economic security. Mr. N has worked since his arrival in Britain in a company affiliated with the one where he was employed in Jamaica before migrating.

Just before their marriage the Ns bought a small short-lease house in Brixton on a site due for later demolition by the London County Council. They have kept one room and a kitchen for themselves, and let all the rest to other migrants ('most of them Bajans,[1] who are quiet and good payers'). The house is clean and well decorated. The N family's joint income from wages and rents is probably in the neighbourhood of £25 per week. They live well, unlike many other Jamaican single-house landlords. Their own room and kitchen are on the ground floor, and they have a television set as well as a radiogram.

[1] Barbadians.

Laurel was taken up by a white sponsor on her arrival and is clearly making an effort to establish herself in the middle class. As yet the couple have no children, although it is not clear whether this is the result of conscious family limitation. They intend to return to Jamaica in a few years, when they have accumulated a sufficiently large nest-egg. Mr. N would like to buy a farm, whereas Laurel would prefer a business in Kingston.

They spend their free time decorating the house, watching television, or sight-seeing. Their friends are mainly coloured, but their relationships with the white neighbours are excellent and they occasionally attend formal social get-togethers of the white and coloured intelligentsia organized by Laurel's white sponsor and friend.

9. 'MRS.' DOROTHY K

Dorothy K is in her thirties – albinoid with ash-coloured, frizzy hair, broad features, and a freckled skin. She has been semi-blind in both eyes from birth. She is of middle-class antecedents, was born 'in a good part of Kingston', and spent her earliest years 'in a nice house with a garden'. Then her father, an Englishman, died and her mother moved into a single room. Later her mother, who is light brown with European features, was married again to a 'brown' man, and the family moved into a 'nice bungalow'; according to Dorothy's account it had four rooms, a bathroom, telephone, a small garden, and there was even a servant.

Dorothy had two full brothers who died. The remainder of the family consists of her younger half-brothers and sisters, all light brown and handsome in appearance. All but Dorothy received secondary education; because of her eyesight she went only to elementary school and she was not allowed to do much cooking or housework. Dorothy says she was teased at the public school for being 'fair', as 'fair' people are supposed to be upper class and therefore well-to-do.

After the death of Dorothy's stepfather the family's resources shrank again. The mother worked as a cleaner in a hospital, where she too encountered hostility as a result of her light colour. One half-sister worked as a secretary in Kingston; another as a dance hostess in one of the smart night clubs, until she won a beauty-contest title and began to travel (see Dolores G's case history); the third half-sister married a well-to-do American Negro and lives in New York. The family are Anglican by denomination but are not particularly zealous church-goers.

The household was not, it would seem, a very happy or secure

321

The migrant settlement from within

one. Her half-sisters were not always kind to Dorothy. Despite her fairness, which would normally be a great social asset, Dorothy says that they regarded her as ugly, stupid, and awkward, and would ask her to stay away when their smarter friends called, or pretend that she was the servant. On the other hand, they would often pretend that her blonde and attractive children were theirs. When Dorothy left for Britain in 1955, the household consisted of: her mother, her stepsister, Dolores G, and her stepbrother; Dorothy's own children, a daughter aged 7 and two boys aged 5 and 2 respectively (she does not talk about their father, to whom she was not married); one baby, the child of Dolores; and an illegitimate child of the eldest married half-sister, the one living in America, who sent and continues to send regular contributions home.

Dorothy left Kingston for the United Kingdom in mid-1955 by sea. Her fare was paid with money borrowed from three different sources – all relatives or friends. She gives as her reason for coming the fact that her mother was badly off and getting too old to work, and that in letters from earlier migrants she had heard that 'in England there is work for even the halt, the maimed, and the blind'. Dorothy commented later: 'People gave a wrong impression of their life here. They boasted but didn't tell of the high taxes, insurance, and cost of living. One woman said she worked as an usherette, another as a barmaid, but I found they were both working as cleaners.'

When Dorothy landed she had no friends to meet her and was picked up at the station by a 'dark' Jamaican who offered her a bed. She went with him to a room in Somerleyton Road, where within weeks he 'made her a baby' and then left her. When the landlord discovered that she was pregnant, he told her to go. She found another room in the same street, which she shared with another woman, each paying 25s. per week.

Before the baby was born, a moral welfare worker arranged for Dorothy to go to a mother-and-baby home. Just before she went into this home, she met an elderly Englishman who befriended her, apparently because of his affection for a Jamaican woman friend of hers who had died. This man owned several rooming-houses in North-East London, and when she came out of the home he collected her by car and took her there. This relationship seems to have remained one of altruistic friendship.

Dorothy then paid 35s. for a large front ground-floor room, nicely furnished with a gas oven, sink, and radio. Some lodgers in the house are coloured, others white. Neighbours are mainly white, though more coloured faces are now to be seen in the street.
322

Dorothy prefers white people, as 'my own people haven't been good to me', and says that she has no desire to return to Brixton. She wears a wedding ring and calls herself 'Mrs.' K at the request of the landlord, who thinks it is more respectable.

Dorothy has never been able to find a regular job in Britain because of her eyesight, although efforts have been made to train her and give her work which she can do at home. She is unable to read public notices and is consequently afraid to use public transport. She receives £6 8*s*. a week (National Assistance, children's allowance, and blind person's allowance), out of which she pays her rent, food, and heating, and sends regular small remittances home to her mother. Alone of the West Indian women whom I encountered in Brixton, Dorothy is somewhat shabby and buys second-hand clothes on hire-purchase for herself and the children. The half-sister in America also helps by sending clothes parcels for the children.

Despite her financial circumstances and physical disability, Dorothy has succeeded in bringing over all three of her older children from Kingston, raising their air fares by further borrowing.

As these three children are all light enough to pass for white, Dorothy feels they will have a better chance in a British school where their background is less known. As for the fourth child, the baby girl born in March 1956, Dorothy would have liked to have her adopted or placed in a home because of her dark colour. She was afraid to write home to her mother and family about this child's birth, not because it was born out of wedlock but because it was dark. When her mother did hear about it from Dolores, after the latter's arrival in London, she wrote saying that she would rather not have it at home: 'You never wanted a black man in Jamaica. Now you go all the way to England to make a baby for one there.' Dorothy has not been able to get the baby adopted because 'they don't like us here'; but lately has expressed pleasure in the fact that the baby's skin appears to be 'getting a little clearer, though she still make one feel embarrassed and her hair never going to be good'. She is very good and affectionate with the baby, tending it most carefully and hygienically; she often kisses it with the words: 'O you wicked little black thing!'

Later, Dorothy moved to two first-floor rooms in a house in the same street, also owned by her original benefactor. Despite her apparently hopeless and helpless situation she seems to have achieved a *modus vivendi*. She is on good terms with a number of white neighbours, and goes occasionally to an Anglican church nearby. She says she would like to go back to Jamaica one day, but has no hope of paying back the money she borrowed for the fares, nor of getting a job there to help support her mother and her children. The children are, she considers, better off here, where they will get free secondary education, and she has the National Assistance and other allowances on which to keep them. She appreciates all the social services, and takes the baby to the clinic once a week. She would not like to have any more children, and has expressed an interest in contraceptive methods. She cannot see any possibility of change in her situation until the children grow up and begin to earn money.

She is reasonably satisfied with her life and finds most English people friendly. Somebody has always helped her to keep going. She has had difficulties with other West Indians because 'if you've a fair skin they say you too proud to talk to them'. The thing she dislikes most about England is the cold weather – 'I didn't guess what it would be like or I wouldn't have come.'

10. MISS DOLORES G

Dolores is a half-sister of 'Mrs.' Dorothy K (see above). She was born in wedlock in Kingston in 1933. Her father was a little darker than her light-skinned mother. She worked as a dance hostess in a Kingston night club and won various beauty contests, including a Caribbean title. She then visited Cuba, Haiti, and the United States, leaving her young illegitimate baby with her mother. In May 1956 she came to Britain on one of the *Queens,* with a large wardrobe of dance dresses, and soon found her way to a coloured West End dance club, where she worked as a hostess. During a sudden illness she went to live with her half-sister to save rent. According to Dorothy, her half-sister contributed little if anything to the housekeeping expenses, and she was a difficult and often disagreeable guest, arriving home about 5 am., sleeping late, and doing no chores. I also heard her commenting frequently and acidly on Dorothy's shabbiness and on the new baby's dark colour. Dorothy also complained that although her half-sister was earning very good money at West End clubs (£5 a week plus large commissions) she did not send any regular contributions to their mother, but only an occasional £5 or £10. After some months Dorothy asked Dolores to leave and she went off to the Riviera with some English friends. On her return she took a room elsewhere, and finally a two-roomed flat at the back of a Kensington club where she works. She never visits her half-sister now but Dorothy's two boys sometimes travel over to see their aunt.

Despite her frequently sullen expression, Dolores is extremely attractive and full of sex appeal. She is slightly built, and brown

324

in colour, with fine 'arab' features and straightened black hair. She spends most of her money and leisure time on her appearance and wardrobe, which is colourful and striking. Her profile is introduced to point the contrast with the majority of West Indian women immigrants. She can be said to have adjusted herself as well to the *coulisses* of café society in London as she did earlier to the very similar life in New York or Kingston, the main difference perhaps being that her dark good looks have more of a rarity value in London.

11. MISS BRENDA U

Brenda was born in 1927 in Kingston, Jamaica. She comes from a middle-class, light-coloured, Catholic family and was trained as a secretary at home. In 1953 she became pregnant by a man who then migrated to Britain. To save the family's face she was quickly sent off to Britain on her own. Accommodation was arranged for her with a rector's wife in North London, but the latter did not feel that she could take her once she learned that Brenda was not entirely white. She then went to live with married friends. Her parents sent money for her support and for the confinement. At this time Brenda was reported as 'having no idea at all of the realities of her situation and being quite content to drift'. After the birth of her child, all trace of her was lost.

12. MRS. LENORE O

Mrs. O was born in 1920 in Berbice, British Guiana. She married and bore two children in 1944 and 1945. Her husband died. Later she met another man, lent him money towards his fare to England, then followed him at his request. On arrival she discovered that she was already pregnant by him, but he refused to marry her. She saved money, intending to send the baby home to her older sister in Georgetown, British Guiana. The latter was already caring for her two legitimate children and was very pleased at the prospect of looking after this baby as well. Meanwhile, however, Mrs. O managed to find a foster mother for the child, applied for and got an affiliation order, and finally decided to keep the baby in England. She moved out of the area shortly afterwards and was not heard from again.

13. MRS. NORAH N

Mrs. N is a very light-coloured, heavily built woman with dusty, grey-brown eyes and lightly crimped coppery-grey hair. Her age is about 50 and she comes from a middle-class background in Barbados. Her family was Methodist, but many years ago she 'received the Lord' and became an evangelist. She has long been married to a darker-skinned pentecostal church leader, whom she now helps with his church work in London. Both she and her husband have been in the United States for 'spiritual training', and a son and a daughter are at present at a sectarian academy in California.

Mrs. N came to Britain soon after the war, with her teenage daughter and son. She says that she had a hard time in the early years, and had to take work as a cleaner, although she suffers from fibrositis. She began her religious work in London by organizing prayer meetings at home.

Her husband remained in Barbados and joined her only in 1954. He works in the 'civil service' (Post Office); her daughter, who is fairly light, has taken a secretarial course and works as a clerk. The family are now fairly secure and own their own two-storey house in a 'respectable' street. It is spotlessly clean, and furnished in elaborate Victorian, lower-middle class style, with an upright piano, many photographs, and lace doylies. Most evenings and week-ends are devoted to religious meetings, held either in local halls or in Hyde Park. The couple also visit West Indian newcomers and try to help them, though they deplore their 'moral weakness'. They get on all right with the 'ordinary white people', many of whom are said to attend their services and to 'receive the unadulterated Gospel'. But they are somewhat bitter about the established churches, who they think have made it difficult for them to hire halls in various localities, on the 'false grounds that their activities promote segregation'.

Mr. and Mrs. N and the members of their congregations do not smoke, drink, or dance, and they advocate Christian marriage for all. Spirituals constitute the only music and records in the N household; some of these are, however, very gay and rhythmical. Mr. and Mrs. N do not speak much about returning home to Barbados. They are materially well established and say that they feel a sense of duty to provide spiritual assistance for their fellow-migrants.

14. MRS. 'NANNIE' D

Mrs. D was born eighty years ago in Jamaica, and has lived all her life in an economically secure, middle-class environment. She came to England in 1954 to housekeep for her daughter and son-in-law, who own a four-storey house in a quiet 'respectable' street in Camberwell where there are few other West Indian residents.

Mrs. D's daughter works as a power-machinist, her son-in-law as a telephonist in the GPO. Both have had secondary education and are ambitious; the son-in-law (Mr. N) is preparing his examinations for entrance into the next GPO grade.

When they first arrived in Britain in 1951, Mr. and Mrs. N found a room in a white-owned house in Somerleyton Road. They disliked the house and the district and soon moved to Clapham, where in another white-owned house (they prefer white landlords) they paid £2 10s. per week for a room, shared with another man who slept in a partitioned-off section. The latter paid £1 10s. per week. Later they moved to the Midlands in search of better jobs and housing, but did not like it there.

After returning to London the Ns bought their own house, which they have gradually improved and keep in immaculate condition. They are as strict with their West Indian tenants as the most severe London landlady could be. The family occupy two rooms in the basement and one on the ground floor. Their apartment is well furnished, contains books, telephone, radio, and television set, and has a large new kitchen made out of a former outhouse. The back garden has been reclaimed and is very trim and gay in summer.

The family are fairly dark in colour but are 'white biased' and upwardly mobile. The daughter gets on well with her fellow-workers in the factory. This she attributes to her working ability: 'Most West Indians can't keep up. These English girls sure know how to work, but at first they were not nice with me. I found out there was a bad kind of Jamaican girl there before and they thought we all the same.'

Mrs. D is a woman of great character and humour, and has adjusted herself to all aspects of English life with the exception of the climate. She dreads the idea of each winter here ('the last one nearly kill me and I like to see Jamaica again before I die'). She enjoys her position as an informal doyenne of Jamaicans in the Brixton area, collects press cuttings and photographs about herself and her family, and is always pleased to welcome and talk to a visitor. She remains a staunch Anglican and gets great satisfaction out of her regular church-going and social relationships with the vicar and various members of the local congregation. She spends several afternoons in the week in various kinds of voluntary work at the church and is a loyal member of the Mothers' Union .

15. MRS. DEIRDRE M

Deirdre M and her husband belong to the younger middle-class professional group. As such they differ from the great majority of

the West Indian migrants in Brixton. This biography is included
for the sake of contrast and because the husband has attempted a
leadership role among the working-class migrants in the area.

Deidre was born in Portland Parish, Jamaica, in 1928 of a
respectable middle-class Anglican family. She spent several years
as a trainee teacher in Jamaica and came over to England at her
family's expense in about 1950 to train as a nurse. She is good-
looking and light brown in colour. Her husband is somewhat older
and somewhat darker. He came over from Jamaica early in the war
to join the Air Force and stayed in Britain to train as a draughtsman.
He has a good position with a firm north of the river. He settled
in Brixton for cheapness' sake immediately after the war, staying
in a house in Vassall Road where a friend had managed to find
rooms. They were among the earliest coloured settlers in Brixton.
In 1953–54 he organized a short-lived West Indian social club in
a nearby Anglican church hall and he is a popular master of
ceremonies at local West Indian weddings.

He met Deirdre in 1951 and they were married three years later.
They had 'colour-bar trouble' when looking for a flat north of the
river and decided to take their present Brixton flat, which is quiet
and suits their purse. Deirdre goes once a week to the Brixton
market. Otherwise she shops in Tooting, and does not know many
West Indians in the Brixton area; a lot of them are, she says, 'bad
types' and 'unadjustable', and give the rest a bad name. The couple
have two children, but a few years ago sent them both home to
Deirdre's mother in Jamaica.

Deirdre is not very domesticated but loves nursing. She has taken
this up again, and in addition to midwifery is taking a course in
tropical diseases. The couple draw their friends mainly from the
West Indian intelligentsia living north of the river. They are a little
on the defensive about their 'Brixton' address, and are at pains when
talking to English people to dissociate themselves from the bulk of
working-class West Indian migrants who live there.

The M family are ambitious and energetic. They do not plan to
stay in England, but hope to move on to Liberia, Ghana, or
Canada, or wherever they can be sure of well-paid professional
jobs. Canada presents a difficulty, says Mrs. M, because her husband
is 'too dark to get in easily'. Later, they hope that the West Indies
will develop economically and make it worth while for them to
return there.

The Ms are on good terms with their white neighbours and have
a number of English friends of the professional class. Both say that
they have never encountered any sort of 'colour bar' directed against
them personally. This they attribute to their own lack of a 'chip-
328

on-the-shoulder' attitude, and to the fact that they know English people and what to expect from them, and therefore do not, unlike most of their fellow-countrymen, invite snubs or awkward situations.

16. MRS. EDITH F

Mrs. F is a cheerful, cosy woman with a matching physique. She is in her late thirties and she comes from Kingston. She is the second wife Mr. F, with whom she has had three young children, all born in London. Also living with them is Mr. F's son by an earlier marriage or association, an intelligent, 12-year-old boy whom she has always treated as if he were her own son.

Mr. F, also from Kingston, came to London some seven years ago. He quickly found work as unskilled help and cleaner in a central London firm, where he remained for some years until he took a better-paid and more responsible semi-skilled manual job in a local government office; this job carries a pension and he does not intend to change it. Mrs. F worked as a cleaner and in a laundry until the birth of her first child.

The F family have changed lodgings several times, always in the direction of better and more spacious accommodation. They have never lived in Brixton proper but always in some part of Camberwell. On arrival they moved into two rooms in a rather grimy and dilapidated small house owned by a West Indian friend; the next move was to a clean, Indian-owned house, also small. Here they were joined by Mr. F's parents, who seem to have had some savings in addition to their joint wages, and who shared with the Fs the entire first floor consisting of three rooms and kitchenette. The most recent move was to a two-storied house in a better part of Camberwell, which they own jointly with Mr F's parents. Only one or two lodgers are taken and the entire house, including public ways and toilet facilities, is kept extremely clean and neat. This is indeed one of the few examples of a 'home' among the West Indian migrants. Mrs. F also reports that she has no trouble from her white neighbours and 'gets on very nicely with the two old ladies on one side'.

The F family might on the surface appear to constitute a typically upwardly mobile unit given favourable circumstances. They are, however, a-typical and even more interesting because Mr. F, his parents, and, to a rather lesser extent, Mrs. F are imbued with a strong 'Ethiopian' orientation. Mr. F was in fact the leader of one of the more respectable and reputable locals of the 'conservative' wing of the Ras Tafarian movement in Jamaica, and his declared motive for emigration to England was to earn enough money to

329

take himself and his family to the acknowledged earthly Eden of Ethiopia. His parents actually achieved this aim and spent some two years in Ethiopia and Liberia; thereafter they returned to England, apparently somewhat disillusioned. Mr. F has seemingly renounced this further goal and settled more or less permanently in London. For some years he attempted to organize an 'Ethiopian-oriented' local of a similar type to that which he had led in Kingston. At that time he complained that the migrants were mainly concerned with day-to-day problems of work and living and would not turn out for politically oriented protest meetings; the few who showed some willingness tended to attend religious sectarian meetings. It is perhaps significant that latterly Mrs. F, asked whether she would still go to Africa given the chance, said that she would not leave London (where she appreciates the educational facilities available to the children) except to migrate to the United States, where wages are higher, or to return home with a sufficient amount of savings to start a business and buy a decent home. The coloured photographs of the Emperor Haile Selassie and the uniformed group pictures of the 'Ethiopian' local still remain on the walls of the F family's sitting-room, which also contains a comfortable suite, a colourful carpet, and a television set and radiogram bought on hire-purchase. But the postponement of the journey to the Black Eden suggests that one motivation at least of the Ras Tafarian movement in Jamaica is the frustration experienced by people of potential ability who are forced by economic conditions to drag out their lives without hope of security or opportunity.

MIGRANT FAMILY PATTERNS IN BRIXTON

Unstable concubinage, and the family unit resulting from it, arise out of the same circumstances and needs as they did in the West Indies. Such unions are particularly common among newer arrivals, the younger migrants, the restless, the unsuccessful, and the lonely. In a minority of cases the female partner may be white; but a family unit rarely results from such a union, because the girl is more likely to leave her child in a children's home. Unions of this kind are more frequently found in the Somerleyton-Geneva 'reception area' than in the more 'respectable' peripheral settlements.

In many cases a man with a wife and family in the West Indies takes a woman to live with him here. If she 'makes a baby' for him, he may contribute spasmodically towards its keep. Such contributions usually depend on his goodwill, as few West Indian women will as yet, despite the exhortations of National Assistance officials

330

and welfare workers, take their non-contributing former consorts to the courts to enforce support. The woman's chances of receiving any help from the father are lessened by the fact that he is usually sending money home to his family or to pay his travelling debt, or is saving to buy a house or for his return. Other men move about in search of work, setting up unstable unions in quick succession. The women's chances of support are correspondingly diminished.[1] I did, however, come across one man who had acknowledged six children by one woman in Jamaica, one child by another woman with whom he lived for the most of his time in London, and a recently born baby by a third woman with whom he lived for some months in another part of London; he was sending this last child home to his mother to keep. In another unusual case I was told by a welfare worker of a man who took the baby from its mother and brought his legal wife over from the West Indies to look after it; the wife apparently raised no objections.

Among those younger migrants who have no legal ties in the West Indies, and who are economically successful and socially ambitious, unstable unions often develop into legalized ones. This pattern is commoner among migrants than it seems to have been in the West Indies. A study of the notices posted in South London registrars' offices shows that a very large number of West Indian couples are already living at the same address, and I have myself come across a number of such cases. Among the short biographical sketches, the case of Mrs. Laurel N (No. 8) illustrates this process.

The unstable unit usually consists of a man and a woman living together in a single room for a period of weeks or months. There may be one young baby, but there are rarely more children actually living with the couple. The baby will not necessarily be the child of the present male partner, but the latter usually treats him as his own, at least while the pair are cohabiting. Sometimes the man lives with the woman only part of the time. In the case of Mrs. Beulah F (No. 1), the man lived and worked outside London, but visited her regularly at week-ends for several months, giving her a weekly pound or so towards her rent and maintenance, and his food at the week-end. In such cases the woman may be in a stronger financial position, since she continues to draw National Assistance, and is not

---

[1] In Hyndman (1960, p. 113) reference is made to the difficulties faced by men who send remittances home for the support of their children born out of wedlock. They find it difficult to provide documentary evidence for the British tax authorities that these children really are their dependants, since they cannot while living at such a distance prove that they have 'physical custody' of the children. As a result the men get no allowances for these children, and some gradually lose interest, form new liaisons, and cease to send remittances. It is very difficult for the mothers or the West Indian authorities to trace these errant migrant fathers.

entirely economically dependent on the fitful goodwill of the man. In this particular instance, however, the man started a similar weekend *ménage* with another woman after refusing to marry Mrs. F, and the arrangement soon broke down, leaving a fully matricentral unit once again.

Among the West Indian migrants, the unstable union is clearly more advantageous for the man than for the woman. For the latter, it is even less satisfactory than it was in the West Indies. In Brixton, such unions are more likely to break up and leave a matricentral unit than to settle down into faithful concubinage or a legalized relationship. This is not surprising, for these migrant unions are rarely based on ties of neighbourhood and friendship, or on common interests, as they might have been at home. In Brixton they are often the result of fortuitous encounters on the migrant ship, at the station, or during the woman's subsequent search for work and, above all, for cheap lodgings.[1] In two of the cases described, 'Mrs.' Dorothy K (No. 9), Miss Florence D (No. 7), the women arrived alone without having any friends in this country, and went to live with men who offered them a lodging. In the first case the union broke up within a few weeks at the first indication of pregnancy, and the welfare services took over the immediate role of the woman's family at home. In the second case, the association persisted for some years in a highly unstable way, with one or other partner moving away at irregular intervals, and with the woman maintaining herself by the help of National Assistance, or by short-term low-paid jobs, or by grudging doles extracted from the man during his periods of cohabitation.

The maternal type of elementary family grouping is illustrated by the former situation[2] of Miss Thelma L (No. 2; matricentral) and the present situations of Mrs. Beulah F (No. 1; matrilineal bias), 'Mrs.' Dorothy K (No. 9; matrilineal in transition to matricentral), Dorothy's half-sister, Miss Dolores G (No. 10; matrilineal), and to some extent that of 'Mrs.' Miriam W (No. 6; matricentral).

In the cases of Mrs. Beulah F and 'Mrs.' Dorothy K, the welfare state, various voluntary agencies, and a handful of friends have provided a reasonable substitute for the women's own families. Although these two are in receipt of National Assistance, each has found it possible to send money regularly to her family at home. Indeed, Dorothy K has, with additional help from other members

---

[1] Data made available by various welfare organizations show that a fair number of unmarried female migrants are pregnant on arrival in Britain. Some are joining men with whom they have been living in the West Indies, others are entirely alone. In either case their chances of establishing themselves satisfactorily in Britain are considerably impaired.

[2] Thelma was married after this section was written.

of her family in the United States, actually managed to bring over her three older children to join herself and her youngest child. The cases of Miss Thelma L and 'Mrs.' Miriam W are different. Both are relatively skilled and capable, and can therefore command a good wage in British industry and afford to keep their children with them. All four of these women seem to prefer their relatively independent status to the dubious security afforded them by temporary conjugal partners, although each has at one time or another complained that 'it is hard for a woman on her own in this country'.

The chief problem for the less self-reliant migrant woman on her own is, of course, that with one child, and still more with two or more children, she is usually unable to make enough money to secure or improve her financial situation here, to repay any loans she may have contracted in coming, or to save any appreciable sums towards her eventual return. The situation of a woman involved in an unstable union is often worse, but there is sometimes the possibility that the conjugal partner may achieve financial stability, in which she and any children of the union can share.

The nature of the conjugal and parental ties and the attitudes of the women in the four cases discussed above are reflected in the titles by which they prefer to be known, and in the registered surnames of their children. Dorothy K and her children by both fathers are all known by her maiden name; she has, however, assumed the title of 'Mrs.' and put on a wedding ring since moving into the house of her white benefactor and landlord. Mrs. Beulah F is a widow who retains her status as a married woman and her style of Mrs., using her former husband's name; this surname has also been given to the children born of both abortive betrothals. Miss Thelma L, whose place in the Jamaican social hierarchy was higher than that of most other women contacts, called herself by her own name with no married title until she married in 1960; the baby by her earlier association still bears her own name. Miriam W has added the title 'Mrs.' to her maiden name since she came to England and her daughter bears the same name, although the father lived with them for several years.

The family unit based on faithful concubinage is, as has been said, very much an established pattern throughout the West Indies. Henriques (1953, p. 111) estimated that roughly 25 per cent of all households would come under this heading. Faithful concubinage differs from the unstable union mainly in duration (three to five years being the median duration in Jamaica and some other islands),[1] and perhaps in the age, occupational stability, and attitudes

[1] Cf. D. Ibberson (1956, p. 94).

of the partners. Unstable unions and units seem to be more prevalent among the young and the unsettled.

In the dynamic migrant situation in Brixton, faithful concubinage is less frequently encountered. There has been little time for new relationships of this type to develop, and the large number of existing unstable unions have tended either to break up, leaving a mother-child unit, or to solidify quickly, given favourable economic circumstances, into legalized monogamous unions. Among the unions that are to all appearances legal and monogamous, there may of course be a number in which the partners are not formally married but are simply 'passing' as married, like many of their English neighbours. The essence of faithful concubinage on the West Indian pattern is, however, that while it is not legally sanctioned, it is socially accepted without any attempt to make it seem what it is not.[1] Pseudo-marriages among migrants in Brixton are a response to a different local climate of opinion, and can no longer be equated with faithful concubinage of the West Indian type. It is conceivable that some of the present large total of unstable unions in Brixton could gradually crystallize into faithful concubinage on the West Indian model, if the partners remain together but fail to achieve economic security.

Such family units based on faithful concubinage as are found in Brixton now are usually of pre-migration date. Here again, however, there is a tendency for the relationship to change fairly quickly. In cases where the man has saved sufficient funds to bring his partner over, it is likely that the couple, if they continue to be compatible, will marry and will gradually bring their children over to join them. This happened in the case of Mrs. Tomasina M (No. 5). In other cases, the union may break up. This occurred in the case of Mrs. Beulah F, who came over to join her 'fiancé' at his request, only to have him leave her, newly pregnant, after a few weeks. In Mrs. Miriam W's case the position was reversed; she was well established economically by the time her partner arrived, and accepted his Cheshire cat behaviour and final exit with equanimity.

Improved economic opportunities have, then, resulted in an increased number of formal marriages in this working-class migrant group. Some of these legal monogamous units follow the established West Indian patricentral middle-class and lower-middle-class pattern. To quote Simey's description of formal marriage and the patriarchal or patricentral family in the aspiring working-class group:

'Marriage . . . is without doubt an economic institution in so far as it is regarded by the masses of the people simply as a hall-

[1] See Henriques (1953, p. 106).

mark of economic success and social achievement, only possible
if the man possesses sufficient wealth to support a family on a
paternal basis. The working class all round the West Indies are
firmly convinced that a wife . . . should not be expected to work
for wages outside the family, that the furnishings of the house
should be something approaching lower-middle-class standard
and that the wife should have a servant. The man on his side
expects his wife to be completely faithful to him. . . . The father
of the peasant family is a stern disciplinarian, and the more
closely connected with the Church the family is, the more patriarchal it becomes. Indeed, the relationships between the various
members of the family bear a striking resemblance to those
obtaining in the Victorian era. There is an almost complete lack
of romantic love; a Jamaican peasant marriage is a good practical
arrangement for maintaining family life and making the most of
land or stock. The fact that this type of family appears to the
ordinary man or woman to be the only form which "respectable"
marriage can take prejudices the vast majority of young women
against marriage as such. Marrige is only accepted as a alternative to be preferred to the insecurity of other forms of family
life' (1946, pp. 85 and 87).

The patricentral type of legalized family unit is found among the
Brixton migrants. Examples are the lower-middle-class family of
Mrs. Amabel L (No. 3), where the wife does not work; the urban
lower-class family of Mrs. Edith F (No. 16), despite the fact that she
worked for some years; and that of Mrs. Georgina W (No. 4), where
the patricentral tradition is buttressed by the couple's strong
religious beliefs and the habit of many years of marriage, in spite
of English influences and the wife's considerable contribution to the
family budget.

An egalitarian type of family based on formal marriage is, however, developing under migrant conditions, particularly among the
younger and more ambitious working-class migrants. This is a type
of family unit common enough in contemporary urban Britain, but
restricted in the West Indies to the younger professional group.[1] In
the egalitarian unit both partners contribute financially, and share
responsibility and authority for the children. In such a unit, children
may be sent home to the family of one or other partner in the West
Indies. In a few exceptionally prosperous cases, however, a relative
may be brought over to act as housekeeper and nurse while the
wife continues to work.

This egalitarian type of unit is a new development among the

[1] Cf. Henriques (1953, p. 151).

West Indian working class; among the migrants it is a clear response to the new conditions and opportunities. A good example of such a unit is found in the marriage of Laurel N (No. 8); under West Indian economic conditions this union might never have been legalized. Another example is that of the daughter and son-in-law of Mrs. 'Nannie' D (No. 14): this family is of middle-class origin, and might have been expected to follow the conventional pattern of male authority; Mrs. N's authority may, however, be attributed not only to the fact that she is an equal wage-earner in this country but also to her own dominating character.

In the case of Mrs. Tomasina M (No. 5) a unit based on faithful concubinage of many years' standing was legalized after arrival in Britain and the attaining of economic security here. For several years the unit was an egalitarian one. In 1957, however, it moved nearer to the traditional patricentral pattern, following the wife's pregnancy and the cessation of her contribution as a wage-earner. Later a 16-year-old daughter arrived to take over part of her mother's functions both as wage-earner and as housekeeper. This change was reflected in the attitudes and behaviour of both parents and children. Towards the end of 1957 the wife found domestic life dull and obtained a good job as a power-machinist. This undoubtedly caused a shift away from the pattern of paternal authority, but the former egalitarian pattern has not been fully restored.

The families of Mrs. Deirdre M (No. 15) and Mrs. Norah N (No. 13) cannot really be cited as instances of the trend towards legalized egalitarian family patterns in the migrant situation. Both *ménages* are in fact egalitarian; but the husband and wife in the first unit are both members of the younger middle-class professional group who would probably have adopted a similar pattern at home. In the case of Mrs. Norah N, her extremely forceful personality would probably have prevented the development of a patricentral family pattern in whatever circumstances she chanced to find herself. In the migrant situation she consolidated her status by coming to Britain ahead of her husband and finding a job and a home for him and the children.[1]

It is difficult to assess the relative efficiency or stability of the old patricentral unit and the new egalitarian unit among the West Indian migrants. The egalitarian unit would seem to be more adapted to modern urban conditions, but it is by no means stable among the British themselves. Among lower-class West Indians this pattern is usually not a modification of the old formal patricentral pattern but an extension of the unstable union, or of the not-so-stable 'faithful

[1] This inversion of the migrant sequence is occasionally encountered, usually in middle-class families.

concubinage' unit, as a result of economic progress by individuals who at home regarded permanent and legalized marriage as a vague ideal well beyond their range of possibilities. One experienced West Indian social worker expressed doubts as to the permanency of many of these unions and units, despite the legal tie, and gloomily predicted a harvest of divorces, separations, desertions, and renewed unstable concubinage.[1]

On the other hand, certain factors in the new situation are, as has been noted, working for the stability of the new marriage. Among them are the individual's greater need for companionship and security, in the absence of the rest of his or her kinship group and former circle of friends; the difficulties of finding alternative accommodation; the needs of the children, to which few West Indians of either sex are totally indifferent; the indirect but increasing pressure of uninstitutionalized local public opinion; and pressure by British welfare organizations and West Indian agencies in Britain (whose workers usually accept upper- or middle-class family patterns) to conform to local middle-class norms.

There is no evidence that the widespread Anglo-American ideal of romantic love and marriage is acting as a factor of change among the West Indian migrants. This may perhaps have more influence on the second migrant generation. Among the majority of migrants, an English middle-class observer might indeed be struck by the fact that couples rarely go out together or make any demonstration of affection towards each other, and by the apparent unconcern with which they accept the prospect of months or years of separation in order to fulfil their economic plans.

Seen from the viewpoint of the children's needs, only the two legalized family types have much chance of proving stable and satisfactory among West Indian migrants in Britain, or of aiding their accommodation to British society. Groupings based on faithful concubinage do not seem to be developing to any great extent. As for the majority of unstable and matricentral units, even if they can keep going economically once they are removed from a rural subsistence economy, they may ultimately fail to give both the women and their children the security and companionship provided at home by the mother's family. The National Assistance Board, the welfare workers, the day nurseries, and the schools cannot take the place of this family circle completely or for ever.[2]

---

[1] See also Hyndman (1960, p. 123 f.).

[2] The Moral Welfare Association statistics for Southwark and London (see Appendix VI) give a fair picture of the situation of West Indian unmarried mothers who have been sufficiently lonely and in need to seek outside help. One in every four or five of the mothers helped was found to be pregnant on arrival; the majority have left children in the West Indies; and there is an increasing number

The migrant settlement from within

This fact seems to be gaining recognition among a growing number of West Indian women migrants, as they contemplate an isolated and indefinite future in one small room with one or more young children, separated from their families and perhaps from other children they have borne, eking out an existence on National Assistance, an unskilled wage, or the grudging and irregular doles made by a temporary male partner,[1] who can disappear even more easily in a British city than he can at home.

In such circumstances, a few women have requested repatriation, despite the humiliation of returning home at the government's expense, poorer than when one left it, and with one's debts unpaid and one or more extra mouths to feed.[2] Others have shown a greater willingness to take the man to court or to press for marriage.[3] A few, particularly those who have already borne more than one illegitimate child in this country, have actually gone so far as to ask almoners and welfare workers for information about birth control. Such a step reflects a great change in attitudes, in view of the almost universal desire for children felt by West Indians, and of the woman's usual view that child-bearing is her natural function and that any attempts at prevention are unnatural, unhealthy, and wrong.[4]

with two or even three children born in Britain. Most putative fathers are West Indian but there is a rather larger minority of English or European fathers north of the river. Despite their difficulties, however, very few of the mothers who have sought assistance wish to go home to the West Indies.

[1] Two excellent articles in the *Manchester Guardian* of 2 and 3 January 1957 discussed the plight of West Indian unmarried mothers in Britain as seen from the social worker's viewpoint.

[2] In the years 1957–60 inclusive, 25 women were repatriated to the West Indies.

[3] Edith Clarke (1957, pp. 106 and 108–9) shows how spasmodic payments for the child may be after the man has left its mother, and how much resented and difficult to enforce a maintenance order is likely to be in Jamaica.

[4] Edith Clarke (1957) and Madeline Kerr (1952, p. 26) both agree that contraceptives are little used in Jamaica, but that a few women try to procure abortion by the use of castor oil or bush tea. Edith Clarke writes: '. . . Women are acutely aware of the economic burden which children represent if they have no male support for them. This fear has to be set against the desire for children as an insurance against old age. Once therefore a woman has demonstrated that she is able to bear a child, she may seek to avoid having another by recourse to drugs or "bush" medicines which are supposed to bring on menstruation. Such action is condemned by the men. . . . We were told that some "bad mothers" took their young daughters to the dispenser and asked him to do away with "the stomach", as pregnancy is described. In view of this attitude it was not surprising to find that we have no evidence of any use of contraceptives except in Sugartown, where the men were said to use them in intercourse with the "pinks" (prostitutes), not with the object of avoiding impregnating the woman but of avoiding venereal disease' (p. 96). Birth control was until recently an explosive political and religious issue which no party in power in any West Indian territory could afford to support. In the last two or three years, however, the need for family planning has been discussed more openly (see the Jamaican People's National Party weekly *Public Opinion* (18 January 1958) headed 'Birth Control or Poverty'; and the report of a statement by Sir Grantley Adams, then Prime Minister-designate of the West Indies Federation, on the necessity of planned parenthood, in the same paper (19 April 1958)).

338

Some cases of abortion have been reported, usually among upwardly mobile women such as nurses, but there is no evidence at hand to show whether its incidence among migrant women is greater than in the West Indies. From my own observations among the working-class Brixton migrants, it would seem that a fair number of women with one or more children are refusing to enter into any more unstable unions. This determination to live without men often breaks down, however, as in the case of one upper-lower-class informant, who lamented her new pregnancy to me: 'I could have had many men, Mistress P, but I stay here alone all that time after the other baby born. After what that Percy do to me I so shamed I say I never go with a man again. I not like all these Jamaican girls here but a decent Christian woman. Now Edwin he come and he always want to go to bed but I say, "No, not until we married". Then one night he bring some drink and it happen, and now he don't come any more.'

The position of the migrant woman left on her own with a child or children in Brixton is worse than that of a local girl. For, as was seen in Chapter 13, the West Indian mother can rarely get her child adopted or even find authorized foster parents. The accessible day nurseries are often too expensive or full,[1] while the services of a licensed baby-minder – or of an unlicensed baby-minder, that bane of the social welfare worker – usually absorb an appreciable portion of a small wage-packet already burdened with a high room-rent, high living costs, clothing, and remittances home. The solution of sending the child home to its grandmother or other maternal relative and remitting its keep is not always so simple; most women with young children cannot easily put away the fare money and the escort fee back to the West Indies.[2]

From the child's point of view, it is doubtful which solution is the least unsatisfactory. Authorized fostering and adoption present their own problems for the few that are at present affected. Not all white foster or adoptive mothers are equipped to resolve the frictions that can arise out of colour and cultural differences, while upbringing in a children's home is regarded as a last resort for children even by the authorities.[3] Upbringing in a single room, in a cold climate with

[1] Over 50 per cent of all children in at least two Brixton day nurseries are coloured.

[2] Children under the age of one year pay no fare; over that age they pay an increasing percentage of the adult fare. They are not allowed to travel alone, and £30 has come to be accepted as the established escort fee payable to returning female migrants who are willing to take charge of children and deliver them to their families at the other end.

[3] 'Two years ago the Council reaffirmed its view that, other things being equal, boarding out with foster parents in private homes was the best upbringing for normal boys and girls' (from the 1954 Dr. Barnardo's Homes Report).

339

no outside playground but the street, with a working mother and no male parent other than a succession of 'uncles', is hardly more desirable.[1]

The unsatisfactory nature of this particular situation is accentuated by the West Indian mother's attitude to her child or children. This attitude is the reverse of neglectful, but it often seems to arise out of a general affection for children rather than a parental love focused on an individual child. Such an attitude is more adequate in the West Indian situation, where the child receives love and affection from a number of close kin, who often share in his or her upbringing.[2] It is less so in Brixton, where often the only close relative is the mother.

The traditional West Indian matrilineal solution of sending the child to the maternal family is less satisfactory in the migrant situation. For the migrant mother has no opportunity at all of visiting the child or children as she could do if she were working in a neighbouring town at home. This 'child-shifting' solution has, however, much to commend it, and should not be judged by British values.[3] The more settled migrant families also make use of 'child-shifting' to enable the mother to continue working and because maintenance is cheaper in the West Indies. But it was noted that a number were bringing their children back to Brixton as soon as they reached school-age, in order to give them the benefit of a British education. The following letter from a woman in the West Indies, who was already looking after two legitimate children of her migrant sister in Brixton, gives an impression of the warmth and normalcy frequently found in these transferred relationships and geographically separated family groupings. She was answering a request from her sister that she should take in a third child, born here to a 'fiancé' who had subsequently deserted her:

'. . . Oh dear me I will be more than proud to receive my little nephew. Well your two children will think they get a piece of sugar cake to know and see their little baby brother. I am only

[1] A certain amount of material was collected about the second migrant generation, its upbringing, education, and various problems that might arise now or in the future. It is hoped to incorporate this material later in a separate paper.

[2] It should, however, be noted that migration to Britain is having a considerable effect on the situation of the many children left behind in the West Indies by one or both parents. Davison (1961, Pt. III) quotes the view of an experienced West Indian social worker that the migration represents the final breakdown of family life in Jamaica. The problem of deserted children is rapidly increasing, and it is estimated that up to 95 per cent of the children of migrants are left behind in Jamaica.

[3] Cf. Rodman (1959, pp. 446–7) on the frequency and acceptability of this 'child-shifting' in the West Indian lower class, and the pitfalls faced by observers and social workers who judge it in terms of their own middle-class values.

too proud to hear he will be coming home – you couldn't suggest a better thing let him come I'll be pleased to receive him any day he landed your mind will be more at ease when you are working . . . I know your mother will be very glad to know and to see him Oh dear me I am one full of joy hearing Josh coming.'

In Brixton the majority of conjugal unions and family groupings are within the migrant group. The general effect of this is to ease the overall process of accommodation in the early stages of the migration, and to lessen the danger of competition and conflict between migrants and local men over women. Should the settlement become permanent, however, the presence of a large number of West Indian women and the existence of so many home-oriented family groupings may tend to slow the process of acculturation and eventual social assimilation among both adult immigrants and the second generation. Such a retarding is not necessarily undesirable. Intra-group integration, followed by gradual assimilation, is sometimes a more satisfactory sequence in the case of a group that differs or is held to differ radically from the receiving or majority society in the sociocultural sphere. If the migrant group develops stable family patterns, this not only furthers satisfactory accommodation in other spheres such as that of work, but also makes the group more acceptable in the eyes of the receiving society.

KINSHIP TIES AMONG MIGRANTS

The West Indian literature emphasizes the relative strength among the lower-class majority of the consanguineous kinship link, particularly on the mother's side. This is in contrast to the conjugal tie. The most important link, not only through childhood, but usually throughout adult life, is that between mother (or mother-substitute) and child.[1] A calypso by the Trinidadian singer Lord Kitchener makes the point forcefully:

> *If your mother and your wife are drowning,*
> *I want to know which one you will be saving.*
> *Well for me I'm holding onto my mother,*
> *And my wife she will have to excuse*
> *Kitchener; I can always get another wife*
> *But I can never get another mother in my life.*
>
> *I heard some men saying round the corner,*
> *That they rather their lawful wife than their mother.*

[1] For detailed discussion of this relationship, see Clarke (1957, pp. 156–66); Henriques (1953, pp. 128, 134–5); and Kerr (1952, p. 70 and *passim*). According to Madeline Kerr, the parent-child tie lasts so long that bereaved adults will refer to themselves as orphans.

> *Ask them the reason, this what they answer:*
> *They can romance their wife but not their mother.*
> *Well, my wife can be flourishing in coin and gold,*
> *But my mother comes first in this blessed world,*
> *'Cos I can always get another wife*
> *But I can never get another mother in my life.*[1]

This relationship retains its strength among recent adult migrants in Brixton, although in our case histories the mother is actually present only in the case of Mrs. 'Nannie' D and her family. In a majority of the family units interviewed, however, the woman's mother in the West Indies constituted an invisible but very important member of the unit, whether or not she was actually looking after her daughter's children.

The ideal role of the mother or mother-substitute was expressed by several West Indian women interviewed; when referring to or introducing social workers or sponsors who had helped them in this country, they would say: 'This is Miss M, whom I tell you so much about. She more than my mother.' Or: 'Mrs. A, she like a mother to me.' This mother-child bond is not always fully reciprocal. The child's attachment to the mother usually seems to be stronger and more focused, whereas the mother's attitude is, as I said earlier, often one of rather general affection. London social workers are often somewhat taken aback at the free and easy way in which many West Indian unmarried mothers discuss the disposal of their children. Some propose to 'give them to the government'; others casually and without any formal guarantees hand them over to other West Indian women who are thought to be in a better position to look after them (see, for instance, the case of Mrs. Beulah F).[2]

It is too early as yet to assess the adequacy and tenacity of the West Indian mother-child bond under migrant conditions, where it is no longer buttressed by the constant presence of other close kin, where the child spends more time at school and on the streets with friends, and where his mother has less time and energy to devote to him after the working day. It seems probable that it may be dangerously weakened, with unfavourable consequences in the second migrant generation, particularly in families where there is no father or father-substitute.

[1] From 'Kitch' selection, on Melodisc MLP500.

[2] Edith Clarke (1957, pp. 176–7) points out that there is no adoption law in Jamaica and no legal recognition of the status. She mentions two kinds of informal adoption in the island. The first seems to correspond to the pattern exemplified in Mrs. Beulah F's case: 'A child may be given away, at any age, to strangers for the reason that the mother is too poor to look after him and hopes that he may have a better chance under the new arrangement. Where the child is an infant, the motive behind the adoption may be the adopted mother's childlessness, and love of children, in which case the baby may find a real foster-home.'

In the West Indies, the usual mother-substitute is the maternal grandmother. Edith Clarke (1957, p. 134) found that 88 out of 679 households in the three Jamaican centres studied were grandmother households, and another eight households were great-grandmother households. The great majority of these households were made up of descendants through the female line, and a large proportion of them were based on family land.

Among the Brixton migrants, only two grandmother households, as opposed to families, were encountered. These were somewhat a-typical and closer to English norms; in each case the legal wife brought over her mother to act as housekeeper or child-minder while she herself returned to a well-paid factory job. There are, however, many 'separated' matrilineal family groupings, in which the woman has left or sent back all or most of her children to be cared for by her mother (or sometimes by her sister, aunt, or other female relation), while she earns their keep in London. In view of the longer and unbroken separation between the migrant mother and her children in the West Indies in these cases, the grandmother-grandchild or mother-substitute-child relationship seems likely to become even stronger than it would normally be.

The father-child bond is tenuous, uncertain, or even totally lacking in all but a small minority of West Indian working-class family groupings.[1] Even in this minority, stabilization and legalization of the union do not necessarily occur during the children's most formative years. In consequence, they are often witnesses of the strains and tensions between their parents, and come to lean more heavily on the mother.[2] They may also have to adjust to one or more stepfathers in their biological father's place. Once grown up, the male child of such a family is unlikely to feel parental responsibility for his own children, since he has learned early that children are 'women's business'.

Of the father-child relationship in the relatively stable units, Edith Clarke writes:

'The relationship to the father where he lives in the home is at best ambivalent. He is always more strict, more exacting and infinitely less well-known than the mother. While the mother's violence and threats of dire punishment are one aspect only of a behaviour pattern which includes tenderness and a sense of

[1] Cf. Simey (1946, p. 88); and Edith Clarke (1957, p. 107 and *passim*).

[2] Edith Clarke found that while 543 (73 per cent) out of 747 children in the three centres studied by her team were living in family homes, only 430 (58 per cent) were living with both their parents. The remainder were living with one parent and a step-parent. '. . . The step-relationship is rarely a happy one. Moreover it cannot be assumed that even those who were (then) living with both parents had done so from infancy or would continue in this situation' (1957, p. 141).

security, the father's discipline is often tempered by no such condition and leaves a permanent mark. There were many references to bad fathers but criticism of the mother is rare. There is nothing worse that can be said of a man or woman than that "they would curse even their mother". Fathers are far less tender and their interest in the child more usually centres on his material progress' (1957, p. 159).

Among the migrants, several factors may influence the development of the father-child relationship. On the one hand, legalization of the parent's relationship may occur sooner and in a greater number of cases than it would have done in the West Indies, and the father may reinterpret his role to approximate more closely to local patterns. Several cases have also been noted where the father, having left the mother and married another woman, has sought to take the child to live with him. In two cases, these zealous fathers were admittedly influenced by the wish to claim tax allowances for their children.

In the migrant situation, on the other hand, the West Indian father-child relationship may be expected, as the children and particularly as the boys grow older, to encounter the same sort of difficulties as did the patricentral families of the Polish and other European migrants in the New World. Such paternal authority is no longer the prevailing pattern in the receiving society in South London, and the migrant father also tends to lose status in the eyes of his London-educated children because of his relative lack of education or skills, his 'foreign' accent, his unfamiliarity with or unwillingness to conform to local *mores* and, in the case of children of a 'mixed' union, because of his colour.

Stepparent-stepchild relationships, which in practice usually mean stepfather-stepchild relationships, have had little time to develop among the Brixton migrants as yet. In Jamaica Simey (1946) suggested that 'a man will accept the children of the woman with whom he is living into his household without question, and will bestow on them a degree of care and attention certainly not inferior to that which he bestows on his own children' (p. 16). Edith Clarke found, however, that the number of cases where 'outside' children of either conjugal partner were included in a household was relatively very small. The man's reluctance to take in his wife's or his concubine's children she attributes partly to financial considerations, partly to the general disapproval of the man 'who fathers another man's bastards'.[1] The handful of cases so far noted in Brixton seem

[1] Clarke (1957, p. 175 and p. 118). In homes based on legal marriage and concubinage, she found that 89 per cent of the children were the offspring of the cohabiting couple, 8 per cent were illegitimate children of the woman, and 3 per

to conform to the former rather than the latter situation. After Miss Thelma L married, her husband readily assumed the responsibilities of a father towards her 'outside' child, Gloria; and the relationship of Mrs. Edith F to her legal husband's 'outside' child also seemed to be close and affectionate.

The sibling tie, particularly between sisters or between brother and sister, appears to be fairly strong in the West Indies, and to persist into adult life. In Brixton the sibling ties between settled and incoming migrants would appear to resemble the ties that linked urban and rural siblings in the West Indies.[1] A brother or sister can always count on initial accommodation and assistance from the earlier arrival. Similar assistance is also extended to aunts, uncles, nieces, nephews, cousins, and other kin.[2] Such assistance is visible in the temporary overcrowding of so many single-room units after each large migrant ship comes in, and in the increasing number of house purchases made by migrants for the express purpose of ensuring accommodation for kinsmen who are on the point of migrating.

Kinship ties may indeed be closer among the migrants than they would be at home, in view of the absence of other close relatives and of the general social isolation of the migrant. Also, as in the village communities of the West Indies, there is among the more settled migrants a tendency to use the terms 'cousin' and 'auntie'[3] in relation to close acquaintances of the same generation or to older women. Henriques suggests that this tendency in Jamaican lower-class society to stress relationships between individuals is to be associated with the prevailing social and economic insecurity. If this be accepted, it is not surprising to find the tendency persisting in the general insecurity of the migrant situation, where an acquaintance from the same village or parish may reasonably be accepted as 'cousin' or 'coz'. In the absence of most other associations and ties there may also be a strengthening of bonds with kin still in the West Indies, particularly in cases where the latter have contributed to the migrant's passage-money.

SIMPLE AND 'CELLULAR' HOUSEHOLDS

Among the Brixton migrants, then, the basic social unit is the elementary family grouping, whether it is identical with a simple

cent were illegitimate children of the man. In homes based on concubinage alone, 64 per cent of the children were children of the cohabiting couple, 27 per cent were illegitimate children of the woman, and 9 per cent were illegitimate children of the man.

[1] Cf. Clarke (pp. 172–4).
[2] Cf. Henriques (1953, Chapter 10) and Kerr (1952, p. 71).
[3] 'Uncle' seems to be used more often in a specific economic context (see p. 107).

The migrant settlement from within

household unit or whether, as is more usual, it is geographically extended between Brixton and the West Indies.

There is, however, some evidence of the evolution among the more settled migrants of a locally based social unit which may be termed the multiple or 'cellular'[1] household. Such households are rarely found in the Somerleyton-Geneva area with its shifting population, but develop fairly often in large rooming-houses in the more settled nuclei of coloured settlement. Occasionally a cellular household is wholly or partly linked by kinship ties. More usually, however, it is associated with a landlord or landlady who either lives on the premises or who, though non-resident, exerts a certain control over the type of tenants accepted and over their subsequent conduct. In such houses, groups of fairly congenial individuals and families, usually from the same island,[2] and sometimes even from the same parish or village, tend to come together and to set up an informal community in which services are exchanged and economic and social needs satisfied.

In one household of this type which I visited frequently there resided four couples, all married or purporting to be married, each with one young child. There were also a man of about 50 and his 19-year-old son, one widow and her baby, and one single man. The majority of tenants had lived in the house for a year or more, and spoke of it as a 'good house, almost a home'. All the tenants were from Jamaica, and two had come to lodge in the house following recommendations by a friend of the landlord. The landlord and his wife were brown-skinned Jamaicans, multiple landlords, who owned property elsewhere in South London and also in New York. The room-rents were no higher than elsewhere, but the house had a certain *cachet* in the eyes of both its landlord and its permanent tenants. The former was fond of saying: 'I won't have any bad behaviour or bad language in my house. Anybody try that, out he or she go at once.'

On one occasion, one of my contacts, Miss Florence D (see No. 7), went to lodge in this house with her baby. She had left her Somerleyton Road room after a quarrel with the baby's father. The man subsequently rejoined her, and loud quarrelling and bad language soon began. Miss D, who showed almost a persecution complex in her relationships with other immigrants, alienated fellow-lodgers'

[1] I am indebted to Professor Isaac Schapera for suggesting this term.

[2] Most of the households which I visited in Brixton were all-Jamaican, or Jamaican with one or two white women. Two all-Barbadian houses, two British Guianian houses, and one St. Lucian household were also noted. The last, a French-speaking household, was somewhat dramatically revealed to the outside world when the entire back wall of a house in Trigon Road, Kennington, collapsed one Sunday morning (*South London Press*, 5 November 1957).

346

sympathy by picking noisy quarrels with every other woman in the house, accusing them of stealing her food and laundry, and in general demonstrating that she was what the others called 'a low sort of person who couldn't fit in here'. Within a month the landlord gave her notice and the couple returned to Somerleyton Road. Several of the other residents opined that this was a more suitable area for 'persons of their type'.

Everyday life was greatly eased for the members of this cellular household. The widow minded two babies along with her own for working mothers who could not get a place in the nearby day nursery or who could not afford its rates. 'I take a £1 a week from each – not 30*s*. or £2 like some women take from their own people', she said. She also cooked dinner and mended for the father and son. They, in return, ran errands for her, took her to and from hospital for her confinement, and often helped her financially, although the father was also sending money home regularly to his wife and other children. The widow kept the public parts of the house clean in return for a reduction in rent, and the father acted as rent collector and general representative of the landlords during their frequent absences. The widow was also the agent for a mail-order hire-purchase firm and earned a commission on these transactions.

All permanent residents were linked by a similar network of small services and courtesies. Two of the married couples and the widow would meet for prayers and Bible readings on Sundays and some week-day evenings. Sometimes they would go out together and attend a nearby Baptist church, taking their children with them. Drinking and dancing were rare in this house, but people usually visited each other in the evening for tea, coffee, or a soft drink, to talk or to listen to the wireless or gramophone.

The sense of community and of shared standards in this house was so strong that when the widow became pregnant by a man whom she was to marry in a few weeks' time, and he broke his engagement, refused to acknowledge the baby as his and disappeared, she felt too 'shamed' to stay on where everyone knew the circumstances; she therefore moved to the comparative anonymity of Somerleyton Road and lost touch with most of the other tenants.

The organization of these 'cellular' households is informal, impermanent, and tenuous, like most other forms of migrant association. Nevertheless, in the earlier years of settlement these households may be of more significance than the various voluntary associations, which rarely draw in the women migrants at all, homebound as they are by children or domestic chores.

347

17

Associations — formal and informal

FEW WORKING-CLASS economic migrant groups evolve a stable or complex set of formal associations in the early years of their new life. Where such associations exist, whether they are organized from within or by outside well-wishers, they tend to provide assistance of a material or spiritual nature. Recreational and political associations usually arise later, when the group is more settled in its new environment.

'PARTNERS' ASSOCIATIONS

In nineteenth-century North America, there was little or no public assistance available to newcomers or indeed to any member of society. The first voluntary associations set up by migrants were usually therefore of the mutual aid or fraternal type; they were sometimes linked with the parish organizations proper, but sometimes preceded them.[1] In the welfare state, there is not the same urgent need for the West Indian migrants to set up such associations. In Brixton, however, I noted the existence of a large number of small cooperative savings associations, formal only to the extent that they have a specific membership and a 'banker' or secretary. Their aim is not to duplicate the public services but to assist members to achieve their economic goals more rapidly.

These associations are groups of 'partners', in which each member contributes a regular weekly sum and draws out a lump sum every so often.[2] The accumulation enables him or her to make a down-payment on a house, car, or other large purchase, or to send

[1] Sometimes they were entirely secular and might take the form of 'lodges' with a craft or semi-masonic orientation. Such 'lodges' are a fairly common form of voluntary association in the West Indies but I came across no evidence of them in Brixton, although one or more were said to exist among migrants in North London.

[2] In a case that came before Lambeth County Court in May 1956 (*South London Press*, 3 May 1956) a woman sued the man with whom she had been living for £37, which she claimed to have given him for safe keeping after such a pay-out. She also sued for £6 10s. to compensate for a week's wages lost after he knocked her about when she asked for the return of the money. Judgement was given in her favour.

348

the fare home for a relative. Weekly payments may range up to several pounds, especially in the case of men, who receive higher wages. In some 'partners' or cooperative groups, the 'kitty' seems to be collected by each member in rotation. In others it is apparently apportioned by the drawing of lots, so that an element of chance, agreeable to many West Indians, is introduced.

'Partners' associations exist in the West Indies,[1] but contributions are naturally on a much smaller scale, often in shillings rather than in pounds. In the rural areas, 'partnership' is also the term applied to a reciprocal exchange of labour for day-to-day tasks between two or more individuals. Michael Smith (1956, p. 11f.) discusses this form of 'partners' and the other form of cooperation known as 'morning sport' or 'digging', and calls them the 'basic foundations and forms of labour-exchange among small-settlers'.

'Morning sport' and 'digging' are free work by a large group on another's farm, for the purpose of discharging large emergency tasks such as building a house, or harvesting. Such forms of cooperation may exist among the Brixton migrants, but no evidence of them was found during the present inquiry, over and above the small reciprocal services performed by kin, close friends, and members of the cellular households. In the absence of any wider community consciousness it would indeed be unreasonable to expect the survival in the migrant situation of a form of association rooted not only in economic needs but also in community values.

The Brixton version of 'partners' continues to flourish, particularly among more recent migrants. But given greater familiarity with banks and savings accounts, and the continued high incidence of theft from fellow-lodgers or -tenants which is reported in Brixton, such associations may well fade away after some years.

RELIGIOUS AND POLITICO-RELIGIOUS ASSOCIATIONS

In Jamaica and other parts of the Caribbean there is, as has been said, a correlation between the type of religious association in which an individual participates and his socio-economic status. The denominational churches, and especially the Anglican Church, have always been associated with the upper and middle classes, and with a small number of upwardly mobile lower-class members. The church officials are often either overseas-born or overseas-trained. It was not until December 1955 that a Jamaican, the Rt. Rev.

[1] This is the Jamaican term. Elsewhere they are known by different names, as, for instance, 'sou-sou', 'chitty', or 'syndicate'. Cf. Hyndman (1960, p. 74) and Margaret Katzin (1959, pp. 436-40). For the Nigerian credit institution of *esusu* from which the Trinidad term 'sou-sou' was almost certainly derived, see W. R. Bascom (1952). I am indebted to Dr. Kenneth Little for this reference.

Percival W. Gibson, Bishop Suffragan of Kingston, was elected as Bishop of Jamaica.[1] The rites in these churches do not differ fundamentally from those in the European parent bodies, although services may be better attended, and congregations may participate in them more whole-heartedly. Membership is primarily an index of status, and makes for social solidarity within the community.

In Jamaica denominational fragmentation and sectarianism seem to have developed further than in most other parts of the British Caribbean.[2] Here Professor George Simpson (1956, p. ii, n. a) distinguishes the established sects (for example, Christian Science, Salvation Army, Seventh Day Adventists, Society of Friends) from ordinary sects (Bedwardites, Church of God, Jehovah's Witnesses, Pentecostal) and cults[3] (Revival Zion, Revival, Pocomania, and Cumina).[4]

Classified according to Simpson and Yinger's typology, the denominational position in the island at the time of the 1943 census was as shown in the table opposite (1960 percentages are given in square brackets).

On these figures, the 1943 census report commented: 'It is believed that most of the religious denominations showing the largest number of adherents have considerably less numbers in their church membership. This is due in part to the fact that children are reported as belonging to the denomination of their parents. . . . Again, it is known that considerable numbers of spasmodic churchgoers favour a particular denomination but are in the main not registered members of a church. . . . It is believed, however,

---

[1] 'This took place in the face of strong opposition from most of the English section of the Anglican diocese', according to a report in the *Daily Telegraph* of 15 December 1955.

[2] See Ruck (Ed.) (1960, p. 174, Table IV) for detailed figures.

[3] For an illuminating study of some cult groups operating in the small town of Morant Bay, Jamaica, in 1950, see J. G. Moore (1954). The groups studied in detail included a pocomania group called the 'Black Israelites' and some African-oriented Cumina groups where membership is said to be based on family and clan links.

[4] This distinction is based on the six-step classification of religious associations proposed by J. M. Yinger, according to the criteria of inclusiveness of membership and the degree of emphasis on social integration. According to this classification, the established sect is described as continuing to 'stress ethical protest themes (while) . . . members believe that the major problems are found in the reform of the evils of society'. The ordinary sect is said to stress 'literal obedience, individual perfection and asceticism, tends to be radical, has a small voluntary membership that lacks continuity, is either hostile or indifferent to the state, is lay religion, and is usually associated with the lower classes'. The cult, according to Yinger's classification, is characterized by 'small size, search for a mystical experience, presence of a charismatic leader; it is short-lived and often local. The implications for anarchy are even stronger than in the case of the sect, which is led by its interest in right behaviour (whether the avoidance of individual sin or the establishment of social justice) back to the problem of social integration' (Simpson, 1956, pp. 338–41).

350

Associations – formal and informal

Christian Denominations			Non-Christian Denominations		
Anglican	28.3%	[19.8]	Buddhist	X	[(X)]
Baptist	25.8%	[18.0]	Confucian	2.1%	[(X)]
Methodist	8.9%	[6.7]	Hindu	0.3%	[0.1]
Presbyterian	7.5%	[5.1]	Jewish	0.1%	[X]
Roman Catholic	5.7%	[7.2]			
Moravian	4.1%	[3.3]			
Congregational	1.7%	[1.4]			
	82.0%	[61.5]		2.5%	[0.1]

Established Sects			Sects		
Brethren	0.4%	[0.9]	Bedwardite	X	[(X)]
Christian Scientist	X	[X]	Bible Student	0.1%	[(X)]
Salvation Army	1.1%	[0.7]	Church of God	3.5%	[11.9]
Seventh Day			(Jehovah's Witnesses	X)	[(X)]
Adventists	2.2%	[4.8]	Mission	0.1%	[(X)]
Society of Friends	0.3%	[0.2]	Pentecostal	0.4%	[0.9]
	4.0%	[6.6]		4.1%	[12.8]

Cults			Other		
Pocomania	0.3%	[X]	Non-denominational	1.6%	[0.9]
(Revival	X)	[(X)]	Not specified	0.3%	[5.6]
(Revival Zion	X)	[(X)]	No Religion	4.0%	[11.4]
(Cumina	X)	[(X)]			
	0.3%	[X]		5.9%	[17.9]

X indicates a very small percentage, totalling 1·1 per cent in the two census years.
( ) indicates cults and groups not given separately in the census report.
The 1960 statistics were received only in time for insertion without further comment.

that the census figures do not completely show the extent of the following and practice of the rites of pocomania and similar sects.'[1]

Henriques and Simpson both support the view that the cult membership figures given in the 1943 census are seriously underrated. One reason advanced is that members are often unwilling to admit affiliation, in view of the general condemnation of pocomania by the upper and middle classes; moreover, it is thought that many of those who attend cult meetings are also members of the more socially acceptable sects or even of the orthodox churches.[2] Henriques found a substantial number of working-class Jamaicans attending pocomania meetings in Portland, and Simpson estimated that there were at least 3,000 Revivalist-pocomania devotees in West Kingston alone in 1953. Many of those listed as 'Baptists' or under the head-

[1] Simpson (1956, p. 339, note b).   [2] Simpson (pp. 338–9) and Henriques (1953, p. 78).

ing 'Other' in the census report may also have been sect or cult adherents.

In Jamaica, the cult groups, and to a lesser extent the sects, meet the emotional needs and help to relieve the frustrations of many members of the lower class, although it should not be assumed that all or even most members of this class are necessarily involved in cult membership[1] or the practice of *obeah* (magic).[2] The cults focus the attention of their members on another world, a world of spirits and magic in which the initiated are no longer under-privileged. All members can share in the satisfaction of being part of an *élite* in relation to the rest of the world, while the many leaders and office-holders, all drawn from more or less the same sphere as the ordinary members, gain an additional semi-messianic satisfaction which is denied them in everyday life. And while the close-knit cult groups give their members a feeling of belonging to an elect community, they also provide entertainment, sensuous thrills, and emotional release to people living out a drab, poverty-stricken, and hopeless existence.

Among the cults a dividing line should be drawn between the autocratic, polytheistic, other-worldly, a-political cults such as Revival and pocomania,[3] with their emphasis on spirit possession, witchcraft, and healing; and the Black Utopian, monotheistic, democratically organized politico-religious groupings which fall under the general heading of the Ras Tafari movement. In groups of the latter kind the withdrawal from real life is not to the next world but to a Black African Utopia. The emphasis here is more political, less religious, but it is still negative in that the members have little real chance of changing their present situation. An early exponent of this black secular messianism was Marcus Garvey, founder of the Universal Negro Improvement Association. Its current supporters in Jamaica since the 1930s have been the Ras Tafari groups, whose main centre is in the economically depressed area of West Kingston.

Simpson estimated that there were in 1953 at least a dozen such groups, whose membership ranged from 20 to 150 or more. These groups differed from the Revival-pocomania groups not only in the

[1] Of the associational outlets available in Jamaica, George Simpson wrote: 'Functional alternatives or functional equivalents of Revivalism for other lower-class Jamaicans include: the orthodox Christian churches, the Ras Tafari movement, labour unions, political parties, clubs and cooperative associations.'

[2] See Henriques (1953, pp. 79–80) and Simpson (1956, pp. 343, 382 f., 406 f.) on the subject of *obeah*, which is legally proscribed.

[3] See Simpson (1956, pp. 342 and 402) for a distinction between these two sub-types of cult which seems to depend mainly on the extent of African influence in ritual. Both cults are despised by upper- and middle-class Jamaicans, but pocomania ranks lower than Revival, and pocomania members will rarely admit to membership, preferring to describe themselves as Revivalists or even Baptists.

location of their Utopia and their God ('Ethiopia is Heaven, Haile
Selassie is the Living God'), and in their black-oriented, often anti-
white doctrines, but also in their extremely democratic organization, and in the absence of witchcraft, healing, and spirit possession
in general. The Ras Tafarians felt profound contempt for the 'backwardness' of the Revivalists. They also differed in that their membership contained more men than women (detractors at times link
Ras Tafarism with homosexual practices) and more young people.
By contrast, Simpson estimated that in 1953 approximately three-
quarters of Revival group members were women, and a majority
were middle-aged or old people.

Since 1953 major changes have occurred in Jamaican folk religion, at the expense of the Revival-pocomania groups, particularly
those in urban areas. These are attributed by the authors of the
1960 report on Ras Tafarism primarily to intensified campaigns in
the island by American Protestant missions – notably the sectarian
Church of God movement – and also by the Ethiopian World
Federation. As a result Revival has steadily lost ground, its less
political members and preachers going to the Church of God, its
less religious members out of the cults altogether or in the direction of the Ras Tafari movement. Thus by 1960 the dozen or so
independent groups of Simpson's day had grown to a movement
with a declared membership in Kingston of some ten to fifteen
thousand, and probably with at least an equal number of un-
declared but closely integrated sympathizers among the disaffected
urban lower class. Its organization is loose and its membership
heterogeneous, ranging from the orderly and moderate branches
of the Ethiopian World Federation and some other independent or
semi-independent groups, through Marxist cells, ganja-sellers and
criminal gangs who use the movement as a shield, to the unemployed extremists of the Niyabingi sub-cult and the revolutionaries
of the Rev. C. V. Henry's African Reform Church.[1]

[1] On the history, doctrines, organization, membership, and aims of the Ras
Tafari brethren see Smith, Augier, and Nettleford (1960). The Rev. Claudius
Henry's organization was disavowed by the Ethiopian World Federation in April-
May 1959. In October several hundred of his followers gathered at his home in
Kingston, with 1*s*. certificates which had been issued implying that the bearer
would be able to return to Africa. Many had sold all their belongings in their
elation at the prospect of leaving 'Babylon' (*Public Opinion*, 10 October 1959).
In October 1960 the Rev. Henry's son and two others were condemned to death
for the murder of two other Ras Tafari brethren after a period of subversive
activities and disturbances in which two unarmed British soldiers were also murdered. At the end of the month Henry was sentenced to ten years' imprisonment
for treason and felony. Meanwhile the Jamaican Prime Minister, the Hon. Norman
Manley, agreed to send a team to Africa to explore the possibilities of Jamaican
emigration there (Institute of Race Relations *Newsletter*, November 1960). This
visit took place in 1961 but no concrete results were reported by the year's end.

The migrant settlement from within

The rise of the politico-religious Ras Tafari movement and the decline of the old-style Revival-pocomania cult groups since 1953 are also attributed to the general increase in internal party-political activity, to the general climate of decolonization and the creation of independent African states, to Fidelismo in the Caribbean, and to the socio-economic ferment generated by large-scale West Indian emigration to Britain. Relatively few thorough-going Ras Tafarians seem to have been in a position to migrate but the movement has given a certain air of reality to their dreams of migration to Africa.

Although few West Indian migrants will admit to having belonged to a cult group before migrating, it is likely that a fair number fall within the class of denominational or sectarian members who occasionally attended cult ceremonies at home. For this reason it seemed advisable to describe the nature and aims of the cults in some detail here, since they are not cultural isolates but simply extremes in a politico-religious continuum, and knowledge of their beliefs and ritual sometimes helps to elucidate certain rather obscure features of migrant religious life. And although Revival-pocomania has declined since 1953 in Jamaica, it was still in a position to influence many migrants, particularly those who migrated by the mid-1950s and those from rural areas. Similar cults also appear to persist in the more rural 'small islands' from which so many later migrants have come.

Most Brixton migrants, as we have already seen, rarely or never enter a church except for weddings, christenings, and other special occasions when group or kin solidarity is demonstrated. At home the majority would seem to have belonged to a denominational congregation, usually Methodist or Baptist, or to a sect, though a middle-class or socially ambitious minority were Anglicans or Roman Catholics. In spite of the most discreet and indirect questioning, I met no migrant who would openly admit to any home affiliation with Revival-pocomania or Ras Tafari groups, although I managed to locate a small group of former Ras Tafari members in South London through an introduction provided by a third party who knew of their antecedents.[1] A West Indian social worker also

[1] Early in 1958 a group of bearded and rather conspicuously dressed young men were noted in the Brixton market area. Several local informants confirmed that these were Ras Tafarians but no further information could be obtained then or later.

In considering informants' statements about their earlier religious affiliation, allowance must be made for their natural desire to match their increased prosperity with an advance in social status, and also to present themselves in a favourable light to a white inquirer. For the same reason it proved impossible to get any definite information as to the practice of *obeah* among the Brixton migrants. A West African club manager in Brixton claimed to have heard of it locally, and

354

told me that he had come across a number of former Revival-pocomania cult members in London, and suggested that some of the migrants who now described themselves as Baptists might have been Revival or pocomonia members at home.

The minority of West Indians who continue to participate in religious life in Brixton may be divided into two classes: the more settled and socially mobile lower-middle-class or upper-lower-class group who attend local churches; and the ardent former sect or cult members who set up their own independent pentecostal groups or take over existing congregations.[1] The second class would seem to be at least as important in the social organization of the West Indian settlement in Brixton as any other type of voluntary association.

At least three sectarian groups were in existence in the Brixton area during the two years of this study. Two of them were in fact splinter-groups originating from one pentecostal Church of God congregation. This Church of God congregation is said to have been set up in Brixton in 1954 by a middle-class American Negro woman who had received some sectarian training in the United States. The group was given a meeting-place by the vicar of an Anglican church in Angell Town in the rather naïve hope that after a while its members might come into communion with the Anglican congregation. As soon as this suggestion was made, however, the group moved elsewhere.[2]

At this stage the split occurred. One prominent member of the group, who had been a Church of God worker in Jamaica, refused to accept the pastorate of the appointed successor. Both the successor and the dissident were Jamaicans living in a lower-middle-class district outside the area, and both were of a rather more educated type than the bulk of the congregation. A roughly equal number of members followed each leader. One group, that of the appointed leader, was given the use of a small mission hall in Sussex Road which runs parallel to Geneva Road. This leader is now an Overseer of several congregations of what is called the 'Church of God in Christ'; he and his wife, a forceful woman who shares in his work, live over in Dalston and administer congrega-

a Dominican informant in Fulham had evidence that at least one 'healer' was practising among the migrants there. It seems likely that *obeah*, which is a secret activity offering the individual power over events, might be more persistent in the migrant situation than the open practice of cult rituals.

[1] In about 1959 a Seventh Day Adventist migrant group appears to have more or less 'taken over' the local Brixton church. By 1960 most of the office-holders were West Indian, and in early 1961 this congregation was reported to be building its own new church. This 'take-over' pattern was reported to be fairly common among migrant sectarian groups elsewhere in London, and indeed it nearly occurred in the case of the Unitarian church described below (p. 357).

[2] See p. 257 for further details of this episode.

tions in Brixton, Dalston, Camden Town, Archway, Kensal Rise, and elsewhere. Each congregation is visited in turn by the Overseer, or one of several evangelists, but has its own pastor, elders, and sisters who are responsible for the sacraments and other functions. Several hundred people are said to attend the various services, and fifty or so would seem to be the average for the Brixton congregation.[1] This number includes a few local whites, mainly elderly men and women, who share 'the unadulterated Christian faith'. Most members are Jamaican and some belonged to Church of God congregations at home. But there are said to be no formal organizational links with Jamaica, and so far as could be ascertained the congregations had come together in London and were not based on pre-migration nuclei of worshippers.

No detailed information with regard to formal organizational links with or financial aid from the United States could be obtained. The Brixton pastor had, according to his own statement, been appointed Overseer by an American 'bishop'. He had a rather grand D.D. Certificate hanging in his parlour, issued by an organization called the 'Universal Renown Scholasticatitation International Ministerial Association and Schools of Theology (Universal)'. This body gave various vague and untraceable addresses in London, India, the United States, and Africa. One daughter and one son of the Overseer were at the time of my interviews in the United States, studying to be missionaries at a seminary called the Angelus Temple College in California.

The Overseer gave as his reasons for undertaking such work among the London migrants the discrimination practised against them in the white churches, and the empty formalism and regimentation of these churches' ritual: 'We worship as we feel, and we believe in personal and modern-day salvation, that is, living the way Jesus did in modern conditions – no strong drink, smoking, dancing, or cinemas. The white ministers do many of these things. How can they teach the people to do better? How could we worship with them? They wouldn't feel comfortable. We believe and practise every word of the Bible from cover to cover.'

He went on to speak bitterly of the local established churches. They had, he claimed, tried to stop his congregation getting a hall in Paddington on the ground that his work encouraged segregation. But his group was in fellowship with some white ministers, who were 'real Christians', and from time to time his members attended the services held by these ministers. The congregation at Dalston

---

[1] This sect began in schism, like almost all pentecostal sects, and by late 1960 was reported a victim of further schism. Several congregations had fallen away and the membership of the Brixton congregation was dwindling.

was in communion with a local Baptist church, whose minister had recently preached that it needed 'coloured people to come from Jamaica to teach us how to receive the unadulterated Gospel without compromise or changes'. At Archway, the congregation held services in communion with the Methodists. The Overseer's wife had herself been a Methodist before she 'received the Lord'. Outdoor meetings were held in Hyde Park during the warmer months, and as many as five hundred might attend from all parts of London. Baptism was by 'full immersion', not 'sprinkling'. It was not for children but for those adults who testified and were willing to receive God: 'Otherwise you go down into the water a dry sinner and come up a wet sinner.'

The second break-away congregation, which calls itself the New Covenant Church of God, soon found other premises. A Unitarian minister in the Brixton area told me that about one dozen Jamaicans turned up at his service one Sunday morning in 1955. The next Sunday there were forty or fifty, totally swamping his small regular congregation of some twenty or so. This development presented some problems, because Unitarian worship is restrained, individual, and intellectualistic, and the regular congregation was somewhat disturbed by pious ejaculations, physical demonstrations (shivering and stamping), and revivalist-style hymn-singing. The 'take-over' was averted by letting the West Indian group have the elegant little modern church for a nominal rent for their own services on Sunday evenings. This was a solution preferred by both congregations. Occasionally a few individuals would attend the other congregation's services and inter-congregational relationships were generally friendly.

The leaders of both splinter-sects complained of religious apathy among the great bulk of the migrants. The majority of their members were drawn from those who were regular members of similar sects at home, and there were few younger members. This was attributed to the plentiful secular distractions available in London, and to the impact of everyday duties and long working hours. It may also be that the rigid rules for members (teetotalism, no dancing or smoking, no cohabitation without marriage) would deter most lower-class migrants.

Apart from personalities, the two Church of God sectarian groups seemed not to differ greatly in creed or manner of worship. Possibly the first group was a little more uninhibited in its practice; a local Baptist minister who had lent his church to both groups claimed that this group was doing things of which he 'did not approve and which he had to stop'. Further questioning elicited that he was referring to physical demonstrations and spirit possession. The

357

second group he continued to allow to use his premises, subject to certain rules.

The service described below seemed to be fairly typical of the mode of worship of both groups, but for the incident of the epileptic:

The small narrow hall is nearly full and the service has started. It is to last over three hours. Most men are sitting on the left, women on the right. There are more women than men, and most of those present, apart from a few very young children or babes-in-arms, seem to be in their mid-thirties or over. The women all wear fairly elaborate hats and good sturdy woollen overcoats. Most seem lighter in colour than the men, almost all of whom are very dark-skinned. A few white people are present, mainly elderly women. A friendly, middle-aged, white man shows us to seats at the back of the hall.

On the platform at the end of the hall, behind a table, sits a light-coloured Sister with a strong American accent, dressed in a striking black and yellow ensemble; with her are a tall, dark-skinned Elder in a dark suit, and a smart-looking, brown-skinned young man. Up in front of the table a seedy-looking white youth is testifying rather incoherently. Within a few minutes he has said something, inaudible to us, which offends the bulk of the congregation in the front seats. The women in particular begin to make an uproar and the young man seems to go into some sort of epileptic fit. He is finally overpowered and carried back, rigid and horizontal, by several men and women. The other women are screaming: 'Get the Devil out of him; make him kneel and confess his sins.' The Elder and other men take charge; a well-dressed white man behind me murmurs: 'It's exorcism they mean.' The women continue to stamp and scream, and the former testifier, now standing on his feet, looks somewhat sheepish and subdued. The police arrive, one sergeant and two constables. A number of curious white faces peer in through the doors behind. Calm is restored by the sergeant, who asks everyone to sit down and speaks very courteously to the Elder, asking if he wishes to prefer charges. The Elder says no, provided the man is taken away. This is done and the doors are shut.

The congregation then start up a rhythmic hymn out of the Redemptionist Hymnal; they use tambourines and cymbals and are accompanied by the Elder on his guitar and by the brown young man on the piano. A few excited women come out into the aisle and begin to undulate and stamp. Next comes a testimony from another seedy-looking white boy in the congregation,

358

concerning his sinfulness and the mercy shown him by the Lord Jesus. This testimony is well received by the congregation, with frequent ejaculations of 'Amen' and 'Lord have mercy on us'. After another hymn comes a series of addresses and messages, interspersed with anthems and slower hymns. An offertory is taken by two Sisters who stand up in front, and most members of the congregation go up to make their offerings. Some go up more than once. Then two cheerful-looking Brothers come almost dancing down the aisle to collect from the less forth-coming members of the congregation, while a rather jazzy hymn is being played.

In general, the women dominate the congregation and their behaviour is highly emotional, often almost hysterical. Some weep; the young girl next to me giggles and weeps hysterically for most of the service. The general tenor of the preaching is that each person can be saved if he or she offers his or her heart and soul to Jesus and makes an acceptable sacrifice. Several speakers refer to the Devil in our midst, and cite the first white testifier as an example. The Elder says that we should be gentle with such people as it is not their fault that the Devil is in them. If we force the Devil out of such a person roughly he may settle in one of us. The messages and exhortations are based mainly on the Old Testament, St. Paul, and the Book of Revelation. Some of the speakers cannot read aloud very fluently, but none are inhibited. One hymn contains the core of their belief: 'My know-ledge of the Bible is my College.'

An evangelistic group which purported to be connected with the British and European section of the Californian 'Soul Clinic Inter-national' (described as a 'world-wide soul-winning faith ministry' started in 1943 by the Reverend Fred Jordan, formerly pastor of the First Baptist Church of South Gate, California) was also active in Brixton in 1955–57. This mission relied less on services than on door-to-door visitations, informal home prayer meetings, and a regular twice-weekly night school for would-be active lay workers which was held in a Somerleyton Road basement. Most of the missionaries had been Baptists, but one was an educated British Guianian of Hindu antecedents. He had been 'reborn' before he came to England, and reckoned that 'the Lord would provide' while he pursued his work here among 'his own people', whom he regarded as 'uneducated, immoral, primitive, and greatly in need of the Lord'. This group was operating in cooperation with various local Baptist churches. The missionaries themselves finally passed on to do similar evangelistic work among West Indians in the Midlands, and the evening classes ceased, although one or two ardent lay workers still held home prayer meetings.[1]

It has already been said that no West Indian migrant informants would admit to having been members of any type of cult group. The individual who had been a Ras Tafari leader in Jamaica was also unwilling to discuss his former religio-political activities, although he knew that I was aware of them. In 1955 he joined with former associates from Jamaica to organize a local branch of the Ras Tafari-oriented United Afro-West Indian Brotherhood in London. Shortly after its inception the leaders called at the Woodford Green offices of the *New Times and Ethiopia Times* to explain their aims and pro-Ethiopian sympathies. This visit was reported as follows (in the issue of 11 June 1955):

'They called at the office . . . wearing a soldierly green uniform with shoulder straps of red, yellow, and green, representing the Ethiopian colours, and red and yellow cords. Their caps were ornamented with a badge bearing a crown and stars, and crossed flags embroidered with lions in heraldic style. The uniform had been designed as a tribute to the great Ethiopian nation.

They explained that the Afro-West Indian Brotherhood stands for equality and justice for all, regardless of colour, race, or creed. It believes that a day will come when all Africa will be one vast free nation. It is allied with a number of other organizations in the West Indies, some of which are politically inspired, others purely religious. Among the leaders of their movement they mentioned D. E. Beckford, Henry Dunkley, H. N. Ebert, O. H. Garden, I. O. Gadden, M. O. Scarlett, and W. S. White. They claimed that upwards of 8,000 people are in sympathy with their aims. They are hoping to meet during their residence in London a number of people sympathetic to African aspirations.

They told us that, in the West Indies, Ethiopia and the Emperor Haile Selassie are intensely popular; and that there is a widespread desire to be associated with Ethiopia. In ceremonial processions of the Afro-West Indian Brotherhood, regalia in the Ethiopian colours are worn.'

The Brotherhood did not appear to develop on any large scale in South London over the next two years. As its leader said, the people were taken up with material things and had no time to come out at nights to meetings. At the end of 1957 there was talk of reorganizing the Brotherhood under the name of the Afro-West Indian Friendship League, which was also to be a uniformed organization. The inaugural public meeting was to be held in March

[1] In early 1960 the leading missionary returned to Brixton and began to hold regular meetings in a derelict shed in the Somerleyton Road area.

1958, to coincide with Ghana's freedom celebrations. This meeting did not, however, take place and the Brotherhood continued to exist uneventfully. Recently it has shown certain 'integrative' tendencies (see p. 362) by establishing relationships with local community organizations and leaders.

There is, then, little sign of the persistence of cult groups among the Brixton migrants, even among the minority who participated in such activities at home. In this context, however, it should be remembered that in the West Indies these groups are the product of unemployment, poverty, ignorance, idleness, and frustration. Even more than the sect, the cult represents an escape from the hopelessness of this world to a spiritual or earthly Utopia where the situation will be reversed, and where the chosen people, long down-trodden and persecuted, will at last find their reward.

Except for some of the more revolutionary Ras Tafari groups, the cult groups are basically passive protest organizations. Migration, on the other hand, is a form of active protest against frustrating circumstances. After his arrival in Brixton, the migrant is usually concerned not with the after-life, but with attaining the things of this life, things that are perhaps within his reach for the first time. This economic priority and the other circumstantial problems already enumerated leave the migrant with little energy for non-economic activities, and this applies particularly to the womenfolk who at home made up the backbone of Revival-pocomania cult membership.

Another element which has probably hampered the rise of cults in the migrant situation is that of status. Even at home in the West Indies, cult affiliation is linked with very low social and economic status. The migrant to Britain tends to be upwardly mobile, and is unlikely therefore to associate himself with such activities in the new and more hopeful circumstances. For those migrants who have the time and inclination to join any sort of non-economic association there are other alternatives, secular as well as religious. Those who feel a continued need for membership of a religious association will therefore be most likely to join one of the sects that operate in migrant settlements. It seems likely, indeed, that the occasional cult-style manifestations during sectarian services are due to the presence of a number of former cult members who may begin to 'labour in the spirit'[1] under the influence of the tambourines or guitars. This supposition was supported by the pastor of one sectarian congregation in Brixton, who confirmed that a few members of his flock had admitted to being cult members at home.

[1] For 'labouring in the spirit' see Simpson (1956, pp. 353–4).

361

The migrant settlement from within

If the accommodation of the West Indian migrants in South London continues without any major frictions and setbacks, it is difficult to envisage any startling increase in migrant intra-group religious activity in this generation, and certainly not in the next one. If the economic position of the migrants were to worsen greatly, however, and if they were to be permanently relegated to the status of a lower-class out-group, living in a coloured ghetto, one might perhaps see the rise of cults like those found among the frustrated slum-dwellers of West Kingston. But in view of the secular atmosphere that prevails in the West Indian settlements in London, it is more likely that the migrants would, if they encountered large-scale frustration and discrimination, turn to political protest associations, though not necessarily of a Ras Tafari type.

OTHER FORMS OF MIGRANT ASSOCIATION

In his study of various coloured settlements in Britain, Collins (1957, pp. 20–2) classified the internal associations which he found there as either 'traditional' or 'emergent'. The term 'traditional' is self-explanatory. It refers to associations that are similar to those found in the migrants' country of origin. Such associations are more usually found in highly integrated, non-assimilating communities such as the Moslem, Chinese, and tribal African groups, and they are relatively stable and enduring. 'Emergent' associations Collins described as 'non-traditional groupings organized by the immigrants to meet the needs arising from the peculiar immigrant situation'. They tend, he said, to be unstable and short-lived,[1] to be of a negative or protest type, and to arise among detribalized Africans or lower-class West Indians, who have few or no traditional associations.

Though this general classification of orientation could probably be applied in all migrant situations, Collins's characterization of the emergent type of association would not cover better-organized migrant groups such as the Jews, Poles, or Cypriots. It might therefore be useful to subdivide emergent associations[2] under the two further headings of 'protest' and 'integrative', according to whether their purpose is to protest against their group's position and treatment by the receiving society or to promote intra-group cohesion and integration in the receiving society. It should also be noted

[1] See also Manley (1958, p. 235) on formal associations among the Liverpool migrant group.
[2] In the case of political or religious exile communities, traditional associations too may be of a 'protest' type, the protest usually being directed against those in power in their homeland. In other kinds of migrant group the purpose of the traditional association is presumably to maintain old-country values and norms and to preserve the link between migrants and the parent society.

362

here that such associations are not static; for example, traditional associations, particularly those of an integrative nature, may gradually change their functions and orientation, and become integrative emergent associations.

It has been stressed that in Brixton the migrants' present need for non-economic associational outlets is minimal. In addition, the formation of any such associations is hampered by the dearth of local leaders. We have, however, noted the existence of informal savings associations, similar to those found in the West Indies, but emergent in orientation and integrative in purpose; and of some independent religious associations, again similar to West Indian groupings, but emergent in that they have arisen to meet the needs of the migrant situation. In purpose these pentecostal groups are organizations of 'passive protest' against the receiving society.[1]

A few ephemeral Afro-West Indian political associations of the emergent protest type were reported in the Brixton area during the years of this study. But with one exception, that of the association organized by the former Ras Tafari group, I was unable, despite the most diligent inquiries, to make contact with anyone connected with these associations. The fact that in most cases neither the British Caribbean Welfare Service (later the Migrant Services Division) nor any of my local contacts had ever heard of the existence of such organizations indicated how insignificant and transient they must have been. It also shows how fragmented and unorganized the West Indian migrant group in South London remains. The Notting Hill disturbances stimulated some initiatives among Brixton migrants to form protest or defence organizations, but even these seem to have petered out after a few weeks or months, in the absence of further tension.

The general lack of interest shown by almost all the migrants who were questioned on this point suggests that the bulk of new migrants still feel no need for West Indian or coloured protest associations. Despite difficulties and disillusionments, most new migrants are still preoccupied with their economic life, while their sense of community identification with other West Indians or coloured people in Brixton, London, or Britain as a whole is as yet small. Once the settlement has been established for another few years, one may expect the growth of more emergent protest associations, particularly if the migrants are affected by a major

[1] In early 1961 Dr. Malcolm Calley began to make a study of pentecostal religious groups among West Indian migrants in Britain for the Institute of Race Relations. When this is concluded a great deal more should be known about the history, membership, organization, ritual, and role of these sectarian congregations, whose number Dr. Calley estimated at between 48 and 65 in England in early 1961. For a preliminary report on this study see Calley (1962).

recession. In the meantime, these evanescent associations may be regarded as functioning largely to provide emotional 'ego-gratification' for their handful of organizers.

A small minority of West Indian migrants in Brixton have joined or taken part in the activities of the larger and older-established West Indian and coloured protest associations north of the river: associations such as the League of Coloured Peoples, now defunct, but in 1955–56 attempting to struggle back to life after years of internecine strife and Communist infiltration; the London branch of the extreme left-wing 'Caribbean Labour Congress'; and such lesser associations as the Coloured Workers' Welfare Association, whose main activity appears to be the delivering of inflammatory speeches at Speakers' Corner, Marble Arch. Migrants from Brixton do from time to time visit Speakers' Corner at the week-end, but less in a spirit of active political protest than because it affords free entertainment and a chance to meet West Indians from other parts of London.

A few Dominica-born migrants from South London joined the flourishing London branch of the Dominica Labour Party, which was for years organized by the white Dominican founder of the Labour Party in the island. This association was, however, more of an integrative than a protest type. Thanks to the energy of its sponsor, it performed the functions of a citizens' advice bureau, of a housing and employment agency, and of a social club. Despite the fact that there are far larger numbers of Jamaicans and migrants from other islands in London, this was the only home-based political association which appeared to exist for migrants at this time, either in Brixton or elsewhere.[1]

RECREATIONAL ASSOCIATIONS

In Chapter 13 reference was made to the difficulties encountered by white sponsors in setting up and maintaining their migrant members' interest in recreational and cultural clubs of an interracial type.

It was not therefore surprising to find that the only organized recreational groupings among the Brixton migrants consisted of cricket teams or of drinking and dancing clubs. There was also a mushroom growth of small, informal associations devoted to activities such as unlicensed drinking, gambling, ganja (Indian hemp)-smoking, and poncing and prostitution. In so far as they deviate from the norms of the receiving society, these illicit groupings may

[1] By 1961 there were reports of activity in London by the 'black-biased' Jamaican People's Political Party, which has allegedly some Ras Tafari links and which intervened in the Jamaican federal referendum in late 1961 and in the Jamaican general elections of 1962 (unsuccessfully).

364

be regarded as protest associations. (For further discussion of such illicit associations and activities, see pp. 370–2 below).

Since 1958 the number of licensed West Indian basement drinking clubs in Brixton and adjacent districts has soared, and most of them have, because of noise, late hours, and the congregation of undesirable elements, white as well as coloured, become a source of friction and potential conflict with local residents in the immediate neighbourhood.[1] In earlier years, however, there were only a few of these licensed clubs under coloured management: several of them showed some stability and clearly met certain social needs for a rather specific minority of Brixton migrants who did not feel at home in the local pubs or the interracial groups.

During the greater part of the period of this study, one particular club occupied a pre-eminent position in the Brixton migrant settlement. This was a licensed basement club in the Somerleyton-Geneva Road area. It was owned and run by educated West Africans living outside the area, and was frequented by the more astute or wealthy local West Indians, by a number of white women and girls who were living with coloured men, by West African students from South London hospitals and colleges, and by a handful of local white people of varied background. The price of drinks limited the clientele to the more affluent migrants and to those who found the club useful for conducting business of various kinds.

This club was for most of its six years of life[2] run with considerable superficial propriety and was in good odour with the local police. Conspicuous drunkenness, bad language, and violence were not countenanced. White women were not usually admitted unescorted, and few coloured women frequented the club at all. Only one of my West Indian women contacts had ever been in the club, although one or two had heard reports of it as a haunt of 'bad boys'.

Apart from its basement situation and rather primitive toilet facilities, this club was by no means a 'joint' or 'dive'. It was clean and well decorated, with an attractive bar and red-and-gold papered walls. There was no overt evidence of gambling or of ganja-smoking. The club opened between 3 and 11 p.m., with an extension at week-ends. It was very quiet from Monday to Thursday; the few who came in on those days drank in moderation, read papers, played bridge or dominoes, or danced to records. At week-ends there was a small but excellent calypso band, and fifty or more people would squeeze into the small basement and onto the pocket-handkerchief floor.

At the beginning of 1958 another club was opened in the area by

[1] See p. 198, note 2, and pp. 279–80 above for more on these drinking clubs.
[2] It subsequently deteriorated and in 1960 lost its licence.

one of the leading local West Indians, a multiple landlord who owned a successful West End club. It was felt that the migrants had achieved sufficient economic security to support another such enterprise, particularly one with a more West Indian orientation. The club premises were formerly Jewish-owned and served as a local businessmen's lunch club, and also as a meeting-place for old theatrical 'pros'. After the take-over, this club continued to be run on a more restrained and professional basis than the older West African club. It had no dancing nor week-end orchestra, but incidental music was supplied by a radiogram or by a pianist. Many of the former clientele continued to patronize this club, and relationships between them and the new West Indian members seemed easy and pleasant.

Dancing is such a favourite recreation among West Indians that it is not confined to the clubs, whether intra-group or interracial. The Racial Brotherhood Association has held a number of public dances at the Lambeth Town Hall, drawing an attendance of up to 400, mainly West Indians, from all over London. Dances are also organized on a commercial basis here and in other London districts with large coloured settlements by individual West Indian impresarios. These dances offer employment to the various West Indian bands and cabaret artists in Britain, and give the migrants as a whole the opportunity of meeting other migrants, dressing up, and displaying their material success. The advertisement for one such dance at the Lambeth Town Hall in November 1957 gives the characteristic flavour of these assemblies:

CALLING ALL CATS

It's Brixton vs. Ladbroke Grove

Joe Beck the High Priest
and Skully the Bishop

proudly present

The Big Five Night

to be held at

LAMBETH TOWN HALL, S.W.9

Saturday, 16th November, 1957

Featuring the Five Greatest
Sounding Systems battling
for the 1957 Club Championship
of Sound and Record
Featuring Duke Vin Sound System.

*   *   *   *

Main attraction of the Night
Dance Contest
Of the five greatest dancers in London
Count Busby . . . Sarge the Lion . . . Little Cripple . . .
Duke Batey . . . Lord Priest
Dancing 7 to 12
Refreshments on sale
Curry goat, etc.
Ladies 3/-   Gents 5/- etc.

Cricket is another form of recreation that is particularly attractive to West Indian male migrants. We have already noted that one or two of the interracial associations have found that the provision of cricketing facilities is the surest way to attract and keep members, even over the winter months when club membership often falls away to nothing. Other cricket teams have been set up on a less formal basis by the migrants themselves. By the summer of 1958 there were at least half a dozen such teams playing regularly in the Brixton area and more have been formed since then. The games usually take place on public sports grounds and are therefore easily visible to other migrants. This aids recruitment of new members, and provides a regular meeting-place for fairly large numbers of migrant spectators.

LEADERSHIP

The stability and range of organized associational life within an immigrant settlement or community are obviously influenced by the availability and quality of leaders within the group, and also by what might be called 'followership' – the prevailing attitude of group members towards authority and leadership. Ideologically motivated immigrant groups usually contain or throw up a good supply of leaders, are receptive to leadership, and provide most leaders with sufficient personal satisfaction to keep them attached to the group. The same is true (subject only to the usual dearth of educated, middle-class, potential leaders) of economically motivated immigrant groups of an integrating type – that is to say, groups coming from a closely organized, traditional kind of society and imbued with a strong attachment to old-country values and culture patterns. This is particularly applicable in the case of self-segregating groups with an alien religion and culture, such as the Moslem and Chinese communities in Britain.

In a potentially assimilating migrant group such as the West Indian one, however, there are few traditionally based associations

367

and few or no traditional leaders. The supply of potential leaders is limited not only by the low socio-economic status of the bulk of the migrants but also by the fact that many potential leaders from among the small upper-class *élite* and the white-biased middle and upper-lower classes dissociate themselves from the rest of the group and reject the community leadership role altogether. They tend rather to seek personal advancement and prestige, although they may at times exert influence through the control of essential commodities such as accommodation. As for followership, the majority of West Indians, at home as well as in Britain, display an individualistic, independent, informal, even aggressive attitude in interpersonal relations which makes them extremely difficult to organize and intolerant of any formal, long-term leadership.[1]

So far, the predominantly lower-class West Indian settlement in Brixton has produced only a very small number of formal or informal leaders, most of them 'peripheral' in Kurt Lewin's sense (1948, p. 195). Virtually all the leaders of the few integrative associations are prestige leaders, who in most cases have achieved their present economic and social status since migrating. They include a West End night-club owner, a Post Office engineer, a cabaret singer, a barrister, a journalist, a skilled draughtsman, and a handful of successful businessmen.

The charismatic leaders of the passive protest pentecostal sects are, in Brixton at least, also drawn from an upwardly mobile minority, but their authority, while it lasts, derives from personality rather than prestige. The leaders of the highly ephemeral active protest organizations also appear to rely on personality rather than prestige, since they are usually individuals with aspirations and perhaps educational or other qualifications which exceed their present socio-economic situation or prospects. Some are individuals who, like the former Ras Tafari leader, have already led protest groupings in the West Indies.

The Brixton settlement contains a minority of individuals who exert a certain amount of informal influence on their immediate circle. A few are potential protest leaders; others are influential because of certain extra-legal activities and the sanctions which they or the cliques or gangs around them are thought to be able to enforce. Most of Brixton's informal leaders are, however, prestige leaders. They may be old-timers, professional or artisan, or successful newcomers, notably the multiple landlords. Indeed, the last-named are probably the only migrants at present in a position to

[1] Cf. Manley (1960, pp. 27-9) on 'Community Organization'; see also Manley (1958, pp. 22–34) for an interesting theoretical discussion of types of leadership in migrant groups, with special reference to Negro migrants in Britain.

368

exert influence and even a certain amount of control within the settlement by means of their possession of a scarce commodity.

One of the most important functions of the informal leaders is to act as interpreters between their own people and the local population or authorities. As interpreters, they are the migrant equivalent of the sponsor. There are far more interpreters than formal leaders in the Brixton settlement at present, and their activities, though uninstitutionalized, are of considerable significance in the preliminary stage of accommodation that is now in process. The sphere of influence of these leaders and interpreters should not, however, be overestimated. With the possible exception of the journalist who edits the locally published monthly, *The West Indian Gazette*,[1] no individual or group had even by the end of 1960 achieved the position of being known to the majority of settled migrants, still less of being able to exert any influence on their actions.

The various leaders' influence was confined to a small radius and few of them had even come together to cooperate on a broader organizational basis. On the rare occasions when the local authorities wished to make some contact with the migrant group, they would usually attempt to do this through the professional-class officials of the Migrant Services Division of the West Indian High Commission, who tried to get and keep in touch with all organized migrant organizations, and who provided a certain amount of formal leadership and liaison in Brixton as elsewhere, chiefly through their Community Development Section.[2]

INFORMAL SOCIAL ASSOCIATION AND ACTIVITIES

Informal and uninstitutionalized forms of association are much more widely spread in the Brixton migrant group than are formal associations. This situation would be typical of most immigrant groups in the early years of settlement, but it also seems to be characteristic of the West Indian parent society, and particularly of the lower-class section.[3] Most students of older coloured settlements in Britain seem to have started from the formal associations and to have found their range and membership wide enough to span the whole group. But in the Brixton settlement, which has only a handful of old-timers, all the voluntary associations put together can probably muster a membership of only a few hundred.

[1] This has been published since early 1958 and was in 1961 said to have a country-wide circulation of about 15,000.

[2] Until its dissolution in spring 1962.

[3] Cf. Cohen (1956); Michael Smith (1956, p. 295 f.). It is interesting to note that the main rural lower-class associations in Jamaica tended to be the same as those then found among the migrants in Brixton: informal economic cooperatives, cult groups, and cricket clubs.

The migrant settlement from within

The vast majority of the Brixton migrant population do not seem to feel the need for formal associations. If they wish to worship they do so alone, in a family group, or in household prayer meetings. If they need economic cooperation and assistance, they rely on 'partners' schemes, or loans from relatives, friends, or landlords. If they need recreation and social intercourse, they find this at home (since 1958 an increasing number have become television addicts), visiting their friends,[1] talking in pubs and barbers' shops or on street corners and door-steps; or in private gramophone or dance sessions, 'blues parties', visits to dance halls, cinema-going, social drinking, occasionally in ganja-smoking, legalized gambling (pools, greyhound racing, and bingo) or illegal gambling (poker or dice); and in attending the frequent wedding parties and other private assemblies held in the settlement at week-ends.[2] Sexual intercourse remains, as it was in rural Jamaica, the main recreation for a large number of migrants.

In Brixton, illegal gambling is organized privately and informally in rooms belonging to members of the group. The police are undoubtedly aware of the existence of such groups or schools, but usually step in only when a particular address becomes notorious for drunken, violent, or indecent behaviour, for prostitution, or for ganja-smoking.[3] Illegal gambling offers not only a chance of quick profits but a form of recreation for unattached men. The more settled men tend to concentrate on the legalized forms of gambling, which take up less time, involve less chance of great losses, and are socially approved by the receiving society.

Except among jazz musicians and entertainers, and by no means

[1] The habit of cooking evening meals, mending, and shopping for single male acquaintances seems fairly widespread among West Indian women in Brixton. This arrangement serves to mitigate loneliness on both sides, in addition to any small economic gain which it often brings to the woman. It often, though not invariably, leads to the setting up of a casual union and perhaps of an 'unstable' family unit.

[2] During the week one's tired after work and one do nothing', said a 45-year-old old house-painter living in Angell Town: 'Friday night is pay-day, rent-night, and "letter from home" night. Saturday, we spruce up and step out a bit—go to a wedding or christening party or just visit. You know what the West Africans sing: "Everybody like Saturday night." That's true for us too.'

[3] On 13 September 1957 Chief Superintendent Wilkinson was reported by the *South London Press* as saying in court: 'There has been an appreciable increase in gaming among coloured people in the Brixton area . . . there have been complaints about these premises, particularly about assaults there.' This was after a raid on two rooms in a Somerleyton Road house where eight West Indian men were found playing poker. A month earlier, thirteen men were found gambling with cards in another Somerleyton Road house, in a room which was apparently kept solely for gaming. A man living in yet another Somerleyton Road house pleaded guilty in November 1957 to keeping a 'common gaming house' in a Stepney café; the latter had already been raided seven times in the past year. See also *South London Press*, 7 April 1959, for the raiding of another West Indian-run 'common gaming house' in Railton Road.

among all of them, ganja-smoking does not not appear to be wide-spread among the West Indians in Brixton.[1] Many of the male migrants have indulged in it from time to time, at home or in Britain. Few are, however, addicts, if only for the reason that it is relatively expensive in Britain compared with other and legal stimulants. There is a tendency among immigrants from other parts of the West Indies to attribute the practice to Jamaicans. 'What, you never heard of smoking ganja, man?', said a British Guianese landlord to a newly arrived young friend: 'That's what the Jamaicans do. You'll soon learn it here. You have to try it once in your life.'

Familiarity with the 'weed' and its effects is greater among West Indians of all classes than it is in British society, and disapproving attitudes towards its practice are often correspondingly weaker. Many of the more settled migrants do, however, disapprove of the minority's indulgence in such socially condemned activities as ganja-smoking, poncing, and knife-fighting, on the ground that this gives the whole West Indian group a bad name in Britain. But as yet there is no effective body of public opinion among the West Indian migrants in Brixton which would be strong enough to enforce this condemnation within the group as a whole.[2]

Another form of potentially a-social association among the Brixton migrants is the street-corner gang or clique. In 1955–58 white teddy-boy gangs were a regular feature of the Brixton landscape. They tended to congregate in cafés and billiard halls, and on street corners in the Atlantic Road-Coldharbour Lane area, that is to say, near the central area of the coloured settlement in the Somerleyton-Geneva Road district. It is possible that the few existing West Indian gangs were set up in self-defence but this could not be ascertained. Until its closure in late 1957, the Atlantic Café, run by a Greek Cypriot, was the haunt of several white and coloured gangs of young men and youths. Gang disputes and fights were said to occur frequently in this area, but not always as a result of colour

[1] During the years 1956 and 1957 fewer than ten West Indians in the Brixton and surrounding districts were reported as having been convicted of possessing or trafficking in hemp. In most of the cases the arrests were made in Soho clubs. The two West Indians gaoled for trafficking were: a 23-year-old Jamaican living in Somerleyton Road, who had a criminal record both in Jamaica and in Britain; and a 32-year-old club tout of Landor Road, Clapham, who claimed that the police planted the hemp on him, and said: 'I only carry this in case some coloured Yanks ask me for it'. Of those found in possession of the drug, two claimed that it was planted on them by others in the club. A third was a carpenter and part-time drummer; the hemp was found in his instrument case by the police when he was on his way home from a dance.

[2] By contrast, N'dem (1953, p. 260f.) writes of the strong opposition to antisocial practices among coloured people in Manchester and of the informal ostracism of individuals indulging in marihuana-smoking or -peddling. Gambling is of course far less socially condemned by British society than drug-peddling and drug addiction.

371

differences. In fact, at least one of the gangs appeared to be inter-racial. Most coloured youths in these 'espresso café' cliques were newcomers who had been brought over to join their families here, rather than second-generation West Indians or Anglo-coloureds.

The coloured migrant group in Brixton does not appear to have produced any significant number of teenage or criminal gangs or cliques. To some extent this may be attributed to the fact that the 10–25 age-group is still small in the migrant settlement. Disgruntled tenants do from time to time allege that the better-off landlords have cliques of adult strong-arm bullies who enforce their orders and make life in Brixton untenable for those who oppose them. So far as could be ascertained, however, those cliques that do exist are not sufficiently organized to exert influence or control over the coloured settlement as a whole.

AGGREGATE, GROUP, AND COMMUNITY

MacIver (1917, p. 8)[1] defines a community as a social grouping in which the members consciously share, not particular interests, but the basic conditions of a common life, usually within a definite territorial area which they may or may not share with other group-ings. And Zorbaugh (1929, p. 222), writing about earlier Negro migrants in the Northern United States, takes the definition further:

> 'An area does not become a community merely by having distributed over it a number of people and institutions, or by those people having certain interests in common. Still less does it become a community by virtue of being an administrative or political unit. An area becomes a community only through the common experiences of the people who live in it, resulting in their becoming a cultural group, with traditions, sentiments, and atti-tudes, and memories in common – a focus of belief, feeling and action.'

Clearly the Brixton migrant settlement cannot now be classified as a community, although it may be a potential one. For this reason I have throughout this study used the less precise terms 'migrant settlement' or 'migrant group'. The term 'group' has been used for simplicity and convenience, but in fact the Brixton migrant settle-ment may be held to fall rather into the category of a 'quasi-group'. Professor Morris Ginsberg (1934, p. 40) defines the latter as 'aggre-gates or portions of the community which have no recognizable structure, but whose members have certain interests or modes of

[1] See also MacIver (1937, p. 23) where he stresses the intensity of the common life which characterizes a community.

behaviour in common, which may at any time lead them to form themselves into definite groups'. 'Groups' he defines as 'masses of people in regular contact or communication, and possessing a recognizable structure'.

Migrant groups or quasi-groups may develop into integrated and accepted sub-communities; alternatively, they may be rejected and relegated to out-group status by the receiving society; or again their individual members may gradually be assimilated into this society. The outcome for each group depends, as has been said, on the interplay and relative strength of a large number of factors operating inside and outside the group.

18

Group and community

Some principles of association and dissociation

THIS CHAPTER will be mainly concerned with the main principles of association and dissociation at work within the Brixton migrant settlement, towards or against the evolution of an integrated migrant sub-community. It should not, however, be forgotten that the attitudes and behaviour of the receiving society often play the most important part in conditioning this evolution.

The individual migrant's concentration on economic activities, high residential mobility, and intention to return home within a few years are all factors which have so far impeded the growth of any stable internal social organization. The most important of the other main principles of association and dissociation operating within the Brixton settlement would appear to be those of national, ethnic, and geographical origin, of sociocultural background, of socio-economic class affiliation both here and at home, and of length of settlement.

Unlike some coloured migrant settlements in Britain, the Brixton settlement is fairly homogeneous from the national and ethnic viewpoint. The great majority of the migrants are West Indians, and the minority of West Africans who live in the area usually remain aloof from the other migrants.[1] This social distance may be attributed not only to national and cultural differences, but also to the fact that most of the Africans are students and therefore middle or upper class in both the home and the migrant contexts. Apart from a real incompatibility of interests, cultural traits (including language), and national orientations, most African students have no wish to jeopardize their own status here by too close association with a lower-class group.[2]

---

[1] An even greater social distance is maintained by the scattering of Indians, Anglo-Indians, and Cape Coloured to be found in the area. The first keep aloof mainly because of social and cultural differences, the other two groups because they are aiming at assimilation in the local white community.

[2] The *South London Press* of 31 May 1957 reported a Rent Tribunal case in which a Nigerian tenant appealed against the rent charged by a West Indian landlord in Clapham. The latter complained that his tenant, who was said to be a student

374

Group and community

The real differences between West Indian and West African social and cultural patterns are enhanced by a set of stereotypes or preconceived ideas on either side. West African informants usually characterized West Indians as servile ('after all, they are the descendants of slaves'), racially bastardized, uncouth in behaviour, devoid of a sense of responsibility towards their own children or kin, and in general lacking a culture or traditions of their own. The attainment of independence by Ghana and later by Nigeria and Sierra Leone also seemed to imbue local African migrants with an additional, if temporary, sense of superiority over West Indians and other 'colonials'.

In some coloured migrant settlements in Britain there are so few West Indians that they are forced into some sort of association with other coloured groups, particularly with West Africans. This was not the case in Brixton, where the West Indian majority tend to hold aloof from the few West Africans, and to describe them as primitive, pagan, and uncivilized, in comparison with the Europeanized, Christian, English-speaking people of the British Caribbean.[1]

On both sides there is a feeling that too close an association with the other group may be damaging in British eyes. West Indians have noted that the British tend to associate a black skin with Africa, with the jungle, primitive savagery, pidgin English, and cultural backwardness. 'They think we all like those African boys – we just drop down from the trees in the jungle like black monkeys and never wear shoes before. The foreman ask me how come I speak English so good if I only here two years' – said one West Indian labourer, describing a very common experience. For their part, West Africans feel that the association of dark pigmentation and low status in Britain is derived less from historical contact between whites and their own forebears than from the institution of slavery and the stereotype of the Negro slave which originated in the West Indies and the Americas.[2] This lack of accord between West African and

of engineering and philosophy who planned to return to Nigeria and stand as an M.P., considered himself much superior to the landlord: 'He seems to think I can't be spoken to.' N'dem's study (1953) of the Manchester coloured settlement, where each national group includes both students and workers, suggests that the national barrier is stronger than the class barrier, since neither students nor workers unite across the national divisions.

[1] When Lambeth Council opposed the continued existence of the Havana Club in Coldharbour Lane, a witness said that, while there were clubs for West Indians, this was the only social club for Africans in Brixton. 'When Africans and West Indians mix there is usually trouble. There is a need for this meeting-place for Africans. We have a culture and they haven't. We have our own language and that annoys them' (*South London Press*, 25 November 1960).

[2] In a Brixton drinking club a West Indian landlord and one of the West African proprietors were heard exchanging the following rather barbed jokes: 'Man, you say you all aristocrats and we slaves, but who sell us off to the white man and

375

West Indian migrants is not confined to informal social life. It is reported quite frequently in the employment situation; as was noted earlier, several South London personnel managers have made it a rule to employ only members of one group, or to separate the two groups at work.

Yet there is a potential link between West Indians and West Africans, which sometimes emerges when they are in contact with Europeans or even Asians. This link is to be found in the two peoples' common Negro biological heritage, African antecedents, and former colonial status. In Brixton, awareness of this bond is stimulated, somewhat self-consciously and artificially, by a small minority of African nationalists and 'black-biased' West Indian protest leaders, who like to talk of the 'Negro race' and 'people of African origin' and to stress the solidarity of the 'coloured peoples' in the face of white imperialism and neo-colonialism. Nevertheless, the bonds of dark pigmentation, Negroid antecedents, and national status at present are only potentially a principle of association for the majority of West Indians and West Africans in Brixton, while the very evident social and cultural differences promote dissociation. This situation could, however, change radically with the homogenizing educational process in the second generation, particularly if a large and depressed coloured proletariat were to emerge.

Within the West Indian migrant group we find no very strong and active consciousness of a shared national identity. There has until recently been little contact between the ordinary people who live along the great crescent of islands that scythes round the Caribbean from Jamaica to British Guiana on the South American mainland. Only now are migrants from British Guiana, Trinidad, the Windward and Leeward Islands, Barbados, and Jamaica beginning to mingle in the markets and streets of Brixton. As yet, most know little more of each other than a few common notions or stereotypes. For instance, Trinidadians are considered to be gay, Jamaicans touchy and flamboyant, Barbadians ('Bajans') dull and hard-working.[1] Migrants from the smaller islands hold aloof from the more sophisticated 'Big Island people' of Jamaica and Trinidad. Nor do all West Indians even speak the same language. Working-class migrants from such islands as St. Lucia and Dominica speak not English but a French 'Creole' patois as their first language.

send us there? Yo' own grandfathers. That's why you so well-off today.' 'That's true, man, but we don't sell off any but the bad slaves and the weak tribes. The good people we keep for ourselves.' For a similar exchange and similar attitudes in Manchester, see N'dem (1953, p. 133).

[1] Ira de A. Reid, writing of West Indian migrants in Harlem, says that 'Trinidadians were regarded as "sweet men", Barbadians as "steady", and Jamaicans as "thrifty" ' (1939, p. 229).

In the Brixton area, islanders tend to congregate together residentially. While the lodging-houses in the central settlement area
often contain a mixed bag of transient tenants – coloured and white,
African, Asian, or West Indian – only one instance was found of a
cellular household in which migrants from different islands were
living together. This came about in the rather special case of a
previously white-owned house in which all the tenants were Barbadian; it was sold to a Jamaican couple who continued the arrangement because they considered the Barbadians to be quiet and careful
tenants.

The consciousness of a shared nationality and of a similar social
and cultural inheritance is undoubtedly a potential principle of
association among the West Indians in Brixton, as it has been in
earlier West Indian settlements like that of Harlem. The insularity
and isolation that at present limit its operation may be expected to
decrease, despite the setback to plans of political federation, as the
migrants settle in their new environment. At present, however, West
Indian community sentiment seems to be limited and rather passive,
stirring to activity only on such occasions as the presence of a West
Indian cricket team in Britain.[1]

The bonds between migrants from the same islands are closer and
more spontaneous than the pan-West Indian link. But they are weak
and loose in comparison with the social ties that bind more cohesive
and integrated societies, and their strength may be further weakened
by colour-class divisions and to a lesser extent by ethnic affiliations.[2]

Most West Indian migrants in Brixton have come here with the
aim of improving their economic and social status at home. As yet,
therefore, few aspire to enter the local socio-economic hierarchy,
and the basis of socio-economic stratification within the migrant
group is still derived from West Indian determinants.

The great majority of the Brixton migrants are drawn from the
dark-brown and black lower classes, and socio-economic class affiliation is therefore on the whole a principle of association in the
settlement. In the absence of a lighter-coloured middle and professional class, there is 'room at the top' locally for those migrants who
achieve moderate prosperity. Indeed, the two most successful individuals encountered during this study were very dark in colour and

---

[1] When the West Indian Test team arrived at Waterloo on 14 April 1957 it was
met by two calypso bands and a dense welcoming throng of West Indians. The
Daily Telegraph (15 April 1957) reported: 'Nearly an hour after the cricketers left,
West Indian music still filled Waterloo. The crowd departed with a stamping,
screaming march through the station.' When a West Indian team plays at the
Oval, Kennington, this of course provides an assembly-point for thousands of West
Indians from Brixton and elsewhere in London.

[2] That is to say, by belonging to an incompletely assimilated ethnic sub-group
such as the Chinese, Hindu, or Portuguese groups.

377

of lower-class antecedents. In this connection, one West Indian informant suggested that dark migrants who are economically successful may prefer to stay on in Britain, since they have little to gain by returning home to a society which does not permit them to proceed far up the social ladder whatever their economic gains.[1]

Pigmentation and physiognomy have not, of course, lost all their importance in the migrant situation. The Brixton migrants have come into the lowest stratum[2] of an all-white society, and their habitual if unconscious 'white bias' still causes them to associate improved status with lighter colour. Men usually seem to marry somewhat lighter women, or occasionally white women; while women spend a great deal of time and money at a local beauty establishment which specializes in hair-straightening and skin-lightening, or work on these processes themselves at home. Individual pigmentation and appearance are not a constant subject of conversation, but children are often praised for their 'clear' or 'fair' colour, or for their 'good' hair, while people are usually described for easier recognition as 'dark', 'brown', or 'light', rather than, for example, as 'fat', 'thin', 'tall', or 'short'.

On the whole, skin colour is a principle of association rather than of dissociation within the Brixton West Indian group. On the other hand, it serves to dissociate the working-class migrants in South London from the fairer, better-educated bourgeois intelligentsia residing north of the river, in the eyes of both groups. In her study of the coloured *élite* in London, Violaine Junod (1952) referred to the *élite*'s tendency to stress, in conversation with whites, the social distance between themselves and the 'good-for-nothing (devils) of immigrants'.

In the West Indies, as in other areas without universal compulsory education, the educational level achieved by the individual serves as a particularly important principle of dissociation. In Brixton, however, few if any of the migrants have had any higher education. A minority have some technical or secondary schooling, while the majority are barely more than literate. Like skin colour, therefore, the educational background is a principle of association rather than of dissociation among the local migrant group, though again it dissociates them from the migrant *élite*.

In the West Indies there is a great cleavage between the respectable and socially ambitious lower-middle or upper-lower classes, and the great mass of the rural or urban proletariat. This persists in Brixton as a principle of dissociation. Instead of aspiring to leader-

---

[1] Cf. Henriques (1953, p. 167) on the position in Jamaica.
[2] The fact of working and living side-by-side with lower-class white people could of course detract ultimately from the high status value of a white or lighter skin.

ship within the migrant group, most members of this respectable minority endeavour to dissociate themselves as much as possible from the bulk of the migrants, at work, residentially, and socially. The migrant group is thereby deprived of many of its natural leaders, and remains weak and unintegrated.

One important source of differentiation, though not yet of dissociation, arises out of the new economic opportunities available in the migrant situation. These opportunities are, of course, more easily exploited by migrants who are already differentiated from the rest by a better education and by their socio-economic background. In Brixton, the majority of the multiple landlords, for instance, appear to come from the lower-middle or the respectable upper-lower classes in the West Indies. The same opportunities are, however, available to those whose individual initiative and energy found no outlet in the home conditions.

A loose economic hierarchy seems to be growing up within the migrant group, based primarily on relative economic achievements. At the top come the professional multiple landlords, the licensed night-club owners and gamblers, and a handful of businessmen and successful commission agents. Then come the minority of West Indian technical students and nurses, skilled workers, transport and Post Office employees, and single-house landlords. Below them is the mass of semi-skilled and unskilled workers; and at the bottom the habitually unemployed and the unemployable. Rather to one side, and not fully identified with the group, are the small minority of settled old-timers and of successful professional men and entertainers.

In this group, occupational ranking is at present subsidiary to ranking according to wealth. This is probably due to the fact that the attainment of material prosperity is the basic motivation of the great majority of migrants. In addition, prosperity can easily be displayed and recognized even within a transient and unintegrated group. In Brixton it is displayed by means of such symbols as gaudy two-toned American cars, expensive and colourful clothes,[1] large radiograms and illuminated cocktail bars, and by lavish parties, conspicuous treating of acquaintances in clubs and pubs, and the purchase of better-class property away from the Somerley-ton-Geneva Road area.

This migrant economic hierarchy is a highly fluid one. It is a *nouveau riche* hierarchy, and has not yet produced a corresponding internal social stratification. Such social and cultural differences as

---

[1] The uniform worn by Post Office and transport employees also gives them a certain status among other migrants, since it indicates that the wearer has a secure and relatively well-paid job by migrant standards.

exist between migrants have for the most part been imported from home. High economic status is demonstrated to other members of the group less by changed behaviour, with the single exception of formalizing the conjugal link, than by material display. There would not as yet appear to be any criteria other than financial success, irrespective of the means by which this success was achieved. Thus a successful gambler or shebeen manager may be as highly regarded within the group as is a legitimate businessman.

With one major exception, this modest economic hierarchy is little related to intra-group activities or needs. Education, welfare, commissariat, services, religious and recreational facilities – the great majority of these are provided by the receiving society and its agencies. The exception is found in the new and powerful class of coloured landlords who supply one of the migrants' basic needs, that of accommodation. The landlords are at present the only members of the Brixton migrant group in a position to exert any social control over other members of the group, by renting or refusing accommodation, and by causing difficult or recalcitrant tenants to be black-listed by other landlords. They have in effect a vested interest in continued residential discrimination against coloured migrants, which enables them to maintain the 'colour tax' in rents. A measure of their power was given by the Gallup Poll of February 1955, according to which 58 per cent of the migrant sample had a West Indian landlord. The current percentage in Brixton is probably much higher.

There must be several hundred West Indian landlords or house-owners (the two terms are at present almost synonymous) in Brixton at present. A score or more are multiple landlords, who are known beyond their own clientele and immediate circle. The landlords have helped to create and maintain a geographically cohesive settlement. More often than not, their power and rumoured wealth earn them resentment among the mass of immigrants, and make for dissociation rather than closer association within the group. A prevalent if somewhat exaggerated migrant notion of the multiple landlord was expressed by a character in Samuel Selvon's *The Lonely Londoners*:

> 'It had a Jamaican fellar who living in Brixton, that come to the station to see what tenants he could pick up for the houses that he have in Brixton. This test [coloured man] when he did first come open up a club, and by and by he save up money and buy a house. The next thing you know, he buy out a whole street of houses in Brixton, and let out rooms to the boys, hitting them anything like three or four guineas for a double. When it come to making money, it ain't have anything like "ease me up" or "both

380

of we is countrymen together" in the old London. Sometimes he put bed and chair in two or three big room and tell the fellars they could live in there together but each would have to pay a pound. . . . And whenever a boat-train come in, he hustling down to Waterloo to pick up them fellars who new to London and ain't have place to stay, telling them Brixton is a nice area, that it have plenty Jamaicans down there already, and they would feel at home in the district, because the Mayor on the boys' side and it ain't have plenty prejudice there' (1956, pp.13–14).[1]

For their part the landlords have developed their own attitudes with regard to tenants. They tend to resent the latter's destructiveness, and their constant appeals for loans or hand-outs. 'They think because I have two houses and a car I made of money' – said one artisan landlord; 'nothing but boys coming to me from home and sleeping free and borrowing a pound or two which they never pay back. I got my own family to consider and I'm starting to be harder from now on.'

The circumstances in which these coloured landlords have achieved their present pre-eminence within the West Indian group are likely to be perpetuated only if there is a continued large flow of newcomers into the Brixton area. If the flow decreases again, as it did in 1958–59, the urgent need for accommodation will ease, and the special influence of the coloured landlords will gradually diminish.

Another factor which affects group cohesion is that of length of residence. Some coloured settlements are old-established and organized communities, in which the old-timers are numerous enough to influence and organize newcomers, though not always without a protest from the latter, and to act as interpreters between them and British society. In Brixton, however, there are probably no more than a score or so of old-timers; most of them are West Indians from different territories, residentially scattered, married to English women, and fully or partly assimilated in local society. These old-timers and the few coloured doctors and other professional men who have practised in the area for many years serve as occasional interpreters but play no full-time integrative part in the life of the migrant group.

Potentially, the presence of so many men, women, and children from the same area and the same sort of socio-economic background could lead to the formation of a community. There is a certain continuity and self-selection in the settlement; most newcomers are

[1] At a Rent Tribunal hearing in 1957, a West Indian tenant said of his landlord: 'His only intention is to suck the blood of the coloured people in this country. He doesn't intend to work.'

coming to join their family or friends, and migrants only stay on in the Brixton area if they feel more at home there than in, say, Stepney, Notting Hill, or Earl's Court. The settlement has a few potential leaders; and above all it has already acquired a geographical identity and a geographical focus in Brixton market.

Moreover, Brixton has certain facilities to offer to migrants. Not only can they be fairly sure of finding a room in a West Indian-owned house, but there are also special shopping[1] and recreational amenities, provided either by local people or, increasingly, by migrant entrepreneurs. By 1958 these included some butchers, grocers, and greengrocers, a record shop, a travel and employment agency, a large hairdressing establishment specializing in straightening and bleaching processes, a barber's shop (which also served as an unofficial men's social club), a café serving Caribbean and West African dishes, and several licensed dancing and drinking clubs. Among the many other services available in the migrant settlement are those of part-time dressmakers, tailors, barbers, hairdressers, photographers, caterers, chauffeurs, M.C.s for weddings, 'uncles' or job-finders, and insurance and mail-order agents. And, for a minority of migrants, there are services less socially approved by the receiving society, in the form of gambling houses, shebeens for illicit drinking, ganja-peddling, and poncing.

For the law-abiding majority of migrants, then, Brixton has gradually become a home from home, a place where they can relax and feel at ease. When, in 1956, the wife of Jamaica's Chief Minister, Mrs. Edna Manley, wished to meet as many migrants as possible, she went down to Brixton market on a Saturday morning: 'I ended up by shaking hands with fifty West Indians who recognized me. I was surprised to see them buying sweet potatoes and tinned ackee. . . . It was like a little bit of home.'[2]

The pull of Brixton was confirmed by several of my informants who moved out of the area only to move back. One Jamaican girl told me: 'I'm going up to Birmingham till things get better in the garment trade but I'll be back next year!' In fact she was back within a few months. Another moved out to a more 'select' house in Peckham with her husband and family but returned after six months, saying she had felt lonely 'over there' (the distance was three miles!).

The development of the Brixton migrant settlement into a com-

[1] The Caribbean, African, and Indian foodstuffs now available in Brixton market attract a large number of migrants from other parts of London. I even came across a West Indian professional couple living in Oxford, who would drive down every Saturday to lay in their week's supply of foods which were unobtainable elsewhere.
[2] *Evening News,* 20 February 1956.

munity has also been hampered by the ebb and flow as migrants return home and others arrive to duplicate their achievements. At present the settlement is not much more than an aggregate of recent arrivals, in which the largest social groupings of any stability at all, apart from some elementary family units, are cellular households, 'partners' associations, and a handful of sects. There are no large and stable voluntary associations, few or no effective intra-group social controls except for the limited control exercised by the multiple landlords, and no leaders with influence over more than a small minority of migrants. Common West Indian origins, similarity of intentions, of socio-economic and cultural background, and pigmentation – none of these has so far proved sufficient to evoke more than vague feelings of potential community. And the *laissez-faire* indifference or mild antipathy which are the prevalent attitudes among the local population are too negative and unfocused to drive the Brixton migrants into a closer defensive association.[1] If the local population's attitudes were to harden over a long period as a result of greatly intensified friction over jobs, houses, or social amenities, a defensive migrant community might be forced into being.

It is too early to predict the possible effects of the 1962 Commonwealth Immigrants Act, imposing controls on further immigration, on local attitudes to 'coloured strangers', or on those West Indian migrants who are already here. Some bitter reactions have been noted from migrants, but also some expressions of satisfaction that overcrowding and competition for work will not be increased, and that the newcomers will gain time to settle and improve their position. On the whole, despite its apparent discrimination on grounds of colour, the Act seems more likely to stimulate West Indian newcomers to more active endeavours to accommodate themselves to life in Britain than to huddle together as a resentful out-group community.

---

[1] For a few weeks after the Notting Hill disturbances there were signs of the growth of such a defensive feeling of 'colour community'. One informant said: 'The boys in Somerleyton Road was all for marching over there in a gang to help. Then we heard that the Teds was moving in on the Brixton area and we got ready. But nothing happen. The police here don't want that sort of trouble. They meet the Teds on the outskirts and move them away so we never get to put a finger on them. The boys here really sorry. They organizing in strength, not like the Notting Hill men, who scattered all over.' After a few uneventful months, however, this feeling of community died back to the earlier apathy. In the borough council elections of April 1959, the Norwood Labour Party put up a West Indian candidate for the Herne Hill ward (which contains Somerleyton and Geneva Roads) but the results showed no significant change and it was thought that very few West Indians had troubled to vote even for 'their own candidate'.

Part VI

Present and future

19

Summary of findings

AT THE beginning of this study I spoke of the sense of strangeness which most local people, and I myself, experienced on first seeing large numbers of coloured people in the streets, public places, and factories of Britain.

Today this feeling is gone in most of our larger industrial towns and cities. Coloured people have become an accepted part of the British urban landscape, if not yet of the community. There is likely to be one coloured face or more in most shopping streets, pubs, and post offices; in many building or road gangs; and among the passengers on a bus or tube train (sometimes the conductor or guard may be coloured as well).

So the superficial strangeness has worn off. The local population has 'got used to seeing them about', in the words of many of my Brixton informants. And it may be that many migrants have dispelled part of the strangeness by adopting the heavy dun-coloured plumage of the natives, and by modifying their gay uninhibited chatter to the local monotone. But how much further have such familiarization and acclimatization gone on both sides?

In this study I have tried to show how this process has developed in the Brixton area in three major areas of association: jobs, housing, and social activities. Brixton was chosen, the reader will recall, because, unlike other areas on which published material was – and for the most part still is – available, it is in essence an entirely post-war settlement, in the sort of central urban area where the residents had little or no first-hand experience of coloured people and no very inflexible attitudes to or ideas about them. In this it seems to be fairly similar to most areas of post-war coloured settlement, with the exception of such a-typical areas of social anarchy and flux as Notting Hill and North Kensington. And, while the fluidity and variety of such situations throughout Britain cannot be stressed too often, they are usually influenced by universal factors such as employment opportunities, the housing situation, and the values and norms of the receiving community – factors which seem to operate

387

in a broadly similar manner in Brixton, Willesden, Birmingham, Middlesbrough, Nottingham, and elsewhere.

As field work proceeded it became clear that Brixton had an additional advantage as a terrain of study. Although the coloured settlement is new in the sense of being a post-war one, its beginnings date back for over a decade, and after 1957 it started to show signs of stablilization, both because of the lack of local economic opportunities and because the coloured settlement itself seemed almost 'saturated' in the residential sense. Thus, because of the Brixton settlement's relative age and increasing demographic 'stability', it was possible to note the emergence and development of certain definite trends and patterns in migrant life and migrant-host relationships.

The main object of this study was, as I emphasized in the first chapter, to trace the development of relationships between migrants and the local population at three main points of contact or areas of association, two of them involving competition; these relationships were to be analysed not in the first place in terms of differences of race or colour, as in the more static situations in the Southern United States, South Africa, or even the Caribbean, but in terms of a two-sided process of adaptation and acceptance between immigrants and the local population, sometimes complicated by colour consciousness on the migrant side and by preconceptions associated with colour and an antipathy to all outsiders on the side of the receiving society.

In the early weeks of field work it also became clear that, despite the existence of a shared language, religion, and political authority, the migrants came from a sub-culture and a socio-economic background which differed in many important points from those of modern urban English society. Thus the very tentative and superficial relationships evolving between migrants and local people were hardly susceptible of analysis in terms of the concepts of 'assimilation' or 'integration' as they have been defined in this study. It was therefore found necessary to make use of the concept of 'accommodation'. This I defined as an early phase of adaptation and acceptance in which migrants and local people achieve a minimum *modus vivendi* – the migrant finds work and a place to live, but makes little further effort to adapt his values or norms of behaviour to local patterns.

I have attempted to show the developing processes of this accommodation on both sides, and it may be as well to summarize these findings here. In the first area of competition, that of economic life, most of the West Indian migrants have found and kept jobs, although these are often not the jobs for which they had hoped, nor

388

are the wage-levels always as high as they had been led to expect. The majority of the male migrants have, however, begun to accommodate themselves to the discipline and demands of British industrial life, and have accepted, however unwillingly, their position at the bottom of the ladder as unskilled workers. A small minority of migrants, consisting mainly of skilled workers, have moved into an assimilatory phase in the economic field by managing to detach themselves from the out-group and to win individual acceptance in their places of work. At the other end of the scale a small minority of migrants, mostly single women with young children, have come to rely on National Assistance, but there was no real evidence to support the frequently made charge that this was a major attraction for the majority of would-be migrants or even that as many as were entitled to apply for assistance were in fact doing so.

On the British side, management resistance to a new and strange source of labour has been weakened by the almost chronic post-war shortage of labour and by the consistent sponsoring carried out by certain employment exchanges. Yet few industrial establishments were found in which a 'quota' ranging between 3 per cent and 10 per cent of the labour force was not applied in practice. Conservatism and antipathy towards outsiders in general and coloured people in particular were less conspicuous as a motivation among employers, particularly in the larger and more modern firms, than was economic expediency. Among workers, on the other hand, we noted the persistence of old hatreds and fears of all outside labour, based less on 'prejudice' than on bitter memories of unemployment, undercutting, and dilution. This hostility is sometimes intensified by preconceptions linking up a coloured skin with low status or uncivilized behaviour, but is often mitigated by 'live-and-let-live' attitudes, by a sense of common British nationality, and by high-level union support for international working-class solidarity.

On the whole, it was found that the bulk of West Indian migrant workers had, for the foregoing reasons and because of their lack of industrial background, their low adaptability, their restricted mobility, and their general attitudes to work, failed over the pre-1956 years of full employment to win full acceptance from management or fellow-workers as a permanent part of the labour force. In this they appeared to differ from the migrant Southern Irish who are their frequent rivals for unskilled and manual work in British industry, but who have been an accepted part of the British labour force for many decades. When the moderate recession of 1956–58 came, West Indian workers were the first to feel the cold winds of redundancy even in South London, where the setback was relatively mild. None the less, such redundancy often occurred because the

389

migrants were in fact the last to have been taken on and therefore the first to go. On the positive side, a later check showed that a number of firms whose managements had spoken of the West Indians as 'temporary, stopgap, expendable labour' had in fact retained quite a number of their West Indian employees.

The coloured migrants who suffered most from the 1956–58 recession were usually not those already in employment but the latest arrivals. Most firms refused or were hesitant about taking on more coloured labour when they could hire 'local' people, and the average time taken by the Brixton employment exchange to place new applicants rose from two to six weeks. The sight of large numbers of coloured work-seekers waiting outside the employment exchange provoked considerable local resentment, particularly in an area with few local industries and a permanently high unemployment register. In most of South London, indeed, employment at this stage took the place of housing as the major potential area of friction.

Another consequence of the 1956–58 recession was that West Indians in work ceased to regard their jobs as expendable. As a result, West Indian turnover fell, time-keeping improved, and many employers who had formerly criticized their nonchalant attitude and high mobility gradually came to regard them as more reliable than most other workers in this respect. In addition, West Indians appeared to be talking less about their 'get-rich-quick' intentions and their imminent return home, both of which encouraged or gave a pretext to local employers to regard them as a temporary and expendable source of unskilled labour whose interests should rate lower than those of settled local workers ('our own people' in the common phrase). By 1960, in fact, the Brixton employment exchange evidence indicated that many employers were coming to accept West Indians as part of the local unskilled or semi-skilled labour force (see p. 142).

On the whole, then, it seemed that the accommodation of West Indians in the economic life of South London was, despite some checks, proceeding slowly but not unsatisfactorily in view of all the factors involved. West Indians were joining the unions where this was the general custom; some were participating in sports and social activities organized by their firms; a very few had achieved minor promotion, although this was often to posts of greater responsibility rather than to those involving direct authority over others.

In the British industrial setting, where the work-place is often miles from the workers' homes, relations at work would appear to constitute a separate world from private social relations. This compartmented living seems rather characteristic of the British urban
390

scene, and we noted that there was relatively little carry-over of relationships between the two areas of association, either between Londoners or between migrants and Londoners.

Turning to the second area of competition, that of housing, we found rather more overlapping of attitudes and behaviour between the residential and the social areas of association. Neighbours are rarely friends in the urban scene, but individuals, particularly if they are householders, like to feel that they are surrounded by people who could qualify in socio-economic and cultural background as potential friends or acquaintances. This sociocultural consideration is obviously of great long-term importance. In the field of housing, however, the main immediate factor in conditioning migrant-host relationships was the tremendous and long-standing housing shortage, which has lain heavy on South Londoners since the second world war, well before coloured migrants began to arrive in any numbers. It was seen that the migrants have suffered even more than local people from this shortage; this was particularly true at the outset, since fewer local landlords would let rooms to them, fewer owners would sell, and they had no residential qualifications to enable them to get council housing, except in the case of a very few who lived in houses scheduled for slum clearance. Incidentally, the subsequent rehousing of these few attracted a disproportionate amount of unfavourable comment from the local population, although in fact most local authorities in South London seem to have proceeded with considerable caution in handling applications for council accommodation from coloured migrants, and in using their powers to relieve statutory overcrowding.

In Chapter 9 it was shown how the great majority of the migrants have found their own temporary solution to the problem of living space by buying up large dilapidated, short-lease properties that no longer have any investment value for British buyers. By 1958, West Indians owned several hundred houses in the Brixton area alone, and the majority were letting furnished rooms at higher than average rents to their compatriots. A West Indian newcomer no longer faces the ordeal of a door-to-door search for accommodation or the possible snubs of white landladies. He can be fairly sure of finding some sort of living space with relatives or among fellow-migrants from the day of his arrival. Migrants have also a certain choice as to the type of accommodation, for the coloured settlement pattern is no longer uniform but has evolved three different stages based on internal socio-economic differentiation and possibly on the individual's degree of adaptation to local patterns.

Apart from the friction generated by the actual housing shortage and by the widespread belief among local people that the migrants are crowding them out of accommodation that is already too scarce, real and fancied differences in social and cultural background have emerged as important factors in conditioning migrant-host relationships in the housing sphere.

As in many areas of recent West Indian settlement in Britain, the problems of adaptation and acceptance have been increased by the fact that the 'dark strangers' moving into this area are predominantly a lower-class group moving into a highly status-conscious lower-middle-class or upper-working-class area. Preconceptions linking colour with low social status, as well as with an alien, primitive, and uncultured way of life, have received considerable support from first-hand, though often superficial, observation of the newcomers' behaviour. And in the cases where newcomers and local people live in a shared house, frictions have often arisen as a result of different ideas on privacy, overcrowding, domestic noise, cooking smells, the use and care of shared sanitary facilities, entertaining, and attitudes or behaviour to women. Occasionally these differences have been deliberately accentuated by the West Indian landlord in an attempt to force his local statutory tenants to leave. Such conflicts are usually resolved by the departure of the local tenant, but hard cases have arisen in the case of elderly people and pensioners long resident in cheap, rent-controlled flats in houses recently bought by West Indians. An additional source of friction, arising out of the prevalent local feeling that the migrant group is socially undesirable and culturally alien, was noted in the belief, not always justified, that coloured infiltration into an area leads to lowered property values. More recently, the mushroom growth of coloured basement clubs in residential areas has provided a focus for local resentment.

On the migrant side, local resistance, and the newcomers' own natural desire to avoid difficulties and rebuffs, have helped to limit their choice of rooms to rent or houses to buy to certain areas. This has contributed to the forcing up of rents and prices by what has been dubbed a 'colour tax'. The majority of migrants are housed in a way unlikely to improve their working capacity or general well-being, and are paying rents higher than the local average and out of all proportion to their modest weekly incomes. This has made it difficult for many to achieve their original goal of a prosperous return home, and has brought them under the not always beneficial influence of the powerful new *élite* of West Indian landlords.

By 1959, however, the housing situation of the migrants in Brixton was beginning to show a moderate improvement. The influx of newcomers had slowed as a result of poor employment prospects in the area, and consisted mainly of the families and friends of migrants already established there. The arrival of a large number of women

392

was helping to improve living standards and to increase neighbourly contacts with local residents. Gross overcrowding was on the wane, although the one-family room remained the norm. As more migrants bought their own houses, more rooms became available for West Indian tenants and some competition was arising for the better type of tenant. This resulted in a certain improvement in standards of furniture, cleanliness, and amenities in a number of houses, although not in any general lowering of rents. There was also evidence that an increasing minority of West Indian landlords were beginning to conform to local optimum standards of house maintenance and improvement.

Despite this modest improvement,[1] certain new problems are likely to arise in the future if an appreciable number of migrants decide to settle in Brixton permanently. One of these problems will affect the local housing authorities. As the years go by, more and more West Indian families may qualify for rehousing from the local waiting-list. They are also likely to adopt local standards, and to become more vociferous in their demands for rehousing on the grounds of overcrowding. In addition, a few streets in the central Brixton reception area may, as a result of overcrowding and neglect, gradually deteriorate into slums, and these will then have to be dealt with on a slum-clearance basis.

Another future problem is fraught with social consequences for the West Indian migrants themselves. Their present heavy concentration in certain streets and the outward movement or deliberate rehousing of white residents could lead to the establishment of a coloured ghetto. Such a concentration has of course some advantages in the early years of a migrant settlement. It reduces the chances of friction with the local population, and eases the migrants' lives by providing them with a familiar and relatively congenial environment in which to relax from the day's strains. As the years go by, however, a ghetto may perpetuate social distance long after the inhabitants have ceased to wish for it. The history of an area such as Bute Town, Cardiff,[2] has shown that this is particularly likely to happen in the case of a highly visible group living in a declassed neighbourhood. In Brixton, though, this possibility is lessened by the lack of natural geographical barriers. West Indians are moving away from the central area of settlement all the time;

---

[1] In consequence of the large-scale immigration in 1960 and 1961, some of which was inevitably attracted to Brixton, this process of improvement appears to have been checked at least temporarily as a result of increased overcrowding and corresponding higher rents, lowered standards, and intensified friction with local fellow-tenants and neighbours. The imposition of immigration controls in July 1962 may, however, have eased the pressure again.

[2] See Little (1947) and Collins (1957, Chapter VI).

and it has been shown that even this area has a limited life in its present dilapidated and unattractive form, since it is on land acquired and marked for redevelopment by the local authorities.

The third area of association examined was that of social relationships, ranging from the most casual contacts through organized social activities to informal social intercourse and finally to sexual relationships and intermarriage. With the exception of casual and temporary contacts in public places, this area of social relationships is the one in which there is least contact and least adaptation in the early years of any immigrant settlement. It is in fact one of voluntary association or avoidance, although some competition can arise over women and material amenities. The newcomers and the local people are kept apart by many factors. These include the exigencies of migrant life, with its need to concentrate on getting a living and keeping a roof over one's head in unfamiliar and often difficult circumstances; local unwillingness to admit any strangers to intimate, personal relationships; and the real and anticipated differences of sociocultural background, already seen operating in the housing sphere. Real differences emerged particularly strongly in the matter of values and norms associated with sex and family life, in the migrant preoccupation with colour and class, in religious beliefs and practice, and in such everyday concerns as diet and recreation, in which most migrants as yet felt no compulsion or desire to adapt their ways to local patterns.

Social relationships between migrants and the local population in Brixton are therefore still mainly restricted to casual contacts in the streets, shops, buses, and public houses. A fair degree of accommodation was discernible on both sides, finding expression in the often repeated local statement: 'We didn't fancy it at first but we've got used to seeing them about now. After all, they've got to live somewhere.' The decreasing tendency of the largest local paper, the *South London Press,* to stress the words 'coloured', 'Jamaican', or 'West Indian' in the headlining and reporting of crimes of a violent or sexual nature can also be regarded as a certain index of accommodation. The newcomers have, it was noted, been well received by the local commercial world. A number of food shops in the market area have begun to stock West Indian foods, and the record shops now sell a wide range of calypsos. The electrical equipment and furniture stores are doing a thriving trade in hire-purchase radiograms, cocktail cabinets, sewing-machines, and three-piece suites.

In the public houses, those cliquey refuges of the older cockneys, acceptance has inevitably been slower. In the earlier years there were some incidents, and a few publicans set up temporary colour bars. By now, however, most migrants who drink outside their homes or the migrant clubs have found their own 'locals' where they are sure of a welcome as regular customers. They are still not so sure of a welcome in dance halls where the sexual motivation is more directly involved. Despite occasional clashes between individuals and small groups, local Brixton *mores* would not appear to condone mob violence and there have been no mass disturbances, even at the height of the tension that followed the 1958 riots in Notting Hill and Nottingham.

Turning to the sphere of organized and formal social activities and contacts, in churches, community centres, youth clubs, or recreational associations, it was usual to find apprehension or apathy on the migrant side, and enthusiasm often followed by disillusionment among a local sponsoring minority. This seemed understandable at this early stage of migrant accommodation, in view of the local factors already mentioned, and of the dearth of organized associational life in the migrants' home environment. It was, however, clear that local sponsors could, with tact, sympathy, and an understanding of the migrants' sociocultural background and needs, play a considerable part in promoting accommodation in the social sphere, as indeed in all others.

As for the most intimate social relationship, that of intermarriage or sexual association between white and coloured, this is not yet the norm in Brixton. A minority of male migrants, particularly in the central settlement area, have been associating with white 'misfits' and declassed women, drawn usually from the provinces or other parts of London. There are a handful of mixed marriages, most of them entirely successful, but the norm in Brixton is the all-West Indian *ménage*. Local Brixtonians still tend to regard intermarriage or sexual association with coloured men as socially declassing or at least socially complicated for the female partner and the children. It is too early to say whether this view is likely to be justified. Most of the migrants' children, whether they are the product of all-West Indian unions or of mixed unions, are in the youngest age-groups. In the day nurseries, nursery schools, primary schools, and street play-groups, there is little evidence of friction between local and migrant children, who are growing up together in the same social and cultural environment.

The major part of this study portrays the development of migrant-host relationships at various points of contact or association. Some material was collected also on social organization within the West Indian migrant group, seen both as a response to the requirements of migrant life and as a consequence of incomplete acceptance by the receiving society. The group's internal social organization was found to be weak and amorphous, again as a result of the same set

395

of factors that have influenced and usually hindered migrant adaptation to the receiving society. Chief among these were a low degree of integration in the home background, and impermanent intentions, residential instability, and socio-economic divisions within the group.

Various forms of the elementary family unit have emerged as the basic if not the only social grouping among the Brixton migrants; many such units have proved impermanent, although a higher incidence of formal marriage was noted as a result of increased prosperity and possibly of an increasing desire to adhere to local *mores*. Otherwise the only associations which have so far evolved within the Brixton group consist of some cellular households, a few pentecostal congregations and cricket clubs, and a fair number of small informal economic partnerships, set up to help individuals to save up enough capital to put down a deposit for a house, pay a wife's fare from the West Indies, and so on. A number of small protest organizations sprang up and vanished like mushrooms during the years of this study, because the local population's attitudes and behaviour, while not particularly welcoming, were insufficiently hostile to provide the impetus for them to keep alive for more than a month or so.

The main source of such social control as exists within the group is still the small minority of wealthy multiple landlords. Otherwise the West Indian migrants lack leaders and are divided as well as linked by such criteria as geographical origin, social class, pigmentation, cultural background, economic status, and length of settlement in Britain. Little or no feeling of community is as yet discernible among them, although a clear geographical focus exists in the area immediately round Brixton market, and this will presumably be enhanced in the second generation that is now growing up there.

Trends and Possibilities

A fair degree of migrant accommodation in work, somewhat less in housing, and the modest beginnings of migrant acclimatization and local acquiescence in casual and formal social contacts – this, then, was the general position in Brixton in mid-1959. Nor since then does there seem to have been any reversal of these trends, but rather a slow though not necessarily smooth or uninterrupted progress towards a more complete accommodation on both sides, as local people and migrants alike begin to realize that the latter are here to stay. Whatever one's judgement on the political morality of this particular Act's rather selective provisions, the imposition of controls on immigration from the Commonwealth in July 1962 seems likely to promote the absorptive process by easing local tensions over housing and work, and giving the migrants a breathing-space in which to consolidate their economic position. It is also likely to do away with impermanent intentions and promote a 'settler' mentality among many migrants, in view of the fact that the right of re-entry into this country is not automatic for those who have been away for more than two years or who cannot prove that they are ordinarily resident in the United Kingdom. This change of intention should also further the processes of accommodation.

Looking into the immediate future, one may discern certain general or alternative lines of development in Brixton and indeed elsewhere in Britain. These trends may be more or less susceptible to acceleration or deflection by some form of social action, in the legislative, educational, welfare, and other fields (see Chapter 20). Meanwhile, it must be stressed again that relationships between migrants and the local population do not develop in a vacuum, but are simply a peripheral aspect of social relationships and life in the locality and in the country as a whole.

In the economic sphere, the trend towards greater accommodation and the ultimate integration of the West Indian newcomers in the permanent labour force should continue, with minor temporary set-backs in periods of moderate recession like that of 1956–58. The evidence seems to show that the more settled migrants with jobs are relatively little affected by such a recession, while the news of worsening employment opportunities deters many would-be migrants and so limits the numbers of new arrivals, who are the most difficult work-seekers to place at such a time. However, if a major slump of depression calibre were to occur in the next few years, before the processes of absorption have reached a point of no return, the consequences could be grave not only for the West Indian migrant group but for all identifiable newcomers or outsiders.

Reference has already been made to problems that may emerge in the housing sphere, which in Brixton as elsewhere is one of the main points of contact and potential sources of friction between newcomers and local people. The long-term dangers inherent in the consolidation of 'coloured quarters' are clear, but the present trend seems to be away from any such consolidation,[1] not only in Brixton but in most other central urban areas where West Indian migrants have been settled for some years.

The initial residential concentration could, however, in conjunction with the presence of so many West Indian women and families,

---

[1] The London trend contrasts sharply with the 'black belts' of recent Negro immigrants from the South which are being built up in Chicago and some other cities of the Northern United States as a result of widespread discriminatory covenants which restrict them to slum areas.

favour the development of a temporary social and cultural 'ghetto' among the migrants, whose main effort at adaptation is at present directed to economic ends. It is of course too early to assess trends in the sphere of social relationships and cultural adaptation, in which the processes of accommodation have barely started, particularly on the migrant side. There is a possibility that, as the elements of 'strangeness' and uncertainty cease to influence local attitudes and behaviour, they could be replaced by a more rigid class-colour identification. This would mean that coloured West Indians, particularly if they remain enclosed in such a social ghetto, and fail to adapt themselves at least superficially to local *mores,* would be ranked not outside the social hierarchy but at its foot, a position from which their high visibility would prevent them or their descendants from escaping as easily as less identifiable immigrants could do.[1]

A development of this kind does not, however, seem very likely when we consider such diverse factors as the small size of the present or even the potential West Indian migrant settlement;[2] its relatively wide dispersal; its lack of any strong organizational tradition or community feeling; the upward social mobility of many individuals; the enhanced international status of the decolonized territories from which the migrants come, and the increasing facilities for improving individual newcomers' educational, social, and economic equipment; the shared social and cultural traits which may against an English background (and aided by a shared education in the second generation) outlive the differences so noticeable today; and the potentially 'assimilating' character of the West Indians, in contrast to the 'integrating' character of other immigrant or minority groups in Britain such as the Moslems, Chinese, Poles, or Jews. On the British side, eventual assimilation seems to be favoured by such factors as the existence of a unified and democratic social structure which admits of no institutionalized differentiation between groups; the prevalent feeling that racial prejudice and discrimination are wrong; the low-intensity, 'live-and-let-live' atti-

---

[1] In Brixton, where there are few non-West Indian coloured migrants, the possibility of an eventual blurring of cultural and ethnic barriers between different coloured migrant groups is small. Such a development could however be anticipated if a lower-class ghetto were to evolve in Birmingham, Manchester, and similar areas.

[2] The migrant group's size is obviously dependent not only on accessions by migration but also on accessions by birth. Birth-rates in the Caribbean are higher than in this country, and in view of the West Indian attitude to fertility this may be carried over into the early years of migrant settlement. However, the history of other working-class immigrant groups, both coloured and white, suggests that the difficulties of migrant life and, later, improved economic status, usually result in a lowered birth-rate.

tudes of so many urban British; and the nation's slowly growing awareness and acceptance, despite the occasional bout of 'post-colonial blues', of Britain's changed role and status in a changing and increasingly multiracial world.

Predictions in such matters are always dangerous. On the strength of the Brixton material and the history of past migrant settlements in this country, however, I would be prepared to hazard the guess that over the next decades in Britain the West Indian migrants and their children will follow in the steps of the Irish; they will, though not without the checks and reverses inevitable in such processes, become accepted as a regular and permanent component of the local labour force, gradually raising their living standards and fanning out of the central areas of settlement. An able minority will push upwards into the skilled and professional strata, where a trail has already been blazed by an upper- and middle-class minority who preceded the mass migration from the West Indies. This adaptation and advancement will lead to closer social relationships with the local population, and probably to increased intermarriage and to an at least partial biological absorption of the West Indians in the local population – as happened in the case of over 10,000 freed coloured slaves in nineteenth-century London, and to many thousands of white ex-soldiers, indentured labourers, and settlers in the West Indian islands themselves.

20

Postscript—action for the future

WHAT OF the more distant future and of the second and succeeding generations? The greater part of the three hundred thousand West Indian migrants in Britain at midsummer 1962 will probably settle here for good. Even allowing for further accessions and for a high initial birth-rate among migrant women, an immigrant group of these dimensions can hardly be said to constitute a serious national problem in a country with a population of over 52 millions.[1] Thus, but for certain rather specific considerations, there would be a reasonable case for leaving the usual processes of adaptation and acceptance to proceed with no more than local and voluntary assistance, as was the case with most earlier migrant groups.

This particular migrant situation is, however, clearly not going to be allowed to develop without interference. For it has come to be identified as part of the world-wide 'colour problem', in which the pigmentation frontier more or less corresponds to the universal line-up of the 'have-nots' and the 'haves', and to a lesser extent to the divide between 'anti-colonialists' and 'colonialists'. Thus every aspect of coloured-white relationships and development in Britain is subjected to outside scrutiny and comment, the effect of which is often rather to exacerbate than to soothe the tensions and conflicts which are an inevitable part of migrant-host relationships. Now that the whole equilibrium of world power is changing, and the Commonwealth is, by virtue of conscious British policy, being transformed from a family based on kinship to a wider multiracial, multicultural *familia*, the presence of coloured migrants in Britain presents a moral and a practical challenge. The people of these

---

[1] Further annual reinforcements will presumably be held below earlier peaks by the operation of the Commonwealth Immigrants Act (1962). It should be pointed out, however, that the estimated total population of the entire British Caribbean area is well under four million, so that even if this population were to migrate bodily to Britain it would not present an insoluble problem. This consideration does not, of course, apply in the case of immigration from Indian and Pakistan.

islands face the need not only to reformulate their views of Britain's role and status in such a Commonwealth,[1] but also to apply the new relationship in their dealings with coloured Commonwealth migrants here at home. And not only the colour-conscious migrants themselves, but the newly independent Afro-Asian countries and the outside world as a whole, show an inclination to judge Britain's good faith in international relations by her ability to put her own house in order.

In these circumstances, the traditional *laissez-faire* approach is obviously inadequate, even though it seems to have worked so far in Brixton. Instead, various forms of nation-wide social action are indicated, on both a short-term and a long-term basis. The sooner such action is decided upon and initiated, the better will be its chance of success, since the situation is still fluid, attitudes on both sides are flexible, and behaviour is uncertain and uninstitutionalized.

SOCIAL ACTION TO PROMOTE ADAPTATION AND ACCEPTANCE

This study was conceived within an academic framework and not as a manual of social work. The subject is, however, one of public concern and controversy, and many of those officials and social workers who were kind enough to help me in my field work ended by asking: 'Once you have collected all this material and analysed it, at least give us some suggestions as to what should be done to deal with the main problems and improve relationships.' I have little that is novel to put forward in this sphere, but shall attempt to summarize the main types of action that seem likely to be of use in lessening tensions and promoting migrant-host accommodation in the kind of situation I studied in Brixton.[2]

Before discussing the different types of social action, one should be quite clear about the ultimate aims of such action and the main assumptions on which it is based. The trend in the world as a whole is towards an ideal situation in which 'racial' affiliations, real or alleged, should no longer be a criterion for the allocation of rights, privileges, and responsibilities between groups and individuals; in which the word 'race' should in fact cease to have any but a

---

[1] The decision of the Union of South Africa to withdraw from the Commonwealth in 1961, in the face of majority condemnation of her internal policies, marked not only the change to a *familia* but the change in Britain's status from leadership to *primus inter pares*.

[2] For particularly detailed and useful suggestions in this regard see: Richmond (1960, pp. 14-26); Little (1958); and Banton (1959, Appendix I, pp. 187-94).

biological significance. This trend arises out of basic assumptions concerning the essential equality and unity in diversity of mankind, such as are set forth in the United Nations Declaration of Human Rights, and in statements by supra-national bodies like the World Council of Churches and the Roman Catholic Church.[1] In Britain, the ultimate goal is a society of unity in diversity; a society in which a coloured skin, like a minority creed, a second language, or a sub-culture, should no longer be associated with strangeness, inferiority, or out-group status by either side.

Three main types of social action seem indicated in the field of race relations in Britain. One would be aimed at the reduction and eventual elimination of discriminatory behaviour; the second at the reduction of 'racial' prejudice or antipathy, and finally of 'racial' consciousness in the receiving population and also among the migrants; and the third at furthering the processes of adaptation and acceptance between newcomers and the local population in various areas of association.[2]

The second and third lines of action clearly involve official and voluntary action at all levels over a long period of time. The first type of action, that designed to reduce discrimination,[3] could be taken immediately and on a national level, in the form of anti-discriminatory legislation, supported by reiterated policy statements from political parties, trade unions, employers' associations, churches, voluntary associations, bodies representing the mass media, and other organizations.

LEGISLATIVE ACTION

The purpose and scope of such legislation should be clearly understood. It is not designed to reduce prejudice or antipathy, but simply to reduce or prevent discriminatory behaviour, regardless of the actor's motivation.

To be efficacious it should be confined to universal spheres such as civic and legal rights, education, public housing and property covenants, jobs, and the right to enter hotels, bars, restaurants,

---

[1] Cf. The Unesco series *The Race Question in Modern Science* (1951–53) and *The Race Question and Modern Thought* (1953-54).

[2] For a discussion of the use of educational, information, legal, and civic techniques in combating prejudice and discrimination, see Report of the Second United Nations Conference of Non-Government Organizations interested in the Eradication of Prejudice and Discrimination (Unesco E/NGO/Conf. 2/7, 28 July 1959).

[3] Stern enforcement by the courts of existing legislation aimed against breaches of the peace, violence, etc., would also appear to be efficacious (cf. the four-year prison sentences passed on nine youths who attacked coloured men in the Notting Hill disturbances of 1958).

cinemas, dance halls, and other places of entertainment.[1] These are areas and situations in which legislation is most applicable and likely to succeed, and the Brixton material has shown that they are those in which the great majority of the local population is least inclined to discriminate against newcomers and outsiders[2] and most willing to accept an egalitarian ethic. They are also those which most concern the West Indian migrant in the early years of his settlement.

At the other end of the 'rank order' of discrimination or avoidance in relation to West Indian migrants, the existence of which was noted in Brixton (see Chapter 14, p. 280), come situations involving co-residence, intimate primary groups, social intercourse, and intermarriage. Here discrimination in the form of avoidance is most marked, and the possibility of direct legislative action is virtually non-existent, so that improvement must be achieved through long-term types of social action. Marginal situations do, however, occur in the case of discrimination by landladies of students' lodgings; here legislative action by the university or college licensing authorities could be fairly effective.[3] It should also be possible to prohibit the publication of discriminatory 'To Let' advertisements by the press or their display by tobacconists and other shopkeepers.[4]

It is sometimes argued that anti-discriminatory legislation would be difficult to enforce without the establishment of an elaborate and expensive machinery (in the form of an administrative agency like the New York State Commission against Discrimination), which would not be justified by the relatively small dimensions of the

---

[1] A private anti-discrimination bill was brought before the House of Commons six times (unsuccessfully) by Mr. Fenner Brockway, M.P. On his sixth attempt the bill for the first time omitted any clauses relating to discrimination at work (*Guardian*, 8 December 1960). Mr. Fenner Brockway tried again in December 1961 and March 1962, unsuccessfully on both occasions (see Institute of Race Relations *Newsletter*, January and April 1962). On 2 June 1961 Mr. Fenner Brockway and Sir Leslie Plummer also tabled an anti-discriminatory amendment to the Licensing Bill, but this was debated for a short while in standing committee and withdrawn. On 29 March 1962 Lord Walston, a Labour life peer, introduced a Racial Discrimination Bill. This was rejected on second reading in the House of Lords by 41 votes to 21 on 14 May.

[2] Such legislation should also cover all forms of racial, religious, and other discrimination, thereby weakening the charge that by singling out one or two groups for protection it is in itself discriminatory and likely to provoke resentment and further discrimination.

[3] In face of the grave shortage of accommodation for students, these authorities have so far been loath to take such direct action, but see Institute of Race Relations *Newsletters* (*passim*, 1960–61) for endeavours by students' organizations.

[4] In February 1960 Sir Leslie Plummer, M.P. (Deptford) introduced (unsuccessfully) a private Racial and Religious Insults Bill to make it an offence to insult, or conspire to insult, persons publicly because of their race or religion (*Hansard*, 2 February 1960, p. 796 f.).

problem of discrimination in Britain. There is something to be said for this argument, particularly in the economic field, where detection and enforcement seem particularly difficult. But whether or not such an agency is set up,[1] the passing of limited anti-discriminatory legislation could well be efficacious in Britain. As the Brixton material has shown, attitudes remain fluid and behaviour uncertain; thus even a few successful test-cases in the courts should help to establish a pattern of behaviour for inn-keepers, employers, and others who at present tend to be swayed by what they think 'our regulars' or the 'local people' will say. Legislation would penalize the display of prejudice by a pathological minority and would give a firm lead to the uncertain but not ill-disposed majority in universal areas of association.[2] It seems probable that it would also create a climate of opinion favourable to the reduction of discrimination in private life and to the carrying out of other long-term programmes.

So far, we have been concerned with the utility of anti-discriminatory legislation in influencing the majority society. Yet such legislation is likely to have an even greater and more immediate impact upon the minority groups involved. In the case of the West Indian migrants, it should dispel much of the uncertainty and suspicion that colour their approach to life in this country.[3] They would 'know where they stand' in the most important situations of everyday life. This added certainty should help to dispel the prickly colour consciousness that so often hampers normal relationships with the local population, and thereby promote easier relationships in the areas of intimate association that are not directly susceptible to legislative manipulation. Given this sense of security, the migrants might also be less prone to attribute all their setbacks and shortcomings to 'colour bar' and 'colour prejudice', and more willing to face the need to adjust and adapt to local *mores* in their capacity as immigrants.

[1] For a strong argument in support of the setting up of such an agency or board see Griffith (1960, pp. 176–7). On the capacity of law to affect race relations in general, see also Greenberg (1959, *passim*).

[2] Another argument against anti-discriminatory legislation advances the thesis that legislation must not run ahead of public opinion, which is not thought to be ready for legislation in this matter. But in fact, as Griffith (1960, p. 174) points out, many of Britain's most important social reforms have been put through not in answer to but despite public opinion. United States experience also supports the view that group *mores* and individual feelings can often be influenced and altered by legal prescription, particularly when this is backed by a strong enforcing agency (see Blumer, 1958, pp. 438–9). In any case, the widespread feeling in Britain that racialism is in principle wrong and un-British (reinforced by the shock of the disturbances in Notting Hill and the rowdy, widely publicized meetings organized by neo-fascist and racialist groups in the late summer of 1962) would provide a favourable climate for the operation of such legislation.

[3] On this important point see Ruth Glass (1960, p. 235 f.).

It may be argued that anti-discriminatory legislation would defeat its own ends by provoking an excessive and frivolous response from members of the minority groups whom it seems to protect. In view of the high costs and delays involved in litigation in Britain, however, it seems probable that the majority of such frivolous and litigious-minded petitioners would be deterred by the legal profession or by legal advice bureaux and other agencies from appearing before the courts with anything but a solid case.

THE REDUCTION OF BIAS AND ANTIPATHY

The second type of social action which seems clearly indicated in the sphere of race relations in Britain is a long-term educational programme, aimed at the reduction of racial or religious bias and antipathy and of all unfavourable attitudes short of extreme pathological prejudice.[1] A favourable climate of opinion for such action may be created by anti-discriminatory legislation at a national level, but the onus of initiating such long-term measures must fall largely on a multiplicity of local government, voluntary, and private agencies. The following suggestions are therefore advanced tentatively and in broad outline, since the measures taken must obviously be influenced by specific local possibilities and needs.

The Brixton material has borne out the view that a mild antipathy to all outsiders and strangers is a cultural norm in English society. Much of this mild antipathy or aversion would seem to arise from sheer ignorance[2] or from vague myths and notions derived from simplified historical accounts or from fleeting superficial contacts. In relation to coloured people, the notions are also influenced by the colour-class myths of an outmoded colonial past and occasionally by the pseudo-scientific racialism that arose to justify it.

School textbooks and syllabuses are inevitably slow to reflect new trends of opinion. Even today many British children are still, like their parents before them, being imbued with the notion that Negroes live in African jungles, and are primitive, pagan, and sexually uninhibited. This is happening to them in a period of their lives in which they are most malleable and in which, at least in

[1] Such prejudice is not of course amenable to rational correction, but requires the attention of a psychiatrist.

[2] 'One side of the problem is the complete indifference of the British public to their own great colonial inheritance. Perhaps it is natural for an island people to set little store by the opinions and customs of foreigners, but when the same insularity is applied to the inhabitants of colonial territories the dangers are obvious. The level of ignorance described in this inquiry remains as a standing reproach to the British educational system' (P.E.P. report, cited by Banton, 1959, p. 194).

the earlier years, they show little or no racial antipathy[1] or even consciousness of differences.

One of the most important items in the educational programme, then, is to carry out a thorough revision of textbooks and syllabuses in such subjects as history, geography, scripture, English literature, and possibly even biology. The teaching of history and geography in particular should lose its insular slant. Judicious teaching of human relations might also be considered for older pupils,[2] as might comparative cultural studies showing the functions and interdependence of differing cultures and their contributions to our own way of life.[3]

Such a thorough-going revision of our educational system could achieve its full objects only with the full participation of the teachers. All too often the latter share the misconceptions and antipathies of the rest of the adult population and help to pass them on to the younger generation. Somehow it should be possible to find space in the training-college syllabus for a course in race and human relations.

Measures of this kind may help to dispel ignorance, but they will not necessarily by themselves dispel all hostility or antipathy. The value of second-hand instruction on race relations could be greatly enhanced by the extension of schemes for the international interchange of teachers and of older pupils. The improvement of pupils' attitudes to coloured people after a fortnight's visit by two African teachers recorded in *The Teacher was Black*[4] suggests that a gill of personal contact in a favourable situation is worth a gallon of second-hand knowledge. Personal contacts will also increase as more immigrant children enter the schools. Teachers may of course find that some personal contacts evoke not greater understanding but greater hostility. For instance, a child's family may live in a house that has been bought by a migrant who is determined to get them out. In such cases it may be more difficult to eradicate the habit of generalizing from the particular, and of thinking in terms of 'we' and 'they'.

The work of educating tomorrow's generation to take their place in a multiracial, multicultural Commonwealth and world can be

---

[1] The absence of racial or colour consciousness in young children has been noted even in South Africa. During my Brixton field work I observed this constantly in play-groups, and it was confirmed by all day-nursery matrons, primary school teachers, and managers of children's homes whom I interviewed.

[2] Cf. Little (1958, pp. 26–7).

[3] For a detailed account of actual and desirable ways of teaching race relations in Britain, see report by A. I. Polack presented to the Unesco Expert Meeting on the Promotion of Teaching of Race Questions in Primary and Secondary Schools (Unesco/SS/Conf. 3/5/Paris, 23 August 1955).

[4] H. E. O. James and Cora Tenen (1953).

largely vitiated if the children return every evening to homes where the old climate of ignorance and insular aversion prevails. The mass media, and to a lesser extent the trade unions and the churches, have the best chance of reaching into and influencing these homes. The unions, the churches, and other agencies have already issued declarations of principle and policy at a national level, and at local level many have arranged talks and discussions to acquaint their more active members with the issues involved. Considerably more could be done in this direction.

So far as the mass media are concerned, there is still a tendency to reflect popular misconceptions about race and colour rather than to dispel them and, particularly in the case of the popular press, a trend to emphasize the exotic and violent aspects of racial contacts.[1] In the case of sound radio and television, some systematization might be feasible, perhaps in the form of an agreed code of reference.[2] The press is not by its nature susceptible to centralized directives, but the ball might be set rolling if cases of repeated and blatantly biased reporting involving people of different races or creeds were to be brought before the Press Council. As the general climate of opinion becomes more tolerant, the popular press will of course move with it. It could, however, move ahead and help to lead public opinion, given determined action by individual editors and sub-editors (the latter in the important matter of headlines), and sustained correspondence from sponsoring readers. At present the letter columns are still largely monopolized by the lunatic racialist fringe, with only an occasional protest from the tolerant but passive majority.

INTEGRATIVE SOCIAL ACTION

The final type of social action to be advocated is of a kind more familiar in the traditional countries of immigration than in Britain. It is the most positive of the three types of action, being concerned with furthering the processes of adaptation and acceptance between the migrant group and the receiving society.

Such action will often be concerned with the most elementary stages of individual adjustment and group accommodation to universal roles and in universal areas of association in the new society.

[1] The presentation of racial situations and personalities on the screen is a subject that merits detailed study. The majority of films dealing with such situations are not produced in Britain and consequently do not reflect British attitudes or situations. A certain filtering takes place through the licensing authorities, and the views of film distributors as to the tastes or distastes of their patrons also play a considerable part in determining what is or is not shown on British screens.

[2] See Little (1958, pp. 28–30) for a more detailed discussion of measures which might in his view be initiated by the British Broadcasting Corporation.

407

But its ultimate goal should be kept clearly in mind by the agencies concerned. In the West Indian case, this goal would seem to be not group integration but assimilation: first, because the West Indian migrant group is 'assimilating' in character if not yet in intention; and second, because to promote cohesive group integration beyond a certain stage might, in the present climate of race relations in Britain, lead to the establishment of a highly visible, lower-class, minority group with inferior rights and status. This does not mean that no efforts should be made to promote internal organization and control within the West Indian migrant group, but rather that this should be done as a transitional and not as a final measure.

Among the considerations to be borne in mind by agencies and individuals concerned with this type of social action are: the particular spheres in which such action is most likely to be effective, and the need to recognize and reconcile the differing expectations and values of the migrants and the local population. As the Brixton material has shown, the British are thinking in terms of gradual and modified acceptance, whereas the West Indians expect this acceptance to be immediate and complete. The British are conscious of class and cultural differences, whereas many West Indians are extremely colour conscious and tend to overlook all other differences.

The normal processes of immigrant adaptation and acceptance always involve some tension and conflict, but these could be considerably reduced if the integratory agencies concerned were to understand these differences and to try to impress them on the two groups involved. For if accommodation and ultimately assimilation are to be achieved, the West Indian migrants must face the fact that they have to make a thorough-going and sustained effort to adapt their behaviour and values in all major spheres of life, while the local population must widen its terms of acceptance of newcomers and learn more about their background and ways. As for the spheres in which this type of organized action is likely to be most successful, these will on the whole correspond to the universal areas of association in which, it was suggested above, anti-discriminatory legislation has most chance of success. An additional sphere is that of personal advice and welfare counselling for individual migrants.

Immigrants are perhaps better served in Britain than in most traditional countries of immigration by the all-embracing provisions of the welfare state. There is, however, no single department concerned with the reception and integration of immigrants, whatever their origin. For some years during and after the war a small welfare department in the Colonial Office was maintained to deal with the problems of colonial immigrants; but this was closed down in 1951 and its duties transferred to the various governments concerned.

408

Postscript – action for the future

There is thus no British governmental agency directly or solely concerned with immigrant welfare or integration, although a number of local authorities have recently set up such bodies.[1]

From the migrant side, the West Indian governments,[2] originally headed by Jamaica, between 1955 and 1962 built up a special Migrant Services Division which covered the reception of immigrants,[3] advisory and personal welfare services, industrial relations, community development, and public relations. All those who were in contact with this agency could have nothing but admiration and respect for its staff and its achievements. But even at the time of its greatest development, before its untimely demise along with the West Indian Federation, it needed additional personnel and facilities, particularly in the provinces, to cope with the multifarious and changing needs of the growing migrant group and with the extension of liaison work with various key agencies and individuals on the British side. The smaller agencies that have succeeded the Federal one are unlikely to be able to duplicate its work.

Whereas the Migrant Services Division and its successors are concerned with migrant welfare, most agencies on the British side are concerned with migrant accommodation only peripherally and in so far as this is connected with their normal activities. In this study something has been shown of the work done by welfare organizations, churches, and other bodies, both to promote migrant adaptation and, by informing local opinion, to encourage acceptance of the newcomers. A great deal more could and should be done in this connection, if possible in a more coordinated manner than heretofore.[4] In the Brixton area there has been little coordination of this kind, but the evidence available from such areas as Birmingham, Bristol, and Willesden[5] indicates its potential value. A good case can also be made for the appointment of a liaison or community

[1] In July 1962 a non-statutory Commonwealth Immigrants' Advisory Council was set up by the home secretary to advise upon the integration of immigrants.
[2] This type of service is not as yet remotely paralleled by any of the other Commonwealth governments concerned (India, Pakistan, Ghana, Nigeria, etc.) although some (notably Pakistan) have recently begun to appoint liaison and welfare officers for their own nationals in Britain.
[3] Among the most valuable services performed by this agency was that of providing information to would-be migrants at home on the conditions, possibilities, and difficulties of life in Britain, and on the kind of skills and behaviour required of the migrant. See *Going to Britain?*—a compilation of talks originally given over the BBC Caribbean Service and published by the British Broadcasting Corporation in 1960.
[4] See special issue on 'Race', *London Quarterly and Holborn Review*, January 1961; also *Life of Faith* (19 January 1961) for an article by Eddie N. Burke, a West Indian Methodist layman and recently Advisor on Community Development to the West Indies Commission in the United Kingdom, on ways in which practising Christians could welcome individual West Indians into the community.
[5] See Ruck (Ed.) (1960, Chapter IX); and Maizels (1960).

409

development officer in areas of large-scale migrant settlement,[1] and the setting-up by local authorities of induction courses for newcomers at evening institutes,[2] although those who conduct such courses will have to be prepared for the usual migrant alternation of enthusiasm and apathy.

A small number of British and interracial agencies have also been set up with the specific aim of promoting migrant accommodation in various spheres. Those concerned with recreation and social relationships have, as was seen in Brixton, not always been particularly successful, for a variety of reasons, notably migrant apathy, artificial or patronizing attitudes on the part of local organizers, or simply failure to provide the sort of recreational facilities likely to attract the newcomers. While some recreational facilities should undoubtedly be made available to the migrant, it may be that integrative social action could in the early years of settlement be more fruitfully concentrated on the fields in which the migrant makes his own major effort of adaptation, that is to say, in work and housing. In the former, the trade unions can do a great deal more at local and shop levels. In the field of housing, there would seem to be a considerable need for watch-dog and information services and for the setting-up of housing associations,[3] which could provide some accommodation at a reasonable rental and advise migrant would-be purchasers.

Integrative social action will have an increasingly large and important part to play in relation to one particular section of the migrant group. This is the second immigrant generation, the children who for the most part are not yet in their teens, and whose primary attachments will be increasingly not to their parents' birthplace but to England, the place of their birth or upbringing. If they find themselves relegated to inferior jobs and treated as strangers in their own country, as earlier Anglo-coloured people have been, this will intensify the special pressures and problems found in most second-generation immigrant groups, and may produce a crop of delinquents rather than a marginal group equipped to assist their parents' accommodation to life in this country and to move towards full assimilation for themselves and their own children.

It is easier to pin-point the achievements of sponsoring agencies and groups than those of individual sponsors. But the Brixton

---

[1] See Hyndman (1960, p. 151). In recent years an increasing number of local authorities have begun to cooperate with national ministries and voluntary organizations in coordinating committees concerned with migrant problems (for instance, the London Council of Social Service organizes regular meetings of London borough representatives).

[2] See Richmond (1960, p. 25).

[3] As has been done with considerable success by the Aggrey Society in Leeds.

material has shown what an important part such sponsors play in all kinds of situations, particularly in groups with little internal cohesion or organization. Their activities do not easily lend themselves to coordination, but it should be borne in mind that sponsors in central positions of power and influence are more likely to further migrant acceptance than are those in marginal positions.[1] And, before we leave the subject of sponsorship, it should be added that sponsors are not born but made. There are a large number of people of goodwill who could with judicious encouragement and information be persuaded to translate this goodwill into action. An instance of such encouragement is to be found in a handbook issued by the Anglican Church Assembly:

> 'There is thus a clear case for positive action on the part of Christians. They must overcome their reluctance "to make a fuss" when they encounter discrimination, and they must seek to overcome prejudice in themselves, and in the groups within which they have influence. Since moral courage is involved, the nature of the Christian life, lived as it is not in isolation but in the community of the congregation, should give Christians the power and determination to act creatively in the community at large, whether as housewives or employees, as shopkeepers or consumers, or as councillors or voters.'[2]

Sponsors are most likely to encounter pitfalls in the sphere of informal social relationships, and it is here that goodwill should be tempered by common sense and social sense. Newcomers should not be sponsored into uncongenial groups with whose members they have no common interest or background. On the other hand, highly successful social contacts can be arranged by means of careful selection, as in the case of functions and home invitations arranged locally for overseas students by Rotary and other organizations.

'NO MAN IS AN ISLAND'[3]

By way of conclusion, it must be stressed once again that the development of relationships between West Indian migrants and British hosts is not a self-contained or self-sufficient process, but a relatively

[1] Cf. Collins (1960, pp. 47–51). The supreme importance of sponsors in key positions in the American situation is stressed by Herbert Blumer (1958, pp. 432–3, points 2 and 12).

[2] *Together in Britain* (a Christian Handbook on Race Relations, Church Information Office, 1960, p. 42). See also the set of points drawn up for the Birmingham Christian Social Council, and published in the pamphlet *Your Neighbour* (Church Information Office, 1960). The latter also draws attention to the need to maintain a simple and continuing attitude of friendliness, and to avoid reserve, over-heartiness, and disappointment if the immediate reaction of the migrant is not always as satisfactory as was expected. [3] John Donne, *Devotions* (1624).

411

small sector or aspect of everyday social life in this country. It has been seen how in Brixton relationships have been affected and even determined by extraneous regional or nation-wide problems in the economic or housing spheres. The alleviation of such problems must obviously further the processes of accommodation between migrants and local people,[1] as must the introduction of a less ethnocentric type of education and the extension of first- and second-hand knowledge of the outside world and of other peoples and cultures.

The difficulties presented by existing differences in social and cultural background and in technical qualifications between migrants and hosts are, however, only a facet of the world-wide problem of the 'haves' and 'have-nots'. Economic and technical aid programmes to under-developed countries in Asia, Africa, and the Caribbean will have the secondary effect of reducing the real differences and inequalities between later migrants and the British population, as well as of decreasing the 'push' factor that at present drives the migrants out to any territory which offers the prospect of work and of giving them increased security and status.[2] The bond of the new Commonwealth *familia* could also be considerably strengthened if the coloured migrants settle and are fully accepted in Britain. And this process could in turn be facilitated by a wider levelling-up process within the Commonwealth as a whole, until the coloured members of the new multiracial *familia* feel and are made to feel as much at home economically and socially in Britain and elsewhere as the foundation members of the old white family have long felt. Dark colour must cease to be the badge of the stranger, the un-skilled, and the lower class, just as light colour is ceasing to be the badge of the conqueror, the overseer, and the social *élite* – not only within the Commonwealth but throughout Europe and in the Western world as a whole.

[1] Cf. Benedict (1943, pp. 151–2): 'The fact that to understand race conflict we need fundamentally to understand *conflict* and not *race*, means something much more drastic. It means that all the deep-seated causes of conflict in any group or between groups are involved in any outbreak of race prejudice. Race will be cried up today in a situation where formerly religion would have been cried up. If civilized men expect to end prejudice – whether religious or racial – they will have to remedy major social abuses, in no way connected with religion or race, to the common advantage. Whatever reduces conflict, curtails irresponsible power, and allows people to obtain a decent livelihood will reduce race conflict. Nothing less will accomplish the task.'

[2] Nevertheless, so long as the West Indian population continues to increase at its present rate and the capital investment cost of creating a single new industrial job at home remains so high (£2,000 in relation to £70 for a migrant single fare to Britain, according to *Commonwealth Affairs*, No. 91, May 1961), it is pointless to delude oneself that investment in the West Indies would altogether halt the migrant outflow, in the event of present controls being relaxed. See Roberts (1957b, p. 276f.) for a discussion of the implications of further unchecked population growth in the British Caribbean territories.

412

APPENDICES

APPENDIX I

	1946–48	Annual Average 1946–48	1949	1950	1951	1952	1953
WEST AFRICA	800	267	254(22)	135(72)	113(36)	69(25)	34(59)
Nigeria	267	89	125(7)	90(20)	52(18)	42(6)	17(25)
Gold Coast (Ghana)	213	71	69(9)	19(6)	34(8)	16(5)	15(16)
Sierra Leone	211	70	37(4)	3(37)	13(7)	4(3)	1(4)
Gambia	109	36	23(—)	23(4)	14(3)	6(10)	1(13)
Unspecified	—	—	—(2)	—(5)	—(—)	1(1)	—(1)
WEST INDIES	330	110	78(6)	162(35)	62(19)	75(41)	81(30)
Jamaica	281	94	66(6)	150(25)	51(14)	37(29)	69(25)
Barbados	14	5	4(—)	4(7)	2(—)	—(—)	1(2)
Trinidad	20	7	4(—)	1(2)	4(3)	4(1)	6(2)
British Guiana	15	5	—(—)	3(—)	2(1)	6(3)	1(—)
Elsewhere	—	—	4(—)	4(1)	3(1)	28(8)	4(1)
OTHERS	91	30	31(13)	8(13)	4(20)	15(23)	7(16)
E. and S. Africa	15	5	8(—)	1(—)	—(—)	1(2)	—(2)
British Somaliland	45	15	13(5)	3(2)	4(14)	10(9)	3(13)
Aden	30	10	5(1)	—(5)	—(3)	2(11)	—(1)
Malta	—	—	4(6)	4(3)	—(—)	1(—)	3(—)
Elsewhere	1	—	1(1)	—(3)	—(3)	1(1)	1(—)
TOTAL	1,221	407	363(41)	305(120)	179(75)	159(89)	122(105)

Note: The 1946–53 figures are taken from a table given by Banton (1955, p. 49); those for 1954–60 were kindly made available by the Home Office (Nationality Division). The first figure in each case shows arrivals who were allowed to land. The numbers of stowaways refused leave to land because they could not satisfy

1946–1960

1954	1955	1956	1957	1958	1959	1960	
1(37)	3(10)	4(18)	7(14)	13(9)	12(8)	3(13)	WEST AFRICA
—(14)	3(1)	2(11)	—(3)	—(1)	—(4)	—(—)	Nigeria
1(6)	—(5)	—(4)	1(—)	2(—)	4(—)	1(5)	Gold Coast (Ghana)
—(9)	—(2)	—(1)	—(1)	8(—)	3(1)	—(2)	Sierra Leone
—(8)	—(2)	2(2)	6(10)	3(8)	5(3)	2(6)	Gambia
0(00)	0(00)	0(00)	0(00)	0(00)	0(00)	0(00)	Unspecified
110(21)	65(23)	38(7)	99(14)	72(5)	62(4)	142(21)	WEST INDIES
93(16)	36(20)	17(6)	77(11)	66(2)	22(2)	67(17)	Jamaica
5(3)	—(—)	—(—)	—(—)	—(—)	2(—)	2(—)	Barbados
2(—)	7(2)	9(1)	4(—)	3(2)	3(—)	23(4)	Trinidad
2(—)	8(—)	8(—)	17(1)	3(—)	4(—)	9(—)	British Guiana
8(2)	14(1)	4(—)	1(2)	—(1)	31(2)	41(—)	Elsewhere
10(12)	11(15)	14(14)	8(10)	14(13)	7(13)	5(11)	OTHERS
7(3)	4(3)	6(6)	—(4)	9(4)	5(9)	4(—)	E. and S. Africa
2(7)	4(9)	3(4)	2(3)	1(1)	—(—)	—(—) (until June 1960)	British Somaliland
—(—)	1(1)	—(—)	—(—)	—(2)	—(—)	—(8)	Aden
—(—)	1(—)	2(3)	5(—)	1(—)	2(—)	—(—)	Malta
1(2)	1(2)	3(1)	1(3)	3(6)	—(4)	1(3)	Elsewhere
121(70)	79(48)	56(39)	114(38)	99(27)	81(25)	150(45)	TOTAL

tne Immigration Officer that they were British subjects or British protected persons are shown in brackets. The data for British Somaliland are only up to June 1960 because this territory then became independent and left the Commonwealth.

APPENDIX II

TABLE A. APPROXIMATE NUMBERS OF WEST INDIAN MIGRANTS
ENTERING THE U.K. IN SUBSTANTIAL PARTIES, 1952–61

Year*	Men	Women	Children (under 16)	Unclassified	Total
1952	1,500	700	—	—	2,200
%	68·2	31·8	—	—	100
1953	1,700	600	—	—	2,300
%	73·9	26·1	—	—	100
1954	6,600	2,600	—	—	9,200
%	71·7	28·3	—	—	100
1955	13,900	7,300	300	2,900	24,400
%	57·0	29·9	1·2	11·9	100
1956	13,900	9,400	600	2,500	26,400
%	52·6	35·6	2·3	9·5	100
1957	11,400	9,400	900	800	22,500
%	50·7	41·8	4·0	3·5	100
1958	7,700	7,800	1,000	—	16,500
%	46·7	47·3	6·0	—	100
1959	10,100	8,200	2,100	—	20,400
%	49·5	40·2	10·3	—	100
1960	29,600	19,900	3,200	—	52,700
%	56·3	37·8	5·9	—	100
1961	28,900	27,600	5,100	—	61,600
%	46·8	44·8	8·4	—	100
Total	125,300	93,500	13,200	6,200	238,200
%	52·6	39·3	5·5	2·6	100

* The figures for 1952–54 are taken from an answer given in the House of Lords on 15 February 1956 (*Hansard*, pp. 1038–9). The figures for 1955–61 are those published or kindly made available by the Migrant Services Division, to the nearest 100.

TABLE B. BREAKDOWN OF WEST INDIAN MIGRANT ARRIVALS BY SEX,

Year		Jamaica	Barbados	Trinidad and Tobago	British Guiana	Antigua	Leeward Islands Mont- serrat	St. Kitts- Nevis
1955	M	9,614	1,298	420	188		1,509	
	F	5,253	713	303	137		515	
	C	220	37	48	14		9	
	U	2,808	—	—	6		100	
Total		17,895	2,048	771	345		2,133	
%		73·2	8·3	3·1	1·4		8·7	
1956	M	9,367						
	F	6,340						
	C	391						
	U	—						
Total		16,098						
%		60·9						
1957	M	6,720	976	705	136	319	270	407
	F	5,965	995	534	104	217	250	257
	C	618	61	42	11	11	17	32
	U	456	78	—	—	94	24	83
Total		13,759	2,110	1,281	251	641	561	779
%		61·3	9·4	5·7	1·1	2·8	2·5	3·5
1958	M	4,489	472	524	311	184	143	451
	F	4,922	633	350	181	205	156	397
	C	726	42	65	21	33	24	80
Total		10,137	1,147	939	513	422	323	928
%		61·5	7·0	5·7	3·1	2·5	2·0	5·6
1959	M	6,014	721	463	474	160	212	353
	F	5,273	669	385	236	121	154	291
	C	1,286	124	125	50	72	89	133
Total		12,573	1,514	973	760	353	455	777
%		61·5	7·4	4·9	3·7	1·7	2·2	3·8
1960	M	18,801	3,177	1,590	519	387	269	1,008
	F	12,776	2,091	1,195	361	312	194	751
	C	1,696	339	167	128	92	111	249
Total		33,273	5,607	2,952	1,008	791	574	2,008
%		63·1	10·5	6·3	1·9	1·5	1·0	3·8
1961	M	18,513	2,375	1,095	1,490		1,362	
	F	17,853	2,346	1,006	1,665		1,458	
	C	2,724	315	181	315		709	
Total		39,090	5,036	2,282	3,470		3,529	
%		63·5	8·2	3·7	5·6		5·7	
*Total	M	73,518						
1955–	F	58,383						
1961	C	7,661						
	U	3,264						
Total		142,825						
%		63·6						

Note: M = male, F = female, C = children, U = unclassified (this drops out after 1957).
* Owing to the closing of the federal offices it was unfortunately impossible to get a full breakdown of

418

	Windward Islands			All other		
Dominica	Grenada	St. Lucia	St. Vincent	territories	Total	Year

Dominica	Grenada	St. Lucia	St. Vincent	All other territories	Total	Year	
	894				13,923	1955	M
	402				7,323		F
	5				333		C
	—				2,894		U
	1,301				24,473	Total	
	5·3				100	%	
				4,554	13,921	1956	M
				3,040	9,380		F
				261	652		C
				2,488	2,488		U
				10,343	26,441	Total	
				39·1	100	%	
568	547	407	357		11,412	1957	M
382	282	255	144		9,385		F
34	25	9	7		867		C
35	—	32	7		809		U
1,019	854	703	515		22,473	Total	
4·5	3·8	3·1	2·3		100	%	
309	346	268	165		7,662	1958	M
241	309	245	129		7,768		F
27	25	28	10		1,081		C
577	680	541	304		16,511	Total	
3·5	4·1	3·3	1·8		100	%	
679	316	483	182		10,057	1959	M
354	243	392	101		8,219		F
83	35	95	27		2,119		C
1,116	594	970	310		20,395	Total	
5·5	3·0	4·8	1·5		100	%	
1,310	1,053	764	711		29,589	1960	M
640	660	589	348		19,917		F
146	96	96	29		3,149		C
2,096	1,809	1,449	1,088		52,655	Total	
3·9	3·4	2·7	1·9		100	%	
	4,099				28,934	1961	M
	3,288				27,616		F
	815				5,059		C
	8,202				61,609	Total	
	13·3				100	%	
				41,980	115,498	Total	M
				31,226	89,608	1955–	F
				5,599	13,260	1961	C
				2,927	6,191		U
				81,732	224,557	Total	
				36·4	100	%	

the 1961 arrival totals. For this reason and because of the incomplete breakdowns for 1955 and 1956, the overall totals can be presented only under the headings 'Jamaica' and 'All Other Territories'.

TABLE C. MONTHLY TOTALS OF WEST INDIAN MIGRANT ARRIVALS, 1955–61

Months	1955	1956	1957	1958	1959	1960	1961
January .	1,102	964	364	789	215	1,217	2,412
February .	1,088	1,130	413	857	684	2,602	2,520
March. .	1,993	2,674	1,434	1,802	615	3,293	5,263
April . .	1,379	2,961	2,018	3,360*	1,106	4,510	7,790*
May . .	2,038	2,958	1,017	1,514	1,264	5,132	6,280
June . .	1,046	3,827*	1,704	1,969	1,765	5,257	3,621
July . .	2,313	3,194	2,398	1,479	1,448	4,201	6,131
August .	2,859	2,971	2,835	1,609	2,641	5,343	6,923
September .	2,835	2,257	3,608*	1,375	3,103	8,140*	6,271
October .	3,084*	1,557	3,292	896	3,381*	5,547	5,638
November .	2,868	989	1,863	407	2,614	3,765	5,304
December .	1,868	959	1,527	454	1,559	3,648	3,596
TOTAL .	24,473	26,441	22,473	16,511	20,395	52,655	61,749

* Peak month in each year.

TABLE D. MAJOR WEST INDIAN SETTLEMENTS IN BRITAIN (ESTIMATES)[a]

City, Town, or District[b]	Mid-1955	End 1956	End 1957	End 1958	End 1959	Mid-1960	M 19
London							
Bethnal Green, *Brixton*,							
Camberwell, *Camden Town*,							
Clapham, Fulham,							
Hammersmith, Islington,							
Kensington (*North* and *West*),							
Lewisham, *Paddington*,							
Shepherds Bush, Southwark,							
Stepney, Streatham,							
Wandsworth, Willesden	15,000	28,000	41,000	40,000	51,000	60,000	135,0
Birmingham							
Aston, Balsall Heath,							
Small Heath, Smethwick,							
(W. Bromwich)[c]	8,000	23,000	27,000	27,000	29,000	36,000	67,0
Manchester							
Ardwick Green,							
Chorlton-cum-Hardy,							
Chorlton-cum-Medlock,							
Moss Side, Wythenshaw	2,000	3,500	5,000	4,000	4,500	5,500	7,0
Nottingham	2,000	3,500	4,000	4,000	4,300	5,900	9,:
Wolverhampton ⎫	1,250	4,000	⎰4,000	2,500	3,000	5,000	7,1
Coventry ⎭			⎱2,000	1,500	1,500	2,500	5,0
Derby	1,000	2,500	1,000	1,000	1,000	1,500	3,0
Leeds	1,250	2,000	3,000	2,500	2,500	4,000	5,0

City, Town, or District[b]	Mid-1955	End 1956	End 1957	End 1958	End 1959	Mid-1960	Mid-1962
ffield	1,000	2,000	3,000	2,000	2,300	4,000	5,700
erpool	1,000	2,000	2,000	2,500	2,500	2,500	4,000
stol	200	1,000	1,500	2,000	2,000	3,500	4,800
wich	600	1,000	1,000	1,000	800	1,000	2,200
gby	500	1,000	600	1,000	1,500	1,000	1,100
cester	—	800	1,000	1,500	1,000	2,000	3,700
rdiff ⎱ ansea ⎰	500	500	600	1,000[d]	1,000[d]	2,000[d]	2,800
isgow ⎱ inburgh ⎰	500	500	500	200	200	200	300
fford	500	500	500	200	200	500	900
ading	200	300	500	800	800	1,000	2,100
lton	250	300	900	800	800	800	900
ddersfield	250	350	500	500	1,700	2,000	4,600
dford	—	350	600	1,000	1,000	3,000	4,600
st Bromwich[c]	—	—	1,000	3,000	3,000	4,500	5,800
oucester	—	—	600	800	800	800	2,000
th	—	—	600	600	1,000	1,000	1,100
wcastle-on-Tyne	—	—	100	100	100	100	400
ll	250	350	200	100	100	100	200
ugh	—	300	500	500	500	800	3,000
ston	—	250	500	500	500	500	600
ton	—	250	600	500	500	700	1,200
ncaster	—	150	200	200	200	300	500
rtsmouth	100	100	100	100	100	100	100
ddlesbrough	—	—	300	—	—	—	—
rham	—	—	100	—	—	—	—
adford	—	300	100	—	—	—	—
ippenham ⎱ adford-on-Avon ⎰	150	250	—	—	—	—	—
eter	100	250	500	—	—	—	—
ford	—	—	—	1,000	1,000	1,000	2,300
ithampton	—	—	—	—	—	800	800
indon	—	—	—	—	—	300	500
mbridge	—	—	—	—	—	—	2,000
imated							
Total Settlement[e]	c. 40,000	c. 80,000	c. 102,000	c. 120,000	c. 139,000	c. 161,000	c. 300,000

hese necessarily vary: approximate estimates were made available by the Migrant Services Division. They are based
n the newcomers' declared destinations on ships' manifestos and on subsequent local estimates.
he districts in italics figured in the 1955 estimates. The others were added in later estimates. In 1960 the names of
nother nine boroughs were added.
/as included in the Birmingham estimate in 1955 and 1956.
ardiff alone.
hese totals appear to include the known figure of 15,000 West Indian-born residents in Britain in 1951, plus the
timated arrivals in 1952–54 inclusive of some 13,700 migrants. They do not make any allowance for losses due to
migration, nor do they include British-born children. They do, however, include West Indians living in smaller
ttlements not mentioned above. The dashes do not necessarily signify that no West Indians live in a given area, but
ther that the settlement has not grown appreciably and that it is small and unconcentrated. The estimates are
viously incomplete. Even the 1962 estimates make no specific mention of appreciable settlements of West Indians
Middlesbrough or Dudley, although recent disturbances in both towns have spotlighted the presence of coloured
sidents.

APPENDIX III

On making contact with migrants

IN CHAPTER 2 I referred to the great difficulty I experienced in making any sort of satisfactory contact with West Indian migrants in the first months of field work. It may be useful to say a few more words on this matter here, for it is a problem that confronts not only sociologists but also social workers and others who are concerned with this particular group, especially in the early years of settlement.

My initial move, in late 1955, was to try to make contact with the Brixton migrants through the members of the more settled West Indian professional and intellectual *élite*. It soon emerged, however, that the working-class migrants in Brixton were neither organizationally nor informally linked with this West Indian *élite*, most of whose members live and work north of the river. Only three contacts were in fact made throughout the period of study by means of such introductions. One West Indian welfare worker who was then working in the area was indeed at pains to convince me that he lived north of the river and had no extra-official contacts with anyone in the area.

The next step was to try to make contact with any local migrant leaders or officers of internal or interracial voluntary associations. Some were located through references made in the local press or by various local officials, and one pentecostal sectarian congregation was discovered because its lively and rhythmic form of worship had attracted the attention of local people living near the church hall.

It soon became evident that there were as yet no enduring or large-scale associations within the Brixton migrant group. The contact that was made was limited to very small groups of people, and the bulk of the migrants remained ignorant of the very existence of such associations. The same was true, at that time at least, of the few licensed clubs catering for the migrants. Their clientele was drawn from a small minority of sophisticated migrants, mainly male, with a certain amount of spending money. Contacts with this café-society proved to be of limited value and usually led into a blind alley.

After a few weeks of such attempts, I came to the conclusion that out of the five or six thousand West Indians then living in the Brixton area, only a few hundred at most participated in any form of associational or organized social life, or could be encountered by such means. There remained the problem of how to make contact with a reasonable number of the thousands who did no more than work, shop, and return home.

422

Another source of contact seemed initially promising, but had to be handled with great caution. The West Indian settlement had already produced a small class of affluent multiple landlords, of whom one in particular had achieved a certain local prestige. This individual was most willing to introduce me to all his tenants, but not, as it turned out, to allow a free hand with interviews. After one highly constrained and embarrassing collective interview in which nine tenants were interrogated, mainly by the landlord, it seemed better to seek other contacts and to avoid being labelled as the landlord's protegé. In more stable situations, such willing sponsors may of course present the investigator with an even greater problem, since they are usually *personae gratae* only to a section of their own community, and identification with them may result in the closing of other doors.

A seemingly suitable place to make contact with these economic migrants would be at their work. But apart from other obvious drawbacks, this would have been difficult in the Brixton situation because the great majority of migrants were working outside the area, and at the outset it would have been hard to know where to look for them.

Finally, I decided to seek the help of local intermediaries or sponsors who were already in contact with West Indians and who were trusted by them because of the nature of their work or services. I was particularly anxious to make contact with women migrants, who for various reasons were even less inclined or able to participate in associational life than the men. Following this method of seeking sponsors for myself, I was able to make a number of satisfactory initial contacts by securing introductions to West Indian women from several day-nursery matrons and social workers. Once contact was made with these migrants, they themselves served as my sponsors among their relations, friends, acquaintances, and fellow-tenants, and the main problem of contact was solved. But making contact did not necessarily mean establishing confidence, and in many cases two or more meetings were required before the informant had passed through successive phases of suspicion and prickliness to that of acquiescence, when it was actually possible to ask some direct questions about his or her circumstances and reactions to life in Brixton. Migrants were often more willing to talk about their home life and background in the early stages, and first-hand knowledge of this proved extremely valuable.

APPENDIX IV

Friction between white and coloured railwaymen in the London area

THE FOLLOWING are the major reported cases of friction between white and coloured railwaymen in the London area from the early 1950s up to 1958:

1. *Kings Cross – 31 December 1952*
There was a two-day strike of shunters following the promotion of an Indian. See Chapter 8 (p.162) for the Kings Cross motion put forward at the ASLEF Annual Assembly of Delegates in 1957.

2. *Liverpool Street Station – August 1956*
Seventy night-shift porters threatened a strike unless West Indian labour was withdrawn: this followed an allegation that a Jamaican had stabbed a white railwayman with a nail file during a quarrel. The *Daily Express* of 18 August reported that at this station the bad feeling was such that parcel porters on the night shift would not have the Jamaicans in their mess room. Said a spokesman: 'We want to impress that this is not a colour bar. We have no objection to any coloured people working here except the Jamaicans. We do not think they are to be trusted.' Later a magistrate discharged the Jamaican, saying: 'You were provoked unjustly but in this country you must not attack people with weapons.'

3. *Stratford Depot, East London – October 1956*
A committee sent a commission claiming to represent the majority of the 550 engine-drivers at this depot to the Ministry of Transport, complaining that the coloured firemen employed on their trains were 'incompetent and irresponsible men' and asking for a public inquiry 'in the interests of public safety'.

The petition said that recently a large number of coloured men had been employed at the Stratford depot. These men had been given a small test and placed in a 'school' under the direction of a locomotive driver 'for a very short period'. They were then passed out and immediately came into 'the line of promotion', and were considered fit for locomotive firing duties. 'In our opinion', said the drivers, '90 per cent of these men are unfit to act in this capacity'.

The drivers also maintained that in many cases they could not 'understand these men' and that, since the responsibility for the train rested solely on the driver, an incompetent fireman was an unfair burden on him. 'We

424

are having to do two men's jobs under conditions which only give time to do one properly. We are expected to break rules and regulations laid down for public safety by assisting incompetent and irresponsible men, and thereby endangering the lives of the travelling public.' It added that 'discontent and bad feeling' were now dominant at the Stratford depot.

An official of British Railways later confirmed that there was a shortage of firemen at Stratford depot and 70 vacancies. Altogether 77 coloured workers were employed on footplate duties. A statement issued by the Eastern Region said, in part: 'Coloured persons have been employed on footplate duties for a number of years on British Railways. Before being allowed to undertake such duties they are given training and are required to pass tests to ensure they are capable. . . . The same tests are applied to white and coloured footplate staff.'

Some days later, British Railways announced that no more coloured firemen would 'at present' be recruited at the Stratford depot. On 11 November the *Daily Telegraph* reported that at a mass meeting of engine-drivers at this depot it was reported that, as from 1 January 1957, drivers would not take out an engine with a coloured fireman. Nothing in fact came of this decision, which never received ASLEF support, but the Stratford branch of ASLEF clearly remained dissatisfied and brought the matter up at the 1957 Annual Assembly (see Chapter 8, pp. 161-2, for a more detailed account).

4. *London Bridge – 1956*

White workers in the parcels office refused to take responsibility for working in pairs with three coloured workers introduced there without prior consultation, on the grounds that the latter lacked the necessary geographical knowledge and speed for this work.

APPENDIX V

Examples of West Indian-tenanted houses in the Brixton settlement

OVER ONE HUNDRED coloured-owned or -tenanted dwellings were visited during the course of this inquiry. The following are fairly typical of privately owned accommodation catering for coloured tenants in Brixton and the surrounding areas. The categories 'good', 'medium', and 'bad' refer to such items as the standard of repair and cleanliness of the accommodation; the degree of overcrowding; the type of tenants; and general landlord-tenant relationships. In each case the property was visited more than once, to check if any notable change had occurred in the interval. The rents apply to the 1955–57 period. There was not in fact much change until the large influx of new migrants in 1960–61 caused a renewed shortage of accommodation and permitted landlords to raise their rents again.

1. *Good*

(*a*) Four-storey, eight-roomed house in the Wandsworth Road (basement and three floors). It has one bathroom, two toilets, three cookers on the landings, and two washbasins on the half-landings. The house is about a century old, built in an agreeable, early-Victorian classical style. It has been thoroughly cleaned and repapered, and new linoleum has been put down on the stairs and landings by the owner. Most tenants are from British Guiana, and are either skilled artisans or students. In the basement are a white mother and daughter, who are regarded by the West Indian landlord as rather poor tenants because they do not pay regularly and because the daughter 'brings in too many men of all colours'. The house is not particularly overcrowded. There are about 16 tenants in all, including young children. One woman tenant is paid to clean the shared parts of the house and to look after the large and attractive back garden. It is the intention of this landlord to buy more houses of a similar type, away from the Somerleyton and Geneva Road area, to attract the more settled type of migrants. He proposes to give them decent rooms and furniture, and permit them to bring in women 'only within reason'.

(*b*) Three-roomed, first-floor, semi-furnished flat, rented by a skilled draughtsman and his wife at £4 a week. The wife is a trained nurse. The house, which is owned by a white landlord, is well kept. It is situated in a predominantly white street, pleasant but shabby, on the fringes of Angell Town. The couple have one baby, and rent a room to a cousin who works as a typist. This situation is not really characteristic as regards either the

426

type of accommodation or the type of tenant. The tenants are well educated, light in colour, and socially ambitious. They take pains to dissociate themselves from the coloured Brixton settlement, explaining that they live there rather than in Earl's Court or Bayswater because it is cheaper and just as convenient for work and leisure pursuits.

(c) Small, Indian-owned, two-storey, non-basement house in a largely white street in Peckham. The landlord retains the ground floor for himself, and rents two furnished rooms and a kitchen on the first floor to a Jamaican family for £3 a week. This family now consists of husband, wife, one 9-year-old boy, and a baby. Toilet facilities are shared but are clean. The second room was formerly inhabited by the husband's father and mother, but they have now left and the second room has been retained for extra comfort. Both parents are working. The house is clean and the furniture adequate.

2. *Medium*

(a) A ten-roomed house in Angell Town, with three storeys and basement. There is one bathroom with a toilet; one kitchen with a sink upstairs; and a toilet, basin, and kitchen with sink in the basement. Two rooms have their own sink and cooker; others have their own paraffin heater with a cooking ring, usually installed by the tenant. Rents are average or slightly above. The landlady is an Americanized Jamaican who does not live on the premises. She administers the house by means of small rebates of rent to particular tenants who collect rents or clean the shared parts (the latter rather perfunctorily). Some attempt is made to select tenants of a 'good type'. Most of them are married couples or couples living in stable concubinage with one or more small children. One or two individual tenants have actually been asked to leave because of their personal habits, noisiness, or quarrelsomeness. Tenants all know each other and exchange visits and services. The main difference between 2a and 1a lies in the greater extent of overcrowding, though in only one case is there what would be described as 'indecent occupation'. The second difference is in 2a's grubbiness and relatively poor state of repair, both structurally and superficially. Some interior painting has, however, been done recently and new wallpaper and linoleum have been put in a few rooms. A third difference lies in the relative indifference of the absentee landlady of 2a compared with the attitude of the landlord at 1a. The latter spends several hours a week at this house and his other two houses, makes minor repairs at once, and endeavours to improve his property even to the extent of cultivating the garden.

(b) A six-roomed, two-storey, short-lease house in the Angell Town area, owned by a Jamaican machinist who lives in one room with her six-year-old daughter, her aunt, and her uncle. Until recently this room was shared by the father of her daughter, but he subsequently moved to the house described above (2a); the aunt and uncle are said to be sharing the room until they find some other accommodation.

In the other two small rooms on this floor live two Jamaican couples, one with one child, the other with two children. All share a landing gas-cooker, and a toilet and basin. The stairs are dirty but the rest of the upper part is fairly clean. On the ground floor is a large white family, statutory tenants, with whom relations are strained and whose children the owner does not approve of as playmates for her daughter: 'They're dirty and rude, and don't know how to behave.'

3. *Bad*

(*a*) A three-storey basement house near Somerleyton Road. The top three rooms are occupied by an aggressive, lower-middle-class, white statutory tenant and his wife. The house was recently bought by a Jamaican couple who with their two children occupy the ground floor back. They let the ground floor front to one couple, and the three small basement rooms to two couples and one man whose name the landlady claimed not to know, when interviewed. One of the rooms has no window and the only ventilation is by the door. This room, it was later ascertained, was let at £2 5*s*. per week. When I visited the house there was no bathroom, the single lavatory was in a highly insanitary condition, and the communal basement kitchen had a quarter-inch of greasy dirt on the food shelves, parts of the stove, and the floor, which also showed some mouse tracks. The landlady's own room was clean.

(*b*) Small, two-storey, four-roomed, non-basement house with no frontage, in a narrow street near Lambeth Town Hall. It was coloured-owned before 1939, and was formerly let by the room to students. In the ground floor front, a small room 12 feet by 12 feet which was formerly a shop, and which is ventilated only by door and chimney, live an Irish girl and her African consort with their two children. Some light comes into this room through a pane of glass in the boarded-up shop front. In the ground floor back live a coloured couple. Five adults and one child live on the first floor upstairs. There is no bath; the one dirty lavatory is outside in a cluttered backyard; and the grimy small back kitchen is shared by the ground-floor tenants. When seen, the floor of this kitchen was covered with a thick layer of grease and mud.

SOME PARTICULARS OF WEST INDIAN AND OTHER WOMEN ASSISTED BY SOUTHWARK AND LONDON AND MIDDLESEX DIOCESAN ASSOCIATIONS FOR MORAL WELFARE (1955–60)

Numbers assisted		1955	1956	1957	1958	1959	1960
1.** Total of new cases of illegitimate children and their parents	Southwark	910	1,472	928	1,266	1,203	1,270
	London and Middlesex	1,470	1,968	2,065	2,114	2,281	2,594
	Total	2,380	3,440	2,993	3,380	3,484	3,864
2. All West Indian mothers	Southwark	96	202	231	208	171	194
	London and Middlesex	103	234	225	266	277	328
	Total	199	436	456	474	448	522
3. West Indian mothers naming English or European putative fathers	Southwark	2	4	3	5	9	3
	London and Middlesex	5	11	8	4	8	47
	Total	7	15	11	9	17	50
4. English girls naming West Indian putative fathers	Southwark	12	12	17	18	30	21
	London and Middlesex	25	37	33	56	99	76
	Total	37	49	50	74	129	97
5a. Illegitimate children left in West Indies by West Indian mothers	Southwark	71	143	190	149	116	124
	London and Middlesex	44	132	127	172	151	201
	Total	115	275	317	321	267	325
5b. Illegitimate children of West Indian mothers in England	Southwark	45	90	102	119	125	89
	London and Middlesex	*	137	131	171	211	204
	Total	—	227	233	290	336	293
6. West Indian women pregnant on arrival in England	Southwark	21	56	45	44	30	29
	London and Middlesex	34	69	41	65	30	77
	Total	55	125	86	109	60	106
7. West Indian mothers wishing to return home	Southwark	11	11	11	15	11	6
	London and Middlesex	2	9	10	15	15	10
	Total	13	20	21	30	26	16
8. West Indian women who are expecting or who have had second or third baby in England	Southwark	—	35	22	30	25	21
	London and Middlesex	*	11	21	26	51	55
	Total	—	46	43	56	76	76

* Indicates not available.
** This item, which shows the total numbers helped by the associations each year, is included for purposes of comparison. All other figures are concerned with West Indian parents, and children with at least one West Indian parent.

APPENDIX VII

Brief biographies of two English wives of West Indians

1. *Mrs Betty Y*

MRS Y is small, lively, grey-haired, and attractive. She was born about sixty years ago in London into a lower-middle-class nonconformist family. Her upbringing and family life were in no way insecure or abnormal. After the first world war she met Mr Y, who had served in the army during the war as a volunteer; he was studying law with a view to returning home to the West Indies, where he had political ambitions. He 'courted' her for four years although her family was strongly opposed to his colour – 'My mum used to call him "that bloody nigger".' She admits freely that she did not love him at first but was 'attracted by his mind'; he says that she was 'not properly educated' when he met her and that he gave her books to read. At this period he did not wish to marry her, because he thought that marriage with a white woman would make it difficult for him to pursue nationalist politics in Barbados he also feared that she would be ostracized by the Europeans there. On her side Betty was unwilling to oppose her family's wishes. Finally, however, they fell in love and decided to get married. 'I never kissed her in public while we were engaged, however, to avoid unpleasantness.'

After the marriage, Mr Y gave up his plans to be a barrister and started work in South London as a craftsman. With his wife's help, he has built up a flourishing small business in which several local people are employed. The Ys have one child, a handsome Latin-looking son who now holds a highly paid position in the entertainment world. Both parents have long been active in local Labour Party politics, and Mr Y was involved with Dr Harold Moody in the pioneering days of the League of Coloured Peoples. 'Now it's just a bunch of rabble-rousing intellectuals, out of touch with the masses. I'm not surprised that all the coloured clubs break up. There's no discipline nor training in organization. That's partly the fault of you English, discouraging initiative in the colonies, but we must learn.' Mr Y is also a staunch supporter of the Royal family.

Mrs Y is entirely wrapped up in her husband. 'He's a really wonderful man', she said once when he went out of the room, 'I've never regretted marrying him for a second and I never think of him as coloured or otherwise. But mark you, we don't approve of indiscriminate mixed marriages. Some of the girls going about with coloured men these days are just little floozies.' Mrs Y is militantly opposed to any display of prejudice or dis-

430

crimination, and in the buses or shops turns on anyone she hears speaking slightingly of coloured people: 'Not niggers, coloured ladies and gentlemen, if you please.'

For the last twenty years the Ys have lived in the same flat. They have always lived quietly, but have over the years made a few white friends locally: 'Everyone accepts us as individuals here, but they're not so keen on the Jamaicans who are beginning to move in down the street. I wish they would keep their windows and house-fronts clean; it gives all coloured people a bad name for letting down the district, for no one sees how clean the rooms are inside.'

After some years the breach between the Ys and Mrs Y's parents was healed, and they began to visit each other. One of her sisters, however, remained hostile, and the families did not meet for nearly twenty years. Finally, however, they were reconciled, and their young daughter fell in love with her cousin at first sight and became a regular visitor at the Y home. The Ys opposed the marriage on the grounds that they were first cousins, but after some initial opposition the girl's parents became enthusiastic about the match. The couple married and are said to be extremely happy together.

Mrs Y long ago learned how to make some West Indian dishes, but in the main the household is run on English lines. There is a radio but no television set, and conversation is a highly valued recreation. There are usually one or more coloured student lodgers. The Y household is a friendly, hospitable, and contented one.

2. *Mrs Clara K*

Mrs K is in her mid-thirties, short, plump and unremarkable in appearance, with mousey straight hair and a pale complexion. She is neatly dressed but wears no make-up. She has a shy, pleasant expression and a quiet voice with a trace of country burr. She was born in East Anglia, but spent most of her childhood and adolescence in a children's home. She was in service for some years and then worked for a London catering firm as a cleaner and dishwasher.

She has been married for nearly ten years to Mr K and they have three lively, light-coloured children, all very attractive in appearance and extremely well-dressed. Mr K is a lower-middle-class Jamaican who worked as a clerk at home and has also spent some time in the United States. Here too he has a white-collar job. He is serious, bespectacled, and dark in colour. He is a practising member of the Anglican church, has seen that the children are baptized, sends them to Sunday school, and is on good terms with the local vicar.

Mrs K seems happily married and is entirely dominated by her ambitious husband, who treats her with great courtesy and formality. Mr K already owns his own rather small house in Brixton. He has redecorated and repaired it throughout, installed a bathroom, and remade the back garden, in which he grows his own vegetables. The house is kept spotless, public ways and all, and Mr K is very particular about the type of tenants he takes. He studies at nights, and has little social life. He does not allow his wife or children out unaccompanied after dark, nor are the children

431

permitted to play in the street. 'This is a bad area full of bad types – West Indian and other,' he says, 'and there are plenty of careless white girls about.'

Mr K has no intention of returning to Jamaica, where he sees no prospects for himself or his family. He is ambitious for his children, of whom he is very proud, and considers that the educational facilities here are better.

APPENDIX VIII

Local press reports of incidents concerning coloured men and white women

IT WAS not possible to check over all back numbers of South London papers for the earlier years of the West Indian settlement. Three successive numbers of the *South London Press* in early November 1954 contained reports, appropriately headlined: of a Brixton woman who was fined for performing an abortion on a 15-year-old girl pregnant by a coloured man; of a coloured man and a Battersea tailor who were sentenced to three years' imprisonment for performing an illegal operation on a Brixton girl; and of a fracas headlined 'Coloured men fight over white girl'.

The following headlines and extracts from local papers in the years 1956–59 were taken at random from a sheaf of some fifty cuttings, almost all of which presented the mixed associations in an unfavourable light and in much more detail than similar cases involving local men:

' *"I went to coloured man's room"*, says schoolgirl.'
'A Tooting schoolgirl told South Western Court on Friday how she and a girl friend met two coloured men in Tooting Broadway. . . . They all four then went to his room and had some wine. She then consented to his being intimate with her. He asked her her age and she told him that was her business. Her friend went in another room with D's friend. . . . About a week later she met him again after ringing him up. They bought some drink but she did not know what it was. They then went to D's room where they were intimate again. When she asked what the time was she found it was 1 o'clock. She was too frightened to go home, so she slept with him in his bed. In the morning she left him at Tooting Broadway when he went to work and she went to school. A policewoman called at the school that morning and took her home. . . . On the last occasion she told him she was 17, but she did not tell him she was at school. She had lipstick on when she first met him. . . . The girl's mother, who could not read the oath or sign her deposition, gave evidence.' (*South London Advertiser*, 5 January 1957.)

' *"Coloured men robbed me after 'pick-up'* " – *woman's alleged complaint*.'
This case concerned a 46-year-old Brixton woman who agreed that she frequented Clapham Common and had convictions for soliciting. She was picked up on the Common by two coloured men and agreed to go to the house with them for £2. She accused the men of robbing her with violence. (*South London Advertiser*, 12 and 18 January 1957.)

433

Appendices

'Police raid discovered coloured men and white girls in bedrooms.'
'The vigil kept by police hidden in a church hall on a house resulted in a coloured man, M.W. (43), of Camberwell being jailed for ten weeks at Lambeth for permitting his house to be used as a brothel. Superintendent H.P. said the door was opened by W., and while the officer was speaking to him an 18-year-old girl appeared and W. said she was living with him. The Superintendent then described what he found in the house. . . . In one room he found a coloured man and a white girl in bed. The man was not wearing any clothing and the girl was wearing a vest. "I asked him who paid for the room and the girl said: 'He paid Mr W. £3. He gives me £1.' " In another room he found a coloured man and a white girl in bed. The man said: "I picked her up in the West End" and that he was paying W. and the girl. . . . Sergeant G.H. described a watch on the house, saying he saw 20 men visit it, including the accused, and 19 girls. There were 19 different men, all coloured, and 8 different girls. Once two young girls and two coloured men entered. "They again appeared in the front first-floor bedroom, and as on the previous evening all four were undressed and went to bed in the same room." ' (*South London Press*, 26 February 1957.)

'Torn brassiere shown' and *'Jamaican is cleared of robbing woman'*.
The earlier report read: 'Reported to have threatened a blonde housewife with a knife and robbed her of 30*s.* in Hyde Park at midnight, A.F. (26), a coloured warehouseman of Gurney Street, Walworth, was committed for trial. Mrs. J.T. claimed that after a dispute about money, F. pushed the blade of a large knife against her stomach and threatened to kill her. He chased her and threw her down, kicking her. Mrs. T. produced a torn brassiere and a torn dress which she said were damaged in the struggle. Mrs. R.D. of Westminster said that she was walking near the bandstand with four or five other girls when she heard screams and saw Mrs. T. on the ground with F. bending over her and punching her on the back and arms. They ran to help her, but somebody shouted "He's got a knife". Mrs. D. added: "We got scared and ran towards Hyde Park Corner. . . . I saw him get hold of S.T. but we were frightened and scared of the knife so we kept running." ' The second report recorded a verdict of Not Guilty, and referred to the 'blonde housewife' as a 'prostitute'. (*South London Press*, 10 August and 14 September 1956.)

Woman rushes into street wearing her underwear.'
'The story of how a woman rushed out of her house in her underwear to call police was told at Tower Bridge, when M.S. (30), machinist, a coloured man, was charged with wounding B.T. at Peckham. She, a waitress, said she was divorced and had known M.S. for about two years. For about a year he had lived with her from time to time. He came home late, having been drinking, and they had words. He went to bed and she took him a cup of tea. He then smashed a light bulb and pulled her on the bed and struck her on the face, head and shoulders. . . . S. said Mrs. T. accused him of going with another woman and he accused her of having another

434

man and she threw a cycle lamp at him. . . . Detective Sergeant T. said that S. came from Jamaica and had not been in trouble before.' (*South London Press*, 8 March 1957.)

'*Coloured man pestered bus queue girl.*'
'A Brixton coloured man took hold of a girl's arm in a bus queue – and kept on annoying her although she showed resentment. He was given the maximum penalty at Lambeth on Monday for using insulting behaviour. H.A. (45) pleaded not guilty. A police officer said he saw A. in a bus queue standing behind a teen-age white girl. "I saw her pull her arm away from his hand," said the officer. "I saw him touch her back and place his hand on her shoulder. I could see from the expression on her face that she resented his action." . . . Giving evidence, A. said: "I did not touch her at all. She was wearing something with many names written on, and I was reading them out. William, Joseph, John." He said that the officer grabbed his arm and tried to twist it. The magistrate said: "I have no doubt you were making a nuisance of yourself with the girl." He asked his clerk what was the maximum penalty, and was told it was a £2 fine.' (*South London Advertiser*, 9 March 1959.)

(This last report and a similar report in the *South London Press* of 8 August 1956 differ from the great majority of others in that the white girl is reported as resisting the coloured man's advances. An undertone of approbation of this response is noticeable.)

APPENDIX IX

A migrant wedding in Brixton

THE ACTUAL marriage ceremony is an important event in the migrant situation, just as it is in the West Indies. Its lavishness and show serve to emphasize the couple's attainment of relative security and their aspiration to middle-class status and values. It remains true in the migrant situation that a marriage without such accessory display would be no marriage at all. A pregnant woman immigrant said contemptuously of a social worker's advice to her to marry the putative father: 'She want we should have a seven-and-six (*sic*) registry marriage. If I get married I do it properly.'

In Brixton, therefore, the wedding ceremony takes more or less the following form. Formal invitations are sent out well in advance. The marriage is almost invariably celebrated on a Saturday, to allow more time for the accompanying festivities before the bride and groom and guests return to work on Monday. The couple rarely if ever take a honeymoon, and indeed there is little need for this introduction to married life in the case of the many who have already been living together for some time.

The marriage ceremony is usually performed in a church; in the majority of cases this is for reasons of prestige rather than on religious grounds. In Brixton, Anglican and Methodist churches seem to attract most of the wedding custom – the Anglican being particularly favoured because in West Indian eyes it is an upper- and middle-class denomination.

The bride is almost invariably dressed in elaborate white, whether or not she is pregnant, and is attended by a number of bridesmaids and maids of honour, whose dresses, always brand new and in matching hues of pink, orange, turquoise, mauve, or other bright colours, usually rival hers in splendour. The groom does not present the depressed, subfusc figure of the average English groom on these occasions. He often outshines the bride and her attendants, by wearing an American-style draped dinner jacket and ballooning peg-top trousers in pale blue, bordeaux, or some other gay colour, with as accessories white gloves and an outsize contrasting flower or pompon buttonhole and narrow bow tie.

Guests often meet at the groom's lodgings and are driven to the church by an unofficial fleet of taxis operated by friends of the groom. Time is no matter, to the despair of the officiating English minister, and it is rare for the ceremony to begin less than half an hour late. After the ceremony, in which the bride is usually given away by an older male friend if no male relatives are in England, a number of West Indian amateur photographers take pictures of the couple, the minister, and the more important guests, all

436

Appendices

of whom are dressed elaborately. Then a shuttle service of the same taxis begins, until all guests are conveyed to the locale of the wedding party; however close this may be, prestige considerations enjoin that guests should be driven there.

The reception takes place in one or two rooms, which have been cleared except for a table in the middle, on which stand a large wedding cake and some glasses and bottles of ruby wine – chairs are ranged all round the walls. The party begins slowly and decorously, with speeches, good wishes, the cutting and eating of the cake, and toasts in the wine. After this most of the 'prestige guests', such as the minister and his wife, and other white people such as local officials, social workers, or prominent parishioners, depart; the table is moved back, the rum and other hard liquor brought out, the radiogram is switched up, and the real party begins. with dancing, drinking of rum and Guinness, and a plentiful collation of curried goat and rice. For reasons of distance and space there will not usually be so many kinsmen or other guests at a Brixton wedding as in the West Indies. But the ceremony may cost quite as much, in view of the higher cost of drinks and other incidentals.

Apart from its importance as an indication of the couple's improved status, the marriage ceremony provides one of the few opportunities for the renewal of former ties and for large-scale group association in general among the migrants. Guests include those kinsfolk and former friends and acquaintances who are in London, neighbours, work-mates, and new friends. Slices of wedding cake are sent back in elaborate small cardboard boxes to relatives and friends at home.

The ceremony also provides an opportunity for spare-time economic activities: dressmakers, car-owners, amateur photographers, good pastry cooks, can all make a few shillings on such occasions. Several older women with a flair for organization have become known as wedding organizers, and older or more settled men with a gift for speechifying turn up again and again as toast-masters or M.Cs.

APPENDIX X

Pentecostal sects in Brixton[1]

SINCE 1958, when the field work in Brixton was concluded, pentecostal sects have gained considerable ground among West Indian migrants. This has not been accompanied by an increase in membership of the less evangelical, less ecstatic denominations such as the Church of England. Some West Indians do attend pentecostal churches that were established in England before the beginning of mass migration, but most of those who are interested in religion are members of one or other of the pentecostal sects established in the West Indies. All of these have West Indian clergy and an almost exclusively West Indian membership.

The larger of these sects originated in the 'Bible belt' of the Southern States of America. They seem to have become established in the West Indies (especially Jamaica) during the 1920s. The smaller sects can best be thought of as offshoots of the larger ones. Pentecostal sects in general, and West Indian ones in particular, are very liable to fission; about three independent sects come into being in London each year.

All the West Indian sects are fundamentalist, all place great emphasis on ecstatic experiences, particularly *talking with tongues*. All believe in faith-healing and indulge in it quite frequently. Most of them practice *washing the feet of the saints* as a part of the communion service. The major doctrinal division among them centres on baptism. The Church of God group baptizes *in the name of the Father, Son, and Holy Ghost*, whereas the Apostolic Faith churches baptize *in the name of Jesus only*; they are commonly known as *Jesus Only* churches. The Church of God group is far and away the most important, accounting for about 80 per cent of the West Indian sects in England.

The larger sects exact tithes, which are not nominal but an actual tenth of the member's income. Some of these sects are already showing signs of becoming quite prosperous and are in a position to buy church buildings.

All but one of the major sects are represented in Brixton; the exception, the Church of God of Prophecy, has a meeting-place close by in Camberwell. The following sects were meeting in Brixton in April 1961:

---

[1] I am much indebted for this note on the development of the pentecostal movement among West Indians in Brixton since 1958 to Dr. Malcolm Calley, who is currently making a study of these sects for the Institute of Race Relations, London.

438

Sect	Approximate following	Meeting-place
New Testament Church of God* . . .	150	Allardyce Street
Church of God in Christ*	80	Sussex Road
New Covenant Church of God . . .	40	Effra Road
Church of God (Independent) . . .	20	Effra Road
International Evangelistic Fellowship . .	20	Dulwich Road
Church of the Lord Jesus Christ of the Apostolic Faith (*Jesus Only*)*	10	Overton Road
Pentecostal Churches of the World (*Jesus Only*)*	20	Paulett Road

* These churches are nationally organized, with many congregations in London and other cities, and branches in the United States and the West Indies.

Estimates of attendance are on the conservative side. Besides faithful members, a considerable number of people will attend intermittently, particularly if they are ill (for the sake of faith-healing) or when the sect holds a big rally.

APPENDIX XI

The climatic factor

ONE FACTOR that has exerted a tremendous influence on West Indian migrants both at work and outside is independent of the human element. This is the British climate. Just as few British people can imagine the chill of a Canadian winter or the damp heat of West Africa till they have experienced these extremes, so the West Indians can hardly believe in the reality which they encounter at Plymouth or Dover, as they step ashore into a January sleet storm wearing linen suits, sandals, and perhaps a towel hastily wrapped round their heads to keep out some of the cold.

The effect of the British climate is often intensified by poor living conditions in damp and draughty houses, by working conditions (either outside on building, or inside in alternating fierce or damp heat and cold), and by longer working and travelling hours. The combination of bad climate and long hours often has an adverse effect on the newcomer's efficiency and output at work. It may also disincline the minority who wish to improve their chances from regular attendance at evening classes.

In its warning on the climate, the handbook issued by the Barbadian government to its migrants states somewhat optimistically: 'You will find however that the coolness of the climate will help you to do more work than you could ever do in Barbados, and after you get over the first shock of the cold and dampness then all will be well if you take care of yourself and wear proper clothing.'

Adjustment to a vastly different climate is as much psychological as physical. During these years I met only one migrant, a successful professional man, who was prepared to state that he both felt and worked better in the British climate. Questioned about their 'greatest problem in settling down in Britain' in the British Institute of Public Opinion Poll of 1955, 19 per cent of migrants complained of the climate. This group was second only to the 30 per cent who complained of housing difficulties. The majority of recent migrants cope with the climate by wearing a lot of heavy woollen clothes and warm boots, by hermetically sealing all windows, and by burning smelly and dangerous oil stoves day and night. Very rarely, however, do they adapt their diet of starch, second-grade protein, and tinned fruit and vegetables to one more suitable for a cooler climate. One factory manager summed up the views of many informants in industry:

'They just don't eat properly and are always complaining of stomach troubles. I attribute their lack of energy to that. Most of the women say

440

they have no breakfast before they come in. They don't go to the canteen for lunch, but eat a small sandwich with some cold beans or rice filling. They say they have their main meal in the evening, rice and cabbage and fish all fried up together. But that's not the sort of diet for a working day. As a result they tend to stay away at the least little sniffle or ache and pain.'

The National Association for the Prevention of Tuberculosis has attempted to explain the need for an adequate diet, for warm clothing and room-airing, in an excellent pamphlet called 'A Warm Welcome to a Cold Climate', which includes the following passage:

'Perhaps you wonder why you ever came to Britain from one of the other lands in the British Commonwealth. One of our grim winter days brings a hankering for blue skies and warm breezes. We give here a touch of encouragement and friendly advice – advice about your health . . . your most precious form of capital. . . .

In a colder climate you need more food – because food is partly fuel, to stoke up the furnace inside you and provide you with body heat. In Britain you may need more food than at home. Then, if you are doing hard physical work – or even work to which you are not exactly accustomed – you need a different sort of food. Work that is unfamiliar takes more out of us than work we have always done. Studying hard uses as much energy as manual work, and the student should think over the question of his diet. . . .'

References

For easy reference the more important publications dealing specifically with West Indian migration to Britain have been indicated by asterisks

ALLEN, THOMAS (1826). *The History and Antiquities of Lambeth.* London: J. Allen.

BANTON, MICHAEL (1952). The Economic and Social Position of Negro Immigrants in Britain. *Sociological Review*, New Series, I, 2.

*BANTON, MICHAEL (1955). *The Coloured Quarter.* London: Cape.

BANTON, MICHAEL (1958). Beware of Strangers. *The Listener*, 3 April. British Broadcasting Corporation.

*BANTON, MICHAEL (1959). *White and Coloured.* London: Cape.

BANTON, MICHAEL (1960). Social Distance: A New Appreciation. *Sociological Review*, New Series, 8, 2.

BASCOM, W. R. (1952). The Esusu: A Credit Institution of the Yoruba. *Journal Royal Anthropological Institute*, LXXXII, Part 1.

BENEDICT, RUTH (1943). *Race and Racism.* London: George Routledge.

BERTRAM, G. C. L. (1958). *West Indian Immigration.* London: Eugenics Society Broadsheet.

BLUMER, HERBERT (1958). Recent Research on Race Relations in the United States of America. Unesco: *International Social Science Bulletin*, X, 3.

BOOTH, CHARLES (1903). *Life and Labour of the People in London*, 3rd Series, Vol. IV. London: Macmillan.

BORRIE, W. D. (1950). *The Cultural Integration of Immigrants.* Unesco: Population Studies Supplement.

BRAITHWAITE, LLOYD (1957). Social Stratification in Trinidad. *Social and Economic Studies*, 2, 2 and 3.

BRAITHWAITE, LLOYD (1957). Sociology and Demographic Research. *Social and Economic Studies*, 6, 4.

BRITISH BROADCASTING CORPORATION (1960). *Going to Britain?* BBC Caribbean Service.

BRITISH COUNCIL OF CHURCHES (1955). *Your Neighbour from the West Indies.*

BRONLEY, C. P. (1960). Mass Parties in Jamaica. *Social and Economic Studies*, 9, 4.

BROWN, J. A. C. (1954). *Social Psychology of Industry.* Harmondsworth: Penguin Books.

BURNS, SIR ALLAN (1957). *In Defence of Colonies.* London: Allen & Unwin.

BURT, ROBERT (1960). *Colour Prejudice in Britain.* Unpublished B.A. thesis, Princeton University, U.S.A.

*CALLEY, MALCOLM (1962). Pentecostal Sects among West Indian Migrants. *Race*, III, 2.

443

References

CAMPBELL, ELLA (1953). Industrial Training Methods. *Social and Economic Studies*, **2**, 1.

CAREY, A. T. (1956). *Colonial Students.* London: Secker & Warburg.

CHURCH INFORMATION OFFICE (1960). *Together in Britain.* (A Christian Handbook on Race Relations.) London: CIO.

CHURCH INFORMATION OFFICE (1960). *Your Neighbour.* Published for the Church Assembly Overseas Council. London: CIO.

CLARKE, EDITH (1957). *My Mother Who Fathered Me.* London: Allen & Unwin.

COHEN, YEHUDI A. (1956). Structure and Function: Family Organization in a Jamaican Community. *American Anthropologist*, **58**, 4.

*COLLINS, SYDNEY (1957). *Coloured Minorities in Britain.* London: Lutterworth Press.

COLLINS, SYDNEY (1960). Recent Trends in Race Relations in Britain. *Race Relations Journal.* S. African Institute of Race Relations, **XXVII**, 1.

CONSERVATIVE COMMONWEALTH COUNCIL (1957). Report on West Indian Accommodation Problem in the United Kingdom. 18 March.

CORBETT, DAVID C. (1957). *Canada's Immigration Policy.* Toronto: University of Toronto Press.

CUMPER, G. E. (1953). Two Studies in Jamaican Productivity. *Social and Economic Studies*, **1**, 2.

*DAVISON, R. B. (1961). West Indian Migration to Britain, 1955–61. *The West Indian Economist*, **4**, 1–4.

DE SOUZA, IVO (1960). Arrival. In S. K. Ruck (Ed.), *The West Indian Comes to England.* London: Routledge & Kegan Paul.

DOLLARD, JOHN (1937). *Caste and Class in a Southern Town.* New York: Harper.

DR. BARNARDO'S HOMES (1954). Report.

DYOS, H. J. (1952). *The Suburban Development of Greater London South of the Thames*, 1836–1914. Ph.D. thesis, University of London.

ECONOMIST INTELLIGENCE UNIT (1961). *Studies on Immigration from the Commonwealth.* 1. Basic Statistics.

EGGINTON, JOYCE (1957). *They Seek a Living.* London: Hutchinson.

EISENSTADT, S. N. (1954). *The Absorption of Immigrants.* International Library of Sociology and Social Reconstruction. London: Routledge & Kegan Paul.

FIRTH, RAYMOND (Ed.) (1956). *Two Studies of Kinship in London.* London School of Economics Monographs on Social Anthropology, Vol. 5. University of London: Athlone Press.

FITZPATRICK, J. P. (1959–60). The Adjustment of Puerto Ricans to New York City. *Journal of Inter-Group Relations*, **1**, 1.

GALLUP POLL. *See* SOCIAL SURVEYS.

GINSBERG, MORRIS (1934). *Sociology.* Home University Library. London: Oxford University Press.

GINSBERG, MORRIS (1959). *Prejudice.* Jacques Cohen Memorial Lecture. London: Woburn Press.

444

References

GLASS, RUTH (1960). Newcomers. London: Centre for Urban Studies, and Allen & Unwin.
GLUCKMAN, MAX (1959). How Foreign are you? *The Listener,* 15 January. BBC.
GORER, GEOFFREY (1955). *Exploring English Character.* London: Cresset.
GREENBERG, J. (1959). *Race Relations and American Law.* New York: Columbia University Press.
GREENFIELD, S. M. (1961). Socio-Economic Factors and Family Form. *Social and Economic Studies,* 10, 1.
*GRIFFITH, J. A. G. (1960). Legal Aspects of Immigration. In Institute of Race Relations, *Coloured Immigrants in Britain.* London: Oxford University Press.

*HENDERSON, JUDITH (1960). A Sociological Report. In Institute of Race Relations, *Coloured Immigrants in Britain.* London: Oxford University Press.
HENRIQUES, F. M. (1953). *Family and Colour in Jamaica.* London: Eyre & Spottiswoode.
HILL, CLIFFORD S. (1958). *Black and White in Harmony.* London: Hodder & Stoughton.
HOYT, ELIZABETH E. (1960). Voluntary Unemployment and Unemployability in Jamaica with Special Reference to the Standard of Living. *British Journal of Sociology,* XI, 2.
*HYNDMAN, ALBERT (1960). The West Indian in London. In S. K. Ruck (Ed.), *The West Indian Comes to England.* London: Routledge & Kegan Paul.

IBBERSON, D. (1956). Illegitimacy and the Birth Rate. *Social and Economic Studies,* 5, 1.
*INSTITUTE OF RACE RELATIONS (1960). *Coloured Immigrants in Britain.* London: Oxford University Press.

JACKSON, J. A. (1958). *The Irish Immigrant in England.* Paper read before the British Sociological Association.
JACKSON, J. A. (1961). *The Irish in Britain.* Paper read before the British Association for the Advancement of Science.
JAMES, H. E. O. & TENEN, CORA (1953). *The Teacher was Black.* An experiment in international understanding sponsored by Unesco. London: Heinemann.
JAYAWARDENA, C. (1960). Marital Stability in Two Guianese Sugar Estate Communities. *Social and Economic Studies,* 9, 1.
JUNOD, V. (1952). *The Coloured Élite in London.* MS. in Department of Social Anthropology, University of Edinburgh.

KATZIN, MARGARET (1959). The Jamaican Country Higgler. *Social and Economic Studies,* 8, 4.
KERR, MADELINE (1952). *Personality and Conflict in Jamaica.* Liverpool: University Press of Liverpool.
KERR, MADELINE (1958). *Ship Street.* London: Routledge & Kegan Paul.

LAMMING, GEORGE (1960). *Pleasures of Exile.* London: Michael Joseph.

445

References

*LANDES, RUTH (1952). *A Preliminary Statement of a Survey of Negro-White Relationships in Britain.* Unpublished communication, Royal Anthropological Institute, 6 May.

LEE, FRANK F. (1959). *A Comparative Study in Race Relations: Negroes in the American North and West Indians in Britain.* Paper read at the Fourth World Congress of Sociology, Stresa.

LEWIN, KURT (1948). *Resolving Social Conflicts.* New York: Harper.

*LITTLE, KENNETH (1947). *Negroes in Britain.* International Library of Sociology and Social Reconstruction. London: Kegan Paul.

LITTLE, KENNETH (1958). *Colour and Commonsense.* London: Fabian Society.

LONDON COUNTY COUNCIL (1956). *Survey of London.* Vols. XXIII, XXIV, XXVI. London: Athlone Press.

LOWENTHAL, DAVID (1957). The Population of Barbados. *Social and Economic Studies,* **6**, 4.

LUKE, SIR STEPHEN (1954). *Development and Welfare in the West Indies.* London: H.M.S.O.

MACINNES, COLIN (1957). *City of Spades.* London: MacGibbon & Kee.

MACIVER, R. M. (1917). *Community.* London: Macmillan. Reprinted 1936.

MACIVER, R. M. (1937). *Society.* New York: Rinehart.

*MAIZELS, JOAN (1960). *The West Indian Comes to Willesden.* Duplicated report of a survey made for the Willesden Citizens' Advice Bureau on behalf of the Willesden Borough Council, London.

MALDEN, H. E. (Ed.) (1912). *The Victoria History of the County of Surrey.* Vol. IV. London: Archibald Constable.

*MANLEY, DOUGLAS (1958). *The Social Structure of the Liverpool Negro Community with Special Reference to the Formation of Formal Associations.* Unpublished Ph.D. thesis, University of Liverpool.

*MANLEY, DOUGLAS (1960). The West Indian Background. In S. K. Ruck (Ed.), *The West Indian Comes to England.* London: Routledge & Kegan Paul.

MAUGHAM, SOMERSET (1897). *Liza of Lambeth.* London: T. Fisher Unwin.

*MAUNDER, W. F. (1955). The New Jamaican Emigration. *Social and Economic Studies,* **4**, 1.

MINISTRY OF LABOUR (1957). Annual Report.

MINTZ, SYDNEY W. (1955). Puerto Rican Emigration. *Social and Economic Studies,* **4**, 4.

MOORE, J. G. (1954). *The Religion of Jamaican Negroes.* Unpublished doctoral dissertation, North Western University, U.S.A.

MORGAN, W. JOHN (1960). Gloom on the Iron Road. *New Statesman,* 16 January.

MYRDAL, GUNNAR (1944). *An American Dilemma.* New York: Harper.

*N'DEM, E. B. (1953). *Negro Immigrants in Manchester.* Unpublished M.A. thesis, University of Manchester.

PARRY, CLIVE (1957). *Nationality and Citizenship Laws of the Commonwealth.* London: Stevens.

References

PATTERSON, SHEILA (1953). *Colour and Culture in South Africa.* International Library of Sociology and Social Reconstruction. London: Routledge & Kegan Paul.

PATTERSON, SHEILA (1961). The Way Forward. *London Quarterly & Holborn Review* (January).

PATTERSON, SHEILA (1961). The Polish Exile Community in Britain. *Polish Review*, VI, 3. U.S.A.

PHELPS, O. W. (1960). Rise of the Labour Movement in Jamaica. *Social and Economic Studies*, 9, 4.

PILGRIM, FRANK (1958). Movements of Population. *Royal Commonwealth Society Journal*, I, 3.

POLACK, A. I. (1955). Unesco Expert Meeting on *The Promotion of Teaching of Race Questions in Primary and Secondary Schools.* Unesco/SS/Conf. 3/5/Paris, 23 August.

POLITICAL AND ECONOMIC PLANNING (1955). *Colonial Students in Britain.* London: PEP.

POLITICAL AND ECONOMIC PLANNING (1960–61). *Overseas Students in the United Kingdom.* London Conference on Overseas Students. London: PEP.

REID, IRA DE A. (1939). *The Negro Immigrant.* New York: Columbia University Press.

*REID, JANET (1956). Employment of Negroes in Manchester. *Sociological Review*, 4, 5.

RENIER, C. J. (1931). *The English, Are They Human?* London: Withams & Norgate.

*RICHMOND, ANTHONY (1954). *Colour Prejudice in Britain.* International Library of Sociology and Social Reconstruction. London: Routledge & Kegan Paul.

RICHMOND, ANTHONY (1955). *The Colour Problem.* Harmondsworth: Penguin Books.

*RICHMOND, ANTHONY (1958). Recent Research on Race Relations in Britain. Unesco: *International Social Science Bulletin*, X, 3.

RICHMOND, ANTHONY (1960). Applied Social Science and Public Policy concerning Racial Relations in Britain. *Race*, 1, 2.

ROBERTS, G. W. (1955). Emigration from Barbados. *Social and Economic Studies*, 4, 3.

ROBERTS, G. W. (1957a). *The Population of Jamaica.* London: Cambridge University Press.

ROBERTS, G. W. (1957b). Some Demographic Considerations. *Social and Economic Studies*, 6, 2.

ROBERTS, G. W. & MILLS, D. O. (1958). Report: Study of External Migration affecting Jamaica, 1953–55. *Social and Economic Studies*, Supplement to 7, 2.

RODMAN, HYMAN (1959). On Understanding Lower-Class Behaviour. *Social and Economic Studies*, 8, 4.

ROYAL COMMISSION ON THE ALIEN IMMIGRATION (1903). Report. London: H.M.S.O.

447

References

*RUCK, S. K. (Ed.) (1960). *The West Indian Comes to England*. London: Routledge & Kegan Paul.

RUSSELL, C. & LEWIS, H. S. (1900). *The Jew in London*. London: T. Fisher Unwin.

SAMUEL, RALPH (1960). The Deference Voter. *New Left Review*, **1**, Jan.-Feb.

SELECT COMMITTEE ON EMIGRATION AND IMMIGRATION (FOREIGNERS) (1888). Report. London: H.M.S.O.

SELVON, SAMUEL (1956). *The Lonely Londoners*. London: Wingate.

*SENIOR, CLARENCE & MANLEY, DOUGLAS (1955). *A Report on Jamaican Migration to Great Britain*. Government of Jamaica.

SIMEY, T. S. (1946). *Welfare and Planning in the West Indies*. London: Oxford University Press.

SIMEY, T. S. (1956). Class Conflict and Social Mobility. *Journal of the Royal Society of Arts*, **CIV**.

SIMPSON, G. E. (1956). Jamaican Revivalist Cults. *Social and Economic Studies*, **5**, 4.

SMITH, MICHAEL (1956). *A Report on Labour Supply in Rural Jamaica*. Government Printer, Kingston, Jamaica.

SMITH, M. G. (1956). Community Organization in Rural Jamaica. *Social and Economic Studies*, **5**, 3.

SMITH, M. G. (1960). Education and Occupational Choice in Jamaica. *Social and Economic Studies*, **9**, 3.

SMITH, M. G. (1961). The Plural Framework of Jamaican Society. *British Journal of Sociology*, **XII**, 3.

SMITH, M. G., AUGIER, R. & NETTLEFORD, R. (1960). *The Ras Tafari Movement in Kingston, Jamaica*. Institute of Social & Economic Research.

SMITH, M. G. & KRUIJER, G. J. (1957). *A Sociological Manual for Extension Workers in the Caribbean*. Caribbean Affairs Series, Extra-mural Department, University College of the West Indies.

SMITH, R. T. (1953). Family Organization in British Guiana. *Social and Economic Studies*, **1**, 1.

SMITH, R. T. (1956). *The Negro Family in British Guiana*. International Library of Sociology and Social Reconstruction. London: Routledge & Kegan Paul.

SMITH, R. T. & JAYAWARDENA, C. (1959). Marriage and the Family amongst East Indians in British Guiana. *Social and Economic Studies*, **8**, 4.

SOCIAL AND ECONOMIC STUDIES (1953–). Journal of the Institute of Social and Economic Research, University College of the West Indies.

SOCIAL SURVEYS (GALLUP POLL) LTD. March 1955 (No. 427); June 1958 (No. CQ77); September 1958 (No. 2577); May 1961 (No. 4024). London.

*STEPHENS, LESLIE (1956). *Employment of Coloured Workers in the Birmingham Area*. Institute of Personnel Management, Occasional Paper No. 10. London: IPM.

448

References

TANNAHILL, J. A. (1958). *European Volunteer Workers in Britain*. Manchester: Manchester University Press.
TANSWELL, JOHN (1858). *The History and Antiquities of Lambeth*. London: Frederick Pickton.
THE TIMES BRITISH COLONIES REVIEW (1957).

UNESCO (1951–53). *The Race Question in Modern Science*.
UNESCO (1953–54). *The Race Question and Modern Thought*.
UNESCO (1955). *The Positive Contribution by Immigrants: Population and Culture*.
UNESCO (1959). Report of the Second United Nations Conference of Non-Government Organizations interested in *The Eradication of Prejudice and Discrimination*. Unesco E/NGO/Conf.2/7, 28 July.

WICKENDEN, JAMES (1958). *Colour in Britain*. The Institute of Race Relations. London: Oxford University Press.
WILLIAMS, B. (1956). Overcrowding and Immigration. Society of Housing Managers *Quarterly Bulletin*, **IV**, 1.
WILSON, FRANCESCA (1959). *They Came as Strangers*. London: Hamish Hamilton.

YOUNG MICHAEL & WILLMOTT, PETER (1957). *Family and Kinship in East London*. London: Routledge & Kegan Paul.

ZORBAUGH, H. W. (1929). *The Gold Coast and the Slum*. Chicago: University of Chicago Press; London: Cambridge University Press.
ZUBRZYCKI, J. (1956). *Polish Immigrants in Britain*. The Hague: Martinus Nijhoff.

449

Index

Index

Anglicans, percentage, West Indies, 351
Anglo-Egyptions, refugees after Suez crisis, 66
Anglo-Indians, 53, 99, 106, 113, 128, 293, 375
anthropologist, social, approach, 26
Antigua, migration statistics, 43
antipathy, 7, 228, 388
  definition, 20
  reduction, 405
  attribution to others, 99, 128, 405
  see also friction; prejudice
anti-Semitism, 52
anti-sponsors, 18
  see also sponsors
appearance, 97, 109, 121, 128, 136, 232, 283
  see also clothes; visibility; and various references to colour
apprentices
  in Britain, 99, 113, 116, 163
  in West Indies, 72
approach to the Brixton inquiry, 6, 26, 29
armed forces, West Indians in, 88
arrivals, West Indians, 4, 41, 417, 418, 419, 410
  see also stowaways
assaults, on coloured people, 237, 248
assimilation
  definition, 10
  processes, 9, 11, 12, 16, 373, 388, 398
  factors influencing, 214, 265, 341
Associated Society of Locomotive Engineers and Firemen (ASLEF), and coloured workers, 157, 160
association, areas of, between migrants and receiving society, 16, 396, 408
  housing, 173, 190, 198, 388, 390
  social and cultural, 5, 149, 198, 219, 225, 228, 234, 256, 278, 388, 394, 398

452

at work, 90, 91, 93, 98, 102, 104, 106, 148, 390
  see also workers
  see also contacts
associations
  British
    leisure, 272
    range in Lambeth, 252
    religious, *see* churches
    welfare, 262
  West Indian
    formal and informal, 348
    informal social, 369
    integrative, 12 13, 364, 368
    leisure, 272
    not enthusiastic 'joiners', 275
    'partners', 310, 317, 342
    political, 364
    protest, 225, 330, 360–2
    recreational, 257, 364
      see also clubs; interracial associations; recreation;
    religious, 349, 363
      see also churches; cults; sects
    traditional, 362, 367, 369
Atlantic Café, 371
attitudes
  and behaviour, 20–2, 169, 235
  British
    children, 265
    to coloured neighbours, 191, 279
    to coloured people, 230, 235, 375, 383
    to intermarriage and sexual mingling, 282, 395
    'live-and-let-live', 148, 199, 202
    to marriage, 227, 305
    to outsiders, 7, 20, 65, 228, 388
    to physical appearance, 232
    to religion, 227
    to sex and marriage, 198, 227, 279
    tolerance, 20, 294
    'wog complex', 87, 124, 147, 233

454

Case Histories